A Writer's Reference

with Exercises

SIXTH EDITION

A Writer's Reference

with Exercises

Diana Hacker

Contributing Authors

Nancy Sommers
Tom Jehn
Jane Rosenzweig

Harvard University

Contributing ESL Specialist

Marcy Carbajal Van Horn

Santa Fe Community College

BEDFORD / ST. MARTIN'S   Boston ◆ New York

For Bedford/St. Martin's

Executive Editor: Michelle M. Clark
Senior Production Editor: Anne Noonan
Senior Production Supervisor: Joe Ford
Senior Marketing Manager: John Swanson
Associate Editors: Amy Hurd Gershman and Mara Weible
Editorial Assistant: Jennifer Lyford
Assistant Production Editor: Amy Derjue
Copyeditor: Barbara G. Flanagan
Text Design: Claire Seng-Niemoeller
Cover Design: Donna Lee Dennison
Composition: Monotype, LLC
Printing and Binding: R.R. Donnelley & Sons Company

President: Joan E. Feinberg
Editorial Director: Denise B. Wydra
Editor in Chief: Karen S. Henry
Director of Marketing: Karen Melton Soeltz
Director of Editing, Design, and Production: Marcia Cohen
Managing Editor: Elizabeth M. Schaaf

Library of Congress Control Number: 2007920749

ACKNOWLEDGMENTS

Scott Adams, "Dilbert and the Way of the Weasel." Copyright © 2000 by United Features Syndicate. Reprinted with permission of United Media.
American Heritage Dictionary, definition for "regard" from *The American Heritage Dictionary of the English Language, Fourth Edition.* Copyright © 2000 by Houghton Mifflin Company. Reprinted with permission.

Acknowledgments and copyrights are continued at the back of the book on page 573, which constitutes an extension of the copyright page. It is a violation of the law to reproduce these selections by any means whatsoever without the written permission of the copyright holder.

How to use this book

A Writer's Reference is designed to save you time. As you can see, the book lies flat, making it easy to consult while you are revising and editing a draft. And the book's twelve section dividers will lead you quickly to the information you need.

Here are brief descriptions of the book's major reference aids, followed by a chart summarizing the content of the book's companion Web site.

THE MENU SYSTEM. The main menu inside the front cover displays the book's contents as briefly and simply as possible. Each of the twelve sections in the main menu leads you to a color-coded tabbed divider, on the back of which you will find a more detailed menu. Let's say you have a question about the proper use of commas between items in a series. Your first step is to scan the main menu, where you will find the comma listed as the first item in section P (Punctuation). Next flip the book open to the blue tabbed divider marked P. Now consult the detailed menu for the precise subsection (P1-c) and the exact page number.

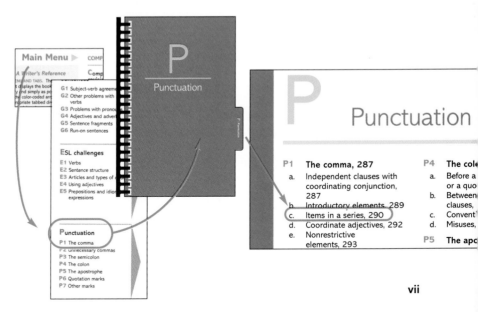

Main Menu ▶   COMP

A Writer's Reference   Comp

...displays the book
...and simply as po
...color-coded and
...opriate tabbed di

G1 Subject-verb agreeme
G2 Other problems with verbs
G3 Problems with pronou
G4 Adjectives and adver
G5 Sentence fragments
G6 Run-on sentences

ESL challenges
E1 Verbs
E2 Sentence structure
E3 Articles and types of
E4 Using adjectives
E5 Prepositions and idio expressions

Punctuation
P1 The comma
P2 Unnecessary commas
P3 The semicolon
P4 The colon
P5 The apostrophe
P6 Quotation marks
P7 Other marks

P   Punctuation

P   **Punctuation**

DETAILED MENU (inside the back cover). A menu more detailed than the main menu appears inside the back cover.

CODES AND REVISION SYMBOLS. Some instructors mark student papers with the codes given on the main menu and detailed menus — section numbers such as S1 or G3-d. When you are revising an essay marked with codes, tracking down information is simple. When you see G3-d, for example, flip to the G tab — and then let the blue tabs at the tops of the pages lead you to G3-d, clear advice about when to use *who* and *whom*. If your instructor uses an abbreviation such as *dm* or *cs* instead of a number, consult the list of revision symbols on the next to last page of the book. There you will find the name of the problem (*dangling modifier*; *comma splice*) and the section number that will help you solve the problem.

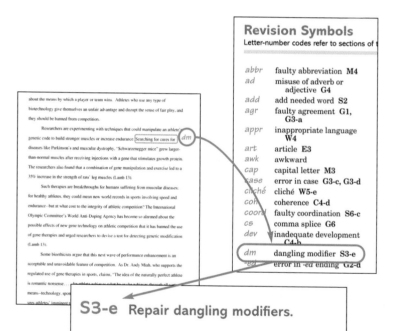

Revision Symbols

Letter-number codes refer to sections of t

abbr	faulty abbreviation **M4**
ad	misuse of adverb or adjective **G4**
add	add needed word **S2**
agr	faulty agreement **G1, G3-a**
appr	inappropriate language **W4**
art	article **E3**
awk	awkward
cap	capital letter **M3**
case	error in case **G3-c, G3-d**
cliché	cliché **W5-e**
coh	coherence **C4-d**
coor	faulty coordination **S6-c**
cs	comma splice **G6**
dev	inadequate development **C4-b**
dm	dangling modifier **S3-e**
-ed	error in -*ed* ending **G2-d**

S3-e Repair dangling modifiers.

A dangling modifier fails to refer logically to any
tence. Dangling modifiers are easy to repair, but t
to recognize, especially in your own writing.

RULES, EXPLANATIONS, AND EXAMPLES. Once you use a code to find a section, such as G1-b, the text presents three main types of help to solve your writing problem. The section number is accompanied by a rule, which is often a revision strategy. The rule is followed by a clear, brief explanation and, in some sections, by one or more hand-edited examples.

Rule

G1-b Make the verb agree with its subject, not with a word that comes between.

Explanation

Word groups often come between the subject and the verb. Such word groups, usually modifying the subject, may contain a noun that at first appears to be the subject. By mentally stripping away such modifiers, you can isolate the noun that is in fact the subject.

The *samples* on the tray in the lab *need* testing.

Examples

▶ High levels of air pollution causes damage to the respiratory tract.

The subject is *levels,* not *pollution.* Strip away the phrase *of air pollution* to hear the correct verb: *levels cause.*

THE INDEX. If you aren't sure what topic to choose from the main menu, consult the index at the back of the book. For example, you may not realize that the issue of whether to use *has* or *have* is a matter of subject-verb agreement (G1 on the main menu). In that case, simply look up "*has* vs. *have*" in the index. The boldface letter in the index entry leads you to the tabbed section G, and the page numbers pinpoint the specific page numbers in G. In addition, a cross-reference suggests another helpful index entry, "Subject-verb agreement."

Each index entry includes a reference to a tab letter and a page number.

THE GLOSSARY OF USAGE. When in doubt about the correct use of a particular word (such as *affect* and *effect* or *among* and *between*), flip to section W1 and consult the alphabetically arranged glossary for the word in question. If the word you are looking for isn't in the glossary of usage, it may be in the index.

The glossary of usage begins on page 131.

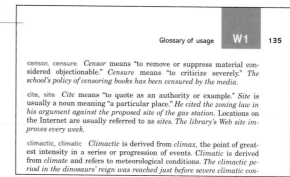

Glossary of usage   **W1**   135

censor, censure *Censor* means "to remove or suppress material considered objectionable." *Censure* means "to criticize severely." *The school's policy of censoring books has been censured by the media.*

cite, site *Cite* means "to quote as an authority or example." *Site* is usually a noun meaning "a particular place." *He cited the zoning law in his argument against the proposed site of the gas station.* Locations on the Internet are usually referred to as *sites. The library's Web site improves every week.*

climactic, climatic *Climactic* is derived from *climax,* the point of greatest intensity in a series or progression of events. *Climatic* is derived from *climate* and refers to meteorological conditions. *The climactic period in the dinosaurs' reign was reached just before severe climatic con-*

THE DIRECTORIES TO DOCUMENTATION MODELS. When you are writing a research paper, you don't need to memorize technical details about handling citations or constructing a list of works you have cited. Instead, you can rely on one of the book's directories to documentation models to help you find examples of the types of citations you will need to provide in your paper. If you are using the Modern Language Association (MLA) system of documentation, flip the book open to the tabbed section marked MLA and then scan the tab menu to find the appropriate directory. If you are using the American Psychological Association (APA) or the *Chicago Manual of Style* (CMS) system, scan the menu on the tab marked APA/CMS.

The directory to MLA works cited models begins on page 421.

Directory to MLA works cited models

COMPANION WEB SITE.   The following chart describes student resources available on the book's companion Web site.

ON THE WEB > dianahacker.com/writersref

▶ Writing exercises

Interactive exercises on topics such as choosing a thesis statement and conducting a peer review — with feedback for every correct and incorrect answer

▶ Grammar exercises

Interactive exercises on grammar, style, and punctuation — with feedback for every correct and incorrect answer

▶ Research exercises

Interactive exercises on topics such as integrating quotations, formatting in-text citations and bibliographic entries, and identifying elements needed for citing sources in MLA, APA, and CMS (*Chicago*) styles — with feedback for every correct and incorrect answer

▶ Language Debates

Brief essays by Diana Hacker that explore controversial issues of grammar and usage, such as split infinitives

▶ ESL help

Resources and strategies to help nonnative speakers improve their college writing skills

▶ Model papers

Annotated sample papers in MLA, APA, CMS (*Chicago*), and CSE styles

▶ Research and Documentation Online

Advice on finding sources and up-to-date guidelines for documenting print and online sources in MLA, APA, CMS (*Chicago*), and CSE styles

▶ Tutorials

Interactive resources that teach essential skills such as navigating *A Writer's Reference*, integrating sources, and making the most of the writing center

▶ Resources for writers and tutors

Handouts, revision checklists, and tips for visiting the writing center

▶ Additional resources

Print-format exercises for practice and links to additional online resources

Tutorials

The following tutorials will give you practice using the book's menus, index, glossary of usage, and MLA directory. Answers to the tutorials begin on page 557.

TUTORIAL 1
Using the menus

Each of the following "rules" violates the principle it expresses. Using the brief menu inside the front cover or the detailed menu inside the back cover, find the section in *A Writer's Reference* that explains the principle. Then fix the problem. Examples:

> *Tutors in*
> ► ~~In~~ the writing center,/ ~~they~~ say that vague pronoun reference
> ^
> is unacceptable. *G3-b*

> *come*
> ► Be alert for irregular verbs that have ~~came~~ to you in the
> ^
> wrong form. *G2-a*

1. A verb have to agree with its subject.
2. Each pronoun should agree with their antecedent.
3. About sentence fragments. You should avoid them.
4. Its important to use apostrophe's correctly.
5. Check for *-ed* verb endings that have been drop.
6. Discriminate careful between adjectives and adverbs.
7. If your sentence begins with a long introductory word group use a comma to separate the word group from the rest of the sentence.
8. Don't write a run-on sentence, you must connect independent clauses with a comma and a coordinating conjunction or with a semicolon.
9. A writer must be careful not to shift your point of view.
10. When dangling, watch your modifiers.

TUTORIAL 2
Using the index

Assume that you have written the following sentences and want to know the answers to the questions in brackets. Use the index at the back of the book to locate the information you need, and edit the sentences if necessary.

1. Each of the candidates have decided to participate in tonight's debate. [Should the verb be *has* or *have* to agree with *Each*?]
2. We had intended to go surfing but spent most of our vacation lying on the beach. [Should I use *lying* or *laying*?]
3. We only looked at two houses before buying the house of our dreams. [Is *only* in the right place?]
4. In Saudi Arabia it is considered ill mannered for you to accept a gift. [Is it okay to use *you* to mean "anyone in general"?]
5. In Canada, Joanne picked up several bottles of maple syrup for her sister and me. [Should I write *for her sister and I*?]

TUTORIAL 3
Using the menu system or the index

Imagine that you are in the following situations. Using either the menus or the index, find the information you need.

1. You are Ray Farley, a community college student who has been out of high school for ten years. You recall learning to put a comma between all items in a series except the last two. But you have noticed that most writers use a comma between all items. You're curious about the current rule. Which section of *A Writer's Reference* will you consult?

2. You are Maria Sanchez, a peer tutor in your university's writing center. Mike Lee, a nonnative speaker of English, has come to you for help. He is working on a rough draft that contains a number of problems with articles (*a, an,* and *the*). You know how to use articles, but you aren't able to explain the complicated rules on their correct use. Which section of *A Writer's Reference* will you and Mike Lee consult?

3. You are John Pell, engaged to marry Sophia Ju. In a note to Sophia's parents, you have written, "Thank you for giving Sophia and myself such a generous contribution toward our honeymoon." You wonder if you should write "Sophia and I" or "Sophia and me." What does *A Writer's Reference* say?

4. You are Selena Young, an intern supervisor at a housing agency. Two of your interns, Jake Gilliam and Aisha Greene, have writing problems involving *-s* endings on verbs. Jake tends to drop *-s* endings; Aisha tends to add them where they don't belong. You suspect that both problems stem from non-standard dialects spoken at home.

    Aisha and Jake are in danger of losing their jobs because your boss thinks that anyone who writes "the tenant refuse" or "the landlords agrees" is beyond hope. You disagree. Aisha and Jake have asked for your help. Where in *A Writer's Reference* can they find the rules they need?

5. You are Owen Thompson, a first-year college student. Your friend Samantha, who has completed two years of college, seems to enjoy correcting your English. Just yesterday she corrected your sentence "I felt badly about her death" to "I felt bad about her death." You're sure you've heard many educated people, including professors, say "I felt badly." Upon consulting *A Writer's Reference*, what do you discover?

TUTORIAL 4
Using the glossary of usage

Consult the glossary of usage (section W1) to see if the italicized words are used correctly. Then edit any sentences containing incorrect usage. If a sentence is correct, write "correct" after it. Example:

▶ The pediatrician gave my daughter ~~a~~ *an* injection for her allergy.

1. Changing attitudes *toward* alcohol have *effected* the beer industry.
2. It is *mankind's* nature to think wisely and act foolishly.
3. This afternoon I plan to *lie* in my hammock and read.
4. Our goal this year is to *grow* our profits by 9 percent.
5. Most sleds are pulled by no *less* than two dogs and no more than ten.

TUTORIAL 5
Using the directory to MLA works cited models

Assume that you have written a short research essay on the origins of hip-hop music. You have cited the following sources in your essay, using MLA documentation, and you are ready to type your list of works cited. Turn to page 421 and use the MLA directory to locate the appropriate models. Then write a correct entry for each source and arrange the entries in a properly formatted list of works cited.

A book by Jeff Chang titled *Can't Stop, Won't Stop: A History of the Hip-Hop Generation.* The book was published in New York by St. Martin's Press in 2005.

An online article by Kay Randall called "Studying a Hip-Hop Nation." The article appeared on the University of Texas at Austin Web site, which you accessed on April 13, 2006. The last update was April 11, 2005, and the URL is <http://www.utexas.edu/features/archive/2003/hiphop.html>.

A journal article by H. Samy Alim titled "360 Degreez of Black Art Comin at You: Sista Sonia Sanchez and the Dimensions of a Black Arts Continuum." The article appears in the journal *BMa: The Sonia Sanchez Literary Review*, which is paginated by issue. The article appears on pages 15–33. The volume number is 6, the issue number is 1, and the year is 2000.

A sound recording entitled "Rapper's Delight" performed by the Sugarhill Gang on the LP *The Sugarhill Gang.* The album was released in 1979 by Sugarhill Records.

A magazine article accessed through the *InfoTrac* database *Expanded Academic ASAP.* The article, "The Roots Redefine Hip-Hop's Past," was written by Kimberly Davis and published in *Ebony* magazine in June 2003. The article appears on pages 162–64. You found this article at the Ray Cosgrove Library at Truman College in Chicago on April 13, 2006, using the URL <http://infotrac.galegroup.com>.

Preface for instructors

Publisher's note

> When Bedford and I invented the quick-reference format — with its main menu, tabbed dividers, and lie-flat binding — ...we had no idea that *A Writer's Reference* would become so popular (or so widely imitated). My goals were more modest. I hoped that the format and the title would send a clear message: *A Writer's Reference* is meant to be consulted as needed; it is not a set of grammar lessons to be studied in a vacuum.... Instructors across the country tell me that their students can and do use the book on their own, keeping it flipped open next to their computers.
>
> Diana Hacker (1942–2004),
> from the Preface for Instructors,
> *A Writer's Reference,* Fifth Edition

In her trademark lucid style, Diana Hacker describes making publishing history. *A Writer's Reference* is not only the most widely adopted English handbook on the market but also the best-selling college textbook of any kind in any discipline. It literally revolutionized the handbook genre. Users of the book routinely tell us that *A Writer's Reference* is the easiest handbook to use — a book that helps students find what they need and understand what they find.

Like all of the innovations that Diana Hacker brought to the genre of handbooks, the innovations of *A Writer's Reference* came from her teaching. She was able to take everything she knew from her thirty-five years of teaching and put it to work on every page of her books. Diana carefully observed how students actually used handbooks — mainly as references — and designed a book that would work better for them. The tabbed dividers and comb binding, which allow *A Writer's Reference* to lie open on any page, make it easier for students to find the information they need as quickly as possible. Once they get to the right page, the information is easy for them to understand on their own. The book's patient, respectful tone; its clear, concise explanations; and its hand-edited examples give students the help they need. Even though many other handbooks have imitated the format, no one understands as Diana did how format and content have to work together to make a truly useful handbook.

Although the first edition grew primarily out of Diana Hacker's own teaching experiences, subsequent editions reflect the experiences of the thousands of instructors using the books in their classrooms and of the millions of students who have found it helpful. For this new edition, we relied on advice from an extraordinary group of reviewers who kept reminding us what their students need. More than five hundred dedicated and experienced composition instructors reviewed the sixth edition. More than thirty of them served as an editorial advisory board; they read and commented on every word of this edition, making sure that it will work as well for their students as it always has and that the new material meets the high standards of a Hacker handbook.

With her team of Bedford editors, Diana had mapped out a plan for the sixth edition. Based on this plan, a talented group of contributing authors revised this edition, putting themselves at the service of the book while bringing their own classroom experience to everything they did. Nancy Sommers, Tom Jehn, and Jane Rosenzweig — all of whom teach in the Harvard Expository Writing Program — helped revise the coverage of the writing process and research. Marcy Carbajal Van Horn, teacher of composition and ESL at Santa Fe Community College (FL), revised the ESL coverage. Diana was a huge fan of Nancy Sommers's work because it focused on student writing, drawing on Nancy's teaching at the University of Oklahoma and Rutgers as well as at Harvard. Diana was eager to have insights from Nancy's recent longitudinal study of student writing in the book. Tom Jehn is the clear and patient writing teacher that Diana always was, especially in helping students work with sources. Jane Rosenzweig is the skilled writer Diana always hoped for in a coauthor. Marcy Carbajal Van Horn creates practical and accessible content for a broad range of students — starting with her own — as Diana always did.

A *Writer's Reference* has always been a team effort between Diana and her editors at Bedford/St. Martin's, and that team is still in place. I was Diana's editor on the first edition of every one of her handbooks, including *A Writer's Reference*, and have been a part of every book since. Special thanks go to Chuck Christensen for understanding what makes a great handbook author and for knowing he had found one in Diana Hacker. At the heart of the Hacker team is Diana's longtime editor, executive editor Michelle Clark, the most skilled, creative editor we could wish for. Development editors Ellen Kuhl and Michelle McSweeney, veterans of many Hacker handbooks, made sure that every word in this book sounds like Diana's voice. Claire Seng-Niemoeller has designed every Hacker handbook since the first and has again retained the clean, uncluttered look of the book while making more use of color. Having copyedited every Hacker handbook, Barbara Flanagan has been hearing Diana's voice for more than twenty years. Diana credited her with the clarity and consistency that is a Hacker hallmark. Senior production editor Anne Noonan kept us all on track with her persistence, sharp eye, and concern for every detail. Assistant production editor Amy Derjue provided detailed assistance throughout the page proof review. Editor in chief Karen Henry and managing editor Elizabeth Schaaf have worked on these books from the beginning and remain committed to Diana's vision. New media editors Mara Weible and Amy Hurd Gershman expanded the new media offerings, making them as easy to use as the book itself. Stellar editorial assistant Jennifer Lyford managed various projects and made sure that we heard from as many users as possible. We all remain committed to maintaining the high level of quality of Hacker handbooks.

The result is a revision that does what *A Writer's Reference* has always done: It works. Our hope is that students will keep flipping it open to find the best answers to their questions about writing.

Joan Feinberg
President, Bedford/St. Martin's

Features of the sixth edition

What's new

NEW VISUALS THAT TEACH CITATION AT A GLANCE.   New full-color, annotated facsimiles of original sources show students where to look for publication information in a book, a periodical, a Web site, and a source accessed in a database. These visuals help students find the information they need to cite print and online materials accurately and responsibly.

ADVICE THAT HELPS STUDENTS MAINTAIN THEIR VOICE WHILE WRITING FROM SOURCES.   Thoroughly revised coverage of integrating sources teaches students how to go beyond patchwork research writing.

Section MLA-3 shows students how to lead into — and get out of — sources while keeping the source material in context and maintaining their own line of argument.

GUIDELINES THAT HELP STUDENTS UNDERSTAND HOW SOURCES CAN FUNCTION IN THEIR WRITING. A new section (MLA-1c) teaches students to consider the varying roles that sources can play in research writing.

NEW CHARTS THAT OFFER PRACTICAL ADVICE FOR USING SOURCES. New quick-reference charts on determining whether a source is "scholarly," on selecting appropriate versions of electronic sources, and on avoiding Internet plagiarism help students meet the challenges of research writing in the digital age.

A NEW EMPHASIS ON ACADEMIC WRITING. A new tabbed section (A) equips students with strategies for writing well in any college course; it brings new chapters on writing about texts and writing in the disciplines together with a revised chapter on argument.

GUIDELINES FOR WRITING ABOUT VERBAL AND VISUAL TEXTS. A new section (A1) provides advice and models for annotating, outlining, summarizing, and analyzing both verbal texts (such as essays and articles) and visual texts (such as advertisements and photographs).

A NEW CHAPTER ON WRITING IN THE DISCIPLINES. *A Writer's Reference* offers more help for students as they write in courses outside of the humanities. It explains the common features of all good college writing and provides practical advice for approaching writing assignments in all disciplines.

MORE HELP WITH WRITING ARGUMENTS. Revised coverage of counterargument teaches students how to strengthen their writing by anticipating and responding to objections.

NEW QUICK-ACCESS CHARTS. The sixth edition features new charts that help writers navigate common writing challenges: understanding a writing assignment, making use of advice from peer reviewers, writing a conclusion, reading actively, and analyzing visuals.

MEETS THE NEEDS OF A BROADER RANGE OF ESL STUDENTS. Thoroughly revised ESL coverage considers the experiences of college students who may be proficient English speakers but who continue to struggle with writing well in English.

MORE HELP FOR THE MOST TROUBLESOME SENTENCE-LEVEL PROBLEMS. Developed with the help of ESL specialists, the sixth edition offers stronger support for using verbs, articles, and prepositions correctly. New charts offer at-a-glance help for nonnative speakers of English.

CRUCIAL ADVICE ON ACADEMIC CONVENTIONS — FOR NATIVE AS WELL AS NONNATIVE SPEAKERS. New boxed tips teach *academic English* — or how to go about writing well at an American college. Throughout the book, these nuggets of advice — on topics such as plagiarism, writing arguments, and understanding writing assignments — help students meet college expectations.

INTEGRATED EXERCISES FOR PRACTICE AND SELF-STUDY. Each of the grammar, style, ESL, punctuation, and mechanics sections is now accompanied by one or more exercise sets for classroom use or independent use. The new edition includes nearly one hundred exercise sets in multiple formats. Most sets begin with five lettered sentences with answers in the back of the book. (A full answer key is available for instructors.) Students who need more practice can visit the book's companion Web site (see p. xi for details) and select "Grammar exercises."

AN UNCLUTTERED PAGE DESIGN. The book's new, more colorful design presents complex material and new visual elements as simply as possible. Because grammar rules and hand-edited examples are highlighted in color, students can easily skim the book's central sections for quick answers to questions. Charts and boxes are easy to find and, just as important, easy to skip.

NEW SAMPLE PAPERS. Four new major papers show good writing and proper formatting: an argument essay; an analysis of an article; an MLA-style research essay; and an APA-style review of the literature.

UPDATED GRAMMAR CHECKER BOXES. A Diana Hacker innovation, the fifty grammar checker boxes have been updated to reflect the way current grammar and spell checker programs work. Students will read helpful advice about the capabilities and limitations of these programs.

FLEXIBLE CONTENT THAT HELPS YOU MEET THE NEEDS OF YOUR STUDENTS. Supplemental content for ESL, writing in the disciplines, visual rhetoric, and writing about literature is available for packaging or for custom publishing to create a handbook that supports your course.

What's the same

We have kept the features that have made *A Writer's Reference* work so well for so many students and instructors. These features, detailed here, will be familiar to users of the previous edition.

COLOR-CODED MAIN MENU AND TABBED DIVIDERS. The main menu directs students to orange, blue, green, and white tabbed dividers; the color coding makes it easy for students to identify and flip to the section they need. The documentation sections are further color-coded: blue for MLA, green for APA, and brown for CMS.

USER-FRIENDLY INDEX. This index, which Diana Hacker wrote herself and which was carefully updated for this edition, helps students find what they are looking for even if they don't know grammatical terminology. When facing a choice between *I* and *me*, for example, students may not know to look up "Case" or even "Pronoun, case of." They are more likely to look up "*I*" or "*me*," so the index includes entries for "*I* vs. *me*" and "*me* vs. *I*." Similar user-friendly entries appear throughout the index.

Index entries include the letter of the tabbed section before the page number of the indexed term (**G**: 201). Users can flip directly to the correct tabbed divider, such as G (for Grammatical sentences) before tracking down the page number.

QUICK-REFERENCE CHARTS. Many of the handbook's charts help students review for common problems in their own writing, such as fragments and subject-verb agreement. Other charts summarize important material: a checklist for global revision, strategies for avoiding sexist language, guidelines for evaluating Web sites, and so on.

DISCIPLINE-SPECIFIC RHETORICAL ADVICE FOR MLA, APA, AND CMS (*CHICAGO*) STYLES. Advice on drafting a thesis, avoiding plagiarism, and integrating sources is illustrated for all three major documentation styles — MLA, APA, and CMS (*Chicago*) — in three color-coded sections. Examples are related to topics appropriate to the disciplines that typically use each style: English and other humanities (MLA), social sciences (APA), and history (CMS).

What's on the companion Web site
<http://dianahacker.com/writersref>

RESOURCES FOR WRITERS AND TUTORS. New writing center resources on the companion Web site offer help for both tutors and writers: checklists for responding to a wide array of assignments, tips for preparing for a visit to the writing center, hints for making the best use of advice from tutors, and helpsheets for common writing problems — the same kinds of handouts students see in the writing center — all available in printable format.

ELECTRONIC GRAMMAR EXERCISES. For online practice, students can access more than one thousand exercise items — on every topic in the handbook — with feedback written by Diana Hacker. Most of the exercises are scorable. Exercises that call for editing are labeled "edit and compare." They ask students to edit sentences and compare their versions with possible revisions.

ELECTRONIC RESEARCH AND WRITING EXERCISES. Scorable electronic exercises on matters such as avoiding plagiarism, integrating sources, documenting sources, and identifying citation elements give students ample practice with these critical topics. Scorable exercises on thesis statements, peer review, point of view, transitions, and other writing topics support students throughout the composing process.

LANGUAGE DEBATES. To encourage students to think about the rationales for a rule and then make their own rhetorical decisions, Diana Hacker wrote twenty brief essays that explore controversial issues of grammar and usage, such as split infinitives and *who* versus *whom*. The Web site for the sixth edition features two additional debates written by style expert Barbara Wallraff.

MODEL PAPERS. Model papers for MLA, APA, CMS (*Chicago*), and CSE styles illustrate both the design and the content of researched writing. Annotations highlight key points about each paper's style, content, and documentation.

RESEARCH AND DOCUMENTATION ONLINE. This online resource helps students conduct research and document their sources. Reference librarian Barbara Fister has updated her advice on finding sources and has provided new links to resources in a variety of disciplines; she continues to maintain the research portion of the site. Guidelines for documenting print and online sources in MLA, APA, CMS (*Chicago*), and CSE styles are also kept up-to-date.

EXTRA HELP FOR ESL WRITERS. For native and nonnative speakers alike, this area of the site offers advice and strategies for understanding college expectations and for writing well on college assignments. Authored by Marcy Carbajal Van Horn (assistant professor of English and ESL at Santa Fe Community College, FL), it includes many helpful charts, exercises and activities, advice for working with sources, and an annotated student essay.

ACCESS TO AN ONLINE E-HANDBOOK. With the purchase of a print version of the handbook, students also have premium access to an electronic version of *A Writer's Reference*, conveniently located at the companion site.

THE INSTRUCTOR SITE. Accessible from the student site, this password-protected Web site offers additional resources such as diagnostic tests and tutorials and serves as a portal for retrieving student exercise results.

Ancillaries for students

PRINT RESOURCES

Developmental Exercises to Accompany A WRITER'S REFERENCE (with answer key)

Working with Sources: Exercises to Accompany A WRITER'S REFERENCE (with answer key)

Research and Documentation in the Electronic Age, Fourth Edition

Language Debates, Second Edition

Writing about Literature

Extra Help for ESL Writers

Writing in the Disciplines: Advice and Models

ONLINE RESOURCES

A Writer's Reference companion Web site (See the On the Web box on p. xi.)

Comment with *A Writer's Reference*

Ancillaries for instructors

PROFESSIONAL RESOURCES FOR INSTRUCTORS

Teaching Composition: Background Readings

The Bedford Guide for Writing Tutors, Fourth Edition

The Bedford Bibliography for Teachers of Writing, Sixth Edition

ONLINE RESOURCES FOR INSTRUCTORS

A Writer's Reference instructor site at <http://dianahacker.com/writersref>

Exercise Masters, print-format versions of all the exercises in the book

Quiz Masters, print-format quizzes on key topics in the book

Electronic Diagnostic Tests, a test bank for instructors' use

Transparency Masters, useful charts, examples, and visuals from the book

Preparing for the CLAST

Preparing for the THEA

In addition, all of the resources within *Re:Writing* <http://bedfordstmartins.com/rewriting> are available for free to users of *A Writer's Reference*. Resources include tutorials, exercises, diagnostics, technology help, and model documents — all written by our most widely adopted authors.

Other composition resources by Bedford/St. Martin's

The following resources are available for packaging with *A Writer's Reference*:

ix visual exercises (CD-ROM), Cheryl E. Ball and Kristin L. Arola. Introduces the fundamentals of visual composition in an interactive medium

i·cite visualizing sources (CD-ROM), Doug Downs. Introduces students to how sources work and provides interactive practice

i·claim visualizing argument (CD-ROM), Patrick Clauss. Introduces argument concepts with a range of multimedia examples; includes assignments

Oral Presentations in the Composition Course: A Brief Guide, Matthew Duncan and Gustav W. Friedrich

For a complete list, contact your sales representative or visit <http://bedfordstmartins.com/composition>.

Course management content

A variety of student and instructor resources developed for *A Writer's Reference* are ready for use in course management systems.

Acknowledgments

Diana Hacker worked with us to map out her goals for the sixth edition. We called on a number of experienced, creative individuals to develop the sixth edition with Diana's plan as the foundation.

Contributing authors

The contributors brought both expertise and enthusiasm to the project. They drafted new content and rethought existing content to make certain that *A Writer's Reference* reaches a broader range of students and meets their varied needs.

Nancy Sommers, Sosland Director of Expository Writing at Harvard University, has also taught composition at Rutgers University and at Monmouth College and has directed the writing program at the University of Oklahoma. A two-time Braddock Award winner, Sommers is well known for her research and publications on student writing. Her articles "Revision Strategies of Student and Experienced Writers" and "Responding to Student Writing" are two of the most widely read in the field. Her recent work involves a longitudinal study of undergraduate writing.

Tom Jehn teaches composition and directs the writing across the disciplines program at Harvard University. A recipient of numerous teaching awards both at Harvard and at the University of Virginia, he also leads professional development seminars on writing instruction for public high school teachers through the Calderwood Writing Fellows Project.

Jane Rosenzweig, a published author of fiction and nonfiction, teaches composition and directs the writing center at Harvard University. She has also taught writing at Yale University and the University of Iowa.

Marcy Carbajal Van Horn, assistant professor of English and ESL at Santa Fe Community College (FL), teaches composition to native and nonnative speakers of English and teaches the advanced ESL writing course. She has also taught university-level academic writing and critical thinking at Instituto Tecnológico y de Estudios Superiores in Mexico.

Editorial Advisory Board

We asked a number of longtime users of the book and several nonusers to serve as editorial advisers. They looked carefully at all new and substantially revised sections of the sixth edition to make certain that the book is still as effective as it has always been in their classrooms. We thank them for their thoughtful and candid reviews.

Joanne Addison, University of Colorado, Denver

Derick Burleson, University of Alaska, Fairbanks

Paige Byam, Northern Kentucky University

Elizabeth Canfield, Virginia Commonwealth University
Richard Carr, University of Alaska, Fairbanks
Michele Cheung, University of Southern Maine, Portland
Jon Cullick, Northern Kentucky University
David Endicott, Tacoma Community College (WA)
Lin Fraser, Sacramento City College (CA)
Hank Galmish, Green River Community College (WA)
Nancy Gish, University of Southern Maine, Portland
Jacqueline Gray, St. Charles Community College (MO)
Barclay Green, Northern Kentucky University
Karen Grossweiner, University of Alaska, Fairbanks
D. J. Henry, Daytona Beach Community College
Kandace Knudson, Sacramento City College (CA)
Tonya Krouse, Northern Kentucky University
Tamara Kuzmenkov, Tacoma Community College (WA)
Cheryl Laz, University of Southern Maine, Portland
Lydia Lynn Lewellen, Tacoma Community College (WA)
Jeanette Lonia, Delaware Technical and Community College
Walter Lowe, Green River Community College (WA)
Michael Mackey, Community College of Denver (CO)
Tammy Mata, Tarrant County College (TX)
Holly McSpadden, Missouri Southern State University
Liora Moriel, University of Maryland, College Park
Patricia Murphy, Missouri Southern State University
Melissa Nicolas, University of Louisiana, Lafayette
Diane Allen O'Heron, Broome Community College (NY)
Sarah Quirk, Waubonsee Community College (IL)
Ann Smith, Modesto Junior College (CA)
Steve Thomas, Community College of Denver (CO)
Nick Tingle, University of California, Santa Barbara
Terry Myers Zawacki, George Mason University (VA)

Reviewers

For their many helpful suggestions, we would like to thank a perceptive group of reviewers. Some answered a detailed questionnaire about the fifth edition; others reviewed manuscript for the sixth edition.

Barry Abrams, Sierra College (CA); Melanie Abrams, California State University, San Bernardino; Susan Achziger, Community College of Aurora (CO); Jo Acres-Devine, University of Alaska, Southeast; D. Michelle Adkerson, Nashville State Technical Community College (TN); Judy Andree, University of Alaska, Southeast; Rebecca Argall, University of Memphis (TN); Marianne Arieux, Empire State College (NY); Diann Arinder, Jackson Preparatory School (MS); Janice Aslanian, Hope College (MI); Greg Barnhisel, Duquesne University (PA); Dana Basinger, Samford University (AL); Dennis Beach, Saint John's University (MN); Diana Bell, University of Alabama, Huntsville; Sally Bell, University of Montevallo (AL); Barbara Bengels, Hofstra University (NY); Rick Beno, Padua Academy (DE); Cameron Bentley, Augusta Technical Institute (GA); Mary Bettley, Lesley University (MA); Nilanjana Bhattacharjya, Cornell University (NY); Desha Bierbaum, Lesley University (MA); Cynthia Bily, Adrian College (MI); Delmar Bishop, Pomona High School (CO); Shalom Black, Catholic University of America (DC); Keva Boone, Barry University (FL); Robin Bott, Adrian College (MI); Kimberly Bovee, Tidewater Community College (VA); Martha Bowden, Kennesaw State (GA); Brad Bowers, Barry University (FL); Mary Boyes, Tusculum College (TN); Molly Boyle, Massachusetts Bay Community College; Karla Braig, Loras College (IA); Angela Branch, John Tyler Community College (VA); Jennifer Brezina, College of the Canyons (CA); Kristi Brock, Northern Kentucky University; Angier Brock Caudle, Virginia Commonwealth University; Elaine Brooks, CUNY Brooklyn College (NY); Barry Brown, Missouri Southern State University; Cheryl Brown, Towson University (MD); Laura Brown, Central Alabama Community College; Shanti Bruce, Indiana University of Pennsylvania; Richard Bullock, Wright State University (OH); William Burgos, Long Island University, Brooklyn (NY); Richard Burke, Lynchburg College (VA); Charles Burm, Monroe Community College (NY); Ellen Butki, University of Texas at Austin; Barb Butler, Bellevue Community College (WA); Candace Byrne, Shasta College (CA); Stephen Calatrello, Calhoun State Community College (AL); Linda Caldwell, Towson University (MD); Catherine Calloway, Arkansas State University, Main Campus; Jorinde Canden Berg, Montgomery College, Germantown (MD); Phyllis Carey, Mount Mary College (WI); Cheryl Carpinello, Alameda Senior High School (CO); Pat Cearley, South Plains College (TX); Sherry Chapman, Modesto Junior College (CA); Nishi Chawla, University of Maryland University College; Marjorie Childers, Elms College (MA); Angela Christman, Loyola College (MD); Greg Clark, Brigham Young University (UT); Anne Clark, St. Cloud State University (MN); Gladys Cleland, SUNY Morrisville (NY); Joanne Clements, University of Rochester Medical School (NY); Cheryl Cobb, Tidewater Community College (VA); Jill Coe, Southwest Texas Junior College; Tammy Conard-Salvo, Purdue University (IA); Magana Conception, Gar-

den City Community College (KS); Linda Conra, Curry College
(MA); Trish Conrad, Hutchinson Community College (KS); Linda
Conway, Howard College (TX); Cheryl Corbiell, Maui Community
College (HI); Jennifer Courtney-Pooler, University of North Car-
olina, Charlotte; Julie Cox, University of California, Santa Cruz;
Michelle Cox, University of New Hampshire; Donna Craine, Front
Range Community College/Westminster (CO); Delmas Crisp, Wes-
leyan College (GA); Beth Crookston, Stark State College of Tech-
nology (OH); Pam Cross, Stockton State College (NJ); Eileen
Crowe, University of North Carolina, Asheville; Debbie Cunning-
ham, Adams State College (CO); Stephen Curley, Texas A&M,
Galveston; Billye Currie, Samford University (AL); Sarah Curtis,
Consumnes River College (CA); Christopher Dainele, Massachu-
setts Bay Community College; Helen Dale, University of Wiscon-
sin, Eau Claire; Sarah Dangelantonio, Franklin Pierce College
(NH); Cynthia Davidson, SUNY Stony Brook (NY); Matthew Davis,
University of Puget Sound (WA); Sister Mary Davlin, Dominican
University (IL); Mary De Nys, George Mason University (VA); Ann
Dean, University of Southern Maine, Portland; Deborah Dean,
Brigham Young University (UT); Renee Dechert, Northwest Col-
lege (WY); Jeffrey Decker, University of California, Los Angeles;
Margie Dernaika, Southwest Tennessee Community College;
Kathryn De Zur, SUNY Delhi (NY); Kristen di Gennaro, Pace Uni-
versity (NY); Theresa Dolan, Los Angeles Trade Technical College
(CA); Lynn Domina, SUNY Delhi (NY); Patricia Don, San Jose
State University (CA); Cecilia Donohue, Madonna University (MI);
Tony D'Souza, Shasta College (CA); Deb Dusek, North Dakota
State College of Science; Chitralekha Duttagupta, Arizona State
University; Scott Earle, Tacoma Community College (WA); Marie
Eckstrom, Rio Hondo College (CA); Martha Edmonds, University of
Richmond (VA); Richard Eichman, Sauk Valley Community College
(IL); Mary Ellen, University of North Carolina, Charlotte; Lynette
Emanuel, Wisconsin Indianhead Technical Institute; Charlene En-
gleking, Lindenwood University (MO); Bill Eppright, Northwestern
College (MN); Douglas Eyman, Michigan State University; Deanna
Fassett, San Jose State University (CA); Deborah Fleming, Ash-
land University (OH); John Fleming, De Anza College (CA);
Maryann Fleming-McCall, Atlantic Cape Community College (NJ);
Jessica Fordham Kidd, University of Alabama; P. Forson-Williams,
McDaniel College (MD); Deanna Foster, Lassen College (CA); Bon-
nie Fox, D'Youville College (NY); Catherine Fraga, California State
University, Sacramento; Martha Francescato, George Mason Uni-
versity (VA); Michael Frank, Bentley College (MA); Traci Freeman,
University of Colorado, Colorado Springs; Christina French, Diablo
Valley College (CA); Steve Frogge, Missouri Western State Univer-
sity; Jacqueline Fulmer, University of California, Berkeley; Karen
Gardiner, University of Alabama; Wayne Garrett, Lipscomb University (TN); Susan Garrett, McDaniel College (MD); Steven

Gehring, SUNY Stony Brook (NY); Dennis Geisler, Columbia College (MO); Gina Genova, University of California, Santa Barbara; James Gifford, Mohawk Valley Community College (NY); Jane Gilligan, Assumption College (MA); Susan Gimprich, Fairleigh Dickinson University (NJ); Tracey Glaessgen, Southwest Missouri State University; Norman Golar, University of Alabama; Bertrand Goldgar, Lawrence University (WI); Amy Goodwin, Randolph-Macon College (VA); Ricia Gordon, Landmark College (VT); Rebecca Gorman, Metropolitan State College of Denver (CO); William Gorski, West Los Angeles College (CA); Susan Gorsky, University of California, Santa Cruz; Gwen Gray Schwartz, University of Arizona; Robert Greenwald, Dominican University (IL); Katie Guest, University of North Carolina, Greensboro; Max Guggenhiemer, Lynchburg College (VA); Diana Gyler, Azusa Pacific University (CA); Joan Haahr, Yeshiva University (NY); Thomas Hackett, CUNY Brooklyn College (NY); Michelle Halbach, Widener University (DE); Susan Halio, Long Island University, Brooklyn (NY); Peggy Hamilton, San Joaquin Delta College (CA); Robin Hammerman, Stevens Institute of Technology (NJ); Kathleen Hammond, Brookdale Community College (NJ); Jefferson Hancock, Cabrillo College (CA); Heidi Hanrahan, University of North Carolina, Greensboro; Katie Hanson, Augustana College (IL); John Hanvey, Barry University (FL); Lisa Harbo, University of Alaska, Fairbanks; Gloria Hardy, Saint John's University (MN); Eunice Hargett, Broward Community College, Central (FL); Mitchell Harris, University of Texas; Terese Hartman, Lynchburg College (VA); Kip Hartvigsen, Brigham Young University, Idaho; Lisa Hastings, Delaware Technical and Community College; Gary Hatch, Brigham Young University (UT); Nancy Hayward, Indiana University of Pennsylvania; Shelly Hedstrom, Palm Beach Community College (FL); Ruth Heller, Eastern Connecticut State University; Diane Henningfeld, Adrian College (MI); Bridgette Henry, University of Missouri, Kansas City; Patricia Henshaw, Sacramento City College (CA); Leah Herman, Pitzer College (CA); Kathleen Hickey, Dominican University (NY); Sharon Hileman, Sul Ross State University (TX); Cheryl Hill, Nova Southeastern University (FL); Vicki Hill, Brewton-Parker College (GA); Lisa Hodgens, Piedmont College (GA); Kathleen Hoffman, Cambridge Community College (MN); John Hogwood, Wayland Baptist University (TX); Deborah Holler, Empire State College (NY); Camille Lee Hornbeck, Tarrant County Community College (TX); Alice Horning, Oakland University (CA); Tai Houser, Broward Community College, North (FL); James Hunter, Gonzaga University (WA); Michael Hustedde, St. Ambrose University (IA); Marie Iglesias-Cardinale, Genessee Community College (NY); Robin Inboden, Wittenberg University (OH); Alyson Indrunas, Everett Community College (WA); James Inman, University of Tennessee, Chattanooga; Sherri Inness, Miami University, Hamilton (OH); Ginger Irwin, Colgate University (NY); James

Isbell, Santiago Canyon College (CA); Kathy Ivey, Lenoir-Rhyne College (NC); Lisa Jackson, University of North Texas; Ian Jacobs, New School University (NY); Dawnelle Jager, Syracuse University (NY); Glenda James, Calhoun State Community College (AL); Susan James, Curry College (MA); Mary Jo Stirling, Santa Monica College (CA); Carol Johnson, Virginia Wesleyan College; Sue Johnson, Sierra College (CA); Nancy Johnson Squaire, Sheridan College (WY); Jennifer Jones, University of Colorado, Boulder; Jay Jordan, Pennsylvania State University; Paul Juhasz, Tarrant County Community College (TX); Demetrios Kapetanakos, Queensborough Community College (NY); Elizabeth Katz, University of New Mexico; Janet Kay, Leeward Community College (HI); Laura Kay, John F. Kennedy University (CA); Joshua Keels, Community College of Vermont, Burlington; Elizabeth Keifer, Tunxis Community College (CT); Sue Keith, Guilford College (NC); Roberta Kelly, Washington State University; Gilda Kelsey, University of Delaware; Jan Kinch, Edinboro University of Pennsylvania; Lola King, Trinity Valley Community College (TX); Liz Kleinfeld, Red Rocks Community College (CO); Matt Kozusko, Ursinus College (PA); Carrie Krantz-Fischer, Washtenaw Community College (MI); Michelle Ladd, California State University, Los Angeles; Gina Ladinsky, Santa Monica College (CA); Lauren LaFauci, University of Michigan, Ann Arbor; John Lang, Emory and Henry College (VA); Margaret Lattimore, Gardner-Webb University (NC); Sally Lavender, Lipscomb University (TN); Joe Law, Wright State University (OH); Amy Lawlor, Pasadena City College (CA); Robert Lawrence, Jefferson Community College (KY); Kathleen Lazarus, Daytona Beach Community College (FL); Andria Leduc, Open Learning Agency (BC); Catharine Lee, Wesleyan College (GA); Michelle Lee, Minnesota State University; Kathy LeGrand, Olympic Heights High School (FL); Lindsay Lewan, Arapahoe Community College (CO); James Livingston, Northern Michigan University; Alice Longaker, University of Northern Colorado; Sonia Maasik, University of California, Los Angeles; Joan Maiers, Marylhurst University (OR); Ceil Malek, University of Colorado, Colorado Springs; Lisa Mallory, Atlanta Metropolitan College (GA); Ajuan Mance, Mills College (CA); Kate Mangelsdorf, University of Texas, El Paso; Travis Mann, Tarrant County Community College (TX); Nicole Marafioti, Cornell University (NY); Annette March, California State University, Monterey Bay; Pete Marcoux, El Camino Community College (CA); Barbara Martin, University of Cincinnati (OH); Joann Martin, Wisconsin Indianhead Technical Institute; Elizabeth Martinez, University of Connecticut; David Maruyama, Long Beach City College (CA); Pat Mathias, Itasca Community College (MN); Leanne Maunu, Palomar Community College (CA); Jennifer McCann, Bay de Noc Community College (MI); Barbara McClain, Contra Costa College (CA); Julia McGregor, Inver Hills Community College (MN); Andrea McKenzie, New York University; James McLaughlin, Master's College and Seminary (CA); Sara McLaughlin, Texas Technical University; Vicky Melograno, Atlantic Cape Community College (NJ); Agnetta Mendoza, Nashville State Technical Community College (TN); Gayle Mercer, Southwest Missouri State; Carol Messing, Northwood University (MI); Allan Metcalf, MacMurray College (IL); Donna Metcalf, Springfield College (IL); Steve Michael, Wayland Baptist University (TX); Marlene Michels, Mid Michigan Community College; Ilene Miele, University of California, Santa Barbara; David Miller, Victor Valley College (CA); Jack Miller, Normandale Community College (MN); Ruth Miller, University of Louisville (KY); Wendy Moffat, Dickinson College (PA); Scott Moncrieff, Andrews University (MI); Jayne Moneysmith, Kent State University (OH); Bryan Moore, Arkansas State University, Main Campus; Matthew Moore, Roberts Wesleyan College (NY); Robert Morace, Daemen College (NY); Dan Morgan, Scott Community College, Bettendorf (IA); Jennifer Morrison, Niagara University (NY); Gala Muench, North Idaho College (ID); Terry Muller, Cambridge College (MA); Deborah Mutnick, Long Island University, Brooklyn (NY); Linda Myers, California State University, Sacramento; Lyndall Nairn, Lynchburg College (VA); James Nash, Montclair State University (NJ); Michelle Nash, Union College (NE); Claire Nava, California State University, Fullerton; Jeffrey Nelson, University of Alabama; Stephen Newmann, Montgomery College, Germantown (MD); Corrine Nicolas, Tusculum College (TN); Jennifer Niester, Central Michigan University; Sylvia Nosworthy, Walla Walla College (WA); Catherine O'Callaghan, Community College of Vermont, Brattleboro; David Okamura-Wilson, East Carolina University (NC); Ben Opipari, Colgate College (NY); Scott Orme, Spokane Community College (WA); Christina Ortmeier-Hooper, University of New Hampshire; Mary O'Sullivan, Western Wisco Technical College (WI); Liz Parker, Nashville State Technical Community College (TN); Allison Parker, Southeastern Community College (NC); M. Elizabeth Parker, Nashville State Technical Community College (TN); Joanne Parsons, Eastern Oregon University (OR); Karen Pass, Empire State College (NY); Mary Pat, Dominican University (IL); David Paul, SUNY Morrisville (NY); Craig Payne, Indian Hills Community College (IA); Tammy Peery, Montgomery College, Germantown (MD); Myra Perry, University of North Carolina, Charlotte; Todd Petersen, Southern Utah University; Stephen Petrina, University of British Columbia; Diane Philen, Sinte Gleska University (SD); Christine Pipitone-Herron, Raritan Valley Community College (NJ); Susan Piqueira, Tunxis Community College (CT); Neil Placky, Broward Community College-South (FL); Faith Plvan, Syracuse University (NY); Robert Prescott, Bradley University (IL); Mary Lou Price, University of Texas, Austin; Ben Rafoth, Indiana University of Pennsylvania; Anniqua Rana, Canada College (CA); Vanessa Rasmussen, Rider University (NJ); Kokila Ravi, Atlanta Metropolitan College (GA);

Susan Regan, Cloud County Community College (KS); Paul Reid, Chippewa Valley Technical College (WI); Steven Reynolds, College of the Siskiyous (CA); Angela Ricciardi, Plymouth State College (NH); Clai Rice, University of Louisiana, Lafayette; Jeff Rice, Wayne State University (MI); Aaron Ritzenberg, Brandeis University (MA); Marilyn Roberts, Waynesburg College (PA); Lourdes Rodriguez-Florido, Broward Community College South (FL); Timothy Rogers, Furman University (SC); Teri Rosen, CUNY Hunter College (NY); Michelle Ross, Indiana University (IN); Deborah Rossen-Knill, University of Rochester (NY); Jennifer Rosti, Roanoke College (VA); Henry Ruminski, Wright State University (OH); Carol Russo, SUNY Stony Brook (NY); Leigh Ryan, University of Maryland; Kristen Salsbury, University of California, Irvine; Art Saltzmann, Missouri Southern State University; Mark Sanders, Three Rivers Community College (MO); Mark Sanford, Suffolk University (MA); Lilia Savova, Indiana University of Pennsylvania; Elizabeth Sawin, Missouri Western State University; Suzy Sayre, Towson University (MD); Bret Scaliter, Crafton Hills College (CA); Sandra Scheller, Wayland Baptist University (TX); Sandra Schroeder, Yakima Valley College (WA); Holly Schullo, University of Louisiana, Lafayette; Gloria Scott, Towson University (MD); Laine Scott, La Grange College (GA); Aparna Screenivasan, California State University, Monterey Bay; Michael Sewell, Wayland Baptist University (TX); Jolly Sharp, Cumberland College (KY); Meighan Sharp, Emory and Henry College (VA); Amy Sheldon, SUNY Geneseo (NY); Brandi Shelton, Nashville State Technical Community College (TN); Suzanne Shepard, Broome Community College (NY); Jean Sheridan, University of Southern Maine, Portland; John Silva, LaGuardia Community College (NY); Mary Beth Simmons, Villanova University (PA); Michele Singletary, Nashville State Technical Community College (TN); Beverly Six, Sul Ross State University (TX); Greta Skogseth, Montcalm Community College (MI); Bonnie Smith, Belmont University (TN); Mary Lou Smith, Alexandria Technical University (MN); Sally Smith, Alexandria Technical University (MN); Sean Smith, Ivy Technical Sate College (IN); James Southerland, Brenau College (GA); Sis Spencer, Trinidad State Junior College (CO); Barbara Steele, Towson University (MD); Sharon Steinberg, Tunxis Community College (CT); Lisa Steinman, Reed College (OR); Shari Stenberg, Creighton University (NE); Rebecca Suarez, University of Texas, El Paso; Jo Suzuki, Master's College and Seminary (CA); Kristine Swenson, University of Missouri, Rolla; Peggy Szczesniak, Genessee Community College (NY); Cynthia Taber, Schenectady County Community College (NY); Dean Taciuch, George Mason University (VA); Marguerite Tassi, University of Nebraska, Kearney; Lisa Terasa, Mount Mary College (WI); Matt Theado, Gardner-Webb University (NC); Catherine Thomas, College of Charleston (SC); Cliff Toliver, Missouri Southern State University; Jill Tucker,

San Diego Miramar College (CA); Anita Turpin, Roanoke College (VA); Pat Tyrer, West Texas A&M University; Wanda Umber, Wayland Baptist University (TX); Kim Van Alkamade, Shippensburg University (PA); Thomas Varner, J. Sargeant Reynolds Community College (VA); Angela Vogel, John Tyler Community College (VA); Michelle Von Euw, University of Maryland; Peter Vose, Falmouth High School (ME); Elizabeth Wagoner, Kent State University (OH); Ralph Wahlstrom, SUNY Buffalo (NY); Shelton Waldrep, University of Southern Maine; Teri Waters, Waubonsee Community College (IL); Pamela Watkins, Los Angeles Harbor Community College (CA); Cindy Welch, Carthage College (WI); Vicky Westacott, Alfred University (NY); Jennifer Whetham, Greenriver Community College (WA); Anne Whitney, University of California, Santa Barbara; John Wiltbank, Tidewater Community College (VA); Barbara Winborn, Asbury College (KY); Rosemary Winslow, Catholic University of America (DC); Kelli Wood-Mancha, El Paso Community College (TX); Michael Woodruff, Hargrave Military Academy (VA); Donna Y. Smith, Wayland Baptist University (OK); Ann Yearick, Radford University (VA); Julie Yen, California State University, Sacramento; Jonathan Ying, Cornell University (NY); Joann Yost, Bethel University (MN); Ben Young, Oregon State University; Michael Young, La Roche College (PA); Laura Zam, George Mason University (VA); Robbin Zeff, George Washington University (DC); Trudy Zimmerman, Hutchinson Community College (KS)

Student contributors

We are indebted to the students whose essays appear in this edition — Ned Bishop, Anna Orlov, Emilia Sanchez, Jamal Hammond, and Luisa Mirano — not only for permission to use their work but also for allowing us to adapt it for pedagogical purposes. Our thanks also go to the students who granted permission to use their paragraphs: Rosa Broderick, Connie Hailey, Craig Lee Hetherington, Kathleen Lewis, Laurie McDonough, Kevin Smith, Margaret Smith, Margaret Stack, and David Warren.

C

Composing and Revising

C Composing and Revising

Writing is not a matter of recording already developed thoughts but a process of figuring out what you think. Since it's not possible to think about everything all at once, most experienced writers handle a piece of writing in stages. You will generally move from planning to drafting to revising, but be prepared to return to earlier stages as your ideas develop.

C1

Planning

C1-a Assess the writing situation.

Begin by taking a look at the writing situation in which you find yourself. Consider your subject, the sources of information available to you, your purpose, your audience, and constraints such as length, document design, review sessions, and deadlines or other assignment requirements. It is likely that you will make final decisions about all of these matters later in the writing process — after a first draft, for example. Nevertheless, you can save yourself time by thinking about as many of them as possible in advance. For a quick checklist, see page 5.

> ACADEMIC ENGLISH What counts as good writing varies from culture to culture and even among groups within cultures. In some situations, you will need to become familiar with the writing styles — such as direct or indirect, personal or impersonal, plain or embellished—that are valued by the culture or discourse community for which you are writing.

C1-b Experiment with ways to explore your subject.

Instead of just plunging into a first draft, experiment with one or more techniques for exploring your subject — perhaps talking and listening, annotating texts and taking notes, listing, clustering, freewriting, or asking the journalist's questions. Whatever technique you turn to, the goal is the same: to generate a wealth of ideas that will lead you to a question, a problem, or an issue that you want to explore further. At this early stage of the writing process, don't censor yourself. Sometimes an idea that initially seems trivial or far-fetched will turn out to be worthwhile.

3

Understanding an assignment

Determining the purpose of the assignment

Usually the wording of an assignment will suggest its purpose. You might be expected to do one of the following:

- summarize information from textbooks, lectures, or research
- analyze ideas and concepts
- take a position on a topic and defend it with evidence
- create an original argument by combining ideas from different sources

Understanding how to answer an assignment's questions

Many assignments will ask a *how* or *why* question. Such a question cannot be answered using only facts; you will need to take a position. For example, the question "*What* are the survival rates for leukemia patients?" can be answered by reporting facts. The question "*Why* are the survival rates for leukemia patients in one state lower than in a neighboring state?" must be answered with both facts and interpretation.

If a list of prompts appears in the assignment, be careful — instructors rarely expect you to answer all of the questions in order. Look instead for topics, themes, or ideas that will help you ask your own questions.

Recognizing implied questions

When an assignment asks you to *discuss, analyze, agree or disagree,* or *consider* a topic, your instructor will often expect you to answer a *how* or *why* question. For example, "*Discuss* the effects of the No Child Left Behind Act on special education programs" is another way of saying "*How* has the No Child Left Behind Act affected special education programs?" Similarly, the assignment "*Consider* the recent rise of attention deficit hyperactivity disorder diagnoses" is asking you to answer the question "*Why* are diagnoses of attention deficit hyperactivity disorder rising?"

ON THE WEB > dianahacker.com/writersref
  Writing exercises > E-ex C1–1

ON THE WEB > dianahacker.com/writersref
  Additional resources > Links Library > The writing process

Checklist for assessing the writing situation

Subject

- Has a subject (or a range of possible subjects) been given to you, or are you free to choose your own?
- What interests you about your subject? What questions would you like to explore?
- How broadly can you cover the subject? Do you need to narrow it to a more specific topic (because of length restrictions, for instance)?

Sources of information

- Where will your information come from: Reading? Personal experience? Direct observation? Interviews? Questionnaires?
- What sort of documentation is required?

Purpose and audience

- Why are you writing: To inform readers? To persuade them? To entertain them? To call them to action? Some combination of these?
- Who are your readers? How well informed are they about your subject? How will they benefit from reading your work?
- How interested and attentive are your readers? Will they care about your purpose? Will they resist any of your ideas?
- What is your relationship to them: Student to instructor? Employee to supervisor? Citizen to citizen? Expert to novice? Scholar to scholar?

Length and document design

- Do you have any length specifications? If not, what length seems appropriate, given your subject, purpose, and audience?
- Must you use a particular format for your document? If so, do you have guidelines to follow or examples to consult?

Reviewers and deadlines

- Who will be reviewing your draft in progress: Your instructor? A writing center tutor? Your classmates? A friend? Someone in your family?
- What are your deadlines? How much time will you need to allow for the various stages of writing, including proofreading and printing the final draft?

Talking and listening

Since writing is a process of figuring out what you think about a subject, it can be useful to try out your ideas on other people. Conversation can deepen and refine your ideas before you even begin to set them down on paper. By talking and listening to others, you can also discover what they find interesting, what they are curious about, and where they disagree with you. If you are planning to advance an argument, you can try it out on listeners with other points of view.

Many writers begin by brainstorming ideas in a group, debating a point with friends, or chatting with an instructor. Others turn to themselves for company — by talking into a tape recorder. Some writers exchange ideas by sending e-mails or instant messages, by joining an Internet chat group, or by following a mailing list discussion. If you are part of a networked classroom, you may be encouraged to share ideas with others in an electronic workshop. For example, a student who participated in the following chat was able to refine her argument before she started drafting her essay on presidential campaign funding.

CONVERSATION ABOUT A SUBJECT

Bay State University - Bay State University - Bay State University - Bay State

 The Composition Chat Room

User Name:

Password:

Log In

Forgot your
password?

Help

Quit

Chat Message:

Submit

Mia Borek: My paper is about presidential elections, but I'm not sure where to go next.
Alex Wu: What ideas do you have?
Mia Borek: I've never understood why the government doesn't just pay for the whole presidential campaign.
Alex Wu: Wouldn't that end up costing taxpayers a lot?
Mia Borek: Maybe. But taxes already fund government services like meals programs and road maintenance. Why shouldn't tax money pay for us to get information about presidential candidates?
Alex Wu: Maybe you could interview some taxpayers and see what they think.

There are **2** users logged on.

Annotating texts

When you write about reading, one of the best ways to explore ideas is to mark up the work — on the pages themselves if you own the work, on photocopies or sticky notes if you don't. Annotating a text encourages you to look at it more carefully — to underline key concepts, to note possible contradictions in an argument, to raise questions for further investigation. Here, for example, is a paragraph from an essay on medical ethics as one student annotated it:

What break-
throughs?
Do all break-
throughs have
the same
consequences?

Is everyone
really uneasy?
Is something a
breakthrough if
it creates a
predicament?

Breakthroughs in genetics present us with a promise and a predicament. The promise is that we may soon be able to treat and prevent a host of debilitating diseases. The predicament is that our newfound genetic knowledge may also enable us to manipulate our own nature — to enhance our muscles, memories, and moods; to choose the sex, height, and other genetic traits of our children; to make ourselves "better than well." When science moves faster than moral understanding as it does today, men and women struggle to articulate their unease. In liberal societies they reach first for the language of autonomy, fairness, and individual rights. But this part of our moral vocabulary is ill equipped to address the hardest questions posed by genetic engineering. The genomic revolution has induced a kind of moral vertigo.

— Michael Sandel, "The Case against Perfection"

Stem cell
research?

What does he
mean by "moral
understanding"?

Which ques-
tions? He
doesn't seem to
be taking sides.

Listing

Listing ideas is a good way to figure out what you know and what questions you have. You might simply write ideas in the order in which they occur to you — a technique sometimes known as *brainstorming*. Here is a list one student writer jotted down for an essay about funding for college athletics:

Football receives the most funding of any sport.

Funding comes from ticket sales, fundraisers, alumni contributions.

Biggest women's sport is soccer.

Women's soccer team is only ten years old; football team is fifty years old.

Football graduates have had time to earn more money than soccer graduates.

Soccer games don't draw as many fans.

Should funding be equal for all teams?

Do alumni have the right to fund whatever they want?

Feel free to rearrange ideas, to group them under general categories, to delete some, and to add others. In other words, treat the initial list as a source of ideas and a springboard to new ideas, not as an outline.

Clustering

Unlike listing, the technique of clustering highlights relationships among ideas. To cluster ideas, write your topic in the center of a sheet of paper, draw a circle around it, and surround that circle with related ideas connected to it with lines. If some of the satellite ideas lead to more specific clusters, write them down as well. The writer of the following cluster diagram was exploring ideas for an essay on obesity in children.

CLUSTER DIAGRAM

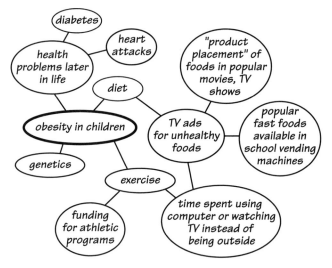

ON THE WEB > dianahacker.com/writersref
Resources for writers and tutors > Tips from writing tutors:
Invention strategies

Freewriting

In its purest form, freewriting is simply nonstop writing. You set aside ten minutes or so and write whatever comes to you, without pausing to think about word choice, spelling, or even meaning. If you get stuck, you can write about being stuck, but you should keep your fingers moving. If nothing much happens, you have lost only ten minutes. It's more likely, though, that something interesting will emerge — an eloquent sentence, an honest expression of feeling, or an idea worth further investigation. To explore ideas on a particular topic, consider using a technique called *focused freewriting*. Again, you write quickly and freely, but this time you focus on a subject and pay attention to the connections among your ideas.

Asking the journalist's questions

By asking relevant questions, you can generate many ideas — and you can make sure that you have adequately surveyed your subject. When gathering material for a story, journalists routinely ask themselves Who? What? When? Where? Why? and How? In addition to helping journalists get started, these questions ensure that they will not overlook an important fact: the date of a prospective summit meeting, for example, or the exact location of a burglary.

Whenever you are writing about events, whether current or historical, asking the journalist's questions is one way to get started. One student, whose subject was the negative reaction in 1915 to D. W. Griffith's silent film *The Birth of a Nation*, began exploring her topic with this set of questions:

Who objected to the film?

What were the objections?

When were the protests first voiced?

Where were protests most strongly expressed?

Why did protesters object to the film?

How did protesters make their views known?

In the academic world, scholars often generate ideas with questions related to a specific discipline: one set of questions for analyzing short stories, another for evaluating experiments in social psychology, still another for reporting field experiences in anthropology. If you are writing in a particular discipline, try to discover the questions that its scholars typically explore (see A4).

C1-c Formulate a tentative thesis.

As you explore your subject and identify questions you would like to investigate, you will begin to see possible ways to focus your material. At this point, try to settle on a tentative central idea. The more complex your topic, the more your focus will change as your drafts evolve.

For many types of writing, you will be able to assert your central idea in a sentence or two. Such a statement, which ordinarily appears in the opening paragraph of your finished essay, is called a *thesis* (see also C2-a). A thesis is often the answer to a question, the resolution of a problem, or a statement that takes a position on a debatable topic. A successful thesis — like the following, all taken from articles in *Smithsonian* magazine — points both the writer and the reader in a definite direction.

> Much maligned and the subject of unwarranted fears, most bats are harmless and highly beneficial.

> The American Revolution was the central event in Washington's life, the crucible for his development as a mature man, a prominent statesman, and a national hero.

> Raging in mines from Pennsylvania to China, coal fires threaten towns, poison air and water, and add to global warming.

The thesis sentence usually contains a key word or controlling idea that limits its focus. The first two example sentences, for instance, use key words to prepare for essays that focus on the *beneficial* aspects of bats and the role of the American Revolution in the *development* of George Washington. The third example uses a controlling idea: the *effects* of coal fires.

It's a good idea to formulate a tentative thesis early in the writing process, perhaps by jotting it on scratch paper, by putting it at the head of a rough outline, or by drafting an introductory paragraph that includes it. This tentative thesis will help you shape your thoughts. Don't worry about the exact wording because your main point may change as you refine your ideas. Here, for example, is one student's early effort:

> In *Rebel without a Cause*, the protagonist, Jim Stark, is often seen literally on the edge of physical danger — walking too close to the swimming pool, leaning over an observation deck, and driving his car toward a cliff.

The thesis that appeared in the student's final draft not only was more polished but also reflected the evolution of the student's ideas.

Testing a tentative thesis

- Is the thesis too obvious? If you cannot come up with interpretations that oppose your own, consider revising your thesis.
- Can you support your thesis with the evidence available?
- Does the thesis require an essay's worth of development? Or will you run out of points too quickly?
- Can you explain why readers will want to read an essay with this thesis?

The scenes in which Jim Stark is seen on the edge of physical danger — walking too close to the swimming pool, leaning over an observation deck, driving his car toward a cliff — suggest that he is becoming more and more agitated by the constraints of family and society.

For a more detailed discussion of thesis, see C2-a.

C1-d Sketch a plan.

Once you have generated some ideas and formulated a tentative thesis, you might want to sketch an informal outline to see how you will support your thesis and to begin to structure your ideas. Informal outlines can take many forms. Perhaps the most common is simply the thesis followed by a list of major ideas.

Thesis: Television advertising should be regulated to help prevent childhood obesity.

- Children watch more television than ever.
- Snacks marketed to children are often unhealthy and fattening.
- Childhood obesity can cause diabetes and other health problems.
- Solving these health problems costs taxpayers billions of dollars.
- Therefore, these ads are actually costing the public money.
- But if advertising is free speech, do we have the right to regulate it?
- We regulate liquor and cigarette ads on television, so why not advertising aimed at children?

If you began by jotting down a list of ideas or drawing a clustering diagram, you may be able to turn that list or diagram into a rough outline by crossing out some ideas, adding others, and putting the ideas in a logical order.

When to use a formal outline

Early in the writing process, rough outlines have certain advantages over their more formal counterparts: They can be produced more quickly, they are more obviously tentative, and they can be revised more easily should the need arise. However, a formal outline may be useful later in the writing process, after you have written a rough draft, especially if your subject matter is complex.

The following formal outline brought order to the research paper that appears in MLA-5b, on Internet surveillance in the workplace. Notice that the student's thesis is an important part of the outline. Everything else in the outline supports it, directly or indirectly.

Thesis: Although companies often have legitimate concerns that lead them to monitor employees' Internet usage — from expensive security breaches to reduced productivity — the benefits of electronic surveillance are outweighed by its costs to employees' privacy and autonomy.

  I. Although employers have always monitored employees, electronic surveillance is more efficient.
    A. Employers can gather data in large quantities.
    B. Electronic surveillance can be continuous.
    C. Electronic surveillance can be conducted secretly, with keystroke logging programs.

 II. Some experts argue that employers have legitimate reasons to monitor employees' Internet usage.
    A. Unmonitored employees could accidentally breach security.
    B. Companies are legally accountable for online actions of employees.

III. Despite valid concerns, employers should value employee morale and autonomy and avoid creating an atmosphere of distrust.
    A. Setting the boundaries for employee autonomy is difficult in the wired workplace.
      1. Using the Internet is the most popular way of wasting time at work.
      2. Employers can't tell easily if employees are working or surfing the Web.
    B. Surveillance can create resentment among employees.
      1. Web surfing can relieve stress, and restricting it can generate tension between managers and workers.
      2. Enforcing Internet usage can seem arbitrary.

IV. Surveillance may not increase employee productivity, and trust may benefit it.

   A. It shouldn't matter to the company how many hours salaried employees work as long as they get the job done.

   B. Casual Internet use can actually benefit companies.

      1. The Internet may spark business ideas.

      2. The Internet may suggest ideas about how to operate more efficiently.

V. Employees' rights to privacy are not well defined by the law.

   A. Few federal guidelines exist on electronic surveillance.

   B. Employers and employees are negotiating the boundaries without legal guidance.

   C. As technological capabilities increase, there will be an increased need to define boundaries.

Guidelines for constructing an outline

1. Put the thesis at the top.

2. Make items at the same level of generality as parallel as possible (see S1).

3. Use sentences unless phrases are clear.

4. Use the conventional system of numbers and letters for the levels of generality.

   I.

      A.

      B.

         1.

         2.

            a.

            b.

   II.

5. Always use at least two subdivisions for a category, since nothing can be divided into fewer than two parts.

6. Limit the number of major sections in the outline; if the list of roman numerals begins to look like a laundry list, find some way of clustering the items into a few major categories with more subcategories.

7. Be flexible; in other words, be prepared to change your outline as your drafts evolve.

C2

Drafting

As you rough out an initial draft, focus your attention on ideas and organization. You can think about sentence structure and word choice later. Writing tends to flow better when it is drafted relatively quickly, without many stops and starts. Keep your prewriting materials — lists, outlines, freewriting, and so on — close at hand. In addition to helping you get started, such notes and blueprints will encourage you to keep moving.

For most kinds of writing, an introduction announces the main point, the body paragraphs develop it, and the conclusion drives it home. You can begin drafting, however, at any point. If you find it difficult to introduce a paper that you have not yet written, try drafting the body first and saving the introduction for later.

ON THE WEB > dianahacker.com/writersref
Resources for writers and tutors > Tips from writing tutors:
Writing introductions and conclusions

C2-a For most types of writing, draft an introduction that includes a thesis.

Your introduction will usually be a paragraph of 50 to 150 words (in a longer paper, it may be more than one paragraph). Perhaps the most common strategy is to open the paragraph with a few sentences that engage the reader, establish your purpose for writing, and conclude with your main point. The sentence stating the main point is called a *thesis*. (See also C1-c.) In the following examples, the thesis has been italicized.

> Credit card companies love to extend credit to college students, especially those just out of high school. Ads for credit cards line campus bulletin boards, flash across commercial Web sites for students, and get stuffed into shopping bags at college bookstores. Why do the companies market their product so vigorously to a population that lacks a substantial credit history and often has no steady source of income? The answer is that significant profits can be earned through high interest rates and assorted penalties and fees. *By granting college students liberal lending arrangements, credit card companies often hook them on a cycle of spending that can ultimately lead to financial ruin.* — Matt Watson, student

As the United States industrialized in the nineteenth century, using desperate immigrant labor, social concerns took a backseat to the task of building a prosperous nation. The government did not regulate industries and did not provide an effective safety net for the poor or for those who became sick or injured on the job. Luckily, immigrants and the poor did have a few advocates. Settlement houses such as Hull-House in Chicago provided information, services, and a place for reform-minded individuals to gather and work to improve the conditions of the urban poor. Alice Hamilton was one of these reformers. *Hamilton's efforts helped to improve the lives of immigrants and drew attention and respect to the problems and people that until then had been virtually ignored.*

— Laurie McDonough, student

Ideally, the sentences leading to the thesis should hook the reader, perhaps with one of the following:

a startling statistic, an unusual fact, or a vivid example

a paradoxical statement

a quotation or a bit of dialogue

a question

an analogy

an anecdote

Whether you are writing for a scholarly audience, a professional audience, or a general audience, you cannot assume your readers' interest in the topic. The hook should spark curiosity and offer readers a reason to continue reading.

Although the thesis frequently appears at the end of the introduction, it can also appear at the beginning. Much work-related writing, in which a straightforward approach is most effective, commonly begins with the thesis.

Flextime scheduling, which has proved its effectiveness at the Library of Congress, should be introduced on a trial basis at the main branch of the Montgomery County Public Library. By offering flexible work hours, the library can boost employee morale, cut down on absenteeism, and expand its hours of operation.

— David Warren, student

For some types of writing, it may be difficult or impossible to express the central idea in a thesis sentence; or it may be unwise or unnecessary to put a thesis sentence in the essay itself. A personal narrative, for example, may have a focus too subtle to be distilled in a single sentence, and such a sentence might ruin the story. Strictly informative writing, like that found in many business memos, may be difficult to summarize in a thesis. In such instances, do not try to force the central idea into a thesis sentence. Instead, think in terms of an overriding purpose, which may or may not be stated directly.

ACADEMIC ENGLISH If you come from a culture that prefers an indirect approach in writing, you may feel that asserting a thesis early in an essay sounds unrefined or even rude. In the United States, however, readers appreciate a direct approach; when you state your point as directly as possible, you show that you value your readers' time.

Characteristics of an effective thesis

An effective thesis sentence is a central idea that requires supporting evidence; it is of adequate scope for an essay of the assigned length; and it is sharply focused.

A thesis must require proof or further development through facts and details; it cannot itself be a fact or a description.

TOO FACTUAL   The polygraph was developed by Dr. John A. Larson in 1921.

REVISED   Because the polygraph has not been proved reliable, even under controlled conditions, its use by employers should be banned.

A thesis should be of sufficient scope for your assignment, not too broad and not too narrow. Unless you are writing a book or a very long research paper, the following thesis is too broad.

TOO BROAD   Mapping the human genome has many implications for health and science.

REVISED   Although scientists can now detect genetic predisposition to specific diseases, not everyone should be tested for these diseases.

A thesis should be sharply focused, not too vague. Avoid fuzzy, hard-to-define words such as *interesting, good,* or *disgusting.*

TOO VAGUE   The way the TV show *ER* portrays doctors and nurses is interesting.

REVISED   In dramatizing the experiences of doctors and nurses as they treat patients, navigate medical bureaucracy, and negotiate bioethical dilemmas, the TV show *ER* portrays health care professionals as unfailingly caring and noble.

In the process of making a too-vague thesis more precise, you may find yourself outlining the major sections of your paper, as in the preceding example. This technique, known as *blueprinting*, helps readers know exactly what to expect as they read on. It also helps you, the writer, control the shape of your essay.

ON THE WEB > dianahacker.com/writersref
Writing exercises > E-ex C2–1 and C2–2

C2-b Draft the body.

The body of an essay develops support for a thesis, so it's important to have at least a tentative thesis before you start writing. What does your thesis promise readers? Try to keep your response to that question in mind as you draft the body.

If you have sketched a preliminary plan, try to block out your paragraphs accordingly. If you do not have a plan, you would be wise to pause a moment and sketch one (see C1-d). Keep in mind that often you might not know what you want to say until you have written a draft. It is possible to begin without a plan — assuming you are prepared to treat your first attempt as a "discovery draft" that will almost certainly be tossed or rewritten once you discover what you really want to say.

For more advice about paragraphs and paragraphing, see C4.

C2-c Draft a conclusion.

A conclusion should remind readers of the essay's main idea without dully repeating it. Often the concluding paragraph can be relatively short. By the end of the essay, readers should already understand your main point; your conclusion simply drives it home and, perhaps, leaves readers with something larger to consider.

In addition to echoing your main idea, a conclusion might briefly summarize the essay's key points, propose a course of action, discuss the topic's wider significance, offer advice, or pose a question for future study. To conclude an essay analyzing the shifting roles of women in the military services, one student discusses her topic's implications for society as a whole:

> As the military continues to train women in jobs formerly reserved for men, our understanding of women's roles in society will no doubt continue to change. When news reports of women

training for and taking part in combat operations become common-place, reports of women becoming CEOs, police chiefs, and even president of the United States will cease to surprise us. Or perhaps we have already reached this point. — Rosa Broderick, student

To make the conclusion memorable, you might include a detail, an example, or an image from the introduction to bring readers full circle; a quotation or a bit of dialogue; an anecdote; or a humorous or ironic comment.

Whatever concluding strategy you choose, keep in mind that an effective conclusion is decisive and unapologetic. Avoid introducing wholly new ideas at the end of an essay. Finally, because the conclusion is so closely tied to the rest of the essay in both content and tone, be prepared to rework it (or even replace it) when you revise.

C3

Revising

Revising is rarely a one-step process. Global matters — focus, purpose, organization, content, and overall strategy — generally receive attention first. Improvements in sentence structure, word choice, grammar, punctuation, and mechanics come later.

C3-a Make global revisions.

By the time you've written a draft, your ideas will probably have gone in directions you couldn't have predicted ahead of time. As a result, global revisions can be quite dramatic. It's possible, for example, that your thesis will evolve as you figure out how your ideas fit together. You might drop whole paragraphs and add others or condense material once stretched over two or three paragraphs. You might rearrange entire sections. You will save time if you handle global revisions before turning to sentence-level issues: There is little sense in revising sentences that may not appear in your final draft.

Many of us resist global revisions because we find it difficult to view our work from our audience's perspective. To distance yourself from a draft, put it aside for a while, preferably overnight or longer. When you return to it, try to play the role of your audience as you

EXAMPLE OF GLOBAL REVISIONS

Big Box Stores Aren't So Bad

In her essay <u>Big Box Stores Are Bad for Main Street</u>, Betsy Taylor shifts

the focus away from the economic effects of these stores to the effects

these stores have on the "soul" of America. She claims that stores like Home

Depot and Target are bad for America, they draw people out of downtown

shopping districts and cause them to focus exclusively on consumption. She

believes that small businesses are good for America because they provide

personal attention, foster community interaction, and make each city

different from the other ones. But Taylor's argument is not strong because it

is based on nostalgic images rather than true assumptions about the roles

that businesses play in consumers lives and communities. Taylor reveals that

she has a nostalgic view of American society and does not understand

economic realities. ~~She focuses~~ on idealized shoppers and shopkeepers

interacting on the quaint Main Streets of America ~~rather than the economic realities of the situation.~~ As a result, she incorrectly assumes that

simply getting rid of big box stores would have a positive effect on us.

For example, in her first paragraph she refers to a big box store as a

"25-acre slab of concrete with a 100,000 square foot box of stuff" that lands

on a town, evoking images of something strong and powerful conquering

something small and weak. But she oversimplifies a complex issue.

She ignores the more complex and economically driven relationship between large chain stores and the communities in which they exist.

read. If possible, enlist the help of reviewers — persons willing to read your draft, focusing on the larger issues, not on the fine points. The checklist for global revision on page 21 may help them get started.

EXAMPLE OF SENTENCE-LEVEL REVISIONS

Rethinking Big-Box Stores
~~Big Box Stores Aren't So Bad~~

In her essay "Big Box Stores Are Bad for Main Street," Betsy Taylor ~~shifts~~
focuses not on   *large chain*   *but on*
~~the focus away from~~ the economic effects of ~~these~~ stores ~~to~~ the effects these
argues
stores have on the "soul" of America. She ~~claims~~ that stores like Home Depot,
and Wal-Mart   *because*
~~and~~ Target, are bad for America ~~/~~ they draw people out of downtown shopping
In contrast, she
districts and cause them to focus exclusively on consumption. ~~She~~ believes

that small businesses are good for America because they provide personal
unique.
attention, foster community interaction, and make each city ~~different from~~
ultimately unconvincing
~~the other ones.~~ But Taylor's argument is ~~not strong~~ because it is based on
nostalgia   *images of a*
~~nostalgic images~~--on idealized ~~shoppers and shopkeepers interacting on the~~
on
quaint Main Streets ~~of America~~--rather than ~~true assumptions about~~ the roles
,   *By ignoring*
that businesses play in consumers' lives and communities. ~~She ignores~~ the

more complex, ~~and~~ economically driven relationship between large chain stores
their   *Taylor*
and ~~the~~ communities, ~~in which they exist. As a result, she~~ incorrectly assumes
America's communities.
that simply getting rid of big box stores would have a positive effect on ~~us.~~
Taylor's colorful use of language
~~Taylor~~ reveals that she has a nostalgic view of American society and does
In   *Taylor*
not understand economic realities. ~~For example, in~~ her first paragraph, ~~she~~

refers to a big box store as a "25-acre slab of concrete with a 100,000 square
a monolithic
foot box of stuff" that lands on a town, evoking images of ~~something strong~~
monster crushing the American way of life (1011).
~~and powerful conquering something small and weak.~~ But she oversimplifies

a complex issue.

TIP: When working on a computer, you might want to print out a hard copy and read the draft as a whole rather than screen by screen. Once you have decided what global revisions may be needed, the computer is an excellent tool for combining or rearranging paragraphs. With little risk, you can explore the possibilities. When a revision misfires, it is easy to return to your original draft.

ON THE WEB > dianahacker.com/writersref
  Writing exercises > E-ex C3–1

Checklist for global revision

Purpose and audience

- Does the draft accomplish its purpose — to inform readers, to persuade them, to entertain them, to call them to action?
- Is the draft appropriate for its audience? Does it account for the audience's knowledge of the subject, level of interest in the subject, and possible attitudes toward the subject?

Focus

- Is the thesis clear? Is it placed prominently? If there is no thesis, is there a good reason for omitting one?
- Do the introduction and conclusion focus clearly on the central idea?
- Are any ideas obviously off the point?

Organization and paragraphing

- Are there enough organizational cues for readers (such as topic sentences or headings)?
- Are ideas presented in a logical order?
- Are any paragraphs too long or too short for easy reading?

Content

- Is the supporting material relevant and persuasive?
- Which ideas need further development?
- Are the parts proportioned sensibly? Do major ideas receive enough attention?
- Where might material be deleted?

Point of view

- Is the draft free of distracting shifts in point of view (from *I* to *you*, for example, or from *it* to *they*)?
- Is the dominant point of view — first person (*I* or *we*), second person (*you*), or third person (*he, she, it, one*, or *they*) — appropriate for your purpose and audience? (See S4-a.)

ON THE WEB > dianahacker.com/writersref
Writing exercises > E-ex C3-2

ON THE WEB > dianahacker.com/writersref
Resources for writers and tutors > Tips from writing tutors:
Revising and editing

C3-b Revise and edit sentences.

Much of the rest of this book offers advice on revising sentences for style and clarity and on editing them for grammar, punctuation, and mechanics. Some writers handle sentence-level revisions directly at the computer, experimenting on-screen with a variety of improvements. Other writers prefer to print out a hard copy of the draft, mark it up, and then return to the computer. Here, for example, is a draft paragraph edited for a variety of sentence-level problems.

Although some cities have found creative ways to improve access to public transportation for physically handicapped passengers, ~~and to fund other programs, there have been problems in~~ our city has struggled with ~~due to the need to address~~ budget constraints and competing ~~needs~~ priorities. ~~This~~ The budget crunch has led citizens to question how funds are distributed.~~?~~ For example, last year ~~when~~ city officials voted to use available funds to support ~~had to choose between allocating funds for accessible transportation or allocating funds to~~ after-school programs rather than transportation upgrades. ~~, they voted for the after-school programs.~~ It is not clear to some citizens why ~~these~~ after-school programs are more important.

The original paragraph was flawed by wordiness, a problem that can be addressed through any number of revisions. This revision would also be acceptable:

> Some cities have funded improved access to public transportation for physically handicapped passengers. Because of budget constraints, our city chose to fund after-school programs rather than transportation programs. As a result, citizens have begun to question how funds are distributed and why certain programs are more important than others.

Some of the paragraph's improvements are not open to debate and must be fixed in any revision. The hyphen in *after-school programs* is necessary; a noun must be substituted for the pronoun *these* in the last sentence; and the question mark in the second sentence must be changed to a period.

> GRAMMAR CHECKERS can help with some but by no means all of the sentence-level problems in a typical draft. Many problems — such as faulty parallelism and misplaced modifiers — require an understanding of grammatical structure that computer programs lack. Such problems often slip right past the grammar checker. Even when the grammar checker makes a suggestion for revision, it is your responsibility as the writer to decide whether the suggestion is more effective than your original.

C3-c Proofread the final manuscript.

After revising and editing, you are ready to prepare the final manuscript. (See C5.) Make sure to allow yourself enough time for proofreading — the final and most important step in manuscript preparation.

Proofreading is a special kind of reading: a slow and methodical search for misspellings, typographical mistakes, and omitted words or word endings. Such errors can be difficult to spot in your own work because you may read what you intended to write, not what is actually on the page. To fight this tendency, try proofreading out loud, articulating each word as it is actually written. You might also try proofreading your sentences in reverse order, a strategy that takes your attention away from the meanings you intended and forces you to focus on one word at a time.

Although proofreading may be dull, it is crucial. Errors strewn throughout an essay are distracting and annoying. A reader may think, If the writer doesn't care about this piece of writing, why should I? A carefully proofread essay, however, sends the message that you value your writing and respect your readers.

> SPELL CHECKERS are more reliable than grammar checkers, but they too must be used with caution. Many typographical errors (such as *quiet* for *quite*) and misused words (such as *effect* for *affect*) slip past the spell checker because the checker flags only words not found in its dictionary.

ON THE WEB > dianahacker.com/writersref
Model papers > MLA paper-in-progress: Watson

C4

Writing paragraphs

Except for special-purpose paragraphs, such as introductions and conclusions (see C2-a and C2-c), paragraphs are clusters of information supporting an essay's main point (or advancing a story's action). Aim for paragraphs that are clearly focused, well developed, organized, coherent, and neither too long nor too short for easy reading.

C4-a Focus on a main point.

A paragraph should be unified around a main point. The point should be clear to readers, and all sentences in the paragraph should relate to it.

Stating the main point in a topic sentence

As a rule, you should state the main point of a paragraph in a topic sentence — a one-sentence summary that tells readers what to expect as they read on. Usually the topic sentence comes first in the paragraph.

> *All living creatures manage some form of communication.* The dance patterns of bees in their hive help to point the way to distant flower fields or announce successful foraging. Male stickleback fish regularly swim upside-down to indicate outrage in a courtship contest. Male deer and lemurs mark territorial ownership by rubbing their own body secretions on boundary stones or trees. Everyone has seen a frightened dog put his tail between his legs and run in panic. We, too, use gestures, expressions, postures, and movement to give our words point. [Italics added.]
> — Olivia Vlahos, *Human Beginnings*

Sometimes the topic sentence is introduced by a transitional sentence linking the paragraph to earlier material, and occasionally it is withheld until the end of the paragraph. And at times a topic sentence is not needed: if a paragraph continues developing an idea clearly introduced in an earlier paragraph, if the details of the paragraph unmistakably suggest its main point, or if the paragraph appears in a narrative of events where generalizations might interrupt the flow of the story.

Sticking to the point

Sentences that do not support the topic sentence destroy the unity of a paragraph. If the paragraph is otherwise well focused, such offending sentences can simply be deleted or perhaps moved elsewhere. In the following paragraph describing the inadequate facilities in a high school, the information about the chemistry instructor (in italics) is clearly off the point.

> As the result of tax cuts, the educational facilities of Lincoln High School have reached an all-time low. Some of the books date back to 1990 and have long since shed their covers. The few computers in working order must share one printer. The lack of lab equipment makes it necessary for four or five students to work at one table, with most watching rather than performing experiments. *Also, the chemistry instructor left to have a baby at the beginning of the semester, and most of the students don't like the substitute.* As for the furniture, many of the upright chairs have become recliners, and the desk legs are so unbalanced that they play seesaw on the floor. [Italics added.]

Sometimes the solution for a disunified paragraph is not as simple as deleting or moving material. Writers often wander into uncharted territory because they cannot think of enough evidence to support a topic sentence. Feeling that it is too soon to break into a new paragraph, they move on to new ideas for which they have not prepared the reader. When this happens, the writer is faced with a choice: Either find more evidence to support the topic sentence or adjust the topic sentence to mesh with the evidence that is available.

ON THE WEB > dianahacker.com/writersref
Writing exercises > E-ex C4–1

C4-b Develop the main point.

Though an occasional short paragraph is fine, particularly if it functions as a transition or emphasizes a point, a series of brief paragraphs suggests inadequate development. How much development is enough? That varies, depending on the writer's purpose and audience.

For example, when she wrote a paragraph attempting to convince readers that it is impossible to lose fat quickly, health columnist Jane Brody knew that she would have to present a great deal of evidence because many dieters want to believe the opposite. She did *not* write:

> When you think about it, it's impossible to lose — as many diets suggest — 10 pounds of *fat* in ten days, even on a total fast. Even a moderately active person cannot lose so much weight so fast. A less active person hasn't a prayer.

This three-sentence paragraph is too skimpy to be convincing. But the paragraph that Brody in fact wrote contains enough evidence to convince even skeptical readers.

> When you think about it, it's impossible to lose — as many . . . diets suggest — 10 pounds of *fat* in ten days, even on a total fast. A pound of body fat represents 3,500 calories. To lose 1 pound of fat, you must expend 3,500 more calories than you consume. Let's say you weigh 170 pounds and, as a moderately active person, you burn 2,500 calories a day. If your diet contains only 1,500 calories, you'd have an energy deficit of 1,000 calories a day. In a week's time that would add up to a 7,000-calorie deficit, or 2 pounds of real fat. In ten days, the accumulated deficit would represent nearly 3 pounds of lost body fat. Even if you ate nothing at all for ten days and maintained your usual level of activity, your caloric deficit would add up to 25,000 calories. . . . At 3,500 calories per pound of fat, that's still only 7 pounds of lost fat.
> — Jane Brody, *Jane Brody's Nutrition Book*

C4-c Choose a suitable pattern of organization.

Although paragraphs may be patterned in any number of ways, certain patterns of organization occur frequently, either alone or in combination: examples and illustrations, narration, description, process, comparison and contrast, analogy, cause and effect, classification and division, and definition. There is nothing particularly magical about these patterns (sometimes called *methods of development*). They simply reflect some of the ways in which we think.

Examples and illustrations

Examples, perhaps the most common pattern of organization, are appropriate whenever the reader might be tempted to ask, "For example?"

Normally my parents abided scrupulously by "The Budget," but several times a year Dad would dip into his battered black strongbox and splurge on some irrational, totally satisfying luxury. Once he bought over a hundred comic books at a flea market, doled out to us thereafter at the tantalizing rate of two a week. He always got a whole flat of pansies, Mom's favorite flower, for us to give her on Mother's Day. One day a boy stopped at our house selling fifty-cent raffle tickets on a sailboat and Dad bought every ticket the boy had left — three books' worth.

— Connie Hailey, student

Illustrations are extended examples, frequently presented in story form.

Part of [Harriet Tubman's] strategy of conducting was, as in all battle-field operations, the knowledge of how and when to retreat. Numerous allusions have been made to her moves when she suspected that she was in danger. When she feared the party was closely pursued, she would take it for a time on a train southward bound. No one seeing Negroes going in this direction would for an instant suppose them to be fugitives. Once on her return she was at a railroad station. She saw some men reading a poster and she heard one of them reading it aloud. It was a description of her, offering a reward for her capture. She took a southbound train to avert suspicion. At another time when Harriet heard men talking about her, she pretended to read a book which she carried. One man remarked, "This can't be the woman. The one we want can't read or write." Harriet devoutly hoped the book was right side up.

— Earl Conrad, *Harriet Tubman*

Narration

A paragraph of narration tells a story or part of a story. The following paragraph recounts one of the author's experiences in the African wild.

One evening when I was wading in the shallows of the lake to pass a rocky outcrop, I suddenly stopped dead as I saw the sinuous black body of a snake in the water. It was all of six feet long, and from the slight hood and the dark stripes at the back of the neck I knew it to be a Storm's water cobra — a deadly reptile for the bite of which there was, at that time, no serum. As I stared at it an incoming wave gently deposited part of its body on one of my feet. I remained motionless, not even breathing, until the wave rolled back into the lake, drawing the snake with it. Then I leaped out of the water as fast as I could, my heart hammering.

— Jane Goodall, *In the Shadow of Man*

Description

A descriptive paragraph sketches a portrait of a person, place, or thing by using concrete and specific details that appeal to one or more senses — sight, sound, smell, taste, and touch. Consider, for example, the following description of the grasshopper invasions that devastated the midwestern landscape in the late 1860s.

> They came like dive bombers out of the west. They came by the millions with the rustle of their wings roaring overhead. They came in waves, like the rolls of the sea, descending with a terrifying speed, breaking now and again like a mighty surf. They came with the force of a williwaw and they formed a huge, ominous, dark brown cloud that eclipsed the sun. They dipped and touched earth, hitting objects and people like hailstones. But they were not hail. These were *live* demons. They popped, snapped, crackled, and roared. They were dark brown, an inch or longer in length, plump in the middle and tapered at the ends. They had transparent wings, slender legs, and two black eyes that flashed with a fierce intelligence.   — Eugene Boe, "Pioneers to Eternity"

Process

A process paragraph is structured in chronological order. A writer may choose this pattern either to describe how something is made or done or to explain to readers, step by step, how to do something. The following paragraph explains how to perform a "roll cast," a popular fly-fishing technique.

> Begin by taking up a suitable stance, with one foot slightly in front of the other and the rod pointing down the line. Then begin a smooth, steady draw, raising your rod hand to just above shoulder height and lifting the rod to the 10:30 or 11:00 position. This steady draw allows a loop of line to form between the rod top and the water. While the line is still moving, raise the rod slightly, then punch it rapidly forward and down. The rod is now flexed and under maximum compression, and the line follows its path, bellying out slightly behind you and coming off the water close to your feet. As you power the rod down through the 3:00 position, the belly of line will roll forward. Follow through smoothly so that the line unfolds and straightens above the water.
>   — *The Dorling Kindersley Encyclopedia of Fishing*

Comparison and contrast

To compare subjects is to draw attention to their similarities, although the word *compare* also has a broader meaning that includes a consideration of differences. To contrast is to focus only on differences.

Whether a paragraph stresses similarities or differences, it may be patterned in one of two ways. The two subjects may be presented one at a time, as in the following paragraph of contrast.

So Grant and Lee were in complete contrast, representing two diametrically opposed elements in American life. Grant was the modern man emerging; beyond him, ready to come on the stage, was the great age of steel and machinery, of crowded cities and a restless, burgeoning vitality. Lee might have ridden down from the old age of chivalry, lance in hand, silken banner fluttering over his head. Each man was the perfect champion of his cause, drawing both his strengths and his weaknesses from the people he led.

— Bruce Catton, "Grant and Lee: A Study in Contrasts"

Or a paragraph may proceed point by point, treating two subjects together, one aspect at a time. The following paragraph uses the point-by-point method to contrast the writer's experiences in an American high school and an Irish convent.

Strangely enough, instead of being academically inferior to my American high school, the Irish convent was superior. In my class at home, *Love Story* was considered pretty heavy reading, so imagine my surprise at finding Irish students who could recite passages from *War and Peace*. In high school we complained about having to study *Romeo and Juliet* in one semester, whereas in Ireland we simultaneously studied *Macbeth* and Dickens's *Hard Times*, in addition to writing a composition a day in English class. In high school, I didn't even begin algebra until the ninth grade, while at the convent seventh graders (or their Irish equivalent) were doing calculus and trigonometry.

— Margaret Stack, student

Analogy

Analogies draw comparisons between items that appear to have little in common. In the following paragraph, physician Lewis Thomas draws an analogy between the behavior of ants and that of humans.

Ants are so much like human beings as to be an embarrassment. They farm fungi, raise aphids as livestock, launch armies into wars, use chemical sprays to alarm and confuse enemies, capture slaves. The families of weaver ants engage in child labor, holding their larvae like shuttles to spin out the thread that sews the leaves together for their fungus gardens. They exchange information ceaselessly. They do everything but watch television.

— Lewis Thomas, "On Societies as Organisms"

Cause and effect

A paragraph may move from cause to effects or from an effect to its causes. The topic sentence in the following paragraph mentions an effect; the rest of the paragraph lists several causes.

> The fantastic water clarity of the Mount Gambier sinkholes results from several factors. The holes are fed from aquifers holding rainwater that fell decades — even centuries — ago, and that has been filtered through miles of limestone. The high level of calcium that limestone adds causes the silty detritus from dead plants and animals to cling together and settle quickly to the bottom. Abundant bottom vegetation in the shallow sinkholes also helps bind the silt. And the rapid turnover of water prohibits stagnation.
>
> — Hillary Hauser, "Exploring a Sunken Realm in Australia"

Classification and division

Classification is the grouping of items into categories according to some consistent principle. The following paragraph classifies species of electric fish.

> Scientists sort electric fishes into three categories. The first comprises the strongly electric species like the marine electric rays or the freshwater African electric catfish and South American electric eel. Known since the dawn of history, these deliver a punch strong enough to stun a human. In recent years, biologists have focused on a second category: weakly electric fish in the South American and African rivers that use tiny voltages for communication and navigation. The third group contains sharks, nonelectric rays and catfish, which do not emit a field but possess sensors that enable them to detect the minute amounts of electricity that leak out of other organisms.
>
> — Anne and Jack Rudloe, "Electric Warfare: The Fish That Kill with Thunderbolts"

Division takes one item and divides it into parts. As with classification, division should be made according to some consistent principle. The following paragraph describes the components that make up a baseball.

> Like the game itself, a baseball is composed of many layers. One of the delicious joys of childhood is to take apart a baseball and examine the wonders within. You begin by removing the red cotton thread and peeling off the leather cover — which comes from the hide of a Holstein cow and has been tanned, cut, printed,

and punched with holes. Beneath the cover is a thin layer of cotton string, followed by several hundred yards of woolen yarn, which makes up the bulk of the ball. Finally, in the middle is a rubber ball, or "pill," which is a little smaller than a golf ball. Slice into the rubber and you'll find the ball's heart — a cork core. The cork is from Portugal, the rubber from southeast Asia, the covers are American, and the balls are assembled in Costa Rica.

— Dan Gutman, *The Way Baseball Works*

Definition

A definition puts a word or concept into a general class and then provides enough details to distinguish it from other members in the same class. In the following paragraph, the writer defines *envy* as a special kind of desire.

Envy is so integral and so painful a part of what animates behavior in market societies that many people have forgotten the full meaning of the word, simplifying it into one of the synonyms of desire. It is that, which may be why it flourishes in market societies: democracies of desire, they might be called, with money for ballots, stuffing permitted. But envy is more or less than desire. It begins with an almost frantic sense of emptiness inside oneself, as if the pump of one's heart were sucking on air. One has to be blind to perceive the emptiness, of course, but that's just what envy is, a selective blindness. *Invidia*, Latin for envy, translates as "non-sight," and Dante has the envious plodding along under cloaks of lead, their eyes sewn shut with leaden wire. What they are blind to is what they have, God-given and humanly nurtured, in themselves.

— Nelson W. Aldrich Jr., *Old Money*

C4-d Make paragraphs coherent.

When sentences and paragraphs flow from one to another without discernible bumps, gaps, or shifts, they are said to be coherent. Coherence can be improved by strengthening the various ties between old information and new. A number of techniques for strengthening those ties are detailed in this section.

Linking ideas clearly

Readers expect to learn a paragraph's main point in a topic sentence early in the paragraph. Then, as they move into the body of the paragraph, they expect to encounter specific facts, details, or examples that support the topic sentence — either directly or indirectly. Consider the following paragraph, in which all of the sentences following the topic sentence directly support it.

> A passenger list of the early years [of the Orient Express] would read like a *Who's Who of the World*, from art to politics. Sarah Bernhardt and her Italian counterpart Eleonora Duse used the train to thrill the stages of Europe. For musicians there were Toscanini and Mahler. Dancers Nijinsky and Pavlova were there, while lesser performers like Harry Houdini and the girls of the Ziegfeld Follies also rode the rails. Violinists were allowed to practice on the train, and occasionally one might see trapeze artists hanging like bats from the baggage racks.
>
> — Barnaby Conrad III, "Train of Kings"

If a sentence does not support the topic sentence directly, readers expect it to support another sentence in the paragraph. The following paragraph begins with a topic sentence. The italicized sentences are direct supports, and the rest of the sentences are indirect supports.

> Though the open-space classroom works for many children, it is not practical for my son, David. *First, David is hyperactive.* When he was placed in an open-space classroom, he became distracted and confused. He was tempted to watch the movement going on around him instead of concentrating on his own work. *Second, David has a tendency to transpose letters and numbers, a tendency that can be overcome only by individual attention from the instructor.* In the open classroom he was moved from teacher to teacher, with each one responsible for a different subject. No single teacher worked with David long enough to diagnose the problem, let alone help him with it. *Finally, David is not a highly motivated learner.* In the open classroom, he was graded "at his own level," not by criteria for a certain grade. He could receive a B in reading and still be a grade level behind, because he was doing satisfactory work "at his own level." [Italics added.]
>
> — Margaret Smith, student

Repeating key words

Repetition of key words is an important technique for gaining coherence. To prevent repetitions from becoming dull, you can use variations of the key word (*hike, hiker, hiking*), pronouns referring to the word (*gamblers . . . they*), and synonyms (*run, spring, race, dash*). In the following paragraph describing plots among indentured servants in the seventeenth century, historian Richard Hofstadter binds sentences together by repeating the key word *plots* and echoing it with variations (italicized).

> *Plots* hatched by several servants to run away together occurred mostly in the plantation colonies, and the few recorded servant *uprisings* were entirely limited to those colonies. Virginia had been forced from its very earliest years to take stringent steps against *mutinous plots*, and severe punishments for *such behavior* were recorded. Most servant *plots* occurred in the seventeenth century: a contemplated *uprising* was nipped in the bud in York County in 1661; apparently led by some left-wing offshoots of the *Great Rebellion*, servants *plotted* an *insurrection* in Gloucester County in 1663, and four leaders were condemned and executed; some discontented servants apparently joined *Bacon's Rebellion* in the 1670's. In the 1680's the planters became newly apprehensive of discontent among the servants "owing to their great necessities and want of clothes," and it was feared they would *rise up* and *plunder* the storehouses and ships; in 1682 there were plant-cutting *riots* in which servants and laborers, as well as some planters, took part. [Italics added.]
>
> — Richard Hofstadter, *America at 1750*

Using parallel structures

Parallel structures are frequently used within sentences to underscore the similarity of ideas (see S1). They may also be used to bind together a series of sentences expressing similar information. In the following passage describing folk beliefs, anthropologist Margaret Mead presents similar information in parallel grammatical form.

> Actually, almost every day, even in the most sophisticated home, something is likely to happen that evokes the memory of some old folk belief. The salt spills. A knife falls to the floor. Your nose tickles. Then perhaps, with a slightly embarrassed smile, the person who spilled the salt tosses a pinch over his left shoulder. Or someone recites the old rhyme, "Knife falls, gentleman calls." Or as you rub your nose you think, That means a letter. I wonder who's writing?   — Margaret Mead, "New Superstitions for Old"

Maintaining consistency

Coherence suffers whenever a draft shifts confusingly from one point of view to another (for example, from *I* to *you* or from *anyone* to *they*). Coherence also suffers when a draft shifts without reason from one verb tense to another (for example, from *swam* to *swims*). For advice on avoiding shifts, see S4.

Providing transitions

Transitions are bridges between what has been read and what is about to be read. Transitions help readers move from sentence to sentence; they also alert readers to more global connections of ideas — those between paragraphs or even larger blocks of text.

> ACADEMIC ENGLISH Choose transitions carefully and vary them appropriately. For instance, avoid using a transition that signals a logical relationship (such as *therefore*) if no clear logical relationship exists. Each transition has a different meaning; if you do not use an appropriate signal, you might confuse your reader.
>
> ▶ Although taking eight o'clock classes may seem unappealing, coming to school early has its advantages. *For example,* ~~Moreover,~~ students who arrive early typically avoid the worst traffic and find the best parking spaces.

SENTENCE-LEVEL TRANSITIONS   Certain words and phrases signal connections between (or within) sentences. Frequently used transitions are included in the chart on page 36.

Skilled writers use transitional expressions with care, making sure, for example, not to use *consequently* when *also* would be more precise. They are also careful to select transitions with an appropriate tone, perhaps preferring *so* to *thus* in an informal piece, *in summary* to *in short* for a scholarly essay.

In the following paragraph, taken from an argument that dinosaurs had the "'right-sized' brains for reptiles of their body size," biologist Stephen Jay Gould uses transitions (italicized) with skill.

I don't wish to deny that the flattened, minuscule head of largebodied *Stegosaurus* houses little brain from our subjective, top-heavy perspective, *but* I do wish to assert that we should not expect more of the beast. *First of all*, large animals have relatively smaller brains than related, small animals. The correlation of brain size with body size among kindred animals (all reptiles, all mammals, *for example*) is remarkably regular. *As* we move from small to large animals, from mice to elephants or small lizards to Komodo dragons, brain size increases, *but* not so fast as body size. *In other words*, bodies grow faster than brains, *and* large animals have low ratios of brain weight to body weight. *In fact*, brains grow only about two-thirds as fast as bodies. *Since* we have no reason to believe that large animals are consistently stupider than their smaller relatives, we must conclude that large animals require relatively less brain to do as well as smaller animals. *If* we do not recognize this relationship, we are likely to underestimate the mental power of very large animals, dinosaurs *in particular.*

— Stephen Jay Gould, "Were Dinosaurs Dumb?"

ON THE WEB > dianahacker.com/writersref
Writing exercises > E-ex C4–2

PARAGRAPH-LEVEL TRANSITIONS Transitions between paragraphs usually link the *first* sentence of a new paragraph with the *first* sentence of the previous paragraph. In other words, the topic sentences signal global connections.

Look for opportunities to allude to the subject of a previous paragraph (as summed up in its topic sentence) in the topic sentence of the next paragraph. In his essay "Little Green Lies," Jonathan H. Alder uses this strategy in the following topic sentences, which appear in a passage describing the benefits of plastic packaging.

> Consider aseptic packaging, the synthetic packaging for the "juice boxes" so many children bring to school with their lunch. One criticism of aseptic packaging is that it is nearly impossible to recycle, yet on almost every other count, aseptic packaging is environmentally preferable to the packaging alternatives. Not only do aseptic containers not require refrigeration to keep their contents from spoiling, but their manufacture requires less than one-10th the energy of making glass bottles.
>
> What is true for juice boxes is also true for other forms of synthetic packaging. The use of polystyrene, which is commonly (and mistakenly) referred to as "Styrofoam," can reduce food waste dramatically due to its insulating properties. (Thanks to these properties, polystyrene cups are much preferred over paper for that morning cup of coffee.) Polystyrene also requires significantly fewer resources to produce than its paper counterpart.

TRANSITIONS BETWEEN BLOCKS OF TEXT In long essays, you may need to alert readers to connections between large blocks of text. You can do this by inserting transitional paragraphs at key points in the essay. On the next page, for example, is a transitional paragraph from a student research paper. It announces that the first part of the paper has come to a close and the second part is about to begin.

Common transitions

TO SHOW ADDITION and, also, besides, further, furthermore, in addition, moreover, next, too, first, second

TO GIVE EXAMPLES for example, for instance, to illustrate, in fact, specifically

TO COMPARE also, in the same manner, similarly, likewise

TO CONTRAST but, however, on the other hand, in contrast, nevertheless, still, even though, on the contrary, yet, although

TO SUMMARIZE OR CONCLUDE in other words, in short, in summary, in conclusion, to sum up, that is, therefore

TO SHOW TIME after, as, before, next, during, later, finally, meanwhile, since, then, when, while, immediately

TO SHOW PLACE OR DIRECTION above, below, beyond, farther on, nearby, opposite, close, to the left

TO INDICATE LOGICAL RELATIONSHIP if, so, therefore, consequently, thus, as a result, for this reason, because, since

Although the great apes have demonstrated significant language skills, one central question remains: Can they be taught to use that uniquely human language tool we call grammar, to learn the difference, for instance, between "ape bite human" and "human bite ape"? In other words, can an ape create a sentence?

C4-e If necessary, adjust paragraph length.

Most readers feel comfortable reading paragraphs that range between one hundred and two hundred words. Shorter paragraphs force too much starting and stopping, and longer ones strain the reader's attention span. There are exceptions to this guideline, however. Paragraphs longer than two hundred words frequently appear in scholarly writing, where they suggest seriousness and depth. Paragraphs shorter than one hundred words occur in newspapers because of narrow columns; in informal essays to quicken the pace; in business letters, where readers routinely skim for main ideas; and in e-mail and on Web sites for ease of reading on the computer screen.

In an essay, the first and last paragraphs will ordinarily be the introduction and conclusion. These special-purpose paragraphs are likely to be shorter than the paragraphs in the body of the essay.

Typically, the body paragraphs will follow the essay's outline: one paragraph per point in short essays, a group of paragraphs per point in longer ones. Some ideas require more development than others, however, so it is best to be flexible. If an idea stretches to a length unreasonable for a paragraph, you should divide the paragraph, even if you have presented comparable points in the essay in single paragraphs.

Paragraph breaks are not always made for strictly logical reasons. Writers use them for all of the following reasons.

REASONS FOR BEGINNING A NEW PARAGRAPH

- to mark off the introduction and the conclusion
- to signal a shift to a new idea
- to indicate an important shift in time or place
- to emphasize a point (by placing it at the beginning or the end, not in the middle, of a paragraph)
- to highlight a contrast
- to signal a change of speakers (in dialogue)
- to provide readers with a needed pause
- to break up text that looks too dense

Beware of using too many short, choppy paragraphs, however. Readers want to see how your ideas connect, and they become irritated when you break their momentum by forcing them to pause every few sentences. Here are some reasons you might have for combining some of the paragraphs in a rough draft.

REASONS FOR COMBINING PARAGRAPHS

- to clarify the essay's organization
- to connect closely related ideas
- to bind together text that looks too choppy

C5

Designing documents

The term *document* is broad enough to describe anything you might write in a college class, in the business world, and in everyday life. How you design a document (format it for the printed page or for a computer screen) will affect how readers respond to it.

Good document design promotes readability, but what *readability* means depends on your purpose and audience and perhaps on other elements of your writing situation, such as your subject and any length restrictions. All of your design choices — layout, word processing options such as margins and fonts, headings, and lists — should be made in light of your writing situation. Likewise, different types of visuals — tables, charts, and images — can support your writing if they are used appropriately.

C5-a Determine layout and format to suit your purpose and audience.

Word processing programs offer abundant options for layout, margins and line spacing, alignment, and fonts. As you use these options to design documents, always keep the purpose of the document and the needs of your readers in mind.

Layout

Most readers have set ideas about how different kinds of documents should look. Advertisements, for example, have a distinctive appearance, as do newsletters, flyers, brochures, and menus. Instructors have expectations about how a college paper should look (see C5-e). Employers expect documents such as letters, résumés, and memos to be presented in standard ways (see C5-f). And anyone who reads your writing online will appreciate a recognizable layout.

Unless you have a compelling reason to stray from convention, it's best to choose a document layout that conforms to your readers' expectations. If you're not sure what readers expect, look at examples of the kind of document you are producing.

Planning a document: Purpose and audience checklist

- What is the purpose of your document? How can your document design help you achieve this purpose?
- Who are your readers? What are their expectations?
- What format is required? What format options — layout, margins, line spacing, alignment, and fonts — will readers expect?
- How can you use visuals — charts, graphs, tables, images — to help you convey information?

Margins and line spacing

Margins help control the look of a page. For most academic and business documents, leave a margin of one to one and a half inches on all sides. These margins create a visual frame for the text and provide room for annotations, such as an instructor's comments or a co-worker's suggestions. Narrower margins generally make a page crowded and difficult to read.

SINGLE-SPACED, UNFORMATTED   **DOUBLE-SPACED, FORMATTED**

ACADEMIC ENGLISH If your word processing program was not purchased in the United States, you may need to change the default settings. From your page setup menu (usually under the file menu) change the paper size to 8.5 × 11 inches (21.5 × 28 cm). In most cases, change your margins to one inch (2.5 or 2.6 cm).

Most manuscripts in progress are double-spaced to allow room for editing. Final copy is often double-spaced as well, since single-spacing is less inviting to read. If you are unsure about margin and spacing requirements, check with your instructor or look at documents similar to the one you are writing. At times, the advantages of double-spacing are offset by other considerations. For example, most business and technical documents are single-spaced, with double-spacing between paragraphs, to save paper and to promote quick scanning. Your document's purpose and context should determine appropriate margins and line spacing.

Alignment

Word processing programs allow you to align text and visuals on a page in four ways: left, right, centered, and justified. Most academic and business documents are left-aligned for easy reading. Although justified margins may seem more professional, they tend to create awkward word spacing and should be avoided.

Fonts

If you have a choice, select a font that fits your writing situation in an easy-to-read size (usually 10–12 points). Although offbeat or decorative fonts, such as those that look handwritten, may seem attractive, they slow readers down and can distract them from your ideas. For example, using comic sans, a font with a handwritten, childish feel, can make an essay seem too informal or unpolished, regardless of how well it is written. Fonts that are easy to read and appropriate for college and workplace documents include the following:

Arial   Tahoma
Courier   Times New Roman
Garamond   Verdana
Georgia

Font styles — such as **boldface**, *italics*, and underlining — can be useful for calling attention to parts of a document. On the whole, it is best to use restraint when selecting font styles. Applying too many different styles within a document results in busy-looking pages and confuses readers.

TIP: Never write a document in all capital or all lowercase letters. Doing so can frustrate or annoy readers. Although some readers have become accustomed to e-mails that omit capital letters entirely, their absence makes a message difficult to read.

ON THE WEB > dianahacker.com/writersref
Links Library > Document design

C5-b Use headings when appropriate.

You will have little need for headings in short essays, especially if you use paragraphing and clear topic sentences to guide readers. In more complex documents, however, such as research papers, grant proposals, business reports, and Web sites, headings can be a useful visual cue for readers.

Headings help readers see at a glance the organization of a document. If more than one level of heading is used, the headings also indicate the hierarchy of ideas — as they do throughout this book.

Headings can serve a number of functions for your readers. When readers are simply looking up information, headings will help them find it quickly. When readers are scanning, hoping to pick up the gist of things, headings will guide them. Even when readers are committed enough to read every word, headings can help. Efficient readers preview a document before they begin reading; when previewing and while reading, they are guided by any visual cues the writer provides.

TIP: While headings can be useful, they cannot substitute for transitions between paragraphs. Keep this in mind as you write college essays.

Phrasing headings

Headings should be as brief and as informative as possible. Certain styles of headings — the most common being *-ing* phrases, noun phrases, questions, and imperative sentences — work better for some purposes, audiences, and subjects than others.

Whatever style you choose, use it consistently. Headings on the same level of organization should be written in parallel structure (see S1), as in the following examples from a report, a history textbook, a financial brochure, and a nursing manual, respectively.

-*ING* HEADINGS

Safeguarding the earth's atmosphere

Charting the path to sustainable energy

Conserving global forests

NOUN PHRASE HEADINGS

The economics of slavery

The sociology of slavery

The psychological effects of slavery

QUESTIONS AS HEADINGS
How do I buy shares?
How do I redeem shares?
What is the history of the fund's performance?

IMPERATIVE SENTENCES AS HEADINGS
Ask the patient to describe current symptoms.
Take a detailed medical history.
Record the patient's vital signs.

Placing and formatting headings

Headings on the same level of organization should be placed and formatted in a consistent way. If you have more than one level of heading, you might center your first-level headings and make them boldface; then you might make the second-level headings left-aligned and italicized, like this:

First-level heading

Second-level heading

A college paper with headings typically has only one level, and the headings are often centered, as in the sample paper on pages 484–88. Business memos often include headings. Important headings can be highlighted by using white space around them. Less important headings can be downplayed by using less white space or by running them into the text.

C5-c   Use lists to guide readers.

Lists are easy to read or scan when they are displayed rather than run into your text. You might choose to display the following kinds of lists:

- steps in a process
- materials needed for a project
- parts of an object
- advice or recommendations
- items to be discussed
- criteria for evaluation (as in checklists)

Lists should usually be introduced with an independent clause followed by a colon (*All mammals share the following five characteristics:*). Periods are not used after items in a list unless the items are complete sentences.

If the order of items is not important, use bullets (circles or squares) or dashes to draw readers' eyes to a list. If you are describing a sequence or a set of steps, number the list with arabic numerals (1, 2, 3) followed by periods.

TIP: Although lists can be useful visual cues, don't overdo them. Too many will clutter a document.

C5-d Add visuals to supplement your text.

Visuals can convey information concisely and powerfully. Charts, graphs, and tables, for example, can simplify complex numerical data. Images — including photographs and diagrams — often express an idea more vividly than words can. With access to the Internet, digital photography, and word processing or desktop publishing software, you can download or create your own visuals to enhance your document. If you download a visual, you must credit your source (see R3).

Choosing appropriate visuals

Use visuals to supplement your writing, not to substitute for it. Always consider how a visual supports your purpose and how your audience might respond to it. A student writing about electronic surveillance in the workplace, for example, used a cartoon to illustrate her point about employees' personal use of the Internet at work (see MLA-5b). Another student, writing about treatments for childhood obesity, created a table to display data she had found in two different sources and discussed in her paper (see APA-5b).

As you draft and revise a document, choose carefully the visuals that support your main point, and avoid overloading your text with too many images. The chart on pages 44–45 describes eight types of visuals and their purposes.

Placing and labeling visuals

A visual may be placed in the text of a document, near a discussion to which it relates, or it can be put in an appendix, labeled, and referred to in the text.

Choosing visuals to suit your purpose

Pie chart

Pie charts compare a part or parts to the whole. The parts are displayed as segments of the pie, represented as percentages of the whole (which is always 100 percent).

Use of the George Mason University writing center, by group, academic year 2003–04

■ Juniors 30%
▨ Seniors 20%
■ First-year students 17%
Sophomores 17%
■ Graduate students 11%
Not indicated 3%
■ Staff / alumni 2%

Line graph

Line graphs highlight trends over a period of time or compare numerical data.

www.mywebsite.com

— 2003
— 2004

January February March April
Number of hits, 2003 and 2004

Bar graph

Bar graphs can be used for the same purpose as line graphs. This bar graph displays the same data as in the line graph above.

www.mywebsite.com

— 2003
— 2004

12 120 27 100 31 161 46 184

January February March April
Number of hits, 2003 and 2004

Table

Tables organize complicated numerical information into an accessible format.

Prices of daily doses of AIDS drugs ($US)

Drug	Brazil	Uganda	Côte d'Ivoire	US
3TC (Lamuvidine)	1.86	3.28	2.95	8.70
ddC (Zalcitabine)	0.24	4.17	3.75	8.80
Didanosine	2.04	5.26	3.48	7.25
Efavirenz	6.96	n/a	6.41	13.13
Indinavir	10.32	12.79	9.07	14.93
Nelfinavir	4.14	4.45	4.39	6.47
Nevirapine	5.04	n/a	n/a	8.48
Saquinavir	6.24	7.37	5.52	6.50
Stavudine	0.56	6.19	4.10	9.07
ZDV/3TC	1.44	7.34	n/a	18.78
Zidovudine	1.08	4.34	2.43	10.12

Source: UNAIDS, 2000

Photograph

Photographs vividly depict people, scenes, or objects discussed in a text.

Diagram

Diagrams, useful in scientific and technical writing, concisely illustrate processes, structures, or interactions.

Map

Maps indicate locations, distances, and demographic information.

Flowchart

Flowcharts show structures or steps in a process. (For another example, see p. 104.)

VISUAL WITH A SOURCE CREDITED

Fig. 6.

Postal Service Size, by Number of Employees

	Among the Global 500			Among US Companies	
Rank	Company	Employees as of 2002	Rank	Company	Employees as of 2002
1	Wal-Mart Stores	1,300,000	1	Wal-Mart Stores	1,300,000
2	China National Petroleum	1,146,194	2	**US Postal Service**	**854,376**
3	Sinopec	917,000	3	McDonald's	413,000
4	**US Postal Service**	**854,376**	4	United Parcel Service	360,000
5	Agricultural Bank of China	490,999	5	Ford Motor	350,321
6	Siemens	426,000	6	General Motors	350,000
7	McDonald's	413,000	7	Intl. Business Machines	315,889
8	Ind. & Comm. Bank of China	405,000	8	General Electric	315,000
9	Carrefour	396,662	9	Target	306,000
10	Compass Group	392,352	10	Home Depot	300,000
11	China Telecomm	365,778	11	Kroger	289,000
12	DaimlerChrysler	365,571	12	Sears Roebuck	289,000
13	United Parcel Service	360,000	13	Tyco International	267,000
14	Ford Motor	350,321	14	Citigroup	252,500
15	General Motors	350,000	15	Verizon Communications	229,497

Source: Number of employees rankings by *Fortune Magazine*, April 14, 2003.

Placing visuals in the text of a document can be tricky. Usually you will want the visual to appear close to the sentences that relate to it, but page breaks won't always allow this placement. At times you may need to insert the visual at a later point and tell readers where it can be found; sometimes, with the help of software, you can make the text flow around the visual. No matter where you place a visual, refer to it in your text. Don't expect visuals to speak for themselves.

Most of the visuals you include in a document will require some sort of label. Labels, which are typically placed above or under the visuals, should be brief but descriptive. Most commonly, a visual is labeled with the word "Figure" or the abbreviation "Fig.," followed by a number: *Fig. 4.* Sometimes a title might be included to explain how the visual relates to the text: *Fig. 4. Voter turnout by age.*

Using visuals responsibly

Most word processing and spreadsheet software will allow you to produce your own visuals. If you create a chart, a table, or a graph using information from your research, you must cite the source of the information even though the visual is your own. The table on page 46 credits the source of its data.

If you download a photograph from the Web or scan an image from a magazine or book, you must credit the person or organization that created it, just as you would cite any other source you use in a college paper (see R3). If your document is written for publication outside the classroom, you will need to request permission to use any visual you borrow.

Guidelines for using visuals vary by academic discipline. See MLA-5a, APA-5a, and CMS-5a for guidelines in English and humanities, social sciences, and history, respectively.

C5-e Use standard academic formatting.

Instructors have certain expectations about how a college paper should look. If your instructor provides guidelines for formatting an essay, report, or research paper, you should follow them. Otherwise, use the manuscript format that is recommended for your academic discipline.

In most English and humanities classes, you will be asked to use the MLA (Modern Language Association) format. The sample on pages 48–49 illustrates this format. For more detailed MLA manuscript guidelines and a sample research paper, see MLA-5. If you have been asked to use APA (American Psychological Association) or CMS (*Chicago Manual of Style*) manuscript guidelines, see APA-5 or CMS-5.

MLA ESSAY FORMAT

1″

¹/₂″

Orlov 1

Anna Orlov

Professor Willis

1″

English 101

17 March 2006

Title is centered.

Online Monitoring:

¹/₂″

A Threat to Employee Privacy in the Wired Workplace

As the Internet has become an integral tool of businesses, company policies on Internet usage have become as common as policies regarding vacation days or sexual harassment. A 2005 study by the American Management Association and ePolicy Institute found that 76% of

Double-spacing is used throughout.

companies monitor employees' use of the Web, and the number of companies that block employees' access to certain Web sites has increased

1″

27% since 2001 (1). Unlike other company rules, however, Internet usage policies often include language authorizing companies to secretly monitor their employees, a practice that raises questions about rights in the workplace. Although companies often have legitimate concerns that lead them to monitor employees' Internet usage--from expensive security breaches to reduced productivity--the benefits of electronic surveillance are outweighed by its costs to employees' privacy and autonomy.

While surveillance of employees is not a new phenomenon, electronic surveillance allows employers to monitor workers with unprecedented efficiency. In his book The Naked Employee, Frederick Lane describes offline ways in which employers have been permitted to intrude on employees' privacy for decades, such as drug testing, background checks, psychological exams, lie detector tests, and in-store video surveillance. The difference, Lane argues, between these old methods of data gathering and electronic surveillance involves quantity:

1″

Technology makes it possible for employers to gather enormous amounts of data about employees, often far beyond what is necessary to satisfy safety or productivity concerns. And the trends that drive technology--faster, smaller, cheaper--make it possible for larger and larger numbers of employers to gather ever-greater amounts of personal data. (3-4)

1″

Marginal annotations indicate MLA-style formatting.

MLA ESSAY FORMAT (continued)

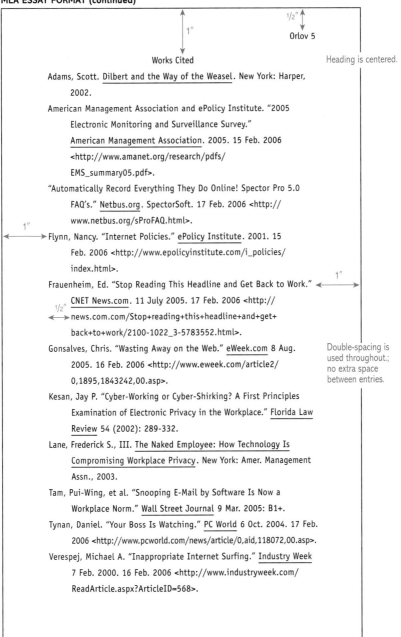

Orlov 5

1″

½″

Works Cited   Heading is centered.

Adams, Scott. Dilbert and the Way of the Weasel. New York: Harper, 2002.

American Management Association and ePolicy Institute. "2005 Electronic Monitoring and Surveillance Survey." American Management Association. 2005. 15 Feb. 2006 <http://www.amanet.org/research/pdfs/ EMS_summary05.pdf>.

"Automatically Record Everything They Do Online! Spector Pro 5.0 FAQ's." Netbus.org. SpectorSoft. 17 Feb. 2006 <http:// www.netbus.org/sProFAQ.html>.

Flynn, Nancy. "Internet Policies." ePolicy Institute. 2001. 15 Feb. 2006 <http://www.epolicyinstitute.com/i_policies/ index.html>.

1″

Frauenheim, Ed. "Stop Reading This Headline and Get Back to Work." CNET News.com. 11 July 2005. 17 Feb. 2006 <http:// news.com/Stop+reading+this+headline+and+get+ back+to+work/2100-1022_3-5783552.html>.

1″

½″

Gonsalves, Chris. "Wasting Away on the Web." eWeek.com 8 Aug. 2005. 16 Feb. 2006 <http://www.eweek.com/article2/ 0,1895,1843242,00.asp>.

Double-spacing is used throughout.; no extra space between entries.

Kesan, Jay P. "Cyber-Working or Cyber-Shirking? A First Principles Examination of Electronic Privacy in the Workplace." Florida Law Review 54 (2002): 289-332.

Lane, Frederick S., III. The Naked Employee: How Technology Is Compromising Workplace Privacy. New York: Amer. Management Assn., 2003.

Tam, Pui-Wing, et al. "Snooping E-Mail by Software Is Now a Workplace Norm." Wall Street Journal 9 Mar. 2005: B1+.

Tynan, Daniel. "Your Boss Is Watching." PC World 6 Oct. 2004. 17 Feb. 2006 <http://www.pcworld.com/news/article/0,aid,118072,00.asp>.

Verespej, Michael A. "Inappropriate Internet Surfing." Industry Week 7 Feb. 2000. 16 Feb. 2006 <http://www.industryweek.com/ ReadArticle.aspx?ArticleID=568>.

C5-f Use standard business formatting.

This section provides advice on preparing business letters, résumés, and memos. For a more detailed discussion of these and other business documents — proposals, reports, executive summaries, and so on — consult a business writing textbook or look at current examples at the organization for which you are writing.

ON THE WEB > dianahacker.com/writersref
Links Library > Document design

BUSINESS LETTER IN FULL BLOCK STYLE

LatinoVoice

March 16, 2005 ⊐├———— Date

Jonathan Ross
Managing Editor   ┐
Latino World Today   ├——— Inside
2971 East Oak Avenue | address
Baltimore, MD 21201   ┘

Dear Mr. Ross: ⊐├———— Salutation

Thank you very much for taking the time yesterday to speak to the University of Maryland's Latino Club. A number of students have told me that they enjoyed your presentation and found your job search suggestions to be extremely helpful.

As I mentioned to you when we first scheduled your appearance, the club publishes a monthly newsletter, *Latino Voice*. Our purpose is to share up-to-date information and expert advice with members of the university's Latino population. Considering how much students benefited from your talk, I would like to publish excerpts from it in our newsletter.

Body ——

I have taken the liberty of transcribing parts of your presentation and organizing them into a question-and-answer format for our readers. When you have a moment, would you mind looking through the enclosed article and letting me know if I may have your permission to print it? I would be happy, of course, to make any changes or corrections that you request. I'm hoping to include this article in our next newsletter, so I would need your response by April 4.

Once again, Mr. Ross, thank you for sharing your experiences with us. You gave an informative and entertaining speech, and I would love to be able to share it with the students who couldn't hear it in person.

Sincerely, ———— Close

Jeffrey Richardson
                                              ———— Signature
Jeffrey Richardson
Associate Editor

Enc.

210 Student Center University of Maryland **College Park MD 20742**

Business letters

In writing a business letter, be direct, clear, and courteous. State your purpose or request at the beginning of the letter and include only relevant information in the body. Being as direct and concise as possible shows that you value your reader's time. For the format of the letter, stick to established business conventions. A sample business letter in *full block* style appears on page 50.

Résumés and cover letters

An effective résumé gives relevant information in a clear, concise form. You may be asked to produce a traditional résumé, a scannable résumé, or a Web résumé. A cover letter gives a prospective employer a reason to look at your résumé. The goal is to present yourself in a favorable light without including unnecessary details and wasting your reader's time.

COVER LETTERS   When you send out your résumé, always include a cover letter that introduces yourself, states the position you seek, and tells where you learned about it. The letter should also highlight past experiences that qualify you for the position and emphasize what you can do for the employer (not what the job will do for you). End the letter with a suggestion for a meeting, and tell your prospective employer when you will be available.

TRADITIONAL RÉSUMÉS   Traditional paper résumés are screened by people, not by computers. Because screeners may face stacks of applications, they often spend very little time looking at each résumé. Therefore, you will need to make your résumé as reader-friendly as possible. Here are a few guidelines. See page 52 for an example.

- Limit your résumé to one page if possible, two pages at the most.

- Organize your information into clear categories — Education, Experience, and so on.

- Present the information in each category in reverse chronological order to highlight your most recent accomplishments.

- Use bulleted lists or some other simple, clear visual device to organize information.

- Use strong, active verbs to emphasize your accomplishments. (Use present-tense verbs, such as *manage,* for current activities and past-tense verbs, such as *managed,* for past activities.)

TRADITIONAL RÉSUMÉ

Jeffrey Richardson
121 Knox Road, #6
College Park, MD 20740
301–555–2651
jrichardson@jrichardson.localhost

OBJECTIVE	To obtain an editorial internship with a magazine

EDUCATION

Fall 2002– present	University of Maryland • BA expected in June 2006 • Double major: English and Latin American studies • GPA: 3.7 (on a 4-point scale)

EXPERIENCE

Fall 2004– present	Associate editor, *Latino Voice*, newsletter of Latino Club • Assign and edit feature articles • Coordinate community outreach
Fall 2003– present	Photo editor, *The Diamondback*, college paper • Shoot and print photographs • Select and lay out photographs and other visuals
Summer 2004	Intern, *The Globe,* Fairfax, Virginia • Wrote stories about local issues and personalities • Interviewed political candidates • Edited and proofread copy • Coedited "The Landscapes of Northern Virginia: A Photoessay"
Summers 2003, 2004	Tutor, Fairfax County ESL Program • Tutored Latino students in English as a Second Language • Trained new tutors
ACTIVITIES	Photographers' Workshop, Latino Club
PORTFOLIO	Available at http://jrichardson.localhost/jrportfolio.htm
REFERENCES	Available upon request

SCANNABLE RÉSUMÉS Scannable résumés might be submitted on paper, by e-mail, or through an online employment service. The prospective employer scans and searches the résumé electronically; a database matches keywords in the employer's job description with keywords in the résumé. A human screener then looks through the résumés filtered out by the database matching. A scannable résumé must be very simply formatted so that the scanner can accurately pick up its content. In general, follow these guidelines when preparing a scannable résumé:

- Include a Keywords section that lists words likely to be searched by a scanner. (Use nouns such as *manager*, not verbs such as *manage*.)

- Use standard résumé headings (Education, Experience, and so on).

- Avoid special characters, graphics, or font styles such as boldface or italics.

WEB RÉSUMÉS Posting your résumé on a Web site is an easy way to provide prospective employers with up-to-date information about your experience and employment goals. Web résumés allow you to present details about yourself without overwhelming your readers. Most guidelines for traditional résumés apply to Web résumés. Always list the date that you last updated the résumé.

ON THE WEB > dianahacker.com/writersref
Model papers > Résumés

Memos

Usually brief and to the point, a memo reports information, makes a request, or recommends an action. The format of a memo, which varies from company to company, is designed for easy distribution, quick reading, and efficient filing.

Most memos display the date, the name of the recipient, the name of the sender, and the subject on separate lines at the top of the page. Many companies have preprinted forms for memos, and some word processing programs allow you to call up a memo template.

The subject line of a memo, on paper or in e-mail, should describe the topic as clearly and concisely as possible, and the introductory paragraph should get right to the point. In addition, the body of the memo should be well organized and easy to skim. To promote skimming, use headings where possible and display any items that deserve special attention by setting them off from the text — in a list, for example, or in boldface.

E-mail

E-mail is fast replacing regular mail in the business world and in most people's personal lives. Especially in business and academic contexts, you will want to show readers that you value their time. Your message may be just one of many that your readers have to wade through. Here are some strategies for writing effective e-mails:

- Fill in the subject line with a meaningful, concise subject to help readers sort through messages and set priorities.

- Put the most important part of your message at the beginning so it will be seen on the first screen.

- For long, detailed messages, consider providing a summary at the beginning.

- Write concisely, and keep paragraphs fairly short, especially if your audience is likely to read your message on the screen.

- Avoid writing in all capital letters or all lowercase letters, a practice that is easy on the writer but hard on the reader.

- Use formatting such as boldface and italics and special characters sparingly; not all e-mail systems handle such elements consistently.

- Proofread for typos and obvious errors that are likely to slow down or annoy readers.

Academic Writing

A Academic Writing

Writing is a fact of college life. No matter what you study, you will be expected to participate in ongoing conversations conducted by other students and scholars. To join in those conversations, you will analyze and respond to texts, evaluate other people's arguments, and put forth your own ideas. Whatever the discipline, the goal of academic writing is to argue a thesis and support it with appropriate evidence.

A1

Writing about texts

The word *texts* can refer to a variety of works: essays, periodical articles, government reports, books, and even visuals such as advertisements and photographs. Most assignments that ask you to respond to a text call for a summary or an analysis or both.

A summary is neutral in tone and demonstrates that you have understood the author's key ideas. Assignments calling for an analysis of a text vary widely, but they will usually ask you to look at how the text's parts contribute to its central argument or purpose, often with the aim of judging its evidence or overall effect.

When you write about a written text, you will need to read it several times to digest its full meaning. Two techniques will help you move beyond a superficial first reading: (1) annotating the text with your observations and questions and (2) outlining the text's key points. The same techniques will help you analyze visual texts.

A1-a Read actively: Annotate the text.

Read actively by jotting down your questions, thoughts, and reactions in the margins of the text or in a notebook. Use a pencil instead of a highlighter; with a pencil you can underline key concepts, mark points, or circle elements that intrigue you. If you change your mind, you can erase your early annotations and replace them with new ones.

ON THE WEB > dianahacker.com/writersref
   Resources for writers and tutors > Tips from writing tutors:
   Benefits of reading

Guidelines for active reading

Familiarize yourself with the basic features and structure of a text.

- What kind of text are you reading? An essay? An editorial? A scholarly article? An advertisement? A photograph?
- What is the author's purpose? To inform? To persuade? To call to action?
- Who is the audience? How does the author attempt to appeal to the audience?
- What is the author's thesis? What question does the text attempt to answer?
- What evidence does the author provide to support the thesis?

Note details that surprise, puzzle, or intrigue you.

- Has the author revealed a fact or made a point that runs counter to what you had assumed was true? What exactly is surprising?
- Has the author made a generalization you disagree with? Can you think of evidence that would challenge the generalization?
- Are there any contradictions or inconsistencies in the text?
- Are there any words, statements, or phrases in the text that you don't understand? If so, what reference materials do you need to consult?

Read and reread to discover meaning.

- What do you notice on a second or third reading that you didn't notice earlier?
- Does the text raise questions that it does not resolve?
- If you could address the author directly, what questions would you pose? Where do you agree and disagree with the author? Why?

Apply critical thinking strategies to visual texts.

- What first strikes you about the image? What elements do you notice immediately?
- Who or what is the main subject of the image?
- What colors and textures dominate?
- What is in the background? In the foreground?
- What role, if any, do words play in the visual text?

Following are an article from a consumer-oriented newsletter and a magazine advertisement, annotated by students. The students, Emilia Sanchez and Albert Lee, were assigned to write a summary and an analysis. Each began by annotating the text.

ANNOTATED ARTICLE

Big Box Stores Are Bad for Main Street
BETSY TAYLOR

There is plenty of reason to be concerned about the proliferation of Wal-Marts and other so-called "big box" stores. The question, however, is not whether or not these types of stores create jobs (although several studies claim they produce a net job loss in local communities) or whether they ultimately save consumers money. The real concern about having a 25-acre slab of concrete with a 100,000 square foot box of stuff land on a town is whether it's good for a <u>community's soul.</u>

Opening strategy — the problem is not x, it's y.

Sentimental — what is a community's soul?

The worst thing about "big boxes" is that they have a tendency to produce Ross Perot's famous "big sucking sound" — sucking the life out of cities and small towns across the country. On the other hand, small businesses are great for a community. They offer more personal service; they won't threaten to pack up and leave town if they don't get tax breaks, free roads and other blandishments; and small-business owners are much more responsive to a customer's needs. (Ever try to complain about bad service or poor quality products <u>to the president</u> of Home Depot?)

Lumps all big boxes together.

Assumes all small businesses are attentive.

Logic problem? Why couldn't customer complain to store manager?

<u>Yet,</u> if big boxes are so bad, why are they so successful? One glaring reason is that (we've become a nation of hyperconsumers,) and the big-box boys know this. Downtown shopping districts comprised of small businesses take some of the efficiency out of overconsumption. There's all that hassle of having to travel from store to store, and having to pull out your credit card so many times. Occasionally, we even find ourselves chatting with the shopkeeper, wandering into a coffee shop to visit with a friend or otherwise wasting precious time that could be spent on acquiring more stuff.

True?

Nostalgia for a time that is long gone or never was.

But let's face it — bustling, thriving city centers are fun. They breathe life into a community. They allow cities and towns to stand out from each other. They provide an atmosphere for people to interact with each other that just cannot be found at Target, or Wal-Mart or Home Depot.

Community vs. economy. What about prices?

Is it anti-American to be against having a retail giant set up shop in one's community? Some people would say so. On the other hand, if you board up Main Street, what's left of America?

Ends with emotional appeal.

ANNOTATED ADVERTISEMENT

What signals is McDonald's giving customers about its menu?

Is McDonald's trying to remake its image with lettuce?

A real customer?

Repetition of "real."

Local vs. corporation, McDonald's as family restaurant.

Open, nothing to hide.

Trying to show its commitment to customer service.

A1-b Try sketching a brief outline of the text.

After reading, rereading, and annotating a text, attempt to outline it. Seeing how the author has constructed a text can help you understand it. As you sketch an outline, pay special attention to the text's thesis (central idea) and its topic sentences. The thesis of a written text usually appears in the introduction, often in the first or second paragraph. Topic sentences can be found at the beginnings of most body paragraphs, where they announce a shift to a new topic. (See C2-a and C4-a.)

In your outline, put the author's thesis and key points in your own words. Here, for example, is the outline that Emilia Sanchez developed as she prepared to write her summary and analysis of the text printed on page 59. Notice that the outline does not simply trace the author's ideas paragraph by paragraph; instead, it sums up the article's central points.

OUTLINE OF "BIG BOX STORES ARE BAD FOR MAIN STREET"

Thesis: Whether or not they take jobs away from a community or offer low prices to consumers, we should be worried about "big-box" stores like Wal-Mart, Target, and Home Depot because they harm communities by taking the life out of downtown shopping districts.

    I. Small businesses are better for cities and towns than big-box stores are.
      A. Small businesses offer personal service and big-box stores do not.
      B. Small businesses don't make demands on community resources as big-box stores do.
      C. Small businesses respond to customer concerns and big-box stores do not.
   II. Big-box stores are successful because they cater to consumption at the expense of benefits to the community.
      A. Buying everything in one place is convenient.
      B. Shopping at small businesses may be inefficient, but it provides opportunities for socializing.
      C. Downtown shopping districts give each city or town a special identity.

Conclusion: While some people say that it's anti-American to oppose big-box stores, actually these stores threaten the communities that make up America by encouraging buying at the expense of the traditional interactions of Main Street.

A visual, of course, doesn't state an explicit thesis or an explicit line of reasoning. Instead, you must infer the meaning beneath the image's surface and interpret its central point and supporting ideas from the elements of its design. One way to outline a visual text is to try to define its purpose and sketch a list of its key elements. Here, for example, are the key features that Albert Lee identified for the advertisement printed on page 60.

> Purpose: To persuade readers that McDonald's is concerned about its customers' health.
>
> Key features:
>
> - A close-up of a fresh, green lettuce leaf makes up the entire background.
> - Near the center there's a comment card with a handwritten question from a "real" McDonald's customer: "What makes your lettuce so crisp?"
> - A photograph of a smiling woman is clipped to the card.
> - Beneath the comment card is the company's response, which emphasizes the farm-fresh quality and purity of its vegetables and urges customers to ask other candid questions.
> - At the bottom of the ad is the McDonald's slogan "I'm lovin' it."

ON THE WEB > dianahacker.com/writersref
Model papers > MLA analysis papers > Albert Lee

A1-c Summarize to demonstrate your understanding.

Your goal in summarizing a text is to state the work's main ideas and key points simply, briefly, and accurately. If you have sketched a brief outline of the text (see A1-b), refer to it as you draft your summary.

To summarize a written text, first find the author's central idea — the thesis. Then divide the whole piece into a few major and perhaps minor ideas. Since a summary must be fairly short, you must make judgments about what is most important. To summarize a visual text, begin with information about who created the visual, who the intended audience is, and when and where the visual appeared. Briefly explain the visual's main point or purpose and point to its key features.

Following is Emilia Sanchez's summary of the article that is printed on page 59.

> In her essay "Big Box Stores Are Bad for Main Street," Betsy Taylor argues that chain stores harm communities by taking the life out of downtown shopping districts. Explaining that a commu-

Guidelines for writing a summary

- In the first sentence, mention the title of the text, the name of the author, and the author's thesis or the visual's central point.
- Maintain a neutral tone; be objective.
- Use the third-person point of view and the present tense.
- Keep your focus on the text. Don't state the author's ideas as if they were your own.
- Put all or most of your summary in your own words; if you borrow a phrase or a sentence from the text, put it in quotation marks and give the page number in parentheses.
- Limit yourself to presenting the text's key points.
- Be concise; make every word count.

nity's "soul" is more important than low prices or consumer convenience, she argues that small businesses are better than stores like Wal-Mart, Target, and Home Depot because they emphasize personal interactions and don't place demands on a community's resources. Taylor asserts that big-box stores are successful because "we've become a nation of hyper-consumers," although the convenience of shopping in these stores comes at the expense of benefits to the community. She concludes by suggesting that it's not "anti-American" to oppose big-box stores because the damage they inflict on downtown shopping districts extends to America itself.

— Emilia Sanchez, student

A1-d Analyze to demonstrate your critical thinking.

Whereas a summary most often answers the question of *what* a text says, an analysis looks at *how* a text makes its point.

Typically, an analysis takes the form of an essay that makes its own argument about a text. Include an introduction that briefly summarizes the text, a thesis that states your own judgment about the text, and body paragraphs that support your thesis with evidence. If you are analyzing an image, examine it as a whole and then reflect on how the individual elements contribute to its overall meaning. If you have written a summary of the text, you may find it useful to refer to the main points of the summary as you write your analysis.

Beginning on the next page is Emilia Sanchez's analysis of the article by Betsy Taylor (see p. 59).

Emilia Sanchez

Professor Goodwin

English 10

22 October 2005

Rethinking Big-Box Stores

In her essay "Big Box Stores Are Bad for Main Street," Betsy Taylor focuses not on the economic effects of large chain stores but on the effects these stores have on the "soul" of America. She argues that stores like Home Depot, Target, and Wal-Mart are bad for America because they draw people out of downtown shopping districts and cause them to focus exclusively on consumption. In contrast, she believes that small businesses are good for America because they provide personal attention, foster community interaction, and make each city unique. But Taylor's argument is ultimately unconvincing because it is based on nostalgia--on idealized images of a quaint Main Street--rather than on the roles that businesses play in consumers' lives and communities. By ignoring the more complex, economically driven relationships between large chain stores and their communities, Taylor incorrectly assumes that simply getting rid of big-box stores would have a positive effect on America's communities.

Taylor's use of colorful language reveals that she has a nostalgic view of American society and does not understand economic realities. In her first paragraph, Taylor refers to a big-box store as a "25-acre slab of concrete with a 100,000 square foot box of stuff" that "lands on a town," evoking images of a monolithic monster crushing the American way of life (1011). But her assessment oversimplifies a complex issue. Taylor does not consider that many downtown business districts failed long before chain stores moved in, when factories and mills closed and workers lost their jobs. In cities with struggling economies, big-box stores can actually provide much-needed jobs. Similarly, while Taylor blames big-box stores for harming local economies by asking for tax breaks, free roads, and other perks, she doesn't acknowledge that these stores also enter into economic partnerships with the surrounding communities by offering financial benefits to schools and hospitals.

Marginal annotations:

Opening summarizes the article's purpose and thesis.

Thesis expresses Sanchez's judgment of Taylor's article.

Signal phrase introduces quotations from the source; Sanchez uses an MLA in-text citation.

Sanchez begins to identify and challenge Taylor's assumptions.

Marginal annotations indicate MLA-style formatting and effective writing.

Sanchez 2

Taylor's assumption that shopping in small businesses is always better for the customer also seems driven by nostalgia for an old-fashioned Main Street rather than by the facts. While she may be right that many small businesses offer personal service and are responsive to customer complaints, she does not consider that many customers appreciate the service at big-box stores. Just as customer service is better at some small businesses than at others, it is impossible to generalize about service at all big-box stores. For example, customers depend on the lenient return policies and the wide variety of products at stores like Target and Home Depot.

Taylor blames big-box stores for encouraging American "hyper-consumerism," but she oversimplifies by equating big-box stores with bad values and small businesses with good values. Like her other points, this claim ignores the economic and social realities of American society today. Big-box stores do not force Americans to buy more. By offering lower prices in a convenient setting, however, they allow consumers to save time and purchase goods they might not be able to afford from small businesses. The existence of more small businesses would not change what most Americans can afford, nor would it reduce their desire to buy affordable merchandise.

Taylor may be right that some big-box stores have a negative impact on communities and that small businesses offer certain advantages. But she ignores the economic conditions that support big-box stores as well as the fact that Main Street was in decline before the big-box store arrived. Getting rid of big-box stores will not bring back a simpler America populated by thriving, unique Main Streets; in reality, Main Street will not survive if consumers cannot afford to shop there.

Clear topic sentence announces a shift to a new topic.

Sanchez refutes Taylor's claim.

Sanchez treats the author fairly.

Conclusion returns to the thesis and shows the wider significance of Sanchez's analysis.

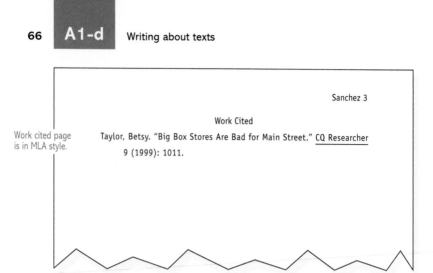

Sanchez 3

Work Cited

Taylor, Betsy. "Big Box Stores Are Bad for Main Street." CQ Researcher
9 (1999): 1011.

Work cited page
is in MLA style.

Guidelines for analyzing a text

Written texts. Instructors who ask you to analyze a written nonfiction text often expect you to address some of the following questions.

- What is the author's thesis or central idea? Who is the audience?
- What questions does the author address (implicitly or explicitly)?
- How does the author structure the text? What are the key parts and how do they relate to one another and to the thesis?
- What strategies has the author used to generate interest in the argument and to persuade readers of its merit?
- What evidence does the author use to support the thesis? How persuasive is the evidence?
- Does the author anticipate objections and counter opposing views?
- Does the author fall prey to any faulty reasoning?

Visual texts. If you are analyzing a visual text, the following additional questions will help you evaluate an image's purpose and meaning.

- What surprises, perplexes, or intrigues you about the image?
- What clues suggest the visual text's intended audience? How does the image appeal to its audience?
- If the text is an advertisement, what product is it selling? Does it attempt to sell an idea or a message as well?
- If the visual text includes words, how do the words contribute to the meaning of the image?
- How do design elements — colors, shapes, perspective, background, foreground — shape the visual text's meaning or serve its purpose?

A2

Constructing reasonable arguments

In writing an argument, you take a stand on a debatable issue. The question being debated might be a matter of public policy:

Should religious groups be allowed to meet on public school property?

What is the least dangerous way to dispose of nuclear waste?

Should a state enact laws rationing medical care?

On such questions, reasonable people may disagree.

Reasonable men and women also disagree about many scholarly issues. Psychologists debate the role of genes and environment in behavior; historians interpret causes of the Civil War quite differently; biologists challenge one another's predictions about the effects of global warming.

When you construct a *reasonable* argument, your goal is not simply to win or to have the last word. Your aim is to explain your understanding of the truth about a subject or to propose the best solution available for solving a problem — without being needlessly combative. In constructing your argument, you join a conversation with other writers and readers. Your aim is to convince readers to reconsider their opinions by offering new reasons to question an old viewpoint.

ACADEMIC ENGLISH Some cultures value writers who argue with force and express their superiority. Other cultures value writers who argue subtly or indirectly, often with an apology. Academic audiences in the United States will expect your writing to be assertive and confident — neither aggressive nor passive. Create an assertive tone by acknowledging different opinions and supporting your view with specific evidence.

TOO AGGRESSIVE	Of course prayer should be discouraged in public schools. Only foolish people think that organized prayer is good for everyone.
TOO PASSIVE	I might be wrong, but I think that organized prayer should be discouraged in public schools.
ASSERTIVE TONE	Organized prayer should be discouraged in public schools because it violates the religious freedom guaranteed by the First Amendment.

If you are uncertain about the tone of your work, ask for help at your school's writing center.

A2-a Examine your issue's social and intellectual contexts.

Arguments appear in social and intellectual contexts. Public policy debates obviously arise in social contexts. Grounded in specific times and places, such debates are conducted among groups with competing values and interests. For example, the debate over nuclear power plants has been renewed in the United States in light of skyrocketing energy costs and terrorism concerns — with environmentalists, nuclear industry officials, and consumers all weighing in on the argument. Most public policy debates also have intellectual dimensions that address scientific or theoretical questions. In the case of the nuclear power issue, physicists, biologists, and economists all contribute their expertise.

Scholarly debates play out in intellectual contexts, but they have a social dimension too. Scholars and researchers rarely work in a vacuum: They respond to the contributions of other specialists in the field, often building on others' views and refining them, but at times challenging them.

Because many of your readers will be aware of the social and intellectual contexts in which your issue is grounded, you need to conduct some research before preparing your argument; consulting even a few sources can help. For example, the student whose paper appears on pages 74–76 became more knowledgeable about his issue — the ethics of performance-enhancing procedures in sports — after consulting a few brief sources.

A2-b View your audience as a panel of jurors.

Do not assume that your audience already agrees with you; instead, envision skeptical readers who, like a panel of jurors, will make up their minds after listening to all sides of the argument. If you are arguing a public policy issue, aim your paper at readers who represent a variety of opinions. In the case of the debate over nuclear power, for example, imagine a jury representative of those who have a stake in the matter: environmentalists, nuclear industry officials, and consumers.

At times, you can deliberately narrow your audience. If you are working within a word limit, for example, you might not have the space in which to address the concerns of all parties to the nuclear energy debate. Or you might be primarily interested in reaching one segment of a general audience, such as consumers. In such instances, you can still view your audience as a panel of jurors; the jury will simply be a less diverse group.

In the case of scholarly debates, you will be addressing readers who share your interest in a discipline such as literature or psychology. Such readers belong to a group with an agreed-upon way of investigating and talking about issues. Though they generally agree about procedures, scholars in an academic discipline often disagree about particular issues. Once you see how they disagree about your issue, you should be able to imagine a jury that reflects the variety of opinions they hold.

A2-c In your introduction, establish credibility and state your position.

When you construct an argument, make sure your introduction contains a thesis sentence that states your position on the issue you have chosen to debate (see also C2-a). In the sentences leading up to the thesis, establish your credibility with readers by showing that you are knowledgeable and fair-minded. If possible, build common ground with readers who may not be in initial agreement with your views and show them why they need to consider your thesis.

In the following introduction, student Kevin Smith presents himself as someone worth listening to. His opening sentence shows that he is familiar with the legal issues surrounding school prayer. His next sentence reveals him to be fair-minded, as he presents the views of both sides. Even Smith's thesis builds common ground: "Prayer is too important to be trusted to our public schools." Because Smith introduces both sides of the debate, readers are likely to approach his essay with an open mind.

> Although the Supreme Court has ruled against prayer in public schools on First Amendment grounds, many people still feel that prayer should be allowed. Such people value prayer as a practice central to their faith and believe that prayer is a way for schools to reinforce moral principles. They also compellingly point out a paradox in the First Amendment itself: at what point does the separation of church and state restrict the freedom of those who wish to practice their religion? What proponents of school prayer fail to realize, however, is that the Supreme Court's decision, although it was made on legal grounds, makes sense on religious grounds as well. Prayer is too important to be trusted to our public schools. — Kevin Smith, student

A good way to test a thesis while drafting and revising is to imagine a counterargument to your argument (see A2-f). If you can't think of an opposing point of view, rethink your thesis or ask friends or classmates to respond to your argument.

A2-d Back up your thesis with persuasive lines of argument.

Arguments of any complexity contain lines of argument that, when taken together, might reasonably persuade readers that the thesis has merit. Here, for example, are the main lines of argument used by a student whose thesis was that athletes' use of biotechnology could constitute an unfair advantage in sports.

> Thesis: Athletes who use any type of biotechnology give themselves an unfair advantage and disrupt the sense of fair play, and they should be banned from competition.
>
> • Athletic achievement nowadays increasingly results from biological and high-tech intervention rather than strictly from hard work.
> • There is a difference between the use of state-of-the-art equipment and drugs and the modification of the body itself.
> • If the rules that guarantee an even playing field are violated, competitors and spectators alike are deprived of a sound basis of comparison on which to judge athletic effort and accomplishment.
> • If we let athletes alter their bodies through biotechnology, we might as well dispense with the human element altogether.

If you sum up your main lines of argument, you will have a rough outline of your essay. The outline will consist of your central claim — the thesis — and any supporting claims that back it up. In your paper, you will provide evidence for each of these claims.

ON THE WEB > dianahacker.com/writersref
  Resources for writers and tutors > Tips from writing tutors:
  Writing arguments; Writing essays in English

A2-e Support your claims with specific evidence.

You will need to support your central claim and any subordinate claims with evidence: facts, statistics, examples and illustrations, expert opinion, and so on. Most debatable topics require that you consult some written sources to gather evidence. Always cite your sources. Documentation gives credit to the authors and shows readers how to locate a source in case they want to assess its credibility or explore the issue further (see R4).

Using facts and statistics

A fact is something that is known with certainty because it has been objectively verified: The capital of Wyoming is Cheyenne.

Carbon has an atomic weight of 12. John F. Kennedy was assassinated on November 22, 1963. Statistics are collections of numerical facts: Alcohol abuse is a factor in nearly 40 percent of traffic fatalities. Almost six out of ten US households own a DVD player. As of 2004, about 48 percent of privately held businesses in the United States were owned by women.

Most arguments are supported at least to some extent by facts and statistics. For example, in the following passage the writer uses statistics to show that college students are granted unreasonably high credit limits.

> A 2001 study by Nellie Mae revealed that while the average credit card debt per college undergraduate is $2,327, more than 20% of undergraduates who have at least one credit card maintain a much higher debt level, from $3,000 to $7,000 (Barrett).

Writers and politicians often use statistics in selective ways to bolster their views. If you suspect that a writer's handling of statistics is not quite fair, read authors with opposing views, who may give you a fuller understanding of the numbers.

Using examples and illustrations

Examples and illustrations (extended examples, often in story form) rarely prove a point by themselves, but when used in combination with other forms of evidence they flesh out an argument and bring it to life. Because examples often are vivid, they can reach readers in ways that statistics cannot.

In a paper arguing that any athletes who use gene therapy should be banned from competition, Jamal Hammond gives a thought-provoking example of how running with genetically modified limbs is no different from riding a motorcycle in a footrace.

Citing expert opinion

Although they are no substitute for careful reasoning of your own, the views of an expert can contribute to the force of your argument. For example, to help him make the case that biotechnology could degrade the meaning of sports, Jamal Hammond quotes the remarks of an expert:

> Thomas Murray, chair of the ethics advisory panel for the World Anti-Doping Agency, says he hopes, not too optimistically, for an "alternative future . . . where we still find meaning in great performances as an alchemy of two factors, natural talents . . . and virtues" (qtd. in Jenkins D11).

When you rely on expert opinion, make sure that your source is an authority in the field you are writing about. In some cases you may need to provide credentials showing why your source is worth listening to. When including expert testimony in your paper, you can summarize or paraphrase the expert's opinion or you can quote the expert's exact words. You will of course need to document the source, as in the example just given (see R4).

A2-f Anticipate objections; counter opposing arguments.

Readers who already agree with you need no convincing, although most welcome a well-argued case for their position on an issue. Indifferent or skeptical readers, however, may resist an argument that conflicts with their point of view. In addition to presenting your own case, therefore, you should acknowledge opposing arguments and any contradictory evidence and explain why your position is stronger.

Countering opposing arguments

To anticipate a possible objection, consider the following questions:

- Could a reasonable person draw a different conclusion from your facts or examples?
- Might a reader question any of your assumptions?
- Could a reader offer an alternative explanation of this issue?

To respond to a potential objection, consider these questions:

- Can you concede the point to the opposition but challenge the point's importance or usefulness?
- Can you explain why readers should consider a new perspective or question a piece of evidence?
- Should you qualify your position in light of contradictory evidence?
- Can you suggest a different interpretation of the evidence?

When you write, use phrasing to signal to readers that you're about to present an objection. Often the signal phrase can go in the lead sentence of a paragraph:

- Critics of this view argue that. . . .
- Some readers might point out that. . . .
- Gray presents compelling challenges to. . . .
- But isn't it possible that . . . ?

There is no best place in an essay to deal with opposing views. Often it is useful to summarize the opposing position early in your essay. After stating your thesis but before developing your own arguments, you might have a paragraph that takes up the most important counterargument. Or you can anticipate objections paragraph by paragraph as you develop your case. Wherever you decide to address opposing points of view, explain the arguments of others accurately and fairly.

A2-g Build common ground.

As you counter opposing arguments, try to build common ground with readers who do not initially agree with your views. If you can show that you share your readers' values, they may be able to switch to your position without giving up what they feel is important. For example, to persuade people opposed to shooting deer, a state wildlife commission would have to show that it too cares about preserving deer and does not want them to die needlessly. Having established these values in common, the commission might be able to persuade critics that a carefully controlled hunting season is good for the deer population because it prevents starvation caused by overpopulation.

People believe that intelligence and decency support their side of an argument. To change sides, they must continue to feel intelligent and decent. Otherwise they will persist in their opposition.

A2-h Sample argument paper

In the following paper, student Jamal Hammond argues that we should ban the use of biotechnology by athletes because the practice degrades the values of hard work and natural ability. Notice that he is careful to present opposing views fairly before providing his counterarguments.

In writing the paper, Hammond consulted three newspaper articles, two in print and one online. When he quotes or uses information from a source, he cites the source with an MLA (Modern Language Association) in-text citation. Citations in the paper refer readers to the list of works cited at the end of the paper. (See MLA-4.)

ON THE WEB > dianahacker.com/writersref
Model papers > MLA papers: Orlov; Daly; Levi

Jamal Hammond

Professor Paschal

English 102

17 March 2006

Performance Enhancement through Biotechnology

Has No Place in Sports

Opening sentences provide background for Hammond's thesis.

The debate over athletes' use of performance-enhancing substances is getting more complicated as biotechnologies such as gene therapy become a reality. The availability of these new methods of boosting performance will force us to decide what we value most in sports--displays of physical excellence developed through hard work or victory at all costs. For centuries, spectators and athletes have cherished the tradition of fairness in sports. While sports competition is, of course, largely about winning, it is also about the means by which a player or team wins.

Thesis states the main point.

Athletes who use any type of biotechnology give themselves an unfair advantage and disrupt the sense of fair play, and they should be banned from competition.

Researchers are experimenting with techniques that could manipulate an athlete's genetic code to build stronger muscles or

Hammond establishes his credibility by summarizing medical research.

increase endurance. Searching for cures for diseases like Parkinson's and muscular dystrophy, scientists at the University of Pennsylvania have created "Schwarzenegger mice," rodents that grew larger-than-normal muscles after receiving injections with a gene that stimulates growth protein. The researchers also found that a combination of gene manipulation and exercise led to a 35% increase in the strength of rats'

Source is cited in MLA style.

leg muscles (Lamb 13).

Such therapies are breakthroughs for humans suffering from muscular diseases; for healthy athletes, they could mean new world records in sports involving speed and endurance--but at what cost to the integrity of athletic competition? The International Olympic Committee's

Hammond uses specific evidence to support his thesis.

World Anti-Doping Agency has become so alarmed about the possible effects of new gene technology on athletic competition that it has banned the use of gene therapies and urged researchers to devise a test for detecting genetic modification (Lamb 13).

Marginal annotations indicate MLA-style formatting **and** effective writing.

Hammond 2

Some bioethicists argue that this next wave of performance enhancement is an acceptable and unavoidable feature of competition. As Dr. Andy Miah, who supports the regulated use of gene therapies in sports, claims, "The idea of the naturally perfect athlete is romantic nonsense. . . . An athlete achieves what he or she achieves through all sorts of means-- technology, sponsorship, support and so on" (qtd. in Rudebeck). Miah, in fact, sees athletes' imminent turn to genetic modification as "merely a continuation of the way sport works; it allows us to create more extraordinary performances" (Rudebeck). Miah's approval of "extraordinary performances" as the goal of competition reflects our culture's tendency to demand and reward new heights of athletic achievement. The problem is that achievement nowadays increasingly results from biological and high-tech intervention rather than strictly from hard work.

Better equipment, such as aerodynamic bicycles and fiberglass poles for pole vaulting, have made it possible for athletes to record achievements unthinkable a generation ago. But athletes themselves must put forth the physical effort of training and practice--they must still build their skills--even in the murky area of legal and illegal drug use (Jenkins D11). There is a difference between the use of state-of-the-art equipment and drugs and the modification of the body itself. Athletes who use medical technology to alter their bodies can bypass the hard work of training by taking on the powers of a machine. If they set new records this way, we lose the opportunity to witness sports as a spectacle of human effort and are left marveling at scientific advances, which have little relation to the athletic tradition of fair play.

Such a tradition has long defined athletic competition. Sports rely on equal conditions to ensure fair play, from regulations that demand similar equipment to referees who evenhandedly apply the rules to all participants. If the rules that guarantee an even playing field are violated, competitors and spectators alike are deprived of a sound basis of comparison on which to judge athletic effort and accomplishment. When major league baseball rules call for solid-wood bats, the player who uses a corked bat enhances his hitting statistics at the expense of players who use regulation equipment. When Ben Johnson tested

Opposing views are presented fairly.

"Qtd. in" is used for an indirect source: words quoted in another source.

Hammond counters opposing arguments.

Hammond develops the thesis.

Transition moves from the writer's main argument to specific examples.

Hammond 3

positive for steroids after setting a world record in the 100-meter dash in the 1988 Olympics, his "achievement" devalued the intense training that his competitors had undergone to prepare for the event--and the International Olympic Committee responded by stripping Johnson of his medal and his world record. Likewise, athletes who use gene therapy to alter their bodies and enhance their performance will create an uneven playing field.

If we let athletes alter their bodies through biotechnology, we might as well dispense with the human element altogether. Instead of watching the 100-meter dash to see who the fastest runner in the world is, we might just as well watch the sprinters mount motorcycles and race across the finish line. The absurdity of such an example, however, points to the damage that we will do to sports if we allow these therapies. Thomas Murray, chair of the ethics advisory panel for the World Anti-Doping Agency, says he hopes, not too optimistically, for an "alternative future . . . where we still find meaning in great performances as an alchemy of two factors, natural talents . . . and virtues" (qtd. in Jenkins D11).

Unless we are willing to organize separate sporting events and leagues--an Olympics, say, for athletes who have opted for a boost from the test tube and another for athletes who have chosen to keep their bodies natural--we should ask from our athletes that they dazzle us less with extraordinary performance and more with the fruits of their hard work.

A vivid example helps the writer make his point.

Conclusion echoes the thesis without dully repeating it.

Hammond 4

Works Cited

Works cited page uses MLA style.

Jenkins, Sally. "The First Item in a Pandora's Box of Moral Ambiguities." Washington Post 4 Dec. 2004: D11.

Lamb, Gregory M. "Will Gene-Altered Athletes Kill Sports?" Christian Science Monitor 23 Aug. 2004: 12-13.

Rudebeck, Clare. "The Eyes Have It." Independent [London] 27 Apr. 2005. 28 Feb. 2006 <http://news.independent.co.uk/world/science_technology/article3597.ece>.

A3

Evaluating arguments

In your reading and in your own writing, evaluate all arguments for logic and fairness. Many arguments can stand up to critical scrutiny. Often, however, a line of argument that at first seems reasonable turns out to be fallacious, unfair, or both.

ON THE WEB > dianahacker.com/writersref
Additional resources > Links Library > Critical thinking

A3-a Distinguish between reasonable and fallacious argumentative tactics.

A number of unreasonable argumentative tactics are known as *logical fallacies*. Most of the fallacies — such as hasty generalizations and false analogies — are misguided or dishonest uses of legitimate argumentative strategies. The examples in this section suggest when such strategies are reasonable and when they are not.

Generalizing (inductive reasoning)

Writers and thinkers generalize all the time. We look at a sample of data and conclude that data we have not observed will most likely conform to what we have seen before. From a spoonful of soup, we conclude just how salty the whole bowl will be. After numerous bad experiences with an airline, we decide to book future flights with one of its competitors instead.

When we draw a conclusion from an array of facts, we are engaged in inductive reasoning. Such reasoning deals in probability, not certainty. For a conclusion to be highly probable, it must be based on evidence that is sufficient, representative, and relevant. (See the chart on p. 79.)

The fallacy known as *hasty generalization* is a conclusion based on insufficient or unrepresentative evidence.

HASTY GENERALIZATION
Deaths from drug overdoses in Metropolis have doubled in the past three years. Therefore, more Americans than ever are dying from drug abuse.

Data from one city do not justify a conclusion about the whole
United States.

A *stereotype* is a hasty generalization about a group. Here are a
few examples.

STEREOTYPES

Women are bad bosses.

Politicians are corrupt.

Asian students are exceptionally intelligent.

Stereotyping is common because of our human tendency to perceive
selectively. We tend to see what we want to see; that is, we notice
evidence confirming our already formed opinions and fail to notice
evidence to the contrary. For example, if you have concluded that
politicians are corrupt, your stereotype will be confirmed by news
reports of legislators being indicted — even though every day the
media describe conscientious officials serving the public honestly
and well.

NOTE: Many hasty generalizations contain words like *all, ever, al-*
ways, and *never*, when qualifiers such as *most, many, usually*, and
seldom would be more accurate.

Drawing analogies

An analogy points out a similarity between two things that are otherwise different. Analogies can be an effective means of arguing a
point. In fact, our system of case law, which relies heavily on prece-
dents, makes extensive use of reasoning by analogy. A prosecutor
may argue, for example, that Z is guilty because his actions resemble those of X and Y, who were judged guilty in previous rulings. In
response, the defense may maintain that the actions of Z bear only
a superficial resemblance to those of X and Y and that in legally
relevant respects they are in fact quite different.

It is not always easy to draw the line between a reasonable and
an unreasonable analogy. At times, however, an analogy is clearly
off-base, in which case it is called a *false analogy*.

FALSE ANALOGY

If we can put humans on the moon, we should be able to find a cure
for the common cold.

The writer has falsely assumed that because two things are alike in
one respect, they must be alike in others. Putting human beings on
the moon and finding a cure for the common cold are both scientific

Testing inductive reasoning

Though inductive reasoning leads to probable and not absolute truth, you can assess a conclusion's likely probability by asking three questions. This chart shows how to apply those questions to a sample conclusion based on a survey.

CONCLUSION   The majority of students on our campus would subscribe to wireless Internet access if it were available.

EVIDENCE   In a recent survey, 923 of 1,515 students questioned say they would subscribe to wireless Internet access.

1. Is the evidence sufficient?
    That depends. On a small campus (say, 3,000 students), the pool of students surveyed would be sufficient for market research, but on a large campus (say, 30,000), 1,515 students are only 5 percent of the population. If that 5 percent were known to be truly representative of the other 95 percent, however, even such a small sample would be sufficient (see question 2).

2. Is the evidence representative?
    The evidence is representative if those responding to the survey reflect the characteristics of the entire student population: age, sex, level of technical expertise, amount of disposable income, and so on. If most of those surveyed are majoring in technical fields, for example, the researchers would be wise to question the survey's conclusion.

3. Is the evidence relevant?
    The answer is yes. The results of the survey are directly linked to the conclusion. A question about the number of hours spent on the Internet, by contrast, would not be relevant, because it would not be about *subscribing to wireless Internet access*.

challenges, but the technical problems confronting medical researchers are quite different from those solved by space scientists.

Tracing causes and effects

Demonstrating a connection between causes and effects is rarely a simple matter. For example, to explain why a chemistry course has a high failure rate, you would begin by listing possible causes: inadequate preparation of students, poor teaching, large class size, lack of qualified tutors, and so on. Next you would investigate each possible cause. To see whether inadequate preparation contributes to the high failure rate, for instance, you might compare the math and science backgrounds of successful and failing students. To see whether large class size is a contributing factor, you might run a pilot program of small classes and compare grades in the small classes with those in the larger ones. Only after investigating the possible causes would you be able to weigh the relative impact of each cause and suggest appropriate remedies.

Because cause-and-effect reasoning is so complex, it is not surprising that writers frequently oversimplify it. In particular, writers sometimes assume that because one event follows another, the first is the cause of the second. This common fallacy is known as *post hoc*, from the Latin *post hoc, ergo propter hoc*, meaning "after this, therefore because of this."

POST HOC FALLACY

Since Governor Cho took office, unemployment of minorities in the state has decreased by 7 percent. Governor Cho should be applauded for reducing unemployment among minorities.

The writer must show that Governor Cho's policies are responsible for the decrease in unemployment; it is not enough to show that the decrease followed the governor's taking office.

Weighing options

Especially when reasoning about problems and solutions, writers must weigh options. To be fair, a writer should mention the full range of options, showing why one is superior to the others or might work well in combination with others.

It is unfair to suggest that there are only two alternatives when in fact there are more. Writers who set up a false choice between their preferred option and one that is clearly unsatisfactory are guilty of the *either . . . or* fallacy.

EITHER . . . OR FALLACY

Our current war against drugs has not worked. Either we should legalize drugs or we should turn the drug war over to our armed forces and let them fight it.

Clearly there are other options, such as increased funding for drug prevention and treatment.

Making assumptions

An assumption is a claim that is taken to be true — without the need of proof. Most arguments are based to some extent on assumptions, since writers rarely have the time and space to prove all of the conceivable claims on which an argument is based. For example, someone arguing about the best means of limiting population growth in developing countries might well assume that the goal of limiting population growth is worthwhile. For most audiences, there would be no need to articulate this assumption or to defend it.

There is a danger, however, in failing to spell out and prove a claim that is clearly controversial. Consider the following short argument, in which a key claim is missing.

ARGUMENT WITH MISSING CLAIM

Violent crime is increasing.

Therefore, we should vigorously enforce the death penalty.

The writer seems to be assuming that the death penalty deters violent criminals — and that most audiences will agree. Obviously, neither is a safe assumption.

When a missing claim is an assertion that few would agree with, we say that a writer is guilty of a *non sequitur* (Latin for "does not follow").

NON SEQUITUR

Mary loves good food; therefore, she will be an excellent chef.

Few people would agree with the missing claim — that lovers of good food always make excellent chefs.

Deducing conclusions (deductive reasoning)

When we deduce a conclusion, we — like Sherlock Holmes — put things together. We establish that a general principle is true, that a specific case is an example of that principle, and that therefore a particular conclusion is a certainty. In real life, such absolute reasoning rarely happens. Approximations of it, however, sometimes occur.

Deductive reasoning can often be structured in a three-step argument called a *syllogism*. The three steps are the major premise, the minor premise, and the conclusion.

1. Anything that increases radiation in the environment is dangerous to public health. (Major premise)
2. Nuclear reactors increase radiation in the environment. (Minor premise)
3. Therefore, nuclear reactors are dangerous to public health. (Conclusion)

The major premise is a generalization. The minor premise is a specific case. The conclusion follows from applying the generalization to the specific case.

Deductive arguments break down if one of the premises is not true or if the conclusion does not logically follow from the premises. In the following short argument, the major premise is very likely untrue.

ARGUMENT WITH A QUESTIONABLE PREMISE

The police do not give speeding tickets to people driving less than five miles per hour over the limit. Sam is driving fifty-nine miles per hour in a fifty-five-mile-per-hour zone. Therefore, the police will not give Sam a speeding ticket.

The conclusion is true only if the premises are true. If the police sometimes give tickets for less than five-mile-per-hour violations, Sam cannot safely conclude that he will avoid a ticket.

In the following argument, both premises might be true, but the conclusion does not follow logically from them.

CONCLUSION DOES NOT FOLLOW

All members of our club ran in this year's Boston Marathon. Jay ran in this year's Boston Marathon. Therefore, Jay is a member of our club.

The fact that Jay ran the marathon is no guarantee that he is a member of the club. Presumably, many runners are nonmembers.

Assuming that both premises are true, the following argument holds up.

CONCLUSION FOLLOWS

All members of our club ran in this year's Boston Marathon. Jay is a member of our club. Therefore, Jay ran in this year's Boston Marathon.

A3-b Distinguish between legitimate and unfair emotional appeals.

There is nothing wrong with appealing to readers' emotions. After all, many issues worth arguing about have an emotional as well as a logical dimension. Even the Greek logician Aristotle lists *pathos* (emotion) as a legitimate argumentative tactic. For example, in an essay criticizing big-box stores, writer Betsy Taylor has a good reason for tugging at readers' emotions: Her subject is the decline of city and town life. In her conclusion, Taylor appeals to readers' emotions by invoking their national pride.

LEGITIMATE EMOTIONAL APPEAL

Is it anti-American to be against having a retail giant set up shop in one's community? Some people would say so. On the other hand, if you board up Main Street, what's left of America?

As we all know, however, emotional appeals are frequently mis-used. Many of the arguments we see in the media, for instance, strive to win our sympathy rather than our intelligent agreement. A TV commercial suggesting that you will be thin and sexy if you drink a certain diet beverage is making a pitch to emotions. So is a political speech that recommends electing a candidate because he is a devoted husband and father who serves as a volunteer firefighter.

The following passage illustrates several types of unfair emo-tional appeals.

UNFAIR EMOTIONAL APPEALS

This progressive proposal to build a ski resort in the state park has been carefully researched by Western Trust, the largest bank in the state; furthermore, it is favored by a majority of the local mer-chants. The only opposition comes from narrow-minded, do-gooder environmentalists who care more about trees than they do about people; one of their leaders was actually arrested for disturbing the peace several years ago.

Words with strong positive or negative connotations, such as *pro-gressive* and *do-gooder*, are examples of *biased language*. Attacking the persons who hold a belief (environmentalists) rather than refut-ing their argument is called *ad hominem*, a Latin term meaning "to the man." Associating a prestigious name (Western Trust) with the writer's side is called *transfer*. Claiming that an idea should be ac-cepted because a large number of people are in favor (the majority of merchants) is called the *bandwagon appeal*. Bringing in irrelevant issues (the arrest) is a *red herring*, named after a trick used in fox hunts to mislead the dogs by dragging a smelly fish across the trail.

A3-c Judge how fairly a writer handles opposing views.

The way in which a writer deals with opposing views is telling. Some writers address the arguments of the opposition fairly, con-ceding points when necessary and countering others, all in a civil spirit. Other writers will do almost anything to win an argument: either ignoring opposing views altogether or misrepresenting such views and attacking their proponents.

In your own writing, you build credibility by addressing oppos-ing arguments fairly. (See also A2-f.) In your reading, you can as-sess the credibility of your sources by looking at how they deal with views not in agreement with their own.

Describing the views of others

Writers and politicians often deliberately misrepresent the views of others. One way they do this is by setting up a "straw man," a character so weak that he is easily knocked down. The *straw man* fallacy consists of an oversimplification or outright distortion of opposing views. For example, in a California debate over attempts to control the mountain lion population, pro-lion groups characterized their opponents as trophy hunters bent on shooting harmless lions and sticking them on the walls of their dens. In truth, such hunters were only one faction of those who saw a need to control the lion population.

In response to the District of Columbia's request for voting representation, some politicians have set up a straw man, as shown in the following example.

STRAW MAN FALLACY

Washington, DC, residents are lobbying for statehood. Giving a city such as the District of Columbia the status of a state would be unfair.

The straw man wants statehood. In fact, most District citizens are lobbying for voting representation in any form, not necessarily through statehood.

Quoting opposing views

Writers often quote the words of writers who hold opposing views. In general, this is a good idea, for it assures some level of fairness and accuracy. At times, though, both the fairness and accuracy are an illusion.

A source may be misrepresented when it is quoted out of context. All quotations are to some extent taken out of context, but a fair writer will explain the context to readers. To select a provocative sentence from a source and to ignore the more moderate sentences surrounding it is both unfair and misleading. Sometimes a writer deliberately distorts a source through the device of ellipsis dots. Ellipsis dots tell readers that words have been omitted from the original source (see P7-g). When those words are crucial to an author's meaning, omitting them is obviously unfair.

ORIGINAL SOURCE

Johnson's *History of the American West* is riddled with inaccuracies and astonishing in its blatantly racist description of the Indian wars.   — B. Smith, reviewer

MISLEADING QUOTATION

According to B. Smith, Johnson's *History of the American West* is "astonishing in its . . . description of the Indian wars."

A4

Writing in the disciplines

College courses expose you to the thinking of scholars in many disciplines, such as the humanities (literature, music, art), the social sciences (psychology, anthropology, sociology), and the sciences (biology, physics, chemistry). Writing in any discipline provides the opportunity to practice the methods used by scholars in these fields and to enter into their debates. Each field has its own questions, evidence, language, and conventions, but all disciplines share certain expectations for good writing.

A4-a Find commonalities across disciplines.

A good paper in any field needs to communicate a writer's purpose to an audience and to explore an engaging question about a subject (see C1-a). All effective writers make an argument and support their claims with evidence (see A2-e). Writers in any field need to show readers the thesis they're developing (or, in the sciences, the hypothesis they're testing) and how they counter opposing explanations or objections of other writers (see A2-f). All disciplines require writers to document where they found their evidence and from whom they borrowed ideas (see A4-e).

A4-b Recognize the questions writers in a discipline ask.

Disciplines are characterized by the kinds of questions their scholars attempt to answer. One way to understand how disciplines ask different questions is to look at assignments on the same topic in various fields. Many disciplines, for example, might be interested in cults. The questions on the next page show how writers in different fields approach the topic of cults.

SOCIOLOGY	What role does gender play in cult leadership?
HISTORY	Why did the cult of Caesar take hold in ancient Rome?
FILM	How does the movie *Fight Club* portray contemporary cults?
BIOLOGY	Do individuals susceptible to cult influence share genetic characteristics?
BUSINESS	How do multilevel marketing (MLM) practices depend on cult techniques for their success?

The questions you will ask in any discipline will form the basis of the thesis for your paper. Questions themselves don't communicate a central idea, but they may lead you to one. For example, the historian who asks "Why did the cult of Caesar take hold in ancient Rome?" might work out a thesis like this: *By raising Caesar to the status of a deity, imperial Rome attempted to unify the various peoples in its far-flung realm into one cult of worship centered on the emperor.*

A4-c Understand the kinds of evidence writers in a discipline use.

Regardless of the discipline in which you're writing, you must support any claims you make with evidence — facts, statistics, examples and illustrations, expert opinion, and so on.

The kinds of evidence used in different disciplines commonly overlap. Students of geography, media studies, and political science, for example, all might use census data to explore different topics. The evidence that one discipline values, however, might not be sufficient to support an interpretation or a conclusion in another field. For example, psychologists, who look for evidence in case studies and in the results of experiments, seldom use expert opinion as evidence. The chart at the top of the next page lists the kinds of evidence typically used in various disciplines.

A4-d Become familiar with a discipline's language conventions.

Every discipline has a specialized vocabulary. As you read the articles and books in a field, you'll notice certain words and phrases that come up repeatedly. Sociologists, for example, use terms like

Evidence typically used in various disciplines

Humanities: Literature, art, film, music, philosophy

- Passages of text or lines of a poem
- Details from an image or a work of art
- Passages of a musical composition
- Essays that analyze original works or put forth theories

Humanities: History

- Firsthand sources such as photographs, letters, maps, and government documents
- Scholarly books and articles that interpret evidence

Social sciences: Psychology, sociology, political science, anthropology

- Data from original experiments
- Results of field research such as interviews, observations, or surveys
- Statistics from government agencies
- Scholarly books and articles that interpret data from original experiments and from other researchers' studies

Sciences: Biology, chemistry, physics

- Data from original experiments
- Scholarly articles that report findings from experiments

---

independent variables, political opportunity resources, and *dyads* to describe social phenomena; computer scientists might refer to *algorithm design* and *loop invariants* to describe programming methods. Practitioners in health fields such as nursing use terms like *treatment plan* and *systemic assessment* to describe patient care. Use discipline-specific terms only when you are certain that you and your readers fully understand their meaning.

In addition to vocabulary, many fields of study have developed specialized conventions for point of view and verb tense. See the chart on the next page.

A4-e Use a discipline's preferred citation style.

In any discipline, you must give credit to those whose ideas or words you have borrowed. Avoid plagiarism by citing sources honestly and accurately (see R4).

Point of view and verb tense in academic writing

Point of view

- Writers of analytical or research essays in the humanities usually use the third-person point of view: *Austen presents* . . . or *Castel describes the battle as.* . . .

- Scientists and most social scientists, who depend on quantitative research to present findings, tend to use the third-person point of view: *The results indicated.* . . .

- Writers in the humanities and in some social sciences occasionally use the first person in discussing their personal experience or in writing a personal narrative: *After spending two years interviewing families affected by the war, I began to understand that* . . . or *Every July as we approached the Cape Cod Canal, we could sense.* . . .

Present or past tense

- Literature scholars use the present tense to discuss a text: *Hughes effectively dramatizes different views of minority assertiveness.* (See MLA-3.)

- Science and social science writers use the past tense to describe experiments and the present tense to discuss the findings: *In 2003, Berkowitz released the first double-blind placebo study.* . . . *These results paint a murky picture.* (See APA-3.)

- Writers in history use the present tense or the present perfect tense to discuss a text: *Shelby Foote describes the scene like this* . . . or *Shelby Foote has described the scene like this.* . . . (See CMS-3.)

While all disciplines emphasize careful documentation, each follows a particular system of citation that its members have agreed on. Writers in the humanities usually use the system established by the Modern Language Association (MLA). Scholars in some social sciences, such as psychology and anthropology, follow the style guidelines of the American Psychological Association (APA); scholars in history and some humanities typically follow *The Chicago Manual of Style.* For guidance on using the MLA, APA, or *Chicago* (CMS) format, see MLA-4, APA-4, or CMS-4, respectively.

Approaching assignments in the disciplines

When you receive a writing assignment, look for key terms that alert you to the purpose of the assignment and to the specialized language of the field. Also determine the kinds of evidence that would be appropriate to support your argument. At first glance, the following four assignments might seem to have nothing in common. A closer look will show that they all use key terms specific to the field, they all use the vocabulary of the field to describe the purpose of the assignment, and they all explain or suggest the kinds of evidence the writers should use.

Environmental science

The El Niño Southern Oscillation (ENSO) is a worldwide climatic oscillation. Evaluate the scientific issues involved in enhancing our ability to predict ENSO events and current limitations to our forecasting ability. Use scientific papers, abstracts, review articles, and course readings to support your conclusions.

1. Key terms
2. Purpose: to summarize and analyze research findings
3. Appropriate evidence: articles, visuals, especially conflicting data

Business

Develop a position in response to the following question: Do corporate takeovers create or destroy value? To determine how these value changes come about, analyze case studies and Securities and Exchange Commission documents.

1. Key terms
2. Purpose: to analyze certain evidence and to argue a position based on that analysis
3. Appropriate evidence: examples of corporate takeovers

→

Approaching assignments in the disciplines (continued)

Anthropology

┌────────2────────┐   ┌────1────┐

Compare and contrast the male rites of passage among the Sambia of

                                        ┌────1────┐

New Guinea and the Maasai of southern Kenya. Consult ethnographic

┌──────────────────3──────────────────┐

descriptions of Sambian and Maasai rituals in course readings.

1. Key terms
2. Purpose: to analyze similarities and differences
3. Appropriate evidence: anthropologists' field research

Nursing

┌─2─┐   ┌────1────┐

Compile a detailed, objective health history for a member of your

        ┌──────────────3──────────────┐

family. Use interview notes and any available health records to build

the patient history.

1. Key term
2. Purpose: to record information
3. Appropriate evidence: interviews, relevant health records

Once you have determined the expectations of a writing assignment, you must be sure to do the following, regardless of the discipline you are writing in.

- Determine your audience and purpose (see C1-a).
- Ask questions appropriate to the field (see A4-b).
- Formulate a thesis (see C2-a).
- Gather evidence. Conduct research if necessary (see R1).
- Identify the required citation style (see R4).

S

Sentence Style

S Sentence Style

S1

Parallelism

If two or more ideas are parallel, they are easier to grasp when expressed in parallel grammatical form. Single words should be balanced with single words, phrases with phrases, clauses with clauses.

> A kiss can be a comma, a question mark, or an exclamation point.
> —Mistinguett

> This novel is not to be tossed lightly aside, but to be hurled with great force.
> —Dorothy Parker

> In matters of principle, stand like a rock; in matters of taste, swim with the current.
> —Thomas Jefferson

GRAMMAR CHECKERS only occasionally flag faulty parallelism. Because the programs cannot assess whether ideas are parallel in grammatical form, they fail to catch the faulty parallelism in sentences such as this: *In my high school, boys were either jocks, preppies, or studied constantly.*

S1-a Balance parallel ideas in a series.

Readers expect items in a series to appear in parallel grammatical form. When one or more of the items violate readers' expectations, a sentence will be needlessly awkward.

▶ Abused children commonly exhibit one or more of the following

symptoms: withdrawal, rebelliousness, restlessness, and *depression.*
~~they are depressed.~~
  ^

The revision presents all of the items as nouns.

▶ Hooked on romance novels, I learned that nothing is more

important than being rich, looking good, and ~~to have~~ a good
         having

time.

The revision uses *-ing* forms for all items in the series.

▶ After assuring us that he was sober, Sam drove down the middle

of the road, ran one red light, and two stop signs.
         went through

The revision adds a verb to make the three items parallel: *drove...,*
ran ..., went through. ...

NOTE: For parallelism in headings and lists, see C5-b and C5-c.

S1-b   Balance parallel ideas presented as pairs.

When pairing ideas, underscore their connection by expressing
them in similar grammatical form. Paired ideas are usually connected in one of these ways:

- with a coordinating conjunction such as *and, but,* or *or*
- with a pair of correlative conjunctions such as *either... or*
  or *not only... but also*
- with a word introducing a comparison, usually *than* or *as*

Parallel ideas linked with coordinating conjunctions

Coordinating conjunctions (*and, but, or, nor, for, so,* and *yet*) link
ideas of equal importance. When those ideas are closely parallel in
content, they should be expressed in parallel grammatical form.

▶ At Lincoln High School, vandalism can result in suspension

or even ~~being expelled~~ from school.
      expulsion

The revision balances the nouns *suspension* and *expulsion.*

▶ Many states are reducing property taxes for home owners and

~~extend~~ financial aid in the form of tax credits to renters.
  extending

The revision balances the *-ing* verb forms *reducing* and *extending.*

Parallel ideas linked with correlative conjunctions

Correlative conjunctions come in pairs: *either. . . or, neither. . . nor, not only. . . but also, both . . . and, whether. . . or.* Make sure that the grammatical structure following the second half of the pair is the same as that following the first half.

▶ Thomas Edison was not only a prolific inventor but also ~~was~~ a

successful entrepreneur.

A prolific inventor follows *not only,* so *a successful entrepreneur* should follow *but also.* Repeating *was* creates an unbalanced effect.

▶ The clerk told me either to change my flight or take the train.

To change my flight, which follows *either,* should be balanced with *to take the train,* which follows *or.*

Comparisons linked with than or as

In comparisons linked with *than* or *as,* the elements being compared should be expressed in parallel grammatical structure.

▶ It is easier to speak in abstractions than ~~grounding~~ one's thoughts

in reality.

To speak in abstractions is balanced with *to ground one's thoughts in reality. Giving* is balanced with *receiving.*

▶ Mother could not persuade me that giving is as much a joy as
receiving.
~~to receive.~~

To speak in abstractions is balanced with *to ground one's thoughts in reality. Giving* is balanced with *receiving.*

NOTE: Comparisons should also be logical and complete. See S2-c.

S1-c Repeat function words to clarify parallels.

Function words such as prepositions (*by, to*) and subordinating conjunctions (*that, because*) signal the grammatical nature of the word groups to follow. Although they can sometimes be omitted, include them whenever they signal parallel structures that might otherwise be missed by readers.

▶ Many hooked smokers try switching to a brand they find

to

distasteful or ⌃ a low tar and nicotine cigarette.

In the original sentence, the prepositional phrase was too complex for easy reading. The repetition of the preposition *to* prevents readers from losing their way.

EXERCISE S1–1 Edit the following sentences to correct faulty parallelism. Revisions of lettered sentences appear in the back of the book. Example:

Rowena began her workday by pouring a cup of coffee and

checking

~~checked~~ her e-mail.
⌃

a. Police dogs are used for finding lost children, tracking criminals, and the detection of bombs and illegal drugs.
b. Hannah told her rock-climbing partner that she bought a new harness and of her desire to climb Otter Cliffs.
c. It is more difficult to sustain an exercise program than starting one.
d. During basic training, I was not only told what to do but also what to think.
e. Jan wanted to drive to the wine country or at least Sausalito.

1. Camp activities include fishing trips, dance lessons, and computers.
2. Arriving at Lake Powell in a thunderstorm, the campers found it safer to remain in their cars than setting up their tents.
3. The streets were not only too steep but also were too narrow for anything other than pedestrian traffic.
4. More digital artists in the show are from the South Shore than the North Shore.
5. To load her toolbox, Anika the Clown gathered hats of different sizes, put in two tubes of face paint, arranged a bundle of extra-long straws, added a bag of colored balloons, and a battery-powered hair dryer.

ON THE WEB > dianahacker.com/writersref
Grammar exercises > Sentence style > E-ex S1–1 through S1–3

S2

Needed words

Do not omit words necessary for grammatical or logical completeness. Readers need to see at a glance how the parts of a sentence are connected.

> **ESL** Languages sometimes differ in the need for certain words. In particular, be alert for missing articles, verbs, subjects, or expletives. See E3, E2-a, and E2-b.

> ✔ GRAMMAR CHECKERS do not flag the vast majority of missing words. They can, however, catch some missing verbs (see G2-e). Although they can flag some missing articles (*a, an,* and *the*), they often suggest that an article is missing when in fact it is not. (See also E3.)

S2-a Add words needed to complete compound structures.

In compound structures, words are often omitted for economy: *Tom is a man who means what he says and* [*who*] *says what he means.* Such omissions are perfectly acceptable as long as the omitted word is common to both parts of the compound structure.

If the shorter version defies grammar or idiom because an omitted word is not common to both parts of the compound structure, the word must be put back in.

> ▶ Some of the regulars are acquaintances whom we see at work or *who*
>
> live in our community.

The word *who* must be included because *whom . . . live in our community* is not grammatically correct.

> ▶ Mayor Davis never has and never will accept a bribe from anyone. *accepted*

Has . . . accept is not grammatically correct.

> ▶ Many South Pacific tribes still believe and live by ancient laws. *in*

Believe . . . by is not idiomatic English.

S2-b Add the word *that* if there is any danger of misreading without it.

If there is no danger of misreading, the word *that* may sometimes be omitted when it introduces a subordinate clause: *The value of a principle is the number of things* [*that*] *it will explain.*

Occasionally, however, a sentence might be misread without *that*.

> Looking out the family room window, Sarah saw ^*that*^ her favorite tree,
>
> which she had climbed so often as a child, was gone.

Sarah didn't see the tree; she saw that the tree was gone. The word *that* tells readers to expect a clause, not just *tree,* as the direct object of *saw.*

S2-c   Add words needed to make comparisons logical and complete.

Comparisons should be made between items that are alike. To compare unlike items is illogical and distracting.

> The forests of North America are much more extensive than ^*those of*^ Europe.

Forests must be compared with forests.

> ~~The graduation rate of our~~ *Our* student athletes ~~is higher~~ *graduate at a higher rate* than the
>
> rest of the student population.

A rate cannot be logically compared with a population. The writer could revise the sentence by inserting *that of* after *than,* but the preceding revision is more concise.

> Some say that Ella Fitzgerald's renditions of Cole Porter's songs
> are better than any other ~~singer.~~ ^*singer's.*^

Ella Fitzgerald's renditions cannot be logically compared with a singer. The revision uses the possessive form *singer's,* with the word *renditions* being implied.

Sometimes the word *other* must be inserted to make a comparison logical.

> Jupiter is larger than any ^*other*^ planet in our solar system.

Jupiter cannot be larger than itself.

Sometimes the word *as* must be inserted to make a comparison grammatically correct.

▶ The city of Lowell is as old, if not older than, the city of Lawrence.
  ^as^

The construction *as old* is not complete without a second *as: as old as . . . the city of Lawrence.*

Comparisons should be complete enough so that readers will understand what is being compared.

INCOMPLETE   Brand X is less salty.

COMPLETE   Brand X is less salty than Brand Y.

Also, comparisons should leave no ambiguity for readers. If more than one interpretation is possible, revise the sentence to state clearly which interpretation you intend. In the following sentence, two interpretations are possible.

AMBIGUOUS   Ken helped me more than my roommate.

CLEAR   Ken helped me more than *he helped* my roommate.

CLEAR   Ken helped me more than my roommate *did.*

S2-d Add the articles *a, an,* and *the* where necessary for grammatical completeness.

Articles are sometimes omitted in recipes and other instructions that are meant to be followed while they are being read. Such omissions are inappropriate, however, in nearly all other forms of writing, whether formal or informal.

▶ Blood can be drawn only by doctor or by authorized person
  ^a^   ^an^
  who has been trained in procedure.
  ^the^   ^

It is not always necessary to repeat articles with paired items: *We bought a computer and printer.* However, if one of the items requires *a* and the other requires *an,* both articles must be included.

▶ We bought a computer and antivirus program at a
  ^an^
  discount.

EXERCISE S2–1 Add any words needed for grammatical or logical completeness in the following sentences. Revisions of lettered sentences appear in the back of the book. Example:

> *that*
> The officer feared the prisoner would escape.
>   ^

a. A good source of vitamin C is a grapefruit or orange.
b. The women entering VMI can expect haircuts as short as the male cadets.
c. Ara stopped the car, only to find one of the new tires had blown.
d. The graphic designers are interested and knowledgeable about producing posters for the balloon race.
e. Reefs are home to more species than any ecosystem in the sea.

1. Very few black doctors were allowed to serve in the Civil War, and their qualifications had to be higher than white doctors.
2. Producers of violent video games are not capable or interested in regulating themselves.
3. Vassily likes mathematics more than his teacher.
4. The inspection team saw many historic buildings had been damaged by the earthquake.
5. American English has borrowed more words from Spanish than from any language.

ON THE WEB > dianahacker.com/writersref
Grammar exercises > Sentence style > E-ex S2–1 and S2–2

S3

Problems with modifiers

Modifiers, whether they are single words, phrases, or clauses, should point clearly to the words they modify. As a rule, related words should be kept together.

GRAMMAR CHECKERS can flag split infinitives, such as *to carefully and thoroughly sift* (S3-d). However, they don't alert you to other misplaced modifiers (*I only ate three radishes*) or dangling modifiers, including danglers like this one: *When a young man, my mother enrolled me in tap dance classes, hoping I would become the next Savion Glover.*

S3-a Put limiting modifiers in front of the words they modify.

Limiting modifiers such as *only, even, almost, nearly,* and *just* should appear in front of a verb only if they modify the verb: *At first I couldn't even touch my toes, much less grasp them.* If they limit the meaning of some other word in the sentence, they should be placed in front of that word.

▶ Lasers ~~only~~ destroy the target, leaving the surrounding healthy
           only

   tissue intact.

   Only limits the meaning of the target, *not* destroy.

▶ The turtle ~~only~~ makes progress when it sticks its neck
             only

   out.

   Only limits the meaning of the when *clause.*

When the limiting modifier *not* is misplaced, the sentence usually suggests a meaning the writer did not intend.

▶ In the United States in 1860, all black southerners were ~~not~~
           not

   slaves.

   The original sentence says that no black southerners were slaves. The revision makes the writer's real meaning clear: Some (but not all) black southerners were slaves.

S3-b Place phrases and clauses so that readers can see at a glance what they modify.

Although phrases and clauses can appear at some distance from the words they modify, make sure that your meaning is clear. When phrases or clauses are oddly placed, absurd misreadings can result.

MISPLACED   The soccer player returned to the clinic where he had undergone emergency surgery in 2004 in a limousine sent by Adidas.

REVISED   Traveling in a limousine sent by Adidas, the soccer player returned to the clinic where he had undergone emergency surgery in 2004.

The revision corrects the false impression that the soccer player underwent emergency surgery in a limousine.

▶ *On the walls*
~~There~~ are many pictures of comedians who have performed at
Gavin's . ~~on the walls.~~

The comedians weren't performing on the walls; the pictures were on the walls.

▶ The robber was described as a *150-pound,* six-foot-tall man with a mustache . ~~weighing 150 pounds.~~

The robber, not the mustache, weighed 150 pounds.

Occasionally the placement of a modifier leads to an ambiguity, in which case two revisions will be possible, depending on the writer's intended meaning.

AMBIGUOUS The exchange students we met for coffee occasionally questioned us about our latest slang.

CLEAR The exchange students we occasionally met for coffee questioned us about our latest slang.

CLEAR The exchange students we met for coffee questioned us occasionally about our latest slang.

In the original version, it was not clear whether the meeting or the questioning happened occasionally. The revisions eliminate the ambiguity.

S3-c Move awkwardly placed modifiers.

As a rule, a sentence should flow from subject to verb to object, without lengthy detours along the way. When a long adverbial element separates a subject from its verb, a verb from its object, or a helping verb from its main verb, the result is often awkward.

▶ *A* ~~Hong Kong,~~ after more than 150 years of British rule, was *Hong Kong* transferred back to Chinese control in 1997.

There is no reason to separate the subject, *Hong Kong,* from the verb, *was transferred,* with a long adverb phrase.

EXCEPTION: Occasionally a writer may choose to delay a verb or an object to create suspense. In the following passage, for example, Robert Mueller inserts the *after* phrase between the subject *women* and the verb *walk* to heighten the dramatic effect.

> I asked a Burmese why women, after centuries of following their men, now walk ahead. He said there were many unexploded land mines since the war. —Robert Mueller

---

ESL English does not allow an adverb to appear between a verb and its object. See E2-f.

▶ Yolanda lifted ~~easily~~ the fifty-pound weight.
  easily

S3-d Avoid split infinitives when they are awkward.

An infinitive consists of *to* plus a verb: *to think, to breathe, to dance.* When a modifier appears between its two parts, an infinitive is said to be "split": *to carefully balance, to completely understand.*

When a long word or a phrase appears between the parts of the infinitive, the result is usually awkward.

▶ ~~Patients~~ should try to ~~if possible~~ avoid going up and down stairs.
  If possible, patients

Attempts to avoid split infinitives can result in equally awkward sentences. When alternative phrasing sounds unnatural, most experts allow—and even encourage—splitting the infinitive.

AWKWARD   We decided actually to enforce the law.

BETTER   We decided to actually enforce the law.

At times, neither the split infinitive nor its alternative sounds particularly awkward. In such situations, you may want to unsplit the infinitive, especially in formal writing.

▶ The candidate decided to ~~formally~~ launch her campaign.
  formally.

ON THE WEB > dianahacker.com/writersref
Language Debates > Split infinitives

EXERCISE S3–1 Edit the following sentences to correct misplaced or awkwardly placed modifiers. Revisions of lettered sentences appear in the back of the book. Example:

> *on college campuses*
> Reports of hazing have been declining since the mid-1990s.
>   ^   ^
> ~~on college campuses.~~

a. More research is needed to effectively evaluate the risks posed by volcanoes in the Pacific Northwest.
b. Many students graduate with debt from college totaling more than fifty thousand dollars.
c. It is a myth that humans only use 10 percent of their brains.
d. A coolhunter is a person who can find in the unnoticed corners of modern society the next wave of fashion.
e. All geese do not fly beyond Narragansett for the winter.

1. The flood nearly displaced half of the city's residents.
2. Most lions at night hunt for medium-sized prey, such as zebra.
3. Several recent studies have encouraged heart patients to more carefully watch their cholesterol levels.
4. The garden's centerpiece is a huge sculpture that was carved by three women called *Walking in Place*.
5. The old Marlboro ads depicted a man on a horse smoking a cigarette.

S3-e   Repair dangling modifiers.

A dangling modifier fails to refer logically to any word in the sentence. Dangling modifiers are easy to repair, but they can be hard to recognize, especially in your own writing.

Recognizing dangling modifiers

Dangling modifiers are usually word groups (such as verbal phrases) that suggest but do not name an actor. When a sentence opens with such a modifier, readers expect the subject of the next clause to name the actor. If it doesn't, the modifier dangles.

> ▶ *When the driver opened*
> ~~Opening~~ the window to let out a huge bumblebee, the car
>   ^
> accidentally swerved into an oncoming car.

The car didn't open the window; the driver did.

> *women have often been denied*
> ▶ After completing seminary training, ~~women's~~ access to the pulpit.
>   ^   ^
> ~~has often been denied.~~

The women (not their access to the pulpit) complete the training.

The following sentences illustrate four common kinds of dangling modifiers.

DANGLING *Deciding to join the navy,* the recruiter enthusiastically pumped Joe's hand. [Participial phrase]

DANGLING *Upon entering the doctor's office,* a skeleton caught my attention. [Preposition followed by a gerund phrase]

DANGLING *To please the children,* some fireworks were set off a day early. [Infinitive phrase]

DANGLING *Though only sixteen,* UCLA accepted Martha's application. [Elliptical clause with an understood subject and verb]

These dangling modifiers falsely suggest that the recruiter decided to join the navy, that the skeleton entered the doctor's office, that the fireworks intended to please the children, and that UCLA is sixteen years old.

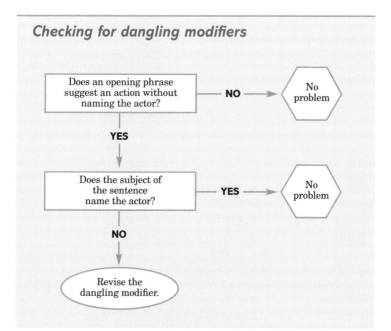

Checking for dangling modifiers

Does an opening phrase suggest an action without naming the actor? — **NO** → No problem

YES ↓

Does the subject of the sentence name the actor? — **YES** → No problem

NO ↓

Revise the dangling modifier.

Although most readers will understand the writer's intended meaning in such sentences, the inadvertent humor can be distracting, and it can make the writer appear somewhat foolish.

ON THE WEB > dianahacker.com/writersref
Language Debates > Dangling modifiers

Repairing dangling modifiers

To repair a dangling modifier, you can revise the sentence in one of two ways:

1. Name the actor in the subject of the sentence, or
2. name the actor in the modifier.

Depending on your sentence, one of these revision strategies may be more appropriate than the other.

ACTOR NAMED IN SUBJECT

▶ Upon entering the doctor's office, a skeleton. *I noticed* ~~caught my attention.~~

▶ To please the children, some fireworks *we set off* ~~were set off~~ a day early.

ACTOR NAMED IN MODIFIER

▶ *When Joe decided* ~~Deciding~~ to join the navy, the recruiter enthusiastically pumped *his* ~~Joe's~~ hand.

▶ Though only sixteen years old, *Martha was* UCLA accepted *her* ~~Martha's~~ application.

NOTE: You cannot repair a dangling modifier just by moving it. Consider, for example, the sentence about the skeleton. If you put the modifier at the end of the sentence (*A skeleton caught my attention upon entering the doctor's office*), you are still suggesting—absurdly, of course—that the skeleton entered the office. The only way to avoid the problem is to put the word *I* in the sentence, either as the subject or in the modifier.

▶ Upon entering the doctor's office, a skeleton. *I noticed* ~~caught my attention.~~

▶ *As I entered* ~~Upon entering~~ the doctor's office, a skeleton caught my attention.

EXERCISE S3–2 Edit the following sentences to correct dangling modifiers. Most sentences can be revised in more than one way. Revisions of lettered sentences appear in the back of the book. Example:

> *a student must complete*
> To acquire a degree in almost any field, two science courses.
> ^   ^
> ~~must be completed.~~

a. At the age of ten, my parents took me on my first balloon ride.
b. To replace the gear mechanism, attached is a form to order the part by mail.
c. Nestled in the cockpit, the pounding of the engine was muffled only slightly by my helmet.
d. After studying polymer chemistry, computer games seemed less complex to Phuong.
e. When a young man, my mother enrolled me in tap dance classes, hoping I would become the next Savion Glover.

1. While working as a ranger in Everglades National Park, a Florida panther crossed the road in front of my truck one night.
2. By following this new procedure, our mailing costs will be reduced significantly.
3. Serving as president of the missionary circle, one of Grandmother's duties is to raise money for the church.
4. After buying an album by Ali Farka Toure, the rich and rolling rhythms of Malian music made more sense to Silas.
5. Understanding the high-tech needs of drivers, the Volkswagen Phaeton has an innovative dashboard design.

ON THE WEB > dianahacker.com/writersref
Grammar exercises > Sentence style > E-ex S3–1 through S3–4

S4

Shifts

GRAMMAR CHECKERS usually do not flag shifts in point of view or in verb tense, mood, or voice. Even obvious errors, like the following shift in tense, slip right past the grammar checker: *My three-year-old fell into the pool and to my surprise she swims to the shallow end.*

Sometimes grammar checkers mark a shift from direct to indirect question or quotation but do not make any suggestions for revision. You must decide where the structure is faulty and determine how to fix it.

S4-a   Make the point of view consistent.

The point of view of a piece of writing is the perspective from which it is written: first person (*I* or *we*), second person (*you*), or third person (*he/she/it/one* or *they*).

The *I* (or *we*) point of view, which emphasizes the writer, is a good choice for informal letters and writing based primarily on personal experience. The *you* point of view, which emphasizes the reader, works well for giving advice or explaining how to do something. The third-person point of view, which emphasizes the subject, is appropriate in formal academic and professional writing.

Writers who are having difficulty settling on an appropriate point of view sometimes shift confusingly from one to another. The solution is to choose a suitable perspective and then stay with it.

▶ One week our class met in a junkyard to practice rescuing a

victim trapped in a wrecked car. We learned to dismantle the car
                We   *our*   *our*

with the essential tools. ~~You~~ were graded on ~~your~~ speed and ~~your~~
                    ^   ^   ^

skill in extricating the victim.

The writer should have stayed with the *we* point of view. *You* is inappropriate because the writer is not addressing readers directly. *You* should not be used in a vague sense meaning "anyone." (See also G3-b.)

You need
▶ ~~One needs~~ a password and a credit card number to access this
  ^

database. You will be billed at an hourly rate.

You is an appropriate choice because the writer is giving advice directly to readers.

Shifts from the third-person singular to the third-person plural are especially common.

Police officers are
▶ ~~A police officer is~~ often criticized for always being there when
  ^

they aren't needed and never being there when they are.

Although the writer might have changed *they* to *he or she* (to match the singular *officer*), the revision in the plural is more concise. (See also G3-a.)

EXERCISE S4–1 Edit the following paragraph to eliminate distracting shifts in point of view (person and number).

When online dating first became available, many people thought that it would simplify romance. We believed that you could type in a list of criteria—sense of humor, college education, green eyes, good job—and a database would select the perfect mate. Thousands of people signed up for services and filled out their profiles, confident that true love was only a few mouse clicks away. As it turns out, however, virtual dating is no easier than traditional dating. I still have to contact the people I find, exchange e-mails and phone calls, and meet him in the real world. Although a database might produce a list of possibilities and screen out obviously undesirable people, you can't predict chemistry. More often than not, people who seem perfect online just don't click in person. Electronic services do help a single person expand their pool of potential dates, but it's no substitute for the hard work of romance.

S4-b Maintain consistent verb tenses.

Consistent verb tenses clearly establish the time of the actions being described. When a passage begins in one tense and then shifts without warning and for no reason to another, readers are distracted and confused.

▶ There was no way I could fight the current. Just as I was losing
          jumped   *swam*
hope, a stranger ~~jumps~~ off a passing boat and ~~swims~~ toward me.
              ^   ^

Writers often encounter difficulty with verb tenses when writing about literature. Because fictional events occur outside the time frames of real life, the past and the present tenses may seem equally appropriate. The literary convention, however, is to describe fictional events consistently in the present tense. (See also G2-f.)

▶ The scarlet letter is a punishment sternly placed on Hester's
                                    is
breast by the community, and yet it ~~was~~ an extremely fanciful and
                                  ^
imaginative product of Hester's own needlework.

EXERCISE S4–2 Edit the following paragraphs to eliminate distracting shifts in tense.

The English colonists who settled in Massachusetts received assistance at first from the local Indian tribes, but by 1675 there had been friction between the English and the Indians for many years. On June 20 of that year, Metacomet, whom the colonists called Philip, leads the Wampanoag tribe in the first of a series of attacks on the colonial settlements. The war, known today as King Philip's War, rages on for over a year and leaves three thousand Indians and six hundred colonists dead. Metacomet's attempt to retain power in his native land failed. Finally he too is killed, and the victorious colonists sell his wife and children into slavery.

The Indians did not leave records of their unfortunate encounters with the English settlers, but the settlers recorded some of their experiences at the hands of the Indians. One of the few accounts to survive was written by a captured colonist, Mrs. Mary Rowlandson. She is a minister's wife who is kidnapped by an Indian war party and held captive for eleven weeks in 1676. Her history, *A Narrative of the Captivity and Restoration of Mrs. Mary Rowlandson,* tells the story of her experiences with the Wampanoags. Although it did not paint a completely balanced picture of the Indians, Rowlandson's narrative, which is considered a classic early American text, showed its author to be a keen observer of life in an Indian camp.

S4-c Make verbs consistent in mood and voice.

Unnecessary shifts in the mood of a verb can be as distracting as needless shifts in tense. There are three moods in English: the indicative, used for facts, opinions, and questions; the imperative, used for orders or advice; and the subjunctive, used for wishes or conditions contrary to fact. (See G2-g.)

The following passage shifts confusingly from the indicative to the imperative mood.

▶ The officers advised us not to allow anyone into our homes
                                    They also suggested that we
without proper identification. ~~Also,~~ alert neighbors to our
                              ^
vacation schedules.

Since the writer's purpose was to report the officers' advice, the revision puts both sentences in the indicative.

A verb may be in either the active voice (with the subject doing the action) or the passive voice (with the subject receiving the action). (See W3-a.) If a writer shifts without warning from one to the other, readers may be left wondering why.

▶ When the tickets are ready, the travel agent notifies the client/,

　lists each ~~files~~

　~~Each~~ ticket ~~is then listed~~ on a daily register form, and a copy of

　the itinerary. ~~is filed.~~

The passage began in the active voice (*agent notifies*) and then switched to the passive (*ticket is listed . . . copy is filed*). Because the active voice is clearer and more direct, the writer changed all the verbs to the active voice.

S4-d　Avoid sudden shifts from indirect to direct questions or quotations.

An indirect question reports a question without asking it: *We asked whether we could visit Mimo.* A direct question asks directly: *Can we visit Mimo?* Sudden shifts from indirect to direct questions are awkward. In addition, sentences containing such shifts are impossible to punctuate because indirect questions must end with a period and direct questions must end with a question mark. (See P7-b.)

▶ I wonder whether Karla knew of the theft and, if so, ~~did~~

　whether she reported

　~~she report~~ it to the police?.

The revision poses both questions indirectly. The writer could also ask both questions directly: *Did Karla know of the theft and, if so, did she report it to the police?*

An indirect quotation reports someone's words without quoting word for word: *Annabelle said that she is a Virgo.* A direct quotation presents the exact words of a speaker or writer, set off with quotation marks: *Annabelle said, "I am a Virgo."* Unannounced shifts from indirect to direct quotations are distracting and confusing, especially when the writer fails to insert the necessary quotation marks, as in the following example.

　　　　　　　　　　　　　　　asked me not to

▶ Mother said that she would be late for dinner and ~~please do not~~

　　　　　　　came

　leave for choir practice until Dad ~~comes~~ home.

The revision reports all of the mother's words. The writer could also quote directly: *Mother said, "I will be late for dinner. Please do not leave for choir practice until Dad comes home."*

EXERCISE S4–3 Edit the following sentences to make the verbs consistent in mood and voice and to eliminate distracting shifts from indirect to direct questions or quotations. Revisions of lettered sentences appear in the back of the book. Example:

> As a public relations intern, I wrote press releases, managed the
>   *fielded all phone calls.*
> Web site, and ~~all phone calls were fielded by me.~~
>   ^

a. An incredibly talented musician, Ray Charles mastered R&B, soul, and gospel styles. Even country music was performed well by him.

b. Environmentalists point out that shrimp farming in Southeast Asia is polluting water and rendering farmlands useless. They warn that action must be taken by governments before it is too late.

c. The samples were observed for five days before we detected any growth.

d. In his famous soliloquy, Hamlet contemplates whether death would be preferable to his difficult life and, if so, is he capable of committing suicide?

e. The lawyer told the judge that Miranda Hale was innocent and allow her to prove the allegations false.

1. When the photographs were taken on the beach at sunset, I intentionally left the foreground out of focus.

2. If the warning sirens sound, evacuate at once. It is not advised that you return to the building until the alarm has stopped.

3. Most baby products warn parents not to leave children unattended. Also, follow all directions carefully.

4. The advertisement promised that results would be seen in five days or consumers could return the product for a full refund.

5. Investigators first need to determine whether there was a forceful entry and then what was the motive?

EXERCISE S4–4 Edit the following sentences to eliminate distracting shifts. Revisions of lettered sentences appear in the back of the book. Example:

> For many first-year engineering students, adjusting to
>   *they*
> rigorous courses can be so challenging that ~~you~~ sometimes
>   ^
> feel overwhelmed.

a. A courtroom lawyer has more than a touch of theater in their blood.

b. The interviewer asked if we had brought our proof of birth and citizenship and did we bring our passports.

c. The reconnaissance scout often has to make fast decisions and use sophisticated equipment to keep their team from detection.

d. After the animators finish their scenes, the production designer arranges the clips according to the storyboard. Synchronization notes must also be made for the sound editor and the composer.

e. Madame Defarge is a sinister figure in Dickens's *A Tale of Two Cities*. On a symbolic level, she represents fate; like the Greek Fates, she knitted the fabric of individual destiny.

1. Everyone should protect yourself from the sun, especially on the first day of extensive exposure.
2. Our neighbors told us that the island was being evacuated because of the coming storm. Also, take the northern route to the mainland.
3. Rescue workers put water on her face and lifted her head gently onto a pillow. Finally, she opens her eyes.
4. In my first tai chi class, the sensei asked if I had ever done yoga stretches and did I have good balance.
5. The artist has often been seen as a threat to society, especially when they refuse to conform to conventional standards of taste.

ON THE WEB > dianahacker.com/writersref
Grammar exercises > Sentence style > E-ex S4–1 through S4–4

S5

Mixed constructions

A mixed construction contains elements that do not sensibly fit together. The mismatch may be a matter of grammar or of logic.

> GRAMMAR CHECKERS can flag *is when, is where,* and *reason . . . is because* constructions (S5-c), but they fail to identify nearly all other mixed constructions, including sentences as tangled as this one: *Depending on our method of travel and our destination determines how many suitcases we are allowed to pack.*

S5-a Untangle the grammatical structure.

Once you head into a sentence, your choices are limited by the range of grammatical patterns in English. (See B2 and B3.) You cannot begin with one grammatical plan and switch without warning to another.

MIXED	For most drivers who have a blood alcohol level of .05 percent double their risk of causing an accident.
REVISED	For most drivers who have a blood alcohol level of .05 percent, the risk of causing an accident is doubled.
REVISED	Most drivers who have a blood alcohol level of .05 percent double their risk of causing an accident.

The writer began with a long prepositional phrase that was destined to be a modifier but then tried to press it into service as the subject of the sentence. A prepositional phrase cannot serve as the subject of a sentence. If the sentence is to begin with the prepositional phrase, the writer must finish the sentence with a subject and verb (*risk . . . is doubled*). The writer who wishes to stay with the original verb (*double*) must head into the sentence another way (*Most drivers . . .*).

▶ *Being*
When an employee is promoted without warning can be exciting
      ^
or alarming.

The adverb clause *When an employee is promoted without warning* cannot serve as the subject of the sentence. The revision replaces the adverb clause with a gerund phrase, a word group that can function as the subject. (See B3-b and B3-e.)

▶ Although the United States is one of the wealthiest nations

in the world, ~~but~~ more than 12 million of our children live in poverty.

The *Although* clause is subordinate, so it cannot be linked to an independent clause with the coordinating conjunction *but*. (If you speak English as a second language, see also E2-e.)

Occasionally a mixed construction is so tangled that it defies grammatical analysis. When this happens, back away from the sentence, rethink what you want to say, and then say it again as clearly as you can.

MIXED	In the whole-word method children learn to recognize entire words rather than by the phonics method in which they learn to sound out letters and groups of letters.
REVISED	The whole-word method teaches children to recognize entire words; the phonics method teaches them to sound out letters and groups of letters.

ESL English does not allow double subjects, nor does it allow an object or an adverb to be repeated in an adjective clause. See E2-c and E2-d. Unlike some languages, English does not allow a noun and a pronoun to be repeated in a sentence if they serve the same grammatical purpose. See E2-c.

▶ My father ~~he~~ moved to North Carolina before he met my

mother.

                         the final exam
▶ ~~The final exam~~ I should really study for it to pass the course.
                                       ^

S5-b Straighten out the logical connections.

The subject and the predicate should make sense together. When they don't, the error is known as *faulty predication.*

                      Tiffany
▶ Reluctantly we decided that ~~Tiffany's welfare~~ would not be safe
                        ^

living with her mother.

Tiffany, not her welfare, may not be safe.

                       double personal exemption for the
▶ Under the revised plan, the elderly, ~~who now receive a double~~
                      ^

~~personal exemption,~~ will be abolished.

The exemption, not the elderly, will be abolished.

An appositive and the noun to which it refers should be logically equivalent. When they are not, the error is known as *faulty apposition.*

       Tax accounting,
▶ ~~The tax accountant,~~ a very lucrative field, requires intelligence,
         ^

patience, and attention to detail.

The tax accountant is a person, not a field.

S5-c Avoid *is when, is where,* and *reason . . . is because* constructions.

In formal English, many readers object to *is when, is where,* and *reason . . . is because* constructions on either logical or grammatical grounds.

a disorder suffered by people who,
► Anorexia nervosa is ~~where people,~~ believing they are too fat, diet
                          ^
to the point of starvation.

Anorexia nervosa is a disorder, not a place.

► ~~The reason~~ I was late ~~is~~ because my motorcycle broke down.

The writer might have replaced the word *because* with *that,* but the
preceding revision is more concise.

EXERCISE S5–1 Edit the following sentences to untangle mixed constructions. Revisions of lettered sentences appear in the back of the book.
Example:

Keeping
~~By keeping~~ your wrists relaxed while rowing will help you
^
avoid injury.

a. Using surgical gloves is a precaution now worn by dentists to prevent
   contact with patients' blood and saliva.
b. A physician, the career my brother is pursuing, requires at least ten
   years of challenging work.
c. The reason the pharaohs had bad teeth was because tiny particles of
   sand found their way into Egyptian bread.
d. Recurring bouts of flu among team members set a record for number of
   games forfeited.
e. In this box contains the key to your future.

1. Early diagnosis of prostate cancer is often curable.
2. Depending on our method of travel and our destination determines
   how many suitcases we are allowed to pack.
3. Dyslexia is where people have a learning disorder that impairs reading ability.
4. Even though Ellen had heard French spoken all her life, yet she could
   not speak it.
5. In understanding artificial intelligence code is a critical skill for computer game designers.

ON THE WEB > dianahacker.com/writersref
Grammar exercises > Sentence style > E-ex S5–1 and S5–2

S6

Sentence emphasis

Within each sentence, emphasize your point by expressing it in the subject and verb of an independent clause, the words that receive the most attention from readers (see S6-a to S6-e).

Within longer stretches of prose, you can draw attention to ideas deserving special emphasis by using a variety of techniques, often involving an unusual twist or some element of surprise (see S6-f).

S6-a Coordinate equal ideas; subordinate minor ideas.

When combining two or more ideas in one sentence, you have two choices: coordination or subordination. Choose coordination to indicate that the ideas are equal or nearly equal in importance. Choose subordination to indicate that one idea is less important than another.

> ☑ GRAMMAR CHECKERS do not catch the problems with coordination and subordination discussed in this section. Not surprisingly, computer programs have no way of sensing the relative importance of ideas.

Coordination

Coordination draws attention equally to two or more ideas. To coordinate single words or phrases, join them with a coordinating conjunction or with a pair of correlative conjunctions (see S1-b). To coordinate independent clauses—word groups that could each stand alone as a sentence—join them with a comma and a coordinating conjunction or with a semicolon. The semicolon is often accompanied by a conjunctive adverb such as *moreover, therefore,* or *however* or by a transitional phrase such as *for example* or *in other words.* (For a longer list, see P3-b.)

Grandmother lost her sight, but her hearing sharpened.

Grandmother lost her sight; however, her hearing sharpened.

Subordination

To give unequal emphasis to two or more ideas, express the major idea in an independent clause and place any minor ideas in subordinate clauses or phrases. (See B3.) Subordinate clauses, which cannot stand alone, typically begin with one of the following subordinating conjunctions or relative pronouns.

after	before	unless	which
although	if	until	while
as	since	when	who
as if	that	where	whom
because	though	whether	whose

Deciding which idea to emphasize is not a matter of right and wrong but is determined by the meaning you intend. Consider the two ideas about Grandmother's sight and hearing.

Grandmother lost her sight. Her hearing sharpened.

If your purpose is to stress your grandmother's acute hearing rather than her blindness, subordinate the idea concerning her blindness.

As Grandmother lost her sight, her hearing sharpened.

To focus on your grandmother's blindness, subordinate the idea about her hearing.

Though her hearing sharpened, Grandmother lost her sight.

EXERCISE S6–1 Use the coordination or subordination technique in brackets to combine each pair of independent clauses. Revisions of lettered sentences appear in the back of the book. Example:

> Ted Williams was one of the best hitters in the history of
> *baseball, but he*
> ~~baseball. He~~ never won a World Series ring. [*Use a comma and a*
> ^
> *coordinating conjunction.*]

a. Williams played for the Boston Red Sox from 1936 to 1960. He managed the Washington Senators and Texas Rangers for several years after retiring as a player. [*Use a comma and a coordinating conjunction.*]

b. In 1941, Williams finished the season with a batting average of .406. No player has hit over .400 for a season since then. [*Use a semicolon.*]

c. Williams acknowledged that Joe DiMaggio was a better all-around player. Williams felt that he was a better hitter than DiMaggio. [*Use the subordinating conjunction* although.]

d. Williams was a stubborn man. He always refused to tip his cap to the crowd after a home run because he claimed that fans were fickle. [*Use a semicolon and the transitional phrase* for example.]

e. Williams's relationship with the media was unfriendly at best. He sarcastically called baseball writers the "knights of the keyboard" in his memoir. [*Use a semicolon.*]

1. Williams took time out from his baseball career to serve in the Marines during World War II. He went on active duty a second time during the Korean War. [*Use a semicolon and the transitional phrase* in addition.]

2. Williams was named most valuable player twice in his career. He was listed as the eighth-best baseball player of all time by the *Sporting News* in 1999. [*Use the relative pronoun* who.]

3. Williams hit a home run in his final at bat in 1960. Then he retired as a player. [*Use a comma and a coordinating conjunction.*]

4. Williams surprised many people with his 1966 Hall of Fame induction speech. It called for the inclusion of Negro League players in the Hall of Fame. [*Use the relative pronoun* which.]

5. At the 1999 All-Star game, Ted Williams returned to Fenway Park in Boston to throw out the ceremonial first pitch. For the first time he waved his hat to the cheering fans. [*Use a comma and a coordinating conjunction.*]

S6-b Combine choppy sentences.

Short sentences demand attention, so you should use them primarily for emphasis. Too many short sentences, one after the other, make for a choppy style.

If an idea is not important enough to deserve its own sentence, try combining it with a sentence close by. Put any minor ideas in subordinate structures such as phrases or subordinate clauses. (See B3.)

▶ We keep our use of insecticides to a minimum/ ~~We~~ are concerned *because we*

about their effect on the environment.

A minor idea is now expressed in a subordinate clause beginning with *because.*

▶ ~~Sister Consilio was~~ ɛnveloped in a black robe with only her face

and hands visible/. ~~She~~ was an imposing figure. *Sister Consilio*

A minor idea is now expressed in a participial phrase beginning with *Enveloped.* (See B3-b.)

▶ My sister owes much of her recovery to a bodybuilding program**/**
that she
~~She~~ began ~~the program~~ three years ago.
                ^

A minor idea is now expressed in an adjective clause beginning with
that. (See B3-e.)

ESL   Unlike Arabic, Farsi, and other languages, English does not repeat
objects or adverbs in adjective clauses. The relative pronoun (*that,*
which, whom) or relative adverb (*where*) in the adjective clause represents the object or adverb. See E2-d.

▶ **The apartment that we rented ~~it~~ needed repairs.**

The pronoun *it* cannot repeat the relative pronoun *that*.

▶ **The small town where my grandfather was born ~~there~~ is now**

a big city.

The adverb *there* cannot repeat the relative adverb *where*.

Although subordination is ordinarily the most effective technique for combining short, choppy sentences, coordination is appropriate when the ideas are equal in importance.

▶ **The hospital decides when patients will sleep and wake./, ~~It~~ dictates**
                                                        ^
and
what and when they will eat./, ~~It~~ tells them when they may be with
                              ^
family and friends.

Equivalent ideas are expressed as parallel elements of a compound
predicate: *decides . . . dictates . . . tells.*

EXERCISE S6–2 Combine the following sentences by subordinating minor
ideas or by coordinating ideas of equal importance. You must decide which
ideas are minor because the sentences are given out of context. Revisions of
lettered sentences appear in the back of the book. Example:

Agnes, ~~was~~ another girl I worked with./, ~~she~~ was a hyperac-
        ^   ^
tive child.

a. The X-Men comic books and Japanese woodcuts of kabuki dancers were part of Marlena's research project on popular culture. They covered the tabletop and the chairs.
b. Our waitress was costumed in a kimono. She had painted her face white. She had arranged her hair in an upswept lacquered beehive.
c. Students can apply for a spot in the foundation's leadership program. The program teaches thinking and communication skills.
d. Shore houses were flooded up to the first floor. Beaches were washed away. Brant's Lighthouse was swallowed by the sea.
e. Laura Thackray is an engineer at Volvo Car Corporation. She designed a pregnant crash-test dummy. She addressed women's safety needs.

1. I noticed that the sky was glowing orange and red. I bent down to crawl into the bunker.
2. The Market Inn is located on North Wharf. It doesn't look very impressive from the outside. The food, however, is excellent.
3. He walked up to the pitcher's mound. He dug his toe into the ground. He swung his arm around backward and forward. Then he threw the ball and struck the batter out.
4. Eryn and Maeve started a business. They have known each other since kindergarten. They will renovate homes for people with disabilities.
5. The first football card set was released by the Goudey Gum Company in 1933. The set featured only three football players. They were Red Grange, Bronko Nagurski, and Knute Rockne.

ON THE WEB > dianahacker.com/writersref
Grammar exercises > Sentence style > E-ex S6–1 and S6–2

S6-c Avoid ineffective coordination.

Coordinate structures are appropriate only when you intend to draw the reader's attention equally to two or more ideas: *Professor Sakellarios praises loudly, and she criticizes softly.* If one idea is more important than another—or if a coordinating conjunction does not clearly signal the relation between the ideas—you should subordinate the lesser idea.

> *After four hours,*
> ▶ ~~Four hours went by, and~~ a rescue truck finally arrived, but
> ^
> by that time the injured swimmer had been evacuated in a
> helicopter.

Three independent clauses were excessive. The least important idea has become a prepositional phrase. (See B3-a.)

EXERCISE S6–3 In the following sentences, ideas have been coordinated (joined with a coordinating conjunction or a semicolon). Restructure the sentences by subordinating minor ideas. You must decide which ideas are minor because the sentences are given out of context. Revisions of lettered sentences appear in the back of the book. Example:

> *where they*
> The crew team finally returned to shore, ~~and~~ had a party on
> *to celebrate*
>   ^
> the beach ~~and celebrated~~ the start of the season.
>   ^

a. These particles are known as "stealth liposomes," and they can hide in the body for a long time without detection.

b. Irena is a competitive gymnast and majors in biochemistry; her goal is to apply her athletic experience and her science degree to a career in sports medicine.

c. Students, textile workers, and labor unions have loudly protested sweatshop abuses, so apparel makers have been forced to examine their labor practices.

d. IRC (Internet Relay Chat) was developed in a European university; it was created as a way for a group of graduate students to talk about projects from their dorm rooms.

e. The cafeteria's new menu has an international flavor, and it includes everything from enchiladas and pizza to pad thai and sauerbraten.

1. Victor switched on his remote-control lawn mower, and it began to shudder and emit clouds of smoke.

2. Iguanas are dependent on ultraviolet rays from the sun, so in the winter months they must be put under ultraviolet-coated lights that can be purchased at most pet stores.

3. The Civil War Trust was founded in 1991; it spearheads a nationwide campaign to protect America's Civil War battlefields.

4. We did not expect to receive so many large orders so quickly, and we are short on inventory.

5. I am certain that Mother spread her love equally among us all, but she had a way of making each of us feel very special in our own way.

S6-d Do not subordinate major ideas.

If a sentence buries its major idea in a subordinate construction, readers may not give the idea enough attention. Express the major idea in an independent clause and subordinate any minor ideas.

> *had polio as a child,*
> ▶ Lanie, who now walks with the help of braces~~/.~~ ~~had polio as a~~
>   ^
> ~~child.~~

The writer wanted to focus on Lanie's ability to walk, but the original sentence buried this idea in an adjective clause. The revision puts the major idea in an independent clause and tucks the less important idea into an adjective clause (*who had polio as a child*). (See B3-e.)

▶ My uncle, ~~noticed~~ *noticing* my frightened look, ~~and~~ told me that the

dentures in the glass were not real teeth.

The less important idea has become a participial phrase modifying the noun *uncle*.

ON THE WEB > dianahacker.com/writersref
Grammar exercises > Sentence style > E-ex S6–3

S6-e   Do not subordinate excessively.

In attempting to avoid short, choppy sentences, writers sometimes move to the opposite extreme, putting more subordinate ideas into a sentence than its structure can bear. If a sentence collapses of its own weight, occasionally it can be restructured. More often, however, such sentences must be divided.

▶ Our job is to stay between the stacker and the tie machine

watching to see if the newspapers jam, *If they do,* ~~in which case~~ we pull the

bundles off and stack them on a skid, because otherwise they

would back up in the stacker.

EXERCISE S6–4 In each of the following sentences, the idea that the writer wished to emphasize is buried in a subordinate construction. Restructure each sentence so that the independent clause expresses the major idea and lesser ideas are subordinated. Revisions of lettered sentences appear in the back of the book. Example:

Although
Catherine has weathered many hardships, ~~although~~ she has

rarely become discouraged. [*Emphasize that Catherine has*

rarely become discouraged.]

a. Gina worked as an aide for the relief agency, distributing food and medical supplies. [*Emphasize distributing food and medical supplies.*]

b. Janbir spent every Saturday learning tabla drumming, noticing with each hour of practice that his memory for complex patterns was growing stronger. [*Emphasize Janbir's memory.*]

c. The rotor hit, gouging a hole about an eighth of an inch deep in my helmet. [*Emphasize that the rotor gouged a hole in the helmet.*]

d. My grandfather, who raised his daughters the old-fashioned way, was born eighty years ago in Puerto Rico. [*Emphasize how the grandfather raised his daughters.*]

e. The Narcan reversed the depressive effect of the drug, saving the patient's life. [*Emphasize that the patient's life was saved.*]

1. Fatima, who studied Persian miniature painting after college, majored in early childhood education. [*Emphasize Fatima's studies after college.*]

2. I was losing consciousness when my will to live kicked in. [*Emphasize the will to live.*]

3. Using a sliding compound miter saw, the carpenter made intricate edges on the cabinets. [*Emphasize the carpenter's use of the saw.*]

4. Ernie was using origami to solve some tricky manufacturing problems when he decided to leave engineering and become an artist. [*Emphasize Ernie's decision.*]

5. As the undulating waves glinted in the sun, the paddlers synchronized their strokes. [*Emphasize the brightness of the waves.*]

S6-f Experiment with techniques for gaining special emphasis.

By experimenting with certain techniques, usually involving some element of surprise, you can draw attention to ideas that deserve special emphasis. Use such techniques sparingly, however, or they will lose their punch. The writer who tries to emphasize everything ends up emphasizing nothing.

Using sentence endings for emphasis

You can highlight an idea simply by withholding it until the end of a sentence. The technique works something like a punch line. In the following example, the sentence's meaning is not revealed until its very last word.

The only completely consistent people are the dead.
—Aldous Huxley

Using parallel structure for emphasis

Parallel grammatical structure draws special attention to paired ideas or to items in a series. (See S1.) When parallel ideas are paired, the emphasis falls on words that underscore comparisons or contrasts, especially when they occur at the end of a phrase or clause.

We must *stop talking* about the *American dream* and *start listening* to the *dreams of Americans.*   —Reubin Askew

In a parallel series, the emphasis falls at the end, so it is generally best to end with the most dramatic or climactic item in the series.

Sister Charity enjoyed passing out writing punishments: translate the Ten Commandments into Latin, type a thousand-word essay on good manners, copy the New Testament with a quill pen.
                                                     —Marie Visosky, student

Using an occasional short sentence for emphasis

Too many short sentences in a row will fast become monotonous (see S6-b), but an occasional short sentence, when played off against longer sentences in the same passage, will draw attention to an idea.

The great secret, known to internists and learned early in marriage by internists' wives [or husbands], but still hidden from the general public, is that most things get better by themselves. Most things, in fact, are better by morning.   —Lewis Thomas

S7

Sentence variety

When a rough draft is filled with too many same-sounding sentences, try to inject some variety—as long as you can do so without sacrificing clarity or ease of reading.

GRAMMAR CHECKERS might tell you when you have used the same word to open several sentences, but sometimes it is a good idea to do so—if you are trying to highlight parallel ideas, for example (see p. 33). It takes a human ear to know when and why sentence variety is needed.

S7-a Use a variety of sentence structures.

A writer should not rely too heavily on simple sentences and compound sentences, for the effect tends to be both monotonous and choppy. (See S6-a and S6-b.) Too many complex sentences, however, can be equally monotonous. If your style tends to one or the other extreme, try to achieve a better mix of sentence types. For a discussion of sentence types, see B4-a.

S7-b Use a variety of sentence openings.

Most sentences in English begin with the subject, move to the verb, and continue to an object, with modifiers tucked in along the way or put at the end. For the most part, such sentences are fine. Put too many of them in a row, however, and they become monotonous.

Adverbial modifiers, being easily movable, can often be inserted at the beginning of the sentence, ahead of the subject. Such modifiers might be single words, phrases, or clauses.

> *Eventually a*
> ▶ A few drops of sap ~~eventually~~ began to trickle from the tree
>   ^
>   into the pail.

> *Just as the sun was coming up, a*
> ▶ A pair of black ducks flew over the lake. ~~just as the sun was~~
>   ^   ^
>   ~~coming up.~~

For variety, adjectives and participial phrases can frequently be moved to the beginning of a sentence without loss of clarity. (See B3-b.)

> *Dejected and withdrawn,*
> ▶ Edward, ~~dejected and withdrawn,~~ nearly gave up his search
>   for a job.

>   *A*   *Roberto and I*
> ▶ ~~Roberto and I,~~ anticipating a peaceful evening, sat cross-legged
>   ^   ^
>   at the campfire to brew a cup of coffee and plan the rest of
>   our hike.

TIP: When beginning a sentence with a participial phrase, make sure that the subject of the sentence names the person or thing described in the introductory phrase. If it doesn't, the phrase will dangle. (See S3-e.)

S7-c Try inverting sentences occasionally.

A sentence is inverted if it does not follow the normal subject-verb-object pattern. Many inversions sound artificial and should be avoided except in the most formal contexts. But if an inversion sounds natural, it can provide a welcome touch of variety.

▶ *Opposite the produce section is a*
A refrigerated case of mouth-watering cheeses. ~~is opposite the~~
  ^   ^
  ~~produce section.~~

▶ *Set at the top two corners of the stage were huge*
~~Huge~~ lavender hearts outlined in bright white lights. ~~were set at~~
  ^   ^
  ~~the top two corners of the stage.~~

EXERCISE S7–1 Edit the following paragraph to increase sentence variety.

Making architectural models is a skill that requires patience and precision. It is an art that illuminates a design. Architects come up with a grand and intricate vision. Draftspersons convert that vision into blueprints. The model maker follows the blueprints. The model maker builds a miniature version of the structure. Modelers can work in traditional materials like wood and clay and paint. Modelers can work in newer materials like Styrofoam and liquid polymers. Some modelers still use cardboard, paper, and glue. Other modelers prefer glue guns, deformable plastic, and thin aluminum and brass wire. The modeler may seem to be making a small mess in the early stages of model building. In the end the modeler has completed a $1/100$-scale structure. Architect Rem Koolhaas has insisted that plans reveal the logic of a design. He has argued that models expose the architect's vision. The model maker's art makes vision real.

W

Word Choice

W Word Choice

W1

Glossary of usage

This glossary includes words commonly confused (such as *accept* and *except*), words commonly misused (such as *aggravate*), and words that are nonstandard (such as *hisself*). It also lists colloquialisms and jargon. Colloquialisms are expressions that may be appropriate in informal speech but are inappropriate in formal writing. Jargon is needlessly technical or pretentious language that is inappropriate in most contexts. If an item is not listed here, consult the index. For irregular verbs (such as *sing, sang, sung*), see G2-a. For idiomatic use of prepositions, see W5-d.

> ✓ GRAMMAR CHECKERS can point out commonly confused words and suggest that you check your usage. It is up to you, however, to determine the correct word for your intended meaning.

ON THE WEB > dianahacker.com/writersref
Language Debates > Absolute concepts such as *unique*
 bad versus *badly*
 however at the beginning of a sentence
 lie versus *lay*
 myself
 that versus *which*
 who versus *which* or *that*
 who versus *whom*
 you

a, an   Use *an* before a vowel sound, *a* before a consonant sound: *an apple, a peach.* Problems sometimes arise with words beginning with *h* or *u*. If the *h* is silent, the word begins with a vowel sound, so use *an: an hour, an honorable deed.* If the *h* is pronounced, the word begins with a consonant sound, so use *a: a hospital, a historian, a hotel.* Words such as *university* and *union* begin with a consonant sound (a *y* sound), so use *a: a union.* Words such as *uncle* and *umbrella* begin with a vowel sound, so use *an: an underground well.* When an abbreviation or an acronym begins with a vowel sound, use *an: an EKG, an MRI, an AIDS patient.*

accept, except   *Accept* is a verb meaning "to receive." *Except* is usually a preposition meaning "excluding." *I will accept all the packages except* *that one. Except* is also a verb meaning "to exclude." *Please except that item from the list.*

adapt, adopt   *Adapt* means "to adjust or become accustomed"; it is usually followed by *to*. *Adopt* means "to take as one's own." *Our family adopted a Vietnamese orphan, who quickly adapted to his new life.*

adverse, averse   *Adverse* means "unfavorable." *Averse* means "opposed" or "reluctant"; it is usually followed by *to*. *I am averse to your proposal because it could have an adverse impact on the economy.*

advice, advise   *Advice* is a noun, *advise* a verb. *We advise you to follow John's advice.*

affect, effect   *Affect* is usually a verb meaning "to influence." *Effect* is usually a noun meaning "result." *The drug did not affect the disease, and it had adverse side effects. Effect* can also be a verb meaning "to bring about." *Only the president can effect such a dramatic change.*

aggravate   *Aggravate* means "to make worse or more troublesome." *Overgrazing aggravated the soil erosion.* In formal writing, avoid the colloquial use of *aggravate* meaning "to annoy or irritate." *Her babbling annoyed* (not *aggravated*) *me.*

agree to, agree with   *Agree to* means "to give consent." *Agree with* means "to be in accord" or "to come to an understanding." *He agrees with me about the need for change, but he won't agree to my plan.*

ain't   *Ain't* is nonstandard. Use *am not, are not* (*aren't*), or *is not* (*isn't*). *I am not* (not *ain't*) *going home for spring break.*

all ready, already   *All ready* means "completely prepared." *Already* means "previously." *Susan was all ready for the concert, but her friends had already left.*

all right   *All right* is written as two words. *Alright* is nonstandard.

all together, altogether   *All together* means "everyone gathered." *Altogether* means "entirely." *We were not altogether certain that we could bring the family all together for the reunion.*

allude   To *allude* to something is to make an indirect reference to it. Do not use *allude* to mean "to refer directly." *In his lecture the professor referred* (not *alluded*) *to several pre-Socratic philosophers.*

allusion, illusion   An *allusion* is an indirect reference. An *illusion* is a misconception or false impression. *Did you catch my allusion to Shakespeare? Mirrors give the room an illusion of depth.*

a lot   *A lot* is two words. Do not write *alot*. *Sam lost a lot of weight.*

among, between   See *between, among.*

amongst   In American English, *among* is preferred.

amoral, immoral *Amoral* means "neither moral nor immoral"; it also means "not caring about moral judgments." *Immoral* means "morally wrong." *Until recently, most business courses were taught from an amoral perspective. Murder is immoral.*

amount, number Use *amount* with quantities that cannot be counted; use *number* with those that can. *This recipe calls for a large amount of sugar. We have a large number of toads in our garden.*

an See *a, an.*

and etc. *Et cetera* (*etc.*) means "and so forth," so *and etc.* is redundant. See also *etc.*

and/or Avoid the awkward construction *and/or* except in technical or legal documents.

angry at, angry with To write that one is *angry at* another person is nonstandard. Use *angry with* instead.

ante-, anti- The prefix *ante-* means "earlier" or "in front of"; the prefix *anti-* means "against" or "opposed to." *William Lloyd Garrison was a leader of the antislavery movement during the antebellum period.* *Anti-* should be used with a hyphen when it is followed by a capital letter or a word beginning with *i.*

anxious *Anxious* means "worried" or "apprehensive." In formal writing, avoid using *anxious* to mean "eager." *We are eager* (not *anxious*) *to see your new house.*

anybody, anyone *Anybody* and *anyone* are singular. (See G1-e and G3-a.)

anymore Reserve the adverb *anymore* for negative contexts, where it means "any longer." *Moviegoers are rarely shocked anymore by profanity.* Do not use *anymore* in positive contexts. Use *now* or *nowadays* instead. *Interest rates are so low nowadays* (not *anymore*) *that more people can afford to buy homes.*

anyone See *anybody, anyone.*

anyone, any one *Anyone,* an indefinite pronoun, means "any person at all." *Any one,* the pronoun *one* preceded by the adjective *any,* refers to a particular person or thing in a group. *Anyone from Chicago may choose any one of the games on display.*

anyplace In formal writing, use *anywhere.*

anyways, anywheres *Anyways* and *anywheres* are nonstandard. Use *anyway* and *anywhere.*

as *As* is sometimes used to mean "because." But do not use it if there is any chance of ambiguity. *We canceled the picnic because* (not *as*) *it began raining. As* here could mean "because" or "when."

as, like See *like, as.*

as to *As to* is jargon for *about*. *He inquired about* (not *as to*) *the job.*

averse See *adverse, averse.*

awful The adjective *awful* and the adverb *awfully* are too colloquial for formal writing.

awhile, a while *Awhile* is an adverb; it can modify a verb, but it cannot be the object of a preposition such as *for.* The two-word form *a while* is a noun preceded by an article and therefore can be the object of a preposition. *Stay awhile. Stay for a while.*

back up, backup *Back up* is a verb phrase. *Back up the car carefully. Be sure to back up your hard drive. Backup* is a noun meaning "a duplicate of electronically stored data." *Keep your backup in a safe place. Backup* can also be used as an adjective. *I regularly create backup disks.*

bad, badly *Bad* is an adjective, *badly* an adverb. (See G4-a and G4-b.) *They felt bad about being early and ruining the surprise. Her arm hurt badly after she slid headfirst into second base.*

being as, being that *Being as* and *being that* are nonstandard expressions. Write *because* instead. *Because* (not *Being as*) *I slept late, I had to skip breakfast.*

beside, besides *Beside* is a preposition meaning "at the side of" or "next to." *Annie Oakley slept with her gun beside her bed. Besides* is a preposition meaning "except" or "in addition to." *No one besides Terrie can have that ice cream. Besides* is also an adverb meaning "in addition." *I'm not hungry; besides, I don't like ice cream.*

between, among Ordinarily, use *among* with three or more entities, *between* with two. *The prize was divided among several contestants. You have a choice between carrots and beans.*

bring, take Use *bring* when an object is being transported toward you, *take* when it is being moved away. *Please bring me a glass of water. Please take these flowers to Mr. Scott.*

burst, bursted; bust, busted *Burst* is an irregular verb meaning "to come open or fly apart suddenly or violently." Its principal parts are *burst, burst, burst.* The past-tense form *bursted* is nonstandard. *Bust* and *busted* are slang for *burst* and, along with *bursted,* should not be used in formal writing.

can, may The distinction between *can* and *may* is fading, but some writers still observe it in formal writing. *Can* is traditionally reserved for ability, *may* for permission. *Can you speak French? May I help you?*

capital, capitol *Capital* refers to a city, *capitol* to a building where lawmakers meet. *Capital* also refers to wealth or resources. *The capitol has undergone extensive renovations. The residents of the state capital protested the development plans.*

censor, censure   *Censor* means "to remove or suppress material considered objectionable." *Censure* means "to criticize severely." *The school's policy of censoring books has been censured by the media.*

cite, site   *Cite* means "to quote as an authority or example." *Site* is usually a noun meaning "a particular place." *He cited the zoning law in his argument against the proposed site of the gas station.* Locations on the Internet are usually referred to as *sites. The library's Web site improves every week.*

climactic, climatic   *Climactic* is derived from *climax,* the point of greatest intensity in a series or progression of events. *Climatic* is derived from *climate* and refers to meteorological conditions. *The climactic period in the dinosaurs' reign was reached just before severe climatic conditions brought on an ice age.*

coarse, course   *Coarse* means "crude" or "rough in texture." *The coarse weave of the wall hanging gave it a three-dimensional quality. Course* usually refers to a path, a playing field, or a unit of study; the expression *of course* means "certainly." *I plan to take a course in car repair this summer. Of course, you are welcome to join me.*

compare to, compare with   *Compare to* means "to represent as similar." *She compared him to a wild stallion. Compare with* means "to examine similarities and differences." *The study compared the language ability of apes with that of dolphins.*

complement, compliment   *Complement* is a verb meaning "to go with or complete" or a noun meaning "something that completes." *Compliment* as a verb means "to flatter"; as a noun it means "flattering remark." *Her skill at rushing the net complements his skill at volleying. Mother's flower arrangements receive many compliments.*

conscience, conscious   *Conscience* is a noun meaning "moral principles." *Conscious* is an adjective meaning "aware or alert." *Let your conscience be your guide. Were you conscious of his love for you?*

continual, continuous   *Continual* means "repeated regularly and frequently." *She grew weary of the continual telephone calls. Continuous* means "extended or prolonged without interruption." *The broken siren made a continuous wail.*

could care less   *Could care less* is a nonstandard expression. Write *couldn't care less* instead. *He couldn't* (not *could*) *care less about his psychology final.*

could of   *Could of* is nonstandard for *could have. We could have* (not *could of*) *taken the train.*

council, counsel   A *council* is a deliberative body, and a *councilor* is a member of such a body. *Counsel* usually means "advice" and can also mean "lawyer"; *counselor* is one who gives advice or guidance. *The* *councilors met to draft the council's position paper. The pastor offered wise counsel to the troubled teenager.*

criteria   *Criteria* is the plural of *criterion,* which means "a standard or rule or test on which a judgment or decision can be based." *The only criterion for the scholarship is ability.*

data   *Data* is a plural noun technically meaning "facts or propositions." But *data* is increasingly being accepted as a singular noun. *The new data suggest* (or *suggests*) *that our theory is correct.* (The singular *datum* is rarely used.)

different from, different than   Ordinarily, write *different from. Your sense of style is different from Jim's.* However, *different than* is acceptable to avoid an awkward construction. *Please let me know if your plans are different than* (to avoid *from what*) *they were six weeks ago.*

differ from, differ with   *Differ from* means "to be unlike"; *differ with* means "to disagree." *She differed with me about the wording of the agreement. My approach to the problem differed from hers.*

disinterested, uninterested   *Disinterested* means "impartial, objective"; *uninterested* means "not interested." *We sought the advice of a disinterested counselor to help us solve our problem. He was uninterested in anyone's opinion but his own.*

don't   *Don't* is the contraction for *do not. I don't want any. Don't* should not be used as the contraction for *does not,* which is *doesn't.* He *doesn't* (not *don't*) *want any.*

due to   *Due to* is an adjective phrase and should not be used as a preposition meaning "because of." *The trip was canceled because of* (not *due to*) *lack of interest. Due to* is acceptable as a subject complement and usually follows a form of the verb *be. His success was due to hard work.*

each   *Each* is singular. (See G1-e and G3-a.)

effect   See *affect, effect.*

e.g.   In formal writing, replace the Latin abbreviation *e.g.* with its English equivalent: *for example* or *for instance.*

either   *Either* is singular. (See G1-e and G3-a.) For *either . . . or* constructions, see G1-d and G3-a.

elicit, illicit   *Elicit* is a verb meaning "to bring out" or "to evoke." *Illicit* is an adjective meaning "unlawful." *The reporter was unable to elicit any information from the police about illicit drug traffic.*

emigrate from, immigrate to   *Emigrate* means "to leave one country or region to settle in another." *In 1900, my grandfather emigrated from Russia to escape the religious pogroms. Immigrate* means "to enter another country and reside there." *Many Mexicans immigrate to the United States to find work.*

eminent, imminent *Eminent* means "outstanding" or "distinguished." *We met an eminent professor of Greek history. Imminent* means "about to happen." *The announcement is imminent.*

enthused Many people object to the use of *enthused* as an adjective. Use *enthusiastic* instead. *The children were enthusiastic* (not *enthused*) *about going to the circus.*

etc. Avoid ending a list with *etc.* It is more emphatic to end with an example, and in most contexts readers will understand that the list is not exhaustive. When you don't wish to end with an example, *and so on* is more graceful than *etc.*

eventually, ultimately Often used interchangeably, *eventually* is the better choice to mean "at an unspecified time in the future" and *ultimately* is better to mean "the furthest possible extent or greatest extreme." *He knew that eventually he would complete his degree. The existentialist considered suicide the ultimately rational act.*

everybody, everyone *Everybody* and *everyone* are singular. (See G1-e and G3-a.)

everyone, every one *Everyone* is an indefinite pronoun. *Every one,* the pronoun *one* preceded by the adjective *every,* means "each individual or thing in a particular group." *Every one* is usually followed by *of. Everyone wanted to go. Every one of the missing books was found.*

except See *accept, except.*

expect Avoid the colloquial use of *expect* meaning "to believe, think, or suppose." *I think* (not *expect*) *it will rain tonight.*

explicit, implicit *Explicit* means "expressed directly" or "clearly defined"; *implicit* means "implied, unstated." *I gave him explicit instructions not to go swimming. My mother's silence indicated her implicit approval.*

farther, further *Farther* usually describes distances. *Further* usually suggests quantity or degree. *Chicago is farther from Miami than I thought. You extended the curfew further than you should have.*

fewer, less *Fewer* refers to items that can be counted; *less* refers to items that cannot be counted. *Fewer people are living in the city. Please put less sugar in my tea.*

finalize *Finalize* is jargon meaning "to make final or complete." Use ordinary English instead. *The architect prepared final drawings* (not *finalized the drawings*).

firstly *Firstly* sounds pretentious, and it leads to the ungainly series *firstly, secondly, thirdly,* and so on. Write *first, second, third* instead.

further See *farther, further.*

get   *Get* has many colloquial uses. In writing, avoid using *get* to mean the following: "to evoke an emotional response" (*That music always gets to me*); "to annoy" (*After a while his sulking got to me*); "to take revenge on" (*I got back at him by leaving the room*); "to become" (*He got sick*); "to start or begin" (*Let's get going*). Avoid using *have got to* in place of *must*. *I must* (not *have got to*) *finish this paper tonight.*

good, well   *Good* is an adjective, *well* an adverb. (See G4.) *He hasn't felt good about his game since he sprained his wrist last season. She performed well on the uneven parallel bars.*

graduate   Both of the following uses of *graduate* are standard: *My sister was graduated from UCLA last year. My sister graduated from UCLA last year.* It is nonstandard, however, to drop the word *from*: *My sister graduated UCLA last year.* Though this usage is common in informal English, many readers object to it.

grow   Phrases such as *to grow the economy* and *to grow a business* are jargon. Usually the verb *grow* is intransitive (it does not take a direct object). *Our business has grown very quickly.* When *grow* is used in a transitive sense, with a direct object, it means "to cultivate" or "to allow to grow." *We plan to grow tomatoes this year. John is growing a beard.*

hanged, hung   *Hanged* is the past-tense and past-participle form of the verb *hang* meaning "to execute." *The prisoner was hanged at dawn. Hung* is the past-tense and past-participle form of the verb *hang* meaning "to fasten or suspend." *The stockings were hung by the chimney with care.*

hardly   Avoid expressions such as *can't hardly* and *not hardly*, which are considerable double negatives. *I can* (not *can't*) *hardly describe my elation at getting the job.* (See G4-d.)

has got, have got   *Got* is unnecessary and awkward in such constructions. It should be dropped. *We have* (not *have got*) *three days to prepare for the opening.*

he   At one time *he* was commonly used to mean "he or she." Today such usage is inappropriate. (See W4-e and G3-a.)

he/she, his/her   In formal writing, use *he or she* or *his or her.* For alternatives to these wordy constructions, see W4-e and G3-a.

hisself   *Hisself* is nonstandard. Use *himself.*

hopefully   *Hopefully* means "in a hopeful manner." *We looked hopefully to the future.* Some usage experts object to the use of *hopefully* as a sentence adverb, apparently on grounds of clarity. To be safe, avoid using *hopefully* in sentences such as the following: *Hopefully, your son will recover soon.* At least some educated readers will want you to indicate who is doing the hoping: *I hope that your son will recover soon.*

however   In the past, some writers objected to *however* at the beginning of a sentence, but current experts advise you to place the word according to your meaning and desired emphasis. Any of the following sentences is correct, depending on the intended contrast. *Pam decided, however, to attend Harvard. However, Pam decided to attend Harvard.* (She had been considering other schools.) *Pam, however, decided to attend Harvard.* (Unlike someone else, Pam opted for Harvard.)

hung   See *hanged, hung.*

i.e.   In formal writing, replace the Latin abbreviation *i.e.* with its English equivalent: *that is.*

if, whether   Use *if* to express a condition and *whether* to express alternatives. *If you go on a trip, whether to Nebraska or New Jersey, remember to bring traveler's checks.*

illusion   See *allusion, illusion.*

immigrate   See *emigrate from, immigrate to.*

imminent   See *eminent, imminent.*

immoral   See *amoral, immoral.*

implement   *Implement* is a pretentious way of saying "do," "carry out," or "accomplish." Use ordinary language instead. *We carried out* (not *implemented*) *the director's orders with some reluctance.*

imply, infer   *Imply* means "to suggest or state indirectly"; *infer* means "to draw a conclusion." *John implied that he knew all about computers, but the interviewer inferred that John was inexperienced.*

in, into   *In* indicates location or condition; *into* indicates movement or a change in condition. *They found the lost letters in a box after moving into the house.*

in regards to   *In regards to* confuses two different phrases: *in regard to* and *as regards.* Use one or the other. *In regard to* (or *As regards*) *the contract, ignore the first clause.*

irregardless   *Irregardless* is nonstandard. Use *regardless.*

is when, is where   These mixed constructions are often incorrectly used in definitions. *A run-off election is a second election held to break a tie* (not *is when a second election breaks a tie*). (See S5-c.)

its, it's   *Its* is a possessive pronoun; *it's* is a contraction for *it is.* (See P5-c and P5-e.) *The dog licked its wound whenever its owner walked into the room. It's a perfect day to walk the twenty-mile trail.*

kind(s)   *Kind* is singular and should be treated as such. Don't write *These kind of chairs are rare.* Write instead *This kind of chair is rare. Kinds* is plural and should be used only when you mean more than one kind. *These kinds of chairs are rare.*

kind of, sort of   Avoid using *kind of* or *sort of* to mean "somewhat." *The movie was somewhat* (not *kind of*) *boring.* Do not put *a* after either phrase. *That kind of* (not *kind of a*) *salesclerk annoys me.*

lay, lie   See *lie, lay.*

lead, led   *Lead* is a metallic element; it is a noun. *Led* is the past tense of the verb *lead. He led me to the treasure.*

learn, teach   *Learn* means "to gain knowledge"; *teach* means "to impart knowledge." *I must teach* (not *learn*) *my sister to read.*

leave, let   *Leave* means "to exit." Avoid using it with the nonstandard meaning "to permit." *Let* (not *Leave*) *me help you with the dishes.*

less   See *fewer, less.*

let, leave   See *leave, let.*

liable   *Liable* means "obligated" or "responsible." Do not use it to mean "likely." *You're likely* (not *liable*) *to trip if you don't tie your shoelaces.*

lie, lay   *Lie* is an intransitive verb meaning "to recline or rest on a surface." Its principal parts are *lie, lay, lain. Lay* is a transitive verb meaning "to put or place." Its principal parts are *lay, laid, laid.* (See G2-b.)

like, as   *Like* is a preposition, not a subordinating conjunction. It can be followed only by a noun or a noun phrase. *As* is a subordinating conjunction that introduces a subordinate clause. In casual speech you may say *She looks like she hasn't slept* or *You don't know her like I do.* But in formal writing, use *as. She looks as if she hasn't slept. You don't know her as I do.* (See also B1-f and B1-g.)

loose, lose   *Loose* is an adjective meaning "not securely fastened." *Lose* is a verb meaning "to misplace" or "to not win." *Did you lose your only loose pair of work pants?*

lots, lots of   *Lots* and *lots of* are colloquial substitutes for *many, much,* or *a lot.* Avoid using them in formal writing.

mankind   Avoid *mankind* whenever possible. It offends many readers because it excludes women. Use *humanity, humans, the human race,* or *humankind* instead. (See W4-e.)

may   See *can, may.*

maybe, may be   *Maybe* is an adverb meaning "possibly." *May be* is a verb phrase. *Maybe the sun will shine tomorrow. Tomorrow may be a brighter day.*

may of, might of   *May of* and *might of* are nonstandard for *may have* and *might have. We may have* (not *may of*) *had too many cookies.*

media, medium   *Media* is the plural of *medium. Of all the media that cover the Olympics, television is the medium that best captures the spectacle of the events.*

most   *Most* is colloquial when used to mean "almost" and should be avoided. *Almost* (not *Most*) *everyone went to the parade.*

must of   See *may of.*

myself   *Myself* is a reflexive or intensive pronoun. Reflexive: *I cut myself.* Intensive: *I will drive you myself.* Do not use *myself* in place of *I* or *me. He gave the flowers to Melinda and me* (not *myself*). (See also G3-c.)

neither   *Neither* is singular. (See G1-e and G3-a.) For *neither . . . nor* constructions, see G1-d and G3-a.

none   *None* may be singular or plural. (See G1-e.)

nowheres   *Nowheres* is nonstandard for *nowhere.*

number   See *amount, number.*

of   Use the verb *have*, not the preposition *of,* after the verbs *could, should, would, may, might,* and *must. They must have* (not *must of*) *left early.*

off of   *Off* is sufficient. Omit *of. The ball rolled off* (not *off of*) *the table.*

OK, O.K., okay   All three spellings are acceptable, but in formal speech and writing avoid these colloquial expressions.

parameters   *Parameter* is a mathematical term that has become jargon for "fixed limit," "boundary," or "guideline." Use ordinary English instead. *The task force was asked to work within certain guidelines* (not *parameters*).

passed, past   *Passed* is the past tense of the verb *pass. Mother passed me another slice of cake. Past* usually means "belonging to a former time" or "beyond a time or place." *Our past president spoke until past midnight. The hotel is just past the next intersection.*

percent, per cent, percentage   *Percent* (also spelled *per cent*) is always used with a specific number. *Percentage* is used with a descriptive term such as *large* or *small,* not with a specific number. *The candidate won 80 percent of the primary vote. Only a small percentage of registered voters turned out for the election.*

phenomena   *Phenomena* is the plural of *phenomenon,* which means "an observable occurrence or fact." *Strange phenomena occur at all hours of the night in that house, but last night's phenomenon was the strangest of all.*

plus   *Plus* should not be used to join independent clauses. *This raincoat is dirty; moreover* (not *plus*), *it has a hole in it.*

precede, proceed   *Precede* means "to come before." *Proceed* means "to go forward." *As we proceeded up the mountain path, we noticed fresh tracks in the mud, evidence that a group of hikers had preceded us.*

principal, principle *Principal* is a noun meaning "the head of a school or an organization" or "a sum of money." It is also an adjective meaning "most important." *Principle* is a noun meaning "a basic truth or law." *The principal expelled her for three principal reasons. We believe in the principle of equal justice for all.*

proceed, precede See *precede, proceed.*

quote, quotation *Quote* is a verb; *quotation* is a noun. Avoid using *quote* as a shortened form of *quotation*. *Her quotations* (not *quotes*) *from Shakespeare intrigued us.*

raise, rise *Raise* is a transitive verb meaning "to move or cause to move upward." It takes a direct object. *I raised the shades*. *Rise* is an intransitive verb meaning "to go up." *Heat rises.*

real, really *Real* is an adjective; *really* is an adverb. *Real* is sometimes used informally as an adverb, but avoid this use in formal writing. *She was really* (not *real*) *angry*. (See G4-a.)

reason . . . is because Use *that* instead of *because*. *The reason she's cranky is that* (not *because*) *she didn't sleep last night.* (See S5-c.)

reason why The expression *reason why* is redundant. *The reason* (not *The reason why*) *Jones lost the election is clear.*

relation, relationship *Relation* describes a connection between things. *Relationship* describes a connection between people. *There is a relation between poverty and infant mortality. Our business relationship has cooled over the years.*

respectfully, respectively *Respectfully* means "showing or marked by respect." *Respectively* means "each in the order given." *He respectfully submitted his opinion to the judge. John, Tom, and Larry were a butcher, a baker, and a lawyer, respectively.*

sensual, sensuous *Sensual* means "gratifying the physical senses," especially those associated with sexual pleasure. *Sensuous* means "pleasing to the senses," especially those involved in the experience of art, music, and nature. *The sensuous music and balmy air led the dancers to more sensual movements.*

set, sit *Set* is a transitive verb meaning "to put" or "to place." Its principal parts are *set, set, set*. *Sit* is an intransitive verb meaning "to be seated." Its principal parts are *sit, sat, sat. She set the dough in a warm corner of the kitchen. The cat sat in the warmest part of the room.*

shall, will *Shall* was once used as the helping verb with *I* or *we*: *I shall, we shall, you will, he/she/it will, they will*. Today, however, *will* is generally accepted even when the subject is *I* or *we*. The word *shall* occurs primarily in polite questions (*Shall I find you a pillow?*) and in legalistic sentences suggesting duty or obligation (*The applicant shall file form 1080 by December 31*).

should of *Should of* is nonstandard for *should have*. *They should have* (not *should of*) *been home an hour ago.*

since Do not use *since* to mean "because" if there is any chance of ambiguity. *Because* (not *Since*) *we won the game, we have been celebrating with a pitcher of root beer. Since* here could mean "because" or "from the time that."

sit See *set, sit.*

site See *cite, site.*

somebody, someone *Somebody* and *someone* are singular. (See G1-e and G3-a.)

something *Something* is singular. (See G1-e.)

sometime, some time, sometimes *Sometime* is an adverb meaning "at an indefinite or unstated time." *Some time* is the adjective *some* modifying the noun *time* and is spelled as two words to mean "a period of time." *Sometimes* is an adverb meaning "at times, now and then." *I'll see you sometime soon. I haven't lived there for some time. Sometimes I run into him at the library.*

suppose to Write *supposed to.*

sure and Write *sure to. We were all taught to be sure to* (not *and*) *look both ways before crossing a street.*

take See *bring, take.*

than, then *Than* is a conjunction used in comparisons; *then* is an adverb denoting time. *That pizza is more than I can eat. Tom laughed, and then we recognized him.*

that See *who, which, that.*

that, which Many writers reserve *that* for restrictive clauses, *which* for nonrestrictive clauses. (See P1-e.)

theirselves *Theirselves* is nonstandard for *themselves. The crash victims pushed the car out of the way themselves* (not *theirselves*).

them The use of *them* in place of *those* is nonstandard. *Please send those* (not *them*) *flowers to the patient in room 220.*

there, their, they're *There* is an adverb specifying place; it is also an expletive. Adverb: *Sylvia is lying there unconscious.* Expletive: *There are two plums left. Their* is a possessive pronoun. *Fred and Jane finally washed their car. They're* is a contraction of *they are. They're later than usual today.*

they The use of *they* to indicate possession is nonstandard. Use *their* instead. *Cindy and Sam decided to sell their* (not *they*) *1975 Corvette.*

this kind See *kind(s).*

to, too, two *To* is a preposition; *too* is an adverb; *two* is a number. *Too many of your shots slice to the left, but the last two were just right.*

toward, towards *Toward* and *towards* are generally interchangeable, although *toward* is preferred in American English.

try and *Try and* is nonstandard for *try to*. *The teacher asked us all to try to* (not *try and*) *write an original haiku.*

ultimately, eventually See *eventually, ultimately.*

unique Avoid expressions such as *most unique, more straight, less perfect, very round.* Either something is unique or it isn't. It is illogical to suggest degrees of uniqueness. (See G4-c.)

usage The noun *usage* should not be substituted for *use* when the meaning is "employment of." *The use* (not *usage*) *of computers dramatically increased the company's profits.*

use to Write *used to.*

utilize *Utilize* means "to make use of." It often sounds pretentious; in most cases, *use* is sufficient. *I used* (not *utilized*) *the laser printer.*

wait for, wait on *Wait for* means "to be in readiness for" or "await." *Wait on* means "to serve." *We're only waiting for* (not *waiting on*) *Ruth to take us to the game.*

ways *Ways* is colloquial when used to mean "distance." *The city is a long way* (not *ways*) *from here.*

weather, whether The noun *weather* refers to the state of the atmosphere. *Whether* is a conjunction referring to a choice between alternatives. *We wondered whether the weather would clear.*

well, good See *good, well.*

where Do not use *where* in place of *that*. *I heard that* (not *where*) *the crime rate is increasing.*

which See *that, which* and *who, which, that.*

while Avoid using *while* to mean "although" or "whereas" if there is any chance of ambiguity. *Although* (not *While*) *Gloria lost money in the slot machine, Tom won it at roulette.* Here *While* could mean either "although" or "at the same time that."

who, which, that Do not use *which* to refer to persons. Use *who* instead. *That,* though generally used to refer to things, may be used to refer to a group or class of people. *The player who* (not *that* or *which*) *made the basket at the buzzer was named MVP. The team that scores the most points in this game will win the tournament.*

who, whom *Who* is used for subjects and subject complements; *whom* is used for objects. (See G3-d.)

who's, whose *Who's* is a contraction of *who is*; *whose* is a possessive pronoun. *Who's ready for more popcorn? Whose coat is this?* (See P5-c and P5-e.)

will See *shall, will.*

would of *Would of* is nonstandard for *would have. She would have* (not *would of*) *had a chance to play if she had arrived on time.*

you In formal writing, avoid *you* in an indefinite sense meaning "anyone." (See G3-b.) *Any spectator* (not *You*) *could tell by the way John caught the ball that his throw would be too late.*

your, you're *Your* is a possessive pronoun; *you're* is a contraction of *you are. Is that your new motorcycle? You're on the list of finalists.* (See P5-c and P5-e.)

EXERCISE W1–1 Edit the following sentences for problems in usage. If a sentence is correct, write "correct" after it. Revisions of lettered sentences appear in the back of the book. Example:

> *an*
> **The pediatrician gave my daughter a̸ injection for her allergy.**
> ^

a. The amount of horses a Comanche warrior had in his possession indicated the wealth of his family.
b. The cat just set there watching his prey.
c. The schoolchildren loved their new principal.
d. What is the capital of Brazil?
e. Chris redesigned the boundary plantings to try and improve the garden's overall design.

1. Will you except the offer?
2. Please phone for an hotel reservation at the Brown Palace in Denver.
3. Gary decided to buy more fruit and less snacks.
4. I usually shop first at the French Market, which is further away, and then stop at Food Mart on my way home.
5. Alan had been lying on the sidewalk unconscious for nearly two hours before help arrived.

W2

Wordy sentences

Long sentences are not necessarily wordy, nor are short sentences always concise. A sentence is wordy if it can be tightened without loss of meaning.

> GRAMMAR CHECKERS flag wordy constructions only occasionally. They
> sometimes alert you to common redundancies, such as *true fact,* but
> they overlook more redundancies than they catch. They may miss
> empty or inflated phrases, such as *in my opinion* and *in order that,*
> and they rarely identify sentences with needlessly complex struc-
> tures. Grammar checkers are very good, however, at flagging and
> suggesting revisions for wordy constructions beginning with *there is*
> and *there are.*

W2-a Eliminate redundancies.

Redundancies such as *cooperate together, close proximity, basic
essentials,* and *true fact* are a common source of wordiness. There is
no need to say the same thing twice.

>   *works*
> ► Daniel ~~is now employed~~ at a private rehabilitation center ~~working~~
>
> as a registered physical therapist.

Though modifiers ordinarily add meaning to the words they
modify, occasionally they are redundant.

> ► Sylvia ~~very hurriedly~~ scribbled her name, address, and phone
>
> number on the back of a greasy napkin.

> ► Joel was determined ~~in his mind~~ to lose weight.
>
> The words *scribbled* and *determined* already contain the notions sug-
> gested by the modifiers *very hurriedly* and *in his mind.*

W2-b Avoid unnecessary repetition of words.

Though words may be repeated deliberately, for effect, repetitions
will seem awkward if they are clearly unnecessary. When a more
concise version is possible, choose it.

> ► Our fifth patient, in room six, is a mentally ill ~~patient.~~
>
>   *grow*
> ► The best teachers help each student to ~~become a better student~~
>
> both academically and emotionally.

W2-c Cut empty or inflated phrases.

An empty phrase can be cut with little or no loss of meaning. Common examples are introductory word groups that apologize or hedge: *in my opinion, I think that, it seems that, one must admit that,* and so on.

▶ ~~In my opinion,~~ Øur current immigration policy is misguided.

Inflated phrases can be reduced to a word or two without loss of meaning.

INFLATED	CONCISE
along the lines of	like
as a matter of fact	in fact
at all times	always
at the present time	now, currently
at this point in time	now, currently
because of the fact that	because
by means of	by
due to the fact that	because
for the purpose of	for
for the reason that	because
have the ability to	can, be able to
in order to	to
in spite of the fact that	although, though
in the event that	if
in the final analysis	finally
in the nature of	like
in the neighborhood of	about
until such time as	until

▶ We will file the appropriate papers ~~in the event that~~ _if_ we are

unable to meet the deadline.

W2-d Simplify the structure.

If the structure of a sentence is needlessly indirect, try simplifying it. Look for opportunities to strengthen the verb.

▶ The CEO claimed that because of volatile market conditions she

could not ~~make an~~ estimate ~~of~~ the company's future profits.

The verb *estimate* is more vigorous and more concise than *make an estimate of.*

The colorless verbs *is, are, was,* and *were* frequently generate excess words. (See also W3-b.)

                 monitors and balances
▶ Eduartina ~~is responsible for monitoring and balancing~~ the
                 ^

budgets for travel and personnel.

The revision is more direct and concise. Actions orginally appearing in subordinate structures have become verbs replacing *is.*

The expletive constructions *there is* and *there are* (or *there was* and *there were*) can also generate excess words. The same is true of expletive constructions beginning with *it.*

          A
▶ ~~There is~~ ₫nother module ~~that~~ tells the story of Charles Darwin
          ^

and introduces the theory of evolution.

                     A   *must*
▶ ~~It is imperative that~~ ₫ll police officers follow strict
                     ^   ^

procedures when apprehending a suspect.

Finally, verbs in the passive voice may be needlessly indirect. When the active voice expresses your meaning as well, use it. (See also W3-a.)

                          our coaches have recruited
▶ All too often, athletes with marginal academic skills. ~~have been~~
                          ^   ^

~~recruited by our coaches.~~

W2-e Reduce clauses to phrases, phrases to single words.

Word groups functioning as modifiers can often be made more compact. Look for any opportunities to reduce clauses to phrases or phrases to single words.

▶ We visited Monticello, ~~which was~~ the home of Thomas Jefferson.

▶ For her birthday we gave Jess a stylish vest.
_^ silk ~~made of silk.~~

EXERCISE W2-1 Edit the following sentences for wordiness. Revisions of lettered sentences appear in the back of the book. Example:

The Wilsons moved into the house ~~in spite of the fact that~~
even though
the back door was only ten yards from the train tracks.

a. Martin Luther King Jr. was a man who set a high standard for future leaders to meet.
b. Anita has been deeply in love with cooking since she was little and could first peek over the edge of a big kitchen tabletop.
c. In my opinion, Bloom's race for the governorship is a futile exercise.
d. It is pretty important in being a successful graphic designer to have technical knowledge and at one and the same moment an eye for color and balance.
e. Your task will be the deliverance of correspondence to all employees in the company.

1. Seeing the barrels, the driver immediately slammed on his brakes.
2. A really well-stocked bookshelf should have classical literature on it as well as important modern works of the current day.
3. China's enormously huge work population has an effect on the global world of high-tech manufacturing of things.
4. A typical autocross course consists of at least two straightaways, and the rest of the course is made up of numerous slaloms and several sharp turns.
5. At breakfast time, Mehrdad always started his day with cantaloupe, lemon yogurt, and black coffee.

EXERCISE W2-2 Edit the following business memo for wordiness.

To: District managers
From: Margaret Davenport, Vice President
Subject: Customer files

It has recently been brought to my attention that a percentage of our sales representatives have been failing to log reports of their client calls in our electronic customer file each and every day. I have also learned that some representatives are not checking the customer file on a routine basis.

Our clients sometimes receive a multiple number of sales calls from us when a sales representative is not cognizant of the fact that the client has been contacted at a previous time. Repeated telephone calls from our representatives annoy our customers. These repeated telephone calls also portray our company as one that is lacking in organization.

Effective as of immediately, direct your representatives to do the following:

- Record each and every customer contact in the electronic file at the end of each day, without fail.
- Check the electronic file at the very beginning of each day to ensure that telephone communications will not be initiated with clients who have already been called.

Let me extend my appreciation to you for cooperating in this important matter.

ON THE WEB > dianahacker.com/writersref
Grammar exercises > Word choice > E-ex W2–1 through W2–3

W3

Active verbs

As a rule, choose an active verb and pair it with a subject that names the person or thing doing the action. Active verbs express meaning more emphatically and vigorously than their weaker counterparts— forms of the verb *be* or verbs in the passive voice. Verbs in the passive voice lack strength because their subjects receive the action instead of doing it (see also B2-b). Forms of the verb *be* (*be, am, is, are, was, were, being, been*) lack vigor because they convey no action.

Although passive verbs and the forms of *be* have legitimate uses, if an active verb can carry your meaning, use it.

PASSIVE   The coolant pumps *were destroyed* by a surge of power.

BE VERB   A surge of power *was* responsible for the destruction of the coolant pumps.

ACTIVE   A surge of power *destroyed* the coolant pumps.

Even among active verbs, some are more active—and therefore more vigorous and colorful—than others. Carefully selected verbs can energize a piece of writing.

▶ The goalie crouched low, ~~reached~~ ^{swept} out his stick, and ~~sent~~ ^{hooked} the rebound away from the mouth of the net.

ACADEMIC ENGLISH Although you may be tempted to avoid the passive voice completely, keep in mind that it is preferred in some writing situations, especially in scientific writing. For appropriate uses of the passive voice, see W3-a; for advice about forming the passive, see E1-c.

GRAMMAR CHECKERS are fairly good at flagging passive verbs, such as *is used.* However, because passive verbs are sometimes appropriate, you—not the computer program—must decide whether to change a verb from passive to active. Grammar checkers tend to suggest revisions only when the passive sentence contains a *by* phrase (*Carbon dating is used by scientists to determine an object's approximate age*). Occasionally they make inappropriate suggestions for revision (*Scientists to determine an object's approximate age use carbon dating*). Only you can determine the most sensible word order for your sentence.

W3-a Use the active voice unless you have a good reason for choosing the passive.

In the active voice, the subject of the sentence does the action; in the passive voice, the subject receives the action. (See also B2-b.)

ACTIVE   Hernando *caught* the fly ball.

PASSIVE   The fly ball *was caught* by Hernando.

In passive sentences, the actor (in this case *Hernando*) frequently disappears from the sentence: *The fly ball was caught.*

In most cases, you will want to emphasize the actor, so you should use the active voice. To replace a passive verb with an active alternative, make the actor the subject of the sentence.

▶ ~~The transformer was struck by a bolt of lightning.~~
 A bolt of lightning struck the transformer.

The active verb (*struck*) makes the point more forcefully than the passive verb (*was struck*).

The passive voice is appropriate if you wish to emphasize the receiver of the action or to minimize the importance of the actor.

> **APPROPRIATE**
> **PASSIVE**
> Many native Hawaiians *are forced* to leave their beautiful beaches to make room for hotels and condominiums.

> **APPROPRIATE**
> **PASSIVE**
> As the time for harvest approaches, the tobacco plants *are sprayed* with a chemical to retard the growth of suckers.

The writer of the first sentence wished to emphasize the receivers of the action, Hawaiians. The writer of the second sentence wished to focus on the tobacco plants, not on the people spraying them.

In much scientific writing, the passive voice properly emphasizes the experiment or process being described, not the researcher.

> **APPROPRIATE**
> **PASSIVE**
> The solution *was heated* to the boiling point, and then it was reduced in volume by 50 percent.

ON THE WEB > dianahacker.com/writersref
Language Debates > Passive voice

W3-b Replace *be* verbs that result in dull or wordy sentences.

Not every *be* verb needs replacing. The forms of *be* (*be, am, is, are, was, were, being, been*) work well when you want to link a subject to a noun that clearly renames it or to an adjective that describes it: *History is a bucket of ashes. Scoundrels are always sociable.* (See B2-b.) And when used as helping verbs before present participles (*is flying, are disappearing*) to express ongoing action, *be* verbs are fine: *Derrick was plowing the field when his wife went into labor.* (See G2-f.)

If using a *be* verb makes a sentence needlessly dull or wordy, however, consider replacing it. Often a phrase following the verb will contain a word (such as *violation*) that suggests a more vigorous, active alternative (*violate*).

> *violate*
> ▶ Burying nuclear waste in Antarctica would ~~be in violation of~~
> ^
> an international treaty.

Violate is less wordy and more vigorous than *be in violation of.*

> *resisted*
> When Rosa Parks ~~was resistant to~~ giving up her seat on the bus,
>   ^
> she became a civil rights hero.

Resisted is stronger than *was resistant to.*

GRAMMAR CHECKERS usually do not flag wordiness caused by *be* verbs: *is in violation of.* Only you can find ways to strengthen your sentences by using vigorous, active verbs in place of *be.*

EXERCISE W3–1 Revise any weak, unemphatic sentences by replacing *be* verbs or passive verbs with active alternatives and, if necessary, by naming in the subject the person or thing doing the action. Some sentences are emphatic; do not change them. Revisions of lettered sentences appear in the back of the book. Example:

> *The ranger doused the campfire before giving us*
> ~~The campfire was doused by the ranger before we were given~~
>   ^
> a ticket for unauthorized use of a campsite.

a. The Prussians were victorious over the Saxons in 1745.
b. The entire operation is managed by Ahmed, the producer.
c. The sea kayaks were awkwardly paddled by the video game programmers.
d. At the crack of rocket and mortar blasts, I jumped from the top bunk and landed on my buddy below, who was crawling on the floor looking for his boots.
e. There were shouting protesters on the courthouse steps.

1. A strange sound was made in the willow tree by the monkey that had escaped from the zoo.
2. Her letter was in acknowledgment of the student's participation in the literacy program.
3. The bomb bay doors rumbled open, and freezing air whipped through the plane.
4. The work of Paul Oakenfold and Sandra Collins was influential in my choice of music for my audition.
5. The only responsibility I was given by my parents was putting gas in the brand-new Mitsubishi they bought me my senior year.

ON THE WEB > dianahacker.com/writersref
Grammar exercises > Word choice > E-ex W3–1 through W3–3

W4

Appropriate language

Language is appropriate when it suits your subject, engages your audience, and blends naturally with your own voice.

W4-a Stay away from jargon.

Jargon is specialized language used among members of a trade, profession, or group. Use jargon only when readers will be familiar with it; even then, use it only when plain English will not do as well.

JARGON   For years the indigenous body politic of South Africa attempted to negotiate legal enfranchisement without result.

REVISED For years the indigenous people of South Africa negotiated in vain for the right to vote.

Broadly defined, jargon includes puffed-up language designed more to impress readers than to inform them. The following are common examples from business, government, higher education, and the military, with plain English translations in parentheses.

ameliorate (improve)   indicator (sign)
commence (begin)   optimal (best, most favorable)
components (parts)   parameters (boundaries, limits)
endeavor (try)   peruse (read, look over)
exit (leave)   prior to (before)
facilitate (help)   utilize (use)
factor (consideration, cause)   viable (workable)
impact (v.) (affect)

Sentences filled with jargon are hard to read, and they are often wordy as well.

▶ All ~~employees functioning in the capacity of~~ work-study students
   must prove that they are currently enrolled.
   ~~are required to give evidence of current enrollment.~~
   ^

                     begin   *improving*
▶ Mayor Summers will ~~commence~~ his term of office by ~~ameliorating~~
                     ^   *poor neighborhoods.*   ^
   living conditions in ~~economically deprived zones.~~
                        ^

EXERCISE W4–1 Edit the following e-mail message to eliminate jargon.

Dear Ms. Jackson:

We members of the Nakamura Reyes team value our external partnering arrangements with Creative Software, and I look forward to seeing you next week at the trade show in Fresno. Per Mr. Reyes, please let me know when you'll have some downtime there so that he and I can conduct a strategizing session with you concerning our production schedule. It's crucial that we all be on the same page re our 2007–2008 product release dates.

Before we have a face-to-face, however, I have some findings to share. Our customer-centric approach to the new products will necessitate that user testing periods trend upward. The enclosed data should help you effectuate any adjustments to your timeline; let me know ASAP if you require any additional information to facilitate the above.

Before we convene in Fresno, Mr. Reyes and I will agendize any further talking points. Thanks for your help.

Sincerely,

Sylvia Nakamura

W4-b Avoid pretentious language, most euphemisms, and "doublespeak."

Hoping to sound profound or poetic, some writers embroider their thoughts with large words and flowery phrases, language that in fact sounds pretentious. Pretentious language is so ornate and often so wordy that it obscures the thought that lies beneath.

>   *parents become old,*
> ▶ When our **progenitors reach their silver-haired and golden years,**
>   ^   *bury*   *old-age*
> we frequently **ensepulcher** them in homes **for senescent beings** as
>   ^   *dead.*   ^
> if they were already **among the deceased.**
>   ^

Euphemisms, nice-sounding words or phrases substituted for words thought to sound harsh or ugly, are sometimes appropriate. It is customary, for example, to say that a couple is "sleeping together" or that someone has "passed away." Most euphemisms, however, are needlessly evasive or even deceitful. Like pretentious language, they obscure the intended meaning.

EUPHEMISM	PLAIN ENGLISH
adult entertainment	pornography
preowned automobile	used car
economically deprived	poor
selected out	fired
negative savings	debts
strategic withdrawal	retreat or defeat
revenue enhancers	taxes
chemical dependency	drug addiction
downsize	lay off
correctional facility	prison

The term *doublespeak* applies to any deliberately evasive or deceptive language, including euphemisms. Doublespeak is especially common in politics, where missiles are named "Peacekeepers," airplane crashes are termed "uncontrolled contact with the ground," and a military retreat is described as "tactical redeployment." Business also gives us its share of doublespeak. When the manufacturer of a pacemaker writes that its product "may result in adverse health consequences in pacemaker-dependent patients as a result of sudden 'no output' failure," it takes an alert reader to grasp the message: The pacemaker might suddenly stop functioning and cause a heart attack or even death.

GRAMMAR CHECKERS rarely identify jargon and only occasionally flag pretentious language. Sometimes they flag language that is acceptable in academic writing. You should be alert to your own use of jargon and pretentious language and simplify it whenever possible. If your grammar checker continually questions language that is appropriate in an academic setting, check to see whether you can set the program to a formal style level.

EXERCISE W4–2 Edit the following sentences to eliminate jargon, pretentious or flowery language, euphemisms, and doublespeak. You may need to make substantial changes in some sentences. Revisions of lettered sentences appear in the back of the book. Example:

After two weeks in the legal department, Sue has ~~worked~~ *mastered*
~~into~~ the routine, *office* ~~of the office,~~ and her ~~functional and self-~~ *performance has*
~~management skills have~~ exceeded all expectations.

a. In my youth, my family was under the constraints of difficult material circumstances.
b. In order that I may increase my expertise in the area of delivery of services to clients, I feel that participation in this conference will be beneficial.
c. Have you ever been accused of flagellating a deceased equine?
d. Governmentally sanctioned investigations into the continued value of after-school programs have begun to indicate a perceived need in the public realm at large.
e. Passengers should endeavor to finalize the customs declaration form prior to exiting the aircraft.

1. The mayor engaged in a creative transfer of employees' pension funds.
2. After a cursory examination of brand-new research materials on textiles, Patricia and the members of her team made the decision to engage in a series of visits to fashion manufacturers in the local vicinity.
3. The nurse announced that there had been a negative patient-care outcome due to a therapeutic misadventure on the part of the surgeon.
4. A generally leisurely pace at the onset of tai chi exercises can yield a variety of beneficial points within a short period of time.
5. The bottom line is that the company is experiencing a negative cash flow.

ON THE WEB > dianahacker.com/writersref
Grammar exercises > Word choice > E-ex W4–1

W4-c In most contexts, avoid slang, regional expressions, and nonstandard English.

Slang is an informal and sometimes private vocabulary that expresses the solidarity of a group such as teenagers, rock musicians, or football fans; it is subject to more rapid change than standard English. For example, the slang teenagers use to express approval changes every few years; *cool, groovy, neat, awesome, phat,* and *sweet* have replaced one another within the last three decades. Sometimes slang becomes so widespread that it is accepted as standard vocabulary. *Jazz,* for example, started as slang but is now generally accepted to describe a style of music.

Although slang has a certain vitality, it is a code that not everyone understands, and it is very informal. Therefore, it is inappropriate in most written work.

▶ If we don't begin studying for the final, a whole semester's work ~~is~~
will be wasted.
~~going down the tubes.~~
^

disgust you.
▶ The government's "filth" guidelines for food will ~~gross you out.~~
^

Regional expressions are common to a group in a geographical area. *Let's talk with the bark off* (for *Let's speak frankly*) is an expression in the southern United States, for example. Regional expressions have the same limitations as slang and are therefore inappropriate in most writing.

▶ John was four blocks from the house before he remembered to ~~cut~~ *turn on*

the headlights ~~on.~~

▶ I'm not ~~for~~ sure, but I think the dance has been postponed.

Standard English is the language used in all academic, business, and professional fields. Nonstandard English is spoken by people with a common regional or social heritage. Although nonstandard English may be appropriate when spoken within a close group, it is out of place in most formal and informal writing.

▶ The counselor ~~have~~ *has* so many problems in her own life that she *doesn't* ~~don't~~ know how to advise anyone else.

If you speak a nonstandard dialect, try to identify the ways in which your dialect differs from standard English. Look especially for the following features of nonstandard English, which commonly cause problems in writing:

Misuse of verb forms such as *began* and *begun* (See G2-a.)

Omission of *-s* endings on verbs (See G2-c.)

Omission of *-ed* endings on verbs (See G2-d.)

Omission of necessary verbs (See G2-e.)

Double negatives (See G4-d.)

You might also scan the Glossary of Usage (W1), which alerts you to nonstandard words and expressions such as *ain't, could of, hisself, theirselves, them* (meaning "those"), *they* (meaning "their"), and so on.

W4-d Choose an appropriate level of formality.

In deciding on a level of formality, consider both your subject and your audience. Does the subject demand a dignified treatment, or is a relaxed tone more suitable? Will the audience be put off if you assume too close a relationship with them, or might you alienate them by seeming too distant?

For most college and professional writing, some degree of formality is appropriate. In a letter applying for a job, for example, it is a mistake to sound too breezy and informal.

TOO INFORMAL	I'd like to get that technician job you've got in the paper.
MORE FORMAL	I would like to apply for the technician position listed in the *Peoria Journal Star*.

Informal writing is appropriate for private letters, business correspondence between close associates, articles in popular magazines, and personal narratives. In such writing, formal language can seem out of place.

> *began*
> Bob's pitching lesson ~~commenced~~ with his famous sucker
> *which he threw*^
> pitch, ~~implemented~~ as a slow ball coming behind a fast windup.
> ^

Formal words such as *commenced* and *implemented* clash with appropriate informal terms such as *sucker pitch* and *fast windup*.

✓ GRAMMAR CHECKERS rarely flag slang and informal language. They do, however, flag contractions. If your ear tells you that a contraction such as *isn't* or *doesn't* strikes the right tone, stay with it.

EXERCISE W4–3 Revise the following passage so that the level of formality is appropriate for a letter to the editor of a major newspaper.

In pop culture, college grads who return home to live with the folks are seen as good-for-nothing losers who mooch off their family. And many older adults seem to feel that the trend of moving back home after school, which was rare in their day, is becoming too commonplace today. But society must realize that times have changed. Most young adults want to live on their own ASAP, but they graduate with heaps of debt and they need some time to get back on their feet. College tuition and the cost of housing have increased way more than salary increases in the past fifty years. Also, the job market is tighter and more jobs require advanced degrees than in the past. So before people go off on college graduates who move back in to their parents' house for a spell, they'd better consider all the facts.

W4-e Avoid sexist language.

Sexist language is language that stereotypes or demeans men or women, usually women. Being aware of sexist language and avoiding it in your writing will show respect for and sensitivity to the feelings of others.

GRAMMAR CHECKERS are good at flagging obviously sexist terms, such as *mankind* and *fireman,* but they do not flag language that might be demeaning to women (*woman doctor*) or stereotypical (referring to assistants as women and lawyers as men, for instance). They also have no way of identifying the generic use of *he* or *his* (*An obstetrician needs to be available to his patients anytime, day or night*). You must use your common sense to tell when a word or a construction is offensive.

ON THE WEB > dianahacker.com/writersref
Language Debates > Sexist language

Recognizing sexist language

Some sexist language is easy to recognize because it reflects genuine contempt for women: referring to a woman as a "chick," for example, or calling a lawyer a "lady lawyer," or saying in an advertisement, "If our new sports car were a lady, it would get its bottom pinched."

Other forms of sexist language are less blatant. The following practices, while they may not result from conscious sexism, reflect stereotypical thinking: referring to nurses as women and doctors as men, using different conventions when naming or identifying women and men, or assuming that all subjects or all readers are men.

STEREOTYPICAL LANGUAGE

After the nursing student graduates, *she* must face a difficult state board examination. [Not all nursing students are women.]

Running for city council are Jake Stein, an attorney, and *Mrs.* Cynthia Jones, a professor of English *and mother of three.* [The title *Mrs.* and the phrase *and mother of three* are irrelevant.]

Wives of senior government officials are required to report any gifts they receive that are valued at more than $100. [Not all senior government officials are men.]

Still other forms of sexist language result from outmoded traditions. The pronouns *he, him,* and *his,* for instance, were traditionally used to refer generically to persons of either sex.

GENERIC *HE* OR *HIS*

When a senior physician is harassed by managed care professionals, *he* may be tempted to leave the profession.

A journalist is stimulated by *his* deadline.

Today, however, such usage is widely viewed as sexist because it excludes women and encourages sex-role stereotyping—the view that men are somehow more suited than women to be doctors, journalists, and so on.

Like the pronouns *he, him,* and *his,* the nouns *man* and *men* were once used indefinitely to refer to persons of either sex. Current usage demands gender-neutral terms instead.

INAPPROPRIATE	APPROPRIATE
anchorman	anchor
chairman	chairperson, moderator, chair, head
clergyman	member of the clergy, minister, pastor
congressman	member of Congress, representative, legislator
fireman	firefighter
foreman	supervisor
mailman	mail carrier, postal worker, letter carrier
(to) man	to operate, to staff
mankind	people, humans
manpower	personnel
policeman	police officer
salesman	sales associate, sales representative
weatherman	weather forecaster, meteorologist
workman	worker, laborer

Revising sexist language

When revising sexist language, be sparing in your use of the wordy constructions *he or she* and *his or her.* Although these constructions are fine in small doses, they become awkward when repeated throughout an essay. A better revision strategy, many writers have discovered, is to write in the plural; yet another strategy is to recast the sentence so that the problem does not arise.

SEXIST

When a senior physician is harassed by managed care professionals, *he* may be tempted to leave the profession.

A journalist is stimulated by *his* deadline.

ACCEPTABLE BUT WORDY

When a senior physician is harassed by managed care professionals, *he or she* may be tempted to leave the profession.

A journalist is stimulated by *his or her* deadline.

BETTER: USING THE PLURAL

When senior *physicians* are harassed by managed care professionals, *they* may be tempted to leave the profession.

Journalists are stimulated by *their* deadlines.

BETTER: RECASTING THE SENTENCE

When harassed by managed care professionals, *a senior physician* may be tempted to leave the profession.

A journalist is stimulated by *a* deadline.

For more examples of these revision strategies, see G3-a.

EXERCISE W4–4 Edit the following sentences to eliminate sexist language or sexist assumptions. Revisions of lettered sentences appear in the back of the book. Example:

> *Scholarship athletes*   *their*
> A scholarship athlete must be as concerned about his
> ^
>   *they are*   *their*   ^
> academic performance as he is about his athletic
>   ^   ^
> performance.

a. Mrs. Geralyn Farmer, who is the mayor's wife, is the chief surgeon at University Hospital. Dr. Paul Green is her assistant.

b. Every applicant wants to know how much he will make.

c. An elementary school teacher should understand the concept of nurturing if she intends to be a success.

d. Every student of high-tech architecture picks his favorite when he studies such inspirational architects as Renzo Piano and Zaha Hadid.

e. If man does not stop polluting his environment, mankind will perish.

1. A fireman must always be on call even when he is off duty.

2. The chairman for the new program in digital art is Ariana Tamlin, an accomplished portrait painter, computer programmer, and cookie baker.

3. In the gubernatorial race, Lena Weiss, a defense lawyer and mother of two, easily defeated Harvey Tower, an architect.

4. Recent military history has shown that lady combat helicopter pilots are as skilled, reliable, and resourceful as men.

5. An emergency room head nurse must know how to use sophisticated digital equipment if she is to keep track of all her patients' data and guide her medical team.

EXERCISE W4–5 Eliminate sexist language or sexist assumptions in the following job posting for an elementary school teacher.

We are looking for qualified women for the position of elementary school teacher. The ideal candidate should have a bachelor's degree, a state teaching certificate, and one year of student teaching. She should be knowledgeable in all elementary subject areas, including science and math. While we want our new teacher to have a commanding presence in the classroom, we are also looking for motherly characteristics such as patience and trustworthiness. She must be able to both motivate an entire classroom and work with each student one-on-one to assess his individual needs. She must also be comfortable communicating with the parents of her students. For salary and benefits information, including maternity leave policy, please contact the Martin County School Board. Any qualified applicant should submit her résumé by March 15.

ON THE WEB > dianahacker.com/writersref
Grammar exercises > Word choice > E-ex W4–2

W4-f Revise language that may offend groups of people.

Obviously it is impolite to use offensive terms such as *Polack* or *redneck*. But biased language can take more subtle forms. Because language evolves over time, names once thought acceptable may become offensive. When describing groups of people, choose names that the groups currently use to describe themselves.

▶ North Dakota takes its name from the ~~Indian~~ *Lakota* word meaning

"friend" or "ally."

▶ Many ~~Oriental~~ *Asian* immigrants have recently settled in our small

town in Tennessee.

Negative stereotypes (such as "drives like a teenager" or "haggard as an old crone") are of course offensive. But you should avoid stereotyping a person or a group even if you believe your generalization to be positive.

▶ It was no surprise that Greer, ~~a Chinese American,~~ was selected
　　　　　　　　　　　　　　　　　　　　　^
　　an excellent math and science student,
for the honors chemistry program.

W5

Exact language

Two reference works (or their online equivalents) will help you find words to express your meaning exactly: a good dictionary, such as *The American Heritage Dictionary* or *Merriam-Webster's Collegiate Dictionary,* and a book of synonyms and antonyms such as *Roget's International Thesaurus.* (See W6.)

> GRAMMAR CHECKERS flag some nonstandard idioms, such as *comply to,* but few clichés. They do not identify commonly confused words, such as *principal* and *principle,* or misused word forms, such as *significance* and *significant.* You must be alert for such words and use your dictionary if you are unsure of the correct form. Grammar checkers are of little help with the other problems discussed in W5: choosing words with appropriate connotations, using concrete language, and using figures of speech appropriately.

W5-a　Select words with appropriate connotations.

In addition to their strict dictionary meanings (or *denotations*), words have *connotations,* emotional colorings that affect how readers respond to them. The word *steel* denotes "made of or resembling commercial iron that contains carbon," but it also calls up a cluster of images associated with steel, such as the sensation of touching it. These associations give the word its connotations—cold, smooth, unbending.

If the connotation of a word does not seem appropriate for your purpose, your audience, or your subject matter, you should change the word. When a more appropriate synonym does not come quickly to mind, consult a dictionary or a thesaurus. (See W6.)

>   *slender*
> The model was ~~skinny~~ and fashionable.
>
> The connotation of the word *skinny* is too negative.

>   *sweat*
> As I covered the boats with marsh grass, the ~~perspiration~~ I had
>
> worked up evaporated in the wind, and the cold morning air
>
> seemed even colder.
>
> The term *perspiration* is too dainty for the context, which suggests vigorous exercise.

W5-b Prefer specific, concrete nouns.

Unlike general nouns, which refer to broad classes of things, specific nouns point to definite and particular items. *Film,* for example, names a general class, *fantasy film* names a narrower class, and *Lord of the Rings: Return of the King* is more specific still.

Unlike abstract nouns, which refer to qualities and ideas (*justice, beauty, realism, dignity*), concrete nouns point to immediate, often sensory experience and to physical objects (*steeple, asphalt, lilac, stone, garlic*).

Specific, concrete nouns express meaning more vividly than general or abstract ones. Although general and abstract language is sometimes necessary to convey your meaning, ordinarily prefer specific, concrete alternatives.

> The senator spoke about the challenges of the future: ~~the~~
> *famine, pollution, dwindling resources, and terrorism.*
> ~~environment and world peace.~~

Nouns such as *thing, area, factor,* and *individual* are especially dull and imprecise.

>   *rewards.*
> A career in city planning offers many ~~things.~~

>   *experienced technician.*
> Try pairing a trainee with an ~~individual with technical experience.~~

W5-c Do not misuse words.

If a word is not in your active vocabulary, you may find yourself misusing it, sometimes with embarrassing consequences. When in doubt, check the dictionary.

▶ The fans were ~~migrating~~ *climbing* up the bleachers in search of good seats.

▶ The Internet has so ~~diffused~~ *permeated* our culture that it touches all segments of society.

Be especially alert for misused word forms—using a noun such as *absence, significance,* or *persistence,* for example, when your meaning requires the adjective *absent, significant,* or *persistent.*

▶ Most dieters are not ~~persistence~~ *persistent* enough to make a permanent change in their eating habits.

EXERCISE W5-1 Edit the following sentences to correct misused words. Revisions of lettered sentences appear in the back of the book. Example:

The training required for a ballet dancer is ~~all-absorbent.~~ *all-absorbing.*

a. We regret this delay; thank you for your patients.
b. Ada's plan is to require education and experience to prepare herself for a position as property manager.
c. Tiger Woods, the penultimate competitor, has earned millions of dollars just in endorsements.
d. Many people take for granite that public libraries have up-to-date networked computer systems.
e. The affect of Gao Xinjian's novels on Chinese exiles is hard to gauge.

1. Waste, misuse of government money, security and health violations, and even pilfering have become major dilemmas in some government agencies.
2. Designers of handheld devices have to understand that changes in ambience temperatures can damage the tiny circuit boards.
3. Grand Isle State Park is surrounded on three sides by water.
4. The Old World nuance of the restaurant intrigued us.
5. The person who complained to the human resources manager wishes to remain unanimous.

ON THE WEB > dianahacker.com/writersref
Grammar exercises > Word choice > E-ex W5–1

W5-d Use standard idioms.

Idioms are speech forms that follow no easily specified rules. The English say "Maria went *to hospital*," an idiom strange to American ears, which are accustomed to hearing *the* in front of *hospital*. Native speakers of a language seldom have problems with idioms, but prepositions sometimes cause trouble, especially when they follow certain verbs and adjectives. When in doubt, consult a good desk dictionary: Look up the word preceding the troublesome preposition.

UNIDIOMATIC	IDIOMATIC
abide with (a decision)	abide by (a decision)
according with	according to
agree to (an idea)	agree with (an idea)
angry at (a person)	angry with (a person)
capable to	capable of
comply to	comply with
desirous to	desirous of
different than (a person or thing)	different from (a person or thing)
intend on doing	intend to do
off of	off
plan on doing	plan to do
preferable than	preferable to
prior than	prior to
superior than	superior to
sure and	sure to
try and	try to
type of a	type of

ESL Because idioms follow no particular rules, you must learn them individually. You may find it helpful to keep a list of idioms that you frequently encounter in your reading. For idiomatic combinations of adjectives and prepositions (such as *afraid of*), see E5-c. For idiomatic combinations of verbs and prepositions (such as *search for*), see E5-d.

EXERCISE W5–2 Edit the following sentences to eliminate errors in the use of idiomatic expressions. If a sentence is correct, write "correct" after it. Answers to lettered sentences appear in the back of the book. Example:

> by
> We agreed to abide ~~with~~ the decision of the judge.
>   ^

a. Queen Anne was so angry at Sarah Churchill that she refused to see her again.
b. Jean-Pierre's ambitious travel plans made it impossible for him to comply with the graduate program's residency requirement.
c. The parade moved off of the street and onto the beach.
d. The frightened refugees intend on making the dangerous trek across the mountains.
e. What type of a wedding are you planning?

1. Be sure and report on the danger of releasing genetically engineered bacteria into the atmosphere.
2. Why do you assume that embezzling bank assets is so different than robbing the bank?
3. The wilderness guide seemed capable to show us where the trail of petroglyphs was located.
4. In Evan's cautious mind, packing his own parachute seemed preferable to letting an indifferent teenager fold all that silk and cord into a small pack.
5. Andrea plans on joining the Peace Corps after graduation.

ON THE WEB > dianahacker.com/writersref
Grammar exercises > Word choice > E-ex W5–2

W5-e Do not rely heavily on clichés.

The pioneer who first announced that he had "slept like a log" no doubt amused his companions with a fresh and unlikely comparison. Today, however, that comparison is a cliché, a saying that has lost its dazzle from overuse. No longer can it surprise.

To see just how predictable clichés are, put your hand over the right-hand column in the following list and then finish the phrases given on the left.

cool as a	cucumber
beat around	the bush
blind as a	bat
busy as a	bee, beaver

crystal	clear
dead as a	doornail
out of the frying pan and	into the fire
light as a	feather
like a bull	in a china shop
playing with	fire
nutty as a	fruitcake
selling like	hotcakes
starting out at the bottom	of the ladder
water under the	bridge
white as a	sheet, ghost
avoid clichés like the	plague

The cure for clichés is frequently simple: Just delete them. When this won't work, try adding some element of surprise. One student, for example, who had written that she had butterflies in her stomach, revised her cliché like this:

> If all of the action in my stomach is caused by butterflies, there must be a horde of them, with horseshoes on.

The image of butterflies wearing horseshoes is fresh and unlikely, not dully predictable like the original cliché.

ON THE WEB > dianahacker.com/writersref
Language Debates > Clichés

W5-f Use figures of speech with care.

A figure of speech is an expression that uses words imaginatively (rather than literally) to make abstract ideas concrete. Most often, figures of speech compare two seemingly unlike things to reveal surprising similarities.

In a *simile,* the writer makes the comparison explicitly, usually by introducing it with *like* or *as:* "By the time cotton had to be picked, grandfather's neck was as red as the clay he plowed." In a *metaphor,* the *like* or *as* is omitted, and the comparison is implied. For example, in the Old Testament Song of Solomon, a young woman compares the man she loves to a fruit tree: "With great delight I sat in his shadow, and his fruit was sweet to my taste."

Although figures of speech are useful devices, writers sometimes use them without thinking through the images they evoke.

The result is sometimes a *mixed metaphor,* the combination of two or more images that don't make sense together.

> Crossing Utah's salt flats in his new convertible, my father flew
> *at jet speed.*
> ~~under a full head of steam.~~
> ^

Flew suggests an airplane, while *under a full head of steam* suggests a steamboat or a train. To clarify the image, the writer should stick with one comparison or the other.

> Our office had decided to put all controversial issues on a back
>
> burner. ~~in a holding pattern.~~
>   ^

Here the writer is mixing stoves and airplanes. Simply deleting one of the images corrects the problem.

EXERCISE W5-3 Edit the following sentences to replace worn-out expressions and clarify mixed figures of speech. Revisions of lettered sentences appear in the back of the book. Example:

>   *the color drained from his face.*
> When he heard about the accident, ~~he turned white as a~~
>   ^
> ~~sheet.~~

a. John stormed into the room like a bull in a china shop.
b. Some people insist that they'll always be there for you, even when they haven't been before.
c. The Cubs easily beat the Mets, who were in the soup early in the game today at Wrigley Field.
d. We ironed out the sticky spots in our relationship.
e. My mother accused me of beating around the bush when in fact I was just talking off the top of my head.

1. Patricia was used to burning the candle at both ends to get her assignments done.
2. No matter how many books he reads, André can never seem to quench his hunger for knowledge.
3. In an era of cutbacks and outsourcing, the best high-tech workers discover that being a jack of all trades is a solid gold key to continued success.
4. There are too many cooks in the broth at corporate headquarters.
5. Juanita told Kyle that keeping skeletons in the closet would be playing with fire.

ON THE WEB > dianahacker.com/writersref
    Grammar exercises > Word choice > E-ex W5-3

W6

The dictionary and thesaurus

W6-a The dictionary

A good dictionary, whether print or online—such as *The American Heritage Dictionary of the English Language, The Random House College Dictionary, Merriam-Webster's Collegiate Dictionary,* or *Webster's New World Dictionary of the American Language*—is an indispensable writer's aid.

The entry on page 172 is taken from *The American Heritage Dictionary.* Labels show where various kinds of information about a word can be found in that dictionary. A sample entry from an online dictionary, *Merriam-Webster Online,* appears on page 173.

Spelling, word division, and pronunciation

The main entry (*re·gard* in the sample entries) shows the correct spelling of the word. When there are two correct spellings of a word (as in *collectible, collectable,* for example), both are given, with the preferred spelling usually appearing first.

The main entry also shows how the word is divided into syllables. The dot between *re* and *gard* separates the word's two syllables. When a word is compound, the main entry shows how to write it: as one word (*crossroad*), as a hyphenated word (*cross-stitch*), or as two words (*cross section*).

The word's pronunciation is given just after the main entry. The accents indicate which syllables are stressed; the other marks are explained in the dictionary's pronunciation key. In print dictionaries this key usually appears at the bottom of every page or every other page. Many online entries include an audio link to a person's voice pronouncing the word. And most online dictionaries have an audio pronunciation guide.

Word endings and grammatical labels

When a word takes endings to indicate grammatical functions (called *inflections*), the endings are listed in boldface, as with *-garded, -garding,* and *-gards* in the sample print entry.

PRINT DICTIONARY ENTRY

Grammatical
label

Pronunciation

Word   Part of   Word endings   Usage label
division   speech label (inflections)

Spelling —— **re•gard** (rĭ-gärd′) *v.* **-gard•ed, -gard•ing, -gards** —*tr.* **1.** To look
at attentively; observe closely. **2.** To look upon or consider in a particular
way: *I regard him as a fool.* **3.** To hold in esteem or respect: *She regards*
her teachers highly. **4.** To relate or refer to; concern: *This item regards their*

Meanings —— *liability.* **5.** To take into account; consider. **6.** *Obsolete* To take care of.
—*intr.* **1.** To look or gaze. **2.** To give heed; pay attention. ❖ *n.* **1.** A look
or gaze. **2.** Careful thought or attention; heed: *She gives little regard to*
her sister's teasing. **3a.** Respect, affection, or esteem: *He has high regard*
for your work. **b. regards** Good wishes expressing such sentiment: *Give*
the family my best regards. **4.** A particular point or aspect; respect: *She*
was lucky in that regard. **5.** Basis for action; motive. **6.** *Obsolete* Appear-

Idioms —— ance or aspect. —***idioms: as regards*** Concerning. **in** (or **with**)
regard to With respect to. [Middle English *regarden,* from Old French
regarder : re-, re- + *guarder,* to guard (of Germanic origin; see GUARD).]

Synonyms *regard, esteem, admiration, respect* These nouns refer to a
feeling based on perception of and approval for the worth of a person or
thing. *Regard* is the most general: *"I once thought you had a kind of regard*
for her" (George Borrow). *Esteem* connotes considered appraisal and positive regard: *"The near-unanimity of esteem he enjoyed during his lifetime*

Synonyms —— *has by no means been sustained since"* (Will Crutchfield). *Admiration* is a
feeling of keen approbation: *"Greatness is a spiritual condition worthy to*
excite love, interest, and admiration" (Matthew Arnold). *Respect* implies
appreciative, often deferential regard resulting from careful assessment:
"I have a great respect for any man who makes his own way in life" (Win-
ston Churchill). See also synonyms at **consider.**

Usage Note *Regard* is traditionally used in the singular in the phrase
in regard (not *in regards*) *to. Regarding* and *as regards* are also standard in

Usage note —— the sense "with reference to." In the same sense *with respect to* is acceptable, but *respecting* is not. • *Respects* is sometimes considered preferable
to *regards* in the sense of "particulars": *In some respects* (not *regards*) *the*
books are alike.

Word origin ——
(etymology)

Labels for the parts of speech and for other grammatical terms
are sometimes abbreviated, as they are in the print entry. The most
commonly used abbreviations are these:

n.	noun	adj.	adjective
pl.	plural	adv.	adverb
sing.	singular	pron.	pronoun
v.	verb	prep.	preposition
tr.	transitive verb	conj.	conjunction
int.	intransitive verb	interj.	interjection

ONLINE DICTIONARY ENTRY

Merriam-Webster Online Dictionary

Thesaurus

3 entries found for **regard**.
To select an entry, click on it.

Alternative entries ——————— regard[1.noun]   Go
regard[2.verb]
self-regard ▾

Audio pronunciation link

Spelling and word division ———

Pronunciation ———————

Part of speech label ————

Usage label ————

Main Entry: ¹**re·gard** ◀»
Pronunciation: ri-'gärd
Function: *noun*
Etymology: Middle English, from Middle
French, from Old French, from *regarder*

Etymology
(word origin)

1 *archaic* : APPEARANCE
2 a : ATTENTION, CONSIDERATION <due
regard should be given to all facets of the
question> **b** : a protective interest : CARE
<ought to have more *regard* for his health>
3 : LOOK, GAZE
4 a : the worth or estimation in which
something or someone is held <a man of
small *regard*> **b** (1) : a feeling of respect and
affection : ESTEEM <his hard work won him
the *regard* of his colleagues> (2) *plural* :
friendly greetings implying such feeling <give
him my *regards*>
5 : a basis of action or opinion : MOTIVE
6 : an aspect to be taken into consideration :
RESPECT <is a small school, and is fortunate
in this *regard*>
7 *obsolete* : INTENTION
- **in regard to** : with respect to :
CONCERNING
- **with regard to** : in regard to

Meanings (synonyms
shown as hyperlinks)

Idioms ———————

Meanings, word origin, synonyms, and antonyms

Each meaning for the word is given a number. Occasionally a
word's use is illustrated in a quoted sentence.

Sometimes a word can be used as more than one part of speech
(*regard,* for instance, can be used as either a verb or a noun). In
such a case, all the meanings for one part of speech are given before all the meanings for another, as in the sample entries. The entries also give idiomatic uses of the word.

The origin of the word, called its *etymology,* appears in brackets after all the meanings in the print version; in the online version, it appears before the meanings.

Synonyms, words similar in meaning to the main entry, are frequently listed. In the sample print entry, the dictionary draws distinctions in meaning among the various synonyms. In the online entry, synonyms appear as hyperlinks. Antonyms, which do not appear in the sample entries, are words having a meaning opposite from that of the main entry.

Usage

Usage labels indicate when, where, or under what conditions a particular meaning for a word is appropriately used. Common labels are *informal* (or *colloquial*), *slang, nonstandard, dialect, obsolete, archaic, poetic,* and *British.* In the sample print entry, two meanings of *regard* are labeled *obsolete* because they are no longer in use. The online entry has meanings labeled both *archaic* and *obsolete.*

Dictionaries sometimes include usage notes as well. In the sample print entry, the dictionary offers advice on several uses of *regard* not specifically covered by the meanings. Such advice is based on the opinions of many experts and on actual usage in current magazines, newspapers, and books.

W6-b   The thesaurus

When you are looking for just the right word, you may want to consult a book of synonyms and antonyms such as *Roget's International Thesaurus* (or its online equivalent). Look up (or click on) the adjective *still,* for example, and you will find synonyms such as *tranquil, quiet, quiescent, reposeful, calm, pacific, halcyon, placid,* and *unruffled.* Unless your vocabulary is better than average, the list will contain words you've never heard of or with which you are only vaguely familiar. Whenever you are tempted to use one of these words, look it up in the dictionary first to avoid misusing it.

On discovering the thesaurus, many writers use it for the wrong reasons, so a word of caution is in order. Do not turn to a thesaurus in search of exotic, fancy words—such as *halcyon*— with which to embellish your essays. Look instead for words that express your meaning exactly. Most of the time these words will be familiar to both you and your readers. The first synonym on the list—*tranquil*—was probably the word you were looking for all along.

G

Grammatical Sentences

G Grammatical Sentences

G1

Subject-verb agreement

Native speakers of standard English know by ear that *he teaches,* *she has,* and *it doesn't* (not *he teach, she have,* and *it don't*) are standard subject-verb combinations. For such speakers, problems with subject-verb agreement arise only in certain tricky situations, which are detailed in G1-b to G1-k.

If you don't trust your ear — perhaps because you speak English as a second language or because you speak or hear nonstandard English in your community — you will need to learn the standard forms explained in G1-a. Even if you do trust your ear, take a quick look at G1-a to see what "subject-verb agreement" means.

> GRAMMAR CHECKERS are fairly good at flagging subject-verb agreement problems. They occasionally flag a correct sentence, usually because they misidentify the subject, the verb, or both. Sometimes they miss an agreement problem because they don't recognize a pronoun's antecedent. In the following sentence, for example, the grammar checker did not detect that *eggs* is the antecedent of *which*: *Some animal rights groups oppose eating eggs, which comes from animals.* Because *eggs* is plural, the correct verb is *come.*

G1-a Consult this section for standard subject-verb combinations.

In the present tense, verbs agree with their subjects in number (singular or plural) and in person (first, second, or third). The present-tense ending *-s* (or *-es*) is used on a verb if its subject is third-person singular; otherwise the verb takes no ending. Consider, for example, the present-tense forms of the verb *love,* given at the beginning of the chart on page 178.

The verb *be* varies from this pattern; unlike any other verb, it has special forms in *both* the present and the past tense. These forms appear at the end of the chart on page 178.

If you aren't confident that you know the standard forms, use the charts on pages 178 and 179 as you proofread for subject-verb agreement. You may also want to look at G2-c, on *-s* endings.

Subject-verb agreement at a glance

Present-tense forms of *love* and *try* (typical verbs)

	SINGULAR		PLURAL	
FIRST PERSON	I	love	we	love
SECOND PERSON	you	love	you	love
THIRD PERSON	he/she/it	loves	they	love

	SINGULAR		PLURAL	
FIRST PERSON	I	try	we	try
SECOND PERSON	you	try	you	try
THIRD PERSON	he/she/it	tries	they	try

Present-tense forms of *have*

	SINGULAR		PLURAL	
FIRST PERSON	I	have	we	have
SECOND PERSON	you	have	you	have
THIRD PERSON	he/she/it	has	they	have

Present-tense forms of *do*

	SINGULAR		PLURAL	
FIRST PERSON	I	do/don't	we	do/don't
SECOND PERSON	you	do/don't	you	do/don't
THIRD PERSON	he/she/it	does/doesn't	they	do/don't

Present-tense and past-tense forms of *be*

	SINGULAR		PLURAL	
FIRST PERSON	I	am/was	we	are/were
SECOND PERSON	you	are/were	you	are/were
THIRD PERSON	he/she/it	is/was	they	are/were

When to use the -s (or -es) form of a present-tense verb

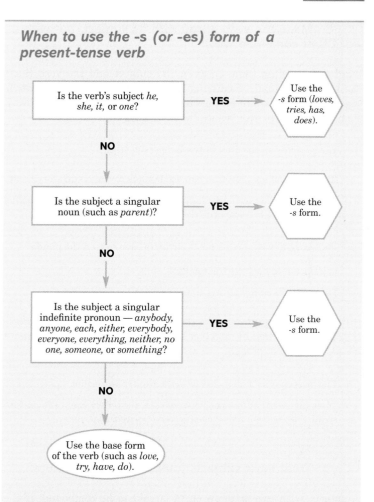

Is the verb's subject *he, she, it,* or *one*? — **YES** → Use the -s form (*loves, tries, has, does*).

NO ↓

Is the subject a singular noun (such as *parent*)? — **YES** → Use the -s form.

NO ↓

Is the subject a singular indefinite pronoun — *anybody, anyone, each, either, everybody, everyone, everything, neither, no one, someone,* or *something*? — **YES** → Use the -s form.

NO ↓

Use the base form of the verb (such as *love, try, have, do*).

EXCEPTION: Choosing the correct present-tense form of *be* (*am, is,* or *are*) is not quite so simple. See the chart on the previous page for both present- and past-tense forms of *be*.

ESL TIP: Do not use the -s form of a verb that follows a modal or another helping verb such as *can, must,* or *do.* (See E1-b.)

G1-b Make the verb agree with its subject, not with a word that comes between.

Word groups often come between the subject and the verb. Such word groups, usually modifying the subject, may contain a noun that at first appears to be the subject. By mentally stripping away such modifiers, you can isolate the noun that is in fact the subject.

The *samples* on the tray in the lab *need* testing.

▶ High levels of air pollution causes damage to the respiratory tract.

The subject is *levels,* not *pollution.* Strip away the phrase *of air pollution* to hear the correct verb: *levels cause.*

▶ The slaughter of pandas for their pelts ~~have~~ *has* caused the panda population to decline drastically.

The subject is *slaughter,* not *pandas* or *pelts.*

NOTE: Phrases beginning with the prepositions *as well as, in addition to, accompanied by, together with,* and *along with* do not make a singular subject plural.

▶ The governor as well as his press secretary ~~were~~ *was* shot.

To emphasize that two people were shot, the writer could use *and* instead: *The governor and his press secretary were shot.*

G1-c Treat most subjects joined with *and* as plural.

A subject with two or more parts is said to be compound. If the parts are connected by *and,* the subject is nearly always plural.

Leon and Jan often *jog* together.

▶ Jill's natural ability and her desire to help others ~~has~~ *have* led to a career in the ministry.

Ability and desire is a plural subject, so its verb should be *have.*

EXCEPTIONS: When the parts of the subject form a single unit or refer to the same person or thing, treat the subject as singular.

Strawberries and cream was a last-minute addition to the menu.

Sue's friend and adviser was surprised by her decision.

When a compound subject is preceded by *each* or *every,* treat the subject as singular.

Each tree, shrub, and vine needs to be sprayed.

This exception does not apply when a compound subject is followed by *each*: *Alan and Marcia each have different ideas.*

G1-d With subjects joined with *or* or *nor* (or with *either . . . or* or *neither . . . nor*), make the verb agree with the part of the subject nearer to the verb.

A driver's *license* or credit *card is* required.

A driver's *license* or two credit *cards are* required.

▶ If an infant or a child ~~are~~ *is* having difficulty breathing, seek medical

attention immediately.

▶ Neither the teacher nor the students ~~was~~ *were* in the lab.

The verb must be matched with the part of the subject closer to it: *child is* in the first sentence, *students were* in the second.

NOTE: If one part of the subject is singular and the other is plural, put the plural one last to avoid awkwardness.

G1-e Treat most indefinite pronouns as singular.

Indefinite pronouns are pronouns that do not refer to specific persons or things. The following commonly used indefinite pronouns are singular: *anybody, anyone, anything, each, either, everybody, everyone, everything, neither, nobody, no one, somebody, someone, something.*

Everyone on the team *supports* the coach.

▶ Each of the furrows ~~have~~ *has* been seeded.

▶ Everybody who signed up for the ski trip ~~were~~ *was* taking lessons.

The subjects of these sentences are *Each* and *Everybody*. These indefinite pronouns are third-person singular, so the verbs must be *has* and *was*.

A few indefinite pronouns (*all, any, none, some*) may be singular or plural depending on the noun or pronoun they refer to.

Some of our *luggage was* lost. *None* of his *advice makes* sense.

Some of the *rocks are* slippery. *None* of the *eggs were* broken.

NOTE: When the meaning of *none* is emphatically "not one," *none* may be treated as singular: *None* [meaning "Not one"] *of the eggs was broken.* However, some experts advise using *not one* instead: *Not one of the eggs was broken.*

ON THE WEB > dianahacker.com/writersref
Language Debates > *none*

G1-f Treat collective nouns as singular unless the meaning is clearly plural.

Collective nouns such as *jury, committee, audience, crowd, class, troop, family,* and *couple* name a class or a group. In American English, collective nouns are usually treated as singular: They emphasize the group as a unit. Occasionally, when there is some reason to draw attention to the individual members of the group, a collective noun may be treated as plural. (See also G3-a.)

SINGULAR   The *class respects* the teacher.

PLURAL   The *class are* debating among themselves.

To underscore the notion of individuality in the second sentence, many writers would add a clearly plural noun such as *members*: *The members of the class are debating among themselves.*

▶ The board of trustees ~~meet~~ *meets* in Denver twice a year.

  The board as a whole meets; there is no reason to draw attention to its individual members.

▶ A young couple ~~was~~ *were* arguing about politics while holding hands.

  The meaning is clearly plural. Only individuals can argue and hold hands.

NOTE: Treat *the number* as singular, *a number* as plural.

SINGULAR   *The number* of school-age children *is* declining.

PLURAL   *A number* of children *are* attending the wedding.

NOTE: In general, when units of measurement are used with a singular noun, treat them as singular; when they are used with a plural noun, treat them as plural.

SINGULAR   *Three-fourths* of the pie *has* been eaten.

PLURAL   *One-fourth* of the truck drivers *were* women.

G1-g Make the verb agree with its subject even when the subject follows the verb.

Verbs ordinarily follow subjects. When this normal order is reversed, it is easy to become confused. Sentences beginning with *there is* or *there are* (or *there was* or *there were*) are inverted; the subject follows the verb.

There *are* surprisingly few *children* in our neighborhood.

Occasionally you may decide to invert a sentence for variety or effect. When you do so, check to make sure that your subject and verb agree.

► At the back of the room ~~is~~ a small aquarium and an enormous

terrarium.

The subject, *aquarium and terrarium,* is plural, so the verb must be *are.* If the correct sentence seems awkward, begin with the subject: *A small aquarium and an enormous terrarium are at the back of the room.*

G1-h Make the verb agree with its subject, not with a subject complement.

One sentence pattern in English consists of a subject, a linking verb, and a subject complement: *Jack is a securities lawyer.* (See B2-b.) Because the subject complement names or describes the subject, it is sometimes mistaken for the subject.

▶ A tent and a sleeping bag ~~is~~ *are* the required equipment.

    Tent and bag is the subject, not *equipment.*

▶ A major force in today's economy ~~are~~ *is* women — as earners,

consumers, and investors.

    Force is the subject, not *women.* If the corrected version seems awkward, make *women* the subject: *Women are a major force in today's economy — as earners, consumers, and investors.*

G1-i   *Who, which,* and *that* take verbs that agree with their antecedents.

Like most pronouns, the relative pronouns *who, which,* and *that* have antecedents, nouns or pronouns to which they refer. Relative pronouns used as subjects of subordinate clauses take verbs that agree with their antecedents. (See B3-e.)

Take a *suit that travels* well.

Constructions such as *one of the students who* [or *one of the things that*] cause problems for writers. Do not assume that the antecedent must be *one.* Instead, consider the logic of the sentence.

▶ Our ability to use language is one of the things that sets us apart

from animals.

    The antecedent of *that* is *things,* not *one.* Several things set us apart from animals.

When the word *only* comes before *one,* you are safe in assuming that *one* is the antecedent of the relative pronoun.

▶ Veronica was the only one of the first-year Spanish students who
  was
~~were~~ fluent enough to apply for the exchange program.

    The antecedent of *who* is *one,* not *students.* Only one student was fluent enough.

ON THE WEB > dianahacker.com/writersref
Language Debates > *one of those who* (or *that*)

G1-j Words such as *athletics, economics, mathematics, physics, statistics, measles,* and *news* are usually singular, despite their plural form.

▶ Statistics ~~are~~ *is* among the most difficult courses in our program.

EXCEPTION: When they describe separate items rather than a collective body of knowledge, words such as *athletics, mathematics, physics,* and *statistics* are plural: *The statistics on steroid use are alarming.*

G1-k Titles of works, company names, words mentioned as words, and gerund phrases are singular.

▶ *Lost Cities* ~~describe~~ *describes* the discoveries of many ancient civilizations.

▶ Delmonico Brothers ~~specialize~~ *specializes* in organic produce and

additive-free meats.

▶ *Controlled substances* ~~are~~ *is* a euphemism for illegal drugs.

A gerund phrase consists of an *-ing* verb form followed by any objects, complements, or modifiers. (See B3-b.) Treat gerund phrases as singular.

▶ Encountering busy signals ~~are~~ *is* troublesome to our clients,

so we have hired two new switchboard operators.

EXERCISE G1-1 For each sentence in the following passage, underline the subject (or compound subject) and then select the verb that agrees with it. (If you have trouble identifying the subject, consult B2-a.)

Loggerhead sea turtles (migrate / migrates) thousands of miles before returning to their nesting location every two to three years. The nesting season for loggerhead turtles (span / spans) the hottest months of the summer. Although the habitat of Atlantic loggerheads (range / ranges) from Newfoundland to Argentina, nesting for these turtles (take / takes) place primarily along the southeastern coast of the United States. Female turtles that have reached sexual maturity (crawl / crawls) ashore at night to lay their eggs. The cavity that serves as a nest for the eggs (is / are) dug out with the female's strong flippers. Deposited into each nest (is / are) anywhere from fifty to two hundred spherical eggs, also known as a *clutch*. After a two-month incubation period, all eggs in the clutch (begin / begins) to hatch, and within a few days the young turtles attempt to make their way into the ocean. A major cause of the loggerhead's decreasing numbers (is / are) natural predators such as raccoons, birds, and crabs. Beach erosion and coastal development also (threaten / threatens) the turtles' survival. For example, a crowd of curious humans or lights from beachfront residences (is / are) enough to make the female abandon her nesting plans and return to the ocean. Since only one in one thousand loggerheads survives to adulthood, special care should be taken to protect this threatened species.

EXERCISE G1-2 Edit the following sentences to eliminate problems with subject-verb agreement. If a sentence is correct, write "correct" after it. Answers to lettered sentences appear in the back of the book. Example:

> *were*
> Jack's first days in the infantry ~~was~~ grueling.

a. One of the main reasons for elephant poaching are the profits received from selling the ivory tusks.

b. Not until my interview with Dr. Hwang were other possibilities opened to me.

c. A number of students in the seminar was aware of the importance of joining the discussion.

d. Batik cloth from Bali, blue and white ceramics from Delft, and a bocce ball from Turin has made Angelie's room the talk of the dorm.

e. The board of directors, ignoring the wishes of the neighborhood, has voted to allow further development.

1. Measles is a contagious childhood disease.

2. Adorning a shelf in the lab is a Vietnamese figurine, a set of Korean clay gods, and an American plastic village.

3. The presence of certain bacteria in our bodies is one of the factors that determines our overall health.

4. Sheila is the only one of the many applicants who has the ability to step into this job.

5. Neither the explorer nor his companions was ever seen again.

ON THE WEB > dianahacker.com/writersref
Grammar exercises > Grammatical sentences > E-ex G1–1 through G1–3

G2

Other problems with verbs

The verb is the heart of the sentence, so it is important to get it right. Section G1 deals with the problem of subject-verb agreement, and section W3 offers advice on active and passive verbs. This section describes other potential problems with verbs:

   a. irregular verb forms (such as *drive, drove, driven*)
   b. *lie* and *lay*
   c. *-s* (or *-es*) endings on verbs
   d. *-ed* endings on verbs
   e. omitted verbs
   f. tense
   g. subjunctive mood

> **ESL** If English is not your native language, see also E1 for more help with verbs.

G2-a Choose standard English forms of irregular verbs.

Except for the verb *be,* all main verbs in English have five forms. The following list shows the five forms and provides a sample sentence in which each might appear.

BASE FORM	Usually I (*walk, ride*).
PAST TENSE	Yesterday I (*walked, rode*).
PAST PARTICIPLE	I have (*walked, ridden*) many times before.
PRESENT PARTICIPLE	I am (*walking, riding*) right now.
-S FORM	He/she/it (*walks, rides*) regularly.

For regular verbs, the past-tense and past-participle forms end in *-ed* or *-d*: *walked, walked.* For irregular verbs, the past tense and past participle are formed differently: *rode, ridden*; *began, begun.*

The past-tense form always occurs alone, without a helping verb. It expresses action that occurred entirely in the past: *I rode to work yesterday. I walked to work last Tuesday.* The past participle is used with a helping verb. It forms the perfect tenses with *has, have,* or *had*; it forms the passive voice with *be, am, is are, was, were, being,* or *been.* (See B1-c for a complete list of helping verbs and G2-f for a survey of tenses.)

PAST TENSE   Last July, we *went* to Paris.

HELPING VERB + **PAST PARTICIPLE**   We *have gone* to Paris twice.

The list of common irregular verbs beginning on page 189 will help you distinguish between past tense and past participle. Choose the past-participle form if the verb in your sentence requires a helping verb; choose the past-tense form if the verb does not require a helping verb.

▶ Yesterday we ~~seen~~ *saw* an unidentified flying object.

▶ The reality of the situation ~~sunk~~ *sank* in.

The past-tense forms *saw* and *sank* are required.

▶ The truck was apparently ~~stole~~ *stolen* while the driver ate lunch.

▶ By Friday, the stock market had ~~fell~~ *fallen* two hundred points.

Because of the helping verbs, the past-participle forms are required: *was stolen, had fallen.*

GRAMMAR CHECKERS sometimes flag misused irregular verbs in sentences, such as *I had drove the car to school* and *Lucia seen the movie already.* But you cannot rely on grammar checkers to identify problems with irregular verbs — they miss about twice as many errors as they find.

Common irregular verbs

When in doubt about the standard English forms of irregular verbs, consult the following list or look up the base form of the verb in the dictionary, which also lists any irregular forms. (If no additional forms are listed in the dictionary, the verb is regular, not irregular.)

BASE FORM	PAST TENSE	PAST PARTICIPLE
arise	arose	arisen
awake	awoke, awaked	awaked, awoke
be	was, were	been
beat	beat	beaten, beat
become	became	become
begin	began	begun
bend	bent	bent
bite	bit	bitten, bit
blow	blew	blown
break	broke	broken
bring	brought	brought
build	built	built
burst	burst	burst
buy	bought	bought
catch	caught	caught
choose	chose	chosen
cling	clung	clung
come	came	come
cost	cost	cost
deal	dealt	dealt
dig	dug	dug
dive	dived, dove	dived
do	did	done
drag	dragged	dragged
draw	drew	drawn
dream	dreamed, dreamt	dreamed, dreamt
drink	drank	drunk
drive	drove	driven
eat	ate	eaten
fall	fell	fallen
fight	fought	fought
find	found	found
fly	flew	flown
forget	forgot	forgotten, forgot
freeze	froze	frozen
get	got	gotten, got
give	gave	given
go	went	gone
grow	grew	grown

BASE FORM	PAST TENSE	PAST PARTICIPLE
hang (suspend)	hung	hung
hang (execute)	hanged	hanged
have	had	had
hear	heard	heard
hide	hid	hidden
hurt	hurt	hurt
keep	kept	kept
know	knew	known
lay (put)	laid	laid
lead	led	led
lend	lent	lent
let (allow)	let	let
lie (recline)	lay	lain
lose	lost	lost
make	made	made
prove	proved	proved, proven
read	read	read
ride	rode	ridden
ring	rang	rung
rise (get up)	rose	risen
run	ran	run
say	said	said
see	saw	seen
send	sent	sent
set (place)	set	set
shake	shook	shaken
shoot	shot	shot
shrink	shrank	shrunk, shrunken
sing	sang	sung
sink	sank	sunk
sit (be seated)	sat	sat
slay	slew	slain
sleep	slept	slept
speak	spoke	spoken
spin	spun	spun
spring	sprang	sprung
stand	stood	stood
steal	stole	stolen
sting	stung	stung

BASE FORM	PAST TENSE	PAST PARTICIPLE
strike	struck	struck, stricken
swear	swore	sworn
swim	swam	swum
swing	swung	swung
take	took	taken
teach	taught	taught
throw	threw	thrown
wake	woke, waked	waked, woken
wear	wore	worn
wring	wrung	wrung
write	wrote	written

ON THE WEB > dianahacker.com/writersref
Grammar exercises > Grammatical sentences > E-ex G2–1

G2-b Distinguish among the forms of *lie* and *lay*.

Writers and speakers frequently confuse the various forms of *lie* (meaning "to recline or rest on a surface") and *lay* (meaning "to put or place something"). *Lie* is an intransitive verb; it does not take a direct object: *The tax forms lie on the table.* The verb *lay* is transitive; it takes a direct object: *Please lay the tax forms on the table.* (See B2-b.)

In addition to confusing the meaning of *lie* and *lay*, writers and speakers are often unfamiliar with the standard English forms of these verbs.

BASE FORM	PAST TENSE	PAST PARTICIPLE	PRESENT PARTICIPLE
lie	lay	lain	lying
lay	laid	laid	laying

                        lay
▶ Sue was so exhausted that she ~~laid~~ down for a nap.

The past-tense form of *lie* ("to recline") is *lay.*

                 lain
▶ The patient had ~~laid~~ in an uncomfortable position all night.

The past-participle form of *lie* ("to recline") is *lain.* If the correct English seems too stilted, recast the sentence: *The patient had been lying in an uncomfortable position all night.*

▶ The prosecutor ~~lay~~ *laid* the pistol on a table close to the jurors.

The past-tense form of *lay* ("to place") is *laid*.

▶ Letters dating from the Civil War were ~~laying~~ *lying* in the corner of the chest.

The present participle of *lie* ("to rest on a surface") is *lying*.

ON THE WEB > dianahacker.com/writersref
Language Debates > *lie* versus *lay*

EXERCISE G2-1 Edit the following sentences to eliminate problems with irregular verbs. If a sentence is correct, write "correct" after it. Answers to lettered sentences appear in the back of the book. Example:

Was it you I ~~seen~~ *saw* last night at the concert?

a. When I get the urge to exercise, I lay down until it passes.
b. Grandmother had drove our new SUV to the sunrise church service on Savage Mountain, so we were left with the station wagon.
c. A pile of dirty rags was laying at the bottom of the stairs.
d. How did the computer know that the gamer had went from the room with the blue ogre to the hall where the gold was heaped?
e. Abraham Lincoln took good care of his legal clients; the contracts he drew for the Illinois Central Railroad could never be broke.

1. The burglar must have gone immediately upstairs, grabbed what looked good, and took off.
2. Have you ever dreamed that you were falling from a cliff or flying through the air?
3. Tomás reached for the pen, signed the title page of his novel, and then laid the book on the table for the first customer in line.
4. In her junior year, Cindy run the 440-yard dash in 51.1 seconds.
5. Larry claimed that he had drank a bad soda, but Esther suspected the truth.

G2-c Use -s (or -es) endings on present-tense verbs that have third-person singular subjects.

When the subject of a sentence is third-person singular, its verb takes an *-s* or *-es* ending in the present tense. (See also G1-a and the charts on pp. 178–79.)

	SINGULAR		PLURAL	
FIRST PERSON	I	know	we	know
SECOND PERSON	you	know	you	know
THIRD PERSON	he/she/it	knows	they	know
	child	knows	parents	know
	everyone	knows		

All singular nouns (such as *child*) and the pronouns *he, she,* and *it* are third-person singular; indefinite pronouns (such as *everyone*) are also third-person singular.

In nonstandard speech, the *-s* ending required by standard English is sometimes omitted.

▶ Sulfur dioxide ~~turn~~ *turns* leaves yellow, ~~dissolve~~ *dissolves* marble, and ~~eat~~ *eats* away iron and steel.

> The subject, *sulfur dioxide*, is third-person singular, so the verbs must end in *-s*.

TIP: Do not add the *-s* ending to the verb if the subject is not third-person singular.

▶ I prepares program specifications and logic diagrams.

> The writer mistakenly concluded that the *-s* ending belongs on present-tense verbs used with *all* singular subjects, not just *third-person* singular subjects. The pronoun *I* is first-person singular, so its verb does not require the *-s*.

▶ The dirt floors requires continual sweeping.

> The writer mistakenly thought that the *-s* ending on the verb indicated plurality. The *-s* goes on present-tense verbs used with third-person *singular* subjects.

In nonstandard speech, the *-s* verb form *has, does,* or *doesn't* is sometimes replaced with *have, do,* or *don't*. In standard English, use *has, does,* or *doesn't* with a third-person singular subject. (See also G1-a.)

▶ This respected musician always ~~have~~ *has* a message in his work.

▶ ~~Do~~ *Does* she know the correct procedure for the experiment?

▶ My uncle ~~don't~~ *doesn't* want to change jobs right now.

> ☑ GRAMMAR CHECKERS are fairly good at catching missing *-s* endings on
> verbs and some misused *-s* forms of the verb, consistently flagging
> errors such as *The training session take place later today* and *The*
> *careful camper learn to feel the signs of a coming storm.* (See the
> grammar checker advice on p. 177 for more information about
> subject-verb agreement.)

G2-d Do not omit *-ed* endings on verbs.

Speakers who do not fully pronounce *-ed* endings sometimes omit
them unintentionally in writing. Failure to pronounce *-ed* endings
is common in many dialects and in informal speech. In the following frequently used words and phrases, for example, the *-ed* ending
is not always fully pronounced.

advised	developed	prejudiced	supposed to
asked	fixed	pronounced	used to
concerned	frightened	stereotyped	

When a verb is regular, both the past tense and the past participle are formed by adding *-ed* to the base form of the verb.

Past tense

Use an *-ed* or *-d* ending to express the past tense of regular verbs.
The past tense is used when the action occurred entirely in the
past.

▶ Over the weekend, Ed ~~fix~~ his brother's skateboard and tuned up
   ^ *fixed*

his mother's 1977 Cougar.

▶ Last summer my counselor ~~advise~~ me to ask my family for help.
   ^ *advised*

Past participles

Past participles are used in three ways: (1) following *have, has,* or
had to form one of the perfect tenses; (2) following *be, am, is, are,*
was, were, being, or *been* to form the passive voice; and (3) as adjectives modifying nouns or pronouns. The perfect tenses are listed on
page 198, and the passive voice is discussed in W3-a. For a discussion of participles functioning as adjectives, see B3-b.

▶ Robin has *asked* ~~ask~~ me to go to California with her.

Has asked is present perfect tense (*have* or *has* followed by a past participle).

▶ Though it is not a new phenomenon, domestic violence is *publicized* ~~publicize~~ more frequently than before.

Is publicized is in the passive voice (a form of *be* followed by a past participle).

▶ All aerobics classes end in a cool-down period to stretch *tightened* ~~tighten~~ muscles.

Tightened is a participle used as an adjective to modify the noun *muscles*.

✓ GRAMMAR CHECKERS flag missing *-ed* endings on verbs more often than not. Unfortunately, they often suggest an *-ing* ending (*passing*) rather than the missing *-ed* ending (*passed*), as in the following sentence: *The law was pass last week.*

G2-e   Do not omit needed verbs.

Although standard English allows some linking verbs and helping verbs to be contracted, at least in informal contexts, it does not allow them to be omitted.

Linking verbs, used to link subjects to subject complements, are frequently a form of *be*: *be, am, is, are, was, were, being, been.* (See B2-b.) Some of these forms may be contracted (*I'm, she's, we're*), but they should not be omitted altogether.

▶ Alvin *is* a man who can defend himself.

Helping verbs, used with main verbs, include forms of *be, do,* and *have* and the modal verbs *can, will, shall, could, would, should, may, might,* and *must.* (See B1-c.) Some helping verbs may be contracted (*he's leaving, we'll celebrate, they've been told*), but they should not be omitted altogether.

▶ Do you know someone who *would* be good for the job?

> **ESL** Several languages, including Russian and Turkish, do not require a linking verb between a subject and its complement. English, however, requires a verb in every sentence. See E2-a.
>
>   *am*
> ▶ **Every night, I read a short book to my daughter. When I too**
>   ^
> **busy, my husband reads to her.**

> ✔ GRAMMAR CHECKERS flag omitted verbs about half the time — but they often miss needed helping verbs. For example, a grammar checker caught the missing verb in this sentence: *We seen the* Shrek *sequel three times already.* However, this sentence went unflagged: *The plot built around a family reunion.*

EXERCISE G2–2 Edit the following sentences to eliminate problems with *-s* and *-ed* verb forms and with omitted verbs. If a sentence is correct, write "correct" after it. Answers to lettered sentences appear in the back of the book. Example:

                             covers
The Pell Grant sometimes ~~cover~~ the student's full tuition.
                             ^

a. The glass sculptures of the Swan Boats was prominent in the brightly lit lobby.
b. Visitors to the glass museum were not suppose to touch the exhibits.
c. Our church has all the latest technology, even a close-circuit television.
d. Christos didn't know about Marlo's promotion because he never listens. He always talking.
e. Most psychologists agree that no one performs well under stress.

1. Have there ever been a time in your life when you were too depressed to get out of bed?
2. My days in this department have taught me to do what I'm told without asking questions.
3. We have change our plan and are waiting out the storm before leaving.
4. Winter training for search-and-rescue divers consist of building up a tolerance to icy water temperatures.
5. How would you feel if a love one had been a victim of a crime like this?

ON THE WEB > dianahacker.com/writersref
Grammar exercises > Grammatical sentences > E-ex G2–2

G2-f   Choose the appropriate verb tense.

Tenses indicate the time of an action in relation to the time of the speaking or writing about that action.

The most common problem with tenses — shifting from one tense to another — is discussed in S4-b. Other problems with tenses are detailed in this section, after the following survey of tenses.

ESL   For additional help with verb tense, see E1-a.

Survey of tenses

Tenses are classified as present, past, and future, with simple, perfect, and progressive forms for each.

The simple tenses indicate relatively simple time relations. The simple present tense is used primarily for actions occurring at the time of the speaking or for actions occurring regularly. The simple past tense is used for actions completed in the past. The simple future tense is used for actions that will occur in the future. In the following table, the simple tenses are given for the regular verb *walk,* the irregular verb *ride,* and the highly irregular verb *be.*

SIMPLE PRESENT

SINGULAR		PLURAL	
I	walk, ride, am	we	walk, ride, are
you	walk, ride, are	you	walk, ride, are
he/she/it	walks, rides, is	they	walk, ride, are

SIMPLE PAST

SINGULAR		PLURAL	
I	walked, rode, was	we	walked, rode, were
you	walked, rode, were	you	walked, rode, were
he/she/it	walked, rode, was	they	walked, rode, were

SIMPLE FUTURE

I, you, he/she/it, we, they	will walk, ride, be

More complex time relations are indicated by the perfect tenses. A verb in one of the perfect tenses (a form of *have* plus the past participle) expresses an action that was or will be completed at the time of another action.

PRESENT PERFECT

I, you, we, they	have walked, ridden, been
he/she/it	has walked, ridden, been

PAST PERFECT

I, you, he/she/it, we, they	had walked, ridden, been

FUTURE PERFECT

I, you, he/she/it, we, they	will have walked, ridden, been

The simple and perfect tenses just discussed have progressive forms that describe actions in progress. A progressive verb consists of a form of *be* followed by a present participle. The progressive forms are not normally used with mental activity verbs such as *believe, know,* and *think.*

PRESENT PROGRESSIVE

I	am walking, riding, being
he/she/it	is walking, riding, being
you, we, they	are walking, riding, being

PAST PROGRESSIVE

I, he/she/it	was walking, riding, being
you, we, they	were walking, riding, being

FUTURE PROGRESSIVE

I, you, he/she/it, we, they	will be walking, riding, being

PRESENT PERFECT PROGRESSIVE

I, you, we, they	have been walking, riding, being
he/she/it	has been walking, riding, being

PAST PERFECT PROGRESSIVE

I, you, he/she/it, we, they	had been walking, riding, being

FUTURE PERFECT PROGRESSIVE

I, you, he/she/it, we, they	will have been walking, riding, being

Special uses of the present tense

Use the present tense when expressing general truths, when writing about literature, and when quoting, summarizing, or paraphrasing an author's views.

General truths or scientific principles should appear in the present tense, unless such principles have been disproved.

>   *revolves*
> ▶ Galileo taught that the earth ~~revolved~~ around the sun.
>   ^

Since Galileo's teaching has not been discredited, the verb should be in the present tense. The following sentence, however, is acceptable: *Ptolemy taught that the sun revolved around the earth.*

When writing about a work of literature, you may be tempted to use the past tense. The convention, however, is to describe fictional events in the present tense.

>   *reaches*
> ▶ In Masuji Ibuse's *Black Rain*, a child ~~reached~~ for a pomegranate
>   ^   *is*
>   in his mother's garden, and a moment later he ~~was~~ dead, killed by
>   ^
>   the blast of the atomic bomb.

When you are quoting, summarizing, or paraphrasing the author of a nonliterary work, use present-tense verbs such as *writes, reports, asserts,* and so on. This convention is usually followed even when the author is dead (unless a date or the context specifies the time of writing).

>   *writes*
> ▶ Baron Bowan of Colwood ~~wrote~~ that "a metaphysician is one who
>   ^
>   goes into a dark cellar at midnight without a light, looking for a
>   black cat that is not there."

EXCEPTION: When you are documenting a paper with the APA (American Psychological Association) style of in-text citations, use past-tense verbs such as *reported* or *demonstrated* or present perfect verbs such as *has reported* or *has demonstrated.*

E. Wilson (1994) reported that positive reinforcement alone was a less effective teaching technique than a mixture of positive reinforcement and constructive criticism.

The past perfect tense

The past perfect tense consists of a past participle preceded by *had* (*had worked, had gone*). This tense is used for an action already completed by the time of another past action or for an action already completed at some specific past time.

Everyone *had spoken* by the time I arrived.

Everyone *had spoken* by 10:00 a.m.

Writers sometimes use the simple past tense when they should use the past perfect.

▶ We built our cabin high on a pine knoll, forty feet above an
had been
abandoned quarry that ~~was~~ flooded in 1920 to create a lake.
⌃

The building of the cabin and the flooding of the quarry both occurred in the past, but the flooding was completed before the time of building.

had
▶ By the time dinner was served, the guest of honor left.
⌃

The past perfect tense is needed because the action of leaving was completed at a specific past time (by the time dinner was served).

Some writers tend to overuse the past perfect tense. Do not use the past perfect if two past actions occurred at the same time.

▶ When we arrived in Paris, Pauline ~~had~~ met us at the train station.

Sequence of tenses with infinitives and participles

An infinitive is the base form of a verb preceded by *to*. (See B3-b.) Use the present infinitive to show action at the same time as or later than the action of the verb in the sentence.

raise
▶ The club had hoped to ~~have raised~~ a thousand dollars by April 1.
⌃

The action expressed in the infinitive (*to raise*) occurred later than the action of the sentence's verb (*had hoped*).

Use the perfect form of an infinitive (*to have* followed by the past participle) for an action occurring earlier than that of the verb in the sentence.

have joined
▶ Dan would like to ~~join~~ the navy, but he did not pass the physical.
⌃

The liking occurs in the present; the joining would have occurred in the past.

Like the tense of an infinitive, the tense of a participle is governed by the tense of the sentence's verb. Use the present participle (ending in *-ing*) for an action occurring at the same time as that of the sentence's verb.

Hiking the Appalachian Trail in early spring, we spotted many wildflowers.

Use the past participle (such as *given* or *helped*) or the present perfect participle (*having* plus the past participle) for an action occurring before that of the verb.

> *Discovered* off the coast of Florida, the *Atocha* yielded many treasures.

> *Having worked* her way through college, Lee graduated debt-free.

G2-g Use the subjunctive mood in the few contexts that require it.

There are three moods in English: the *indicative,* used for facts, opinions, and questions; the *imperative,* used for orders or advice; and the *subjunctive,* used in certain contexts to express wishes, requests, or conditions contrary to fact. Of these moods, the subjunctive is most likely to cause problems for writers.

Forms of the subjunctive

In the subjunctive mood, present-tense verbs do not change form to indicate the number and person of the subject (see G1-a). Instead, the subjunctive uses the base form of the verb (*be, drive, employ*) with all subjects.

> It is important that you *be* [not *are*] prepared for the interview.

> We asked that she *drive* [not *drives*] more slowly.

Also, in the subjunctive mood, there is only one past-tense form of *be: were* (never *was*).

> If I *were* [not *was*] you, I'd proceed more cautiously.

Uses of the subjunctive

The subjunctive mood appears in only a few contexts: in contrary-to-fact clauses beginning with *if* or expressing a wish; in *that* clauses following verbs such as *ask, insist, recommend, request,* and *suggest*; and in certain set expressions.

IN CONTRARY-TO-FACT CLAUSES BEGINNING WITH *IF* When a subordinate clause beginning with *if* expresses a condition contrary to fact, use the subjunctive mood.

> *were*
> If I ~~was~~ a member of Congress, I would vote for that bill.
>   ^

> *were*
> We could be less cautious if Jake ~~was~~ more trustworthy.
>   ^

The verbs in these sentences express conditions that do not exist: The writer is not a member of Congress, and Jake is not trustworthy.

Do not use the subjunctive mood in *if* clauses expressing conditions that exist or may exist.

If Dana *wins* the contest, she will leave for Spain in June.

IN CONTRARY-TO-FACT CLAUSES EXPRESSING A WISH   In formal English, the subjunctive is used in clauses expressing a wish or desire; in informal speech, however, the indicative is more commonly used.

FORMAL   I wish that Dr. Vaughn *were* my professor.

INFORMAL   I wish that Dr. Vaughn *was* my professor.

IN *THAT* CLAUSES FOLLOWING VERBS SUCH AS *ASK, INSIST, RECOMMEND, REQUEST,* AND *SUGGEST*   Because requests have not yet become reality, they are expressed in the subjunctive mood.

> *be*
> Professor Moore insists that her students ~~are~~ on time.
>   ^

> *file*
> We recommend that Lambert ~~files~~ form 1050 soon.
>   ^

IN CERTAIN SET EXPRESSIONS   The subjunctive mood, once more widely used, remains in certain set expressions: *be that as it may, as it were, far be it from me,* and so on.

EXERCISE G2–3 Edit the following sentences to eliminate errors in verb tense or mood. If a sentence is correct, write "correct" after it. Answers to lettered sentences appear in the back of the book. Example:

> *had been*
> After the path ~~was~~ plowed, we were able to walk through the park.
>   ^

a. The palace of Knossos in Crete is believed to have been destroyed by fire around 1375 BCE.

b. Watson and Crick discovered the mechanism that controlled inheritance in all life: the workings of the DNA molecule.

c. When Hitler decided to kill the Jews in 1941, did he know that Himmler and his SS had mass murder in mind since 1938?

d. Tonight's concert begins at 9:30. If it were earlier, I'd consider going.

e. As soon as my aunt applied for the position of pastor, the post was filled by an inexperienced seminary graduate who had been so hastily snatched that his mortarboard was still in midair.

1. Don Quixote, in Cervantes's novel, was an idealist ill suited for life in the real world.
2. Visiting the technology museum inspired the high school seniors and had reminded them that science could be fun.
3. I would like to have been on the *Mayflower* but not to have lived through the first winter.
4. When the director yelled "Action!" I forgot my lines, even though I practiced my part every waking hour for three days.
5. If midday naps were a regular practice in American workplaces, employees would be far more productive.

ON THE WEB > dianahacker.com/writersref
Grammar exercises > Grammatical sentences > E-ex G2–3

☑ GRAMMAR CHECKERS only sometimes flag problems with the subjunctive mood. What they catch is very spotty, so you must be alert to the correct uses of the subjunctive in your own writing.

G3

Problems with pronouns

Pronouns are words that substitute for nouns (see B1-b). Four frequently encountered problems with pronouns are discussed in this section:

a. pronoun-antecedent agreement (singular vs. plural)
b. pronoun reference (clarity)
c. pronoun case (personal pronouns such as *I* vs. *me, she* vs. *her*)
d. pronoun case (*who* vs. *whom*)

For other problems with pronouns, consult the glossary of usage (W1).

G3-a Make pronouns and antecedents agree.

Many pronouns have antecedents, nouns or pronouns to which they refer. A pronoun and its antecedent agree when they are both singular or both plural.

SINGULAR   *Dr. Ava Berto* finished *her* rounds.

PLURAL   The *hospital interns* finished *their* rounds.

ESL The pronouns *he, his, she, her, it,* and *its* must agree in gender (masculine, feminine, or neuter) with their antecedents (the words they refer to), not with the words that follow them.

> ▶ Elvis Presley had an unusually close bond with ~~her~~ mother.
> his ^

Because the pronoun refers to the masculine noun *Elvis Presley,* the pronoun must also be masculine.

✔ GRAMMAR CHECKERS do not flag problems with pronoun-antecedent agreement. It takes a human eye to see that a plural pronoun, such as *their,* does not agree with a singular antecedent, such as *logger,* in a sentence like this: *The logger in the Northwest relies on the old forest growth for their living.*

When grammar checkers do flag agreement problems, they often suggest (correctly) substituting the singular phrase *his or her* for the plural pronoun *their.* For alternatives to the wordy *his or her* construction, see "Revising sexist language" on page 161.

Indefinite pronouns

Indefinite pronouns refer to nonspecific persons or things. Even though some of the following indefinite pronouns may seem to have plural meanings, treat them as singular in formal English: *anybody, anyone, anything, each, either, everybody, everyone, everything, neither, nobody, no one, nothing, somebody, someone, something.*

In this class *everyone* performs at *his or her* [not *their*] fitness level.

When a plural pronoun refers mistakenly to a singular indefinite pronoun, you can usually choose one of three options for revision.

1. Replace the plural pronoun with *he or she* (or *his or her*).
2. Make the antecedent plural.
3. Rewrite the sentence so that no problem of agreement exists.

▶ When someone has been drinking, ~~they are~~ *he or she is* likely to speed.

▶ When ~~someone has~~ *drivers have* been drinking, they are likely to speed.

▶ ~~When someone~~ *A driver who* has been drinking/ ~~they are~~ *is* likely to speed.

Because the *he or she* construction is wordy, often the second or third revision strategy is more effective.

NOTE: The traditional use of *he* (or *his*) to refer to persons of either sex is now widely considered sexist (see W4-e).

Generic nouns

A generic noun represents a typical member of a group, such as a typical student, or any member of a group, such as any lawyer. Although generic nouns may seem to have plural meanings, they are singular.

Every *runner* must train vigorously if *he or she* wants [not *they want*] to excel.

When a plural pronoun refers mistakenly to a generic noun, you will usually have the same three revision options as mentioned at the top of this page for indefinite pronouns.

▶ A medical student must study hard if ~~they want~~ *he or she wants* to succeed.

▶ ~~A medical student~~ *Medical students* must study hard if they want to succeed.

▶ A medical student must study hard ~~if they want~~ to succeed.

Collective nouns

Collective nouns such as *jury, committee, audience, crowd, class, troop, family, team,* and *couple* name a class or group. Ordinarily the group functions as a unit, so the noun should be treated as singular; if the members of the group function as individuals, however, the noun should be treated as plural.

AS A UNIT The planning *committee* granted *its* permission to build.

AS INDIVIDUALS The *committee* put *their* signatures on the document.

When treating a collective noun as plural, many writers prefer to add a clearly plural antecedent such as *members* to the sentence: *The members of the committee put their signatures on the document.*

To some extent, you can choose whether to treat a collective noun as singular or plural depending on your meaning. Make sure, however, that you are consistent.

▶ The jury has reached ~~their~~ *its* decision.

> There is no reason to draw attention to the individual members of the jury, so *jury* should be treated as singular. Notice also that the writer treated the noun as singular when choosing the verb *has,* so for consistency the pronoun must be *its.*

Compound antecedents

Treat compound antecedents joined by *and* as plural.

> *Joanne and John* moved to Luray, where *they* built a log cabin.

With compound antecedents joined by *or* or *nor,* make the pronoun agree with the nearer antecedent.

> Either *Bruce* or *Tom* should receive first prize for *his* poem.

> Neither the *mouse* nor the *rats* could find *their* way through the maze.

NOTE: If one of the antecedents is singular and the other plural, as in the second example, put the plural one last to avoid awkwardness.

EXCEPTION: If one antecedent is male and the other female, do not follow the traditional rule. The sentence *Either Bruce or Anita should receive first prize for her story* makes no sense. The best solution is to recast the sentence: *The prize for best story should go to Bruce or Anita.*

ON THE WEB > dianahacker.com/writersref
Language Debates > Pronoun-antecedent agreement

EXERCISE G3–1 Edit the following sentences to eliminate problems with pronoun-antecedent agreement. Most of the sentences can be revised in more than one way, so experiment before choosing a solution. If a sentence is correct, write "correct" after it. Revisions of lettered sentences appear in the back of the book. Example:

> *Recruiters*
> ~~The recruiter~~ may tell the truth, but there is much that they
> ^
> choose not to tell.

a. Every presidential candidate must appeal to a wide variety of ethnic and social groups if they want to win the election.
b. David lent his motorcycle to someone who allowed their friend to use it.
c. The aerobics teacher motioned for everyone to move their arms in wide, slow circles.
d. The parade committee was unanimous in its decision to allow all groups and organizations to join the festivities.
e. The applicant should be bilingual if they want to qualify for this position.

1. If a driver refuses to take a blood or breath test, he or she will have their licenses suspended for six months.
2. Why should anyone learn a second language? One reason is to sharpen their minds.
3. The Department of Education issued new guidelines for school security. They were trying to anticipate problems and avert disaster.
4. Seven qualified Hispanic agents applied, each hoping for a career move that would let them use their language and cultural training on more than just translations.
5. If anyone notices any suspicious activity, they should report it to the police.

EXERCISE G3–2 Edit the following paragraph to eliminate problems with pronoun-antecedent agreement or sexist language.

A common practice in businesses is to put each employee in their own cubicle. A typical cubicle resembles an office, but their walls don't reach the ceiling. Many office managers feel that a cubicle floor plan has its advantages. Cubicles make a large area feel spacious. In addition, they can be moved around so that each new employee can be accommodated in his own work area. Of course, the cubicle model also has problems. The typical employee is not as happy with a cubicle as they would be with a traditional office. Also, productivity can suffer. Neither a manager nor a frontline worker can ordinarily do their best work in a cubicle because of noise and lack of privacy. Each worker can hear his neighbors tapping on computer keyboards, making telephone calls, and muttering under their breath.

ON THE WEB > dianahacker.com/writersref
Grammar exercises > Grammatical sentences > E-ex G3–1 through G3–3

G3-b Make pronoun references clear.

Pronouns substitute for nouns; they are a kind of shorthand. In a sentence like *After Andrew intercepted the ball, he kicked it as hard as he could,* the pronouns *he* and *it* substitute for the nouns *Andrew* and *ball.* The word a pronoun refers to is called its *antecedent.*

GRAMMAR CHECKERS do not flag problems with faulty pronoun reference. Although a computer program can identify pronouns, it has no way of knowing which words, if any, they refer to. For example, grammar checkers miss the fact that the pronoun *it* has an ambiguous reference in the following sentence: *The thief stole the woman's purse and her car and then destroyed it.* Did the thief destroy the purse or the car? It takes human judgment to realize that readers might be confused.

Ambiguous reference

Ambiguous pronoun reference occurs when a pronoun could refer to two possible antecedents.

▶ *The pitcher broke when Gloria set it*
  ~~When Gloria set the pitcher~~ on the glass-topped table~~, it broke.~~

▶ *"You have*
  Tom told James*,* ~~that he had~~ won the lottery*."*

What broke — the table or the pitcher? Who won the lottery — Tom or James? The revisions eliminate the ambiguity.

Implied reference

A pronoun must refer to a specific antecedent, not to a word that is implied but not present in the sentence.

▶ After braiding Ann's hair, Sue decorated ~~them~~ *the braids* with brightly

colored ribbons.

The pronoun *them* referred to Ann's braids (implied by the term *braiding*), but the word *braids* did not appear in the sentence.

Modifiers, such as possessives, cannot serve as antecedents. A modifier may strongly imply the noun that the pronoun might logically refer to, but it is not itself that noun.

▶ In ~~Mary Gordon's~~ *Mary Gordon* *The Shadow Man,* ~~she~~ writes about her

father's mysterious and startling past.

The pronoun *she* cannot refer logically to the possessive modifier *Mary Gordon's.* The revision substitutes the noun *Mary Gordon* for the pronoun *she,* thereby eliminating the problem.

ON THE WEB > dianahacker.com/writersref
Language Debates > Possessives as antecedents

Broad reference of this, that, which, *and* it

For clarity, the pronouns *this, that, which,* and *it* should ordinarily refer to specific antecedents rather than to whole ideas or sentences. When a pronoun's reference is needlessly broad, either replace the pronoun with a noun or supply an antecedent to which the pronoun clearly refers.

▶ More and more often, we are finding ourselves victims of serious crimes. We learn to accept ~~this~~ *our fate* with minor complaints.

For clarity, the writer substituted a noun (*fate*) for the pronoun *this,* which referred broadly to the idea expressed in the preceding sentence.

▶ Romeo and Juliet were both too young to have acquired much wisdom, *a fact* which accounts for their rash actions.

Indefinite reference of they, it, *or* you

Do not use *they* to refer indefinitely to persons who have not been specifically mentioned. The pronoun *they* should refer to a specific antecedent.

▶ In 2001, ~~they~~ shut down all government agencies for more than a
    Congress

month until the budget crisis was resolved.

The word *it* should not be used indefinitely in constructions such as "In the article it says that. . . ."

▶ ~~In the~~ encyclopedia ~~it~~ states that male moths can smell female
    The

moths from several miles away.

The pronoun *you* is appropriate when the writer is addressing the reader directly: *Once you have kneaded the dough, let it rise in a warm place.* Except in very informal contexts, however, the indefinite *you* (meaning "anyone in general") is inappropriate.

▶ Ms. Pickersgill's *Guide to Etiquette* stipulates that ~~you~~ should not
    a guest

arrive at a party too early or leave too late.

The writer could have replaced *you* with *one,* but in American English the pronoun *one* can seem stilted.

ON THE WEB > dianahacker.com/writersref
Language Debates > *you*

EXERCISE G3–3 Edit the following sentences to correct errors in pronoun reference. In some cases you will need to decide on an antecedent that the pronoun might logically refer to. Revisions of lettered sentences appear in the back of the book. Example:

> Following the breakup of AT&T, many other companies began
> to offer long-distance phone service. ~~This~~ led to lower
>   *The competition*
> long-distance rates.

a. They say that an engineering student should have hands-on experience with dismantling and reassembling machines.

b. She had decorated her living room with posters from chamber music festivals. This led her date to believe that she was interested in classical music. Actually she preferred rock.

c. In Ethiopia, you don't need much property to be considered well-off.

d. Marianne told Jenny that she was worried about her mother's illness.

e. Though Lewis cried for several minutes after scraping his knee, eventually it subsided.

1. Our German conversation group is made up of six people, three of which I had never met before.

2. Many people believe that the polygraph test is highly reliable if you employ a licensed examiner.

3. Parent involvement is high at Mission San Jose High School. They participate in many committees and activities that affect all aspects of school life.

4. Because of Paul Robeson's outspoken attitude toward fascism, he was labeled a Communist.

5. In the report it points out that lifting the ban on Compound 1080 would prove detrimental, possibly even fatal, to the bald eagle.

EXERCISE G3–4 Edit the following passage to correct errors in pronoun reference. In some cases you will need to decide on an antecedent that the pronoun might logically refer to.

Since the Internet's inception in the 1980s, it has grown to be one of the largest forums for communicating in the world. The Internet was created by a team of academics who were building on a platform that government scientists had started developing in the 1950s. They initially viewed it as a noncommercial enterprise that would serve only the needs of the academic and technical communities. But with the introduction of user-friendly browser technology in the 1990s, it expanded tremendously. By the late 1990s, many businesses were connecting to the Internet with high-speed broadband and fiber-optic connections, which is also true of many home users today. Accessing information, shopping, and communicating are easier than ever before. This, however, can lead to some possible downfalls. You can be bombarded with spam and pop-up ads or attacked by harmful viruses and worms. They say that the best way to protect home computers from harm is to keep antivirus protection programs up-to-date and to shut them down when not in use.

ON THE WEB > dianahacker.com/writersref
Grammar exercises > Grammatical sentences > E-ex G3–4 through G3–6

G3-c Distinguish between pronouns such as *I* and *me*.

The personal pronouns in the following chart change what is known as case form according to their grammatical function in a sentence. Pronouns functioning as subjects (or subject complements) appear in the *subjective* case; those functioning as objects appear in the *objective* case; and those functioning as possessives appear in the *possessive* case.

	SUBJECTIVE CASE	OBJECTIVE CASE	POSSESSIVE CASE
SINGULAR	I	me	my
	you	you	your
	he/she/it	him/her/it	his/her/its
PLURAL	we	us	our
	you	you	your
	they	them	their

This section explains the difference between the subjective and objective cases; then it alerts you to certain structures that may tempt you to choose the wrong pronoun. Finally, it describes a special use of possessive-case pronouns.

> GRAMMAR CHECKERS sometimes flag incorrect pronouns and suggest using the correct form: *I* or *me, he* or *him, she* or *her, we* or *us, they* or *them*. A grammar checker flagged *we* in the following sentence and correctly advised using *us* instead: *I say it is about time for we parents to revolt.* Grammar checkers miss more incorrect pronouns than they catch, however, and their suggestions for revision are sometimes off the mark. A grammar checker caught the error in the following sentence: *I am a little jealous that my dog likes my neighbor more than I.* But instead of suggesting changing the final *I* to *me* (*. . . more than me*), it suggested adding *do* (*. . . more than I do*), which does not fit the meaning of the sentence.

Subjective case

When a pronoun functions as a subject or a subject complement, it must be in the subjective case (*I, we, you, he, she, it, they*).

SUBJECT	Sylvia and *he* shared the award.
SUBJECT COMPLEMENT	Greg announced that the winners were Sylvia and *he*.

Subject complements — words following linking verbs that complete the meaning of the subject — frequently cause problems for writers, since we rarely hear the correct form in casual speech. (See B2-b.)

▶ **During the Lindbergh trial, Bruno Hauptmann repeatedly denied**

that the kidnapper was ~~him~~.
he.
^

If *kidnapper was he* seems too stilted, rewrite the sentence: *During the Lindbergh trial, Bruno Hauptmann repeatedly denied that he was the kidnapper.*

Objective case

When a personal pronoun is used as a direct object, an indirect object, or the object of a preposition, it must be in the objective case (*me, us, you, him, her, it, them*).

DIRECT OBJECT	Bruce found Tony and brought *him* home.
INDIRECT OBJECT	Alice gave *me* a surprise party.
OBJECT OF A PREPOSITION	Jessica wondered if the call was for *her*.

Compound word groups

When a subject or an object appears as part of a compound structure, you may occasionally become confused. To test for the correct pronoun, mentally strip away all of the compound word group except the pronoun in question.

▶ **Joel ran away from home because his stepfather and ~~him~~ had**
he
^

quarreled.

His stepfather and he is the subject of the verb *had quarreled.* If we strip away the words *his stepfather and,* the correct pronoun becomes clear: *he had quarreled* (not *him had quarreled*).

▶ **The most traumatic experience for her father and ~~I~~ occurred long**
me
^

after her operation.

Her father and me is the object of the preposition *for.* Strip away the words *her father and* to test for the correct pronoun: *for me* (not *for I*).

When in doubt about the correct pronoun, some writers try to avoid making the choice by using a reflexive pronoun such as *myself.* Such evasions are nonstandard, even though they are used by some educated persons.

> ▶ The Indian cab driver gave my husband and ~~myself~~ ^{me} some good
>
> tips on traveling in New Delhi.

My husband and me is the indirect object of the verb *gave.* For correct uses of *myself,* see the glossary of usage (W1).

ON THE WEB > dianahacker.com/writersref
Language Debates > *myself*

Appositives

Appositives are noun phrases that rename nouns or pronouns. A pronoun used as an appositive has the same function (usually subject or object) as the word(s) it renames.

> ▶ The chief strategists, Dr. Bell and ~~me,~~ ^{I,} could not agree on a plan.

The appositive *Dr. Bell and I* renames the subject, *strategists.* Test: *I could not agree* (not *me could not agree*).

> ▶ The reporter interviewed only two witnesses, the bicyclist and ~~I.~~ ^{me.}

The appositive *the bicyclist and me* renames the direct object *witnesses.* Test: *interviewed me* (not *interviewed I*).

We or us before a noun

When deciding whether *we* or *us* should precede a noun, choose the pronoun that would be appropriate if the noun were omitted.

> ▶ ~~Us~~ ^{We} tenants would rather fight than move.

> ▶ Management is shortchanging ~~we~~ ^{us} tenants.

No one would say *Us would rather fight than move* or *Management is shortchanging we.*

Comparisons with than or as

Sentence parts, usually verbs, are often omitted in comparisons beginning with *than* or *as.* To test for the correct pronoun, mentally complete the sentence.

► Even though he is sometimes ridiculed by the other boys,
                                        they.
  Norman is much better off than ~~them.~~
                                     ^

They is the subject of the verb *are,* which is understood: *Norman is much better off than they [are].* If the correct English seems too formal, you can always add the verb.

► We respected no other candidate for the city council as much
      her.
  as ~~she.~~
       ^

This sentence means that we respected no other candidate as much as *we respected her. Her* is the direct object of the understood verb *respected.*

Subjects and objects of infinitives

An infinitive is the word *to* followed by the base form of a verb. (See B3-b.) Subjects of infinitives are an exception to the rule that subjects must be in the subjective case. Whenever an infinitive has a subject, it must be in the objective case. Objects of infinitives also are in the objective case.

                        me   *her*
► Ms. Wilson asked John and ~~I~~ to drive the senator and ~~she~~ to
                              ^   ^
  the airport.

John and me is the subject of the infinitive *to drive; senator and her* is the direct object of the infinitive.

Possessive case to modify a gerund

A pronoun that modifies a gerund or a gerund phrase should appear in the possessive case (*my, our, your, his, her, its, their*). A gerund is a verb form ending in *-ing* that functions as a noun. Gerunds frequently appear in phrases, in which case the whole gerund phrase functions as a noun. (See B3-b.)

                    your
► The chances against ~~you~~ being hit by lightning are about two
                        ^
  million to one.

Your modifies the gerund phrase *being hit by lightning.*

Nouns as well as pronouns may modify gerunds. To form the possessive case of a noun, use an apostrophe and an *-s* (*victim's*) or just an apostrophe (*victims'*). See P5-a.

▶ The old order in France paid a high price for the ~~aristocracy~~ *aristocracy's*

exploiting the lower classes.

The possessive noun *aristocracy's* modifies the gerund phrase *exploiting the lower classes*.

ON THE WEB > dianahacker.com/writersref
Language Debates > Possessive before a gerund

EXERCISE G3-5 Edit the following sentences to eliminate errors in pronoun case. If a sentence is correct, write "correct" after it. Answers to lettered sentences appear in the back of the book. Example:

Grandfather cuts down trees for neighbors much younger
than ~~him.~~ *he.*

a. Rick applied for the job even though he heard that other candidates were more experienced than he.
b. The volleyball team could not believe that the coach was she.
c. She appreciated him telling the truth in such a difficult situation.
d. The director has asked you and I to draft a proposal for a new recycling plan.
e. Five close friends and myself rented a station wagon, packed it with food, and drove two hundred miles to Mardi Gras.

1. The squawk of the brass horns nearly overwhelmed us oboe and bassoon players.
2. Ushio, the last rock climber up the wall, tossed Teri and she the remaining pitons and carabiners.
3. The programmer realized that her and the interface designers were creating an entirely new Web application.
4. My desire to understand classical music was aided by me working as an usher at Symphony Hall.
5. The shower of sinking bricks caused he and his diving partner to race away from the collapsing seawall.

EXERCISE G3-6 Choose the correct pronoun in each set of parentheses.

We may blame television for the number of products based on characters in children's TV shows—from Big Bird to SpongeBob—but in fact merchandising that capitalizes on a character's popularity started long before television. Raggedy Ann began as a child's rag doll, and a few years later books about (she / her) and her brother, Raggedy Andy, were published. A cartoonist named Johnny Gruelle painted a cloth face on a family doll and applied for a patent in 1915. Later Gruelle began writing and illustrating stories about Raggedy Ann, and in 1918 (he / him) and a publisher teamed up to publish the books and sell the dolls. He was not the only one to try to sell products linked to children's stories. Beatrix Potter published the first of many Peter Rabbit picture books in 1902, and no one was better than (she / her) at making a living from spin-offs. After Peter Rabbit and Benjamin Bunny became popular, Potter began putting pictures of (they / them) and their little animal friends on merchandise. Potter had fans all over the world, and she understood (them / their) wanting to see Peter Rabbit not only in books but also on teapots and plates and lamps and other furnishings for the nursery. Potter and Gruelle, like countless others before and since, knew that entertaining children could be a profitable business.

ON THE WEB > dianahacker.com/writersref
Grammar exercises > Grammatical sentences > E-ex G3–7 and G3–8

G3-d   Distinguish between *who* and *whom*.

The choice between *who* and *whom* (or *whoever* and *whomever*) occurs primarily in subordinate clauses and in questions. *Who* and *whoever,* subjective-case pronouns, are used for subjects and subject complements. *Whom* and *whomever,* objective-case pronouns, are used for objects.

An exception to this general rule occurs when the pronoun functions as the subject of an infinitive. See page 219.

> GRAMMAR CHECKERS catch misuses of *who* and *whom* (*whoever* and *whomever*) only about half the time. A grammar checker flagged the incorrect use of *whomever* in the sentence *Daniel always volunteers this information to whomever will listen,* recognizing that *whoever* is required as the subject of the verb *will listen.* But it did not flag the incorrect use of *who* in this sentence: *My cousin Sylvie, who I am teaching to fly a kite, watches us every time we compete.*

In subordinate clauses

The case of a relative pronoun in a subordinate clause is determined by its function *within the subordinate clause it introduces.*

▶ The prize goes to the runner ~~whom~~ collects the most points.
(who)

The subordinate clause is *who collects the most points.* The verb of the clause is *collects,* and its subject is *who.*

When it functions as an object in a subordinate clause, *whom* appears out of order, before both the subject and the verb. To choose the correct pronoun, you can mentally restructure the clause.

▶ You will work with our senior engineers, ~~who~~ you will meet later.
(whom)

The subordinate clause is *whom you will meet later.* The subject of the clause is *you* and the verb is *will meet. Whom* is the direct object of the verb. The correct choice becomes clear if you mentally restructure the clause: *you will meet whom.*

When functioning as the object of a preposition in a subordinate clause, *whom* is often separated from its preposition.

▶ The tutor ~~who~~ I was assigned to was very supportive.
(whom)

Whom is the object of the preposition *to.* If the correct English seems too formal, drop *whom: The tutor I was assigned to. . . .*

NOTE: Inserted expressions such as *they know, I think,* and *she says* should be ignored in determining whether to use *who* or *whom.*

▶ All of the school bullies want to take on a big guy ~~whom~~ they
(who)

know will not hurt them.

Who is the subject of *will hurt,* not the object of *know.*

In questions

The case of an interrogative pronoun is determined by its function within the question.

▶ ~~Whom~~ was responsible for creating that computer virus?
(Who)

Who is the subject of the verb *was.*

When *whom* functions as an object in a question, it appears out of normal order, before both the subject and the verb. To choose the correct pronoun, you must mentally restructure the question.

> *Whom*
> ~~Who~~ did the Democratic Party nominate in 1992?
> ^

Whom is the direct object of the verb *did nominate*. This becomes clear if you restructure the question: *The Democratic Party did nominate whom in 1992?*

For subjects or objects of infinitives

An infinitive is the word *to* followed by the base form of a verb. (See B3-b.) Subjects of infinitives are an exception to the rule that subjects must be in the subjective case. Whenever an infinitive has a subject, it must be in the objective case. Objects of infinitives also are in the objective case.

> *whom*
> On the subject of health care, I don't know ~~who~~ to believe.
> ^

ON THE WEB > dianahacker.com/writersref
Language Debates > *who* versus *whom*

EXERCISE G3–7 Edit the following sentences to eliminate errors in the use of *who* and *whom* (or *whoever* and *whomever*). If a sentence is correct, write "correct" after it. Answers to lettered sentences appear in the back of the book. Example:

> *whom*
> What is the address of the artist ~~who~~ Antonio hired?
> ^

a. The roundtable featured scholars who I had never heard of.
b. Arriving late for rehearsal, we had no idea who was supposed to dance with whom.
c. Whom did you support in the last presidential election?
d. Daniel always gives a holiday donation to whomever needs it.
e. So many singers came to the audition that Natalia had trouble deciding who to select for the choir.

1. My cousin Sylvie, who I am teaching to fly a kite, watches us every time we compete.
2. Who decided to research the history of Hungarians in New Brunswick?
3. According to the Greek myth, the Sphinx devoured those who could not answer her riddles.
4. The people who ordered their medications from Canada were retirees whom don't have health insurance.
5. Who did the committee select?

ON THE WEB > dianahacker.com/writersref
Grammar exercises > Grammatical sentences > E-ex G3–9
and G3–10

G4

Adjectives and adverbs

Adjectives ordinarily modify nouns or pronouns; occasionally they function as subject complements following linking verbs. Adverbs modify verbs, adjectives, or other adverbs.

Many adverbs are formed by adding *-ly* to adjectives (*normal, normally*). But don't assume that all words ending in *-ly* are adverbs or that all adverbs end in *-ly*. Some adjectives end in *-ly* (*lovely, friendly*) and some adverbs don't (*always, here, there*). When in doubt, consult a dictionary.

ESL In English, adjectives are not pluralized to agree with the words they modify: *The red* [not *reds*] *roses were a wonderful surprise.*

 GRAMMAR CHECKERS can flag a number of problems with adjectives and adverbs: some misuses of *bad* or *badly* and *good* or *well*; some double comparisons, such as *more meaner*; some absolute comparisons, such as *most unique*; and some double negatives, such as *can't hardly*. However, the programs miss more problems than they find. Programs ignored errors like these: *could have been handled more professional* and *hadn't been bathed regular.*

G4-a   Use adverbs, not adjectives, to modify verbs, adjectives, and adverbs.

When adverbs modify verbs (or verbals), they nearly always answer the question When? Where? How? Why? Under what conditions? How often? or To what degree? When adverbs modify adjectives or other adverbs, they usually qualify or intensify the meaning of the word they modify.

Adjectives are often used incorrectly in place of adverbs in casual or nonstandard speech.

▶ The manager must see that the office runs ~~smooth~~ and ~~efficient.~~
  smoothly   efficiently.

The adverbs *smoothly* and *efficiently* modify the verb *runs.*

▶ In the early 1970s, chances for survival of the bald eagle looked ~~real~~ slim.
  really

Only adverbs can be used to modify adjectives or other adverbs. *Really* intensifies the meaning of the adjective *slim.*

NOTE: The incorrect use of the adjective *good* in place of the adverb *well* to modify a verb is especially common in casual and nonstandard speech. Use *well,* not *good,* to modify a verb in your writing.

▶ We were glad that Sanya had done ~~good~~ on the CPA exam.
  well

The adverb *well* should be used to modify the verb *had done.*

The word *well* is an adjective, however, when it means "healthy," "satisfactory," or "fortunate": *I feel very well today. All is well. It is just as well.*

ESL The placement of adverbs varies from language to language. Unlike some languages, such as French and Spanish, English does not allow an adverb between a verb (*poured*) and its direct object (*the liquid*). See E2-f.

▶ In the last stage of our experiment, we poured ~~slowly~~ the
  slowly

liquid into the container.

G4-b Use adjectives, not adverbs, as subject complements.

Adjectives ordinarily precede nouns, but they can also function as subject complements following linking verbs (see B2-b). When an adjective functions as a subject complement, it describes the subject.

Justice is *blind.*

Problems can arise with verbs such as *smell, taste, look,* and *feel,* which sometimes, but not always, function as linking verbs. If the word following one of these verbs describes the subject, use an adjective; if it modifies the verb, use an adverb.

ADJECTIVE   The detective looked *cautious.*

ADVERB   The detective looked *cautiously* for fingerprints.

The adjective *cautious* describes the detective; the adverb *cautiously* modifies the verb *looked.*

Linking verbs suggest states of being, not actions. Notice, for example, the different meanings of *looked* in the preceding examples. To look cautious suggests the state of being cautious; to look cautiously is to perform an action in a cautious way.

▶ The lilacs in our backyard smell especially ~~sweetly~~ this year.
      sweet
      ∧

▶ Lori looked ~~well~~ in her new go-go boots.
      good
      ∧

▶ We felt ~~badly~~ upon hearing of your grandmother's death.
      bad
      ∧

The verbs *smell, looked,* and *felt* suggest states of being, not actions. Therefore, they should be followed by adjectives, not adverbs.

ON THE WEB > dianahacker.com/writersref
Language Debates > *bad* versus *badly*

G4-c   Use comparatives and superlatives with care.

Most adjectives and adverbs have three forms: the positive, the comparative, and the superlative.

POSITIVE	COMPARATIVE	SUPERLATIVE
soft	softer	softest
fast	faster	fastest
careful	more careful	most careful
bad	worse	worst
good	better	best

Comparative versus superlative

Use the comparative to compare two things, the superlative to compare three or more.

▶ Which of these two low-carb drinks is ~~best?~~ *better?*

▶ Though Shaw and Jackson are impressive, Hobbs is the ~~more~~ *most*
qualified of the three candidates running for mayor.

Form of comparatives and superlatives

To form comparatives and superlatives of most one- and two-syllable adjectives, use the endings *-er* and *-est*: *smooth, smoother, smoothest; easy, easier, easiest.* With longer adjectives, use *more* and *most* (or *less* and *least* for downward comparisons): *exciting, more exciting, most exciting; less helpful, least helpful.*

Some one-syllable adverbs take the endings *-er* and *-est* (*fast, faster, fastest*), but longer adverbs and all of those ending in *-ly* form the comparative and superlative with *more* and *most* (or *less* and *least*).

The comparative and superlative forms of the following adjectives and adverbs are irregular: *good, better, best; well, better, best; bad, worse, worst; badly, worse, worst.*

▶ The Kirov was the ~~talentedest~~ *most talented* ballet company we had ever seen.

▶ Lloyd's luck couldn't have been ~~worser~~ *worse* than David's.

Double comparatives or superlatives

Do not use double comparatives or superlatives. When you have added *-er* or *-est* to an adjective or adverb, do not also use *more* or *most* (or *less* or *least*).

▶ All the polls indicated that Gore was more ~~likelier~~ *likely* to win than Bush.

▶ Of all her family, Julia is the ~~most~~ happiest about the move.

Absolute concepts

Avoid expressions such as *more straight, less perfect, very round,* and *most unique.* Either something is unique or it isn't. It is illogical to suggest that absolute concepts come in degrees.

▶ That is the most ~~unique~~ *unusual* wedding gown I have ever seen.

> *valuable*
> The painting would have been even more ~~priceless~~ had it been
> �
> signed.

ON THE WEB > dianahacker.com/writersref
Language Debates > Absolute concepts such as *unique*

G4-d Avoid double negatives.

Standard English allows two negatives only if a positive meaning
is intended: *The orchestra was not unhappy with its performance.*
Double negatives used to emphasize negation are nonstandard.

Negative modifiers such as *never, no,* and *not* should not be
paired with other negative modifiers or with negative words such
as *neither, none, no one, nobody,* and *nothing.*

> *anything*
> Management is not doing ~~nothing~~ to see that the trash is
> �
> picked up.

The double negative *not . . . nothing* is nonstandard.

The modifiers *hardly, barely,* and *scarcely* are considered negatives in standard English, so they should not be used with other
negatives such as *not, no one,* and *never.*

> *can*
> Maxine is so weak from her surgery she ~~can't~~ hardly climb stairs.

EXERCISE G4–1 Edit the following sentences to eliminate errors in the
use of adjectives and adverbs. If a sentence is correct, write "correct" after
it. Answers to lettered sentences appear in the back of the book. Example:

> *well*
> We weren't surprised by how ~~good~~ the sidecar racing team
> �
> flowed through the tricky course.

    a. Did you do good on last week's chemistry exam?
    b. With the budget deadline approaching, our office hasn't hardly had
       time to handle routine correspondence.
    c. Some flowers smell surprisingly bad.
    d. The customer complained that he hadn't been treated nice.
    e. Of all my relatives, Uncle Roberto is the most cleverest.

1. When you answer the phone, speak clear and courteous.
2. Who was more upset about the loss? Was it the coach or the quarterback or the owner of the team?
3. To a novice skateboarder, even the basic ollie seems real challenging.
4. After checking how bad I had been hurt, my sister dialed 911.
5. If the college's Web page had been updated more regular, students would have learned about the new course offerings.

EXERCISE G4–2 Edit the following passage to eliminate errors in the use of adjectives and adverbs.

　　Doctors recommend that to give skin the most fullest protection from ultraviolet rays, people should use plenty of sunscreen, limit sun exposure, and wear protective clothing. The commonest sunscreens today are known as "broad spectrum" because they block out both UVA and UVB rays. These lotions don't feel any differently on the skin from the old UVA-only types, but they work best at preventing premature aging and skin cancer. Many sunscreens claim to be waterproof, but they won't hardly provide adequate coverage after extended periods of swimming or perspiring. To protect good, even waterproof sunscreens should be reapplied liberal and often. All areas of exposed skin, including ears, backs of hands, and tops of feet, need to be coated good to avoid burning or damage. Some people's skin reacts bad to PABA, or para-aminobenzoic acid, so PABA-free (hypoallergenic) sunscreens are widely available. In addition to recommending sunscreen, doctors almost unanimously agree that people should stay out of the sun when rays are the most strongest — between 10:00 a.m. and 3:00 p.m. — and limit time in the sun. They also suggest that people wear long-sleeved shirts, broad-rimmed hats, and long pants whenever possible.

ON THE WEB > dianahacker.com/writersref
Grammar exercises > Grammatical sentences > E-ex G4–1
and G4–2

G5

Sentence fragments

A sentence fragment is a word group that pretends to be a sentence. Sentence fragments are easy to recognize when they appear out of context, like these:

On the old wooden stool in the corner of my grandmother's kitchen.

And immediately popped their flares and life vests.

When fragments appear next to related sentences, however, they are harder to spot.

On that morning I sat in my usual spot. On the old wooden stool in the corner of my grandmother's kitchen.

The pilots ejected from the burning plane, landing in the water not far from the ship. And immediately popped their flares and life vests.

GRAMMAR CHECKERS can flag as many as half of the sentence fragments in a sample; but that means, of course, that they miss half or more of them. If fragments are a serious problem for you, you will still need to proofread for them.

Sometimes the grammar checker will identify "false positives," sentences that have been flagged but are not fragments. For example, a grammar checker flagged this complete sentence as a possible fragment: *I bent down to crawl into the bunker.* When a program spots a possible fragment, you should check to see if it is really a fragment by using the flowchart on page 228.

ESL Unlike some languages, English requires a subject and a verb in every sentence (except in commands, where the subject *you* is understood but not present: *Sit down*). See E2-a and E2-b.

   It is
▶ ~~Is~~ often hot and humid during the summer.
   ^

      are
▶ Students usually very busy at the end of the semester.
     ^

Recognizing sentence fragments

To be a sentence, a word group must consist of at least one full independent clause. An independent clause has a subject and a verb, and it either stands alone or could stand alone.

To test a word group for sentence completeness, use the flowchart on page 228. For example, by using the flowchart, you can see exactly why *On the old wooden stool in the corner of my grand-*

mother's kitchen is a fragment: It lacks both a subject and a verb. *And immediately popped their flares and life vests* is a fragment because it lacks a subject.

Repairing sentence fragments

You can repair most fragments in one of two ways: Either pull the fragment into a nearby sentence or turn the fragment into a sentence.

▶ On that morning I sat in my usual spot, ~~On~~ *on* the old wooden

stool in the corner of my grandmother's kitchen.

▶ The pilots ejected from the burning plane, landing in the water

not far from the ship. ~~And~~ *They* immediately popped their flares and

life vests.

G5-a Attach fragmented subordinate clauses or turn them into sentences.

A subordinate clause is patterned like a sentence, with both a subject and a verb, but it begins with a word that marks it as subordinate. The following words commonly introduce subordinate clauses: *after, although, because, before, if, though, unless, until, when, where, who, which,* and *that.* (See B3-e.)

Most fragmented subordinate clauses beg to be pulled into a sentence nearby.

▶ Americans have come to fear the West Nile virus, ~~Because~~ *because*

it is transmitted by the common mosquito.

Because introduces a subordinate clause. (For punctuation of a subordinate clause appearing at the end of a sentence, see P2-f.)

If a fragmented clause cannot be attached to a nearby sentence or if you feel that attaching it would be awkward, try turning it into a sentence. The simplest way to do this is to delete the opening word or words that mark it as subordinate.

▶ Population increases and uncontrolled development are taking a

deadly toll on the environment. ~~So that in~~ *In* many parts of the

world, fragile ecosystems are collapsing.

Test for sentence completeness

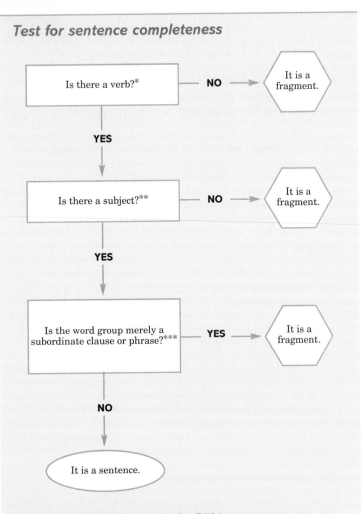

*Do not mistake verbals for verbs. (See B3-b.)

**The subject of a sentence may be *you,* understood. (See B2-a.)

***A sentence may open with a subordinate clause or phrase, but the sentence must also include an independent clause. (See B3.)

If you find any fragments, try one of these methods of revision:

1. Attach the fragment to a nearby sentence.

2. Turn the fragment into a sentence.

G5-b Attach fragmented phrases or turn them into sentences.

Like subordinate clauses, phrases function within sentences as adjectives, as adverbs, or as nouns. They cannot stand alone. Fragmented phrases are often prepositional or verbal phrases; sometimes they are appositives, words or word groups that rename nouns or pronouns. (See B3-a, B3-b, and B3-c.)

Often a fragmented phrase may simply be pulled into a nearby sentence.

▶ The archaeologists worked slowly/, ~~Examining~~ *examining* and labeling

every pottery shard they uncovered.

The word group beginning with *Examining* is a verbal phrase.

▶ Mary is suffering from agoraphobia/, ~~A~~ *a* fear of the outside

world.

A fear of the outside world is an appositive renaming the noun *agoraphobia.*

If a fragmented phrase cannot be pulled into a nearby sentence effectively, turn the phrase into a sentence. You may need to add a subject, a verb, or both.

▶ In the training session, Jamie explained how to access our

new database. ~~Also~~ *She also taught us* how to submit expense reports and

request vendor payments.

The revision turns the fragmented phrase into a sentence by adding a subject and a verb.

G5-c Attach other fragmented word groups or turn them into sentences.

Other word groups that are commonly fragmented include parts of compound predicates, lists, and examples introduced by *such as, for example,* or similar expressions.

Parts of compound predicates

A predicate consists of a verb and its objects, complements, and modifiers. A compound predicate includes two or more predicates joined by a coordinating conjunction such as *and, but,* or *or.* Because the parts of a compound predicate have the same subject, they should appear in the same sentence.

> The woodpecker finch of the Galápagos Islands carefully selects a
>
> twig of a certain size and shape/ And then uses this tool to pry out
>
> grubs from trees.

Notice that no comma appears between the parts of a compound predicate. (See P2-a.)

Lists

When a list is mistakenly fragmented, it can often be attached to a nearby sentence with a colon or a dash. (See P4-a and P7-d.)

> It has been said that there are only three indigenous American art
>
> forms/: Jazz, musical comedy, and soap opera.

Examples introduced by such as, for example, or similar expressions

Expressions that introduce examples (or explanations) can lead to unintentional fragments. Although you may begin a sentence with some of the following words or phrases, make sure that what you have written is a sentence, not a fragment.

also	especially	in addition	namely	that is
and	for example	like	or	
but	for instance	mainly	such as	

Sometimes fragmented examples can be attached to the preceding sentence.

> In the twentieth century, the South produced some great
>
> American writers/. Such as Flannery O'Connor, Eudora Welty,
>
> William Faulkner, Alice Walker, and Thomas Wolfe.

At times, however, it may be necessary to turn the fragment into a sentence.

▶ If Eric doesn't get his way, he goes into a fit of rage. For example,
he lies
~~lying~~ on the floor screaming or ~~opening~~ *opens* the cabinet doors and
then ~~slamming~~ *slams* them shut.
^

The writer corrected this fragment by adding a subject — *he* — and substituting verbs — *lies, opens,* and *slams* — for the verbals *lying, opening,* and *slamming.*

G5-d Exception: Fragments may be used for special purposes.

Skilled writers occasionally use sentence fragments for the following special purposes.

FOR EMPHASIS	Following the dramatic Americanization of their children, even my parents grew more publicly confident. *Especially my mother.* — Richard Rodriguez
TO ANSWER A QUESTION	Are these new drug tests 100 percent reliable? *Not in the opinion of most experts.*
AS A TRANSITION	*And now the opposing arguments.*
EXCLAMATIONS	*Not again!*
IN ADVERTISING	*Fewer carbs. Improved taste.*

Although fragments are sometimes appropriate, writers and readers do not always agree on when they are appropriate. Therefore, you will find it safer to write in complete sentences.

EXERCISE G5–1 Repair any fragment by attaching it to a nearby sentence or by rewriting it as a complete sentence. If a word group is correct, write "correct" after it. Revisions of lettered sentences appear in the back of the book. Example:

> *a*
> One Greek island that should not be missed is Mykonos~~.~~ ~~A~~
> ^
> vacation spot for Europeans and a playground for the rich
> and famous.

a. Listening to the CD her sister had sent, Mia was overcome with a mix of emotions. Happiness, homesickness, nostalgia.

b. Cortés and his soldiers were astonished when they looked down from the mountains and saw Tenochtitlán. The magnificent capital of the Aztecs.

c. Although my spoken Spanish is not very good. I can read the language with ease.

d. There are several reasons for not eating meat. One reason being that dangerous chemicals are used throughout the various stages of meat production.

e. To learn how to sculpt beauty from everyday life. This is my intention in studying art and archaeology.

1. The panther lay motionless behind the rock. Waiting silently for its unsuspecting prey.

2. Mother loved to play all our favorite games. Canasta, Monopoly, hide-and-seek, and even kick-the-can.

3. With machetes, the explorers cut their way through the tall grasses to the edge of the canyon. Then they began to lay out the tapes for the survey.

4. The owners of the online grocery store rented a warehouse in the Market district. An area catering to small businesses.

5. If a woman from the desert tribe showed anger toward her husband, she was whipped in front of the whole village. And shunned by the rest of the women.

EXERCISE G5–2 Repair each fragment in the following passage by attaching it to a sentence nearby or by rewriting it as a complete sentence.

Browsing the Web has become a way of life, but some people think it is destroying a way of life. That we will never recover. Our grandparents and parents feared that the age of television — starting with *Howdy Doody* and progressing through MTV and *America's Next Top Model* — would create generations of viewers who were content to sit for hours and hours. Passively watching images flit before their eyes. Cable television now offers far more passive entertainment than previous generations could ever have imagined. Hundreds of channels and an endless supply of round-the-clock programming. The World Wide Web has the potential to top even cable television's reach. Making access to information easy and available to people anywhere in the world at any time.

One major risk that our grandparents and parents feared is still an issue today. In a culture based on images, the written word may become an endangered species. As our brains eventually adapt to greater and greater levels of stimulation. Will we continue to be able to focus on a page of print? Before we send out too many alarms, however, we should remember that the World Wide Web is based more on words than television ever was. There is some evidence that those who spend time browsing the Web are doing more, not less, reading. Unlike TV viewers. Some Web surfers prefer to run their eyes over the words on the screen. An activity that is, after all, reading. Others download information and read the printouts. While it is true that television has reduced our nation's level of literacy, the World Wide Web could well advance it. Only the future will tell.

ON THE WEB > dianahacker.com/writersref
Grammar exercises > Grammatical sentences > E-ex G5–1
through G5–3

G6

Run-on sentences

Run-on sentences are independent clauses that have not been joined correctly. An independent clause is a word group that can stand alone as a sentence. (See B4.) When two independent clauses appear in one sentence, they must be joined in one of these ways:

- with a comma and a coordinating conjunction (*and, but, or, nor, for, so, yet*)

- with a semicolon (or occasionally with a colon or a dash)

Recognizing run-on sentences

There are two types of run-on sentences. When a writer puts no mark of punctuation and no coordinating conjunction between independent clauses, the result is called a *fused sentence*.

> ┌─────────── INDEPENDENT CLAUSE ───────────┐
> **FUSED** Gestures are a means of communication for everyone
>
> ┌─────────── INDEPENDENT CLAUSE ──────────┐
> they are essential for the hearing-impaired.

A far more common type of run-on sentence is the *comma splice —* two or more independent clauses joined by a comma without a coordinating conjunction. In some comma splices, the comma appears alone.

> **COMMA** Gestures are a means of communication for everyone,
> **SPLICE** they are essential for the hearing-impaired.

In other comma splices, the comma is accompanied by a joining word that is *not* a coordinating conjunction. There are only seven coordinating conjunctions in English: *and, but, or, nor, for, so,* and *yet.* Notice that all of these words are short — only two or three letters long. (See also G6-a.)

COMMA   Gestures are a means of communication for everyone,
SPLICE   however, they are essential for the hearing-impaired.

However is a transitional expression, not a coordinating conjunction.

To review your writing for possible run-on sentences, use the flowchart on page 236.

ON THE WEB > dianahacker.com/writersref
Language Debates > Comma splices

GRAMMAR CHECKERS flag fewer than half the run-on sentences in a sample. They usually suggest a semicolon as a method of revision, but you can consult G6-a through G6-d for other revision strategies that might be more suitable in a particular situation. If you have repeated problems with run-ons, the flowchart on page 236 will help you identify them.

Revising run-on sentences

To revise a run-on sentence, you have four choices:

1. Use a comma and a coordinating conjunction (*and, but, or, nor, for, so, yet*).

   ▶ Gestures are a means of communication for everyone, _{but} they are essential for the hearing-impaired.

2. Use a semicolon (or, if appropriate, a colon or a dash). A semicolon may be used alone; it can also be accompanied by a transitional expression (see also G6-b and P3-b).

   ▶ Gestures are a means of communication for everyone; they are essential for the hearing-impaired.

   ▶ Gestures are a means of communication for everyone; however, they are essential for the hearing-impaired.

3. Make the clauses into separate sentences.

   ▶ Gestures are a means of communication for everyone. They ~~they~~ are essential for the hearing-impaired.

4. Restructure the sentence, perhaps by subordinating one of the clauses.

> *Although gestures*
> ▶ ~~Gestures~~ are a means of communication for everyone, they are
> ^
> essential for the hearing-impaired.

One of these revision techniques will often work better than the others for a particular sentence. The fourth technique, the one requiring the most extensive revision, is frequently the most effective.

G6-a Consider separating the clauses with a comma and a coordinating conjunction.

There are seven coordinating conjunctions in English: *and, but, or, nor, for, so,* and *yet.* When a coordinating conjunction joins independent clauses, it is usually preceded by a comma. (See P1-a.)

> *and*
> ▶ The paramedic asked where I was hurt, as soon as I motioned
> ^
> toward my pain, he cut up the leg of my favorite pair of jeans.

> ▶ Many government officials privately admit that the polygraph
> *yet*
> is unreliable, ~~however,~~ they continue to use it as a security
> ^
> measure.

However is a transitional expression, not a coordinating conjunction, so it cannot be used with only a comma to join independent clauses.

G6-b Consider separating the clauses with a semicolon (or, if appropriate, with a colon or a dash).

When the independent clauses are closely related and their relation is clear without a coordinating conjunction, a semicolon is an acceptable method of revision. (See P3-a.)

> ▶ Tragedy depicts the individual confronted with the fact of death;
> ^
> comedy depicts the adaptability of human society.

Recognizing run-on sentences

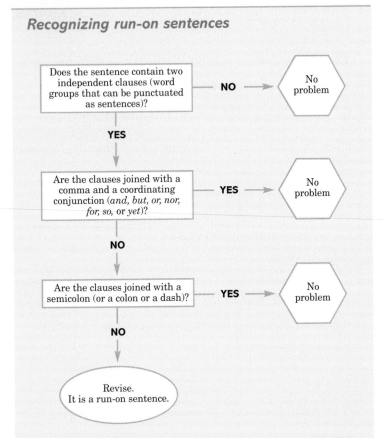

Does the sentence contain two independent clauses (word groups that can be punctuated as sentences)? — **NO** → No problem

YES ↓

Are the clauses joined with a comma and a coordinating conjunction (*and, but, or, nor, for, so,* or *yet*)? — **YES** → No problem

NO ↓

Are the clauses joined with a semicolon (or a colon or a dash)? — **YES** → No problem

NO ↓

Revise. It is a run-on sentence.

If you find an error, choose an effective method of revision. See G6-a through G6-d for revision strategies.

A semicolon is required beween independent clauses that have been linked with a transitional expression (such as *however, therefore, moreover, in fact,* or *for example*). For a longer list, see P3-b.

▶ Handheld PDAs are gaining in popularity,/; however, they are

not nearly as popular as cell phones.

If the first independent clause introduces the second or if the second clause summarizes or explains the first, a colon or a dash may be an appropriate method of revision. (See P4-b and P7-d.) In formal writing, the colon is usually preferred to the dash.

► Nuclear waste is hazardous ~~this~~ is an indisputable fact. *: This*

► The female black widow spider is often a widow of her own making, she has been known to eat her partner after mating.

If the first independent clause introduces a quoted sentence, a colon is an appropriate method of revision.

► Carolyn Heilbrun has this to say about the future, "Today's shocks are tomorrow's conventions."

G6-c Consider making the clauses into separate sentences.

► Why should we spend money on expensive space exploration,? *We* ~~we~~ have enough underfunded programs here on Earth.

Since one independent clause is a question and the other is a statement, they should be separate sentences.

► I gave the necessary papers to the police officer, ~~then~~ he said I would have to accompany him to the police station, where a counselor would talk with me and call my parents. *Then*

Because the second independent clause is quite long, a sensible revision is to use separate sentences.

NOTE: When two quoted independent clauses are divided by explanatory words, make each clause its own sentence.

► "It's always smart to learn from your mistakes," quipped my supervisor, "~~it's~~ even smarter to learn from the mistakes of others." *"It's*

G6-d Consider restructuring the sentence, perhaps by subordinating one of the clauses.

If one of the independent clauses is less important than the other, turn it into a subordinate clause or phrase. (See S6-a.)

▶ *Although many*
~~Many~~ scholars dismiss the abominable snowman of the Himalayas
︿

as a myth, others claim it may be a kind of ape.

▶ Of the many geysers in Yellowstone National Park, the most
which
famous is Old Faithful, ~~it~~ sometimes reaches 150 feet in height.
︿

▶ Mary McLeod Bethune, ~~was~~ the seventeenth child of former
︿

slaves, ~~she~~ founded the National Council of Negro Women in 1935.

Minor ideas in these sentences are now expressed in subordinate clauses or phrases.

EXERCISE G6–1 Revise any run-on sentences using the method of revision suggested in brackets. Revisions of lettered sentences appear in the back of the book. Example:

Because
Orville had been obsessed with his weight as a teenager, he
︿

rarely ate anything sweet. [*Restructure the sentence.*]

a. The city had one public swimming pool, it stayed packed with children all summer long. [*Restructure the sentence.*]
b. The building is being renovated, therefore at times we have no heat, water, or electricity. [*Use a comma and a coordinating conjunction.*]
c. The view was not what the travel agent had described, where were the rolling hills and the shimmering rivers? [*Make two sentences.*]
d. All those gnarled equations looked like toxic insects, maybe I was going to have to rethink my major. [*Use a semicolon.*]
e. The city government had good reason to fear a major earthquake, most of the business district was built on landfill. [*Use a colon.*]

1. The car was hardly worth trading, the frame was twisted and the block was warped. [*Restructure the sentence.*]
2. The next time an event is canceled because of bad weather, don't blame the meteorologist, blame nature. [*Make two sentences.*]
3. Ray was fluent in American Sign Language he could sign as easily as he could speak. [*Restructure the sentence.*]

4. Susanna arrived with a stack of her latest hats she hoped the gift shop would place a big winter order. [*Restructure the sentence.*]

5. There was one major reason for John's wealth, his grandfather had been a multimillionaire. [*Use a colon.*]

EXERCISE G6–2 Revise any run-on sentences using a technique that you find effective. If a sentence is correct, write "correct" after it. Revisions of lettered sentences appear in the back of the book. Example:

> Crossing so many time zones on an eight-hour flight, I knew
>
>   *but*
> I would be tired when I arrived, ~~however,~~ I was too excited
>   ^
>
> to sleep on the plane.

a. Wind power for the home is a supplementary source of energy, it can be combined with electricity, gas, or solar energy.

b. Aidan viewed Sofia Coppola's *Lost in Translation* three times and then wrote a paper describing the film as the work of a mysterious modern painter.

c. In the Middle Ages, the streets of London were dangerous places, it was safer to travel by boat along the Thames.

d. "He's not drunk," I said, "he's in a state of diabetic shock."

e. Are you able to endure boredom, isolation, and potential violence, then the army may well be the adventure for you.

1. Death Valley National Monument, located in southern California and Nevada, is one of the hottest places on earth, temperatures there have soared as high as 134 degrees Fahrenheit.

2. Anamaria opened the boxes crammed with toys, out sprang griffins, dragons, and phoenixes.

3. Subatomic physics is filled with strange and marvelous particles, tiny bodies of matter that shiver, wobble, pulse, and flatten to no thickness at all.

4. As his first major project, landscape architect Frederick Law Olmsted designed New York City's Central Park, this park is one of the most beautiful urban spaces in the United States.

5. The neurosurgeon explained that the medication could have one side effect, it might cause me to experience temporary memory loss.

EXERCISE G6–3 In the following rough draft, revise any run-on sentences.

> Some parents and educators argue that requiring uniforms in public schools would improve student behavior and performance. They think that uniforms give students a more professional attitude toward school, moreover, they believe that uniforms help create a sense of community

among students from diverse backgrounds. But parents and educators should consider the drawbacks to requiring uniforms in public schools.

Uniforms do create a sense of community, they do this, however, by stamping out individuality. Youth is a time to express originality, it is a time to develop a sense of self. One important way young people express their identities is through the clothes they wear. Of course, it could be argued that the self-patrolled dress code of high school students is stricter than any school-imposed code, nevertheless, trying to control dress habits from above will only lead to resentment or to mindless conformity.

If children are going to act like adults, they need to be treated like adults, they need to be allowed to make their own choices. Telling young people what to wear to school merely prolongs their childhood. Requiring uniforms undermines the educational purpose of public schools, which is not just to teach facts and figures but to help young people grow into adults who are responsible for making their own choices.

ON THE WEB > dianahacker.com/writersref
Grammar exercises > Grammatical sentences > E-ex G6–1
through G6–3

E

ESL Challenges

E   ESL Challenges

This section of *A Writer's Reference* is primarily for multilingual writers. You may find this section helpful if you learned English as a second language (ESL) or if you speak a language other than English with your friends and family.

ON THE WEB > dianahacker.com/writersref
    ESL help

E1

Verbs

Both native and nonnative speakers of English encounter the following challenges with verbs, which are treated elsewhere in this book:

    making subjects and verbs agree (G1)

    using irregular verb forms (G2-a)

    leaving off verb endings (G2-c, G2-d)

    choosing the correct verb tense (G2-f)

    avoiding inappropriate uses of the passive voice (W3-a)

This section focuses on the major challenges that verbs can cause for multilingual writers.

ON THE WEB > dianahacker.com/writersref
    Grammar exercises > ESL challenges > E-ex E1–1 through E1–4

E1-a Use the appropriate verb form and tense.

This section offers a brief review of the various English verb forms and tenses. See the chart on pages 251–53 for an overview of verb usage. For additional help with verb form and tense, see G2-f and B1-c.

Basic verb forms

VERB FORM	REGULAR VERB *HELP*	IRREGULAR VERB *GIVE*	IRREGULAR VERB *BE*
BASE FORM	help	give	be
PAST TENSE	helped	gave	was, were
PAST PARTICIPLE	helped	given	been
PRESENT PARTICIPLE	helping	giving	being
-S FORM	helps	gives	is

Basic verb forms

Every main verb in English has five forms, which are used to create all of the verb tenses in standard English. The chart at the top of this page shows these forms for the regular verb *help* and the irregular verbs *give* and *be*. (*Be* has the six forms listed in the chart as well as *am* and *are*, used in the present tense. See G2-a for a list of common irregular verbs.)

Simple tenses for general facts, states of being, habitual actions

SIMPLE PRESENT (BASE FORM OR *-S* FORM) Simple present tense shows general facts, constant states, or habitual or repetitive actions. It is also used for scheduled future events. (For uses of the present tense in writing about literature, see G2-f.)

> We *donate* to a different charity each year.

> The sun *rises* in the east and *sets* in the west.

> The plane *leaves* tomorrow at 6:30 p.m.

SIMPLE PAST (BASE FORM + *-ED* OR *-D* OR IRREGULAR FORM) Simple past tense expresses actions that happened at a specific time or during a specific period in the past. It can also show states of being and repetitive actions that have ended. It is often accompanied by a word (such as *ago* or *yesterday*) or a phrase (*in 1902, last year*) that indicates a specific past time. (See G2-a for irregular past-tense forms.)

> She *drove* to Montana three years ago.

> When I *was* young, I usually *walked* to school with my sister.

SIMPLE FUTURE (*WILL* + BASE FORM)   Simple future tense expresses actions that will happen at some time in the future as well as promises or predictions of future events.

> I *will call* you next week.

Simple progressive forms for continuing actions

PRESENT PROGRESSIVE (*AM, IS, ARE* + PRESENT PARTICIPLE)   Present progressive verbs show actions that are in progress at the present time but are not expected to remain constant or to continue indefinitely. Present progressive forms of verbs such as *leave, go, come,* and *move* are also used to express future actions.

> Carlos *is building* his house on a cliff overlooking the ocean.

> We *are going* to the circus tomorrow.

PAST PROGRESSIVE (*WAS, WERE* + PRESENT PARTICIPLE)   Past progressive verbs express actions that were in progress at a specific past time. They often indicate a continuing action that was interrupted by another action. The past progressive form *was going to* or *were going to* is used for past plans that did not happen.

> Roy *was driving* a brand-new red Corvette yesterday.

> When my roommate walked in, we *were planning* her party.

> We *were going to* spend spring break in Florida, but we went to New York instead.

FUTURE PROGRESSIVE (*WILL* + *BE* + PRESENT PARTICIPLE)   Future progressive verbs show actions that will be in progress at a certain time in the future.

> Naomi *will be flying* home tomorrow.

TIP: Certain verbs are not usually used in the progressive sense in English. In general, these verbs express a state of being or mental activity, not a dynamic action. Common examples are *appear, believe, belong, contain, have, hear, know, like, need, see, seem, taste, think, understand,* and *want.*

>   *want*
> ▶ I ~~am wanting~~ to see August Wilson's *Gem of the Ocean.*

Some of these verbs, however, have special uses in which progressive forms are normal (*We are thinking about going to the Bahamas*). You should note exceptions as you encounter them.

Perfect tenses for actions that happened or will happen before another time

PRESENT PERFECT (*HAVE, HAS* + PAST PARTICIPLE)   Present perfect tense expresses actions that began in the past and continue to the present or actions that happened at an unspecific time in the past.

> An-Mei *has* not *spoken* Chinese since she was a child.

> My parents *have traveled* to South Africa twice.

PAST PERFECT (*HAD* + PAST PARTICIPLE)   The past perfect tense conveys actions that began in the past and continued to a more recent past time. It is also used for an action that happened at an unspecific time before another past event. (For uses of the past perfect in conditional sentences, see E1-e.)

> By the time Hakan was fifteen, he *had* already *learned* to drive.

> I *had* just *finished* the test when the professor announced that time was up.

FUTURE PERFECT (*WILL* + *HAVE* + PAST PARTICIPLE)   The future perfect tense expresses actions that will be completed before or at a specified future time.

> By the time I graduate, I *will have taken* five composition classes.

Perfect progressive forms for continuous past actions before another time

PRESENT PERFECT PROGRESSIVE (*HAVE, HAS* + *BEEN* + PRESENT PARTICIPLE)   Present perfect progressive verbs express continuous actions that began in the past and continue to the present.

> My sister *has been living* in Oregon since 2001.

PAST PERFECT PROGRESSIVE (*HAD* + *BEEN* + PRESENT PARTICIPLE)   Past perfect progressive verbs convey actions that began and continued in the past until some other past action.

> By the time I moved to Georgia, I *had been supporting* myself for five years.

FUTURE PERFECT PROGRESSIVE (*WILL* + *HAVE* + *BEEN* + PRESENT PARTICIPLE)   Future perfect progressive verbs indicate actions that are or will be in progress before a specified time in the future.

> By the time we reach the register, we *will have been waiting* in line for two full hours.

EXERCISE E1-1 Revise any sentences to correct errors in verb forms and verb tenses. You may need to look at the list in G2-a to determine the correct form of some irregular verbs. Answers to lettered sentences appear in the back of the book. Example:

> *begins*
> The meeting ~~begin~~ tonight at 7:30.
> ^

a. In the past, tobacco companies deny any connection between smoking and health problems.
b. There is nothing in the world that TV has not touch on.
c. I am wanting to register for a summer tutoring session.
d. By the end of the year, the state will have test 139 birds for avian flu.
e. The benefits of eating fruits and vegetables have been promoting by health care providers.

1. By the time he was twelve years old, Mozart had compose an entire opera.
2. A serious accident was happened at the corner of Main Street and First Avenue last night.
3. My family has been gone to Sam's restaurant ever since we moved to this neighborhood.
4. I have ate Thai food only once before.
5. The bear is appearing to be sedated.

E1-b Use the base form of the verb after a modal.

A modal verb—*can, could, may, might, must, shall, should, will,* or *would*—is used with the base form of a verb to show certainty, necessity, or possibility. Modals do not change form to indicate tense. For a summary of modals and their meanings, see the chart beginning on this page. (Along with forms of *have, do,* and *be,* modals are also called *helping verbs.* See B1-c.)

▶ My cousin will sends us photographs from her wedding when she returns from Portugal.

> *speak*
▶ We could ~~spoke~~ Portuguese when we were young.
> ^

TIP: Do not use *to* in front of a main verb that follows a modal.

▶ Gina can ~~to~~ drive us home from the party if we miss the last subway train.

For the use of modals in conditional sentences, see E1-e.

Modals and their meanings

Can

■ General ability (present)

Valerie *can sing.*

Jorge *can run* the marathon faster than his brother.

■ Informal requests or permission

Can you *tell* me where the bookstore is?

You *can borrow* my calculator until Wednesday.

Could

■ General ability (past)

Hilit *could speak* three languages when she was only five years old.

■ Polite, informal requests or suggestions

Could you *give* me that pen?

May

■ Formal requests or permission

May I *use* your pen?

Students *may park* only in the yellow zone.

■ Possibility

I *may try* to finish my homework tonight, or I *may wake up* early and finish it tomorrow.

Might

■ Possibility

The population of New Delhi *might reach* thirteen million by 2010.

Must

■ Necessity (present or future)

To be effective, welfare-to-work programs *must provide* access to job training.

→

■ Strong possibility or near certainty (present or past)

> Amy doesn't look well this morning. She *must be* sick. [She is probably sick.]

> I *must have left* my wallet at home. [I probably left my wallet at home.]

Should

■ Suggestions or advice

> Frank *should join* student government.

> You *should drink* plenty of water every day.

■ Obligations or duties

> The government *should protect* the rights of citizens.

■ Expectations

> The books *should arrive* soon. [We expect the books to arrive soon.]

Will

■ Certainty

> If you don't leave now, you *will be* late.

■ Requests

> *Will* you *help* me study for my history test?

■ Promises and offers

> I *will arrange* the carpool.

NOTE: *Shall* traditionally was the modal used with *I* or *we* in place of *will*. It is now used mainly for polite requests or in very formal contexts (*Shall I call you soon?*).

Would

■ Polite requests

> *Would* you *help* me carry these books?

> I *would like* some coffee. [Polite for *want*.]

■ Habitual or repeated actions (past)

> Whenever I needed help with sewing, I *would call* my aunt.

EXERCISE E1–2 Edit the following sentences to correct errors in the use of verb forms with modals. If a sentence is correct, write "correct" after it. Answers to lettered sentences appear in the back of the book. Example:

> We should ~~to~~ order pizza for dinner.

a. A major league pitcher can to throw a baseball over ninety-five miles per hour.
b. The writing center tutors will helps you to revise your essay.
c. A reptile must adjusted its body temperature to its environment.
d. In some states, individuals may renew a driver's license online.
e. My uncle, a caricature artist, could sketched a face in less than two minutes.

1. Working more than twelve hours a day might to contribute to insomnia, according to researchers.
2. A wasp will carry its immobilized prey back to the nest.
3. Hikers should not wandered too far from the trail.
4. When we turn in electronic files, should we continued to submit hard copies of our essays?
5. Surgery may to cure patients with carpal tunnel syndrome.

E1-c Use a form of *be* with the past participle to write a verb in the passive voice.

When a sentence is written in the passive voice, the subject receives the action instead of doing it. (See B2-b.)

> ┌────── S ──────┐ ┌── V ──┐
> The control group was given a placebo.

> Melissa *was taken* to the hospital.

To form the passive voice, use a form of *be — am, is, are, was, were, being, be,* or *been* — followed by the past participle of the main verb.

>   *written*
> ▶ **Dreaming in Cuban was** ~~writing~~ **by Cristina García.**

The past participle *written*, not the present participle *writing*, must be used following *was* (the past tense of *be*) in the passive voice.

> ▶ **If we can trust the polls, we are confident that Senator Dixon**
>   *be*
> **will ᴧ defeated.**

The passive voice requires a form of *be* before the past participle.

> The child was being ~~tease.~~ *teased.*

The past participle *teased*, not the base form *tease*, must be used with *was being* to form the passive voice.

For details on forming the passive in various tenses, consult the chart at the bottom of this page. (For appropriate uses of the passive voice, see W3-a.)

TIP: Only transitive verbs, those that take direct objects, may be used in the passive voice. Intransitive verbs such as *occur, happen, sleep, die,* and *fall* are not used in the passive. (See B2-b.)

> The accident ~~was~~ happened suddenly.

Verbs at a glance

Simple tenses

	ACTIVE VOICE	PASSIVE VOICE
Simple present • general facts • states of being • habitual, repetitive actions	**Base form or -s form** College students often *study* late at night.	*am, is, are* + past participle Breakfast *is served* daily at 8:00.
Simple past • completed past actions • facts or states of being in the past	**Base form + -ed or -d or irregular form** The storm *destroyed* their property.	*was, were* + past participle He *was punished* for being late.
Simple future • future actions, promises, or predictions	***will* + base form** I *will exercise* tomorrow.	*will be* + past participle The governor *will be elected* next week.

→

Simple progressive forms

	ACTIVE VOICE	PASSIVE VOICE
Present progressive • actions in progress at the present time • future actions (with *leave*, *go*, *come*, *move*, etc.)	*am*, *is*, *are* + **present participle** The students *are taking* an exam in Room 105. I *am leaving* tomorrow morning.	*am*, *is*, *are* + *being* + **past participle** Dinner *is being served* now. Jo *is being moved* to a new class next month.
Past progressive • actions in progress at a specific time in the past	*was*, *were* + **present participle** They *were swimming* when the storm struck.	*was*, *were* + *being* + **past participle** We thought we *were being followed*.
Future progressive • actions in progress at a specific time in the future	*will* + *be* + **present participle** Brad *will be cooking* when his parents arrive.	[Future progressive is usually not used in the passive voice.]

Perfect tenses

	ACTIVE VOICE	PASSIVE VOICE
Present perfect • repetitive or constant actions that began in the past and continue to the present • actions that happened at an unknown or unspecific time in the past	*has*, *have* + **past participle** I *have loved* cats since I was a child. Steph *has visited* Wales three times.	*has*, *have* + *been* + **past participle** Wars *have been fought* throughout history.
Past perfect • actions that began or occurred before another time in the past	*had* + **past participle** She *had* just *crossed* the street when the runaway car plowed into the building.	*had* + *been* + **past participle** He *had been given* all the hints he needed to complete the puzzle.

→

	ACTIVE VOICE	PASSIVE VOICE
	will + have + past	
Future perfect	**participle**	
• actions that will be completed before or at a specific future time	By the end of this year, I *will have seen* three concerts.	[Future perfect is usually not used in the passive voice.]

Perfect progressive forms

ACTIVE VOICE

Present perfect progressive
- continuous actions that began in the past and continue to the present

has, have + been + present participle
My sister *has been trying* to get a job in Boston for five years.

Past perfect progressive
- actions that began and continued in the past until some other past action

had + been + present participle
By the time I entered high school, I *had been taking* piano lessons for eight years.

Future perfect progressive
- actions that are or will be in progress before a specified future time

will + have + been + present participle
When Carol is eighty years old, she *will have been living* in Vermont for sixty-two years.

E1-d To make negative verb forms, add *not* in the appropriate place.

If the verb is the simple present or past tense of *be* (*am, is, are, was, were*), add *not* after the verb.

Mario *is not* a member of the club.

For simple present-tense verbs other than *be*, use *do* or *does* plus *not* before the base form of the verb. (For the correct use of *do* and *does*, see the chart in G1-a.)

► Mariko ~~no~~ want more dessert.
does not

► Mariko does not want~~s~~ more dessert.

For simple past-tense verbs other than *be*, use *did* plus *not* before the base form of the verb.

► They did not ~~planted~~ corn this year.
plant

In a verb phrase consisting of one or more helping verbs and a present or past participle (*is watching, were living, has played, could have been driven*), use the word *not* after the first helping verb.

► Inna should have ~~not~~ gone dancing last night.
not

► Bonnie is ~~no~~ singing this weekend.
not

NOTE: The word *not* can be contracted to *n't* when used with some forms of *be* (*is, are, was, were*) and with other helping verbs and modals. Use *isn't* for *is not*, *don't* for *do not*, *doesn't* for *does not*, *shouldn't* for *should not*, and so on. *Won't* is the contracted form of *will not*. The contracted form of *am not*, used only in questions, is *aren't*.

English allows only one negative in an independent clause to express a negative idea; using more than one is an error known as a *double negative* (see also G4-d). Double negatives can be corrected by eliminating one of the two negative words or by replacing one of them with an article or another noun marker such as *any*.

► I don't have ~~no~~ homework this weekend.

► We could not find ~~no~~ books about the history of our school.
any

► The smoke detector doesn't have ~~no~~ battery in it.
a

E1-e In a conditional sentence, choose verb tenses according to the type of condition expressed in the sentence.

Conditional sentences contain two clauses: a subordinate clause (usually starting with *if, when,* or *unless*) and an independent clause. The subordinate clause (sometimes called the *if* or *unless* clause) states the condition or cause; the independent clause states the result or effect.

Verb tenses in conditional sentences usually express the nature of the condition rather than the time of an action or event. Present tenses typically express factual or true conditions, and past tenses typically express speculative or imaginary conditions.

Three kinds of conditional sentences are discussed in this section: factual, predictive, and speculative. In each example, the subordinate clause is marked SUB, and the independent clause is marked IND.

Factual

Factual conditional sentences express factual relationships. If the relationship is a scientific truth, use the present tense in both clauses.

┌──────── SUB ────────┐ ┌─IND─┐
If water *cools* to 32°, it *freezes*.

If the sentence describes a condition that is (or was) habitually true, use the same tense in both clauses.

┌──────────── SUB ────────────┐ ┌──────── IND ────────┐
When Sue *jogs* along the canal, her dog *runs* ahead of her.

┌──────────── SUB ────────────┐ ┌──── IND ────┐
Whenever the coach *asked* for help, I *volunteered*.

Predictive

Predictive conditional sentences are used to predict the future or to express future plans or possibilities. To form a predictive sentence, use a present-tense verb in the subordinate clause; in the independent clause, use the modal *will*, *can*, *may*, *should*, or *might* plus the base form of the verb.

┌──────── SUB ────────┐ ┌──────── IND ────────┐
If you *practice* regularly, your tennis game *should improve*.

┌──────────── IND ────────────┐ ┌──── SUB ────┐
We *will lose* our remaining wetlands unless we *act* now.

TIP: In all types of conditional sentences (factual, predictive, and speculative), *if* or *unless* clauses do not use the modal verb *will*.

▶ If Jenna ~~will pass~~ her history test, she will graduate this year.
      passes

Speculative

Speculative conditional sentences, sometimes called *unreal conditionals*, show unlikely, contrary-to-fact, or impossible conditions. To show distance from truth or reality, English uses past or past perfect tense in the *if* clause, even for conditions in the present and future.

UNLIKELY POSSIBILITIES   If the condition is possible but unlikely in the present or future, use the past tense in the subordinate clause; in the independent clause, use *would, could,* or *might* plus the base form of the verb.

> ┌────── SUB ──────┐ ┌────── IND ──────┐
> If I *won* the lottery, I *would travel* to Egypt.

The writer does not expect to win the lottery. Because this is a possible but unlikely present or future situation, the subordinate clause uses the past tense.

CONDITIONS CONTRARY TO FACT   In conditions that are currently unreal or contrary to fact, use the past-tense verb *were* (not *was*) in the *if* clause for all subjects. (See G2-g for more details.)

> ▸ If I ~~was~~ president, I would make children's issues a priority.
>   ^*were*

The writer is not president, so *were* is correct in the *if* clause.

EVENTS THAT DID NOT HAPPEN   In a conditional sentence that speculates about an event that did not happen or was impossible in the past, use the past perfect tense in the *if* clause; in the independent clause, use *would have, could have,* or *might have* with the past participle. (See also past perfect tense, p. 246.)

> ┌────── SUB ──────┐ ┌────── IND ──────┐
> If I *had saved* enough money, I *would have visited* Senegal last year.

The writer did not save enough money and did not travel to Senegal. This sentence shows a possibility that did not happen.

> ┌────── SUB ──────┐ ┌── IND ──┐
> If Aunt Grace *had been* alive for your graduation, she *would have*
> ┌──────────┐
> *been* very proud.

Aunt Grace was not alive at the time of the graduation. This sentence shows an impossible situation in the past.

EXERCISE E1–3 Edit the following conditional sentences for problems with verbs. In some cases, more than one revision is possible. Suggested revisions of lettered sentences appear in the back of the book. Example:

> *had*
> If I ~~have~~ time, I would study Russian next semester.
>   ^

a. The electrician might have discovered the broken circuit if she went through the modules one at a time.
b. If Verena wins a scholarship, she would go to graduate school.
c. Whenever there is a fire in our neighborhood, everybody came out to watch.
d. Sarah will take the paralegal job unless she would get a better offer.
e. If I live in Budapest with my cousin Szusza, she would teach me Hungarian cooking.

1. If the science fiction festival starts Monday, we wouldn't need to plan entertainment for our visitors.
2. If everyone has voted in the last election, the results would have been very different.
3. The tenants will not pay the rent unless the landlord fixed the furnace.
4. When dark gray clouds appeared on a hot summer afternoon, a thunderstorm often follows.
5. Our daughter would have drowned if Officer Blake didn't risk his life to save her.

E1-f Become familiar with verbs that may be followed by gerunds or infinitives.

A gerund is a verb form that ends in *-ing* and is used as a noun: *sleeping, dreaming.* (See B3-b.) An infinitive is the word *to* plus the base form of the verb: *to sleep, to dream.* The word *to* is not a preposition in this use but an infinitive marker.

A few verbs may be followed by either a gerund or an infinitive; others may be followed by a gerund but not by an infinitive; still others may be followed by an infinitive but not by a gerund.

Verb + gerund or infinitive (no change in meaning)

The following commonly used verbs may be followed by a gerund or an infinitive, with little or no difference in meaning:

begin	hate	love
continue	like	start

I love *skiing.* I love *to ski.*

Verb + gerund or infinitive (change in meaning)

With a few verbs, the choice of a gerund or an infinitive changes the meaning dramatically:

> forget   remember   stop   try

> She stopped *speaking* to Lucia. [She no longer spoke to Lucia.]
>
> She stopped *to speak* to Lucia. [She paused so that she could speak to Lucia.]

Verb + gerund

These verbs may be followed by a gerund but not by an infinitive:

admit	enjoy	postpone	resist
appreciate	escape	practice	risk
avoid	finish	put off	suggest
deny	imagine	quit	tolerate
discuss	miss	recall	

> Bill enjoys *playing* [not *to play*] the piano.
>
> Jamie quit *smoking*.

Verb + infinitive

These verbs may be followed by an infinitive but not by a gerund:

agree	expect	need	refuse
ask	help	offer	wait
beg	hope	plan	want
claim	manage	pretend	wish
decide	mean	promise	would like

> Jill has offered *to water* [not *watering*] the plants while we are away.
>
> Joe finally managed *to find* a parking space.
>
> The man refused *to join* the rebellion.

A few of these verbs may be followed either by an infinitive directly or by a noun or pronoun plus an infinitive:

ask	help	promise	would like
expect	need	want	

We asked *to speak* to the congregation.

We asked *Rabbi Abrams to speak* to our congregation.

Alex expected *to get* the lead in the play.

Ira expected *Alex to get* the lead in the play.

Verb + noun or pronoun + infinitive

With certain verbs in the active voice, a noun or pronoun must come between the verb and the infinitive that follows it. The noun or pronoun usually names a person who is affected by the action.

advise	convince	order	tell
allow	encourage	persuade	urge
cause	have ("own")	remind	warn
command	instruct	require	

V   N   ⌐INF⌐
The class encouraged Luis to tell the story of his escape.

The counselor *advised Haley to take* four courses instead of five.

Professor Howlett *instructed us to write* our names on the left side of the paper.

Verb + noun or pronoun + unmarked infinitive

An unmarked infinitive is an infinitive without *to*. A few verbs (often called *causative verbs*) may be followed by a noun or pronoun and an unmarked infinitive.

have ("cause")   help   let ("allow")   make ("force")

Jorge *had the valet park* his car.

▶ Please let me ~~to~~ pay for the tickets.

▶ Frank made me ~~to~~ carry his book for him.

NOTE: *Help* can be followed by a noun or pronoun and either an unmarked or a marked infinitive: *Emma helped Brian wash the dishes. Emma helped Brian to wash the dishes.*

EXERCISE E1–4 Form sentences by adding gerund or infinitive constructions to the following sentence openings. In some cases, more than one kind of construction may be possible. Possible answers to lettered items appear in the back of the book. Example:

Please remind ˄ *your sister to call me.*

a. I enjoy
b. The tutor told Samantha
c. The team hopes
d. Ricardo and his brothers miss
e. The babysitter let

1. Pollen makes
2. The club president asked
3. Next summer we plan
4. My supervisor intends
5. Please stop

E2

Sentence structure

Although their structure can vary widely, sentences in English generally flow from subject to verb to object or complement: *Bears eat fish*. This section focuses on the major challenges that multilingual students face when writing sentences in English. For more details on the parts of speech and how they work together to form sentences, consult B, Basic Grammar.

ON THE WEB > dianahacker.com/writersref
    Grammar exercises > ESL challenges > E-ex E2–1 and E2–2

E2-a Use a linking verb between a subject and its complement.

Some languages, such as Russian and Turkish, do not use linking verbs (*is, are, was, were*) between subjects and complements (nouns or adjectives that rename or describe the subject). Every English sentence, however, must include a verb. For more on linking verbs, see G2-e.

▶ *is*
 Jim ⌃ intelligent.

▶ *are*
 Many streets in San Francisco ⌃ very steep.

E2-b Include a subject in every sentence.

Some languages, such as Spanish and Japanese, do not require a subject in every sentence. Every English sentence, however, needs a subject. An exception is commands, in which the subject *you* is understood but not present (*Give to the poor*).

▶ *She seems*
 Your aunt is very energetic. ~~Seems~~ young for her age.
 ⌃

The word *it* is used as the subject of a sentence describing the weather or temperature, stating the time, indicating distance, or suggesting an environmental fact.

▶ *It is*
 ~~Is~~ raining in the valley and snowing in the mountains.
 ⌃

▶ *it*
 In July, ⌃ is very hot in Arizona.

▶ *It is*
 ~~Is~~ 9:15 a.m.
 ⌃

▶ *It is*
 ~~Is~~ three hundred miles to Chicago.
 ⌃

▶ *It gets*
 ~~Gets~~ noisy in our dorm on weekends.
 ⌃

In most English sentences, the subject appears before the verb. Some sentences, however, are inverted: The subject comes after the verb. In these sentences, a placeholder called an *expletive* (*there* or *it*) often comes before the verb.

EXP   V ┌──— S —──┐   ┌──── S —──┐ V
There are many people here today. (Many people are here today.)

▶ *There is*
 ~~Is~~ an apple in the refrigerator.
 ⌃

▶ *there are*
 As you know, ⌃ many religious sects in India.

Notice that the verb agrees with the subject that follows it: *apple is, sects are.* (See G1-g.)

In inverted sentences that have an infinitive (*to work*) or a noun clause (*that she is intelligent*) as the subject, the placeholder *it* is needed to open the sentence. *It* is followed by a linking verb (*is, was, seems,* and so on), an adjective, and then the subject. (See B3-b and B3-e.)

EXP V   ┌—S—┐   ┌—S—┐   V
It is important to study daily. (To study daily is important.)

> *It is*
> ~~Is~~ healthy to eat fruit and grains.
> ^

> *It is*
> ~~Is~~ clear that we must change our approach.
> ^

TIP: The words *here* and *there* are not used as subjects. When they mean "in this place" (*here*) or "in that place" (*there*), they are adverbs — not nouns.

> *It*   *there.*
> I just returned from a vacation in Japan. ~~There~~ is very beautiful /
> ^   ^

> *This school*   *that school*
> ~~Here~~ offers a master's degree in physical therapy; ~~there~~ has only
> ^   ^
>
> a bachelor's program.

GRAMMAR CHECKERS can flag some sentences with a missing expletive, or placeholder (*there* or *it*), but they often misdiagnose the problem, suggesting that if a sentence opens with a word such as *Is* or *Are*, it may need a question mark at the end. Consider this sentence, which a grammar checker flagged as requiring a question mark: *Are two grocery stores on Elm Street.* The sentence is missing the placeholder *there*, whether it is phrased as a question or as a statement: *There are two grocery stores on Elm Street. Are there two grocery stores on Elm Street?*

E2-c Do not use both a noun and a pronoun to perform the same grammatical function in a sentence.

English does not allow a subject to be repeated in its own clause.

> The doctor ~~she~~ advised me to cut down on salt.

> Andrea ~~she~~ is late all the time.

> The pronoun *she* cannot repeat the subject, *doctor*, in the first sentence or the subject, *Andrea*, in the second.

Do not add a pronoun even when a word group comes between the subject and the verb.

▶ **The watch that had been lost on vacation i̶t̶ was in my**

backpack.

The pronoun *it* cannot repeat the subject, *watch.*

Some languages allow "topic fronting," or placing a word or phrase (a "topic") at the beginning of a sentence and following it with an independent clause that explains something about the topic. This form is not allowed in English.

```
           ┌─ TOPIC ─┐ ┌──── IND CLAUSE ────┐
```
INCORRECT   The seeds I planted them last fall.

The pronoun *them* repeats the "topic," *the seeds.* The sentence can be revised by replacing *them* with *the seeds.*

　　　　　　　　　　　the seeds
▶ T̶h̶e̶ ̶s̶e̶e̶d̶s̶ I planted t̶h̶e̶m̶ last fall.
　　　　　　　　　　　　　　 ^

E2-d Do not repeat an object or an adverb in an adjective clause.

Adjective clauses begin with relative pronouns (*who, whom, whose, which, that*) or relative adverbs (*when, where*). Relative pronouns usually serve as subjects or objects in the clauses they introduce; another word in the clause cannot serve the same function. Relative adverbs should not be repeated by other adverbs later in the clause.

```
                      ┌──────── ADJ CLAUSE ────────┐
```
The cat ran under the car that was parked on the street.

▶ **The cat ran under the car that i̶t̶ was parked on the street.**

The relative pronoun *that* is the subject of the adjective clause, so the pronoun *it* cannot be added as the subject.

▶ **Myrna enjoyed the investment seminars that she attended t̶h̶e̶m̶**

last week.

The relative pronoun *that* is the object of the verb *attended.* The pronoun *them* cannot also serve as object.

Even when the relative pronoun has been omitted, do not add another word with its same function.

▶ Myrna enjoyed the investment seminars she attended ~~them~~ last week.

The relative pronoun *that* is understood even though it is not present in the sentence.

If the clause begins with a relative adverb, do not use another adverb with the same meaning later in the clause.

▶ The office where I work ~~there~~ is one hour from the city.

The adverb *there* cannot repeat the relative adverb *where*.

✓ GRAMMAR CHECKERS usually fail to mark sentences with repeated subjects or objects. One program flagged some sentences with repeated subjects, such as this one: *The yarn that she ordered it will arrive next Monday.* But the program misdiagnosed the problem and did not recognize that *it* repeats the subject, *yarn*.

EXERCISE E2–1 In the following sentences, add needed subjects or expletives (placeholders) and delete any repeated subjects, objects, or adverbs. Answers to lettered sentences appear in the back of the book. Example:

The new geology professor is the one whom we saw ~~him~~ on

TV this morning.

a. Are some cartons of ice cream in the freezer.
b. I don't use the subway because am afraid.
c. The prime minister she is the most popular leader in my country.
d. We tried to get in touch with the same manager whom we spoke to him earlier.
e. Recently have been a number of earthquakes in Turkey.

1. We visited an island where several ancient ruins are being excavated there.
2. In this city is difficult to find a high-paying job.
3. Beginning knitters they are often surprised that their fingers are sore at first.
4. Is a banyan tree in our backyard.
5. The CD that teaches Italian for opera lovers it was stolen from my backpack.

E2-e Do not mix *although* or *because* with other linking words that serve the same purpose in a sentence.

A word group that begins with *although* cannot be linked to a word group that begins with *but* or *however* (both words have the same meaning as *although*). Similarly, a word group that begins with *because* cannot be linked to a word group that begins with *so* or *therefore*.

If you want to keep *although* or *because,* drop the other linking word.

▶ Although the sales figures look impressive, ~~but~~ the company is

losing money.

▶ Because finance laws are not always enforced, ~~therefore~~ investing

in the former Soviet Union can be very risky.

If you want to keep the other linking word, omit *although* or *because.*

▶ ~~Because finance~~ Finance laws are not always enforced~~,~~; therefore,

investing in the former Soviet Union can be very risky.

▶ ~~Although the~~ The sales figures look impressive, but the company is

losing money.

For advice about using commas and semicolons with linking words, see P1-a and P3-b.

E2-f Do not place an adverb between a verb and its direct object.

Adverbs modifying verbs can appear in various positions:

- at the beginning or end of the sentence

  Slowly, we drove along the rain-slick road.

  Mother wrapped the gift *carefully.*

- before or after the verb

Martin *always* wins our tennis matches.

Christina is *rarely* late for our lunch dates.

- between a helping verb and a main verb

My daughter has *often* spoken of you.

The election results were being *closely* followed by analysts.

However, an adverb cannot appear between a verb and its direct object.

▶ Mother wrapped ~~carefully~~ the gift.
    carefully (^)

The adverb *carefully* may be placed at the beginning or at the end of this sentence or before the verb, *wrapped*. It cannot appear after the verb because the verb is followed by a direct object, *the gift*.

EXERCISE E2–2 Edit the following sentences for proper sentence structure. If a sentence is correct, write "correct" after it. Answers to lettered sentences appear in the back of the book. Example:

She peeled ~~slowly~~ the banana.
                  slowly. (^)

a. Although freshwater freezes at 32 degrees Fahrenheit, however ocean water freezes at 28 degrees Fahrenheit.

b. Because we switched Internet service providers, so our e-mail address has changed.

c. The competitor mounted confidently his skateboard and executed expertly a kickflip.

d. My sister performs well the *legong*, a Balinese dance.

e. Because product development is behind schedule, we will have to launch the product next spring.

1. The teller counted methodically the stack of one-dollar bills.

2. As I dashed toward shelter, I gasped when I saw the lightning strike repeatedly the barn.

3. Although hockey is traditionally a winter sport, but many towns offer skills programs all year.

4. Because salmon can survive in both freshwater and salt water, so they are classified as anadromous fish.

5. A surveyor determines precisely the boundaries between adjacent pieces of property.

E3

Articles and types of nouns

Articles (*a, an, the*) are part of a category of words known as *noun markers* or *determiners*. Standard English uses noun markers to help identify the nouns that follow. In addition to articles, noun markers include

- possessive nouns, such as *Elena's* (See P5-a.)
- possessive pronoun/adjectives: *my, your, his, her, its, our, their* (See B1-b.)
- demonstrative pronoun/adjectives: *this, that, these, those* (See B1-b.)
- quantifiers: *all, any, each, either, every, few, many, more, most, much, neither, several, some,* and so on (See E3-e.)
- numbers: *one, two,* and so on

ON THE WEB > dianahacker.com/writersref
Grammar exercises > ESL challenges > E-ex E3–1 and E3–2

E3-a Be familiar with articles and other noun markers.

Articles and other noun markers always appear before nouns. If you use an adjective with a noun, put the article before the adjective.

ART N
Felix is reading a book about mythology.

ART ADJ N
We took an exciting trip to Alaska last summer.

In most cases, do not use an article with another noun marker, such as *Natalie's* or *this.*

▶ When did you buy ~~the~~ this round pine table?

▶ ~~The~~ Natalie's older brother lives in Wisconsin.

Types of articles

Indefinite articles

Indefinite articles (*a, an*) are used with nouns that are not specific. See E3-d.

a   *A* means "one" or "one among many." Use *a* before a consonant sound: *a banana, a tree, a picture, a hand, a happy child.*

an   *An* also means "one" or "one among many." Use *an* before a vowel sound: *an eggplant, an occasion, an uncle, an hour, an honorable person.*

NOTE: Words beginning with *h* and *u* can have either a consonant sound (*a hand, a happy baby, a university, a union*) or a vowel sound (*an hour, an honorable person, an umbrella, an uncle*). (See also W1.)

Definite article

The definite article (*the*) is used with specific nouns. See E3-c.

the   *The* makes nouns specific; it does not refer to a number or amount. Use *the* with one or more than one specific thing: *the newspaper, the soldiers.*

EXCEPTION: Expressions like *a few, the most,* and *all the* are exceptions. See E3-e.

Did you bring *all the books* with you?

We got *the most snow* ever in January.

E3-b Understand the different types of nouns.

To choose an appropriate article for a noun, you must first determine whether the noun is common or proper, specific or general, count or noncount, and singular or plural.

Common or proper

Common nouns name general persons, places, things, or ideas. Proper nouns, which are marked in English with capital letters, name specific persons, places, things, or ideas. (See also M3.)

- common: religion, student, country
- proper: Hinduism, Philip, Vietnam

Specific (definite) or general (indefinite)

Specific or definite nouns represent persons, places, things, or ideas that can be identified within a group of nouns of the same type. General or indefinite nouns represent whole categories in general; they can also name nonspecific persons, places, things, or ideas that represent a group.

SPECIFIC	The *students* in Professor Martin's class should study harder. [The specific students in the class]
GENERAL	*Students* should study. [All students, students in general]
SPECIFIC	The *airplane* carrying Senator Chen took off at 1:30. [The specific airplane carrying the senator]
GENERAL	The *airplane* has made commuting between major cities easy. [All airplanes as a category of transportation]

Count or noncount

Count nouns refer to persons, places, things, or ideas that can be counted. Only count nouns have plural forms. Noncount nouns refer to things or abstract ideas that cannot be counted or made plural.

- count: *one girl, two girls*; *one city, three cities*; *one goose, four geese*; *one philosophy, five philosophies*
- noncount: *water, silver, air, furniture, patience, knowledge*

Some nouns can be used in both a count and a noncount sense.

COUNT	NONCOUNT
I'll have *a coffee.*	I'll have *coffee.*
There are many *democracies* in the world.	We learned that *democracy* originated in ancient Greece.

Some nouns (such as *advice* and *information*) may be countable in some languages but not in English. If you do not know whether a noun is count or noncount, refer to the chart on page 270 or consult an ESL dictionary.

Singular or plural

Singular nouns represent one person, place, thing, or idea; plural nouns represent more than one. Only count nouns can be made plural. (For more information on forming plural nouns, see M1-a.)

- singular: *backpack, country, woman, achievement*
- plural: *backpacks, countries, women, achievements*

GRAMMAR CHECKERS rarely flag missing or misused articles. They cannot distinguish when *a* or *an* is appropriate and when *the* is correct, nor can they tell when an article is missing.

E3-c Use *the* with most specific common nouns.

The definite article *the* is used with most nouns—both count and noncount—that the reader can identify specifically. Usually the identity will be clear to the reader for one of the following reasons.

1. The noun has been previously mentioned.

▶ A truck cut in front of our van. When ~~the~~ truck skidded a few seconds

later, we almost crashed into it.

The article *A* is used before *truck* when the noun is first mentioned. When the noun is mentioned again, it needs the article *the* because readers can now identify which truck skidded.

Commonly used noncount nouns

Food and drink

beef, bread, butter, candy, cereal, cheese, cream, meat, milk, pasta, rice, salt, sugar, water, wine

Nonfood substances

air, cement, coal, dirt, gasoline, gold, paper, petroleum, plastic, rain, silver, snow, soap, steel, wood, wool

Abstract nouns

advice, anger, beauty, confidence, courage, employment, fun, happiness, health, honesty, information, intelligence, knowledge, love, poverty, satisfaction, wealth

Other

biology (and other areas of study), clothing, equipment, furniture, homework, jewelry, luggage, machinery, mail, money, news, poetry, pollution, research, scenery, traffic, transportation, violence, weather, work

NOTE: A few noncount nouns can also be used as count nouns: *You can't buy love. He had two loves: music and archery.*

2. A phrase or clause following the noun restricts its identity.

>   *the*
> ▶ Bryce warned me that͜ computer on his desk had just
>
> crashed.

The phrase *on his desk* identifies the specific computer.

NOTE: Descriptive adjectives do not necessarily make a noun specific. A specific noun is one that readers can identify within a group of nouns of the same type.

>   *a*
> ▶ If I win the lottery, I will buy ~~the~~ brand-new bright red
>
> sports car.

The reader cannot identify which specific brand-new bright red sports car the writer will buy. Even though *car* has many adjectives in front of it, it is a general noun in this sentence.

3. A superlative adjective such as *best* or *most intelligent* makes the noun's identity specific. (See also G4-c on comparatives and superlatives.)

>   *the*
> ▶ Our petite daughter dated͜ tallest boy in her class.

The superlative *tallest* makes the noun *boy* specific. Although there might be several tall boys, only one boy can be the tallest.

4. The noun describes a unique person, place, or thing.

>   *the*
> ▶ During an eclipse, one should not look directly at͜ sun.

There is only one sun in our solar system, so its identity is clear.

5. The context or situation makes the noun's identity clear.

>   *the*
> ▶ Please don't slam͜ door when you leave.

Both the speaker and the listener know which door is meant.

6. The noun is singular and refers to a scientific class or category of items (most often animals, musical instruments, and inventions).

>   *The assembly*
> ▶ ͜~~Assembly~~ line transformed manufacturing in America.

The writer is referring to the assembly line as an invention.

Choosing articles for common nouns

This chart summarizes the most frequent uses of articles with common nouns. For help choosing articles with proper nouns, see E3-g.

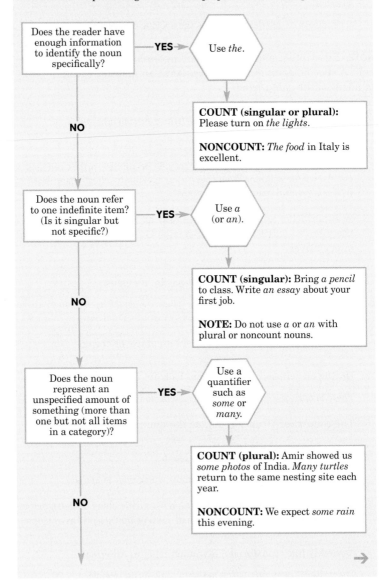

Does the reader have enough information to identify the noun specifically?

YES → Use *the*.

COUNT (singular or plural): Please turn on *the lights*.

NONCOUNT: *The food* in Italy is excellent.

NO

Does the noun refer to one indefinite item? (Is it singular but not specific?)

YES → Use *a* (or *an*).

COUNT (singular): Bring *a pencil* to class. Write *an essay* about your first job.

NOTE: Do not use *a* or *an* with plural or noncount nouns.

NO

Does the noun represent an unspecified amount of something (more than one but not all items in a category)?

YES → Use a quantifier such as *some* or *many*.

COUNT (plural): Amir showed us *some photos* of India. *Many turtles* return to the same nesting site each year.

NONCOUNT: We expect *some rain* this evening.

NO

*A singular count noun is occasionally used with *the* to refer to all items in a class or a specific category. See E3-f.

E3-d Use *a* (or *an*) with common singular count nouns that refer to "one" or "any."

If a count noun refers to one unspecific item (not a whole category), use the indefinite article *a* (or *an*). *A* and *an* usually mean "one among many" but can also mean "any one."

▶ My English professor asked me to bring $\overset{a}{\wedge}$dictionary to class.

The noun *dictionary* refers to "one unspecific dictionary" or "any dictionary."

▶ We want to rent $\overset{an}{\wedge}$apartment close to the lake.

The noun *apartment* refers to "any apartment close to the lake," not a specific apartment.

E3-e Use a quantifier such as *some* or *more*, not *a* (or *an*), with a noncount noun to express an approximate amount.

Do not use *a* (or *an*) with noncount nouns. Also do not use numbers or words such as *several* or *many* because they must be used with plural nouns, and noncount nouns do not have plural forms.

▶ Dr. Snyder gave us ~~an~~ information about the Peace Corps.

▶ Do you have ~~many~~ money with you?

You can use quantifiers such as the following to suggest approximate amounts or nonspecific quantities of noncount nouns.

QUANTIFIER	NONCOUNT NOUN
a little	salt, rain, knowledge, time
any	sugar, homework
enough	bread, wood, money
less	meat, violence
more	coffee, information
much (*or* a lot of)	snow, pollution
plenty of	paper, lumber
some	tea, news, work

▶ Claudia's mother told her that she had *some* ~~a~~ news that would surprise her.

E3-f Do not use articles with nouns that refer to all of something or something in general.

When a noncount noun refers to all of its type or to a concept in general, it is not marked with an article.

▶ ~~The~~ *Kindness* ~~kindness~~ is a virtue.

The noun represents kindness in general; it does not represent a specific type of kindness.

▶ In some parts of the world, ~~the~~ rice is preferred to all other grains.

The noun *rice* represents rice in general, not a specific type or serving of rice.

In most cases, when you use a count noun to represent a general category, make the noun plural. Do not use unmarked singular count nouns to represent whole categories.

▶ *Fountains are* ~~Fountain is~~ an expensive element of landscape design.

Fountains is a count noun that represents fountains in general.

EXCEPTION: In some cases, *the* can be used with singular count nouns to represent a class or specific category: *The American alligator is no longer listed as an endangered species.* Also see number 6 in E3-c.

E3-g Do not use articles with most singular proper nouns. Use *the* with most plural proper nouns.

Since singular proper nouns are already specific, they typically do not need an article: *Prime Minister Blair, Jamaica, Lake Huron, Mount Etna.*

There are, however, many exceptions. In most cases, if the proper noun consists of a common noun with modifiers (adjectives or an *of* phrase), use *the* with the proper noun.

Using *the* with geographical nouns

When to omit *the*

streets, squares, parks	Ivy Street, Union Square, Denali National Park
cities, states, counties	Miami, New Mexico, Bee County
most countries, continents	Italy, Nigeria, China, South America, Africa
bays, single lakes	Tampa Bay, Lake Geneva
single mountains, islands	Mount Everest, Crete

When to use *the*

country names with *of* phrase	the United States (of America), the People's Republic of China
large regions, deserts	the East Coast, the Sahara
peninsulas	the Iberian Peninsula, the Sinai Peninsula
oceans, seas, gulfs	the Pacific Ocean, the Dead Sea, the Persian Gulf
canals and rivers	the Panama Canal, the Amazon
mountain ranges	the Rocky Mountains, the Alps
groups of islands	the Solomon Islands

► We visited *the* Great Wall of China last year.

► Rob wants to be a translator for *the* Central Intelligence Agency.

The is used with most plural proper nouns: *the McGregors, the Bahamas, the Finger Lakes, the United States.*

Geographical names create problems because there are so many exceptions to the rules. When in doubt, consult the chart on page 275, check a dictionary, or ask a native speaker.

EXERCISE E3–1 Edit the following sentences for proper use of articles and nouns. If a sentence is correct, write "correct" after it. Answers to lettered sentences appear in the back of the book. Example:

~~The~~ Josefina's dance routine was flawless.

a. Doing volunteer work often brings a satisfaction.
b. As I looked out the window of the plane, I could see the Cape Cod.
c. Melina likes to drink her coffees with lots of cream.
d. Recovering from abdominal surgery requires patience.
e. I completed the my homework assignment quickly.

1. The attorney argued that her client should receive a money for emotional suffering.
2. Please check to see if there is a mail in the mailbox.
3. The Times Square in New York City is known for its billboards and theaters.
4. A cement is one of the components in concrete.
5. I took all the boys on the roller coaster after lunch.

EXERCISE E3–2 Articles have been omitted from the following story, adapted from *Zen Flesh, Zen Bones,* compiled by Paul Reps. Insert the articles *a, an,* and *the* where English requires them, and be prepared to explain the reasons for your choices.

Moon Cannot Be Stolen

Ryokan, who was Zen master, lived simple life in little hut at foot of mountain. One evening thief visited hut only to discover there was nothing in it to steal.

Ryokan returned and caught him. "You may have come long way to visit me," he told prowler, "and you should not return empty-handed. Please take my clothes as gift." Thief was bewildered. He took Ryokan's clothes and slunk away. Ryokan sat naked, watching moon. "Poor fellow," he mused. "I wish I could give him this beautiful moon."

E4

Using adjectives

E4-a Distinguish between present participles and past participles used as adjectives.

Both present and past participles may be used as adjectives. The present participle always ends in *-ing*. Past participles usually end in *-ed, -d, -en, -n,* or *-t.* (See G2-a.)

PRESENT PARTICIPLES   confusing, speaking, boring

PAST PARTICIPLES   confused, spoken, bored

Like all other adjectives, participles can come before nouns; they also can follow linking verbs, in which case they describe the subject of the sentence. (See B2-b.)

ADJ   N
It was a depressing movie.

V   ADJ
The movie was depressing.

The *confused tourists* stared at the map.

The *tourists* were *confused* by the map.

Use a present participle to describe a person or thing *causing or stimulating an experience.*

The *boring lecture* put us to sleep. [The lecture caused boredom; it didn't experience it.]

Use a past participle to describe a person or thing *undergoing an experience.*

The *audience* was *bored* by the lecture. [The audience experienced boredom; it didn't cause boredom.]

Participles that describe emotions or mental states often cause the most confusion.

▶ Our hike was ~~exhausted.~~
      exhausting.

Exhausting describes how the hike made us feel.

▶ The ~~exhausting~~ hikers reached camp at sunset.
      exhausted

Exhausted describes how the hikers felt.

Choosing the present or past participle

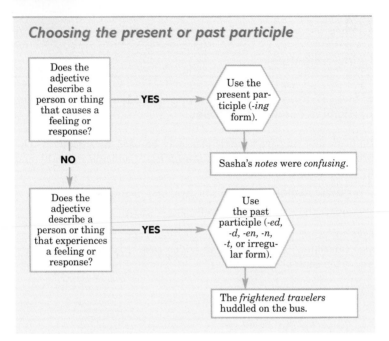

Does the adjective describe a person or thing that causes a feeling or response? —— **YES** ——> Use the present participle (-*ing* form).

NO

Sasha's *notes* were *confusing*.

Does the adjective describe a person or thing that experiences a feeling or response? —— **YES** ——> Use the past participle (-*ed*, -*d, -en, -n, -t,* or irregular form).

The *frightened travelers* huddled on the bus.

The chart at the top of this page can help you use these participles correctly.

annoying/annoyed   exhausting/exhausted
boring/bored   fascinating/fascinated
confusing/confused   frightening/frightened
depressing/depressed   satisfying/satisfied
exciting/excited   surprising/surprised

> ✓ GRAMMAR CHECKERS do not flag problems with present and past participles used as adjectives. Not surprisingly, the programs have no way of knowing the meaning a writer intends.

EXERCISE E4–1 Edit the following sentences for proper use of present and past participles. If a sentence is correct, write "correct" after it. Answers to lettered sentences appear in the back of the book. Example:

excited
Danielle and Monica were very ~~exciting~~ to be going to a
                                    ^
Broadway show for the first time.

a. Listening to everyone's complaints all day was irritated.
b. The long flight to Singapore was exhausted.
c. His skill at chess is amazing.
d. After several years of painstaking research, the scientist made a fascinated discovery.
e. That blackout was one of the most frightened experiences I've ever
   had.

1. I couldn't concentrate on my homework because I was distracted.
2. The directions to the new board game seem extremely complicating.
3. How interested are you in visiting Civil War battlefields?
4. The aerial view of the devastated villages was depressing.
5. Even after the lecturer went over the main points again, the students
   were still confusing.

ON THE WEB > dianahacker.com/writersref
Grammar exercises > ESL challenges > E-ex E4–1 and E4–2

E4-b Place cumulative adjectives in an appropriate order.

Adjectives usually come before the nouns that they modify and may
also come after linking verbs. (See B1-d, B1-e, and B2-b.)

ADJ   N   V   ADJ
Janine wore a new necklace. Janine's necklace was new.

Cumulative adjectives, which cannot be joined by the word *and*
or separated by commas, must come in a particular order. If you use
cumulative adjectives before a noun, see the chart on page 280. The
chart is only a guide; don't be surprised if you encounter exceptions.
(See also P2-d.)

smelly red plastic
► My dorm room has only a small desk and a ~~plastic red smelly~~
                                           ^
chair.

clear blue
► Nice weather, ~~blue clear~~ water, and ancient monuments attract
                ^
many people to Italy.

Order of cumulative adjectives

FIRST   **ARTICLE OR OTHER NOUN MARKER**   a, an, the, her, Joe's, two, many, some

       EVALUATIVE WORD   attractive, dedicated, delicious, ugly, disgusting

       SIZE   large, enormous, small, little

       LENGTH OR SHAPE   long, short, round, square

       AGE   new, old, young, antique

       COLOR   yellow, blue, crimson

       NATIONALITY   French, Peruvian, Vietnamese

       RELIGION   Catholic, Protestant, Jewish, Muslim

       MATERIAL   silver, walnut, wool, marble

LAST   **NOUN/ADJECTIVE**   tree (as in *tree* house)

THE NOUN MODIFIED   house, sweater, bicycle, bread, woman, priest

My long green wool coat is in the attic.

Ana's collection includes *four small antique silver* coins.

EXERCISE E4–2 Using the chart at the top of this page, arrange the following modifiers and nouns in their proper order. Answers to lettered items appear in the back of the book. Example:

> *two new French racing bicycles*
> **new, French, two, bicycles, racing**

   a. woman, young, an, Vietnamese, attractive
   b. dedicated, a, priest, Catholic
   c. old, her, sweater, blue, wool
   d. delicious, Joe's, Scandinavian, bread
   e. many, boxes, jewelry, antique, beautiful

   1. oval, nine, brass, lamps, miniature
   2. several, yellow, tulips, tiny
   3. the, tree, gingko, yellow, ancient, Mongolian
   4. courtyard, a, square, small, brick
   5. charming, restaurants, Italian, several

E5

Prepositions and idiomatic expressions

E5-a Become familiar with prepositions that show time and place.

The most frequently used prepositions in English are *at, by, for, from, in, of, on, to,* and *with.* Prepositions can be difficult to master because the differences among them are subtle and idiomatic. The following chart is limited to three troublesome prepositions that show time and place: *at, on,* and *in.*

At, on, *and* in *to show time and place*

Showing time

AT   *at* a specific time: *at* 7:20, *at* dawn, *at* dinner

ON   *on* a specific day or date: *on* Tuesday, *on* June 4

IN   *in* a part of a 24-hour period: *in* the afternoon, *in* the daytime [but *at* night]

      in a year or month: *in* 1999, *in* July

      in a period of time: finished *in* three hours

Showing place

AT   *at* a meeting place or location: *at* home, *at* the club

      at the edge of something: sitting *at* the desk

      at the corner of something: turning *at* the intersection

      at a target: throwing the snowball *at* Lucy

ON   *on* a surface: placed *on* the table, hanging *on* the wall

      on a street: the house *on* Spring Street

      on an electronic medium: *on* television, *on* the Internet

IN   *in* an enclosed space: *in* the garage, *in* an envelope

      in a geographic location: *in* San Diego, *in* Texas

      in a print medium: *in* a book, *in* a magazine

Not every possible use is listed in the chart, so don't be surprised when you encounter exceptions and idiomatic uses that you must learn one at a time. For example, in English we ride *in* a car but *on* a bus, plane, train, or subway.

▶ My first class starts ~~on~~ 8:00 a.m.
  <small>*at*</small>

▶ The farmers go to market ~~in~~ Wednesday.
  <small>*on*</small>

▶ I want to work at one of the biggest companies ~~on~~ the world.
  <small>*in*</small>

ON THE WEB > dianahacker.com/writersref
Grammar exercises > ESL challenges > E-ex E5–1

EXERCISE E5–1 In the following sentences, replace prepositions that are not used correctly. If a sentence is correct, write "correct" after it. Answers to lettered sentences appear in the back of the book. Example:

> The play begins ~~on~~ 7:20 p.m.
> <small>*at*</small>

a. Whenever we eat at the Centerville Diner, we sit at a small table on the corner of the room.

b. At the beginning of the dotcom wave, students created new businesses in record numbers.

c. In Thursday, Nancy will attend her first Pilates class at the community center.

d. Alex began looking for her lost mitten in another location.

e. We decided to go to a restaurant because there was no fresh food on the refrigerator.

1. I don't feel safe walking on my neighborhood in night.

2. If the train is on time, it will arrive on six o'clock at the morning.

3. In the corner of the room is a large bookcase with a pair of small Russian dolls standing at the top shelf.

4. She licked the stamp, stuck it in the envelope, put the envelope on her pocket, and walked to the nearest mailbox.

5. The mailbox was in the intersection of Park Avenue and Oak Street.

E5-b Use nouns (including *-ing* forms) after prepositions.

In a prepositional phrase, use a noun (not a verb) after the preposition. Sometimes the noun will be a gerund, the *-ing* verb form that functions as a noun (see B3-b).

>   *saving*
> ▶ Our student government is good at ~~save~~ money.

Distinguish between the preposition *to* and the infinitive marker *to*. If *to* is a preposition, it should be followed by a noun or a gerund.

>   *helping*
> ▶ We are dedicated to ~~help~~ the poor.

If *to* is an infinitive marker, it should be followed by the base form of the verb.

>   *help*
> ▶ We want to ~~helping~~ the poor.

TIP: To test whether *to* is a preposition or an infinitive marker, insert a word that you know is a noun after the word *to*. If the noun sounds right in that position, *to* is a preposition.

>   Zoe is addicted to _____.

In this case, a noun (such as *magazines*) makes sense after *to*, so *to* is a preposition and should be followed by a noun or a gerund: *Zoe is addicted to magazines. Zoe is addicted to reading.*

>   They are planning to _____.

In this case, a noun (such as *house*) does not make sense after *to*, so *to* is an infinitive marker and must be followed by the base form of the verb: *They are planning to build a new house.*

E5-c Become familiar with common adjective + preposition combinations.

Some adjectives appear only with certain prepositions. These expressions are idiomatic and may be different from the combinations used in your native language.

>   *to*
> ▶ Paula is married ~~with~~ Jon.

Check an ESL dictionary for combinations that are not listed in the chart on page 284.

Adjective + preposition combinations

accustomed to	connected to	interested in	proud of
addicted to	covered with	involved in	responsible for
afraid of	dedicated to	involved with	satisfied with
angry with	devoted to	known as	scared of
ashamed of	different from	known for	similar to
aware of	engaged to	made of (*or*	tired of
committed to	excited about	made from)	worried about
concerned about	familiar with	married to	
concerned with	full of	opposed to	
	guilty of	preferable to	

E5-d Become familiar with common verb + preposition combinations.

Many verbs and prepositions appear together in idiomatic phrases. Pay special attention to the combinations that are different from the combinations used in your native language.

> ►　Your success depends ~~of~~ your effort.
>
> *on*

　　Check an ESL dictionary for combinations that are not listed in the following chart.

Verb + preposition combinations

agree with	compare with	forget about	speak to (*or* speak with)
apply to	concentrate on	happen to	stare at
approve of	consist of	hope for	succeed at
arrive in	count on	insist on	succeed in
arrive at	decide on	listen to	take advantage of
ask for	depend on	participate in	take care of
believe in	differ from	rely on	think about
belong to	disagree with	reply to	think of
care about	dream about	respond to	wait for
care for	dream of	result in	wait on
compare to	feel like	search for	

P

Punctuation

P Punctuation

P1

The comma

The comma was invented to help readers. Without it, sentence parts can collide into one another unexpectedly, causing misreadings.

CONFUSING   If you cook Elmer will do the dishes.

CONFUSING   While we were eating a rattlesnake approached our campsite.

Add commas in the logical places (after *cook* and *eating*), and suddenly all is clear. No longer is Elmer being cooked, the rattlesnake being eaten.

Various rules have evolved to prevent such misreadings and to speed readers along through complex grammatical structures. Those rules are detailed in this section.

GRAMMAR CHECKERS rarely flag missing or misused commas. They sometimes recognize that a comma belongs before a *which* clause but not before a *that* clause (see P1-e). For all other uses of the comma — after introductory word groups, between items in a series, between coordinate adjectives, around appositives, and so on — they are unreliable. When a grammar checker does note a missing comma, its suggested revision is often incorrect and sometimes even amusing. One program, for example, suggested a comma after the word *delivery* in the following sentence: *While I was driving a huge delivery truck ran through a red light.*

P1-a Use a comma before a coordinating conjunction joining independent clauses.

When a coordinating conjunction connects two or more independent clauses — word groups that could stand alone as separate sentences — a comma must precede it. There are seven coordinating conjunctions in English: *and, but, or, nor, for, so,* and *yet.*

A comma tells readers that one independent clause has come to a close and that another is about to begin.

▶ Nearly everyone has heard of love at first sight‸but I fell in love at first dance.

EXCEPTION: If the two independent clauses are short and there is no danger of misreading, the comma may be omitted.

The plane took off and we were on our way.

TIP: As a rule, do *not* use a comma to separate coordinate word groups that are not independent clauses. (See P2-a.)

▶ A good money manager controls expenses⁄and invests surplus dollars to meet future needs.

The word group following *and* is not an independent clause; it is the second half of a compound predicate.

EXERCISE P1–1 Add or delete commas where necessary in the following sentences. If a sentence is correct, write "correct" after it. Answers to lettered sentences appear in the back of the book. Example:

Negative campaigning is designed to make an opponent look bad‸ and it usually takes the focus away from relevant issues.

a. *Chinatown* is generally considered to be part of the hard-boiled detective genre, but it contains many conventions that make it unlike other detective films.
b. As an intern, I learned about all aspects of the broadcasting industry, and trained specifically in fundraising efforts.
c. J. R. R. Tolkien finished writing his draft of *The Lord of the Rings* trilogy in 1949 but the first book in the series wasn't published until 1954.
d. German shepherds can be gentle guide dogs or they can be fierce attack dogs.
e. Some former professional cyclists claim that performance-enhancing drug use is widespread in cycling and they argue that no rider can be competitive without doping.

1. Reptiles are cold-blooded, and are covered with scales.
2. The low-key lighting effect known as *chiaroscuro* was first used in German Expressionist filmmaking, and was later seen in American film noir.
3. Freedom is an important value for many Americans, so it is a central theme in much of our political rhetoric.
4. Advertisers use a variety of techniques to grab the audience's attention and to imprint their messages into consumers' minds.

5. Many musicians of Bach's time played several instruments but few mastered them as early or played with as much expression as Bach.

P1-b Use a comma after an introductory word group.

The most common introductory word groups are clauses and phrases functioning as adverbs. Such word groups usually tell when, where, how, why, or under what conditions the main action of the sentence occurred. (See B3-a, B3-b, and B3-e.)

A comma tells readers that the introductory clause or phrase has come to a close and that the main part of the sentence is about to begin.

▶ When Irwin was ready to iron, his cat tripped on the cord.

Without the comma, readers may have Irwin ironing his cat. The comma signals that *his cat* is the subject of a new clause, not part of the introductory one.

▶ Near a small stream at the bottom of the canyon, the park

rangers discovered an abandoned mine.

The comma tells readers that the introductory prepositional phrase has come to a close.

EXCEPTION: The comma may be omitted after a short adverb clause or phrase if there is no danger of misreading.

In no time we were at 2,800 feet.

Sentences also frequently begin with participial phrases describing the noun or pronoun immediately following them. The comma tells readers that they are about to learn the identity of the person or thing described; therefore, the comma is usually required even when the phrase is short. (See also B3-b.)

▶ Thinking his motorcade drive through Dallas was routine,

President Kennedy smiled and waved at the crowds.

▶ Buried under layers of younger rocks, the earth's oldest rocks

contain no fossils.

NOTE: Other introductory word groups include transitional expressions and absolute phrases. (See P1-f.)

EXERCISE P1–2 Add or delete commas where necessary in the following sentences. If a sentence is correct, write "correct" after it. Answers to lettered sentences appear in the back of the book. Example:

> **Because we had been saving molding for a few weeks, we had**
>
> **enough wood to frame all thirty paintings.**

a. Considered a classic of early animation *The Adventures of Prince Achmed* used hand-cut silhouettes against colored backgrounds.

b. In the first two minutes of its ascent, the space shuttle had broken the sound barrier and reached a height of over twenty-five miles.

c. If you complete the enclosed evaluation form, you will receive a free breakfast during your next stay.

d. After retiring from the New York City Ballet in 1965 legendary dancer Maria Tallchief went on to found the Chicago City Ballet.

e. Because the car had been sitting idle for so long the battery was completely dead.

1. After successfully navigating the dangerous rapids, we sat back and drifted on more tranquil waters.

2. To be considered for the position candidates must demonstrate initiative and strong communication skills.

3. Lit by bright halogen lamps hundreds of origami cranes sparkled like diamonds in the sunlight.

4. Preying on the ignorance of the public, advertisers insist that antibacterial hand soaps are the best way to prevent the spread of disease.

5. By the end of the first quarter the operating budget will be available online.

P1-c   Use a comma between all items in a series.

When three or more items are presented in a series, those items should be separated from one another with commas. Items in a series may be single words, phrases, or clauses.

> ► **Bubbles of air, leaves, ferns, bits of wood, and insects are often**
>
> **found trapped in amber.**

Although some publications omit the comma between the last two items, be aware that its omission can result in ambiguity or misreading.

▶ My uncle willed me all of his property, houses, and warehouses.

Did the uncle will his property *and* houses *and* warehouses — or simply his property, consisting of houses and warehouses? If the first meaning is intended, a comma is necessary to prevent ambiguity.

▶ The activities include a search for lost treasure, dubious

financial dealings, much discussion of ancient heresies, and

midnight orgies.

Without the comma, the people seem to be discussing orgies, not participating in them. The comma makes it clear that *midnight orgies* is a separate item in the series.

ON THE WEB > dianahacker.com/writersref
Language Debates > Commas with items in a series

EXERCISE P1–3 Add or delete commas where necessary in the following sentences. If a sentence is correct, write "correct" after it. Answers to lettered sentences appear in the back of the book. Example:

Good social workers excel in patience, diplomacy, and positive

thinking.

a. A baseball player achieves the triple crown by having the highest batting average, the most home runs, and the most runs batted in during the regular season.
b. A complete diagnostic of the system revealed that the trouble was neither electrical, nor mechanical.
c. Love, vengeance, greed and betrayal are common themes in Western literature.
d. Two increasingly popular sources of alternative energy are solar panels that are installed in homes or office buildings and wind farms in open areas.
e. In Sherman's march to the sea, the Union army set fire to all crops, killed all livestock and destroyed all roads and bridges in its path.

1. The film's primary message is that global warming is real, it is the result of human activity, and it should not be ignored.
2. For breakfast the children ordered cornflakes, English muffins with peanut butter and cherry Cokes.
3. At the age of twenty-two, my father graduated from college, got married and joined the military.

4. After two broken arms, three cracked ribs and one concussion, Ken quit the varsity football team.

5. Animation master Hironobu Sakaguchi makes computer-generated scenes look realistic, vivid and seductive.

P1-d Use a comma between coordinate adjectives not joined by *and*. Do not use a comma between cumulative adjectives.

When two or more adjectives each modify a noun separately, they are *coordinate*.

> Roberto is a *warm, gentle, affectionate* father.

Adjectives are coordinate if they can be joined with *and* (warm *and* gentle *and* affectionate).

Two or more adjectives that do not modify the noun separately are cumulative.

> *Three large gray* shapes moved slowly toward us.

Beginning with the adjective closest to the noun *shapes,* these modifiers lean on one another, piggyback style, with each modifying a larger word group. *Gray* modifies *shapes, large* modifies *gray shapes,* and *three* modifies *large gray shapes.* Cumulative adjectives cannot be joined with *and* (three *and* large *and* gray shapes).

COORDINATE ADJECTIVES

▶ Patients with severe‸ irreversible brain damage should not be put

on life support systems.

CUMULATIVE ADJECTIVES

▶ Ira ordered a rich⁄chocolate⁄layer cake.

EXERCISE P1–4 Add or delete commas where necessary in the following sentences. If a sentence is correct, write "correct" after it. Answers to lettered sentences appear in the back of the book. Example:

> The cold‸ impersonal atmosphere of the office was unbearable.

a. NASA's rovers on Mars are equipped with special cameras that can take close-up high-resolution pictures of the terrain.
b. Teenage cliques expect absolute, unswerving loyalty from their members.

c. If it does not get enough sunlight, a healthy green lawn can turn into a shriveled brown mess within a matter of days.
d. Many experts believe that shark attacks on surfers are a result of the sharks' mistaking surfboards for small, injured seals.
e. Cyril was clad in a luminous orange rain suit and a brilliant white helmet.

1. Milk that comes from grass-fed steroid-free cows has been gaining market share.
2. The *1812 Overture* is a stirring, magnificent piece of music.
3. The three, handmade, turquoise bracelets brought in the most money at the charity auction.
4. Former athletes often suffer debilitating, joint pain late in life.
5. Matisse is well known for his vibrant colorful prints that have been reproduced extensively on greeting cards and posters.

P1-e Use commas to set off nonrestrictive elements. Do not use commas to set off restrictive elements.

Word groups describing nouns or pronouns (adjective clauses, adjective phrases, and appositives) are restrictive or nonrestrictive. A *restrictive* element defines or limits the meaning of the word it modifies and is therefore essential to the meaning of the sentence. Because it contains essential information, a restrictive element is not set off with commas.

RESTRICTIVE For camp the children need clothes *that are washable.*

If you remove a restrictive element from a sentence, the meaning changes significantly, becoming more general than you intended. The writer of the example sentence does not mean that the children need clothes in general. The intended meaning is more limited: The children need *washable* clothes.

A *nonrestrictive* element describes a noun or pronoun whose meaning has already been clearly defined or limited. Because it contains nonessential or parenthetical information, a nonrestrictive element is set off with commas.

NONRESTRICTIVE For camp the children need sturdy shoes, *which are expensive.*

If you remove a nonrestrictive element from a sentence, the meaning does not change dramatically. Some meaning is lost, to be sure, but the defining characteristics of the person or thing described remain the same as before. The children need *sturdy shoes,* and these happen to be expensive.

NOTE: Often it is difficult to tell whether a word group is restrictive or nonrestrictive without seeing it in context and considering the writer's meaning. Both of the following sentences are grammatically correct, but their meaning is slightly different.

> The dessert made with fresh raspberries was delicious.

> The dessert, made with fresh raspberries, was delicious.

In the example without commas, the phrase *made with fresh raspberries* tells readers which of two or more desserts the writer is referring to. In the example with commas, the phrase merely adds information about the particular dessert.

Adjective clauses

Adjective clauses are patterned like sentences, containing subjects and verbs, but they function within sentences as modifiers of nouns or pronouns. They always follow the word they modify, usually immediately. Adjective clauses begin with a relative pronoun (*who, whom, whose, which, that*) or with a relative adverb (*where, when*).

Nonrestrictive adjective clauses are set off with commas; restrictive adjective clauses are not.

NONRESTRICTIVE CLAUSE

▶ Ed's house‸which is located on thirteen acres‸was furnished

with bats in the rafters and mice in the kitchen.

The clause *which is located on thirteen acres* does not restrict the meaning of *Ed's house,* so the information is nonessential.

RESTRICTIVE CLAUSE

▶ Ramona's cat⁄ that just had kittens⁄ became defensive around the

other cats in the house.

Because the adjective clause *that just had kittens* identifies the particular cat, the information is essential.

NOTE: Use *that* only with restrictive clauses. Many writers prefer to use *which* only with nonrestrictive clauses, but usage varies.

ON THE WEB > dianahacker.com/writersref
Language Debates > *that* versus *which*

Phrases functioning as adjectives

Prepositional or verbal phrases functioning as adjectives may be restrictive or nonrestrictive. Nonrestrictive phrases are set off with commas; restrictive phrases are not.

NONRESTRICTIVE PHRASE

► The helicopter͵with its million-candlepower spotlight

illuminating the area͵ circled above.

The *with* phrase is nonessential because its purpose is not to specify which of two or more helicopters is being discussed.

RESTRICTIVE PHRASE

► One corner of the attic was filled with newspapers͵/dating from

the turn of the century.

Dating from the turn of the century restricts the meaning of *newspapers,* so the comma should be omitted.

Appositives

An appositive is a noun or noun phrase that renames a nearby noun. Nonrestrictive appositives are set off with commas; restrictive appositives are not.

NONRESTRICTIVE APPOSITIVE

► Darwin's most important book͵ *On the Origin of Species͵* was the

result of many years of research.

Most important restricts the meaning to one book, so the appositive *On the Origin of Species* is nonrestrictive and should be set off with commas.

RESTRICTIVE APPOSITIVE

► The song͵/ "Vertigo͵/" was blasted out of huge amplifiers.

Once they've read *song,* readers still don't know precisely which song the writer means. The appositive following *song* restricts its meaning.

EXERCISE P1–5 Add or delete commas where necessary in the following sentences. If a sentence is correct, write "correct" after it. Answers to lettered sentences appear in the back of the book. Example:

My youngest sister, who plays left wing on the soccer
⌃
team, now lives at The Sands, a beach house near Los Angeles.
⌃   ⌃

a. Choreographer Alvin Ailey's best-known work *Revelations* is more than just a crowd pleaser.
b. Twyla Tharp's contemporary ballet *Push Comes to Shove* was made famous by Russian dancer Baryshnikov. [Tharp has written more than one contemporary ballet.]
c. The glass sculptor sifting through hot red sand explained her technique to the other glassmakers.
d. A member of an organization, that provides housing for AIDS patients, was also appointed to the commission.
e. Brian Eno who began his career as a rock musician turned to meditative compositions in the late seventies.

1. I had the pleasure of talking to a woman who had just returned from India where she had lived for ten years.
2. Patrick's oldest sister Fiona graduated from MIT with a degree in aerospace engineering.
3. The artist painting a portrait of Aung San Suu Kyi, the Burmese civil rights leader, was once a political prisoner himself.
4. *The Polar Express,* the 1986 Caldecott Medal winner, is my nephew's favorite book.
5. The flame crawled up a few blades of grass to reach a low-hanging palmetto branch which quickly ignited.

P1-f Use commas to set off transitional and parenthetical expressions, absolute phrases, and contrasted elements.

Transitional expressions

Transitional expressions serve as bridges between sentences or parts of sentences. They include conjunctive adverbs such as *however, therefore,* and *moreover* and transitional phrases such as *for example, as a matter of fact,* and *in other words.* (For more complete lists, see P3-b.)

When a transitional expression appears between independent clauses in a compound sentence, it is preceded by a semicolon and is usually followed by a comma.

▶ Minh did not understand our language; moreover, he was
⌃

unfamiliar with our customs.

When a transitional expression appears at the beginning of a sentence or in the middle of an independent clause, it is usually set off with commas.

► As a matter of fact‸ American football was established by fans

who wanted to play a more organized game of rugby.

► Natural foods are not always salt free; celery‸ for example‸

contains more sodium than most people would imagine.

EXCEPTION: If a transitional expression blends smoothly with the rest of the sentence, calling for little or no pause in reading, it does not need to be set off with commas. Expressions such as *also, at least, certainly, consequently, indeed, of course, no doubt, perhaps, then,* and *therefore* do not always call for a pause.

Alice's bicycle is broken; *therefore* you will need to borrow Sue's.

Alice's bicycle is broken; you will *therefore* need to borrow Sue's.

Parenthetical expressions

Expressions that are distinctly parenthetical should be set off with commas. Providing supplemental information, they interrupt the flow of a sentence or appear at the end as afterthoughts.

► Evolution‸ so far as we know‸ doesn't work this way.

► The bass weighed twelve pounds‸ give or take a few

ounces.

Absolute phrases

An absolute phrase, which modifies the whole sentence, usually consists of a noun followed by a participle or participial phrase. (See B3-d.) Absolute phrases may appear at the beginning or at the end of a sentence. Wherever they appear, they should be set off with commas.

► The sun appearing for the first time in a week‸ we were at last

able to begin the archaeological dig.

► Elvis Presley made music industry history in the 1950s‸ his

records having sold more than ten million copies.

TIP: Do not insert a comma between the noun and the participle in an absolute construction.

▶ The next contestant‸ being five years old, the emcee adjusted the

height of the microphone.

Contrasted elements

Sharp contrasts beginning with words such as *not, never,* and *unlike* are set off with commas.

▶ The Epicurean philosophers sought mental‸ not bodily‸pleasures.

▶ Unlike Robert‸Celia loved dance contests.

P1-g Use commas to set off nouns of direct address, the words *yes* and *no*, interrogative tags, and mild interjections.

▶ Forgive us‸Dr. Atkins‸for having rolls with dinner.

▶ Yes‸the loan will probably be approved.

▶ The film was faithful to the book‸wasn't it?

▶ Well‸cases like these are difficult to decide.

P1-h Use commas with expressions such as *he said* to set off direct quotations. (See also P6-f.)

▶ Naturalist Arthur Cleveland Bent once remarked‸ "In part

the peregrine declined unnoticed because it is not adorable."

▶ "Convictions are more dangerous foes of truth than lies‸" wrote

philosopher Friedrich Nietzsche.

P1-i Use commas with dates, addresses, titles, and numbers.

Dates

In dates, the year is set off from the rest of the sentence with a pair of commas.

▶ On December 12, 1890, orders were sent out for the arrest of
   Sitting Bull.

EXCEPTIONS: Commas are not needed if the date is inverted or if
only the month and year are given.

   The recycling plan went into effect on 15 April 2002.
   January 2004 was an extremely cold month.

Addresses

The elements of an address or a place name are separated by commas. A zip code, however, is not preceded by a comma.

▶ John Lennon was born in Liverpool, England, in 1940.

▶ Please send the package to Greg Tarvin at 708 Spring Street,
   Washington, Illinois 61571.

Titles

If a title follows a name, separate it from the rest of the sentence
with a pair of commas.

▶ Sandra Belinsky, MD, has been appointed to the board of
   trustees.

Numbers

In numbers more than four digits long, use commas to separate the
numbers into groups of three, starting from the right. In numbers
four digits long, a comma is optional.

       3,500 [or 3500]
     100,000
   5,000,000

EXCEPTIONS: Do not use commas in street numbers, zip codes, telephone numbers, or years.

P1-j Use a comma to prevent confusion.

In certain contexts, a comma is necessary to prevent confusion. If the writer has omitted a word or phrase, for example, a comma may be needed to signal the omission.

▶ To err is human; to forgive, divine.

If two words in a row echo each other, a comma may be needed for ease of reading.

▶ All of the catastrophes that we had feared might happen, happened.

Sometimes a comma is needed to prevent readers from grouping words in ways that do not match the writer's intention.

▶ Patients who can, walk up and down the halls several times a day.

EXERCISE P1–6 Major uses of the comma This exercise covers the major uses of the comma detailed in P1. Add or delete commas where necessary. If a sentence is correct, write "correct" after it. Answers to lettered sentences appear in the back of the book. Example:

Even though Pavel had studied Nigella Lawson's recipes for a

week, he underestimated how long it would take to juice

two hundred lemons.

a. Cricket, which originated in England is also popular in Australia, South Africa and India.
b. At the sound of the starting pistol the horses surged forward toward the first obstacle, a sharp incline three feet high.
c. After seeing an exhibition of Western art Gerhard Richter escaped from East Berlin, and smuggled out many of his notebooks.
d. Corrie's new wet suit has an intricate, blue pattern.
e. The cookies will keep for two weeks in sturdy airtight plastic containers.

1. Research on Andean condors has shown that high levels of the chemical pesticide chlorinated hydrocarbon can cause the thinning of eggshells.
2. Founded in 1868 Hampton University was one of the first colleges for African Americans.
3. Aunt Emilia was an impossible demanding guest.
4. The French Mirage, a high-tech fighter, is an astonishing machine to fly.
5. At the bottom of the ship's rusty hold sat several, well-preserved trunks, reminders of a bygone era of sea travel.

EXERCISE P1–7 **All uses of the comma** Add or delete commas where necessary in the following sentences. If a sentence is correct, write "correct" after it. Answers to lettered sentences appear in the back of the book. Example:

"Yes, dear, you can have dessert," my mother said.

    a. On January 15, 2004 our office moved to 29 Commonwealth Avenue, Mechanicsville VA 23111.
    b. The coach having bawled us out thoroughly, we left the locker room with his harsh words ringing in our ears.
    c. Ms. Carlson you are a valued customer whose satisfaction is very important to us.
    d. Mr. Mundy was born on July 22, 1939 in Arkansas, where his family had lived for four generations.
    e. Her board poised at the edge of the half-pipe, Nina waited her turn to drop in.

    1. President Lincoln's original intention was to save the Union, not to destroy slavery.
    2. For centuries people believed that Greek culture had developed in isolation from the world. Today however scholars are acknowledging the contributions made by Egypt and the Middle East.
    3. Putting together a successful fundraiser, Patricia discovered, requires creativity and good timing.
    4. Fortunately science is creating many alternatives to research performed on animals.
    5. While the machine was printing the oversize paper jammed.

ON THE WEB > dianahacker.com/writersref
Grammar exercises > Punctuation > E-ex P1–1 through P1–3

P2

Unnecessary commas

P2-a Do not use a comma between compound elements that are not independent clauses.

Though a comma should be used before a coordinating conjunction joining independent clauses (see P1-a), this rule should not be extended to other compound word groups.

▶ Marie Curie discovered radium,/and later applied her work on radioactivity to medicine.

And links two verbs in a compound predicate: *discovered* and *applied.*

▶ Jake still does not realize that his illness is serious,/and that he will have to alter his diet to improve.

And links two subordinate clauses, each beginning with *that.*

P2-b Do not use a comma to separate a verb from its subject or object.

A sentence should flow from subject to verb to object without unnecessary pauses. Commas may appear between these major sentence elements only when a specific rule calls for them.

▶ Zoos large enough to give the animals freedom to roam,/are becoming more popular.

The comma should not separate the subject, *zoos,* from the verb, *are becoming.*

▶ Francesca explained to him,/that she was busy and would see him later.

The comma should not separate the verb, *explained,* from its object, the subordinate clause *that she was busy and would see him later.*

P2-c Do not use a comma before the first or after the last item in a series.

Though commas are required between items in a series (see P1-c), do not place them either before or after the whole series.

▶ Other causes of asthmatic attacks are,/stress, change in temperature, and cold air.

▶ Ironically, this job that appears so glamorous, carefree, and easy,/carries a high degree of responsibility.

P2-d Do not use a comma between cumulative adjectives, between an adjective and a noun, or between an adverb and an adjective.

Though commas are required between coordinate adjectives (those that can be joined with *and*), they do not belong between cumulative adjectives (those that cannot be joined with *and*). (For a full discussion, see P1-d.)

▶ In the corner of the closet we found an old/ maroon hatbox from Sears.

A comma should never be used to separate an adjective from the noun that follows it.

▶ It was a senseless, dangerous/ mission.

Nor should a comma be used between an adverb and an adjective that follows it.

▶ The Hurst Home is unsuitable as a mental facility for severely/ disturbed youths.

P2-e Do not use commas to set off restrictive or mildly parenthetical elements.

Restrictive elements are modifiers or appositives that restrict the meaning of the nouns they follow. Because they are essential to the meaning of the sentence, they are not set off with commas. (For a full discussion, see P1-e.)

▶ Drivers/ who think they own the road/ make cycling a dangerous sport.

The modifier *who think they own the road* restricts the meaning of *Drivers* and is therefore essential to the meaning of the sentence. Putting commas around the *who* clause falsely suggests that all drivers think they own the road.

▶ Margaret Mead's book/ *Coming of Age in Samoa/* stirred up considerable controversy when it was published in 1928.

Since Mead wrote more than one book, the appositive contains information essential to the meaning of the sentence.

Although commas should be used with distinctly parenthetical expressions (see P1-f), do not use them to set off elements that are only mildly parenthetical.

▶ Charisse believes that the Internet is/ essentially/ one giant

billboard.

P2-f Do not use a comma to set off a concluding adverb clause that is essential to the meaning of the sentence.

When adverb clauses introduce a sentence, they are nearly always followed by a comma (see P1-b). When they conclude a sentence, however, they are not set off by commas if their content is essential to the meaning of the earlier part of the sentence. Adverb clauses beginning with *after, as soon as, before, because, if, since, unless, until,* and *when* are usually essential.

▶ Don't visit Paris at the height of the tourist season/ unless

you have booked hotel reservations.

Without the concluding *unless* clause, the meaning of the sentence would be broader than the writer intended.

When a concluding adverb clause is nonessential, it should be preceded by a comma. Clauses beginning with *although, even though, though,* and *whereas* are usually nonessential.

▶ The lecture seemed to last only a short time, although the clock

said it had gone on for more than an hour.

P2-g Avoid other common misuses of the comma.

Do not use a comma in the following situations.

AFTER A COORDINATING CONJUNCTION (*AND, BUT, OR, NOR, FOR, SO, YET*)

▶ I have an iPod, but/ I don't have a sound dock.

AFTER *SUCH AS* OR *LIKE*

▶ Many shade-loving plants, such as/ begonias, impatiens, and

coleus, can add color to a shady garden.

BEFORE *THAN*

▶ Touring Crete was more thrilling for us/ than visiting the Greek islands frequented by rich Europeans.

AFTER *ALTHOUGH*

▶ Although/ the air was balmy, the water was too cold for swimming.

BEFORE A PARENTHESIS

▶ At Nextel Sylvia began at the bottom/ (with only three and a half walls and a swivel chair), but within five years she had been promoted to supervisor.

TO SET OFF AN INDIRECT (REPORTED) QUOTATION

▶ Samuel Goldwyn once said/ that a verbal contract isn't worth the paper it's written on.

WITH A QUESTION MARK OR AN EXCLAMATION POINT

▶ "Why don't you try it?/" she coaxed.

EXERCISE P2–1 Delete commas where necessary in the following sentences. If a sentence is correct, write "correct" after it. Answers to lettered sentences appear in the back of the book. Example:

In his Silk Road Project, Yo-Yo Ma has incorporated work by musicians such as/ Kayhan Kahlor and Richard Danielpour.

a. After the morning rains cease, the swimmers emerge from their cottages.
b. Tricia's first artwork was a big, blue, clay dolphin.
c. Some modern musicians, (trumpeter John Hassell is an example) blend several cultural traditions into a unique sound.
d. Myra liked hot, spicy foods such as, chili, jambalaya, and buffalo wings.
e. On the display screen, was a soothing pattern of light and shadow.

1. Mesquite, the hardest of the softwoods, grows primarily in the Southwest.
2. Jolie's parents encouraged independent thinking, but required respect for others' opinions.
3. Miranda told her boss, that she had discovered a new plastic as strong as metal.

4. The streets that three hours later would be bumper to bumper with commuters, were quiet and empty except for a few prowling cats.

5. Some first-year architecture students, expect to design intricate structures immediately.

EXERCISE P2–2 Delete commas where necessary in the following passage.

Each spring since 1970, New Orleans has hosted the Jazz and Heritage Festival, an event that celebrates the music, food, and culture, of the region. Although, it is often referred to as "Jazz Fest," the festival typically includes a wide variety of musical styles such as, gospel, Cajun, blues, zydeco, and, rock and roll. Famous musicians who have appeared regularly at Jazz Fest, include Dr. John, B. B. King, and Aretha Franklin. Large stages are set up throughout the fairgrounds in a way, that allows up to ten bands to play simultaneously without any sound overlap. Food tents are located throughout the festival, and offer popular, local dishes like crawfish Monica, jambalaya, and fried, green tomatoes. In 2006, many doubted whether New Orleans could put on Jazz Fest, after the horrific destruction from Hurricane Katrina just six months before. But the festival went on as scheduled, and helped to raise spirits throughout the city by celebrating its great heritage.

ON THE WEB > dianahacker.com/writersref
Grammar exercises > Punctuation > E-ex P2–1

P3

The semicolon

The semicolon is used to connect major sentence elements of equal grammatical rank.

GRAMMAR CHECKERS flag some, but not all, misused semicolons (P3-d). In addition, they can alert you to some run-on sentences (G6). However, they miss more run-on sentences than they identify, and they sometimes flag correct sentences as possible run-ons. (See also the grammar checker advice in G6.)

P3-a Use a semicolon between closely related independent clauses not joined with a coordinating conjunction.

When related independent clauses appear in one sentence, they are ordinarily linked with a comma and a coordinating conjunction (*and, but, or, nor, for, so, yet*). The coordinating conjunction signals the relation between the clauses. If the clauses are closely related and the relation is clear without the conjunction, they may be linked with a semicolon instead.

> Injustice is relatively easy to bear; what stings is justice.
> — H. L. Mencken

A semicolon must be used whenever a coordinating conjunction has been omitted between independent clauses. To use merely a comma creates a kind of run-on sentence known as a comma splice. (See G6.)

▶ In 1800, a traveler needed six weeks to get from New York City to Chicago, in 1860, the trip by railroad took two days.

TIP: Do not overuse the semicolon as a means of revising run-on sentences. For other revision strategies, see G6.

P3-b Use a semicolon between independent clauses linked with a transitional expression.

Transitional expressions include conjunctive adverbs and transitional phrases.

CONJUNCTIVE ADVERBS

accordingly	finally	meanwhile	similarly
also	furthermore	moreover	specifically
anyway	hence	nevertheless	still
besides	however	next	subsequently
certainly	indeed	nonetheless	then
consequently	instead	now	therefore
conversely	likewise	otherwise	thus

TRANSITIONAL PHRASES

after all	even so	in fact
as a matter of fact	for example	in other words
as a result	for instance	in the first place
at any rate	in addition	on the contrary
at the same time	in conclusion	on the other hand

When a transitional expression appears between independent clauses, it is preceded by a semicolon and usually followed by a comma.

▶ Many corals grow very gradually ̸; in fact, the creation of a coral

reef can take centuries.

When a transitional expression appears in the middle or at the end of the second independent clause, the semicolon goes *between the clauses.*

Most singers gain fame through hard work and dedication; Evita, however, found other means.

Transitional expressions should not be confused with the coordinating conjunctions *and, but, or, nor, for, so,* and *yet,* which are preceded by a comma when they link independent clauses. (See P1-a and G6-a.)

P3-c Use a semicolon between items in a series containing internal punctuation.

▶ Classic science fiction sagas are *Star Trek,* with Mr. Spock

and his large pointed ears ̸; *Battlestar Galactica,* with its Cylon

Raiders ̸; and *Star Wars,* with Han Solo, Luke Skywalker, and

Darth Vader.

Without the semicolons, the reader must sort out the major groupings, distinguishing between important and less important pauses according to the logic of the sentence. By inserting semicolons at the major breaks, the writer does this work for the reader.

P3-d Avoid common misuses of the semicolon.

Do not use a semicolon in the following situations.

BETWEEN A SUBORDINATE CLAUSE AND THE REST OF THE SENTENCE

▶ Unless you brush your teeth within ten or fifteen minutes after

eating,̷ brushing does almost no good.

BETWEEN AN APPOSITIVE AND THE WORD IT REFERS TO

▶ The scientists were fascinated by the species *Argyroneta*

acquatica,̷ a spider that lives underwater.

TO INTRODUCE A LIST

▶ Some of my favorite film stars have home pages on the Web,̷:

Uma Thurman, Billy Bob Thornton, and Halle Berry.

BETWEEN INDEPENDENT CLAUSES JOINED BY *AND, BUT, OR, NOR, FOR, SO,*
OR *YET*

▶ Five of the applicants had worked with spreadsheets,̷ but only

one was familiar with database management.

EXCEPTIONS: If at least one of the independent clauses contains internal punctuation, you may use a semicolon even though the clauses are joined with a coordinating conjunction.

> As a vehicle [the model T] was hard-working, commonplace, and heroic; and it often seemed to transmit those qualities to the person who rode in it. — E. B. White

Although a comma would also be correct in this sentence, the semicolon is more effective, for it indicates the relative weights of the pauses.

Occasionally, a semicolon may be used to emphasize a sharp contrast or a firm distinction between clauses joined with a coordinating conjunction.

> We hate some persons because we do not know them; and we will not know them because we hate them. — Charles Caleb Colton

EXERCISE P3–1 Add commas or semicolons where needed in the following well-known quotations. If a sentence is correct, write "correct" after it. Answers to lettered sentences appear in the back of the book. Example:

> **If an animal does something, we call it instinct; if we do the**
>
> **same thing, we call it intelligence.**   — Will Cuppy

a. Do not ask me to be kind just ask me to act as though I were.
    — Jules Renard
b. When men talk about defense they always claim to be protecting women and children but they never ask the women and children what they think.   — Pat Schroeder
c. When I get a little money I buy books if any is left I buy food and clothes.   — Desiderius Erasmus
d. America is a country that doesn't know where it is going but is determined to set a speed record getting there.   — Lawrence J. Peter
e. Wit has truth in it wisecracking is simply calisthenics with words.
    — Dorothy Parker

1. Standing in the middle of the road is very dangerous you get knocked down by the traffic from both sides.   — Margaret Thatcher
2. I do not believe in an afterlife, although I am bringing a change of underwear.   — Woody Allen
3. Once the children were in the house the air became more vivid and more heated every object in the house grew more alive.
    — Mary Gordon
4. We don't know what we want but we are ready to bite someone to get it.   — Will Rogers
5. I've been rich and I've been poor rich is better.   — Sophie Tucker

EXERCISE P3–2 Edit the following sentences to correct errors in the use of the comma and the semicolon. If a sentence is correct, write "correct" after it. Answers to lettered sentences appear in the back of the book. Example:

> **Love is blind; envy has its eyes wide open.**

a. Strong black coffee will not sober you up, the truth is that time is the only way to get alcohol out of your system.
b. It is not surprising that our society is increasingly violent, after all, television desensitizes us to brutality at a very early age.
c. There is often a fine line between right and wrong; good and bad; truth and deception.

d. At Weight Watchers, we believe that being fat is not hereditary; it is a choice.

e. Severe, unremitting pain is a ravaging force; especially when the patient tries to hide it from others.

1. Another delicious dish is the chef's special; a roasted duck rubbed with spices and stuffed with wild rice.
2. Martin Luther King Jr. had not intended to be a preacher, initially, he had planned to become a lawyer.
3. We all assumed that the thief had been Jean's boyfriend; even though we had seen him only from the back.
4. The Victorians avoided the subject of sex but were obsessed with death, our contemporaries are obsessed with sex but avoid thinking about death.
5. Some educators believe that African American history should be taught in separate courses, others prefer to see it integrated into survey courses.

ON THE WEB > dianahacker.com/writersref
Grammar exercises > Punctuation > E-ex P3–1 and P3–2

P4

The colon

The colon is used primarily to call attention to the words that follow it. In addition, the colon has some conventional uses.

> ✓ GRAMMAR CHECKERS are fairly good at flagging colons that incorrectly follow a verb (*The office work includes: typing, filing, and answering the phone*). They also point out semicolons used where colons are needed, although they don't suggest revisions.

P4-a Use a colon after an independent clause to direct attention to a list, an appositive, or a quotation.

A LIST

The daily routine should include at least the following: twenty knee bends, fifty sit-ups, fifteen leg lifts, and five minutes of running in place.

AN APPOSITIVE

My roommate is guilty of two of the seven deadly sins: gluttony and sloth.

A QUOTATION

Consider the words of John F. Kennedy: "Ask not what your country can do for you; ask what you can do for your country."

For other ways of introducing quotations, see P6-f.

P4-b Use a colon between independent clauses if the second summarizes or explains the first.

Faith is like love: It cannot be forced.

NOTE: When an independent clause follows a colon, it may begin with a capital or a lowercase letter. (See M3-f.)

P4-c Use a colon after the salutation in a formal letter, to indicate hours and minutes, to show proportions, between a title and subtitle, and between city and publisher in bibliographic entries.

Dear Sir or Madam:

5:30 p.m.

The ratio of women to men was 2:1.

The Glory of Hera: Greek Mythology and the Greek Family

Boston: Bedford, 2005

NOTE: In biblical references, a colon is ordinarily used between chapter and verse (Luke 2:14). The Modern Language Association recommends a period instead (Luke 2.14).

P4-d Avoid common misuses of the colon.

A colon must be preceded by a full independent clause. Therefore, avoid using it in the following situations.

BETWEEN A VERB AND ITS OBJECT OR COMPLEMENT

▶ Some important vitamins and minerals in vegetables are⁄

vitamin A, thiamine, niacin, and vitamin C.

BETWEEN A PREPOSITION AND ITS OBJECT

▶ The heart's two pumps each consist of⁄ an upper chamber, or

atrium, and a lower chamber, or ventricle.

AFTER *SUCH AS, INCLUDING,* OR *FOR EXAMPLE*

▶ The trees on our campus include many fine Japanese specimens

such as⁄ black pines, ginkgos, and weeping cherries.

EXERCISE P4–1 Edit the following sentences to correct errors in the use of the comma, the semicolon, or the colon. If a sentence is correct, write "correct" after it. Answers to lettered sentences appear in the back of the book. Example:

Lifting the cover gently, Luca found the source of the odd sound⁄:
∧
a marble in the gears.

a. We always looked forward to Thanksgiving in Vermont: It was our only chance to see our Grady cousins.
b. If we have come to fight, we are far too few, if we have come to die, we are far too many.
c. The travel package includes: a round-trip ticket to Athens, a cruise through the Cyclades, and all hotel accommodations.
d. The media portray my generation as lazy; although polls show that we work as hard as the twentysomethings before us.
e. Fran Lebowitz has this advice for parents, "Never allow your child to call you by your first name. He hasn't known you long enough."

1. Harry Potter prevails against pain and evil for one reason, his heart is pure.
2. While traveling through France, Rose visited: the Loire Valley, Chartres, the Louvre, and the McDonald's stand at the foot of the Eiffel Tower.
3. There are three types of leave; annual leave, used for vacations, sick leave, used for medical appointments and illness, and personal leave, used for a variety of personal reasons.
4. Carl Sandburg once asked these three questions, "Who paid for my freedom? What was the price? And am I somehow beholden?"
5. Amelie had four goals: to be encouraging, to be effective, to be efficient, and to be elegant.

ON THE WEB > dianahacker.com/writersref
Grammar exercises > Punctuation > E-ex P4–1

P5

The apostrophe

> GRAMMAR CHECKERS flag only some missing or misused apostrophes. They catch missing apostrophes in contractions, such as *don't*. They also flag problems with possessives (*sled dogs feet, a babys eyes*), although they miss as many problems as they identify. Only you can decide when to add an apostrophe and whether to put it before or after the *-s* in possessives.

P5-a Use an apostrophe to indicate that a noun is possessive.

Possessive nouns usually indicate ownership, as in *Tim's hat* or *the lawyer's desk*. Frequently, however, ownership is only loosely implied: *the tree's roots, a day's work*. If you are not sure whether a noun is possessive, try turning it into an *of* phrase: *the roots of the tree, the work of a day*.

When to add -'s

If the noun does not end in *-s*, add *-'s*.

> Roy managed to climb out on the driver's side.

> Thank you for refunding the children's money.

If the noun is singular and ends in *-s* or an *s* sound, add *-'s*.

> Lois's sister spent last year in India.

> Her article presents an overview of Marx's teachings.

EXCEPTION: To avoid potentially awkward pronunciation, some writers use only the apostrophe with a singular noun ending in *-s*: *Sophocles'*.

ON THE WEB > dianahacker.com/writersref
Language Debates > -'s for singular nouns ending in -s
or an s sound

When to add only an apostrophe

If the noun is plural and ends in *-s,* add only an apostrophe.

> Both diplomats' briefcases were searched by guards.

Joint possession

To show joint possession, use *-'s* (or *-s'*) with the last noun only; to show individual possession, make all nouns possessive.

> Have you seen Joyce and Greg's new camper?

> Hernando's and Maria's expectations of marriage couldn't have been more different.

Joyce and Greg jointly own one camper. Hernando and Maria individually have different expectations.

Compound nouns

If a noun is compound, use *-'s* (or *-s'*) with the last element.

> Her father-in-law's sculpture won first place.

P5-b   Use an apostrophe and *-s* to indicate that an indefinite pronoun is possessive.

Indefinite pronouns refer to no specific person or thing: *everyone, someone, no one, something.* (See B1-b.)

> Someone's raincoat has been left behind.

P5-c   Use an apostrophe to mark contractions.

In contractions, the apostrophe takes the place of missing letters.

> It's a shame that Frank can't go on the tour.

It's stands for *It is* and *can't* for *cannot.*
> The apostrophe is also used to mark the omission of the first two digits of a year (*the class of '99*) or years (*the '60s generation*).

P5-d An apostrophe is often optional in plural numbers, letters, abbreviations, and words mentioned as words.

An apostrophe typically is not used to pluralize numbers, letters, abbreviations, and words mentioned as words. Note the few exceptions and be consistent throughout your paper.

PLURAL NUMBERS   Omit the apostrophe in the plural of all numbers, including decades.

> Oksana skated nearly perfect figure 8s.

> The 1920s are known as the Jazz Age.

PLURAL LETTERS   Italicize the letter and use roman (regular) font style for the *-s* ending. Do not italicize academic grades. Use of an apostrophe is usually optional; the Modern Language Association recommends the apostrophe for the plural of both capital and lowercase letters.

> Two large *J*s (*or J*'s) were painted on the door.

PLURAL ABBREVIATIONS   Do not use an apostrophe to pluralize an abbreviation.

> We collected only four IOUs out of forty.

> Marco earned two PhDs before his thirtieth birthday.

PLURAL OF WORDS MENTIONED AS WORDS   Generally, omit the apostrophe to form the plural of words mentioned as words. If the word is italicized, the *-s* ending appears in roman type.

> We've heard enough *maybe*s.

Words mentioned as words may also appear in quotation marks. When you choose this option, use the apostrophe: *We've heard enough "maybe's."*

P5-e Avoid common misuses of the apostrophe.

Do not use an apostrophe in the following situations.

WITH NOUNS THAT ARE NOT POSSESSIVE

> ▶ Some ~~outpatient's~~ *outpatients* are given special parking permits.

IN THE POSSESSIVE PRONOUNS *ITS, WHOSE, HIS, HERS, OURS, YOURS,*
AND *THEIRS*

▶ Each area has ~~it's~~ *its* own conference room.

It's means "it is." The possessive pronoun *its* contains no apostrophe
despite the fact that it is possessive.

EXERCISE P5–1 Edit the following sentences to correct errors in the use
of the apostrophe. If a sentence is correct, write "correct" after it. Answers to
lettered sentences appear in the back of the book. Example:

> We rented an art studio above a barbecue restaurant, Poor
> ~~Richards~~ *Richard's* Ribs.

   a. This diet will improve almost anyone's health.
   b. The innovative shoe fastener was inspired by the designers young son.
   c. Each days menu features a different European country's dish.
   d. Sue worked overtime to increase her families earnings.
   e. Ms. Jacobs is unwilling to listen to students complaints about computer failures and damaged disks.

  1. Siddhartha sat by the river and listened to its many voices.
  2. Three teenage son's can devour about as much food as four full-grown field hands. The only difference is that they dont do half as much work.
  3. We handle contracts with NASA and many other government agency's.
  4. Patience and humor are key tools in a travelers survival kit.
  5. My sister-in-law's quilts are being shown at the Fendrick Gallery.

EXERCISE P5–2 Edit the following passage to correct errors in the use of
the apostrophe.

> Its never too soon to start holiday shopping. In fact, some people
> choose to start shopping as early as January, when last seasons left-
> over's are priced at their lowest. Many stores try to lure customers in
> with promise's of savings up to 90 percent. Their main objective, of
> course, is to make way for next years inventory. The big problem with
> postholiday shopping, though, is that there isnt much left to choose
> from. Store's shelves have been picked over by last-minute shoppers
> desperately searching for gifts. The other problem is that its hard to
> know what to buy so far in advance. Next year's hot items are anyones
> guess. But proper timing, mixed with lot's of luck and determination,
> can lead to good purchases at great price's.

ON THE WEB > dianahacker.com/writersref
Grammar exercises > Punctuation > E-ex P5–1

P6

Quotation marks

> ✓ GRAMMAR CHECKERS are no help with quotation marks. They do not recognize direct and indirect quotations, they fail to identify quotation marks used incorrectly inside periods and commas, and they do not point out a missing quotation mark in a pair.

P6-a Use quotation marks to enclose direct quotations.

Direct quotations of a person's words, whether spoken or written, must be in quotation marks.

> "A foolish consistency is the hobgoblin of little minds," wrote Ralph Waldo Emerson.

CAUTION: Do not use quotation marks around indirect quotations. An indirect quotation reports someone's ideas without using that person's exact words.

> Ralph Waldo Emerson believed that consistency for its own sake is the mark of a small mind.

NOTE: In dialogue, begin a new paragraph to mark a change in speaker.

> "Mom, his name is Willie, not William. A thousand times I've told you, it's *Willie.*"
> "Willie is a derivative of William, Lester. Surely his birth certificate doesn't have Willie on it, and I like calling people by their proper names."
> "Yes, it does, ma'am. My mother named me Willie K. Mason."
> — Gloria Naylor

If a single speaker utters more than one paragraph, introduce each paragraph with quotation marks, but do not use closing quotation marks until the end of the speech.

P6-b Set off long quotations of prose or poetry by indenting.

The guidelines in this section are those of the Modern Language Association (MLA). The American Psychological Association (APA) and *The Chicago Manual of Style* (CMS) have slightly different guidelines (see APA-2a and CMS-2a).

When a quotation of prose runs to more than four typed lines in your paper, set it off by indenting one inch (or ten spaces) from the left margin. Quotation marks are not required because the indented format tells readers that the quotation is taken word-for-word from a source. Long quotations are ordinarily introduced by a sentence ending with a colon.

> After studying the historical record, James Horan evaluates Billy the Kid like this:
>> The portrait that emerges of [the Kid] from the thousands of pages of affidavits, reports, trial transcripts, his letters, and his testimony is neither the mythical Robin Hood nor the stereotyped adenoidal moron and pathological killer. Rather Billy appears as a disturbed, lonely young man, honest, loyal to his friends, dedicated to his beliefs, and betrayed by our institutions and the corrupt, ambitious, and compromising politicians of his time. (158)

The number in parentheses is a citation handled according to the Modern Language Association style. (See MLA-4a.)

NOTE: When you quote two or more paragraphs from the source, indent the first line of each paragraph an additional one-half inch (or five spaces).

When you quote more than three lines of a poem, set the quoted lines off from the text by indenting one inch (or ten spaces) from the left margin. Use no quotation marks unless they appear in the poem itself. (To quote two or three lines of poetry, see P7-h.)

> Although many anthologizers "modernize" her punctuation, Emily Dickinson relied heavily on dashes, using them, perhaps, as a musical device. Here, for example, is the original version of the opening stanza from "The Snake":
>> A narrow Fellow in the Grass
>> Occasionally rides--
>> You may have met Him--did you not
>> His notice sudden is--

P6-c Use single quotation marks to enclose a quotation within a quotation.

> According to Paul Eliott, Eskimo hunters "chant an ancient magic song to the seal they are after: 'Beast of the sea! Come and place yourself before me in the early morning!'"

P6-d Use quotation marks around the titles of short works: newspaper and magazine articles, poems, short stories, songs, episodes of television and radio programs, and chapters or subdivisions of books.

> Katherine Mansfield's "The Garden Party" provoked a lively discussion in our short-story class last night.

NOTE: Titles of books, plays, Web sites, television and radio programs, films, magazines, and newspapers are put in italics or underlined. (See M6-a.)

P6-e Quotation marks may be used to set off words used as words.

Although words used as words are ordinarily italicized (see M6-d), quotation marks are also acceptable. Just be sure to follow consistent practice throughout a paper.

> The words "accept" and "except" are frequently confused.

> The words *accept* and *except* are frequently confused.

P6-f Use punctuation with quotation marks according to convention.

This section describes the conventions used by American publishers in placing various marks of punctuation inside or outside quotation marks. It also explains how to punctuate when introducing quoted material.

Periods and commas

Place periods and commas inside quotation marks.

> "This is a stick-up," said the well-dressed young couple. "We want all your money."

This rule applies to single quotation marks as well as double quotation marks. (See P6-c.) It also applies to all uses of quotation marks: for quoted material, for titles of works, and for words used as words.

EXCEPTION: In the Modern Language Association's style of parenthetical in-text citations (see MLA-4a), the period follows the citation in parentheses.

> James M. McPherson comments, approvingly, that the Whigs "were not averse to extending the blessings of American liberty, even to Mexicans and Indians" (48).

Colons and semicolons

Put colons and semicolons outside quotation marks.

> Harold wrote, "I regret that I am unable to attend the fundraiser for AIDS research"; his letter, however, contained a substantial contribution.

Question marks and exclamation points

Put question marks and exclamation points inside quotation marks unless they apply to the sentence as a whole.

> Contrary to tradition, bedtime at my house is marked by "Mommy, can I tell you a story now?"
>
> Have you heard the old proverb "Do not climb the hill until you reach it"?

In the first sentence, the question mark applies only to the quoted question. In the second sentence, the question mark applies to the whole sentence.

NOTE: In MLA style for a quotation that ends with a question mark or an exclamation point, the parenthetical citation and a period should follow the entire quotation: *Rosie Thomas asks, "Is nothing in life ever straight and clear, the way children see it?" (77).*

Introducing quoted material

After a word group introducing a quotation, choose a colon, a comma, or no punctuation at all, whichever is appropriate in context.

FORMAL INTRODUCTION   If a quotation has been formally introduced, a colon is appropriate. A formal introduction is a full independent clause, not just an expression such as *he said* or *she remarked.*

> Morrow views personal ads in the classifieds as an art form: "The personal ad is like a haiku of self-celebration, a brief solo played on one's own horn."

EXPRESSION SUCH AS *HE SAID*   If a quotation is introduced with an expression such as *he said* or *she remarked* — or if it is followed by such an expression — a comma is needed.

> Stephen Leacock once said, "I am a great believer in luck, and I find the harder I work the more I have of it."
>
> "You can be a little ungrammatical if you come from the right part of the country," writes Robert Frost.

BLENDED QUOTATION   When a quotation is blended into the writer's own sentence, either a comma or no punctuation is appropriate, depending on the way in which the quotation fits into the sentence structure.

> The future champion could, as he put it, "float like a butterfly and sting like a bee."
>
> Charles Hudson noted that the prisoners escaped "by squeezing through a tiny window eighteen feet above the floor of their cell."

BEGINNING OF SENTENCE   If a quotation appears at the beginning of a sentence, set it off with a comma unless the quotation ends with a question mark or an exclamation point.

> "We shot them like dogs," boasted Davy Crockett, who was among Jackson's troops.
>
> "What is it?" I asked, bracing myself.

INTERRUPTED QUOTATION   If a quoted sentence is interrupted by explanatory words, use commas to set off the explanatory words.

> "A great many people think they are thinking," wrote William James, "when they are merely rearranging their prejudices."

If two successive quoted sentences from the same source are interrupted by explanatory words, use a comma before the explanatory words and a period after them.

"I was a flop as a daily reporter," admitted E. B. White. "Every piece had to be a masterpiece — and before you knew it, Tuesday was Wednesday."

P6-g Avoid common misuses of quotation marks.

Do not use quotation marks to draw attention to familiar slang, to disown trite expressions, or to justify an attempt at humor.

▶ Between Thanksgiving and Super Bowl Sunday, many American wives become ~~"football widows."~~

Do not use quotation marks around indirect quotations. (See also P6-a.)

▶ After leaving the scene of the domestic quarrel, the officer said that ~~"~~he was due for a coffee break.~~"~~

Do not use quotation marks around the title of your own essay.

EXERCISE P6–1 Add or delete quotation marks as needed and make any other necessary changes in punctuation in the following sentences. If a sentence is correct, write "correct" after it. Answers to lettered sentences appear in the back of the book. Example:

Gandhi once said, ⌄"An eye for an eye only ends up making the whole world blind. "⌄

a. As for the advertisement "Sailors have more fun", if you consider chipping paint and swabbing decks fun, then you will have plenty of it.
b. Even after forty minutes of discussion, our class could not agree on an interpretation of Robert Frost's poem "The Road Not Taken."
c. Accepting the check for her lottery winnings, Juanita said that "she would give half the money to charity."
d. After the movie, Vicki said, "The reviewer called this flick "trash of the first order." I guess you can't believe everything you read."
e. "Cleaning your house while your kids are still growing," quipped Phyllis Diller, "is like shoveling the walk before it stops snowing."

1. "That's the most beautiful seashell I've ever seen!", shouted Alexa.
2. "Get your head in the game, and the rest will come" advised the coach just before the whistle.

3. Gloria Steinem once twisted an old proverb like this, "A woman without a man is like a fish without a bicycle."
4. "Even when freshly washed and relieved of all obvious confections," says Fran Lebowitz, "children tend to be sticky."
5. Have you heard the Cowboy Junkies' cover of Hank Williams's "I'm So Lonesome I Could Cry?"

EXERCISE P6–2 Add or delete quotation marks as needed and make any other necessary changes in punctuation in the following passage. Citations should conform to MLA style (see MLA-4).

In his article The Moment of Truth, former vice president Al Gore argues that global warming is a genuine threat to life on earth and that we must act now to avoid catastrophe. Gore points out that in Chinese two symbols form the character for the word crisis. The first of those symbols means "danger", and the second means "opportunity." Gore calls our situation a "true *planetary emergency*" and cites scientific evidence of the greenhouse effect and its consequences (170–71). "What is at stake, Gore insists, is the survival of our civilization and the habitability of the Earth (197)." With such a grim predicament at hand, Gore questions why so many political and economic leaders are reluctant to act. "Is it simply more convenient to ignore the warnings," he asks (171)?

The crisis, of course, will not go away if we just pretend it isn't there. As with the Chinese symbol for crisis, however, Gore claims that the danger we face is accompanied by what he has termed "unprecedented opportunity." (172) Gore contends that throughout history, we have won battles against seemingly unbeatable evils such as slavery and fascism, and we did so by facing the truth and choosing the moral high ground. Gore's final appeal is to our humanity:

> "Ultimately, [the fight to end global warming] is not about any scientific discussion or political dialogue; it is about who we are as human beings. It is about our capacity to transcend our limitations, to rise to this new occasion. To see with our hearts, as well as our heads, the response that is now called for." (244)

Gore feels that the fate of our world rests in our own hands, and his hope is that we will make the choice to save the planet.

—Quotations are from Al Gore,
"The Moment of Truth," *Vanity Fair* May 2006: 170+.

ON THE WEB > dianahacker.com/writersref
Grammar exercises > Punctuation > E-ex P6–1

P7

Other marks

> ✓ GRAMMAR CHECKERS occasionally flag sentences beginning with words like *Why* or *Are* and suggest that a question mark may be needed. On the whole, however, grammar checkers are of little help with end punctuation. Most notably, they neglect to tell you when your sentence is missing end punctuation.

P7-a The period

Use a period to end all sentences except direct questions or genuine exclamations. Also use periods in abbreviations according to convention.

To end sentences

Everyone knows that a period should be used to end most sentences. The only problems that arise concern the choice between a period and a question mark or between a period and an exclamation point.

If a sentence reports a question instead of asking it directly, it should end with a period, not a question mark.

▶ Joelle asked whether the picnic would be canceled?.

If a sentence is not a genuine exclamation, it should end with a period, not an exclamation point.

▶ After years of working her way through school, Geeta finally

graduated with high honors!.

In abbreviations

A period is conventionally used in abbreviations such as these:

Mr.	i.e.	a.m. (or AM)
Ms.	e.g.	p.m. (or PM)
Dr.	etc.	

NOTE: If a sentence ends with a period marking an abbreviation, do not add a second period.

A period is not used in US Postal Service abbreviations for states: MD, TX, CA.

Current usage is to omit the period in abbreviations of organization names, academic degrees, and designations for eras.

NATO	UNESCO	UCLA	BS	BC
IRS	AFL-CIO	NIH	PhD	AD
USA	NAACP	SEC	RN	BCE

P7-b The question mark

Obviously a direct question should be followed by a question mark.

What is the horsepower of a 777 engine?

If a polite request is written in the form of a question, it may be followed by a period.

Would you please send me your catalog of lilies.

CAUTION: Do not use a question mark after an indirect question, one that is reported rather than asked directly. Use a period instead.

▶ He asked me who was teaching the mythology course?.
                                                      ^

NOTE: Questions in a series may be followed by question marks even when they are not complete sentences.

We wondered where Calamity had hidden this time. Under the sink? Behind the furnace? On top of the bookcase?

P7-c The exclamation point

Use an exclamation point after a word group or sentence to express exceptional feeling or to provide special emphasis.

When Gloria entered the room, I switched on the lights and we all yelled "Surprise!"

TIP: Do not overuse the exclamation point.

▶ In the fisherman's memory the fish lives on, increasing in length

and weight with each passing year, until at last it is big enough to

shade a fishing boat!.
　　　　　　 ∧

This sentence doesn't need to be pumped up with an exclamation point.
It is emphatic enough without it.

▶ Whenever I see Venus lunging forward to put away an

overhead smash, it might as well be me!. She does it just the
　　　　　　　　　　　　　　　　　∧

way I would!

The first exclamation point should be deleted so that the second one
will have more force.

EXERCISE P7-1 Add appropriate end punctuation where it is missing in
the following paragraph.

　　Although I am generally rational, I am superstitious I never walk
under ladders or put shoes on the table If I spill the salt, I go into fren-
zied calisthenics picking up the grains and tossing them over my left
shoulder As a result of these curious activities, I've always wondered
whether knowing the roots of superstitions would quell my irrational
responses Superstition has it, for example, that one should never place
a hat on the bed This superstition arises from a time when head lice
were common and placing a guest's hat on the bed stood a good chance
of spreading lice through the host's bed Doesn't this make good sense
And doesn't it stand to reason that if I know that my guests don't have
lice I shouldn't care where their hats go Of course it does It is fair to
ask, then, whether I have changed my ways and place hats on beds Are
you kidding I wouldn't put a hat on a bed if my life depended on it

P7-d The dash

When typing, use two hyphens to form a dash (--). Do not put
spaces before or after the dash. (If your word processing program
has what is known as an "em-dash," you may use it instead, with no
space before or after it.) Dashes are used for the following purposes.

To set off parenthetical material that deserves emphasis

　　Everything that went wrong — from the peeping Tom at her window
last night to my head-on collision today — we blamed on our move.

To set off appositives that contain commas

An appositive is a noun or noun phrase that renames a nearby noun. Ordinarily most appositives are set off with commas (see P1-e), but when the appositive itself contains commas, a pair of dashes helps readers see the relative importance of all the pauses.

> In my hometown the basic needs of people — food, clothing, and shelter — are less costly than in a big city like Los Angeles.

To prepare for a list, a restatement, an amplification, or a dramatic shift in tone or thought

> Along the wall are the bulk liquids — sesame seed oil, honey, safflower oil, maple syrup, and peanut butter.

> Consider the amount of sugar in the average person's diet — 104 pounds per year, 90 percent more than that consumed by our ancestors.

> Everywhere we looked there were little kids — a box of Cracker Jacks in one hand and mommy's or daddy's sleeve in the other.

> Kiere took a few steps back, came running full speed, kicked a mighty kick — and missed the ball.

In the first two examples, the writer could also use a colon. (See P4-a.) The colon is more formal than the dash and not quite as dramatic.

CAUTION: Unless there is a specific reason for using the dash, avoid it. Unnecessary dashes create a choppy effect.

> ▶ Insisting that our young people learn to use computers as instructional tools ⟋ for information retrieval ⟋ makes good sense.
>
> Herding them ⟋ sheeplike ⟋ into computer technology does not.

P7-e Parentheses

Use parentheses to enclose supplemental material, minor digressions, and afterthoughts.

> After taking her vital signs (temperature, pulse, and blood pressure), the nurse made Becky as comfortable as possible.

The weights James was first able to move (not lift, mind you) were measured in ounces.

Use parentheses to enclose letters or numbers labeling items in a series.

Regulations stipulated that only the following equipment could be used on the survival mission: (1) a knife, (2) thirty feet of parachute line, (3) a book of matches, (4) two ponchos, (5) an *E* tool, and (6) a signal flare.

TIP: Do not overuse parentheses. Rough drafts are likely to contain more afterthoughts than necessary. As writers head into a sentence, they often think of additional details, occasionally working them in as best they can with parentheses. Such sentences should be revised so that the additional details no longer seem to be afterthoughts.

▶ Researchers have said that ~~thirteen million (estimates run as~~ *from thirteen to eighteen million*
⌃
~~high as eighteen million)~~ Americans have diabetes.

P7-f Brackets

Use brackets to enclose any words or phrases that you have inserted into an otherwise word-for-word quotation.

Audubon reports that "if there are not enough young to balance deaths, the end of the species [California condor] is inevitable."

The sentence quoted from the *Audubon* article did not contain the words *California condor* (since the context made clear what species was meant), so the writer needed to add the name in brackets.

The Latin word "sic" in brackets indicates that an error in a quoted sentence appears in the original source.

According to the review, Nelly Furtado's performance was brilliant, "exceding [sic] the expectations of even her most loyal fans."

Do not overuse "sic," however, since calling attention to others' mistakes can appear snobbish. The preceding quotation, for example, might have been paraphrased instead: *According to the review, even Nelly Furtado's most loyal fans were surprised by the brilliance of her performance.*

P7-g The ellipsis mark

The ellipsis mark consists of three spaced periods. Use an ellipsis mark to indicate that you have deleted material from an otherwise word-for-word quotation.

> Reuben reports that "when the amount of cholesterol circulating in the blood rises over . . . 300 milligrams per 100, the chances of a heart attack increase dramatically."

If you delete a full sentence or more in the middle of a quoted passage, use a period before the three ellipsis dots.

> "Most of our efforts," writes Dave Erikson, "are directed toward saving the bald eagle's wintering habitat along the Mississippi River. . . . It's important that the wintering birds have a place to roost, where they can get out of the cold wind."

TIP: Ordinarily, do not use the ellipsis mark at the beginning or at the end of a quotation. Readers will understand that the quoted material is taken from a longer passage. If you have cut some words from the end of the final sentence quoted, however, MLA requires an ellipsis mark, as in the second example on page 405.

In quoted poetry, use a full line of dots to indicate that you have dropped a line or more from the poem:

> Had we but world enough, and time,
> This coyness, lady, were no crime.
> .   .   .   .
> But at my back I always hear
> Time's wingèd chariot hurrying near;
>
> — Andrew Marvell

The ellipsis mark may also be used to mark a hesitation or an interruption in speech or to suggest unfinished thoughts.

> "The apartment building next door . . . it's going up in flames!" yelled Marcia.

> Before falling into a coma, the victim whispered, "It was a man with a tattoo on his . . ."

P7-h The slash

Use the slash to separate two or three lines of poetry that have been run into your text. Add a space both before and after the slash.

In the opening lines of "Jordan," George Herbert pokes gentle fun at popular poems of his time: "Who says that fictions only and false hair / Become a verse? Is there in truth no beauty?"

More than three lines of poetry should be handled as an indented quotation. (See P6-b.)

The slash may occasionally be used to separate paired terms such as *pass/fail* and *producer/director.* Do not use a space before or after the slash.

Roger, the producer/director, announced a casting change.

Be sparing, however, in this use of the slash. In particular, avoid the use of *and/or, he/she,* and *his/her.*

EXERCISE P7–2 Edit the following sentences to correct errors in punctuation, focusing especially on appropriate use of the dash, parentheses, brackets, ellipsis mark, and slash. If a sentence is correct, write "correct" after it. Answers to lettered sentences appear in the back of the book. Example:

Social insects/—bees, for example,/— are able to communicate
⌃ ⌃
quite complicated messages to one another.

a. A client has left his/her cell phone in our conference room.
b. The films we made of Kilauea—on our trip to Hawaii Volcanoes National Park—illustrate a typical spatter cone eruption.
c. Samantha selected the pass/fail option for Chemistry 101.
d. Masahiro poked through his backpack—laptop, digital camera, guidebook—to make sure he was ready for a day's study at the Ryoanji Temple garden.
e. Of three engineering fields, chemical, mechanical, and materials, Keegan chose materials engineering for its application to toy manufacturing.

1. The old Valentine verse we used to chant says it all: "Sugar is sweet,/And so are you."
2. In studies in which mothers gazed down at their infants in their cribs but remained facially unresponsive, for example, not smiling, laughing, or showing any change of expression, the infants responded with intense weariness and eventual withdrawal.
3. Remember these three points of etiquette in poker: 1. always allow someone to cut the cards, 2. don't forget to ante up, and 3. never stack your chips.
4. In *Lifeboat,* Alfred Hitchcock appears [some say without his knowledge] in a newspaper advertisement for weight loss.

5. The writer Chitra Divakaruni explained her work with other Indian American immigrants: "Many women who came to Maitri [a women's support group in San Francisco] needed to know simple things like opening a bank account or getting citizenship. . . . Many women in Maitri spoke English, but their English was functional rather than emotional. They needed someone who understands their problems and speaks their language."

ON THE WEB > dianahacker.com/writersref
Grammar exercises > Punctuation > E-ex P7–1

M
_____

Mechanics

M Mechanics

M1

Spelling

You learned to spell from repeated experience with words in both reading and writing, but especially writing. Words have a look, a sound, and even a feel to them as the hand moves across the page. As you proofread, you can probably tell if a word doesn't look quite right. In such cases, the solution is obvious: Look up the word in the dictionary. (See W6-a.)

 SPELL CHECKERS are useful alternatives to a dictionary, but only to a point. A spell checker will not tell you how to spell words not listed in its dictionary; nor will it help you catch words commonly confused, such as *accept* and *except,* or some typographical errors, such as *own* for *won.* You will still need to proofread, and for some words you may need to turn to the dictionary.

M1-a Become familiar with the major spelling rules.

i *before* e *except after* c

Use *i* before *e* except after *c* or when sounded like *ay,* as in *neighbor* and *weigh.*

I BEFORE *E*	relieve, believe, sieve, niece, fierce, frieze
E BEFORE *I*	receive, deceive, sleigh, freight, eight
EXCEPTIONS	seize, either, weird, height, foreign, leisure

Suffixes

FINAL SILENT *-E*   Generally, drop a final silent *-e* when adding a suffix that begins with a vowel. Keep the final *-e* if the suffix begins with a consonant.

combine, combination	achieve, achievement
desire, desiring	care, careful
prude, prudish	entire, entirety
remove, removable	gentle, gentleness

Words such as *changeable, judgment, argument,* and *truly* are exceptions.

FINAL -Y   When adding -*s* or -*d* to words ending in -*y*, ordinarily change -*y* to -*ie* when the -*y* is preceded by a consonant but not when it is preceded by a vowel.

comedy, comedies   monkey, monkeys
dry, dried   play, played

With proper names ending in -*y*, however, do not change the -*y* to -*ie* even if it is preceded by a consonant: *the Dougherty family, the Doughertys.*

FINAL CONSONANTS   If a final consonant is preceded by a single vowel *and* the consonant ends a one-syllable word or a stressed syllable, double the consonant when adding a suffix beginning with a vowel.

bet, betting   occur, occurrence
commit, committed

Plurals

-S OR -ES   Add -*s* to form the plural of most nouns; add -*es* to singular nouns ending in -*s, -sh, -ch,* and -*x.*

table, tables   church, churches
paper, papers   dish, dishes

Ordinarily add -*s* to nouns ending in -*o* when the -*o* is preceded by a vowel. Add -*es* when it is preceded by a consonant.

radio, radios   hero, heroes
video, videos   tomato, tomatoes

OTHER PLURALS   To form the plural of a hyphenated compound word, add -*s* to the chief word even if it does not appear at the end.

mother-in-law, mothers-in-law

English words derived from other languages such as Latin or French sometimes form the plural as they would in their original language.

medium, media   chateau, chateaux
criterion, criteria

ESL Spelling may vary slightly among English-speaking countries. If you studied British, Australian, or Canadian English before you began studying American English, be aware of the different forms listed here. Consult a dictionary for others.

AMERICAN	BRITISH
canceled, traveled	cancelled, travelled
color, humor	colour, humour
judgment	judgement
check	cheque
realize, apologize	realise, apologise
defense	defence
anemia, anesthetic	anaemia, anaesthetic
theater, center	theatre, centre
fetus	foetus
mold, smolder	mould, smoulder
civilization	civilisation
connection, inflection	connexion, inflexion
licorice	liquorice

NOTE: For rules on pluralizing numbers, letters, abbreviations, and words mentioned as words, see P5-d.

M1-b Discriminate between words that sound alike but have different meanings.

Words that sound alike or nearly alike but have different meanings and spellings are called *homophones*. The following sets of words are so commonly confused that a good proofreader will double-check their every use.

affect (verb: to exert an influence)
effect (verb: to accomplish; noun: result)

its (possessive pronoun: of or belonging to it)
it's (contraction for *it is*)

loose (adjective: free, not securely attached)
lose (verb: to fail to keep, to be deprived of)

principal (adjective: most important; noun: head of a school)
principle (noun: a general or fundamental truth)

their (possessive pronoun: belonging to them)
they're (contraction for *they are*)
there (adverb: that place or position)

who's (contraction for *who is*)
whose (possessive form of *who*)

your (possessive form of *you*)
you're (contraction of *you are*)

To check for correct use of these and other commonly confused words, consult the Glossary of Usage in this book (W1).

ON THE WEB > dianahacker.com/writersref
Links Library > Grammar, style, punctuation, and usage

EXERCISE M1–1   The following memo has been run through a spell checker. Proofread it carefully, editing the spelling and typographical errors that remain.

November 1, 2006

To: Patricia Wise
cc: Richard Chang
From: Constance Mayhew
Subject: Express Tours annual report

Thank you for agreeing to draft the annual report for Express Tours. Before you begin you're work, let me outline the initial steps.

First, its essential for you to include brief profiles of top management. Early next week, I'll provide profiles for all manages accept Samuel Heath, who's biographical information is being revised. You should edit these profiles carefully, than format them according to the enclosed in-structions. We may ask you to include other employee's profiles at some point.

Second, you should arrange to get complete financial information for fiscal year 2006 from our comptroller, Richard Chang. (Helen Boyes, to, can provide the necessary figures.) When you get this information, pre-cede according tot he plans we discuss in yesterday's meeting. By the way, you will notice from the figures that the sale of our Charterhouse division did not significantly effect net profits.

Third, you should submit first draft of the report by December 15. I as-sume that you won a laser printer, but if you don't, you can submit a disk and we'll print out a draft here. Of coarse, you should proofread you writing.

I am quiet pleased that you can take on this project. If I or anyone else at Express Tours can answers questions, don't hesitate to call.

M2

The hyphen

> GRAMMAR CHECKERS can flag some, but not all, missing or misused hyphens. For example, the programs can often tell you that a hyphen is needed in compound numbers, such as *sixty-four*. They can also tell you how to spell certain compound words, such as *breakup* (not *break-up*).

M2-a Consult the dictionary to determine how to treat a compound word.

The dictionary will tell you whether to treat a compound word as a hyphenated compound (*water-repellent*), one word (*waterproof*), or two words (*water table*). If the compound word is not in the dictionary, treat it as two words.

▶ The prosecutor chose not to cross‑examine any witnesses.

▶ Imogene kept her sketches in a small note⁻book.

▶ Alice walked through the looking⁄glass into a backward world.

M2-b Use a hyphen to connect two or more words functioning together as an adjective before a noun.

▶ Mrs. Douglas gave Toshiko a seashell and some newspaper‑

wrapped fish to take home to her mother.

▶ Richa Gupta is not yet a well‑known candidate.

Newspaper-wrapped and *well-known* are adjectives used before the nouns *fish* and *candidate*.

Generally, do not use a hyphen when such compounds follow the noun.

▶ After our television campaign, Richa Gupta will be well/known.

Do not use a hyphen to connect *-ly* adverbs to the words they modify.

▶ A slowly/moving truck tied up traffic.

NOTE: In a series, hyphens are suspended.

Do you prefer first-, second-, or third-class tickets?

M2-c Hyphenate the written form of fractions and of compound numbers from twenty-one to ninety-nine.

▶ One-fourth of my salary goes to pay my child care expenses.

M2-d Use a hyphen with the prefixes *all-*, *ex-*, and *self-* and with the suffix *-elect*.

▶ The charity is funneling more money into self-help projects.

▶ Anne King is our club's president-elect.

M2-e A hyphen is used in some words to avoid ambiguity or to separate awkward double or triple letters.

Without the hyphen there would be no way to distinguish between words such as *re-creation* and *recreation*.

Bicycling in the city is my favorite form of recreation.

The film was praised for its astonishing re-creation of nineteenth-century London.

Hyphens are sometimes used to separate awkward double or triple letters in compound words (*anti-intellectual, cross-stitch*). Always check a dictionary for the standard form of the word.

M2-f If a word must be divided at the end of a line, divide it correctly.

Divide words between syllables; never divide a one-syllable word.

▶ When I returned from my semester overseas, I didn't ~~reco~~*recog-*
  nize
  ~~gnize~~ one face on the magazine covers.

▶ He didn't have the courage or the ~~stren~~-
  strength
  ~~gth~~ to open the door.

Never divide a word so that a single letter stands alone at the end of a line or fewer than three letters begin a line.

▶ She'll bring her brother with her when she comes ~~a-~~
  again.
  ~~gain.~~

▶ As audience to the play *The Mousetrap,* Hamlet is a ~~watch~~-
  watcher
  ~~er~~ watching watchers.

When dividing a compound word at the end of a line, either make the break between the words that form the compound or put the whole word on the next line.

▶ My niece Marielena is determined to become a long-~~dis~~-
  distance
  ~~tance~~ runner when she grows up.

To divide long e-mail and Internet addresses (URLs), do not use a hyphen. Break an e-mail address after the @ symbol or before a period. Break a URL after a colon, a slash, or a double slash or before a period or other punctuation mark.

I repeatedly e-mailed Janine at janine.r.rose@dunbaracademy .org before I gave up and called her cell phone.

To find a zip code quickly, I always use the United States Postal Service Web site at http://zip4.usps.com/zip4/ welcome.jsp.

NOTE: For breaks in URLs in MLA and APA documentation styles, see MLA-5 and APA-5.

EXERCISE M2–1 Edit the following sentences to correct errors in hyphenation. If a sentence is correct, write "correct" after it. Answers to lettered sentences appear in the back of the book. Example:

> **Zola's first readers were scandalized by his slice-of-life novels.**
> ^   ^

a. Gold is the seventy-ninth element in the periodic table.

b. The swiftly-moving tugboat pulled alongside the barge and directed it away from the oil spill in the harbor.

c. The Moche were a pre-Columbian people who established a sophisticated culture in ancient Peru.

d. Your dog is well-known in our neighborhood.

e. Road-blocks were set up along all the major highways leading out of the city.

1. We knew we were driving too fast when our tires skidded on the rain slick surface.

2. The Black Death reduced the population of some medieval villages by two thirds.

3. Sewing forty-eight sequined tutus for the ballet recital nearly made Karyn cross-eyed.

4. Olivia had hoped to find a pay as you go plan to finance the construction of her observatory.

5. Gail Sheehy writes that at age twenty five many people assume that the choices they make are irrevocable.

ON THE WEB > dianahacker.com/writersref
Grammar exercises > Mechanics > E-ex M2–1

M3

Capitalization

In addition to the rules in this section, a good dictionary can tell you when to use capital letters.

> GRAMMAR CHECKERS remind you that sentences should begin with capital letters and that some words, such as *Cherokee,* are proper nouns. Many words, however, should be capitalized only in certain contexts, and you must determine when to do so.

M3-a Capitalize proper nouns and words derived from them; do not capitalize common nouns.

Proper nouns are the names of specific persons, places, and things. All other nouns are common nouns. The following types of words are usually capitalized: names for the deity, religions, religious followers, sacred books; words of family relationship used as names; particular places; nationalities and their languages, races, tribes; educational institutions, departments, degrees, particular courses; government departments, organizations, political parties; historical movements, periods, events, documents; specific electronic sources; and trade names.

PROPER NOUNS	COMMON NOUNS
God (used as a name)	a god
Book of Common Prayer	a book
Uncle Pedro	my uncle
Father (used as a name)	my father
Lake Superior	a picturesque lake
the Capital Center	a center for advanced studies
the South	a southern state
Wrigley Field	a baseball stadium
University of Wisconsin	a good university
Geology 101	geology
Environmental Protection Agency	a federal agency
Phi Kappa Psi	a fraternity
a Democrat	an independent
the Enlightenment	the eighteenth century
the Declaration of Independence	a treaty
the World Wide Web, the Web	a home page
the Internet, the Net	a computer network
Advil	a painkiller

Months, holidays, and days of the week are treated as proper nouns; the seasons and numbers of the days of the month are not.

Our academic year begins on a Tuesday in early September, right after Labor Day.

My mother's birthday is in early summer, on the second of June.

EXCEPTION: Capitalize Fourth of July (or July Fourth) when referring to the holiday.

Names of school subjects are capitalized only if they are names of languages. Names of particular courses are capitalized.

> This semester Austin is taking math, geography, geology, French, and English.

> Professor Obembe offers Modern American Fiction 501 to graduate students.

TIP: Do not capitalize common nouns to make them seem important. *Our company is currently hiring computer programmers* [not *Company, Computer Programmers*].

M3-b Capitalize titles of persons when used as part of a proper name but usually not when used alone.

> Prof. Margaret Barnes; Dr. Sinyee Sein; John Scott Williams Jr.; Anne Tilton, LLD

> District Attorney Marshall was reprimanded for badgering the witness.

> The district attorney was elected for a two-year term.

Usage varies when the title of an important public figure is used alone. *The president* [or *President*] *vetoed the bill.*

M3-c Capitalize the first, last, and all major words in titles and subtitles of works such as books, articles, songs, and online documents.

In both titles and subtitles, major words such as nouns, pronouns, verbs, adjectives, and adverbs should be capitalized. Minor words such as articles, prepositions, and coordinating conjunctions are not capitalized unless they are the first or last word of a title or subtitle. Capitalize the second part of a hyphenated term in a title if it is a major word but not if it is a minor word.

> *Seizing the Enigma: The Race to Break the German U-Boat Codes*
> "Fire and Ice"
> "I Want to Hold Your Hand"
> *The Canadian Green Page*

Capitalize chapter titles and the titles of other major divisions of a work following the same guidelines used for titles of complete works.

"Work and Play" in Santayana's *The Nature of Beauty*

"Size Matters" on the Web site *Discovery Channel Online*

M3-d Capitalize the first word of a sentence.

Obviously the first word of a sentence should be capitalized.

When lightning struck the house, the chimney collapsed.

When a sentence appears within parentheses, capitalize its first word unless the parentheses appear within another sentence.

Early detection of breast cancer significantly increases survival rates. (See table 2.)

Early detection of breast cancer significantly increases survival rates (see table 2).

M3-e Capitalize the first word of a quoted sentence but not a quoted phrase.

In *Time* magazine Robert Hughes writes, "There are only about sixty Watteau paintings on whose authenticity all experts agree."

Russell Baker has written that in our country, sports are "the opiate of the masses."

If a quoted sentence is interrupted by explanatory words, do not capitalize the first word after the interruption. (See also P6-f.)

"If you want to go out," he said, "tell me now."

When quoting poetry, copy the poet's capitalization exactly. Many poets capitalize the first word of every line of poetry; a few contemporary poets dismiss capitalization altogether.

When I consider everything that grows
Holds in perfection but a little moment   — Shakespeare

it was the week   that
i felt the city's narrow breezes rush about
me   — Don L. Lee

M3-f Capitalize the first word after a colon if it begins an independent clause.

I came to a startling conclusion: The house must be haunted.

NOTE: MLA and CMS styles use a lowercase letter to begin an independent clause following a colon; APA style uses a capital letter.

Use lowercase after a colon to introduce a list or an appositive.

The students were divided into two groups: residents and commuters.

M3-g Capitalize abbreviations for departments and agencies of government, other organizations, and corporations; capitalize the call letters of radio and television stations.

EPA, FBI, OPEC, IBM, WCRB, KNBC-TV

EXERCISE M3–1 Edit the following sentences to correct errors in capitalization. If a sentence is correct, write "correct" after it. Answers to lettered sentences appear in the back of the book. Example:

> On our trip to the West we visited the grand canyon and the
> great salt desert.

a. Assistant dean Shirin Ahmadi recommended offering more world language courses.

b. We went to the Mark Taper Forum to see a production of *Angels in America.*

c. Kalindi has an ambitious semester, studying differential calculus, classical hebrew, brochure design, and greek literature.

d. Lydia's Aunt and Uncle make modular houses as beautiful as modernist works of art.

e. We amused ourselves on the long flight by discussing how Spring in Kyoto stacks up against Summer in London.

1. When the Ducati will not start, I try a few tricks with the ignition key: Jiggling it to the left, pulling it out a quarter of an inch, and gently pulling down on it.

2. When you slowly bake a clove of garlic, the most amazing thing happens: It loses its bitter tang and becomes sweet and buttery.

3. After World War II, aunt Helena left Poland to study in Italy.

4. When we drove through the south last summer, we were amazed to see kudzu growing wild along the road.

5. Following in his sister's footsteps, Leonid is pursuing a degree in Marketing Research.

ON THE WEB > dianahacker.com/writersref
Grammar exercises > Mechanics > E-ex M3–1

M4

Abbreviations

 GRAMMAR CHECKERS can flag a few inappropriate abbreviations, such as *Xmas* and *e.g.,* but do not assume that a program will catch all problems with abbreviations.

M4-a Use standard abbreviations for titles immediately before and after proper names.

TITLES BEFORE PROPER NAMES	TITLES AFTER PROPER NAMES
Mr. Rafael Zabala	William Albert Sr.
Ms. Nancy Linehan	Thomas Hines Jr.
Mrs. Edward Horn	Anita Lor, PhD
Dr. Margaret Simmons	Robert Simkowski, MD
the Rev. John Stone	Margaret Chin, LLD
Prof. James Russo	Polly Stein, DDS

Do not abbreviate a title if it is not used with a proper name.

> My history ~~prof.~~ is an expert on race relations in South Africa.
  ^professor^

Avoid redundant titles such as *Dr. Amy Day, MD.* Choose one title or the other: *Dr. Amy Day* or *Amy Day, MD.*

M4-b Use abbreviations only when you are sure your readers will understand them.

Familiar abbreviations, written without periods, are acceptable.

CIA, FBI, AFL-CIO, NAACP, IBM, UPI, CBS, USA, IOU, CD-ROM, ESL

The YMCA has opened a new gym close to my office.

NOTE: When using an unfamiliar abbreviation (such as NASW for National Association of Social Workers) throughout a paper, write the full name followed by the abbreviation in parentheses at the first mention of the name. Then use the abbreviation throughout the rest of the paper.

M4-c Use BC, AD, a.m., p.m., No., and $ only with specific dates, times, numbers, and amounts.

The abbreviation BC ("before Christ") follows a date, and AD ("*anno Domini*") precedes a date. Acceptable alternatives are BCE ("before the common era") and CE ("common era"), both of which follow a date.

40 BC (or 40 BCE)	4:00 a.m. (or AM)	No. 12 (or no. 12)
AD 44 (or 44 CE)	6:00 p.m. (or PM)	$150

Avoid using a.m., p.m., No., or $ when not accompanied by a specific figure.

▶ We set off for the lake early in the ~~a.m.~~ *morning.*

M4-d Be sparing in your use of Latin abbreviations.

Latin abbreviations are acceptable in footnotes and bibliographies and in informal writing for comments in parentheses.

cf. (Latin *confer,* "compare")
e.g. (Latin *exempli gratia,* "for example")
et al. (Latin *et alii,* "and others")
etc. (Latin *et cetera,* "and so forth")
i.e. (Latin *id est,* "that is")
N.B. (Latin *nota bene,* "note well")

Harold Simms et al., *The Race for Space*

Alfred Hitchcock directed many classic thrillers (e.g., *Psycho, Rear Window,* and *Vertigo*).

In formal writing, use the appropriate English phrases.

▶ Many obsolete laws remain on the books, ~~e.g.,~~ *for example,* a law in Vermont forbidding an unmarried man and woman to sit closer than six inches apart on a park bench.

M4-e Avoid inappropriate abbreviations.

In formal writing, abbreviations for the following are not commonly accepted: personal names, units of measurement, days of the week, holidays, months, courses of study, divisions of written works, states and countries (except in addresses and except Washington, DC). Do not abbreviate *Company* and *Incorporated* unless their abbreviated forms are part of an official name.

PERSONAL NAME   Charles (*not* Chas.)

UNITS OF MEASUREMENT   pound (*not* lb.)

DAYS OF THE WEEK   Monday (*not* Mon.)

HOLIDAYS   Christmas (*not* Xmas)

MONTHS   January, February, March (*not* Jan., Feb., Mar.)

COURSES OF STUDY   political science (*not* poli. sci.)

DIVISIONS OF WRITTEN WORKS   chapter, page (*not* ch., p.)

STATES AND COUNTRIES   Massachusetts (*not* MA or Mass.)

PARTS OF A BUSINESS NAME   Adams Lighting Company (*not* Adams Lighting Co.); Kim and Brothers, Inc. (*not* Kim and Bros., Inc.)

▶ Eliza promised to buy me one l̶b̶.̶ of Godiva chocolate for my
  pound

birthday, which was last F̶r̶i̶.̶
  Friday.

EXERCISE M4–1 Edit the following sentences to correct errors in abbreviations. If a sentence is correct, write "correct" after it. Answers to lettered sentences appear in the back of the book. Example:

  Christmas   *Tuesday.*
This year X̶m̶a̶s̶ will fall on a T̶u̶e̶s̶.̶

a. Since its inception, the BBC has maintained a consistently high standard of radio and television broadcasting.
b. Some combat soldiers are trained by govt. diplomats to be sensitive to issues of culture, history, and religion.
c. "Mahatma" Gandhi has inspired many modern leaders, including Martin Luther King Jr.
d. How many lb. have you lost since you began running four miles a day?
e. Denzil spent all night studying for his psych. exam.

1. My favorite prof., Dr. Barker, is on sabbatical this semester.
2. When we visited NYU in early September, we were charmed by the lull of summer crickets in Washington Square Park.

3. Some historians think that the New Testament was completed by AD 100.
4. My mother's birthday was on Fri. the 13th this year.
5. Many first-time users of Flash panic before the complex menus—i.e., some develop a blank stare and the tingling of a migraine.

ON THE WEB > dianahacker.com/writersref
Grammar exercises > Mechanics > E-ex M4–1

M5

Numbers

 GRAMMAR CHECKERS can tell you to spell out certain numbers, such as *thirty-three* and numbers that begin a sentence, but they won't help you understand when it is acceptable to use figures.

M5-a Spell out numbers of one or two words or those that begin a sentence. Use figures for numbers that require more than two words to spell out.

▶ It's been 8̸ years since I visited Peru.
    eight

▶ I counted ~~one hundred seventy-six~~ DVDs on the shelf.
    176

If a sentence begins with a number, spell out the number or rewrite the sentence.

▶ ~~150~~ children in our program need expensive dental treatment.
    One hundred fifty

Rewriting the sentence will also correct the error and may be less awkward if the number is long: *In our program 150 children need expensive dental treatment.*

EXCEPTIONS: In technical and some business writing, figures are preferred even when spellings would be brief, but usage varies. When in doubt, consult the style guide of the organization for which you are writing.

When several numbers appear in the same passage, many writers choose consistency rather than strict adherence to the rule.

When one number immediately follows another, spell out one and use figures for the other: *three 100-meter events, 25 four-poster beds.*

M5-b Generally, figures are acceptable for dates, addresses, percentages, fractions, decimals, scores, statistics and other numerical results, exact amounts of money, divisions of books and plays, pages, identification numbers, and the time.

DATES July 4, 1776, 56 BC, AD 30

ADDRESSES 77 Latches Lane, 519 West 42nd Street

PERCENTAGES 55 percent (or 55%)

FRACTIONS, DECIMALS ½, 0.047

SCORES 7 to 3, 21–18

STATISTICS average age 37, average weight 180

SURVEYS 4 out of 5

EXACT AMOUNTS OF MONEY $105.37, $106,000

DIVISIONS OF BOOKS volume 3, chapter 4, page 189

DIVISIONS OF PLAYS act 3; scene 3 (*or* act III, scene iii)

IDENTIFICATION NUMBERS serial number 10988675

TIME OF DAY 4:00 p.m., 1:30 a.m.

▶ Several doctors put up ~~two hundred fifty-five thousand dollars~~ for

                $255,000

the construction of a golf course.

NOTE: When not using a.m. or p.m., write out the time in words (*four o'clock in the afternoon, twelve noon, seven in the morning*).

EXERCISE M5–1 Edit the following sentences to correct errors in the use of numbers. If a sentence is correct, write "correct" after it. Answers to lettered sentences appear in the back of the book. Example:

By the end of the evening, Ashanti had only ~~three dollars and~~ ~~six cents~~ left.

$3.06

a. The carpenters located 3 maple timbers, 21 sheets of cherry, and 10 oblongs of polished ebony for the theater set.
b. The program's cost is well over one billion dollars.
c. The score was tied at 5–5 when the momentum shifted and carried the Standards to a decisive 12–5 win.
d. 8 students in the class had been labeled "learning disabled."
e. The Vietnam Veterans Memorial in Washington, DC, had fifty-eight thousand one hundred thirty-two names inscribed on it when it was dedicated in 1982.

1. One of my favorite scenes in Shakespeare is the property division scene in act 1 of *King Lear.*
2. The botany lecture will begin at precisely 3:30 p.m.
3. 50 percent of the gamers who play *The Sims* are female.
4. In two thousand and four, Fox TV's *American Idol* earned more advertising dollars than any other reality show.
5. On a normal day, I spend at least 4 to 5 hours surfing the Internet.

ON THE WEB > dianahacker.com/writersref
Grammar exercises > Mechanics > E-ex M5–1

M6

Italics (underlining)

Italics, a slanting font style used in printed material, can be produced by word processing programs. In handwritten or typed papers, underlining is used instead. Some instructors prefer underlining even though their students can produce italics.

NOTE: Some e-mail systems do not allow for italics or underlining. Many people indicate words that should be italicized by preceding and ending them with underscore marks or asterisks. Punctuation should follow the coding.

> I am planning to write my senior thesis on _Memoirs of a Geisha_.

In less formal e-mail messages, normally italicized words aren't marked at all.

> I finally finished reading Memoirs of a Geisha--what a story!

TIP: In World Wide Web documents, underlining indicates a hot link. When creating a Web document, use italics, not underlining, for the conventions described in this section.

> ✓ GRAMMAR CHECKERS do not flag problems with italics or underlining.

M6-a   Underline or italicize the titles of works according to convention.

Titles of the following works, including electronic works, should be underlined or italicized.

TITLES OF BOOKS   *The Color Purple, Middlesex, Encarta*

MAGAZINES   *Time, Scientific American, Salon.com*

NEWSPAPERS   the *Baltimore Sun,* the *New York Times on the Web*

PAMPHLETS   *Common Sense, Facts about Marijuana*

LONG POEMS   *The Waste Land, Paradise Lost*

PLAYS   *King Lear, Rent*

FILMS   *Casablanca, American Beauty*

TELEVISION PROGRAMS   *Survivor, 60 Minutes*

RADIO PROGRAMS   *All Things Considered*

MUSICAL COMPOSITIONS   *Porgy and Bess*

CHOREOGRAPHIC WORKS   *Brief Fling*

WORKS OF VISUAL ART   Rodin's *The Thinker*

COMIC STRIPS   *Dilbert*

ELECTRONIC DATABASES   *InfoTrac*

WEB SITES   *ZDNet, Google*

ELECTRONIC GAMES   *Free Cell, Zuma*

The titles of other works, such as short stories, essays, episodes of radio or television programs, songs, and short poems, are enclosed in quotation marks. (See P6-d.)

NOTE: Do not use underlining or italics when referring to the Bible, titles of books in the Bible (Genesis, not *Genesis*), or titles of legal documents (the Constitution, not the *Constitution*). Do not underline the titles of computer software (WordPerfect, Photoshop). Do not underline the title of your own paper.

M6-b Underline or italicize the names of spacecraft, aircraft, ships, and trains.

Challenger, Spirit of St. Louis, Queen Mary 2, Silver Streak

▶ The success of the Soviets' <u>Sputnik</u> galvanized the US space program.

M6-c Underline or italicize foreign words in an English sentence.

▶ Caroline's <u>joie de vivre</u> should be a model for all of us.

EXCEPTION: Do not underline or italicize foreign words that have become part of the English language—"laissez-faire," "fait accompli," "modus operandi," and "per diem," for example.

M6-d Underline or italicize words, letters, and numbers mentioned as themselves.

▶ Tim assured us that the howling probably came from his bloodhound, Hill Billy, but his <u>probably</u> stuck in our minds.

▶ Sarah called her father by his given name, Johnny, but she was unable to pronounce the <u>J</u>.

▶ A big <u>3</u> was painted on the door.

NOTE: Quotation marks may be used instead of underlining or italics to set off words mentioned as words. (See P6-e.)

M6-e Avoid excessive underlining or italics for emphasis.

Frequent underlining or italicizing to emphasize words or ideas is distracting and should be used sparingly.

▶ In-line skating is a popular sport that has become almost

an addiction.
~~////////~~

EXERCISE M6–1 Edit the following sentences to correct errors in the use of italics. If a sentence is correct, write "correct" after it. Answers to lettered sentences appear in the back of the book. Example:

We had a lively discussion about Gini Alhadeff's memoir <u>The Sun at Midday.</u>

a. Howard Hughes commissioned the Spruce Goose, a beautifully built but thoroughly impractical wooden aircraft.

b. The old man *screamed* his anger, *shouting* to all of us, "I will not leave my money to you worthless layabouts!"

c. I learned the Latin term ad infinitum from an old nursery rhyme about fleas: "Great fleas have little fleas upon their back to bite 'em, / Little fleas have lesser fleas and so on ad infinitum."

d. Cinema audiences once gasped at hearing the word *damn* in *Gone with the Wind.*

e. Neve Campbell's lifelong interest in ballet inspired her involvement in the film "The Company," which portrays a season with the Joffrey Ballet.

1. Yasmina spent a year painting white flowers in imitation of Georgia O'Keeffe's Calla Lilies.

2. On the monastery walls are murals depicting scenes from the book of Kings and the book of Proverbs.

3. My per diem allowance was two hundred dollars.

4. Cecily watched in amazement as the tattoo artist made angles and swooping loops into the Gothic letter G.

5. The blend of poetic lyrics and progressive instruments on Seal's "Human Being" makes it one of my favorite CDs.

ON THE WEB > dianahacker.com/writersref
Grammar exercises > Mechanics > E-ex M6–1

R

Researching

R Researching

College research assignments ask you to pose a question worth exploring, to read widely in search of possible answers, to interpret what you read, to draw reasoned conclusions, and to support those conclusions with valid and well-documented evidence. The process takes time: time for researching and time for drafting, revising, and documenting the paper in the style recommended by your instructor (see the tabbed dividers marked MLA and APA/CMS). Before beginning a research project, set a realistic schedule of deadlines. One student created a calendar to map out her tasks for a paper assigned on October 3 and due October 31.

SAMPLE CALENDAR FOR A RESEARCH ASSIGNMENT

2	3	4	5	6	7	8
	Receive assignment.	Pose questions worth exploring.	Talk with a librarian; plan a search strategy.		Settle on a topic. Locate sources.	
9	10	11	12	13	14	15
		Read and take notes.		Draft a tentative thesis and an outline.	Draft the paper.	
16	17	18	19	20	21	22
	Draft the paper.		Visit the writing center to get help with ideas for revision.	Do further research if necessary.		
23	24	25	26	27	28	29
Revise the paper.					Prepare a list of works cited.	
30	31					
Proofread the final draft.	**Final draft due.**					

R1

Conducting research

Throughout this tabbed section, you will encounter examples related to three sample research papers:

- A paper on the dangers of Internet surveillance in the workplace, written by a student in an English composition class (see p. 450). The student, Anna Orlov, uses the MLA (Modern Language Association) style of documentation.

- A paper on the limitations of medications to treat childhood obesity, written by a student in a psychology class (see p. 493). The student, Luisa Mirano, uses the APA (American Psychological Association) style of documentation.

- A paper on the extent to which Civil War general Nathan Bedford Forrest can be held responsible for the Fort Pillow massacre, written by a student in a history class (see p. 526). The student, Ned Bishop, uses the CMS (*Chicago Manual of Style*) documentation system.

R1-a Pose possible questions worth exploring.

Working within the guidelines of your assignment, pose a few questions that seem worth researching. Here, for example, are some preliminary questions jotted down by students enrolled in a variety of classes in different disciplines.

- Should the FCC broaden its definition of indecent programming to include violence?

- Which geological formations are the safest repositories for nuclear waste?

- What was Marcus Garvey's contribution to the fight for racial equality?

- How can governments and zoos help preserve Asia's endangered snow leopard?

- Why was amateur archaeologist Heinrich Schliemann such a controversial figure in his own time?

As you formulate possible questions, make sure that they are appropriate lines of inquiry for a research paper. Choose questions that are narrow (not too broad), challenging (not too bland), and grounded (not too speculative).

Choosing a narrow question

If your initial question is too broad, given the length of the paper you plan to write, look for ways to restrict your focus. Here, for example, is how two students narrowed their initial questions.

TOO BROAD

What are the hazards of fad diets?

Is the United States seriously addressing the problem of prisoner abuse?

NARROWER

What are the hazards of low-carbohydrate diets?

To what extent has the US military addressed the problem of prisoner abuse since the Abu Ghraib discoveries?

Choosing a challenging question

Your research paper will be more interesting to both you and your audience if you base it on an intellectually challenging line of inquiry. Avoid bland questions that fail to provoke thought or engage readers in a debate.

TOO BLAND

What is obsessive-compulsive disorder?

How does DNA testing work?

CHALLENGING

What treatments for obsessive-compulsive disorder show the most promise?

How reliable is DNA testing?

You may need to address a bland question in the course of answering a more challenging one. For example, if you were writing about promising treatments for obsessive-compulsive disorder, you would no doubt answer the question "What is obsessive-compulsive disorder?" at some point in your paper. It would be a mistake, however, to use the bland question as the focus for the whole paper.

Choosing a grounded question

Finally, you will want to make sure that your research question is grounded, not too speculative. Although speculative questions — such as those that address philosophical, ethical, or religious issues — are worth asking and may receive some attention in a research paper, they are inappropriate central questions. The central argument of a research paper should be grounded in facts; it should not be based entirely on beliefs.

TOO SPECULATIVE

Is it wrong to share music files on the Internet?

Do medical scientists have the right to experiment on animals?

GROUNDED

How has Internet file sharing affected the earning potential of musicians?

How have technology breakthroughs made medical experiments on animals increasingly unnecessary?

ON THE WEB > dianahacker.com/writersref
Research exercises > E-ex R1–1

R1-b   Map out a search strategy.

A search strategy is a systematic plan for tracking down sources. To create a search strategy appropriate for your research question, consult a reference librarian and take a look at your library's Web site, which will give you an overview of available resources.

> ACADEMIC ENGLISH Whether it is your first or fiftieth time writing a research paper, you may initially feel overwhelmed by the number of resources available to you both in print and online. Instead of turning immediately to a popular search engine like *Google*, step back and think about the best way to find the right information for your purpose. You can start by consulting the advice in this section.

Getting started

Reference librarians are information specialists who can save you time by steering you toward relevant and reliable sources. With the help of an expert, you can make the best use of electronic databases, Web search engines, and other reference tools.

When you ask a reference librarian for help, be prepared to answer a number of questions:

- What is your assignment?
- In which academic discipline are you writing?
- What is your tentative research question?
- How long will the paper be?
- How much time can you spend on the project?

It's a good idea to bring a copy of the assignment with you.

In addition to speaking with a reference librarian, take some time to explore your library's Web site. You will typically find links to the library's catalog and to a variety of databases and electronic sources that you can access from any networked computer. In addition, you may find resources listed by subject, research guides, information about interlibrary loans, and links to Web sites selected by librarians for their quality. Many libraries also offer online reference assistance.

LIBRARY HOME PAGE

Address ⬛ http://www.columbia.edu/cu/lweb/

LibraryWeb

[   ] [Search LWeb]

COLUMBIA UNIVERSITY LIBRARIES | **CU Homepage** | **Contacts** | **Hours** | **Ask Us**

Library News

Columbia University Librarians Awarded ARL Fellowships in New Program.

Librarians Create New Inventory Tool for Special Collections.

Limited Edition Catalog of Libraries' "Treasures" Now Available.

Spotlight

The Herbert H. Lehman Suite and Papers

• *Text-only homepage*

Catalogs

- CLIO (Columbia's online catalog)
- Other catalogs at CU and nearby
- A-to-Z List of library catalogs
- Course Reserves

Electronic Resources

- Databases (reference works & indexes)
- E-Journals
- E-Books
- E-News
- E-Images
- E-Data
- Subject Guides
- Digital Library Projects
- Internet Search Engines

Request It Online

- Books & Articles
- BorrowDirect
- Ask Us Now
- More...

Services

- Access
- Borrowing
- Classes & Workshops
- Computing
- Reference Services
- More...

Columbia's Libraries

- Library Homepages
- Locations & Phones
- Hours of Operation
- More...

For Visitors | Jobs | Alumni & Friends | Help | Suggestions

© Columbia University Libraries

Including the library in your plan

Resist the temptation to do all of your work on the Internet. Most college assignments will require using at least some formally published sources, and libraries offer a wider range of quality materials than the Web does. Although you can locate some newspaper, magazine, and journal articles online, you may have to pay a fee to access them. Most libraries subscribe to databases that will give you unlimited access to these materials as well as scholarly resources that won't turn up in a Web search. Keep in mind that databases don't always include full-text articles of everything they cite. Often you'll need to track down print copies in your library's stacks or request them through interlibrary loan.

Choosing an appropriate search strategy

No single search strategy works for every topic. For some topics, it may be appropriate to search for information in newspapers, magazines, and Web sites. For others, the best sources might be found in scholarly journals and books and specialized reference works. Still other topics might be enhanced by field research — interviews, surveys, or direct observation. With the help of a reference librarian, each of the students mentioned on page 360 constructed a search strategy appropriate for his or her research question.

ANNA ORLOV Anna Orlov's topic, the dangers of Internet surveillance in the workplace, was so current that books were an unlikely source. To find up-to-date information on her topic, Orlov decided to

- search a general database for articles in magazines, newspapers, and journals
- use Web search engines, such as *Google*, to locate relevant sites, online articles, and government publications

LUISA MIRANO Luisa Mirano's topic, the limitations of medications for childhood obesity, has recently become the subject of psychological studies as well as articles in the popular press (newspapers and magazines aimed at the general public). Thinking that both popular and scholarly works would be appropriate, Mirano decided to

- locate books through the library's online catalog
- check a specialized encyclopedia, *Encyclopedia of Psychology*
- search a general database for popular articles
- search a specialized database, *PsycINFO*, for scholarly articles

NED BISHOP   Ned Bishop's topic, the role played by Nathan Bedford Forrest in the Fort Pillow massacre, is an issue that has been investigated and debated by professional historians. Given the nature of his historical topic, Ned Bishop decided to

- locate books through the library's online catalog
- locate scholarly articles by searching a specialized database, *America: History and Life*
- locate newspaper articles from 1864 by using a print index
- search the Web for other historical primary sources

R1-c To locate articles, search a database or consult a print index.

Libraries subscribe to a variety of electronic databases (sometimes called *periodical databases*) that give students access to articles and other materials without charge. Because many databases are limited to relatively recent works, you may need to consult a print index as well.

What databases offer

Your library has access to databases that can lead you to articles in newspapers, magazines, and scholarly or technical journals. Some databases cover several subjects; others cover one subject in depth. Your library might subscribe to some of the following resources.

GENERAL DATABASES

EBSCOhost. A portal to more than one hundred databases that include periodical articles, government documents, pamphlets, and other types of documents.

InfoTrac. A collection of databases, some of which index periodical articles.

LexisNexis. A set of databases that are particularly strong in coverage of news, business, legal, and political topics.

ProQuest. A database of periodical articles.

SUBJECT-SPECIFIC DATABASES

ERIC. An education database.

PubMed. A database offering abstracts of medical research studies.

MLA Bibliography. A database of literary criticism.

PsycINFO. A database of psychology research.

Refining keyword searches in databases and search engines

Although command terms and characters vary among electronic databases and Web search engines, some of the most commonly used functions are listed here.

- Use quotation marks around words that are part of a phrase: "Broadway musicals".

- Use AND to connect words that must appear in a document: Ireland AND peace. Some search engines require a plus sign instead: Ireland +peace.

- Use NOT in front of words that must not appear in a document: Titanic NOT movie. Some search engines require a minus sign (hyphen) instead: Titanic -movie.

- Use OR if only one of the terms must appear in a document: "mountain lion" OR cougar.

- Use an asterisk as a substitute for letters that might vary: "marine biolog*" (to find *marine biology* or *marine biologist,* for example).

- Use parentheses to group a search expression and combine it with another: (cigarettes OR tobacco OR smok*) AND lawsuits.

NOTE: Many search engines and databases offer an advanced search option that makes it easy to refine your search.

Many databases include the full text of at least some articles; others list only citations or citations with short summaries called *abstracts*. When full text is not available, the citation will give you enough information to track down an article.

How to search a database

To find articles on your topic in a database, start with a keyword search. If the first keyword you try results in no matches, experiment with synonyms or ask a librarian for suggestions. For example, if you're searching for sources on a topic related to education, you might also want to try the terms *teaching, learning, pedagogy,* and *curriculum.* If your keyword search results in too many matches, narrow it by using one of the strategies in the chart at the top of this page.

For her paper on Internet surveillance in the workplace, Anna Orlov conducted a keyword search in a general periodical database.

DATABASE SCREEN: RESULTS OF A KEYWORD SEARCH

She typed in *employee* and *privacy* and *"internet use"* and *surveillance*; her search brought up nineteen possible articles, some of which looked promising (see the screen above).

When to use a print index

If you want to search for articles published before the 1980s, you may need to turn to a print index. For example, Ned Bishop consulted the *New York Times Index* to locate newspaper articles written in April 1864, just after the battle at Fort Pillow. To find older magazine articles, consult the *Readers' Guide to Periodical Literature* or *Poole's Index to Periodical Literature* or ask a librarian for help.

R1-d   To locate books, consult the library's catalog.

The books your library owns are listed in its computer catalog, along with other resources such as videos. You can search the catalog by author, title, or topic keywords.

Don't be surprised if your first search calls up too few or too many results. If you have too few results, try different keywords or search for books on broader topics. If a search gives you too many results, use the strategies in the chart on page 366 or try an advanced search tool to combine concepts and limit your results. If those strategies don't work, ask a librarian for suggestions.

When Luisa Mirano, whose topic was childhood obesity, entered the term *obesity* into the computer catalog, she was faced with an unmanageable number of hits. She narrowed her search by adding two more specific terms to *obesity*: *child** (to include the terms *child*, *children*, and *childhood*) and *treatment*. When she still got too many results, she limited the first two terms to subject searches to find books that had obesity in children as their primary subject (see screen 1). Screen 2 shows the complete record for one of the books she found. The call number, listed beside *Availability*, is the book's address on the library shelf. (When you're retrieving a book from the shelf, scan other books in the area since they are likely to be on the same topic.)

LIBRARIAN'S TIP: The record for a book lists related subject headings. These headings are a good way to locate other books on your subject. For example, the record in screen 2 lists the terms *obesity in children* and *obesity in adolescence* as related subject headings. By clicking on these new terms, Mirano found a few more books on her subject.

LIBRARY CATALOG SCREEN 1: ADVANCED SEARCH

LIBRARY CATALOG SCREEN 2: COMPLETE RECORD FOR A BOOK

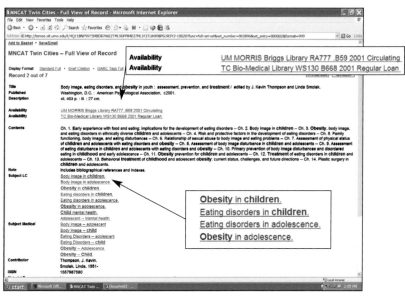

R1-e To locate a wide variety of sources, turn to the Web.

For some (but not all) topics, the Web is an excellent resource. For example, government agencies post information on the Web, and the sites of many organizations are filled with information about the issues they cover. Museums and libraries often post digital versions of primary sources, such as photographs, political speeches, and classic literary texts.

Although the Web can be a rich source of information, some of which can't be found anywhere else, it lacks quality control. Anyone can publish on the Web, so you'll need to evaluate online sources with special care (see R2).

This section describes the following Web resources: search engines, directories, digital archives, government and news sites, and discussion forums.

ON THE WEB > dianahacker.com/writersref
    Additional resources > Links Library > Conducting research

Search engines

Search engines take your search terms and seek matches among millions of Web pages. Some search engines go into more depth than others, but none can search the entire Web. Often it is a good idea to try more than one search engine, since each locates sources in its own way. For current information about search engines, visit *Search Engine Showdown* at <http://www.searchengineshowdown.com>. This site classifies search engines, evaluates them, and provides updates on new search features. Following are some popular search engines:

Google <http://www.google.com>

MSN Search <http://search.msn.com>

Teoma <http://www.teoma.com>

Yahoo! <http://www.yahoo.com>

In using a search engine, focus your search as narrowly as possible. You can sharpen your search by using many of the tips listed in the chart on page 366 or by using the search engine's advanced search form.

SEARCH ENGINE SCREEN: RESULTS OF AN ADVANCED SEARCH

Web Results 1 - 5 of about 9 over the past 3 months for "Internet surveillance" employee "workplace privacy" site:.org (0.44 seconds)

Tip: Try removing quotes from your search to get more results.

EPIC/PI - Privacy & Human Rights 2000
Now the supervision of **employee**'s performance, behavior and... [89]Information and
Privacy Commissioner/Ontario, **Workplace Privacy**: The Need for a..
www.privacyinternational.org/survey/phr2000/threats.html - 131k Cached - Similar pages

Privacy and Human Rights 2003: Threats to Privacy
Other issues that raise **workplace privacy** concerns are employer requirements that
employees complete medical tests, questionnaires, and polygraph tests..
www.privacyinternational.org/survey/phr2003/threats.htm - 279k Cached - Similar pages
[More results from www.privacyinternational.org]

[PDF] Monitoring **Employee** E-Mail And Internet Usage: Avoiding The..
File Format: PDF/Adobe Acrobat - View as HTML
Internet surveillance by employers in the American workplace. At present, US **employees**
in the private workplace have no constitutional, common law or statu
lsr.nellco.org/cgi/viewcontent.cgi?article=1006&context=suffolk/ip - Similar pages

Previous EPIC Top News
The agencies plan to use RFID to track **employees**' movements and in ID cards... For more
information on **workplace privacy**, see the EPIC **Workplace Privacy** ...
www.epic.org/news/2005.html - 163k Cached - Similar pages

For her paper on Internet surveillance in the workplace, Anna Orlov had difficulty restricting the number of hits. When she typed the words *internet, surveillance, workplace,* and *privacy* into a search engine, she got more than 80,000 matches. To narrow her search, Orlov tried typing in the phrases *"internet surveillance",* *employee,* and *"workplace privacy"*. The result was 422 matches, still too many, so Orlov clicked on Advanced Search and restricted her search to sites with URLs ending in *.org* and to those updated only in the last three months. (See the screen on p. 370.)

Directories

Unlike search engines, which hunt for Web pages automatically, directories are put together by information specialists who choose reputable sites and arrange them by topic: education, health, politics, and so on.

Some directories are more selective and therefore more useful for scholarly research than the directories that typically accompany a search engine. For example, the directory for the *Internet Scout Project* was created for a research audience; it includes annotations that are both descriptive and evaluative. The following directories are especially useful for scholarly research:

Internet Scout Project <http://scout.wisc.edu/Archives>

Librarian's Internet Index <http://www.lii.org>

Open Directory Project <http://www.dmoz.org>

WWW Virtual Library <http://www.vlib.org>

Digital archives

Archives may contain the texts of poems, books, speeches, political cartoons, and historically significant documents such as the Declaration of Independence and the Emancipation Proclamation. The materials in these sites are usually limited to official documents and older works because of copyright laws. The following online archives are impressive collections:

American Memory <http://memory.loc.gov>

Archival Research Catalog <http://www.archives.gov/research/arc>

Avalon Project <http://www.yale.edu/lawweb/avalon/avalon.htm>

Electronic Text Center <http://etext.lib.virginia.edu>

Eurodocs <http://library.byu.edu/~rdh/eurodocs>

Internet History Sourcebooks <http://www.fordham.edu/halsall>

Online Books Page <http://digital.library.upenn.edu/books>

Government and news sites

For current topics, both government and news sites can prove useful. Many government agencies at every level provide online information. Government-maintained sites include resources such as legal texts, facts and statistics, government reports, and searchable reference databases. Here are just a few government sites:

Census Bureau <http://www.census.gov>

Fedstats <http://www.fedstats.gov>

FirstGov <http://www.firstgov.gov>

GPO Access <http://www.gpoaccess.gov>

United Nations <http://www.un.org>

Many news organizations offer up-to-date information on the Web. These online services often allow nonsubscribers to read current stories for free. Some allow users to log on as guests and search archives without cost, but to read actual articles users typically must pay a fee. Check with your library to see if it subscribes to a news archive that you can access at no charge. The following are some free news sites:

Google News <http://news.google.com>

Kidon Media-Link <http://www.kidon.com/media-link>

NewsLink <http://newslink.org>

Discussion forums

The Web offers various ways of communicating with experts and others who have an interest in your topic. You might join an online mailing list, for example, to send and receive e-mail messages relevant to your topic. Or you may wish to search a newsgroup's postings. Newsgroups resemble bulletin boards on which messages are posted and connected through "threads" as others respond. In addition, you might log on to real-time discussion forums. To find mailing lists, newsgroups, and forums, try one of these sites:

CataList <http://www.lsoft.com/catalist.html>

Google Groups <http://groups.google.com>

Tile.Net <http://tile.net/lists>

NOTE: Be aware that many of the people you contact in discussion forums will not be experts on your topic. Although you are more likely to find serious and worthwhile commentary in moderated mailing lists and scholarly discussion forums than in more free-wheeling newsgroups, it is difficult to guarantee the credibility of anyone you meet online.

R1-f Use other search tools.

In addition to articles, books, and Web sources, you may want to consult reference works such as encyclopedias and almanacs. Bibliographies (lists of works written on a topic) and citations in scholarly works can lead you to additional sources.

Reference works

The reference section of the library holds both general and specialized encyclopedias, dictionaries, almanacs, atlases, and biographical references, some available in electronic format. Such works often serve as a good overview of a subject and include references to the most significant works on a topic. Check with a reference librarian to see which works are most appropriate for your project.

GENERAL REFERENCE WORKS   General reference works are good places to check facts and get basic information. Here are a few frequently used general references:

American National Biography

National Geographic Atlas of the World

The New Encyclopaedia Britannica

The Oxford English Dictionary

Statistical Abstract of the United States

World Almanac and Book of Facts

Although general encyclopedias are often a good place to find background about your topic, you should rarely use them in your final paper. Most instructors expect you to rely on more specialized sources.

SPECIALIZED REFERENCE WORKS   Specialized reference works often go into a topic in depth, sometimes in the form of articles written by leading authorities. Many specialized works are available, including these:

> *Contemporary Authors*
>
> *Encyclopedia of Applied Ethics*
>
> *Encyclopedia of Crime and Justice*
>
> *Encyclopedia of Psychology*
>
> *McGraw-Hill Encyclopedia of Science and Technology*

ON THE WEB > dianahacker.com/writersref
Research and Documentation Online > Finding sources

Bibliographies and scholarly citations

Bibliographies are lists of works written on a particular topic. They include enough information about each work (author's name, title, publication data) so that you can locate the book or article. In some cases bibliographies are annotated: They contain abstracts giving a brief overview of each work's contents.

In addition to book-length bibliographies, scholarly books and articles list the works the author has cited, usually at the end. These lists are useful shortcuts. For example, most of the scholarly articles Luisa Mirano consulted contained citations to related research studies; through these citations, she quickly located additional relevant sources on her topic, treatments for childhood obesity.

R1-g   Conduct field research, if appropriate.

Writing projects may be enhanced by, and sometimes focused on, your own field research. For a composition class, for example, you might want to interview a local politician about some aspect of a current issue, such as the use of cell phones while driving. For a sociology class, you might decide to conduct a survey regarding campus trends in community service. At work, you might need to learn how food industry executives have responded to reports that their products are contributing to health problems.

R2

Evaluating sources

With electronic search tools, you can often locate dozens or even hundreds of potential sources for your topic — far more than you will have time to read. Your challenge will be to determine what kinds of sources you need and to zero in on a reasonable number of quality sources, those truly worthy of your time and attention.

Later, once you have decided on some sources worth consulting, your challenge will be to read them with an open mind and a critical eye.

R2-a Determine how a source will contribute to your writing.

Before you even begin to research your topic, think about how the sources you encounter could help you make your argument. How you plan to use a source will affect how you will evaluate it. Not every source must directly support your thesis. Sources can have various functions in a paper. They can

- provide background information or context for your topic
- explain terms or concepts that your readers might not understand
- provide evidence for your argument
- lend authority to your argument
- offer counterevidence and alternative interpretations to your argument

For examples of how student writers use sources for a variety of purposes, see MLA-3a, APA-3a, and CMS-3a.

R2-b Select sources worth your time and attention.

The chart on page 366 shows how to refine your searches in the library's book catalog, in databases, and in search engines. This section explains how to scan through the results for the most promising sources and how to preview them — without actually reading them — to see whether they are likely to live up to your expectations and meet your needs.

Scanning search results

You will need to use somewhat different strategies when scanning search results from a book catalog, a database, and a Web search engine.

BOOK CATALOGS   The library's book catalog usually gives you a fairly short list of hits. A book's title and date of publication will often be your first clues as to whether the book is worth consulting. If a title looks interesting, you can click on it for further information: the book's subject matter and its length, for example.

DATABASES   Most databases, such as *ProQuest* and *LexisNexis*, list at least the following information, which can help you decide if a source is relevant, current, scholarly enough (see the chart on p. 378), and a suitable length for your purposes.

> Title and brief description (How relevant?)
>
> Date (How current?)
>
> Name of periodical (How scholarly?)
>
> Length (How extensive in coverage?)

At the bottom of this page are just a few of the hits Ned Bishop came up with when he consulted a general database for articles on the Fort Pillow massacre, using the search term *Fort Pillow*.

By scanning the titles, Bishop saw that only one contained the words *Fort Pillow*. This title and the name of the periodical, *Jour-*

☐ **Black, blue and gray: the other Civil War; African-American soldiers, sailors and**
Mark **spies were the unsung heroes.** *Ebony* Feb 1991 v46 n4 p96(6)
    View <u>text and retrieval choices</u>

☐ **The Civil War.** (movie reviews) Lewis Cole. *The Nation* Dec 3, 1990 v251 n19 p694(5)
Mark   View <u>text and retrieval choices</u>

☐ **The hard fight was getting into the fight at all.** (black soldiers in the Civil War)
Mark   Jack Fincher. *Smithsonian* Oct 1990 v21 n7 p46(13)
    View <u>text and retrieval choices</u>

☑ **The Fort Pillow massacre: a statistical note.** John Cimprich, Robert C. Mainfort Jr..
Mark   *Journal of American History* Dec 1989 v76 n3 p830(8)
    View <u>extended citation and retrieval choices</u>

nal of American History, suggested that the source was scholarly. The 1989 publication date was not a problem, since currency is not necessarily a key issue for historical topics. The article's length (eight pages) is given in parentheses at the end of the citation. While the article may seem short, the topic — a statistical note — is narrow enough to ensure adequate depth of coverage. Bishop decided the article was worth consulting.

Bishop chose not to consult the other sources. The first is a brief article in a popular magazine, the second is a movie review, and the third surveys a topic that is far too broad, "black soldiers in the Civil War."

WEB SEARCH ENGINES   Anyone can publish on the Web, and unreliable sites often masquerade as legitimate sources of information. As you scan through search results, look for the following clues about the probable relevance, currency, and reliability of a site — but be aware that the clues are by no means foolproof.

Title, keywords, and lead-in text (How relevant?)

A date (How current?)

An indication of the site's sponsor or purpose (How reliable?)

The URL, especially the domain name: .com, .edu, .gov, or .org (How relevant? How reliable?)

The following are a few of the results that Luisa Mirano retrieved after typing the keywords *childhood obesity* into a search engine; she limited her search to works with those words in the title.

American **Obesity** Association - **Childhood Obesity**
Childhood Obesity. **Obesity** in children ... Note: The term "**childhood obesity**" may refer to both **children** and adolescents. In general, we ...
www.**obesity**.org/subs/**childhood**/ - 17k - Jan 8, 2005 - Cached - Similar pages

Childhood Obesity
KS Logo, **Childhood Obesity**. advertisement. Source. ERIC Clearinghouse on Teaching and Teacher Education. Contents. ... Back to the Top Causes of **Childhood Obesity**. ...
www.kidsource.com/kidsource/content2/**obesity**.html - 18k - Cached - Similar pages

Childhood Obesity, June 2002 Word on Health - National Institutes ...
Childhood Obesity on the Rise, an article in the June 2002 edition of The NIH Word on Health - Consumer Information Based on Research from the National ...
www.nih.gov/news/WordonHealth/ jun2002/**childhoodobesity**.htm - 22k - Cached - Similar pages

MayoClinic.com - **Childhood obesity**: Parenting advice
... **Childhood obesity**: Parenting advice By Mayo Clinic staff. ... Here are some other tips to help your **obese child** — and yourself: Be a positive role model. ...
www.mayoclinic.com/invoke.cfm?id=FL00058 - 42k - Jan 8, 2005 - Cached - Similar pages

Determining if a source is scholarly

For many college assignments, you will be asked to use scholarly sources. These are written by experts for a knowledgeable audience and usually go into more depth than books and articles written for a general audience. (Scholarly sources are sometimes called *refereed* or *peer-reviewed* because the work is evaluated by experts in the field before publication.) To determine if a source is scholarly, look for the following:

- Formal language and presentation
- Authors who are academics or scientists, not journalists
- Footnotes or a bibliography documenting the works cited by the author in the source
- Original research and interpretation (rather than a summary of other people's work)
- Quotations from and analysis of primary sources (in humanities disciplines such as literature, history, and philosophy)
- A description of research methods or a review of related research (in the sciences and social sciences)

NOTE: In some databases, searches can be limited to refereed or peer-reviewed journals.

Mirano found the first site, which was sponsored by a research-based organization, promising enough to explore for her paper. The second and fourth sites held less promise, because they seemed to offer popular rather than scholarly information. In addition, the *KidSource* site was populated by advertisements. Mirano rejected the third source not because of its reliability — in fact, research from the National Institutes of Health was what she was looking for — but because a quick skim of its contents revealed that the information was too general for her purposes.

Selecting appropriate versions of electronic sources

An electronic source may appear as an abstract, an excerpt, or a full-text article or book. It is important to distinguish among these versions and to use a complete source, preferably one with page numbers, for your research.

Abstracts and excerpts are shortened versions of complete works. An abstract — a summary of a work's contents — might ap-

DATABASE RECORD WITH AN ABSTRACT

LINCC, Library Information Network for Community Colleges
Expanded Academic ASAP

—— Article 1 of 2 —— ▶

☐ *Civil War History*, June 1996 v42 n2 p116(17)
Mark

"These devils are not fit to live on God's earth": war crimes and the Committee on the Conduct of the War, 1864-1865. *Bruce Tap.*

Abstract: The Committee on the Conduct of the War's report on the April 1864 Fort Pillow massacre of black Union soldiers by Confederate forces influenced public opinion against the atrocities of the Confederate troops and accelerated the reconstruction program. Hostility against blacks and abolition in the South prompted the Confederates to target black troops and deny them prisoner of war status. Investigation exposed the barbaric act and the Northern prisoners' suffering in Southern prisons. The report helped the inclusion of black troops in the prisoner exchange program.

Article A18749078

pear in a database record for a periodical article (see above) or in a catalog listing for a book. An excerpt is the first few sentences or paragraphs (the *lead*) of a newspaper or magazine article and usually appears in a list of hits in an online search (see the example on p. 380). Abstracts or excerpts can give you clues about the usefulness of an article for your paper, but by themselves they do not contain enough information to cite. To understand an author's argument and use it in your own paper, you must track down and read the complete article. (See R1-c and R1-d.)

A full-text work may appear online as a PDF (for *portable document format*) file or as an HTML file (sometimes called a *text file*). A PDF file is usually an exact copy of the pages of a periodical article as they appeared in print, including the page numbers. Some corporate and government reports are presented online as PDF files, and these too are usually paginated. A full-text document that appears as an HTML or a text file is not paginated. If your source is available in both formats, choose the PDF file for your research because you will be able to cite specific page numbers.

SEARCH RESULT WITH AN EXCERPT

▾ **BOSTON GLOBE ARCHIVES**

Your search for ((**fort** AND **pillow** AND **massacre**)) returned **1** article(s) matching your terms. To purchase the full-text of an article, follow the link that says "Click for complete article."

| Perform a new search |

Your search results:

TALES OF BLACKS IN THE CIVIL WAR, FOR ALL AGES
Published on March 23, 1998
Author(s):   Scott Alarik, Globe Correspondent

For African Americans, the Civil War was always two wars. It was, of course, the war to save the union and destroy slavery, but for the nearly 180,000 black soldiers who served in the Union Army, it was also a war to establish their rights as citizens and human beings in the United States. Their role in defeating the Confederacy is grandly chronicled in two new books, the massively complete "Like Men of War" and the superbly readable children's book "Black, Blue and
Click for complete article *(782 words)*

R2-c Read with an open mind and a critical eye.

As you begin reading the sources you have chosen, keep an open mind. Do not let your personal beliefs prevent you from listening to new ideas and opposing viewpoints. Your research question — not a snap judgment about the question — should guide your reading.

When you read critically, you are not necessarily judging an author's work harshly; you are simply examining its assumptions, assessing its evidence, and weighing its conclusions.

> ACADEMIC ENGLISH When you research on the Web, it is easy to ignore views different from your own. Web pages that appeal to you will often link to other pages that support the same viewpoint. If your sources all seem to agree with you — and with one another — seek out opposing views and evaluate them with an open mind.

Distinguishing between primary and secondary sources

As you begin assessing evidence in a source, determine whether you are reading a primary or a secondary source. Primary sources are original documents such as letters, diaries, legislative bills, laboratory studies, field research reports, and eyewitness accounts. Secondary sources are commentaries on primary sources — another source's opinions about or interpretation of a primary source. A primary source for Ned Bishop was Nathan Bedford Forrest's official report on the battle at Fort Pillow. Bishop also consulted a number of secondary sources, some of which relied heavily on primary sources such as letters.

Although a primary source is not necessarily more reliable than a secondary source, it has the advantage of being a firsthand account. Naturally, you can better evaluate what a secondary source says if you have first read any primary sources it discusses.

Being alert for signs of bias

Both in print and online, some sources are more objective than others. If you were exploring the conspiracy theories surrounding John F. Kennedy's assassination, for example, you wouldn't look to a supermarket tabloid, such as the *National Enquirer*, for answers. Even publications that are considered reputable can be editorially biased. For example, *USA Today*, *National Review*, and *Ms.* are all credible sources, but they are also likely to interpret events quite

---

Evaluating all sources

CHECKING FOR SIGNS OF BIAS

- Does the author or publisher have political leanings or religious views that could affect objectivity?
- Is the author or publisher associated with a special-interest group, such as Greenpeace or the National Rifle Association, that might see only one side of an issue?
- Are alternative views presented and addressed? How fairly does the author treat opposing views?
- Does the author's language show signs of bias?

ASSESSING AN ARGUMENT

- What is the author's central claim or thesis?
- How does the author support this claim — with relevant and sufficient evidence or with just a few anecdotes or emotional examples?
- Are statistics consistent with those you encounter in other sources? Have they been used fairly? Does the author explain where the statistics come from? (It is possible to "lie" with statistics by using them selectively or by omitting mathematical details.)
- Are any of the author's assumptions questionable?
- Does the author consider opposing arguments and refute them persuasively? (See A3-c.)
- Does the author fall prey to any logical fallacies? (See A3-a.)

Evaluating Web sources

AUTHORSHIP

- Does the Web site or document have an author? You may need to do some clicking and scrolling to find the author's name. If you have landed directly on an internal page of a site, for example, you may need to navigate to the home page or find an "about this site" link.

- If there is an author, can you tell whether he or she is knowledge-able and credible? When the author's qualifications aren't listed on the site itself, look for links to the author's home page, which may provide evidence of his or her interests and expertise.

SPONSORSHIP

- Who, if anyone, sponsors the site? The sponsor of a site is often named and described on the home page.

- What does the URL tell you? The URL ending often specifies the type of group hosting the site: commercial (.com), educational (.edu), nonprofit (.org), governmental (.gov), military (.mil), or net-work (.net). URLs may also indicate a country of origin: uk (United Kingdom) or jp (Japan), for instance.

PURPOSE AND AUDIENCE

- Why was the site created: To argue a position? To sell a product? To inform readers?

- Who is the site's intended audience? If you do not fit the audience profile, is information on the site still relevant to your topic?

CURRENCY

- How current is the site? Check for the date of publication or the latest update, often located at the bottom of the home page or at the beginning or end of an internal page.

- How current are the site's links? If many of the links no longer work, the site may be too dated for your purposes.

TIP: If the authorship and the sponsorship of a site are both unclear, think twice about using the site for your research.

TIP: To discover a site's sponsor, you may have to truncate, or shorten, the URL. For example, to find the sponsor of a Web site featuring an article on environmentally friendly neighborhood development, you might need to shorten the full URL <http://www.bankofamerica.com/environment/dex.cfm?template=env_reports_speeches&context=smartgrowth> to its base URL <http://www.bankofamerica.com> to find that the sponsor is Bank of America.

differently from one another. If you are uncertain about a periodical's special interests, consult *Magazines for Libraries*. To check for bias in a book, see *Book Review Digest*. A reference librarian can help you locate these resources.

Like publishers, some authors are more objective than others. If you have reason to believe that a writer is particularly biased, you will want to assess his or her arguments with special care. For a list of questions worth asking, see the chart on page 381.

Assessing the author's argument

In nearly all subjects worth writing about, there is some element of argument, so don't be surprised to encounter experts who disagree. When you find areas of disagreement, you will want to read each source's arguments with special care, testing them with your own critical intelligence. For a list of questions worth asking, see the chart on page 381.

R2-d Assess Web sources with special care.

Web sources can be deceptive. Sophisticated-looking sites can be full of dubious information, and the identities of those who created a site are often hidden, along with their motives for having created it. Even hate sites may be cleverly disguised to look legitimate. In contrast, sites with reliable information can stand up to careful scrutiny. For a checklist on evaluating Web sources, see page 382.

In researching her topic on Internet surveillance and workplace privacy, Anna Orlov encountered sites that raised her suspicions. In particular, some sites were authored by surveillance software companies, which have an obvious interest in focusing on the benefits of such software to company management.

R3

Managing information; avoiding plagiarism

An effective researcher is a good record keeper. Whether you decide to keep records on paper or on your computer — or both — your challenge as a researcher will be to find systematic ways of managing information. More specifically, you will need methods for maintaining a working bibliography (see R3-a), keeping track of source materials (see R3-b), and taking notes without plagiarizing (stealing from) your sources (see R3-c).

R3-a Maintain a working bibliography.

Keep a record of any sources you decide to consult. You will need this record, called a *working bibliography*, when you compile the list of sources that will appear at the end of your paper. (The format of this list depends on the documentation style you are using. For MLA style, see MLA-4b; for APA style, see APA-4b; for *Chicago* style, see CMS-4c.) Your working bibliography will probably contain more sources than you will actually include in your list of works cited.

Most researchers print or save bibliographic information from the library's computer catalog, its periodical databases, and the Web. The information you need to collect is given in the chart on page 385. If you download a visual, you must gather the same information as for a print source.

For Web sources, some bibliographic information may not be available, but spend time looking for it before assuming that it doesn't exist. When information isn't available on the home page, you may have to drill into the site, following links to interior pages. Look especially for the author's name, the date of publication (or latest update), and the name of any sponsoring organization. Do not omit such information unless it is genuinely unavailable.

Once you have created a working bibliography, you can annotate it. Writing several brief sentences summarizing key points of a source will help you to identify the source's role in your paper. Also, clarifying the source's ideas at this stage will help you avoid plagiarizing them later.

ON THE WEB > dianahacker.com/writersref
Model papers > Annotated bibliography (MLA)

R3-b Keep track of source materials.

The best way to keep track of source materials is to photocopy them or print them out. Many database subscription services will allow you to e-mail citations or full copies of articles to yourself. Some researchers choose to save these and online sources on a computer or disk.

Information for a working bibliography

FOR A BOOK

- All authors; any editors or translators
- Title and subtitle
- Edition (if not the first)
- Publication information: city, publisher, and date

FOR A PERIODICAL ARTICLE

- All authors of the article
- Title and subtitle of the article
- Title of the magazine, journal, or newspaper
- Date; volume, issue, and page numbers, if available

FOR A PERIODICAL ARTICLE RETRIEVED FROM A DATABASE (IN ADDITION TO PRECEDING INFORMATION)

- Name of the database and an item number, if available
- Name of the subscription service
- URL of the subscription service (for an online database)
- Library where you retrieved the source
- Date you retrieved the source

NOTE: Use particular care when printing or saving articles in PDF files. These may not include some of the elements you need to cite the electronic source properly.

FOR A WEB SOURCE (INCLUDING VISUALS)

- All authors, editors, or creators of the source
- Editor or compiler of the Web site, if there is one
- Title and subtitle of the source and title of the longer work, if applicable
- Title of the site, if available
- Publication information for the source, if available
- Page or paragraph numbers, if any
- Date of online publication (or latest update), if available
- Sponsor of the site
- Date you accessed the source
- The site's URL

NOTE: For the exact bibliographic format to use in the final paper, see MLA-4b, APA-4b, or CMS-4c.

Working with photocopies, printouts, and electronic files — as opposed to relying on memory or hastily written notes — has several benefits. You save time spent in the library. You can highlight key passages, perhaps even color-coding them to reflect topics in your outline. You can annotate the source in the margins and get a head start on note taking. Finally, you reduce the chances of unintentional plagiarism, since you will be able to compare your use of a source in your paper with the actual source, not just with your notes (see R3-c).

NOTE: It's especially important to keep print or electronic copies of Web sources, which may change or even become inaccessible. Make sure that your copy includes the site's URL and your date of access, information needed for your list of works cited.

R3-c   As you take notes, avoid unintentional plagiarism.

When you take notes and jot down ideas, be very careful not to borrow language from your sources. Even if you half-copy the author's sentences — either by mixing the author's phrases with your own without using quotation marks or by plugging your synonyms into the author's sentence structure — you are committing plagiarism, a serious academic offense. (For examples of this kind of plagiarism, see MLA-2, APA-2, and CMS-2.)

To prevent unintentional borrowing, resist the temptation to look at the source as you take notes — except when you are quoting. Keep the source close by so you can check for accuracy, but don't try to put ideas in your own words with the source's sentences in front of you. When you need to quote the exact words of a source, make sure you copy the words precisely and put quotation marks around them.

ACADEMIC ENGLISH Even when you are in the early stages of note taking, it is important to keep in mind that, in the United States, written texts are considered to be an author's property. (This "property" isn't a physical object, so it is often referred to as *intellectual property*.) The author (or publisher) owns the language as well as any original ideas contained in the writing, whether the source is published in print or electronic form. When you use another author's property in your own writing, you are required to follow certain conventions or risk committing the ethical and legal offense known as *plagiarism*.

There are three kinds of note taking: summarizing, paraphrasing, and quoting. Be sure to include exact page references for all three types of notes, since you will need the page numbers later if you use the information in your paper.

Summarizing without plagiarizing

A summary condenses information, perhaps reducing a chapter to a short paragraph or a paragraph to a single sentence. A summary should be written in your own words; if you use phrases from the source, put them in quotation marks.

Here is a passage from an original source read by student John Garcia in researching a paper on mountain lions. Following the passage is Garcia's summary of the source.

ORIGINAL SOURCE

In some respects, the increasing frequency of mountain lion encounters in California has as much to do with a growing *human* population as it does with rising mountain lion numbers. The scenic solitude of the western ranges is prime cougar habitat, and it is falling swiftly to the developer's spade. Meanwhile, with their ideal habitat already at its carrying capacity, mountain lions are forcing younger cats into less suitable terrain, including residential areas. Add that cougars have generally grown bolder under a lengthy ban on their being hunted, and an unsettling scenario begins to emerge.

— Ray Rychnovsky, "Clawing into Controversy," p. 40

SUMMARY

Source: Rychnovsky, "Clawing into Controversy" (40)

Encounters between mountain lions and humans are on the rise in California because increasing numbers of lions are competing for a shrinking habitat. As the lions' wild habitat shrinks, older lions force younger lions into residential areas. These lions have lost some of their fear of humans because of a ban on hunting.

Paraphrasing without plagiarizing

Like a summary, a paraphrase is written in your own words; but whereas a summary reports significant information in fewer words than the source, a paraphrase retells the information in roughly the same number of words. If you retain occasional choice phrases from the source, use quotation marks so you will know later which phrases are not your own.

As you read the following paraphrase of the original source (see p. 387), notice that the language is significantly different from that in the original.

PARAPHRASE

> Source: Rychnovsky, "Clawing into Controversy" (40)
>
> Californians are encountering mountain lions more frequently because increasing numbers of humans and a rising population of lions are competing for the same territory. Humans have moved into mountainous regions once dominated by the lions, and the wild habitat that is left cannot sustain the current lion population. Therefore, the older lions are forcing younger lions into residential areas. And because of a ban on hunting, these younger lions have become bolder — less fearful of encounters with humans.

Using quotation marks to avoid plagiarizing

A quotation consists of the exact words from a source. In your notes, put all quoted material in quotation marks; do not assume that you will remember later which words, phrases, and passages you have quoted and which are your own. When you quote, be sure to copy the words of your source exactly, including punctuation and capitalization. In the following example, John Garcia quotes from the original source on page 387.

QUOTATION

> Source: Rychnovsky, "Clawing into Controversy" (40)
>
> Rychnovsky explains that as humans expand residential areas into mountain ranges, the cougar's natural habitat "is falling swiftly to the developer's spade."

Avoiding Internet plagiarism

Understand what plagiarism is. When you use another author's intellectual property — language, visuals, or ideas — in your own writing without giving proper credit, you commit a kind of academic theft called *plagiarism*.

Treat Web sources in the same way you treat print sources. Any language that you find on the Internet must be carefully cited, even if the material is in the public domain or is publicly accessible on free sites. When you use material from Web sites authored by federal, state, or municipal governments (.gov sites) and by nonprofit organizations (.org sites), you must acknowledge that material, too, as intellectual property owned by those agencies.

Keep track of which words come from sources and which are your own. To prevent unintentional plagiarism when you copy passages from Web sources to an electronic file, put quotation marks around any text that you have inserted into your own work. In addition, during note taking and drafting, you might use a different color font or your word processor's highlighting feature to indicate text taken from sources — so that source material stands out unmistakably as someone else's writing.

Avoid Web sites that bill themselves as "research services" and sell essays. When you use Web search engines to research a topic, you will often see links to sites that appear to offer legitimate writing support but that actually sell term papers. Of course, submitting a paper that you have purchased is cheating, but even using material from one counts as plagiarizing.

R4

Choosing a documentation style

The various academic disciplines use their own editorial style for citing sources and for listing the works that are cited in a paper. *A Writer's Reference* describes three commonly used styles: MLA (Modern Language Association), APA (American Psychological Association), and CMS (*Chicago Manual of Style*). See the appropriate tabbed section for each style. For a list of style manuals in a variety of disciplines, see R4-b.

R4-a Select a style appropriate for your discipline.

In researched writing, sources are cited for several reasons. First, it is important to acknowledge the contributions of others. If you fail to credit sources properly, you commit plagiarism, a serious academic offense. Second, choosing good sources will add credibility to your work; in a sense, you are calling on authorities to serve as expert witnesses. The more care you have taken in choosing reliable sources, the stronger your argument will be. Finally — and most importantly — you are helping to build knowledge by showing readers where they can pursue your topic in greater depth.

All of the academic disciplines cite sources for these same reasons. However, the different styles for citing sources are based on the values and intellectual goals of scholars in different disciplines.

MLA and APA in-text citations

The Modern Language Association (MLA) style and the American Psychological Association (APA) style both use citations in the text of a paper that refer to a list of works at the end of the paper. The systems work somewhat differently, however, because MLA style was created for scholars in English composition and literature, and APA style was created for researchers in the social sciences.

MLA IN-TEXT CITATION

Brandon Conran argues that the story is written from "a bifocal point of view" (111).

APA IN-TEXT CITATION

As researchers Yanovski and Yanovski (2002) have explained, obesity was once considered "either a moral failing or evidence of underlying psychopathology" (p. 592).

While MLA and APA styles work in a similar way, some basic disciplinary differences show up in these key elements:

- author's name
- date of publication
- page numbers
- verb tense in signal phrases

MLA style, which gives the author's full name on first mention, reflects the respect that English scholars have for authors of written words. APA style usually uses last names only, not out of disrespect but to emphasize the objectivity of scientific inquiry. APA style, which gives a date after the author's name, reflects the social scientist's concern with the currency of experimental results. MLA style omits the date in the text citation because English scholars are less concerned with currency; what someone had to say a century ago may be as significant as the latest contribution to the field.

Both styles include page numbers for quotations. MLA style requires page numbers for summaries and paraphrases as well; with a page number, readers can easily find the exact passage that has been summarized or paraphrased. While APA does not require page numbers for summaries and paraphrases, it recommends that writers use a page number if doing so would help readers find the passage in a longer work.

Finally, MLA style uses the present tense (such as *argues*) to introduce cited material, whereas APA style uses the past or present perfect tense (such as *argued* or *have argued*). The present tense evokes the timelessness of a literary text; the past or present perfect tense emphasizes that an experiment was conducted in the past.

CMS footnotes or endnotes

Most historians and many scholars in the humanities use the style of footnotes or endnotes recommended by *The Chicago Manual of Style* (CMS). Historians base their work on a wide variety of primary and secondary sources, all of which must be cited. The CMS note system has the virtue of being relatively unobtrusive; even when a paper or an article is thick with citations, readers will not be overwhelmed. In the text of the paper, only a raised number appears. Readers who are interested can consult the accompanying numbered note, which is given either at the foot of the page or at the end of the paper.

TEXT

Historian Albert Castel quotes several eyewitnesses on both the Union and the Confederate sides as saying that Forrest ordered his men to stop firing.[7]

NOTE

7. Albert Castel, "The Fort Pillow Massacre: A Fresh Examination of the Evidence," *Civil War History* 4, no. 1 (1958): 44–45.

The CMS system gives as much information as the MLA or APA system, but less of that information appears in the text of the paper.

R4-b If necessary, consult a style manual.

Following is a list of style manuals used in a variety of disciplines.

BIOLOGY (See <http://dianahacker.com/resdoc> for more information.)

Council of Science Editors. *Scientific Style and Format: The CSE Manual for Authors, Editors, and Publishers.* 7th ed. Reston: Council of Science Eds., 2006.

BUSINESS

American Management Association. *The AMA Style Guide for Business Writing.* New York: AMACOM, 1996.

CHEMISTRY

Dodd, Janet S., ed. *The ACS Style Guide: A Manual for Authors and Editors.* 2nd ed. Washington: Amer. Chemical Soc., 1997.

ENGINEERING

Institute of Electrical and Electronics Engineers. *IEEE Standards Style Manual.* Rev. ed. New York: IEEE, 2005 <http://standards.ieee.org/guides/style/2005Style.pdf>.

ENGLISH AND THE HUMANITIES (See MLA-1 to MLA-5.)

Gibaldi, Joseph. *MLA Handbook for Writers of Research Papers.* 6th ed. New York: MLA, 2003.

GEOLOGY

Bates, Robert L., Rex Buchanan, and Marla Adkins-Heljeson, eds. *Geowriting: A Guide to Writing, Editing, and Printing in Earth Science.* 5th ed. Alexandria: Amer. Geological Inst., 1995.

GOVERNMENT DOCUMENTS

Garner, Diane L. *The Complete Guide to Citing Government Information Resources: A Manual for Social Science and Business Research.* 3rd ed. Bethesda: Congressional Information Service, 2002.

United States Government Printing Office. *Style Manual.* Washington: GPO, 2000.

HISTORY (See CMS-1 to CMS-5.)

The Chicago Manual of Style. 15th ed. Chicago: U of Chicago P, 2003.

JOURNALISM

Goldstein, Norm, ed. *Associated Press Stylebook and Briefing on Media Law.* Rev. ed. New York: Associated Press, 2005.

LAW

Harvard Law Review et al. *The Bluebook: A Uniform System of Citation.* 18th ed. Cambridge: Harvard Law Rev. Assn., 2005.

LINGUISTICS

Linguistic Society of America. "LSA Style Sheet." Published annually in the December issue of the *LSA Bulletin.*

MATHEMATICS

American Mathematical Society. *Author Resource Center* <http://www.ams.org/authors>.

MEDICINE

Iverson, Cheryl, et al. *American Medical Association Manual of Style: A Guide for Authors and Editors.* 9th ed. Baltimore: Williams, 1998.

MUSIC

Holoman, D. Kern, ed. *Writing about Music: A Style Sheet from the Editors of* 19th-Century Music. Berkeley: U of California P, 1988.

PHYSICS

American Institute of Physics. *Style Manual: Instructions to Authors and Volume Editors for the Preparation of AIP Book Manuscripts.* 5th ed. New York: AIP, 1995.

POLITICAL SCIENCE

American Political Science Association. *Style Manual for Political Science.* Rev. ed. Washington: APSA, 2001.

PSYCHOLOGY AND OTHER SOCIAL SCIENCES (See APA-1 to APA-5.)

American Psychological Association. *Publication Manual of the American Psychological Association.* 5th ed. Washington: APA, 2001.

SCIENCE AND TECHNICAL WRITING

American National Standards Institute. *American National Standard for the Preparation of Scientific Papers for Written or Oral Presentation.* New York: ANSI, 1979.

Microsoft Corporation. *Microsoft Manual of Style for Technical Publications.* 3rd ed. Redmond: Microsoft, 2004.

Rubens, Philip, ed. *Science and Technical Writing: A Manual of Style.* 2nd ed. New York: Routledge, 2001.

SOCIAL WORK

National Association of Social Workers. *Writing for the NASW Press: Information for Authors* <http://naswpress.org/resources/tools/01-write/guidelines_toc.htm>.

MLA

MLA Papers

MLA

MLA Papers

MLA Papers

Most English instructors and some humanities instructors will ask you to document your sources with the Modern Language Association (MLA) system of citations described in MLA-4. When writing an MLA paper that is based on sources, you face three main challenges: (1) supporting a thesis, (2) citing your sources and avoiding plagiarism, and (3) integrating quotations and other source material.

Examples in this tabbed section are drawn from research a student conducted on online monitoring of employees' computer use. Anna Orlov's research paper, which argues that electronic surveillance in the workplace threatens employees' privacy and autonomy, appears on pages 450–54.

MLA-1

Supporting a thesis

Most research assignments ask you to form a thesis, or main idea, and to support that thesis with well-organized evidence.

MLA-1a Form a tentative thesis.

Once you have read a variety of sources and considered all sides of your issue, you are ready to form a tentative thesis: a one-sentence (or occasionally a two-sentence) statement of your central idea (see C2-a). In a research paper, your thesis will answer the central research question you posed earlier (see R1-a). Here, for example, are Anna Orlov's research question and her tentative thesis statement.

ORLOV'S RESEARCH QUESTION

Should employers monitor their employees' online activities in the workplace?

ORLOV'S TENTATIVE THESIS

Employers should not monitor their employees' online activities because electronic surveillance can compromise workers' privacy.

After you have written a rough draft and perhaps done more reading, you may decide to revise your tentative thesis, as did Orlov.

ORLOV'S REVISED THESIS

Although companies often have legitimate concerns that lead them to monitor employees' Internet usage--from expensive security breaches to reduced productivity--the benefits of electronic surveillance are outweighed by its costs to employees' privacy and autonomy.

The thesis usually appears at the end of the introductory paragraph. To read Anna Orlov's thesis in the context of her introduction, see page 450.

ON THE WEB > dianahacker.com/writersref
Research exercises > E-ex MLA 1–1

MLA-1b Organize your evidence.

The body of your paper will consist of evidence in support of your thesis. Instead of getting tangled up in a complex, formal outline, sketch an informal plan that organizes your ideas in bold strokes. Anna Orlov, for example, used this simple plan to outline the structure of her argument:

- Electronic surveillance allows employers to monitor workers more efficiently than older types of surveillance.
- Some experts have argued that companies have important financial and legal reasons to monitor employees' Internet usage.
- But monitoring employees' Internet usage may lower worker productivity when the threat to privacy creates distrust.
- Current laws do little to protect employees' privacy rights, so employees and employers have to negotiate the potential risks and benefits of electronic surveillance.

After you have written a rough draft, a more formal outline can be a useful way to shape the complexities of your argument. See C1-d for an example.

MLA-1c Use sources to inform and support your argument.

Used thoughtfully, the source materials you have gathered will make your argument more complex and convincing for readers.

Sources can play several different roles as you develop your points.

Providing background information or context

You can use facts and statistics to support generalizations or to establish the importance of your topic, as student writer Anna Orlov does in her introduction.

> As the Internet has become an integral tool of businesses, company policies on Internet usage have become as common as policies regarding vacation days or sexual harassment. A 2005 study by the American Management Association and ePolicy Institute found that 76% of companies monitor employees' use of the Web, and the number of companies that block employees' access to certain Web sites has increased 27% since 2001 (1).

Explaining terms or concepts

If readers are unlikely to be familiar with a word, a phrase, or an idea important to your topic, you must explain it for them. Quoting or paraphrasing a source can help you define terms and concepts in neutral, accessible language.

> One popular monitoring method is keystroke logging, which is done by means of an undetectable program on employees' computers. . . . As Lane explains, these programs record every key entered into the computer in hidden directories that can later be accessed or uploaded by supervisors; at their most sophisticated, the programs can even scan for keywords tailored to individual companies (128-29).

Supporting your claims

As you draft your argument, make sure to back up your assertions with facts, examples, and other evidence from your research (see also A2-e). Orlov, for example, uses an anecdote from one of her sources to support her claim that limiting computer access causes resentment among a company's staff.

> Monitoring online activities can have the unintended effect of making employees resentful. . . . Kesan warns that "prohibiting personal use can seem extremely arbitrary and can seriously harm morale. . . . Imagine a concerned parent who is prohibited from checking on a sick child by a draconian company policy" (315-16). As this analysis indicates, employees can become disgruntled when Internet usage policies are enforced to their full extent.

Lending authority to your argument

Expert opinion can give weight to your argument (see also A2-e). But don't rely on experts to make your argument for you. Construct your argument in your own words and, when appropriate, cite the judgment of an authority in the field to support your position.

> Additionally, many experts disagree with employers' assumption that online monitoring can increase productivity. Employment law attorney Joseph G. Schmitt argues that, particularly for employees who are paid a salary rather than by the hour, "a company shouldn't care whether employees spend one or 10 hours on the Internet as long as they are getting their jobs done--and provided that they are not accessing inappropriate sites" (qtd. in Verespej).

Anticipating and countering objections

Do not ignore sources that seem contrary to your position or that offer arguments different from your own. Instead, use them to give voice to opposing points of view and to state potential objections to your argument before you counter them (see A-2f). Anna Orlov, for example, cites conflicting evidence to acknowledge that readers may disagree with her position that online monitoring is bad for businesses.

> On the one hand, computers and Internet access give employees powerful tools to carry out their jobs; on the other hand, the same technology offers constant temptations to avoid work. As a 2005 study by Salary.com and America Online indicates, the Internet ranked as the top choice among employees for ways of wasting time on the job; it beat talking with co-workers--the second most popular method--by a margin of nearly two to one (Frauenheim).

MLA-2

Citing sources; avoiding plagiarism

Your research paper is a collaboration between you and your sources. To be fair and ethical, you must acknowledge your debt to the writers of those sources. If you don't, you commit plagiarism, a serious academic offense.

Three different acts are considered plagiarism: (1) failing to cite quotations and borrowed ideas, (2) failing to enclose borrowed language in quotation marks, and (3) failing to put summaries and paraphrases in your own words.

MLA-2a Cite quotations and borrowed ideas.

You must of course cite all direct quotations. You must also cite any ideas borrowed from a source: summaries and paraphrases; statistics and other specific facts; and visuals such as cartoons, graphs, and diagrams.

The only exception is common knowledge — information your readers could easily find in any number of general sources. For example, it is well known that Toni Morrison won the Nobel Prize in literature in 1993 and that Emily Dickinson published only a handful of her many poems during her lifetime.

As a rule, when you have seen information repeatedly in your reading, you don't need to cite it. However, when information has appeared in only one or two sources or when it is controversial, you should cite the source. If a topic is new to you and you are not sure what is considered common knowledge or what is controversial, ask someone with expertise. When in doubt, cite the source.

The Modern Language Association recommends a system of in-text citations. Here, briefly, is how the MLA citation system usually works:

1. The source is introduced by a signal phrase that names its author.
2. The material being cited is followed by a page number in parentheses.
3. At the end of the paper, a list of works cited (arranged alphabetically according to authors' last names) gives complete publication information about the source.

IN-TEXT CITATION

Legal scholar Jay Kesan points out that the law holds employers liable for employees' actions such as violations of copyright laws, the distribution of offensive or graphic sexual material, and illegal disclosure of confidential information (312).

ENTRY IN THE LIST OF WORKS CITED

Kesan, Jay P. "Cyber-Working or Cyber-Shirking? A First Principles Examination of Electronic Privacy in the Workplace." Florida Law Review 54 (2002): 289-332.

Handling an MLA citation is not always this simple. For a detailed discussion of possible variations, see MLA-4.

MLA-2b Enclose borrowed language in quotation marks.

To indicate that you are using a source's exact phrases or sentences, you must enclose them in quotation marks unless they have been set off from the text by indenting (see p. 406). To omit the quotation marks is to claim — falsely — that the language is your own. Such an omission is plagiarism even if you have cited the source.

ORIGINAL SOURCE

Without adequate discipline, the World Wide Web can be a tremendous time sink; no other medium comes close to matching the Internet's depth of materials, interactivity, and sheer distractive potential.

— Frederick Lane, *The Naked Employee*, p. 142

PLAGIARISM

Frederick Lane points out that if people do not have adequate discipline, the World Wide Web can be a tremendous time sink; no other medium comes close to matching the Internet's depth of materials, interactivity, and sheer distractive potential (142).

BORROWED LANGUAGE IN QUOTATION MARKS

Frederick Lane points out that for those not exercising self-control, "the World Wide Web can be a tremendous time sink; no other medium comes close to matching the Internet's depth of materials, interactivity, and sheer distractive potential" (142).

MLA-2c Put summaries and paraphrases in your own words.

A summary condenses information from a source; a paraphrase repeats the information in about the same number of words. When you summarize or paraphrase, it is not enough to name the source; you must restate the source's meaning using your own language. (See also R3-c.) You commit plagiarism if you half-copy the author's sentences — either by mixing the author's phrases with your own without using quotation marks or by plugging your synonyms into the author's sentence structure.

The first paraphrase of the following source is plagiarized — even though the source is cited — because too much of its language is borrowed from the original. The underlined strings of words have been copied word-for-word (without quotation marks). In addition, the writer has closely echoed the sentence structure of the source, merely substituting some synonyms (*restricted* for *limited, modern era* for *computer age, monitoring* for *surveillance,* and *inexpensive* for *cheap*).

ORIGINAL SOURCE

In earlier times, surveillance was limited to the information that a supervisor could observe and record firsthand and to primitive counting devices. In the computer age surveillance can be instantaneous, unblinking, cheap, and, maybe most importantly, easy.

— Carl Botan and Mihaela Vorvoreanu, "What Do Employees Think about Electronic Surveillance at Work?" p. 126

PLAGIARISM: UNACCEPTABLE BORROWING

Scholars Carl Botan and Mihaela Vorvoreanu argue that in earlier times monitoring of employees was restricted to the information that a supervisor could observe and record firsthand. In the modern era, monitoring can be instantaneous, inexpensive, and, most importantly, easy (126).

To avoid plagiarizing an author's language, resist the temptation to look at the source while you are summarizing or paraphrasing. Close the book, write from memory, and then open the book to check for accuracy. This technique prevents you from being captivated by the words on the page.

ACCEPTABLE PARAPHRASE

Scholars Carl Botan and Mihaela Vorvoreanu claim that the nature of workplace surveillance has changed over time. Before the arrival of computers, managers could collect only small amounts of information about their employees based on what they saw or heard. However, because computers are now standard workplace technology, employers can monitor employees efficiently (126).

ON THE WEB > dianahacker.com/writersref
Research exercises > E-ex MLA 2–1 through MLA 2–6

MLA-3

Integrating sources

Quotations, summaries, paraphrases, and facts will help you make your argument, but they cannot speak for you. You can use several strategies to integrate information from research sources into your paper while maintaining your own voice.

MLA-3a Limit your use of quotations.

Using quotations appropriately

Although it is tempting to insert many quotations in your paper and to use your own words only for connecting passages, do not quote excessively. It is almost impossible to integrate numerous long quotations smoothly into your own text.

Except for the following legitimate uses of quotations, use your own words to summarize and paraphrase your sources and to explain your own ideas.

WHEN TO USE QUOTATIONS

- When language is especially vivid or expressive

- When exact wording is needed for technical accuracy

- When it is important to let the debaters of an issue explain their positions in their own words

- When the words of an important authority lend weight to an argument

- When language of a source is the topic of your discussion (as in an analysis or interpretation)

It is not always necessary to quote full sentences from a source. To reduce your reliance on the words of others, you can often integrate language from a source into your own sentence structure. (For the use of signal phrases in integrating quotations, see MLA-3b.)

> Kizza and Ssanyu observe that technology in the workplace has been accompanied by "an array of problems that needed quick answers" such as electronic monitoring to prevent security breaches (4).

Using the ellipsis mark and brackets

Two useful marks of punctuation, the ellipsis mark and brackets, allow you to keep quoted material to a minimum and to integrate it smoothly into your text.

THE ELLIPSIS MARK To condense a quoted passage, you can use the ellipsis mark (three periods, with spaces between) to indicate that you have omitted words. What remains must be grammatically complete.

> Lane acknowledges the legitimate reasons that many companies have for monitoring their employees' online activities, particularly management's concern about preventing "the theft of information that can be downloaded to a . . . disk, e-mailed to oneself . . . , or even posted to a Web page for the entire world to see" (12).

The writer has omitted from the source the words *floppy or Zip* before *disk* and *or a confederate* after *oneself.*

On the rare occasions when you want to omit one or more full sentences, use a period before the three ellipsis dots.

> Charles Lewis, director of the Center for Public Integrity, points out that "by 1987, employers were administering nearly 2,000,000 polygraph tests a year to job applicants and employees. . . . Millions of workers were required to produce urine samples under observation for drug testing . . ." (22).

Ordinarily, do not use an ellipsis mark at the beginning or at the end of a quotation. Your readers will understand that the quoted material is taken from a longer passage, so such marks are not necessary. The only exception occurs when words have been dropped at the end of the final quoted sentence. In such cases, put three ellipsis dots before the closing quotation mark and parenthetical reference, as in the previous example.

Do not use an ellipsis mark to distort the meaning of your source.

BRACKETS Brackets allow you to insert your own words into quoted material. You can insert words in brackets to explain a confusing reference or to keep a sentence grammatical in your context.

Legal scholar Jay Kesan notes that "a decade ago, losses [from employees' computer crimes] were already mounting to five billion dollars annually" (311).

To indicate an error such as a misspelling in a quotation, insert [sic] after the error.

Johnson argues that "while online monitoring is often imagined as harmles [sic], the practice may well threaten employees' rights to privacy" (14).

Setting off long quotations

When you quote more than four typed lines of prose or more than three lines of poetry, set off the quotation by indenting it one inch (or ten spaces) from the left margin.

Long quotations should be introduced by an informative sentence, usually followed by a colon. Quotation marks are unnecessary because the indented format tells readers that the words are taken word-for-word from the source.

> Botan and Vorvoreanu examine the role of gender in company practices of electronic surveillance:
>> There has never been accurate documentation of the extent of gender differences in surveillance, but by the middle 1990s, estimates of the proportion of surveilled employees that were women ranged from 75% to 85%. . . . Ironically, this gender imbalance in workplace surveillance may be evening out today because advances in surveillance technology are making surveillance of traditionally male dominated fields, such as long-distance truck driving, cheap, easy, and frequently unobtrusive. (127)

Notice that at the end of an indented quotation the parenthetical citation goes outside the final mark of punctuation. (When a quotation is run into your text, the opposite is true. See the sample citations on p. 405.)

MLA-3b Use signal phrases to integrate sources.

Whenever you include a paraphrase, summary, or direct quotation of another writer in your paper, prepare your readers for it with an introduction called a *signal phrase*. A signal phrase names the author of the source and often provides some context for the source material.

Using signal phrases in MLA papers

To avoid monotony, try to vary both the language and the placement of your signal phrases.

Model signal phrases

In the words of researchers Greenfield and Davis, "..."

As legal scholar Jay Kesan has noted, "..."

The ePolicy Institute, an organization that advises companies about reducing risks from technology, reported that "..."

"...," writes Daniel Tynan, "..."

"...," claims attorney Schmitt.

Kizza and Ssanyu offer a persuasive counterargument: "..."

Verbs in signal phrases

acknowledges	comments	endorses	reasons
adds	compares	grants	refutes
admits	confirms	illustrates	rejects
agrees	contends	implies	reports
argues	declares	insists	responds
asserts	denies	notes	suggests
believes	disputes	observes	thinks
claims	emphasizes	points out	writes

When you write a signal phrase, choose a verb that is appropriate for the way you are using the source (see MLA-1c). Are you providing background, explaining a concept, supporting a claim, lending authority, or refuting a belief? See the chart at the top of this page for a list of verbs commonly used in signal phrases. Note that MLA style calls for present-tense verbs (*argues*) to introduce source material unless a date specifies the time of writing.

Marking boundaries

Readers need to move from your words to the words of a source without feeling a jolt. Avoid dropping quotations into the text without warning. Instead, provide clear signal phrases, including at least the author's name, to indicate the boundary between your words and the source's words.

DROPPED QUOTATION

Some experts have argued that a range of legitimate concerns justifies employer monitoring of employee Internet usage. "Employees could accidentally (or deliberately) spill confidential corporate information . . . or allow worms to spread throughout a corporate network" (Tynan).

QUOTATION WITH SIGNAL PHRASE

Some experts have argued that a range of legitimate concerns justifies employer monitoring of employee Internet usage. As PC World columnist Daniel Tynan explains, companies that don't monitor network traffic can be penalized for their ignorance: "Employees could accidentally (or deliberately) spill confidential information . . . or allow worms to spread throughout a corporate network."

Establishing authority

Good research writing uses evidence from reliable sources. The first time you mention a source, briefly include the author's title, credentials, or experience — anything that would help your readers recognize the source's authority.

SOURCE WITH NO CREDENTIALS

Jay Kesan points out that the law holds employers liable for employees' actions such as violations of copyright laws, the distribution of offensive or graphic sexual material, and illegal disclosure of confidential information (312).

SOURCE WITH CREDENTIALS

Legal scholar Jay Kesan points out that the law holds employers liable for employees' actions such as violations of copyright laws, the distribution of offensive or graphic sexual material, and illegal disclosure of confidential information (312).

When you establish your source's authority, as with the phrase *Legal scholar* in the previous example, you also signal to readers your own credibility as a responsible researcher, one who has located trustworthy sources.

Introducing summaries and paraphrases

Introduce most summaries and paraphrases with a signal phrase that names the author and places the material in the context of your argument. Readers will then understand that everything between the signal phrase and the parenthetical citation summarizes or paraphrases the cited source.

Without the signal phrase (underlined) in the following example, readers might think that only the quotation at the end is being cited, when in fact the whole paragraph is based on the source.

> <u>Frederick Lane believes that</u> the personal computer has posed new challenges for employers worried about workplace productivity. Whereas early desktop computers were primitive enough to prevent employees from using them to waste time, the machines have become so sophisticated that they now make non-work-related computer activities easy and inviting. Many employees enjoy adjusting and readjusting features of their computers, from the desktop wallpaper to software they can quickly download. Many workers spend considerable company time playing games on their computers. But perhaps most problematic from the employer's point of view, Lane asserts, is giving employees access to the Internet, "roughly the equivalent of installing a gazillion-channel television set for each employee" (15-16).

There are times when a summary or paraphrase does not require a signal phrase. Readers will understand, for example, that the citation at the end of the following passage applies to the entire paragraph, not just part of it.

> In 2005, the American Management Association and the ePolicy Institute cosponsored a survey on electronic surveillance in the workplace, including the monitoring of employees' use of e-mail, instant messaging, the Web, and voice mail. The organizations received responses to a detailed questionnaire from 526 companies, with nearly half of the respondents representing companies employing up to five hundred workers (12).

Putting direct quotations in context

Because a source cannot reveal its meaning or function by itself, you must make the connection between a source and your own ideas. A signal phrase can show readers how a quotation supports or challenges a point you are making.

Efforts by the music industry to stop Internet file sharing have been unsuccessful and, worse, divisive. Industry analysts share this view. <u>Salon's</u> Scott Rosenberg, for example, writes that the only thing the music industry's "legal strategy has accomplished is to radicalize the community of online music fans and accelerate the process of technological change" (2).

Readers should not have to guess why a quotation appears in your paper. If you use another writer's words, you must explain how they contribute to your point. It's a good idea to embed a quotation — especially a long one — between sentences of your own. In addition to introducing it with a signal phrase, follow it with interpretive comments that link the quotation to your paper's argument.

QUOTATION WITH INSUFFICIENT CONTEXT

The difference, Lane argues, between these old methods of data gathering and electronic surveillance involves quantity:

> Technology makes it possible for employers to gather enormous amounts of data about employees, often far beyond what is necessary to satisfy safety or productivity concerns. And the trends that drive technology--faster, smaller, cheaper--make it possible for larger and larger numbers of employers to gather ever-greater amounts of personal data. (3-4)

QUOTATION WITH EFFECTIVE CONTEXT

The difference, Lane argues, between these old methods of data gathering and electronic surveillance involves quantity:

> Technology makes it possible for employers to gather enormous amounts of data about employees, often far beyond what is necessary to satisfy safety or productivity concerns. And the trends that drive technology--faster, smaller, cheaper--make it possible for larger and larger numbers of employers to gather ever-greater amounts of personal data. (3-4)

Lane points out that employers can collect data whenever employees use their computers--for example, when they send e-mail, surf the Web, or even arrive at or depart from their workstations.

Integrating statistics and other facts

When you are citing a statistic or other specific fact, a signal phrase is often not necessary. In most cases, readers will understand that the citation refers to the statistic or fact (not the whole paragraph).

> According to a 2002 survey, 60% of responding companies reported disciplining employees who had used the Internet in ways the companies deemed inappropriate; 30% had fired their employees for those transgressions (Greenfield and Davis 347).

There is nothing wrong, however, with using a signal phrase to introduce a statistic or other fact.

ON THE WEB > dianahacker.com/writersref
Research exercises > E-ex MLA 3–1 through MLA 3–4

Reviewing an MLA paper: Use of sources

Use of quotations

- Is quoted material enclosed within quotation marks (unless it has been set off from the text)? (See MLA-2b.)
- Is quoted language word-for-word accurate? If not, do brackets or ellipsis marks indicate the changes or omissions? (See pp. 405–06.)
- Does a clear signal phrase (usually naming the author) prepare readers for each quotation and for the purpose the quotation serves? (See MLA-3b.)
- Does a parenthetical citation follow each quotation? (See MLA-4a.)
- Is each quotation put in context? (See pp. 409–10.)

Use of summaries and paraphrases

- Are summaries and paraphrases free of plagiarized wording — not copied or half-copied from the source? (See MLA-2c.)
- Are summaries and paraphrases documented with parenthetical citations? (See MLA-4a.)
- Do readers know where the cited material begins? In other words, does a signal phrase mark the boundary between your words and the summary or paraphrase, unless the context makes clear exactly what you are citing? (See pp. 409–10.)
- Does a clear signal phrase prepare readers for the purpose the summary or paraphrase has in your argument?

Use of statistics and other facts

- Are statistics and facts (other than common knowledge) documented with parenthetical citations? (See MLA-2a.)
- If there is no signal phrase, will readers understand exactly which facts are being cited? (See MLA-3b.)

MLA-4

Documenting sources

In English and in some humanities classes, you will be asked to use the MLA (Modern Language Association) system for documenting sources, which is set forth in the *MLA Handbook for Writers of Research Papers,* 6th ed. (New York: MLA, 2003). MLA recommends in-text citations that refer readers to a list of works cited.

An in-text citation names the author of the source, often in a signal phrase, and gives the page number in parentheses. At the end of the paper, a list of works cited provides publication information about the source; the list is alphabetized by authors' last names (or by titles for works without authors). There is a direct connection between the in-text citation and the alphabetical listing. In the following example, that link is highlighted in orange.

IN-TEXT CITATION

Jay Kesan notes that even though many companies now routinely monitor employees through electronic means, "there may exist less intrusive safeguards for employers" (293).

ENTRY IN THE LIST OF WORKS CITED

Kesan, Jay P. "Cyber-Working or Cyber-Shirking? A First Principles Examination of Electronic Privacy in the Workplace." Florida Law Review 54 (2002): 289–332.

For a list of works cited that includes this entry, see page 454.

NOTE: If your instructor allows italics for the titles of long works and for the names of publications, substitute italics for underlining in all the models in this section.

MLA-4a   MLA in-text citations

MLA in-text citations are made with a combination of signal phrases and parenthetical references. A signal phrase indicates that something taken from a source (a quotation, summary, paraphrase, or fact) is about to be used; usually the signal phrase includes the author's name. The parenthetical reference, which comes

Directory to MLA in-text citation models

after the cited material, normally includes at least a page number. In the models in this section, the elements of the in-text citation are shown in orange.

IN-TEXT CITATION

Kwon points out that the Fourth Amendment does not give employees any protections from employers' "unreasonable searches and seizures" (6).

Readers can look up the author's last name in the alphabetized list of works cited, where they will learn the work's title and other publication information. If readers decide to consult the source, the page number will take them straight to the passage that has been cited.

Basic rules for print and electronic sources

The MLA system of in-text citations, which depends heavily on authors' names and page numbers, was created in the early 1980s with print sources in mind. Because some of today's electronic sources have unclear authorship and lack page numbers, they present a special challenge. Nevertheless, the basic rules are the same for both print and electronic sources.

The models in this section (items 1–5) show how the MLA system usually works and explain what to do if your source has no author or page numbers.

■ **1. AUTHOR NAMED IN A SIGNAL PHRASE** Ordinarily, introduce the material being cited with a signal phrase that includes the author's name. In addition to preparing readers for the source, the signal phrase allows you to keep the parenthetical citation brief.

> Frederick Lane reports that employers do not necessarily have to use software to monitor how their employees use the Web: employers can "use a hidden video camera pointed at an employee's monitor" and even position a camera "so that a number of monitors [can] be viewed at the same time" (147).

The signal phrase — *Frederick Lane reports that* — names the author; the parenthetical citation gives the page number of the book in which the quoted words may be found.

Notice that the period follows the parenthetical citation. When a quotation ends with a question mark or an exclamation point, leave the end punctuation inside the quotation mark and add a period after the parentheses: ". . . ?" (8). (See also the note on p. 321.)

■ **2. AUTHOR NAMED IN PARENTHESES** If a signal phrase does not name the author, put the author's last name in parentheses along with the page number.

> Companies can monitor employees' every keystroke without legal penalty, but they may have to combat low morale as a result (Lane 129).

Use no punctuation between the name and the page number.

■ **3. AUTHOR UNKNOWN** Either use the complete title in a signal phrase or use a short form of the title in parentheses. Titles of books are underlined; titles of articles are put in quotation marks.

> A popular keystroke logging program operates invisibly on workers' computers yet provides supervisors with details of the workers' online activities ("Automatically").

TIP: Before assuming that a Web source has no author, do some detective work. Often the author's name is available but is not easy to find. For example, it may appear at the end of the source, in tiny print. Or it may appear on another page of the site, such as the home page.

NOTE: If a source has no author and is sponsored by a corporate entity, such as an organization or a government agency, name the corporate entity as the author (see item 9 on p. 417).

■ **4. PAGE NUMBER UNKNOWN** You may omit the page number if a work lacks page numbers, as is the case with many Web sources. Although printouts from Web sites usually show page numbers, print-ers don't always provide the same page breaks; for this reason, MLA recommends treating such sources as unpaginated.

> As a 2005 study by Salary.com and America Online indicates, the Internet ranked as the top choice among employees for ways of wasting time on the job; it beat talking with co-workers--the second most popular method--by a margin of nearly two to one (Frauenheim).

When the pages of a Web source are stable (as in PDF files), however, supply a page number in your in-text citation. (For ex-ample, the source cited in the first paragraph of the student paper is a PDF file with stable pages, so a page number is included in the citation. See p. 450.)

NOTE: If a Web source numbers its paragraphs or screens, give the abbreviation "par." or "pars." or the word "screen" or "screens" in the parentheses: (Smith, par. 4).

■ **5. ONE-PAGE SOURCE** If the source is one page long, MLA al-lows (but does not require) you to omit the page number. Many in-structors will want you to supply the page number because without it readers may not know where your citation ends or, worse, may not realize that you have provided a citation at all.

> *No page number given*
>
> Anush Yegyazarian reports that in 2000 the National Labor Relations Board's Office of the General Counsel helped win restitution for two workers who had been dismissed because their employers were displeased by the employees' e-mails about work-related issues. The case points to the ongoing struggle to define what constitutes protected speech in the workplace.

> *Page number given*
>
> Anush Yegyazarian reports that in 2000 the National Labor Relations Board's Office of the General Counsel helped win restitution for two workers who had been dismissed because their employers were displeased by the employees' e-mails about work-related issues (62). This case points to the ongoing struggle to define what constitutes protected speech in the workplace.

Variations on the basic rules

This section describes the MLA guidelines for handling a variety of situations not covered by the basic rules just given. These rules on in-text citations are the same for both traditional print sources and electronic sources.

■ **6. TWO OR MORE TITLES BY THE SAME AUTHOR** If your list of works cited includes two or more titles by the same author, mention the title of the work in the signal phrase or include a short version of the title in the parentheses.

> The American Management Association and ePolicy Institute have tracked employers' practices in monitoring employees' e-mail use. The groups' 2003 survey found that one-third of companies had a policy of keeping and reviewing employees' e-mail messages ("2003 E-mail" 2); in 2005, more than 55% of companies engaged in e-mail monitoring ("2005 Electronic" 1).

Titles of articles and other short works are placed in quotation marks, as in the example just given. Titles of books are underlined.

In the rare case when both the author's name and a short title must be given in parentheses, separate them with a comma.

> A 2004 survey found that 20% of employers responding had employees' e-mail "subpoenaed in the course of a lawsuit or regulatory investigation," up 7% from the previous year (Amer. Management Assn. and ePolicy Inst., "2004 Workplace" 1).

■ **7. TWO OR THREE AUTHORS** Name the authors in a signal phrase, as in the following example, or include their last names in the parenthetical reference: (Kizza and Ssanyu 2).

> Kizza and Ssanyu note that "employee monitoring is a dependable, capable, and very affordable process of electronically or otherwise recording all employee activities at work and also increasingly outside the workplace" (2).

When three authors are named in the parentheses, separate the names with commas: (Alton, Davies, and Rice 56).

■ **8. FOUR OR MORE AUTHORS** Name all of the authors or include only the first author's name followed by "et al." (Latin for "and others"). Make sure that your citation matches the entry in the list of works cited (see item 2 on p. 422).

> The study was extended for two years, and only after results were reviewed by an independent panel did the researchers publish their findings (Blaine et al. 35).

■ **9. CORPORATE AUTHOR** When the author is a corporation, an organization, or a government agency, name the corporate author either in the signal phrase or in the parentheses.

> According to a 2001 survey of human resources managers by the American Management Association, more than three-quarters of the responding companies reported disciplining employees for "misuse or personal use of office telecommunications equipment" (2).

In the list of works cited, the American Management Association is treated as the author and alphabetized under *A*.

When a government agency is treated as the author, it will be alphabetized in the list of works cited under the name of the government, such as "United States" (see item 3 on p. 423). For this reason, you must name the government in your in-text citation.

> The United States Department of Transportation provides nationwide statistics on traffic fatalities.

■ **10. AUTHORS WITH THE SAME LAST NAME** If your list of works cited includes works by two or more authors with the same last name, include the author's first name in the signal phrase or first initial in the parentheses.

> Estimates of the frequency with which employers monitor employees' use of the Internet each day vary widely (A. Jones 15).

■ **11. INDIRECT SOURCE (SOURCE QUOTED IN ANOTHER SOURCE)** When a writer's or a speaker's quoted words appear in a source written by someone else, begin the parenthetical citation with the abbreviation "qtd. in."

> Researchers Botan and McCreadie point out that "workers are objects of information collection without participating in the process of exchanging the information . . ." (qtd. in Kizza and Ssanyu 14).

■ **12. ENCYCLOPEDIA OR DICTIONARY** Unless an encyclopedia or a dictionary has an author, it will be alphabetized in the list of works cited under the word or entry that you consulted — not under the title of the reference work itself (see item 13 on p. 426). Either in your text or in your parenthetical reference, mention the word or the entry. No page number is required, since readers can easily look up the word or entry.

> The word crocodile has a surprisingly complex etymology ("Crocodile").

■ **13. MULTIVOLUME WORK** If your paper cites more than one volume of a multivolume work, indicate in the parentheses the volume you are referring to, followed by a colon and the page number.

> In his studies of gifted children, Terman describes a pattern of accelerated
> language acquisition (2: 279).

If your paper cites only one volume of a multivolume work, you will include the volume number in the list of works cited and will not need to include it in the parentheses.

■ **14. TWO OR MORE WORKS** To cite more than one source in the parentheses, give the citations in alphabetical order and separate them with a semicolon.

> The effects of sleep deprivation have been well documented (Cahill 42;
> Leduc 114; Vasquez 73).

Multiple citations can be distracting, however, so you should not overuse the technique. If you want to alert readers to several sources that discuss a particular topic, consider using an information note instead (see MLA-4c).

■ **15. AN ENTIRE WORK** Use the author's name in a signal phrase or a parenthetical reference. There is of course no need to use a page number.

> Lane explores the evolution of surveillance in the workplace.

■ **16. WORK IN AN ANTHOLOGY** Put the name of the author of the work (not the editor of the anthology) in the signal phrase or the parentheses.

> In "A Jury of Her Peers," Mrs. Hale describes both a style of quilting and a
> murder weapon when she utters the last words of the story: "We call it--knot
> it, Mr. Henderson" (Glaspell 210).

In the list of works cited, the work is alphabetized under Glaspell, not under the name of the editor of the anthology.

Glaspell, Susan. "A Jury of Her Peers." Literature and Its Writers: A Compact
    Introduction to Fiction, Poetry, and Drama. Ed. Ann Charters and Samuel
    Charters. 3rd ed. Boston: Bedford, 2004. 194-210.

■ **17. LEGAL SOURCE** For well-known historical documents, such as articles of the United States Constitution, and for laws in the United States Code, provide a parenthetical citation in the text: (US Const., art. 1, sec. 2) or (12 USC 3412, 2000). There is no need to provide a works cited entry.

Legislative acts and court cases are included in the works cited list (see item 53 on p. 444). Your in-text citation should name the act or case either in a signal phrase or in parentheses. In the text of a paper, names of acts are not underlined, but names of cases are.

> The Jones Act of 1917 granted US citizenship to Puerto Ricans.

> In 1857, Chief Justice Roger B. Taney declared in the case of Dred Scott v. Sandford that blacks, whether enslaved or free, could not be citizens of the United States.

Literary works and sacred texts

Literary works and sacred texts are usually available in a variety of editions. Your list of works cited will specify which edition you are using, and your in-text citation will usually consist of a page number from the edition you consulted (see item 18).

However, MLA suggests that when possible you should give enough information — such as book parts, play divisions, or line numbers — so that readers can locate the cited passage in any edition of the work (see items 19–21).

■ **18. LITERARY WORKS WITHOUT PARTS OR LINE NUMBERS** Many literary works, such as most short stories and many novels and plays, do not have parts or line numbers that you can refer to. In such cases, simply cite the page number.

> At the end of Kate Chopin's "The Story of an Hour," Mrs. Mallard drops dead upon learning that her husband is alive. In the final irony of the story, doctors report that she has died of a "joy that kills" (25).

■ **19. VERSE PLAYS AND POEMS** For verse plays, MLA recommends giving act, scene, and line numbers that can be located in any edition of the work. Use arabic numerals, and separate the numbers with periods.

> In Shakespeare's King Lear, Gloucester, blinded for suspected treason, learns a profound lesson from his tragic experience: "A man may see how this world goes / with no eyes" (4.2.148-49).

For a poem, cite the part (if there are a number of parts) and the line numbers, separated by a period.

> When Homer's Odyssey comes to the hall of Circe, he finds his men
> "mild / in her soft spell, fed on her drug of evil" (10.209-10).

For poems that are not divided into parts, use line numbers. For a first reference, use the word "lines": (lines 5-8). Thereafter use just the numbers: (12-13).

■ **20. NOVELS WITH NUMBERED DIVISIONS** When a novel has numbered divisions, put the page number first, followed by a semicolon, and then indicate the book, part, or chapter in which the passage may be found. Use abbreviations such as "bk." and "ch."

> One of Kingsolver's narrators, teenager Rachel, pushes her vocabulary beyond
> its limits. For example, Rachel complains that being forced to live in the
> Congo with her missionary family is "a sheer tapestry of justice" because her
> chances of finding a boyfriend are "dull and void" (117; bk. 2, ch. 10).

■ **21. SACRED TEXTS** When citing a sacred text such as the Bible or the Qur'an, name the edition you are using in your works cited entry (see item 14 on p. 427). In your parenthetical citation, give the book, chapter, and verse (or their equivalent), separated by periods. Common abbreviations for books of the Bible are acceptable.

> Consider the words of Solomon: "If your enemies are hungry, give them
> food to eat. If they are thirsty, give them water to drink" (Holy Bible,
> Prov. 25.21).

ON THE WEB > dianahacker.com/writersref
Research exercises > E-ex MLA 4–1 and MLA 4–2

MLA-4b MLA list of works cited

An alphabetized list of works cited, which appears at the end of your research paper, gives publication information for each of the sources you have cited in the paper. (For information about preparing the list, see p. 448; for a sample list of works cited, see p. 454.)

NOTE: Unless your instructor asks for them, omit sources not actually cited in the paper, even if you read them.

Directory to *MLA works cited models*

ON THE WEB > dianahacker.com/writersref
Research and Documentation Online > Humanities: Documenting
sources (MLA)

General guidelines for listing authors

Alphabetize entries in the list of works cited by authors' last names
(if a work has no author, alphabetize it by its title). The author's
name is important because citations in the text of the paper refer to
it and readers will be looking for it at the beginning of an entry in
the alphabetized list.

NAME CITED IN TEXT

According to Nancy Flynn, . . .

BEGINNING OF WORKS CITED ENTRY

Flynn, Nancy.

Items 1–5 show how to begin an entry for a work with a single
author, multiple authors, a corporate author, an unknown author,
and multiple works by the same author. What comes after this first
element of your citation will depend on the kind of source you are
citing. (See items 6–60.)

NOTE: For a book, an entry in the works cited list will sometimes
begin with an editor (see item 9 on p. 424).

■ **1. SINGLE AUTHOR** For a work with one author, begin with the
author's last name, followed by a comma; then give the author's
first name, followed by a period.

Tannen, Deborah.

■ **2. MULTIPLE AUTHORS** For works with two or three authors,
name the authors in the order in which they are listed in the
source. Reverse the name of only the first author.

Walker, Janice R., and Todd Taylor.

Wilmut, Ian, Keith Campbell, and Colin Tudge.

For a work with four or more authors, either name all of the
authors or name the first author, followed by "et al." (Latin for "and
others").

Sloan, Frank A., Emily M. Stout, Kathryn Whetten-Goldstein, and Lan Liang.

Sloan, Frank A., et al.

■ **3. CORPORATE AUTHOR** When the author of a print document or Web site is a corporation, a government agency, or some other organization, begin your entry with the name of the group.

First Union.

United States. Bureau of the Census.

American Management Association.

NOTE: Make sure that your in-text citation also treats the organization as the author (see item 9 on p. 417).

■ **4. UNKNOWN AUTHOR** When the author of a work is unknown, begin with the work's title. Titles of articles and other short works, such as brief documents from Web sites, are put in quotation marks. Titles of books and other long works, such as entire Web sites, are underlined.

Article or other short work
"Media Giants."

Book or other long work
Atlas of the World.

Before concluding that the author of a Web source is unknown, check carefully (see the tip on p. 414). Also remember that an organization may be the author (see item 3 at the top of this page).

■ **5. TWO OR MORE WORKS BY THE SAME AUTHOR** If your list of works cited includes two or more works by the same author, use the author's name only for the first entry. For other entries, use three hyphens followed by a period. The three hyphens must stand for exactly the same name or names as in the first entry. List the titles in alphabetical order (ignoring the article *A, An,* or *The* at the beginning of a title).

García, Cristina. The Agüero Sisters. New York: Ballantine, 1998.

---. Monkey Hunting. New York: Ballantine, 2003.

Books

Items 6–19 apply to print books. For online books, see item 29.

■ **6. BASIC FORMAT FOR A BOOK** For most books, arrange the information into three units, each followed by a period and one space: the author's name; the title and subtitle, underlined; and the place of publication, the publisher, and the date.

Tan, Amy. The Bonesetter's Daughter. New York: Putnam, 2001.

Take the information about the book from its title page and copyright page. Use a short form of the publisher's name; omit terms such as *Press, Inc.*, and *Co.* except when naming university presses (Harvard UP, for example). If the copyright page lists more than one date, use the most recent one.

■ **7. AUTHOR WITH AN EDITOR** Begin with the author and title, followed by the name of the editor. In this case the abbreviation "Ed." means "Edited by," so it is the same for one or multiple editors.

Plath, Sylvia. The Unabridged Journals of Sylvia Plath. Ed. Karen V. Kukil.
    New York: Anchor-Doubleday, 2000.

■ **8. AUTHOR WITH A TRANSLATOR** Begin with the name of the author. After the title, write "Trans." (for "Translated by") and the name of the translator.

Allende, Isabel. Zorro. Trans. Margaret Sayers Peden. London: Fourth Estate, 2005.

■ **9. EDITOR** An entry for a work with an editor is similar to that for a work with an author except that the name is followed by a comma and the abbreviation "ed." for "editor" (or "eds." for "editors").

Craig, Patricia, ed. The Oxford Book of Travel Stories. Oxford: Oxford UP, 1996.

■ **10. WORK IN AN ANTHOLOGY** Begin with (1) the name of the author of the selection, not with the name of the editor of the anthology. Then give (2) the title of the selection; (3) the title of the anthology; (4) the name of the editor (preceded by "Ed." for "Edited by"); (5) publication information; and (6) the pages on which the selection appears.

┌─── 1 ──┐ ┌──── 2 ────┐ ┌──────── 3 ────────┐
Desai, Anita. "Scholar and Gypsy." The Oxford Book of Travel Stories.

┌──── 4 ────┐ ┌──── 5 ────┐ ┌─6─┐
    Ed. Patricia Craig. Oxford: Oxford UP, 1996. 251-73.

Citation at a glance: Book (MLA)

To cite a book in MLA style, include the following elements:

1 Author
2 Title and subtitle
3 City of publication
4 Publisher
5 Date of publication

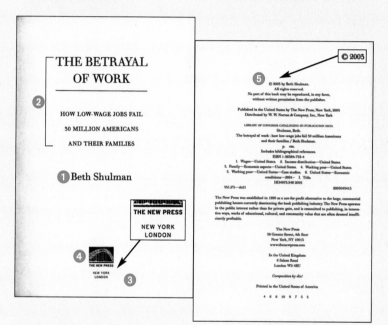

WORKS CITED ENTRY FOR A BOOK

Shulman, Beth. The Betrayal of Work: How Low-Wage Jobs Fail 30

Million Americans and Their Families. New York: New, 2003.

For more on citing books in MLA style, see pages 424–28.

If you wish, you may cross-reference two or more works from the same anthology. Provide an entry for the anthology (see item 9 on p. 424). Then in separate entries list the author and title of each selection, followed by the last name of the editor of the anthology and the page numbers on which the selection appears.

Desai, Anita. "Scholar and Gypsy." Craig 251-73.

Malouf, David. "The Kyogle Line." Craig 390-96.

Alphabetize the entry for the anthology under the name of its editor (Craig); alphabetize the entries for the selections under the names of the authors (Desai, Malouf).

■ **11. EDITION OTHER THAN THE FIRST** If you are citing an edition other than the first, include the number of the edition after the title (or after the names of any translators or editors that appear after the title): 2nd ed., 3rd ed., and so on.

Auletta, Ken. The Underclass. 2nd ed. Woodstock: Overlook, 2000.

■ **12. MULTIVOLUME WORK** Include the total number of volumes before the city and publisher, using the abbreviation "vols."

Conway, Jill Ker, ed. Written by Herself. 2 vols. New York: Random, 1996.

If your paper cites only one of the volumes, give the volume number before the city and publisher and give the total number of volumes after the date.

Conway, Jill Ker, ed. Written by Herself. Vol. 2. New York: Random, 1996. 2 vols.

■ **13. ENCYCLOPEDIA OR DICTIONARY ENTRY** When an encyclopedia or a dictionary is well known, simply list the author of the entry (if there is one), the title of the entry, the title of the reference work, the edition number (if any), and the date of the edition.

Posner, Rebecca. "Romance Languages." The Encyclopaedia Britannica:
    Macropaedia. 15th ed. 1987.

"Sonata." The American Heritage Dictionary of the English Language. 4th ed.
    2000.

Volume and page numbers are not necessary because the entries in the source are arranged alphabetically and therefore are easy to locate.

If a reference work is not well known, provide full publication information as well.

■ **14. SACRED TEXT** Give the title of the edition of the sacred text (taken from the title page), underlined; the editor's or translator's name (if any); and publication information.

Holy Bible. Wheaton: Tyndale, 2005.

The Qur'an: Translation. Trans. Abdullah Yusuf Ali. Elmhurst: Tahrike, 2000.

■ **15. FOREWORD, INTRODUCTION, PREFACE, OR AFTERWORD** Begin with the author of the foreword or other book part, followed by the name of that part. Then give the title of the book; the author of the book, preceded by the word "By"; and the editor of the book (if any). After the publication information, give the page numbers for the part of the book being cited.

Morris, Jan. Introduction. Letters from the Field, 1925-1975. By Margaret Mead.
New York: Perennial-Harper, 2001. xix-xxiii.

If the book part being cited has a title, include it in quotation marks immediately after the author's name.

Ozick, Cynthia. "Portrait of the Essay as a Warm Body." Introduction. The Best
American Essays 1998. Ed. Ozick. Boston: Houghton, 1998. xv-xxi.

■ **16. BOOK WITH A TITLE IN ITS TITLE** If the book title contains a title normally underlined, neither underline the internal title nor place it in quotation marks.

King, John N. Milton and Religious Controversy: Satire and Polemic in Paradise
Lost. Cambridge: Cambridge UP, 2000.

If the title within the title is normally put in quotation marks, retain the quotation marks and underline the entire title.

Knight, Denise D., and Cynthia J. Davis. Approaches to Teaching Gilman's "The
Yellow Wall-Paper" and Herland. New York: Mod. Lang. Assn., 2003.

■ **17. BOOK IN A SERIES** Before the publication information, cite the series name as it appears on the title page, followed by the series number, if any.

Malena, Anne. The Dynamics of Identity in Francophone Caribbean Narrative.
Francophone Cultures and Lits. Ser. 24. New York: Lang, 1998.

■ **18. REPUBLISHED BOOK** After the title of the book, cite the original publication date, followed by the current publication information. If the republished book contains new material, such as an introduction or afterword, include information about the new material after the original date.

Hughes, Langston. <u>Black Misery</u>. 1969. Afterword Robert O'Meally. New York:

Oxford UP, 2000.

■ **19. PUBLISHER'S IMPRINT** If a book was published by an imprint (a division) of a publishing company, link the name of the imprint and the name of the publisher with a hyphen, putting the imprint first.

Truan, Barry. <u>Acoustic Communication</u>. Westport: Ablex-Greenwood, 2000.

Articles in periodicals

This section shows how to prepare works cited entries for articles in magazines, scholarly journals, and newspapers. In addition to consulting the models in this section, you will at times need to turn to other models as well:

- More than one author: see item 2
- Corporate author: see item 3
- Unknown author: see item 4
- Online article: see item 32
- Article from a subscription service: see item 31

NOTE: For articles appearing on consecutive pages, provide the range of pages (see items 21 and 22). When an article does not appear on consecutive pages, give the number of the first page followed by a plus sign: 32+.

■ **20. ARTICLE IN A MAGAZINE** List, in order, separated by periods, the author's name; the title of the article, in quotation marks; and the title of the magazine, underlined. Then give the date and the page numbers, separated by a colon. If the magazine is issued monthly, give just the month and year. Abbreviate the names of the months except May, June, and July.

Fay, J. Michael. "Land of the Surfing Hippos." <u>National Geographic</u> Aug. 2004:

100+.

If the magazine is issued weekly, give the exact date.

Lord, Lewis. "There's Something about Mary Todd." US News and World Report
   19 Feb. 2001: 53.

▨ **21. ARTICLE IN A JOURNAL PAGINATED BY VOLUME** Many scholarly
journals continue page numbers throughout the year instead of beginning each issue with page 1; at the end of the year, the issues
are collected in a volume. To find an article, readers need only the
volume number, the year, and the page numbers.

Ryan, Katy. "Revolutionary Suicide in Toni Morrison's Fiction." African American
   Review 34 (2000): 389-412.

▨ **22. ARTICLE IN A JOURNAL PAGINATED BY ISSUE** If each issue of
the journal begins with page 1, you need to indicate the number of
the issue. After the volume number, put a period and the issue
number.

Wood, Michael. "Broken Dates: Fiction and the Century." Kenyon Review 22.3
   (2000): 50-64.

▨ **23. ARTICLE IN A DAILY NEWSPAPER** Begin with the name of the
author, if known, followed by the title of the article. Next give the
name of the newspaper, the date, and the page numbers (including
the section letter). Use a plus sign (+) after the page number if the
article does not appear on consecutive pages.

Brummitt, Chris. "Indonesia's Food Needs Expected to Soar." Boston Globe 1 Feb.
   2005: A7.

If the section is marked with a number rather than a letter,
handle the entry as follows:

Wilford, John Noble. "In a Golden Age of Discovery, Faraway Worlds Beckon."
   New York Times 9 Feb. 1997, late ed., sec. 1: 1+.

When an edition of the newspaper is specified on the mast-
head, name the edition after the date and before the page reference
(eastern ed., late ed., natl. ed., and so on), as in the example just
given.

If the city of publication is not obvious, include it in brackets
after the name of the newspaper: City Paper [Washington, DC].

Citation at a glance: Article in a periodical (MLA)

To cite an article in a periodical in MLA style, include the following elements:

1 Author
2 Title of article
3 Name of periodical
4 Date of publication
5 Page numbers

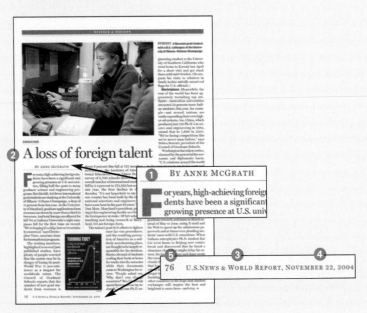

WORKS CITED ENTRY FOR AN ARTICLE IN A PERIODICAL

————1———— ————2———————— ————————3————————
McGrath, Anne. "A Loss of Foreign Talent." <u>US News and World Report</u>

————4———— ——5—
22 Nov. 2004: 76.

For more on citing periodical articles in MLA style, see pages 428–31.

■ **24. EDITORIAL IN A NEWSPAPER** Cite an editorial as you would an article with an unknown author, adding the word "Editorial" after the title.

"All Wet." Editorial. Boston Globe 12 Feb. 2001: A14.

■ **25. LETTER TO THE EDITOR** Name the writer, followed by the word "Letter" and the publication information for the periodical in which the letter appears.

Shrewsbury, Toni. Letter. Atlanta Journal-Constitution 17 Feb. 2001: A13.

■ **26. BOOK OR FILM REVIEW** Name the reviewer and the title of the review, if any, followed by the words "Rev. of" and the title and author or director of the work reviewed. Add the publication information for the periodical in which the review appears.

Gleick, Elizabeth. "The Burdens of Genius." Rev. of The Last Samurai, by Helen
    DeWitt. Time 4 Dec. 2000: 171.

Denby, David. "On the Battlefield." Rev. of The Hurricane, dir. Norman Jewison.
    New Yorker 10 Jan. 2000: 90-92.

Electronic sources

This section shows how to prepare works cited entries for a variety of electronic sources, including Web sites, online books, articles in online periodicals and databases, blogs, e-mail, and Web postings.

NOTE: When a Web address in a works cited entry must be divided at the end of a line, MLA recommends that you break it after a slash. Do not insert a hyphen.

■ **27. AN ENTIRE WEB SITE** Begin with the name of the author or corporate author (if known) and the title of the site, underlined. Then give the names of any editors, the date of publication or last update, the name of any sponsoring organization, the date you accessed the source, and the URL in angle brackets. Provide as much of this information as is available.

With author
Peterson, Susan Lynn. The Life of Martin Luther. 2002. 24 Jan. 2006
    <http://www.susanlynnpeterson.com/luther/home.html>.

With corporate (group) author

United States. Environmental Protection Agency. Drinking Water Standards. 8 July
2004. 24 Jan. 2006 <http://www.epa.gov/safewater/standards.html>.

Author unknown

Margaret Sanger Papers Project. 18 Oct. 2000. History Dept., New York U. 6 Feb.
2006 <http://www.nyu.edu/projects/sanger>.

With editor

Internet Modern History Sourcebook. Ed. Paul Halsall. 22 Sept. 2001. Fordham U.
22 Feb. 2006 <http://www.fordham.edu/HALSALL/mod/modsbook.html>.

NOTE: If the site has no title, substitute a description, such as
"Home page," for the title. Do not underline the words or put them
in quotation marks.

Yoon, Mina. Home page. 29 Sept. 2004. 12 Jan. 2005 <http://www.pa.msu.edu/
~mnyoon>.

■ **28. SHORT WORK FROM A WEB SITE**   Short works are those that
appear in quotation marks in MLA style: articles, poems, and other
documents that are not book length. For a short work from a Web
site, include as many of the following elements as apply and as are
available: author's name; title of the short work, in quotation
marks; title of the site, underlined; date of publication or last update; sponsor of the site (if not named as the author or given as the
title of the site); date you accessed the source; and the URL in angle
brackets.

Usually at least some of these elements will not apply or will
be unavailable. In the following example, no sponsor or date of publication was available. (The date given is the date on which the researcher accessed the source.) For an annotated example, see pages
434–35.

With author

Shiva, Vandana. "Bioethics: A Third World Issue." NativeWeb. 22 Feb. 2006
<http://www.nativeweb.org/pages/legal/shiva.html>.

Author unknown

"Media Giants." Frontline: The Merchants of Cool. 2001. PBS Online. 7 Feb. 2006
<http://www.pbs.org/wgbh/pages/frontline/shows/cool/giants>.

NOTE: When the URL for a short work from a Web site is very long, you may give the URL for the home page and indicate the path by which readers can access the source.

"US Obesity Trends 1985-2004." Centers for Disease Control and Prevention.

3 Jan. 2003. 17 Feb. 2006 <http://www.cdc.gov>. Path: A-Z Index;

Overweight and Obesity; Obesity Trends; US Obesity Trends 1985 to 2004.

■ **29. ONLINE BOOK** When a book or a book-length work such as a play or a long poem is posted on the Web as its own site, give as much publication information as is available, followed by your date of access and the URL. (See also the models for print books: items 6–19.)

Rawlins, Gregory J. E. Moths to the Flame. Cambridge: MIT P, 1996. 17 Jan. 2006

<http://mitpress.mit.edu/e-books/Moths/contents.html>.

If the book-length work is posted on a scholarly Web site, provide information about that site.

Jacobs, Harriet Ann. Incidents in the Life of a Slave Girl. Boston, 1861.

Documenting the American South: The Southern Experience in Nineteenth-

Century America. Ed. Ji-Hae Yoon and Natalia Smith. 1998. Academic Affairs

Lib., U of North Carolina, Chapel Hill. 3 Mar. 2006 <http://docsouth.unc.edu/

jacobs/jacobs.html>.

■ **30. PART OF AN ONLINE BOOK** Place the part title before the book's title. If the part is a short work such as a poem or an essay, put its title in quotation marks. If the part is an introduction or other division of the book, do not use quotation marks.

Adams, Henry. "Diplomacy." The Education of Henry Adams. Boston: Houghton,

1918. Bartleby.com: Great Books Online. 1999. 8 Jan. 2005

<http://bartleby.com/159/8.html>.

■ **31. WORK FROM A SERVICE SUCH AS *INFOTRAC*** For sources retrieved from a library's subscription database service, give as much of the following information as is available: publication information for the source (see items 20–26); the name of the database, underlined; the name of the service; the name and location of the library where you retrieved the source; your date of access; and the URL of the service.

The following models are for articles retrieved through three popular library subscription services. The *InfoTrac* source is a

Citation at a glance: Short work from a Web site (MLA)

To cite a short work from a Web site in MLA style, include the following elements:

1 Author
2 Title of short work
3 Title of Web site
4 Date of publication or latest update

5 Sponsor of site
6 Date of access
7 URL

ON-SCREEN VIEW OF SHORT WORK

LINKS PAGE ON WEB SITE FOR SHORT WORK

BROWSER PRINTOUT OF SHORT WORK

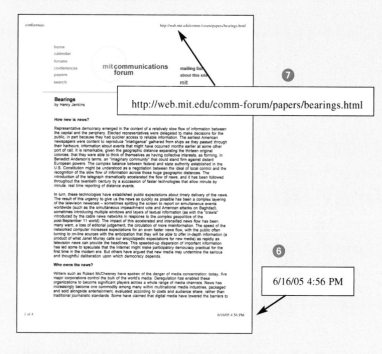

WORKS CITED ENTRY FOR A SHORT WORK FROM A WEB SITE

┌──1──┐ ┌──2──┐ ┌──────3──────┐ ┌──4──┐
Jenkins, Henry. "Bearings." <u>MIT Communications Forum</u>. 19 Feb. 2002.

    ┌5┐ ┌───6───┐ ┌────────7────────┐
    MIT. 16 June 2005 <http://web.mit.edu/comm-forum/papers/

    bearings.html>.

For more on citing sources from Web sites in MLA style, see pages 431–33.

scholarly article in a journal paginated by volume (see item 21); the
EBSCOhost source is an article in a bimonthly magazine (see item
20); and the *ProQuest* source is an article in a daily newspaper (see
item 23). An annotated example appears on pages 438–39.

InfoTrac

Johnson, Kirk. "The Mountain Lions of Michigan." <u>Endangered Species Update</u>

19.2 (2002): 27+. <u>Expanded Academic Index</u>. InfoTrac. U of Michigan Lib.,

Ann Arbor. 26 Nov. 2005 <http://infotrac.galegroup.com>.

EBSCOhost

Barrera, Rebeca María. "A Case for Bilingual Education." <u>Scholastic Parent and</u>

<u>Child</u> Nov.-Dec. 2004: 72-73. <u>Academic Search Premier</u>. EBSCOhost.

St. Johns River Community Coll. Lib., Palatka, FL. 1 Feb. 2006

<http://search.epnet.com>.

ProQuest

Kolata, Gina. "Scientists Debating Future of Hormone Replacement." <u>New York</u>

<u>Times</u> 23 Oct. 2002: A20. ProQuest. Drew U Lib., Madison, NJ. 26 Nov. 2005

<http://www.proquest.com>.

NOTE: When you access a work through a personal subscription service such as *America Online,* give the information about the source,
the name of the service, the date of access, and the keyword used to
retrieve the source.

Conniff, Richard. "The House That John Built." <u>Smithsonian</u> Feb. 2001. America

Online. 11 Mar. 2006. Keyword: Smithsonian Magazine.

32. ARTICLE IN AN ONLINE PERIODICAL When citing online articles, follow the guidelines for printed articles (see items 20–26), giving whatever information is available in the online source. End the
citation with your date of access and the URL.

NOTE: In some online articles, paragraphs are numbered. For such
articles, include the total number of paragraphs in your citation, as
in the next example.

From an online scholarly journal

Belau, Linda. "Trauma and the Material Signifier." <u>Postmodern Culture</u> 11.2 (2001):

37 pars. 20 Feb. 2006 <http://muse.jhu.edu/journals/postmodern_culture/

toc/pmc11.2.html#articles>.

From an online magazine

Morgan, Fiona. "Banning the Bullies." Salon.com 15 Mar. 2001. 21 Jan. 2006

    <http://www.salon.com/news/feature/2001/03/15/bullying/index.html>.

From an online newspaper

Rubin, Joel. "Report Faults Charter School." Los Angeles Times 22 Jan. 2005.

    24 Jan. 2005 <http://pqasb.pqarchiver.com/latimes/search.html>.

▦ **33. AN ENTIRE WEBLOG (BLOG)** To cite an entire Weblog, give the author's name; the title of the Weblog, underlined; the word "Weblog"; the date of most recent update; the sponsor of the site, if any; the date of access; and the URL. Note that MLA currently provides no guidelines for documenting a blog. Items 33 and 34 are based on MLA's guidelines for Web sites and short works from Web sites.

Mayer, Caroline. The Checkout. Weblog. 27 Apr. 2006. Washingtonpost.com.

    29 Apr. 2006 <http://blog.washingtonpost.com/thecheckout>.

▦ **34. AN ENTRY IN A WEBLOG (BLOG)** To cite an entry or a comment (a response to an entry) in a Weblog, give the author of the entry or comment; the title, if any, in quotation marks; the words "Weblog post" or "Weblog comment"; and the information about the entire blog as in item 33.

Mayer, Caroline. "Some Surprising Findings about Identity Theft." Weblog post.

    The Checkout. 28 Feb. 2006. Washingtonpost.com. 2 Mar. 2006

    <http://blog.washingtonpost.com/thecheckout/02/

    some_surprising_findings_about.html>.

Burdick, Dennis. Weblog comment. The Checkout. 28 Feb. 2006.

    Washingtonpost.com. 2 Mar. 2006 <http://blog.washingtonpost.com/

    thecheckout/02/some_surprising_findings_about.html#comments>.

▦ **35. CD-ROM** Treat a CD-ROM as you would any other source, but name the medium before the publication information.

"Pimpernel." The American Heritage Dictionary of the English Language. 4th ed.

    CD-ROM. Boston: Houghton, 2000.

Wattenberg, Ruth. "Helping Students in the Middle." American Educator 19.4

    (1996): 2-18. ERIC. CD-ROM. SilverPlatter. Sept. 1996.

Citation at a glance: Article from a database (MLA)

To cite an article from a database in MLA style, include the following elements:

1 Author
2 Title of article
3 Name of periodical, volume and issue numbers
4 Date of publication
5 Inclusive pages
6 Name of database

7 Name of subscription service
8 Library at which you retrieved the source
9 Date of access
10 URL of service

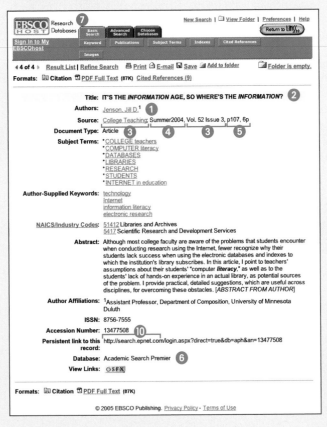

WORKS CITED ENTRY FOR AN ARTICLE FROM A DATABASE

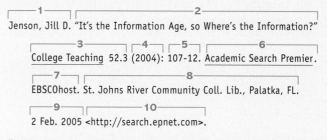

Jenson, Jill D. "It's the Information Age, so Where's the Information?"
College Teaching 52.3 (2004): 107-12. Academic Search Premier.
EBSCOhost. St. Johns River Community Coll. Lib., Palatka, FL.
2 Feb. 2005 <http://search.epnet.com>.

For more on citing articles from a database in MLA style, see pages 433 and 436.

■ **36. E-MAIL** To cite an e-mail, begin with the writer's name and the subject line. Then write "E-mail to" followed by the name of the recipient. End with the date of the message.

Lowe, Walter. "Review questions." E-mail to the author. 15 Mar. 2006.

■ **37. POSTING TO AN ONLINE LIST, FORUM, OR GROUP** When possible, cite archived versions of postings. If you cannot locate an archived version, keep a copy of the posting for your records. Begin with the author's name, followed by the title or subject line; the words "Online posting"; the date of the posting; the name of the list, forum, or newsgroup; and your date of access. For a discussion list, give the URL of the list if it is available; otherwise give the e-mail address of the list moderator. For a Web forum, give the network address. For a Usenet group, use the prefix "news:" followed by the name of the newsgroup.

Discussion list posting

Edwards, David. "Media Lens." Online posting. 20 Dec. 2001. Media Lens Archives.
    10 Apr. 2002 <http://groups.yahoo.com/group/medialens/message/25>.

Web forum posting

Brown, Oliver. "Welcome." Online posting. 8 Oct. 2002. Chester Coll. Students
    Web Forum. 20 Feb. 2003 <http://www.voy.com/113243>.

Newsgroup posting

Reedy, Tom. "Re: Macbeth an Existential Nightmare?" Online posting.
    9 Mar. 2002. 8 Apr. 2002 <news:humanities.lit.authors.shakespeare>.

■ **38. POSTING TO A MUD OR A MOO**   Include the writer's name (if relevant), a description and date of the event, the title of the forum, the date of access, and the electronic address, beginning with the prefix "telnet://." If possible, cite an archived version of the posting.

Carbone, Nick. Planning for the future. 1 Mar. 2001. TechRhet's Thursday night

MOO. 1 Mar. 2001 <telnet://connections.moo.mud.org:3333>.

Multimedia sources (including online versions)

Multimedia sources include visuals (such as works of art), audio works (such as sound recordings), audiovisuals (such as films), podcasts, and live events.

When citing multimedia sources that you retrieved online, consult the appropriate model in this section and give whatever information is available for the online source; then end the citation with your date of access and the URL. (See items 39, 42, 46, and 48 for examples.)

■ **39. WORK OF ART**   Cite the artist's name, followed by the title of the artwork, usually underlined, and the institution and city in which the artwork can be found. If you want to indicate the work's date, include it after the title. For a work of art you viewed online, end your citation with your date of access and the URL.

Constable, John. <u>Dedham Vale</u>. Victoria and Albert Museum, London.

van Gogh, Vincent. <u>The Starry Night</u>. 1889. Museum of Mod. Art, New York. 3 Feb.

2006 <http://moma.org/collection/browse_results.php?object_id=79802>.

■ **40. CARTOON**   Begin with the cartoonist's name, the title of the cartoon (if it has one) in quotation marks, the word "Cartoon," and the publication information for the publication in which the cartoon appears.

Sutton, Ward. "Why Wait 'til November?" Cartoon. <u>Village Voice</u> 7-13 July 2004: 6.

■ **41. ADVERTISEMENT**   Name the product or company being advertised, followed by the word "Advertisement." Give publication information for the source in which the advertisement appears.

Truth by Calvin Klein. Advertisement. <u>Vogue</u> Dec. 2000: 95-98.

■ **42. MAP OR CHART**   Cite a map or a chart as you would a book or a short work within a longer work. Add the word "Map" or "Chart" following the title.

Serbia. Map. 2 Feb. 2001. 17 Mar. 2006 <http://www.biega.com/serbia.html>.

Joseph, Lori, and Bob Laird. "Driving While Phoning Is Dangerous." Chart.
USA Today 16 Feb. 2001: 1A.

▨ **43. MUSICAL COMPOSITION** Cite the composer's name, followed
by the title of the work. Underline the title of an opera, a ballet, or
a composition identified by name, but do not underline or use quotation marks around a composition identified by number or form.

Ellington, Duke. Conga Brava.

Haydn, Franz Joseph. Symphony no. 88 in G.

▨ **44. SOUND RECORDING** Begin with the name of the person you
want to emphasize: the composer, conductor, or performer. For a long
work, give the title, underlined, followed by names of pertinent
artists (such as performers, readers, or musicians) and the orchestra
and conductor (if relevant). End with the manufacturer and the date.

Bizet, Georges. Carmen. Perf. Jennifer Laramore, Thomas Moser, Angela
Gheorghiu, and Samuel Ramey. Bavarian State Orch. and Chorus. Cond.
Giuseppe Sinopoli. Warner, 1996.

For a song, put the title in quotation marks. If you include the
name of the album or CD, underline it.

Blige, Mary J. "Be without You." The Breakthrough. Geffen, 2005.

▨ **45. FILM OR VIDEO** Begin with the title, underlined. For a film,
cite the director and the lead actors or narrator ("Perf." or "Narr."),
followed by the name of the distributor and the year of the film's release. For a videotape or DVD, add "Videocassette" or "DVD" before
the name of the distributor.

Finding Neverland. Dir. Marc Forster. Perf. Johnny Depp, Kate Winslet, Julie
Christie, Radha Mitchell, and Dustin Hoffman. Miramax, 2004.

High Fidelity. Dir. Stephen Frears. Perf. John Cusack, Iben Hjejle, Jack Black, and
Todd Louiso. 2000. Videocassette. Walt Disney Video, 2001.

▨ **46. RADIO OR TELEVISION PROGRAM** Begin with the title of the
radio segment or television episode (if there is one) in quotation
marks, followed by the title of the program, underlined. Next give
relevant information about the program's writer ("By"), director
("Dir."), performers ("Perf."), or host ("Host"). Then name the

network, the local station (if any), and the date the program was broadcast.

"Monkey Trial." American Experience. PBS. WGBH, Boston. 18 Mar. 2003.

"Live at NPR: The Music and Life of Richard Thompson." Fresh Air. Natl. Public
    Radio. 17 Feb. 2006. 22 Feb. 2006 <http://www.npr.org/templates/story/
    story.php?storyId=5221211>.

If there is a series title, include it after the title of the program, neither underlined nor in quotation marks.

Mysteries of the Pyramids. On the Inside. Discovery Channel. 7 Feb. 2001.

■ **47. RADIO OR TELEVISION INTERVIEW** Begin with the name of the person who was interviewed, followed by the word "Interview." End with the information about the program as in item 46.

McGovern, George. Interview. Charlie Rose. PBS. WNET, New York. 1 Feb. 2001.

■ **48. PODCAST** A podcast can refer to digital audio content — downloadable lectures, interviews, or essays — or to the method of delivery. In an entry for a podcast, include as many of the following elements as apply and as are available: the author's (or speaker's) name; the title of the podcast, in quotation marks; the word "Podcast"; the names of the performers or the host; the title of the site on which it appears, underlined; the date of posting; the sponsor of the site; the date you accessed the source; and the URL.

Patterson, Chris. "Will School Consolidation Improve Education?" Podcast. Host
    Michael Quinn Sullivan. Texas PolicyCast. 13 Apr. 2006. Texas Public Policy
    Foundation. 27 Apr. 2006 <http://www.texaspolicy.com/texaspolicycast.php>.

NOTE: The Modern Language Association currently provides no guidelines for documenting a podcast. The model shown here is based on MLA's guidelines for a short work from a Web site.

■ **49. LIVE PERFORMANCE** For a live performance of a play, a ballet, an opera, or a concert, begin with the title of the work performed. Then name the author or composer of the work (preceded by the word "By"), followed by as much information about the performance as is available: the director ("Dir."), choreographer ("Chor."), or conductor ("Cond."); the major performers ("Perf."); the theater, ballet, or opera company; the theater and its city; and the date of the performance.

Art. By Yasmina Reza. Dir. Matthew Warchus. Perf. Philip Franks, Leigh Lawson,
and Simon Shephard. Whitehall Theatre, London. 3 Dec. 2001.

Cello Concerto no. 2. By Eric Tanguy. Cond. Seiji Ozawa. Perf. Mstislav
Rostropovich. Boston Symphony Orch. Symphony Hall, Boston. 5 Apr. 2002.

■ **50. LECTURE OR PUBLIC ADDRESS** Cite the speaker's name, followed by the title of the lecture (if any), the organization sponsoring the lecture, the location, and the date.

Wellbery, David E. "On a Sentence of Franz Kafka." Franke Inst. for the
Humanities. Gleacher Center, Chicago. 1 Feb. 2006.

■ **51. PERSONAL INTERVIEW** To cite an interview that you conducted, begin with the name of the person interviewed. Then write "Personal interview," followed by the date of the interview.

Akufo, Dautey. Personal interview. 11 Aug. 2006.

Other sources (including online versions)

This section includes a variety of traditional print sources not covered elsewhere. For sources obtained on the Web, consult the appropriate model in this section and give whatever information is available for the online source; then end the citation with the date on which you accessed the source and the URL. (See the second example under item 52.)

■ **52. GOVERNMENT PUBLICATION** Treat the government agency as the author, giving the name of the government followed by the name of the agency.

United States. Dept. of Labor. America's Dynamic Workforce. Washington: US
Dept. of Labor, 2004.

For government documents published online, give as much publication information as is available and end your citation with the date of access and the URL.

United States. Dept. of Transportation. Natl. Highway Traffic Safety Administration.
An Investigation of the Safety Implications of Wireless Communications in
Vehicles. Nov. 1999. 20 May 2006 <http://www.nhtsa.dot.gov/people/
injury/research/wireless>.

■ **53. LEGAL SOURCE** For articles of the United States Constitution and laws in the United States Code, no works cited entry is required; instead, simply give an in-text citation (see item 17 on p. 419).

For a legislative act, begin with the name of the act. Then provide the act's Public Law number, its date of enactment, and its Statutes at Large number.

Electronic Freedom of Information Act Amendments of 1996. Pub. L. 104-418.

2 Oct. 1996. Stat. 3048.

For a court case, name the first plaintiff and first defendant. Then give the case number, the court name, and the date of the decision. In a works cited entry, the name of the case is not underlined.

Utah v. Evans. No. 01-714. Supreme Ct. of the US. 20 June 2002.

■ **54. PAMPHLET** Cite a pamphlet as you would a book.

Commonwealth of Massachusetts. Dept. of Jury Commissioner. A Few Facts about

Jury Duty. Boston: Commonwealth of Massachusetts, 2004.

■ **55. DISSERTATION** Begin with the author's name, followed by the dissertation title in quotation marks, the abbreviation "Diss.," the name of the institution, and the year the dissertation was accepted.

Jackson, Shelley. "Writing Whiteness: Contemporary Southern Literature in Black

and White." Diss. U of Maryland, 2000.

For dissertations that have been published in book form, underline the title. After the title and before the book's publication information, add the abbreviation "Diss.," the name of the institution, and the year the dissertation was accepted.

Damberg, Cheryl L. Healthcare Reform: Distributional Consequences of an

Employer Mandate for Workers in Small Firms. Diss. Rand Graduate School,

1995. Santa Monica: Rand, 1996.

■ **56. ABSTRACT OF A DISSERTATION** Cite an abstract as you would an unpublished dissertation. After the dissertation date, give the abbreviation *DA* or *DAI* (for *Dissertation Abstracts* or *Dissertation Abstracts International*), followed by the volume number, the date of publication, and the page number.

Chen, Shu-Ling. "Mothers and Daughters in Morrison, Tan, Marshall, and Kincaid."

Diss. U of Washington, 2000. DAI 61 (2000): 2289.

■ **57. PUBLISHED PROCEEDINGS OF A CONFERENCE** Cite published conference proceedings as you would a book, adding information about the conference after the title.

Kartiganer, Donald M., and Ann J. Abadie. Faulkner at 100: Retrospect and
Prospect. Proc. of Faulkner and Yoknapatawpha Conf., 27 July-1 Aug. 1997,
U of Mississippi. Jackson: UP of Mississippi, 2000.

■ **58. PUBLISHED INTERVIEW** Name the person interviewed, followed by the title of the interview (if there is one). If the interview does not have a title, include the word "Interview" followed by a period after the interviewee's name. Give publication information for the work in which the interview was published.

Armstrong, Lance. "Lance in France." Sports Illustrated 28 June 2004: 46+.

If the name of the interviewer is relevant, include it after the name of the interviewee.

Prince. Interview with Bilge Ebiri. Yahoo! Internet Life 7.6 (2001):
82-85.

■ **59. PERSONAL LETTER** To cite a letter that you have received, begin with the writer's name and add the phrase "Letter to the author," followed by the date.

Primak, Shoshana. Letter to the author. 6 May 2006.

■ **60. ENTRY IN A WIKI** A wiki is an online reference that is openly edited by its users. Treat it as you would a short work from a Web site (see item 28 on p. 432). Because wiki content is, by definition, collectively edited and continually updated, do not include an author. Include the title of the entry; the name of the wiki; the date of last update; the sponsor of the wiki, if any; your date of access; and the URL.

"Hip Hop Music." Wikipedia. 2 Mar. 2006. Wikimedia Foundation. 18 Mar. 2006
<http://en.wikipedia.org/wiki/Hip_hop_music>.

"Negation in Languages." UniLang.org. 22 Apr. 2006. UniLang. 9 June 2006
<http://home.unilang.org/wiki3/index.php/Negation_in_languages>.

ON THE WEB > dianahacker.com/writersref
Research exercises > E-ex MLA 4-4 through MLA 4-6

MLA-4c MLA information notes (optional)

Researchers who use the MLA system of parenthetical documentation (see MLA-4a) may also use information notes for one of two purposes:

1. to provide additional material that might interrupt the flow of the paper yet is important enough to include
2. to refer readers to any sources not discussed in the paper

Information notes may be either footnotes or endnotes. Footnotes appear at the foot of the page; endnotes appear on a separate page at the end of the paper, just before the list of works cited. For either style, the notes are numbered consecutively throughout the paper. The text of the paper contains a raised arabic numeral that corresponds to the number of the note.

TEXT

In the past several years, employees have filed a number of lawsuits against employers because of online monitoring practices.[1]

NOTE

[1] For a discussion of federal law applicable to electronic surveillance in the workplace, see Kesan 293.

MLA-5

Manuscript format; sample paper

MLA-5a Manuscript format

The following guidelines are consistent with advice given in the *MLA Handbook for Writers of Research Papers*, 6th ed. (New York: MLA, 2003). For a sample MLA paper, see MLA-5b.

Formatting the paper

Papers written in MLA style should be formatted as follows.

MATERIALS Use good-quality 8½″ × 11″ white paper. Secure the pages with a paper clip. Unless your instructor suggests otherwise, do not staple or bind the pages.

TITLE AND IDENTIFICATION MLA does not require a title page. On the first page of your paper, place your name, your instructor's name, the course title, and the date on separate lines against the left margin. Then center your title. (See p. 450 for a sample first page.)

If your instructor requires a title page, ask for guidelines on formatting it. A format similar to the one on page 493 may be acceptable.

PAGINATION Put the page number preceded by your last name in the upper right corner of each page, one-half inch below the top edge. Use arabic numerals (1, 2, 3, and so on).

MARGINS, LINE SPACING, AND PARAGRAPH INDENTS Leave margins of one inch on all sides of the page. Left-align the text.

Double-space throughout the paper. Do not add extra line spaces above or below the title of the paper or between paragraphs.

Indent the first line of each paragraph one-half inch (or five spaces) from the left margin.

LONG QUOTATIONS When a quotation is longer than four typed lines of prose or three lines of verse, set it off from the text by indenting the entire quotation one inch (or ten spaces) from the left margin. Double-space the indented quotation, and don't add extra space above or below it.

Quotation marks are not needed when a quotation has been set off from the text by indenting. See page 450 for an example.

WEB ADDRESSES When a Web address (URL) mentioned in the text of your paper must be divided at the end of a line, do not insert a hyphen (a hyphen could appear to be part of the address). For MLA rules on dividing Web addresses in your list of works cited, see page 448.

HEADINGS MLA neither encourages nor discourages the use of headings and currently provides no guidelines for their use. If you would like to insert headings in a long essay or research paper, check first with your instructor.

VISUALS MLA classifies visuals as tables and figures (figures include graphs, charts, maps, photographs, and drawings). Label each table with an arabic numeral (Table 1, Table 2, and so on) and provide a clear caption that identifies the subject. The label and caption should appear on separate lines above the table, flush left. Below the table, give its source in a note like this one:

Source: David N. Greenfield and Richard A. Davis, "Lost in Cyberspace: The Web @ Work," Cyberpsychology and Behavior 5 (2002): 349.

For each figure, place a label and a caption below the figure, flush left. They need not appear on separate lines. The word "Figure" may be abbreviated to "Fig." Include source information following the caption.

Visuals should be placed in the text, as close as possible to the sentences that relate to them unless your instructor prefers them in an appendix. See page 452 for an example of a visual in the text of a paper.

Preparing the list of works cited

Begin the list of works cited on a new page at the end of the paper. Center the title Works Cited about one inch from the top of the page. Double-space throughout. See page 454 for a sample list of works cited.

ALPHABETIZING THE LIST Alphabetize the list by the last names of the authors (or editors); if a work has no author or editor, alphabetize by the first word of the title other than *A, An,* or *The.*

If your list includes two or more works by the same author, use the author's name only for the first entry. For subsequent entries use three hyphens followed by a period. List the titles in alphabetical order. See item 5 on page 423.

INDENTING Do not indent the first line of each works cited entry, but indent any additional lines one-half inch (or five spaces). This technique highlights the names of the authors, making it easy for readers to scan the alphabetized list.

WEB ADDRESSES Do not insert a hyphen when dividing a Web address (URL) at the end of a line. Break the line after a slash. Also insert angle brackets around the URL.

For advice about how to cite sources with long URLs, see the note at the top of page 433.

If your word processing program automatically turns Web addresses into hot links (by underlining them and highlighting them in color), turn off this feature.

ON THE WEB > dianahacker.com/writersref
Additional resources > Formatting help

MLA-5b Sample MLA research paper

On the following pages is a research paper on the topic of electronic surveillance in the workplace, written by Anna Orlov, a student in a composition class. Orlov's paper is documented with MLA-style in-text citations and list of works cited. Annotations in the margins of the paper draw your attention to Orlov's use of MLA style and her effective writing.

ON THE WEB > dianahacker.com/writersref
Model papers > MLA papers: Orlov; Daly; Levi
> MLA annotated bibliography: Orlov

Orlov 1

Anna Orlov

Professor Willis

English 101

17 March 2006

Online Monitoring:

A Threat to Employee Privacy in the Wired Workplace

As the Internet has become an integral tool of businesses, company policies on Internet usage have become as common as policies regarding vacation days or sexual harassment. A 2005 study by the American Management Association and ePolicy Institute found that 76% of companies monitor employees' use of the Web, and the number of companies that block employees' access to certain Web sites has increased 27% since 2001 (1). Unlike other company rules, however, Internet usage policies often include language authorizing companies to secretly monitor their employees, a practice that raises questions about rights in the workplace. Although companies often have legitimate concerns that lead them to monitor employees' Internet usage--from expensive security breaches to reduced productivity--the benefits of electronic surveillance are outweighed by its costs to employees' privacy and autonomy.

While surveillance of employees is not a new phenomenon, electronic surveillance allows employers to monitor workers with unprecedented efficiency. In his book The Naked Employee, Frederick Lane describes offline ways in which employers have been permitted to intrude on employees' privacy for decades, such as drug testing, background checks, psychological exams, lie detector tests, and in-store video surveillance. The difference, Lane argues, between these old methods of data gathering and electronic surveillance involves quantity:

> Technology makes it possible for employers to gather enormous amounts of data about employees, often far beyond what is necessary to satisfy safety or productivity concerns. And the trends that drive technology--faster, smaller, cheaper--make it possible for larger and larger numbers of employers to gather ever-greater amounts of personal data. (3-4)

Title is centered.

Opening sentences provide background for thesis.

Thesis asserts Orlov's main point.

Summary and long quotation are introduced with a signal phrase naming the author.

Long quotation is set off from the text; quotation marks are omitted.

Page number is given in parentheses after the final period.

Marginal annotations indicate MLA-style formatting and effective writing.

Orlov 2

Lane points out that employers can collect data whenever employees use their computers--for example, when they send e-mail, surf the Web, or even arrive at or depart from their workstations.

Another key difference between traditional surveillance and electronic surveillance is that employers can monitor workers' computer use secretly. One popular monitoring method is keystroke logging, which is done by means of an undetectable program on employees' computers. The Web site of a vendor for Spector Pro, a popular keystroke logging program, explains that the software can be installed to operate in "Stealth" mode so that it "does not show up as an icon, does not appear in the Windows system tray, . . . [and] cannot be uninstalled without the Spector Pro password which YOU specify" ("Automatically"). As Lane explains, these programs record every key entered into the computer in hidden directories that can later be accessed or uploaded by supervisors; at their most sophisticated, the programs can even scan for keywords tailored to individual companies (128-29).

Some experts have argued that a range of legitimate concerns justifies employer monitoring of employee Internet usage. As PC World columnist Daniel Tynan explains, companies that don't monitor network traffic can be penalized for their ignorance: "Employees could accidentally (or deliberately) spill confidential information . . . or allow worms to spread throughout a corporate network." The ePolicy Institute, an organization that advises companies about reducing risks from technology, reported that breaches in computer security cost institutions $100 million in 1999 alone (Flynn). Companies also are held legally accountable for many of the transactions conducted on their networks and with their technology. Legal scholar Jay Kesan points out that the law holds employers liable for employees' actions such as violations of copyright laws, the distribution of offensive or graphic sexual material, and illegal disclosure of confidential information (312).

These kinds of concerns should give employers, in certain instances, the right to monitor employee behavior. But employers rushing to adopt surveillance programs might not be adequately weighing the effect such programs can have on employee morale.

Clear topic sentences, like this one, are used throughout the paper.

Source with an unknown author is cited by a shortened title.

Orlov anticipates objections and provides sources for opposing views.

Transition helps readers move from one paragraph to the next.

Fig. 1. Scott Adams, Dilbert and the Way of the Weasel (New York: Harper, 2002) 106.

Illustration has figure number and source information.

Employers must consider the possibility that employees will perceive surveillance as a breach of trust that can make them feel like disobedient children, not responsible adults who wish to perform their jobs professionally and autonomously.

Orlov treats both sides fairly; she provides a transition to her own argument.

Yet determining how much autonomy workers should be given is complicated by the ambiguous nature of productivity in the wired workplace. On the one hand, computers and Internet access give employees powerful tools to carry out their jobs; on the other hand, the same technology offers constant temptations to avoid work. As a 2005 study by Salary.com and America Online indicates, the Internet ranked as the top choice among employees for ways of wasting time on the job; it beat talking with co-workers--the second most popular method--by a margin of nearly two to one (Frauenheim). Chris Gonsalves, an editor for eWeek.com, argues that the technology has changed the terms between employers and employees: "While bosses can easily detect and interrupt water-cooler chatter," he writes, "the employee who is shopping at Lands' End or IMing with fellow fantasy baseball managers may actually appear to be working." The gap between behaviors that are observable to managers and the employee's actual activities when sitting behind a computer has created additional motivations for employers to invest in surveillance programs. "Dilbert," a popular cartoon that spoofs office culture, aptly captures how rampant recreational Internet use has become in the workplace (see Fig. 1).

No page number is available for this Web source.

But monitoring online activities can have the unintended effect of making employees resentful. As many workers would be quick to point out, Web surfing and other personal uses of the Internet can provide needed outlets in the stressful work environment; many scholars have

Orlov counters opposing views and provides support for her argument.

Orlov 4

argued that limiting and policing these outlets can exacerbate tensions between employees and managers. Kesan warns that "prohibiting personal use can seem extremely arbitrary and can seriously harm morale. . . . Imagine a concerned parent who is prohibited from checking on a sick child by a draconian company policy" (315-16). As this analysis indicates, employees can become disgruntled when Internet usage policies are enforced to their full extent.

> Orlov uses a brief signal phrase to move from her argument to the words of a source.

Additionally, many experts disagree with employers' assumption that online monitoring can increase productivity. Employment law attorney Joseph Schmitt argues that, particularly for employees who are paid a salary rather than by the hour, "a company shouldn't care whether employees spend one or 10 hours on the Internet as long as they are getting their jobs done--and provided that they are not accessing inappropriate sites" (qtd. in Verespej). Other experts even argue that time spent on personal Internet browsing can actually be productive for companies. According to Bill Coleman, an executive at Salary.com, "Personal Internet use and casual office conversations often turn into new business ideas or suggestions for gaining operating efficiencies" (qtd. in Frauenheim). Employers, in other words, may benefit from showing more faith in their employees' ability to exercise their autonomy.

> Orlov cites an indirect source: words quoted in another source.

Employees' right to privacy and autonomy in the workplace, however, remains a murky area of the law. Although evaluating where to draw the line between employee rights and employer powers is often a duty that falls to the judicial system, the courts have shown little willingness to intrude on employers' exercise of control over their computer networks. Federal law provides few guidelines related to online monitoring of employees, and only Connecticut and Delaware require companies to disclose this type of surveillance to employees (Tam et al.). "It is unlikely that we will see a legally guaranteed zone of privacy in the American workplace," predicts Kesan (293). This reality leaves employees and employers to sort the potential risks and benefits of technology in contract agreements and terms of employment. With continuing advances in technology, protecting both employers and employees will require greater awareness of these programs, better disclosure to employees, and a more public discussion about what types of protections are necessary to guard individual freedoms in the wired workplace.

> Orlov sums up her argument and suggests a course of action.

Orlov 5

Heading is centered.

Works Cited

Adams, Scott. Dilbert and the Way of the Weasel. New York: Harper, 2002.

List is alphabetized by authors' last names (or by title when a work has no author).

American Management Association and ePolicy Institute. "2005 Electronic Monitoring and Surveillance Survey." American Management Association. 2005. 15 Feb. 2006 <http://www.amanet.org/research/pdfs/EMS_summary05.pdf>.

The URL is broken after a slash. No hyphen is inserted.

"Automatically Record Everything They Do Online! Spector Pro 5.0 FAQ's." Netbus.org. SpectorSoft. 17 Feb. 2006 <http://www.netbus.org/sProFAQ.html>.

Flynn, Nancy. "Internet Policies." ePolicy Institute. 2001. 15 Feb. 2006 <http://www.epolicyinstitute.com/i_policies/index.html>.

First line of each entry is at the left margin; extra lines are indented ½" (or five spaces).

Frauenheim, Ed. "Stop Reading This Headline and Get Back to Work." CNET News.com. 11 July 2005. 17 Feb. 2006 <http://news.com.com/Stop+reading+this+headline+and+get+back+to+work/2100-1022_3-5783552.html>.

Double-spacing is used throughout.

Gonsalves, Chris. "Wasting Away on the Web." eWeek.com 8 Aug. 2005. 16 Feb. 2006 <http://www.eweek.com/article2/0,1895, 1843242,00.asp>.

Kesan, Jay P. "Cyber-Working or Cyber-Shirking? A First Principles Examination of Electronic Privacy in the Workplace." Florida Law Review 54 (2002): 289-332.

Lane, Frederick S., III. The Naked Employee: How Technology Is Compromising Workplace Privacy. New York: Amer. Management Assn., 2003.

A work with four authors is listed by the first author's name and the abbreviation "et al." (for "and others").

Tam, Pui-Wing, et al. "Snooping E-Mail by Software Is Now a Workplace Norm." Wall Street Journal 9 Mar. 2005: B1+.

Tynan, Daniel. "Your Boss Is Watching." PC World 6 Oct. 2004. 17 Feb. 2006 <http://www.pcworld.com/news/article/0,aid,118072,00.asp>.

Verespej, Michael A. "Inappropriate Internet Surfing." Industry Week 7 Feb. 2000. 16 Feb. 2006 <http://www.industryweek.com/ReadArticle.aspx?ArticleID=568>.

APA
CMS

APA and CMS
Papers

APA • CMS
APA/CMS Papers

This tabbed section shows how to document sources in psychology and other social science classes (APA style) and in history and some humanities classes (CMS style). It also includes discipline-specific advice on three important topics: supporting a thesis, citing sources and avoiding plagiarism, and integrating sources. Examples are documented with the appropriate style.

NOTE: For cross-disciplinary advice on finding and evaluating sources and on managing information, see the tabbed section R, Researching.

APA Papers

Most writing assignments in the social sciences are either reports of original research or reviews of the literature written about a research topic. Often an original research report contains a "review of the literature" section that places the writer's project in the context of previous research.

Most social science instructors will ask you to document your sources with the American Psychological Association (APA) system of in-text citations and references described in APA-4. You face three main challenges when writing a social science paper that draws on written sources: (1) supporting a thesis, (2) citing your sources and avoiding plagiarism, and (3) integrating quotations and other source material.

APA-1

Supporting a thesis

Most assignments ask you to form a thesis, or main idea, and to support that thesis with well-organized evidence. In a paper reviewing the literature on a topic, this thesis analyzes the often competing conclusions drawn by a variety of researchers.

APA-1a Form a thesis.

A thesis, which usually appears at the end of the introduction, is a one-sentence (or occasionally a two-sentence) statement of your central idea. You will be reading articles and other sources that address a central research question. Your thesis will express a reasonable answer to that question, given the current state of research in the field. Here, for example, is a research question posed by Luisa Mirano, a student in a psychology class, followed by a thesis that answers the question.

RESEARCH QUESTION

Is medication the right treatment for the escalating problem of childhood obesity?

POSSIBLE THESIS

Understanding the limitations of medical treatments for children highlights the complexity of the childhood obesity problem in the United States and underscores the need for physicians, advocacy groups, and policymakers to search for other solutions.

ON THE WEB > dianahacker.com/writersref
Research exercises > E-ex APA 1–1

APA-1b Organize your evidence.

The American Psychological Association encourages the use of headings to help readers follow the organization of a paper. For an original research report, the major headings often follow a standard model: Method, Results, Discussion. The introduction is not given a heading; it consists of the material between the title of the paper and the first heading.

For a literature review, headings will vary. The student who wrote about treatments for childhood obesity used four questions to focus her research; the questions then became headings in her paper (see pp. 493–501).

APA-1c Use sources to inform and support your argument.

Used thoughtfully, the source materials you have gathered will make your argument more complex and convincing for readers. Sources can play several different roles as you develop your points.

Providing background information or context

You can use facts and statistics to support generalizations or to establish the importance of your topic, as student writer Luisa Mirano does in her introduction.

> In March 2004, U.S. Surgeon General Richard Carmona called attention to a health problem in the United States that, until recently, has been overlooked: childhood obesity. Carmona said that the "astounding" 15% child obesity rate constitutes an "epidemic." Since the early 1980s, that rate has "doubled in children and tripled in adolescents." Now more than 9 million children are classified as obese (paras. 3, 6).

Explaining terms or concepts

If readers are unlikely to be familiar with a word, a phrase, or an idea important to your topic, you must explain it for them. Quoting or paraphrasing a source can help you define terms and concepts in neutral, accessible language.

> Sibutramine suppresses appetite by blocking the reuptake of the neurotransmitters serotonin and norepinephrine in the brain (Yanovski & Yanovski, 2002, p. 594).

Supporting your claims

As you draft your argument, make sure to back up your assertions with facts, examples, and other evidence from your research (see also A2-e). Luisa Mirano, for example, uses one source's findings to support her central idea that the medical treatment of childhood obesity has limitations.

> As journalist Greg Critser (2003) noted in his book *Fat Land,* use of weight-loss drugs is unlikely to have an effect without the proper "support system"-- one that includes doctors, facilities, time, and money (p. 3).

Lending authority to your argument

Expert opinion can give weight to your argument (see also A2-e). But don't rely on experts to make your argument for you. Construct your argument in your own words and, when appropriate, cite the judgment of an authority in the field to support your position.

Both medical experts and policymakers recognize that solutions might come not only from a laboratory but also from policy, education, and advocacy. Indeed, a handbook designed to educate doctors on obesity recommended a notably nonmedical course of action, calling for "major changes in some aspects of western culture" (Hoppin & Taveras, 2004, Conclusion section, para. 1).

Anticipating and countering alternative interpretations

Do not ignore sources that seem contrary to your position or that offer interpretations different from your own. Instead, use them to give voice to opposing points of view and to state potential objections before you counter them (see A2-f). Mirano uses a source to show readers that there is substance to her opponents' position that medication is the preferable approach to treating childhood obesity.

As researchers Yanovski and Yanovski (2002) have explained, obesity was once considered "either a moral failing or evidence of underlying psychopathology" (p. 592). But this view has shifted: Many medical professionals now consider obesity a biomedical rather than a moral condition, influenced by both genetic and environmental factors. Yanovski and Yanovski have further noted that the development of weight-loss medications in the early 1990s showed that "obesity should be treated in the same manner as any other chronic disease . . . through the long-term use of medication" (p. 592).

APA-2

Citing sources; avoiding plagiarism

Your research paper is a collaboration between you and your sources. To be fair and ethical, you must acknowledge your debt to the writers of those sources. If you don't, you commit plagiarism, a serious academic offense.

Three different acts are considered plagiarism: (1) failing to cite quotations and borrowed ideas, (2) failing to enclose borrowed language in quotation marks, and (3) failing to put summaries and paraphrases in your own words.

APA-2a Cite quotations and borrowed ideas.

You must of course cite all direct quotations. You must also cite any ideas borrowed from a source: summaries and paraphrases; statistics and other specific facts; and visuals such as cartoons, graphs, and diagrams.

The only exception is common knowledge—information that your readers may know or could easily locate in any number of reference sources. For example, the current population of the United States is common knowledge among sociologists and economists, and psychologists are familiar with Freud's theory of the unconscious. As a rule, when you have seen certain information repeatedly in your reading, you don't need to cite it. However, when information has appeared in only a few sources, when it is highly specific (as with statistics), or when it is controversial, you should cite the source.

The American Psychological Association recommends an author-date system of citations. Here, very briefly, is how the author-date system usually works. See APA-4 for a detailed discussion of variations.

1. The source is introduced by a signal phrase that includes the last names of the authors followed by the date of publication in parentheses.
2. The material being cited is followed by a page number in parentheses.
3. At the end of the paper, an alphabetized list of references gives complete publication information about the source.

IN-TEXT CITATION

As researchers Yanovski and Yanovski (2002) have explained, obesity was once considered "either a moral failing or evidence of underlying psychopathology" (p. 592).

ENTRY IN THE LIST OF REFERENCES

Yanovski, S. Z., & Yanovski, J. A. (2002). Drug therapy: Obesity [Electronic version]. *The New England Journal of Medicine, 346*, 591-602.

APA-2b Enclose borrowed language in quotation marks.

To indicate that you are using a source's exact phrases or sentences, you must enclose them in quotation marks. To omit the quotation marks is to claim—falsely—that the language is your own. Such an omission is plagiarism even if you have cited the source.

ORIGINAL SOURCE

In an effort to seek the causes of this disturbing trend, experts have pointed to a range of important potential contributors to the rise in childhood obesity that are unrelated to media: a reduction in physical education classes and after-school athletic programs, an increase in the availability of sodas and snacks in public schools, the growth in the number of fast-food outlets across the country, the trend toward "super-sizing" food portions in restaurants, and the increasing number of highly processed high-calorie and high-fat grocery products.

—Henry J. Kaiser Family Foundation,
"The Role of Media in Childhood Obesity" (2004), p. 1

PLAGIARISM

According to the Henry J. Kaiser Family Foundation (2004), experts have pointed to a range of important potential contributors to the rise in childhood obesity that are unrelated to media (p. 1).

BORROWED LANGUAGE IN QUOTATION MARKS

According to the Henry J. Kaiser Family Foundation (2004), "experts have pointed to a range of important potential contributors to the rise in childhood obesity that are unrelated to media" (p. 1).

NOTE: When quoted sentences are set off from the text by indenting, quotation marks are not needed (see p. 465).

APA-2c Put summaries and paraphrases in your own words.

Summaries and paraphrases are written in your own words. A summary condenses information; a paraphrase reports information in about the same number of words as in the source. When you summarize or paraphrase, you must restate the source's meaning using your own language. You commit plagiarism if you half-copy the author's sentences—either by mixing the author's well-chosen phrases with your own without using quotation marks or by plugging your own synonyms into the author's sentence structure. The following paraphrases are plagiarized—even though the source is cited—because their language is too close to that of the source.

ORIGINAL SOURCE

In an effort to seek the causes of this disturbing trend, experts have pointed to a range of important potential contributors to the rise in childhood obesity that are unrelated to media.

—Henry J. Kaiser Family Foundation,
"The Role of Media in Childhood Obesity" (2004), p. 1

UNACCEPTABLE BORROWING OF PHRASES

According to the Henry J. Kaiser Family Foundation (2004), experts have indicated a range of significant potential contributors to the rise in childhood obesity that are not linked to media (p. 1).

UNACCEPTABLE BORROWING OF STRUCTURE

According to the Henry J. Kaiser Family Foundation (2004), experts have identified a variety of significant factors causing a rise in childhood obesity, factors that are not linked to media (p. 1).

To avoid plagiarizing an author's language, set the source aside, write from memory, and consult the source later to check for accuracy. This strategy prevents you from being captivated by the words on the page.

ACCEPTABLE PARAPHRASE

A report by the Henry J. Kaiser Family Foundation (2004) described sources other than media for the childhood obesity crisis.

ON THE WEB > dianahacker.com/writersref
Research exercises > E-ex APA 2–1 through APA 2–5

APA-3

Integrating sources

Quotations, summaries, paraphrases, and facts will support your argument, but they cannot speak for you. You can use several strategies to integrate information from research sources into your paper while maintaining your own voice.

APA-3a Limit your use of quotations.

Using quotations appropriately

Although it is tempting to insert many quotations in your paper and to use your own words only for connecting passages, do not quote excessively. It is almost impossible to integrate numerous long quotations smoothly into your own text.

It is not always necessary to quote full sentences from a source. At times you may wish to borrow only a phrase or to weave part of a source's sentence into your own sentence structure.

> Carmona (2004) advised the subcommittee that the situation constitutes an "epidemic" and that the skyrocketing statistics are "astounding" (para. 3).

> As researchers continue to face a number of unknowns about obesity, it may be helpful to envision treating the disorder, as Yanovski and Yanovski (2002) suggested, "in the same manner as any other chronic disease" (p. 592).

USING THE ELLIPSIS MARK   To condense a quoted passage, you can use the ellipsis mark (three periods, with spaces between) to indicate that you have omitted words. What remains must be grammatically complete.

> Roman (2003) reported that "social factors are nearly as significant as individual metabolism in the formation of . . . dietary habits of adolescents" (p. 345).

The writer has omitted the words *both healthy and unhealthy.*

When you want to omit a full sentence or more, use a period before the three ellipsis dots.

> According to Sothern and Gordon (2003), "Environmental factors may contribute as much as 80% to the causes of childhood obesity. . . . Research suggests that obese children demonstrate decreased levels of physical activity and increased psychosocial problems" (p. 104).

Ordinarily, do not use an ellipsis mark at the beginning or at the end of a quotation. Readers will understand that the quoted material is taken from a longer passage. The only exception occurs when you think that the author's meaning might be misinterpreted without ellipsis marks.

USING BRACKETS   Brackets (square parentheses) allow you to insert your own words into quoted material to explain a confusing reference or to keep a sentence grammatical in your context.

> The cost of treating obesity currently totals $117 billion per year--a price, according to the surgeon general, "second only to the cost of [treating] tobacco use" (Carmona, 2004, para. 9).

To indicate an error in a quotation, insert [*sic*] right after the error. Notice that the term *sic* is italicized and appears in brackets.

SETTING OFF LONG QUOTATIONS   When you quote forty or more words, set off the quotation by indenting it one-half inch (or five spaces) from the left margin. Use the normal right margin and do not single-space.

Long quotations should be introduced by an informative sentence, usually followed by a colon. Quotation marks are unnecessary because the indented format tells readers that the words are taken directly from the source.

> Yanovski and Yanovski (2002) have described earlier treatments of obesity
> that focused on behavior modification:
>
>> With the advent of behavioral treatments for obesity in the 1960s,
>> hope arose that modification of maladaptive eating and exercise habits
>> would lead to sustained weight loss, and that time-limited programs
>> would produce permanent changes in weight. Medications for the
>> treatment of obesity were proposed as short-term adjuncts for
>> patients, who would presumably then acquire the skills necessary to
>> continue to lose weight, reach "ideal body weight," and maintain a
>> reduced weight indefinitely. (p. 592)

APA-3b Use signal phrases to integrate sources.

The information you gather from sources cannot speak for itself. Whenever you include a paraphrase, summary, or direct quotation of another writer in your paper, prepare your readers for it with an introduction called a *signal phrase*. A signal phrase usually names the author of the source and gives the publication date in parentheses.

When the signal phrase includes a verb, choose one that is appropriate for the way you are using the source (see APA-1c). Are you arguing a point, making an observation, reporting a fact, drawing a conclusion, or refuting an argument? By choosing an appropriate verb, you can make your source's role clear. See the chart on page 466 for a list of verbs commonly used in signal phrases.

The American Psychological Association requires using past tense or present perfect tense in phrases that introduce quotations and other source material: *Davis (2005) noted that* or *Davis (2005) has noted that*, not *Davis (2005) notes that*. Use the present tense only for discussing the results of an experiment (*the results show*) or knowledge that has clearly been established (*researchers agree*).

It is generally acceptable in the social sciences to call authors by their last name only, even on a first mention. If your paper refers to two authors with same last name, use initials as well.

Using signal phrases in APA papers

To avoid monotony, try to vary the language and placement of your signal phrases.

MODEL SIGNAL PHRASES

In the words of Carmona (2004), "..."

As Yanovski and Yanovski (2002) have noted, "..."

Hoppin and Taveras (2004), medical researchers, pointed out that "..."

"...," claimed Critser (2003).

"...," wrote Duenwald (2004), "..."

Researchers McDuffie et al. (2003) have offered an odd argument for this view: "..."

Hilts (2002) answered these objections with the following analysis: "..."

VERBS IN SIGNAL PHRASES

admitted	contended	reasoned
agreed	declared	refuted
argued	denied	rejected
asserted	emphasized	reported
believed	insisted	responded
claimed	noted	suggested
compared	observed	thought
confirmed	pointed out	wrote

Marking boundaries

Readers need to move from your words to the words of a source without feeling a jolt. Avoid dropping direct quotations into your text without warning. Instead, provide clear signal phrases, including at least the author's name and the date of publication. A signal phrase indicates the boundary between your words and the source's words and can also tell readers why a source is trustworthy.

DROPPED QUOTATION

Obesity was once considered in a very different light. "For many years, obesity was approached as it if were either a moral failing or evidence of underlying psychopathology" (Yanovski & Yanovski, 2002, p. 592).

QUOTATION WITH SIGNAL PHRASE

As researchers Yanovski and Yanovski (2002) have explained, obesity was once considered "either a moral failing or evidence of underlying psychopathology" (p. 592).

Introducing summaries and paraphrases

As with quotations, you should introduce most summaries and paraphrases with a signal phrase that mentions the author and the date of publication and places the material in context. Readers will then understand where the summary or paraphrase begins.

Without the signal phrase (underlined) in the following example, readers might think that only the last sentence is being cited, when in fact the whole paragraph is based on the source.

Carmona (2004) advised a Senate subcommittee that the problem of childhood obesity is dire and that the skyrocketing statistics--which put the child obesity rate at 15%--are cause for alarm. More than 9 million children, double the number in the early 1980s, are classified as obese. Carmona warned that obesity can cause myriad physical problems that only worsen as children grow older (para. 6).

There are times, however, when a summary or a paraphrase does not require a signal phrase naming the author. When the context makes clear where the cited material begins, omit the signal phrase and include the author's name in the parentheses. Unless the work is short, also include the page number in the parentheses: (Saltzman, 2004, p. D8).

Putting source material in context

Readers need to understand how your source is relevant to your paper's thesis. It's a good idea, in other words, to embed your quotation—especially a long one—between sentences of your own, introducing it with a signal phrase and following it up with interpretive comments that link the source material to your paper's thesis.

QUOTATION WITH INSUFFICIENT CONTEXT

A report by the Henry J. Kaiser Family Foundation (2004) outlined trends that may have contributed to the childhood obesity crisis, including food advertising for children as well as

a reduction in physical education classes . . . , an increase in the availability of sodas and snacks in public schools, the growth in the

number of fast-food outlets . . . , and the increasing number of highly
processed high-calorie and high-fat grocery products. (p. 1)

QUOTATION WITH EFFECTIVE CONTEXT

A report by the Henry J. Kaiser Family Foundation (2004) outlined
trends that may have contributed to the childhood obesity crisis, including
food advertising for children as well as

a reduction in physical education classes . . . , an increase in the
availability of sodas and snacks in public schools, the growth in the
number of fast-food outlets . . . , and the increasing number of highly
processed high-calorie and high-fat grocery products. (p. 1)

Addressing each of these areas requires more than a doctor armed with a
prescription pad; it requires a broad mobilization not just of doctors and
concerned parents but of educators, food industry executives, advertisers,
and media representatives.

Integrating statistics and other facts

When you are citing a statistic or another specific fact, a signal phrase
is often not necessary. In most cases, readers will understand that the
citation refers to the statistic or fact (not the whole paragraph).

In purely financial terms, the drugs cost more than $3 a day on average
(Duenwald, 2004, paras. 33, 36).

There is nothing wrong, however, with using a signal phrase.

Duenwald (2004) reported that the drugs cost more than $3 a day on
average (paras. 33, 36).

ON THE WEB > dianahacker.com/writersref
Research exercises > E-ex APA 3–1 through APA 3–4

APA-4

Documenting sources

In most social science classes, you will be asked to use the APA system for documenting sources, which is set forth in the *Publication
Manual of the American Psychological Association,* 5th ed. (Wash-

ington: APA, 2001). APA recommends in-text citations that refer readers to a list of references.

An in-text citation gives the author of the source (often in a signal phrase), the date of publication, and at times a page number in parentheses. At the end of the paper, a list of references provides publication information about the source (see p. 501). The direct link between the in-text citation and the entry in the reference list is highlighted in green in the following example.

IN-TEXT CITATION

Yanovski and Yanovski (2002) reported that "the current state of the treatment for obesity is similar to the state of the treatment of hypertension several decades ago" (p. 600).

ENTRY IN THE LIST OF REFERENCES

Yanovski, S. Z., & Yanovski, J. A. (2002). Drug therapy: Obesity [Electronic version]. *The New England Journal of Medicine, 346,* 591-602.

For a reference list that includes this entry, see page 501.

Directory to APA in-text citations

APA-4a APA in-text citations

The APA's in-text citations provide at least the author's last name and the date of publication. For direct quotations and some paraphrases, a page number is given as well.

NOTE: APA style requires the use of the past tense or the present perfect tense in signal phrases introducing cited material: *Smith (2005) reported, Smith (2005) has argued.*

■ **1. BASIC FORMAT FOR A QUOTATION** Ordinarily, introduce the quotation with a signal phrase that includes the author's last name followed by the year of publication in parentheses. Put the page number (preceded by "p.") in parentheses after the quotation.

> Critser (2003) noted that despite growing numbers of overweight Americans, many health care providers still "remain either in ignorance or outright denial about the health danger to the poor and the young" (p. 5).

If the author is not named in the signal phrase, place the author's name, the year, and the page number in parentheses after the quotation: (Critser, 2003, p. 5).

NOTE: APA style requires the year of publication in an in-text citation. Do not include a month, even if the source is listed by month and year.

■ **2. BASIC FORMAT FOR A SUMMARY OR A PARAPHRASE** Include the author's last name and the year either in a signal phrase introducing the material or in parentheses following it. A page number or another locator is not required for a summary or a paraphrase, but include one if it would help readers find the passage in a long work.

> According to Carmona (2004), the cost of treating obesity is exceeded only by the cost of treating illnesses from tobacco use (para. 9).

> The cost of treating obesity is exceeded only by the cost of treating illnesses from tobacco use (Carmona, 2004, para. 9).

■ **3. A WORK WITH TWO AUTHORS** Name both authors in the signal phrase or parentheses each time you cite the work. In the parentheses, use "&" between the authors' names; in the signal phrase, use "and."

> According to Sothern and Gordon (2003), "Environmental factors may contribute as much as 80% to the causes of childhood obesity" (p. 104).

> Obese children often engage in limited physical activity (Sothern & Gordon, 2003, p. 104).

■ **4. A WORK WITH THREE TO FIVE AUTHORS** Identify all authors in the signal phrase or parentheses the first time you cite the source.

> In 2003, Berkowitz, Wadden, Tershakovec, and Cronquist concluded, "Sibutramine . . . must be carefully monitored in adolescents, as in adults, to control increases in [blood pressure] and pulse rate" (p. 1811).

In subsequent citations, use the first author's name followed by "et al." in either the signal phrase or the parentheses.

> As Berkowitz et al. (2003) advised, "Until more extensive safety and efficacy data are available, . . . weight-loss medications should be used only on an experimental basis for adolescents" (p. 1811).

5. A WORK WITH SIX OR MORE AUTHORS   Use the first author's name followed by "et al." in the signal phrase or the parentheses.

> McDuffie et al. (2002) tested 20 adolescents, aged 12-16, over a three-month period and found that orlistat, combined with behavioral therapy, produced an average weight loss of 4.4 kg, or 9.7 pounds (p. 646).

6. UNKNOWN AUTHOR   If the author is unknown, mention the work's title in the signal phrase or give the first word or two of the title in the parenthetical citation. Titles of articles and chapters are put in quotation marks; titles of books and reports are italicized.

> Children struggling to control their weight must also struggle with the pressures of television advertising that, on the one hand, encourages the consumption of junk food and, on the other, celebrates thin celebrities ("Television," 2002).

NOTE: In the rare case when "Anonymous" is specified as the author, treat it as if it were a real name: (Anonymous, 2001). In the list of references, also use the name Anonymous as author.

7. ORGANIZATION AS AUTHOR   If the author is a government agency or other organization, name the organization in the signal phrase or in the parenthetical citation the first time you cite the source.

> Obesity puts children at risk for a number of medical complications, including type 2 diabetes, hypertension, sleep apnea, and orthopedic problems (Henry J. Kaiser Family Foundation, 2004, p. 1).

If the organization has a familiar abbreviation, you may include it in brackets the first time you cite the source and use the abbreviation alone in later citations.

FIRST CITATION   (National Institute of Mental Health [NIMH], 2001)

LATER CITATIONS   (NIMH, 2001)

■   **8. TWO OR MORE WORKS IN THE SAME PARENTHESES**   When your parenthetical citation names two or more works, put them in the same order that they appear in the reference list, separated by semicolons.

> Researchers have indicated that studies of pharmacological treatments for childhood obesity are inconclusive (Berkowitz et al., 2003; McDuffie et al., 2003).

■   **9. AUTHORS WITH THE SAME LAST NAME**   To avoid confusion, use initials with the last names if your reference list includes two or more authors with the same last name.

> Research by E. Smith (1989) revealed that . . .

■   **10. PERSONAL COMMUNICATION**   Interviews, memos, letters, e-mail, and similar unpublished person-to-person communications should be cited as follows:

> One of Atkinson's colleagues, who has studied the effect of the media on children's eating habits, has contended that advertisers for snack foods will need to design ads responsibly for their younger viewers (F. Johnson, personal communication, October 20, 2004).

Do not include personal communications in your reference list.

■   **11. AN ELECTRONIC DOCUMENT**   When possible, cite an electronic document as you would any other document (using the author-date style).

> Atkinson (2001) found that children who spent at least four hours a day watching TV were less likely to engage in adequate physical activity during the week.

Electronic sources may lack authors' names or dates. In addition, they may lack page numbers (required in some citations). Here are APA's guidelines for handling sources without authors' names, dates, or page numbers.

Unknown author
If no author is named, mention the title of the document in a signal phrase or give the first word or two of the title in parentheses (see also item 6). (If an organization serves as the author, see item 7.)

> The body's basal metabolic rate, or BMR, is a measure of its at-rest energy requirement ("Exercise," 2003).

Unknown date

When the date is unknown, APA recommends using the abbreviation "n.d." (for "no date").

> Attempts to establish a definitive link between television programming and children's eating habits have been problematic (Magnus, n.d.).

No page numbers

APA ordinarily requires page numbers for quotations, and it recommends them for summaries or paraphrases from long sources. When an electronic source lacks stable numbered pages, your citation should include—if possible—information that will help readers locate the particular passage being cited.

When an electronic document has numbered paragraphs, use the paragraph number preceded by the symbol ¶ or by the abbreviation "para.": (Hall, 2001, ¶ 5) *or* (Hall, 2001, para. 5). If neither a page nor a paragraph number is given and the document contains headings, cite the appropriate heading and indicate which paragraph under that heading you are referring to.

> Hoppin and Taveras (2004) pointed out that several other medications were classified by the Drug Enforcement Administration as having the "potential for abuse" (Weight-Loss Drugs section, para. 6).

NOTE: Electronic files in portable document format (PDF) often have stable page numbers. For such sources, give the page number in the parenthetical citation.

▪ **12. INDIRECT SOURCE** If you use a source that was cited in another source (a secondary source), name the original source in your signal phrase. List the secondary source in your reference list and include it in your parenthetical citation, preceded by the words "as cited in." In the following example, Critser is the secondary source.

> Former surgeon general Dr. David Satcher described "a nation of young people seriously at risk of starting out obese and dooming themselves to the difficult task of overcoming a tough illness" (as cited in Critser, 2003, p. 4).

▪ **13. TWO OR MORE WORKS BY THE SAME AUTHOR IN THE SAME YEAR** When your list of references includes more than one work by the same author in the same year, use lowercase letters ("a," "b," and so on) with the year to order the entries in the reference list. (See item 6 on p. 476.) Use those same letters with the year in the in-text citation.

> Research by Durgin (2003b) has yielded new findings about the role of counseling in treating childhood obesity.

ON THE WEB > dianahacker.com/writersref
Research exercises > E-ex APA 4–1 through APA 4–3

APA-4b   APA references

In APA style, the alphabetical list of works cited, which appears at the end of the paper, is titled "References." Following are models illustrating APA style for entries in the list of references. Observe all details: capitalization, punctuation, use of italics, and so on. For advice on preparing the reference list, see pages 491–92. For a sample reference list, see page 501.

ON THE WEB > dianahacker.com/writersref
Research exercises > E-ex APA 4–4

ON THE WEB > dianahacker.com/writersref
Research and Documentation Online > Social sciences:
Documenting sources (APA)

General guidelines for listing authors

Alphabetize entries in the list of references by authors' last names; if a work has no author, alphabetize it by its title. The first element of each entry is important because citations in the text of the paper refer to it and readers will be looking for it in the alphabetized list. The date of publication appears immediately after the first element of the citation.

NAME AND DATE CITED IN TEXT

Duncan (2006) has reported that . . .

BEGINNING OF ENTRY IN THE LIST OF REFERENCES

Duncan, B. (2006).

Items 1–4 show how to begin an entry for a work with a single author, multiple authors, an organization as author, and an unknown author. Items 5 and 6 show how to begin an entry when your list includes two or more works by the same author or two or more works by the same author in the same year. What comes after the first element of your citation will depend on the kind of source you are citing (see items 7–32).

Directory to APA references (bibliographic entries)

1. SINGLE AUTHOR Begin the entry with the author's last name, followed by a comma and the author's initial(s). Then give the date in parentheses.

Perez, E. (2006).

2. MULTIPLE AUTHORS List up to six authors by last names followed by initials. Use an ampersand (&) between the names of two authors or, if there are more than two authors, before the name of the last author.

DuNann, D. W., & Koger, S. M. (2004).

Sloan, F. A., Stout, E. M., Whetten-Goldstein, K., & Liang, L. (2000).

If there are more than six authors, list the first six and "et al." (meaning "and others") to indicate that there are others.

■ **3. ORGANIZATION AS AUTHOR** When the author is an organization, begin with the name of the organization.

American Psychiatric Association. (2005).

NOTE: If the organization is also the publisher, see item 29.

■ **4. UNKNOWN AUTHOR** Begin the entry with the work's title.
Titles of books are italicized; titles of articles are neither italicized
nor put in quotation marks. (For rules on capitalization of titles, see
p. 491.)

Oxford essential world atlas. (2001).

Omega-3 fatty acids. (2004, November 23).

■ **5. TWO OR MORE WORKS BY THE SAME AUTHOR** Use the author's
name for all entries. List the entries by year, the earliest first.

Schlechty, P. C. (1997).

Schlechty, P. C. (2001).

■ **6. TWO OR MORE WORKS BY THE SAME AUTHOR IN THE SAME YEAR**
List the works alphabetically by title. In the parentheses, following
the year, add "a," "b," and so on. Use these same letters when giving
the year in the in-text citation. (See also p. 491.)

Durgin, P. A. (2003a). At-risk behaviors in children.

Durgin, P. A. (2003b). Treating obesity with psychotherapy.

Articles in periodicals

This section shows how to prepare an entry for an article in a periodical such as a scholarly journal, a magazine, or a newspaper. In
addition to consulting the models in this section, you may need to
refer to items 1–6 (general guidelines for listing authors).

NOTE: For articles on consecutive pages, provide the range of pages
at the end of the citation (see item 7 for an example). When an article does not appear on consecutive pages, give all page numbers:
A1, A17.

■ **7. ARTICLE IN A JOURNAL PAGINATED BY VOLUME** Many professional journals continue page numbers throughout the year instead of beginning each issue with page 1; at the end of the year,

Citation at a glance: Article in a periodical (APA)

To cite an article in a periodical in APA style, include the following elements:

1 Author
2 Date of publication
3 Title of article
4 Name of periodical
5 Volume and issue numbers
6 Page numbers

REFERENCE LIST ENTRY FOR AN ARTICLE IN A PERIODICAL

Hoxby, C. M. (2002). The power of peers. *Education Next, 2*(2), 57-63.

For more on citing periodicals in APA style, see pages 476–79.

the issues are collected in a volume. After the italicized title of the journal, give the volume number (also italicized), followed by the page numbers.

Morawski, J. (2000). Social psychology a century ago. *American Psychologist, 55,*
427-431.

■ **8. ARTICLE IN A JOURNAL PAGINATED BY ISSUE** When each issue of a journal begins with page 1, include the issue number in parentheses after the volume number. Italicize the volume number but not the issue number.

Smith, S. (2003). Government and nonprofits in the modern age. *Society, 40*(4),
36-45.

■ **9. ARTICLE IN A MAGAZINE** In addition to the year of publication, list the month and, for weekly magazines, the day. If there is a volume number, include it (italicized) after the title.

Raloff, J. (2001, May 12). Lead therapy won't help most kids. *Science News, 159,*
292.

■ **10. ARTICLE IN A NEWSPAPER** Begin with the name of the author followed by the exact date of publication. (If the author is unknown, see also item 4.) Page numbers are introduced with "p." (or "pp.").

Lohr, S. (2004, December 3). Health care technology is a promise unfinanced. *The*
New York Times, p. C5.

■ **11. LETTER TO THE EDITOR** Letters to the editor appear in journals, magazines, and newspapers. Follow the appropriate model and insert the words "Letter to the editor" in brackets before the name of the periodical.

Carter, R. (2006, July). Lost in translation? [Letter to the editor]. *Scientific*
American, 295(1), 12.

■ **12. REVIEW** Reviews of books and other media appear in a variety of periodicals. Follow the appropriate model for the periodical. For a review of a book, give the title of the review (if there is one), followed in brackets by the words "Review of the book" and the title of the book.

Gleick, E. (2000, December 14). The burdens of genius [Review of the book *The*
Last Samurai]. *Time, 156,* 171.

For a film review, write "Review of the motion picture," and for a TV review, write "Review of the television program." Treat other media in a similar way.

Books

In addition to consulting the items in this section, you may need to refer to items 1–6 (general guidelines for listing authors).

▨ **13. BASIC FORMAT FOR A BOOK** Begin with the author's name, followed by the date and the book's title. End with the place of publication and the name of the publisher. Take the information about the book from its title page and copyright page. If more than one place of publication is given, use only the first; if more than one date is given, use the most recent one.

Highmore, B. (2001). *Everyday life and cultural theory*. New York: Routledge.

▨ **14. BOOK WITH AN EDITOR** For a book with an editor but no author, begin with the name of the editor (or editors) followed by the abbreviation "Ed." (or "Eds.") in parentheses.

Bronfen, E., & Kavka, M. (Eds.). (2001). *Feminist consequences: Theory for a new century*. New York: Columbia University Press.

For a book with an author and an editor, begin with the author's name. Give the editor's name in parentheses after the title of the book, followed by the abbreviation "Ed." (or "Eds.").

Plath, S. (2000). *The unabridged journals* (K. V. Kukil, Ed.). New York: Anchor.

▨ **15. TRANSLATION** After the title, name the translator, followed by the abbreviation "Trans.," in parentheses. Add the original date of the work's publication in parentheses at the end of the entry.

Steinberg, M. D. (2003). *Voices of revolution, 1917* (M. Schwartz, Trans.). New Haven, CT: Yale University Press. (Original work published 2001)

▨ **16. EDITION OTHER THAN THE FIRST** Include the number of the edition in parentheses after the title.

Helfer, M. E., Keme, R. S., & Drugman, R. D. (1997). *The battered child* (5th ed.). Chicago: University of Chicago Press.

Citation at a glance: Book (APA)

To cite a book in APA style, include the following elements:

1 Author
2 Date of publication
3 Title and subtitle
4 City of publication
5 Publisher

REFERENCE LIST ENTRY FOR A BOOK

Levenstein, H. A. (2003). *Revolution at the table: The transformation of the American diet.* Berkeley: University of California Press.

For more on citing books in APA style, see pages 479–81.

▨ **17. ARTICLE OR CHAPTER IN AN EDITED BOOK** Begin with the author, year of publication, and title of the article or chapter. Then write "In" and give the editor's name, followed by "Ed." in parentheses; the title of the book; and the page numbers of the article or chapter in parentheses. End with the book's publication information.

Luban, D. (2000). The ethics of wrongful obedience. In D. L. Rhode (Ed.), *Ethics in practice: Lawyers' roles, responsibilities, and regulation* (pp. 94-120). New York: Oxford University Press.

▨ **18. MULTIVOLUME WORK** Give the number of volumes after the title.

Luo, J. (Ed.). (2005). *China today: An encyclopedia of life in the People's Republic* (Vols. 1-2). Westport, CT: Greenwood Press.

Electronic sources

This section shows how to prepare reference list entries for a variety of electronic sources, including articles in online periodicals and databases, Web documents, Weblogs, and e-mail.

▨ **19. ARTICLE FROM AN ONLINE PERIODICAL** When citing online articles, follow the guidelines for printed articles (see items 7–12), giving whatever information is available in the online source. If the article also appears in a printed journal, a URL is not required; instead, include "Electronic version" in brackets after the title of the article.

Whitmeyer, J. M. (2000). Power through appointment [Electronic version]. *Social Science Research, 29*, 535-555.

If there is no print version, include the date you accessed the source and the article's URL.

Ashe, D. D., & McCutcheon, L. E. (2001). Shyness, loneliness, and attitude toward celebrities. *Current Research in Social Psychology, 6*(9). Retrieved March 2, 2006, from http://www.uiowa.edu/~grpproc/crisp/crisp.6.9.htm

NOTE: When you have retrieved an article from a newspaper's searchable Web site, give the URL for the site, not for the exact source.

Cary, B. (2001, June 18). Mentors of the mind. *Los Angeles Times.* Retrieved July 5, 2001, from http://www.latimes.com

■ **20. ARTICLE FROM A DATABASE** To cite an article from a library's subscription database, include the publication information from the source (see items 7–12). End the citation with your date of access, the name of the database, and the document number (if applicable).

Holliday, R. E., & Hayes, B. K. (2001). Dissociating automatic and intentional
     processes in children's eyewitness memory. *Journal of Experimental Child
     Psychology, 75(*1), 1-5. Retrieved February 21, 2001, from Expanded
     Academic ASAP database (A59317972).

■ **21. NONPERIODICAL WEB DOCUMENT** To cite a nonperiodical Web document, such as a report, list as many of the following elements as are available.

  Author's name

  Date of publication (if there is no date, use "n.d.")

  Title of document (in italics)

  Date you accessed the source

  A URL that will take readers directly to the source

In the first model, the source has both an author and a date; in the second, the source lacks a date.

Cain, A., & Burris, M. (1999, April). *Investigation of the use of mobile phones
     while driving.* Retrieved January 15, 2000, from http://www.cutr.eng
     .usf.edu/its/mobile_phone_text.htm

Archer, D. (n.d.). *Exploring nonverbal communication.* Retrieved March 2, 2006,
     from http://nonverbal.ucsc.edu

If a source has no author, begin with the title and follow it with the date in parentheses.

NOTE: If you retrieved the source from a university program's Web site, name the program in your retrieval statement.

Cosmides, L., & Tooby, J. (1997). *Evolutionary psychology: A primer.* Retrieved
     March 1, 2006, from the University of California, Santa Barbara, Center for
     Evolutionary Psychology Web site: http://www.psych.ucsb.edu/research/cep/
     primer.html

■ **22. CHAPTER OR SECTION IN A WEB DOCUMENT** Begin with the author, the year of publication, and the title of the chapter or section. Then write "In" and give the title of the document, followed by any identifying information in parentheses. End with your date of access and the URL for the chapter or section.

Heuer, R. J., Jr. (1999). Keeping an open mind. In *Psychology of intelligence analysis* (chap. 6). Retrieved January 7, 2006, from http://www.cia.gov/csi/books/19104/art9.html

■ **23. ENTRY IN A WEBLOG (BLOG)** To cite an entry in a Weblog, give the author's name, the title of the entry, the name of the Weblog, the date on which you retrieved the source, and the URL.

Mayer, C. (2006, February 28). Some surprising findings about identity theft. *The Checkout.* Retrieved March 2, 2006, from http://blog.washingtonpost.com/thecheckout/2006/02/some_surprising_findings_about.html

■ **24. E-MAIL** E-mail messages and other personal communications are not included in the list of references.

■ **25. ONLINE POSTING** If an online posting is not maintained in an archive, cite it as a personal communication in the text of your paper and do not include it in the list of references. If the posting can be retrieved from an archive, give as much information as is available.

Eaton, S. (2001, June 12). Online transactions [Msg 2]. Message posted to news://sci.psychology.psychotherapy.moderated

■ **26. COMPUTER PROGRAM** Add the words "Computer software" in brackets after the title of the program.

Kaufmann, W. J., III, & Comins, N. F. (2003). Discovering the universe (Version 6.0) [Computer software]. New York: Freeman.

Other sources

■ **27. DISSERTATION ABSTRACT**

Yoshida, Y. (2001). Essays in urban transportation (Doctoral dissertation, Boston College, 2001). *Dissertation Abstracts International, 62,* 7741A.

■ **28. GOVERNMENT DOCUMENT**

U.S. Census Bureau. (2006). *Statistical abstract of the United States.* Washington, DC: U.S. Government Printing Office.

Citation at a glance: Article from a database (APA)

To cite an article from a database in APA style, include the following elements:

1 Author
2 Date of publication
3 Title of article
4 Name of periodical
5 Volume and issue numbers

6 Page numbers
7 Date of access
8 Name of database
9 Document number

ON-SCREEN VIEW OF DATABASE RECORD

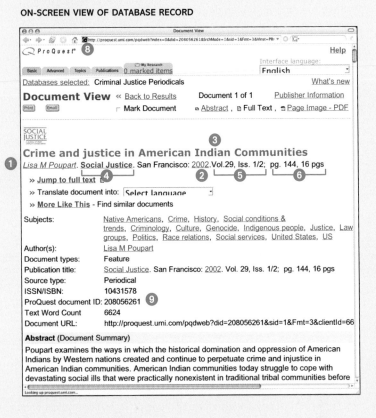

PRINTOUT OF RECORD AND BEGINNING OF ARTICLE

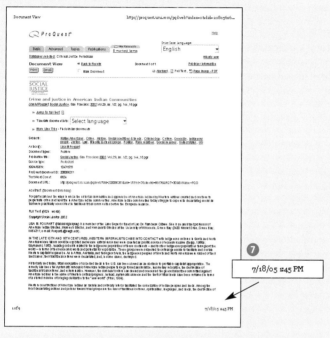

7/18/05 #45 PM

REFERENCE LIST ENTRY FOR AN ARTICLE FROM A DATABASE

Poupart, L. M. (2002). Crime and justice in American Indian communities.

Social Justice, 29(1/2), 144-159. Retrieved July 18, 2005, from

ProQuest database (208056261).

For more on citing articles from a database in APA style, see page 482.

Citation at a glance: Document from a Web site (APA)

To cite a document from a Web site in APA style, include the following elements:

1 Author
2 Date of publication or most recent update
3 Title of document on Web site

4 Title of Web site or section of site
5 Date of access
6 URL of document

BROWSER PRINTOUT OF WEB SITE

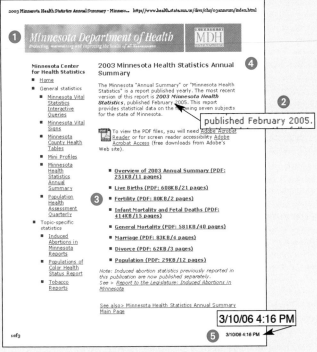

ON-SCREEN VIEW OF DOCUMENT

REFERENCE LIST ENTRY FOR A DOCUMENT FROM A WEB SITE

Minnesota Department of Health. (2005). Fertility. In *2003 Minnesota health*

statistics annual summary. Retrieved March 10, 2006, from

http://www.health.state.mn.us/divs/chs/03annsum/fertility.pdf

For more on citing documents from Web sites in APA style, see pages 481–83.

■   **29. REPORT FROM A PRIVATE ORGANIZATION**   If the publisher and the author are the same, use the word "Author" as the publisher. If a person is named as the author, begin with that person and give the organization as publisher at the end.

American Psychiatric Association. (2000). *Practice guidelines for the treatment of patients with eating disorders* (2nd ed.). Washington, DC: Author.

■   **30. CONFERENCE PROCEEDINGS**

Stahl, G. (Ed.). (2002). *Proceedings of CSCL '02: Computer support for collaborative learning.* Hillsdale, NJ: Erlbaum.

■   **31. MOTION PICTURE**   To cite a motion picture (film, video, or DVD), list the director and the year of the picture's release. Give the title, followed by "Motion picture" in brackets, the country where it was made, and the name of the studio. If the motion picture is difficult to find, include instead the name and address of its distributor.

Gaghan, S. (Director). (2005). *Syriana* [Motion picture]. United States: Warner Brothers Pictures.

Spurlock, M. (Director). (2004). *Super size me* [Motion picture]. (Available from IDP Films, 1133 Broadway, Suite 926, New York, NY 10010)

■   **32. TELEVISION PROGRAM**   To cite a television program, list the producer and the date it was aired. Give the title, followed by "Television broadcast" in brackets, the city, and the television network or service.

Pratt, C. (Executive Producer). (2006, February 19). *Face the nation* [Television broadcast]. Washington, DC: CBS News.

For a television series, use the year in which the series was produced, and follow the title with "Television series" in brackets. For an episode in a series, list the writer and director and the year. After the episode title, put "Television series episode" in brackets. Follow with information about the series.

Janows, J. (Executive Producer). (2000). *Culture shock* [Television series]. Boston: WGBH.

Loeterman, B. (Writer), & Gale, B. (Director). (2000). Real justice [Television series episode]. In M. Sullivan (Executive Producer), *Frontline.* Boston: WGBH.

ON THE WEB > dianahacker.com/writersref
Electronic research exercises > E-ex APA 4–5 and APA 4–6

APA-5

Manuscript format; sample paper

APA-5a Manuscript format

The American Psychological Association makes a number of recommendations for formatting a paper and preparing a list of references. The following guidelines are consistent with advice given in the *Publication Manual of the American Psychological Association,* 5th ed. (Washington: APA, 2001).

Formatting the paper

APA guidelines for formatting a paper are endorsed by many instructors in the social sciences.

MATERIALS AND TYPEFACE   Use good-quality $8\frac{1}{2}'' \times 11''$ white paper. Avoid a typeface that is unusual or hard to read.

TITLE PAGE   The APA manual does not provide guidelines for preparing the title page of a college paper, but most instructors will want you to include one. See page 493 for an example.

PAGE NUMBERS AND RUNNING HEAD   The title page is numbered as page i; the abstract page, if there is one, is numbered as page ii. Use arabic numerals, beginning with 1, for the rest of the paper. In the upper right-hand corner of each page, type a short version of your title, followed by five spaces and the page number. Number all pages, including the title page.

MARGINS, LINE SPACING, AND PARAGRAPH INDENTS   Use margins of one inch on all sides of the page. Left-align the text.

Double-space throughout the paper, but single-space footnotes. Indent the first line of each paragraph one-half inch (or five spaces).

LONG QUOTATIONS AND FOOTNOTES   When a quotation is longer than forty words, set it off from the text by indenting it one-half inch (or five spaces) from the left margin. Double-space the quotation. Quotation marks are not needed when a quotation has been set off from the text. See page 500 for an example.

Place each footnote, if any, at the bottom of the page on which the text reference occurs. Double-space between the last line of text on the page and the footnote. Indent the first line of the footnote one-half inch (or five spaces). Begin the note with the superscript arabic numeral that corresponds to the number in the text. See page 495 for an example.

ABSTRACT   If your instructor requires one, include an abstract immediately after the title page. Center the word Abstract one inch from the top of the page; double-space the abstract as you do the body of your paper.

An abstract is a 100-to-120-word paragraph that provides readers with a quick overview of your essay. It should express your main idea and your key points; it might also briefly suggest any implications or applications of the research you discuss in the paper. See page 494 for an example.

HEADINGS   Although headings are not always necessary, their use is encouraged in the social sciences. For most undergraduate papers, one level of heading will usually be sufficient.

In APA style, major headings are centered. Capitalize the first word of the heading, along with all words except articles, short prepositions, and coordinating conjunctions.

VISUALS   The APA classifies visuals as tables and figures (figures include graphs, charts, drawings, and photographs). Keep visuals as simple as possible. Label each table with an arabic numeral (Table 1, Table 2, and so on) and provide a clear title. The label and title should appear on separate lines above the table, flush left and single-spaced. Below the table, give its source in a note. If any data in the table require an explanatory footnote, use a superscript lowercase letter in the body of the table and in a footnote following the source note. Single-space source notes and footnotes and do not indent the first line of each note. See page 497 for an example.

For each figure, place a label and a caption below the figure, flush left and single-spaced. They need not appear on separate lines.

In the text of your paper, discuss the most significant features of each visual. Place the visual as close as possible to the sentences that relate to it unless your instructor prefers it in an appendix.

Preparing the list of references

Begin your list of references on a new page at the end of the paper. Center the title References one inch from the top of the page. Double-space throughout. For a sample reference list, see page 501.

INDENTING ENTRIES   APA recommends using a hanging indent: Type the first line of an entry flush left and indent any additional lines one-half inch (or five spaces), as shown on page 501.

ALPHABETIZING THE LIST   Alphabetize the reference list by the last names of the authors (or editors); when a work has no author or editor, alphabetize by the first word of the title other than *A, An,* or *The.*

If your list includes two or more works by the same author, arrange the entries by year, the earliest first. If your list includes two or more works by the same author in the same year, arrange them alphabetically by title. Add the letters "a," "b," and so on within the parentheses after the year. Use only the year for articles in journals: (2002a). Use the full date for articles in magazines and newspapers in the reference list: (2005a, July 7). Use only the year in the in-text citation.

AUTHORS' NAMES   Invert all authors' names and use initials instead of first names. With two or more authors, use an ampersand (&) before the last author's name. Separate the names with commas. Include names for the first six authors; if there are additional authors, end the list with "et al." (Latin for "and others").

TITLES OF BOOKS AND ARTICLES   Italicize the titles and subtitles of books. Do not use quotation marks around the titles of articles. Capitalize only the first word of the title and subtitle (and all proper nouns) of books and articles. Capitalize names of periodicals as you would capitalize them normally (see M3-c).

ABBREVIATIONS FOR PAGE NUMBERS   Abbreviations for "page" and "pages" ("p." and "pp.") are used before page numbers of newspaper articles and articles in edited books (see item 10 on p. 478 and item 17 on p. 481) but not before page numbers of articles appearing in magazines and scholarly journals (see items 7–9 on pp. 476–78).

BREAKING A URL   When a URL must be divided, break it after a slash or before a period. Do not insert a hyphen.

See page 501 for an example of how to type your list of references. For information about the exact format of each entry in your list, consult the models on pages 475–88.

APA-5b Sample research paper: APA style

On the following pages is a research paper written by Luisa Mirano, a student in a psychology class. Mirano's assignment was to write a review of the literature paper documented with APA-style citations and references.

ON THE WEB > dianahacker.com/writersref
   Model papers > APA papers: Mirano; Shaw
                  > APA annotated bibliography: Haddad

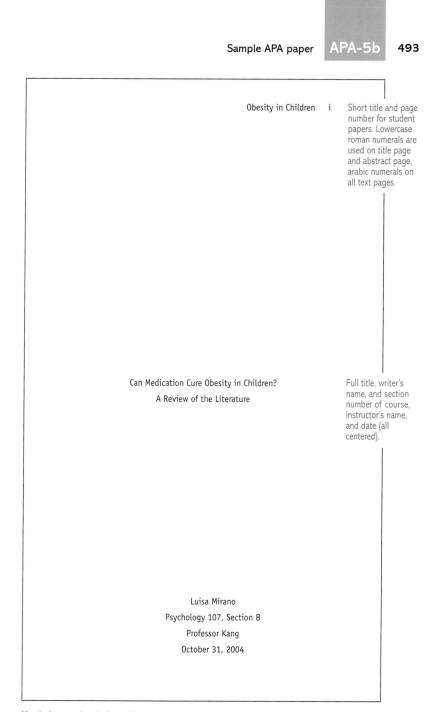

Obesity in Children   i

Short title and page number for student papers. Lowercase roman numerals are used on title page and abstract page, arabic numerals on all text pages.

Can Medication Cure Obesity in Children?

A Review of the Literature

Full title, writer's name, and section number of course, instructor's name, and date (all centered).

Luisa Mirano

Psychology 107, Section B

Professor Kang

October 31, 2004

Marginal annotations indicate APA-style formatting and effective writing.

Abstract appears on a separate page.

Abstract

In recent years, policymakers and medical experts have expressed alarm about the growing problem of childhood obesity in the United States. While most agree that the issue deserves attention, consensus dissolves around how to respond to the problem. This literature review examines one approach to treating childhood obesity: medication. The paper compares the effectiveness for adolescents of the only two drugs approved by the Food and Drug Administration (FDA) for long-term treatment of obesity, sibutramine and orlistat. This examination of pharmacological treatments for obesity points out the limitations of medication and suggests the need for a comprehensive solution that combines medical, social, behavioral, and political approaches to this complex problem.

Can Medication Cure Obesity in Children?

A Review of the Literature

In March 2004, U.S. Surgeon General Richard Carmona called attention to a health problem in the United States that, until recently, has been overlooked: childhood obesity. Carmona said that the "astounding" 15% child obesity rate constitutes an "epidemic." Since the early 1980s, that rate has "doubled in children and tripled in adolescents." Now more than 9 million children are classified as obese (paras. 3, 6).[1] While the traditional response to a medical epidemic is to hunt for a vaccine or a cure-all pill, childhood obesity has proven more elusive. The lack of success of recent initiatives suggests that medication might not be the answer for the escalating problem. This literature review considers whether the use of medication is a promising approach for solving the childhood obesity problem by responding to the following questions:

1. What are the implications of childhood obesity?
2. Is medication effective at treating childhood obesity?
3. Is medication safe for children?
4. Is medication the best solution?

Understanding the limitations of medical treatments for children highlights the complexity of the childhood obesity problem in the United States and underscores the need for physicians, advocacy groups, and policymakers to search for other solutions.

What Are the Implications of Childhood Obesity?

Obesity can be a devastating problem from both an individual and a societal perspective. Obesity puts children at risk for a number of medical complications, including type 2 diabetes, hypertension, sleep apnea, and orthopedic problems (Henry J. Kaiser Family Foundation, 2004, p. 1). Researchers Hoppin and Taveras (2004) have noted that obesity is often associated with psychological issues such as depression, anxiety, and binge eating (Table 4).

[1]Obesity is measured in terms of body-mass index (BMI): weight in kilograms divided by square of height in meters. An adult with a BMI 30 or higher is considered obese. In children and adolescents, obesity is defined in relation to others of the same age and gender. An adolescent with a BMI in the 95th percentile for his or her age and gender is considered obese.

Full title, centered.

The writer sets up her organization by posing four questions.

The writer states her thesis.

Headings, centered, help readers follow the organization.

In a signal phrase, the word "and" links the names of two authors; the date is given in parentheses.

The writer uses a footnote to define an essential term that would be cumbersome to define within the text.

Obesity also poses serious problems for a society struggling to cope with rising health care costs. The cost of treating obesity currently totals $117 billion per year--a price, according to the surgeon general, "second only to the cost of [treating] tobacco use" (Carmona, 2004, para. 9). And as the number of children who suffer from obesity grows, long-term costs will only increase.

Is Medication Effective at Treating Childhood Obesity?

The widening scope of the obesity problem has prompted medical professionals to rethink old conceptions of the disorder and its causes. As researchers Yanovski and Yanovski (2002) have explained, obesity was once considered "either a moral failing or evidence of underlying psychopathology" (p. 592). But this view has shifted: Many medical professionals now consider obesity a biomedical rather than a moral condition, influenced by both genetic and environmental factors. Yanovski and Yanovski have further noted that the development of weight-loss medications in the early 1990s showed that "obesity should be treated in the same manner as any other chronic disease . . . through the long-term use of medication" (p. 592).

The search for the right long-term medication has been complicated. Many of the drugs authorized by the Food and Drug Administration (FDA) in the early 1990s proved to be a disappointment. Two of the medications--fenfluramine and dexfenfluramine--were withdrawn from the market because of severe side effects (Yanovski & Yanovski, 2002, p. 592), and several others were classified by the Drug Enforcement Administration as having the "potential for abuse" (Hoppin & Taveras, 2004, Weight-Loss Drugs section, para. 6). Currently only two medications have been approved by the FDA for long-term treatment of obesity: sibutramine (marketed as Meridia) and orlistat (marketed as Xenical). This section compares studies on the effectiveness of each.

Sibutramine suppresses appetite by blocking the reuptake of the neurotransmitters serotonin and norepinephrine in the brain (Yanovski & Yanovski, 2002, p. 594). Though the drug won FDA approval in 1998, experiments to test its effectiveness for younger patients came considerably later. In 2003, University of Pennsylvania researchers Berkowitz, Wadden, Tershakovec, and Cronquist released the first double-blind placebo study testing the effect of sibutramine on adolescents, aged 13-17, over a 12-month period. Their findings are summarized in Table 1.

Because the author (Carmona) is not named in the signal phrase, his name and the date appear in parentheses, along with the paragraph number of the electronic source.

Ellipsis mark indicates omitted words.

An ampersand links the names of two authors in parentheses.

The writer draws attention to an important article.

Table 1

Effectiveness of Sibutramine and Orlistat in Adolescents

The writer uses a
table to summarize
the findings pre-
sented in two
sources.

Medication	Subjects	Treatment[a]	Side effects	Average weight loss/gain
Sibutra-mine	Control	0-6 mos.: placebo 6-12 mos.: sibutra-mine	Mos. 6-12: increased blood pres-sure; in-creased pulse rate	After 6 mos.: loss of 3.2 kg (7 lb) After 12 mos.: loss of 4.5 kg (9.9 lb)
	Medicated	0-12 mos.: sibutra-mine	Increased blood pres-sure; in-creased pulse rate	After 6 mos.: loss of 7.8 kg (17.2 lb) After 12 mos.: loss of 7.0 kg (15.4 lb)
Orlistat	Control	0-12 mos.: placebo	None	Gain of 0.67 kg (1.5 lb)
	Medicated	0-12 mos.: orlistat	Oily spot-ting; flatu-lence; abdominal discomfort	Loss of 1.3 kg (2.9 lb)

Note. The data on sibutramine are adapted from "Behavior Therapy and Sibutramine for
the Treatment of Adolescent Obesity" [Electronic version], by R. I. Berkowitz, T. A.
Wadden, A. M. Tershakovec, & J. L. Cronquist, 2003, *Journal of the American Medical
Association, 289,* pp. 1807-1809. The data on orlistat are adapted from *Xenical (Orlistat)
Capsules: Complete Product Information,* by Roche Laboratories, December 2003,
retrieved October 11, 2004, from http://www.rocheusa.com/products/xenical/pi.pdf
[a]The medication and/or placebo were combined with behavioral therapy in all groups
over all time periods.

A note gives the
source of the data.

A content note ex-
plains data common
to all subjects.

After 6 months, the group receiving medication had lost 4.6 kg (about 10 pounds) more than the control group. But during the second half of the study, when both groups received sibutramine, the results were more ambiguous. In months 6-12, the group that continued to take sibutramine gained an average of 0.8 kg, or roughly 2 pounds; the control group, which switched from placebo to sibutramine, lost 1.3 kg, or roughly 3 pounds (p. 1808). Both groups received behavioral therapy covering diet, exercise, and mental health.

These results paint a murky picture of the effectiveness of the medication: While initial data seemed promising, the results after one year raised questions about whether medication-induced weight loss could be sustained over time. As Berkowitz et al. (2003) advised, "Until more extensive safety and efficacy data are available, . . . weight-loss medications should be used only on an experimental basis for adolescents" (p. 1811).

A study testing the effectiveness of orlistat in adolescents showed similarly ambiguous results. The FDA approved orlistat in 1999 but did not authorize it for adolescents until December 2003. Roche Laboratories (2003), maker of orlistat, released results of a one-year study testing the drug on 539 obese adolescents, aged 12-16. The drug, which promotes weight loss by blocking fat absorption in the large intestine, showed some effectiveness in adolescents: an average loss of 1.3 kg, or roughly 3 pounds, for subjects taking orlistat for one year, as opposed to an average gain of 0.67 kg, or 1.5 pounds, for the control group (pp. 8-9). See Table 1.

Short-term studies of orlistat have shown slightly more dramatic results. Researchers at the National Institute of Child Health and Human Development tested 20 adolescents, aged 12-16, over a three-month period and found that orlistat, combined with behavioral therapy, produced an average weight loss of 4.4 kg, or 9.7 pounds (McDuffie et al., 2002, p. 646). The study was not controlled against a placebo group; therefore, the relative effectiveness of orlistat in this case remains unclear.

Is Medication Safe for Children?

While modest weight loss has been documented for both medications, each carries risks of certain side effects. Sibutramine has been

When this article was first cited, all four authors were named. In subsequent citations of a work with three to five authors, "et al." is used after the first author's name.

For a source with six or more authors, the first author's surname followed by "et al." is used for the first and subsequent references.

observed to increase blood pressure and pulse rate. In 2002, a consumer group claimed that the medication was related to the deaths of 19 people and filed a petition with the Department of Health and Human Services to ban the medication (Hilts, 2002). The sibutramine study by Berkowitz et al. (2003) noted elevated blood pressure as a side effect, and dosages had to be reduced or the medication discontinued in 19 of the 43 subjects in the first six months (p. 1809).

The main side effects associated with orlistat were abdominal discomfort, oily spotting, fecal incontinence, and nausea (Roche Laboratories, 2003, p. 13). More serious for long-term health is the concern that orlistat, being a fat-blocker, would affect absorption of fat-soluble vitamins, such as vitamin D. However, the study found that this side effect can be minimized or eliminated if patients take vitamin supplements two hours before or after administration of orlistat (p. 10). With close monitoring of patients taking the medication, many of the risks can be reduced.

Is Medication the Best Solution?

The data on the safety and efficacy of pharmacological treatments of childhood obesity raise the question of whether medication is the best solution for the problem. The treatments have clear costs for individual patients, including unpleasant side effects, little information about long-term use, and uncertainty that they will yield significant weight loss.

In purely financial terms, the drugs cost more than $3 a day on average (Duenwald, 2004, paras. 33, 36). In each of the clinical trials, use of medication was accompanied by an expensive regime of behavioral therapies, including counseling, nutritional education, fitness advising, and monitoring. As journalist Greg Critser (2003) noted in his book *Fat Land,* use of weight-loss drugs is unlikely to have an effect without the proper "support system"--one that includes doctors, facilities, time, and money (p. 3). For some, this level of care is prohibitively expensive.

A third complication is that the studies focused on adolescents aged 12-16, but obesity can begin at a much younger age. Little data exist to establish the safety or efficacy of medication for treating very young children.

The writer develops
the paper's thesis.

While the scientific data on the concrete effects of these medications in children remain somewhat unclear, medication is not the only
avenue for addressing the crisis. Both medical experts and policymakers
recognize that solutions might come not only from a laboratory but also
from policy, education, and advocacy. Indeed, a handbook designed to
educate doctors on obesity recommended a notably nonmedical course of
action, calling for "major changes in some aspects of western culture"
(Hoppin & Taveras, 2004, Conclusion section, para. 1). Cultural change
may not be the typical realm of medical professionals, but the handbook
urged doctors to be proactive and "focus [their] energy on public policies
and interventions" (Conclusion section, para. 1).

Brackets indicate a
word not in the
original source.

The solutions proposed by a number of advocacy groups underscore
this interest in political and cultural change. A report by the Henry J.
Kaiser Family Foundation (2004) outlined trends that may have contributed to the childhood obesity crisis, including food advertising for
children as well as

A quotation longer
than 40 words is set
off from the text
without quotation
marks.

> a reduction in physical education classes and after-school athletic
> programs, an increase in the availability of sodas and snacks in
> public schools, the growth in the number of fast-food outlets . . . ,
> and the increasing number of highly processed high-calorie and
> high-fat grocery products. (p. 1)

The writer interprets
the evidence; she
doesn't just report it.

Addressing each of these areas requires more than a doctor armed with a
prescription pad; it requires a broad mobilization not just of doctors and
concerned parents but of educators, food industry executives, advertisers, and media representatives.

The tone of the con-
clusion is objective.

The barrage of possible approaches to combating childhood obe-
sity--from scientific research to political lobbying--indicates both the
severity and the complexity of the problem. While none of the medications currently available is a miracle drug for curing the nation's 9 million obese children, research has illuminated some of the underlying factors that affect obesity and has shown the need for a comprehensive
approach to the problem that includes behavioral, medical, social, and
political change.

References

Berkowitz, R. I., Wadden, T. A., Tershakovec, A. M., & Cronquist, J. L. (2003). Behavior therapy and sibutramine for the treatment of adolescent obesity [Electronic version]. *Journal of the American Medical Association, 289,* 1805-1812.

Carmona, R. H. (2004, March 2). *The growing epidemic of childhood obesity.* Testimony before the Subcommittee on Competition, Foreign Commerce, and Infrastructure of the U.S. Senate Committee on Commerce, Science, and Transportation. Retrieved October 10, 2004, from http://www.hhs.gov/asl/testify/t040302.html

Critser, G. (2003). *Fat land: How Americans became the fattest people in the world.* Boston: Houghton Mifflin.

Duenwald, M. (2004, January 6). Slim pickings: Looking beyond ephedra. *The New York Times,* p. F1. Retrieved October 12, 2004, from LexisNexis.

Henry J. Kaiser Family Foundation. (2004, February). *The role of media in childhood obesity.* Retrieved October 10, 2004, from http://www.kff.org/entmedia/7030.cfm

Hilts, P. J. (2002, March 20). Petition asks for removal of diet drug from market. *The New York Times,* p. A26. Retrieved October 12, 2004, from LexisNexis.

Hoppin, A. G., & Taveras, E. M. (2004, June 25). Assessment and management of childhood and adolescent obesity. *Clinical Update.* Retrieved October 12, 2004, from Medscape Web site: http://www.medscape.com/viewarticle/481633

McDuffie, J. R., Calis, K. A., Uwaifo, G. I., Sebring, N. G., Fallon, E. M., Hubbard, V. S., et al. (2003). Three-month tolerability of orlistat in adolescents with obesity-related comorbid conditions [Electronic version]. *Obesity Research, 10,* 642-650.

Roche Laboratories. (2003, December). *Xenical (orlistat) capsules: Complete product information.* Retrieved October 11, 2004, from http://www.rocheusa.com/products/xenical/pi.pdf

Yanovski, S. Z., & Yanovski, J. A. (2002). Drug therapy: Obesity [Electronic version]. *The New England Journal of Medicine, 346,* 591-602.

List of references begins on a new page. Heading is centered.

List is alphabetized by authors' last names. All authors' names are inverted.

The first line of an entry is at the left margin; subsequent lines indent ½" (or five spaces).

Double-spacing is used throughout.

CMS (*Chicago*) Papers

Most assignments in history and other humanities classes are based to some extent on reading. At times you will be asked to respond to one or two readings, such as essays or historical documents. At other times you may be asked to write a research paper that draws on a wide variety of sources.

Most history instructors and some humanities instructors require you to document sources with footnotes or endnotes based on *The Chicago Manual of Style,* 15th ed. (Chicago: U of Chicago P, 2003). (See CMS-4.)

When you write a paper using sources, you face three main challenges in addition to documenting your sources: (1) supporting a thesis, (2) citing your sources and avoiding plagiarism, and (3) integrating quotations and other source material.

CMS-1

Supporting a thesis

Most assignments ask you to form a thesis, or main idea, and to support that thesis with well-organized evidence.

CMS-1a Form a thesis.

A thesis is a one-sentence (or occasionally a two-sentence) statement of your central idea. Usually your thesis will appear at the end of the first paragraph (as on p. 527), but if you need to provide readers with considerable background information, you may place it in the second paragraph.

The thesis of your paper will be a reasoned answer to the central question you pose. Here is a research question posed by Ned Bishop, a student in a history course, followed by a thesis that answers the question.

RESEARCH QUESTION

To what extent was Confederate Major General Nathan Bedford Forrest responsible for the massacre of Union troops at Fort Pillow?

POSSIBLE THESIS

> Although we will never know whether Nathan Bedford Forrest directly ordered the massacre of Union troops at Fort Pillow, evidence suggests that he was responsible for it.

Notice that the thesis expresses a view on a debatable issue—an issue about which intelligent, well-meaning people might disagree. The writer's job is to convince such readers that this view is worth taking seriously.

ON THE WEB > dianahacker.com/writersref
Research exercises > E-ex CMS 1–1

CMS-1b Organize your evidence.

The body of your paper will consist of evidence in support of your thesis. Instead of getting tangled up in a complex, formal outline, sketch an informal plan that organizes your evidence in bold strokes. Ned Bishop, the student who wrote about Fort Pillow, used a simple list of questions as the blueprint for his paper. In the paper itself, these became headings that help readers follow Bishop's line of argument.

> What happened at Fort Pillow?
>
> Did Forrest order the massacre?
>
> Can Forrest be held responsible for the massacre?

CMS-1c Use sources to inform and support your argument.

Used thoughtfully, the source materials you have gathered will make your argument more complex and convincing for readers. Sources can play several different roles as you develop your points.

Providing background information or context

You can use facts and statistics to support generalizations or to establish the importance of your topic, as student writer Ned Bishop does early in his paper.

Fort Pillow, Tennessee, which sat on a bluff overlooking the Mississippi River, had been held by the Union for two years. It was garrisoned by 580 men, 292 of them from United States Colored Heavy and Light Artillery regiments, 285 from the white Thirteenth Tennessee Cavalry. Nathan Bedford Forrest commanded about 1,500 troops.[1]

Explaining terms or concepts

If readers are unlikely to be familiar with a word, a phrase, or an idea important to your topic, you must explain it for them. Quoting or paraphrasing a source can help you define terms and concepts in neutral, accessible language.

The Civil War practice of giving no quarter to an ememy--in other words "denying [an enemy] the right of survival"--defied Lincoln's mandate for humane and merciful treatment of prisoners.[9]

Supporting your claims

As you draft your argument, make sure to back up your assertions with facts, examples, and other evidence from your research (see also A2-e). Ned Bishop, for example, uses an eyewitness report of the racially motivated violence perpetrated by Nathan Bedford Forrest's troops.

The slaughter at Fort Pillow was no doubt driven in large part by racial hatred. . . . A Southern reporter traveling with Forrest makes clear that the discrimination was deliberate: "Our troops maddened by the excitement, shot down the ret[r]eating Yankees, and not until they had attained t[h]e water's edge and turned to beg for mercy, did any prisoners fall in [t]o our hands-- Thus the whites received quarter, but the negroes were shown no mercy."[19]

Lending authority to your argument

Expert opinion can give weight to your argument (see also A2-e). But don't rely on experts to make your argument for you. Construct your argument in your own words and, when appropriate, cite the judgment of an authority in the field to support your position.

Fort Pillow is not the only instance of a massacre or threatened massacre of black soldiers by troops under Forrest's command. Biographer Brian Steel Wills points out that at Brice's Cross Roads in June 1864, "black soldiers suffered inordinately" as Forrest looked the other way and Confederate soldiers deliberately sought out those they termed "the damned negroes."[21]

Anticipating and countering objections

Do not ignore sources that seem contrary to your position or that offer arguments different from your own. Instead, use them to give voice to opposing points of view and to state potential objections to your arguments before you counter them (see A2-f). Ned Bishop, for example, presents evidence from a source that challenges his thesis.

> Hurst suggests that the temperamental Forrest "may have ragingly ordered a massacre and even intended to carry it out--until he rode inside the fort and viewed the horrifying result" and ordered it stopped.[15] While this is an intriguing interpretation of events, even Hurst would probably admit that it is merely speculation.

CMS-2

Citing sources; avoiding plagiarism

Your research paper is a collaboration between you and your sources. To be fair and ethical, you must acknowledge your debt to the writers of those sources. If you don't, you commit plagiarism, a serious academic offense.

Three different acts are considered plagiarism: (1) failing to cite quotations and borrowed ideas, (2) failing to enclose borrowed language in quotation marks, and (3) failing to put summaries and paraphrases in your own words.

CMS-2a Cite quotations and borrowed ideas.

You must of course cite all direct quotations. You must also cite any ideas borrowed from a source: summaries and paraphrases; statistics and other specific facts; and visuals such as cartoons, graphs, and diagrams.

The only exception is common knowledge—information your readers could easily locate in any number of reference sources. For example, the current population of the United States is common knowledge among sociologists and economists, and historians are familiar with facts such as the date of the Emancipation Proclamation. As a rule, when you have seen certain information repeatedly in your reading, you don't need to cite it. However, when information has appeared in only a few sources, when it is highly specific (as with statistics), or when it is controversial, you should cite the source.

CMS citations consist of superscript numbers in the text of the paper that refer readers to notes with corresponding numbers either at the foot of the page (footnotes) or at the end of the paper (endnotes).

TEXT

Governor John Andrew was not allowed to recruit black soldiers from out of state. "Ostensibly," writes Peter Burchard, "no recruiting was done outside Massachusetts but it was an open secret that Andrew's agents were working far and wide."[1]

NOTE

    1. Peter Burchard, *One Gallant Rush: Robert Gould Shaw and His Brave Black Regiment* (New York: St. Martin's, 1965), 85.

For detailed advice on using CMS-style notes, see CMS-4. When you use footnotes or endnotes, you will usually need to provide a bibliography as well (see CMS-4b).

CMS-2b Enclose borrowed language in quotation marks.

To indicate that you are using a source's exact phrases or sentences, you must enclose them in quotation marks. To omit the quotation marks is to claim—falsely—that the language is your own. Such an omission is plagiarism even if you have cited the source.

ORIGINAL SOURCE

For many Southerners it was psychologically impossible to see a black man bearing arms as anything but an incipient slave uprising complete with arson, murder, pillage, and rapine.

    —Dudley Taylor Cornish, *The Sable Arm*, p. 158

PLAGIARISM

According to Civil War historian Dudley Taylor Cornish, for many Southerners it was psychologically impossible to see a black man bearing arms as anything but an incipient slave uprising complete with arson, murder, pillage, and rapine.[2]

BORROWED LANGUAGE IN QUOTATION MARKS

According to Civil War historian Dudley Taylor Cornish, "For many Southerners it was psychologically impossible to see a black man bearing arms as anything but an incipient slave uprising complete with arson, murder, pillage, and rapine."[2]

NOTE: When quoted sentences are set off from the text by indenting, quotation marks are not needed (see pp. 509–10).

CMS-2c Put summaries and paraphrases in your own words.

Summaries and paraphrases are written in your own words. A summary condenses information; a paraphrase reports information in about the same number of words as in the source. When you summarize or paraphrase, you must restate the source's meaning using your own language. You commit plagiarism if you half-copy the author's sentences—either by mixing the author's well-chosen phrases with your own without using quotation marks or by plugging your own synonyms into the author's sentence structure. The following paraphrase is plagiarized—even though the source is cited—because too much of its language is borrowed from the source without quotation marks. The underlined phrases have been copied word-for-word. In addition, the writer has closely followed the sentence structure of the original source, merely plugging in some synonyms (such as *Fifty percent* for *half* and *savage hatred* for *fierce, bitter animosity*).

ORIGINAL SOURCE

Half of the force holding Fort Pillow were Negroes, former slaves now enrolled in the Union Army. Toward them Forrest's troops had the fierce, bitter animosity of men who had been educated to regard the colored race as inferior and who for the first time had encountered that race armed and fighting against white men. The sight enraged and perhaps terrified many of the Confederates and aroused in them the ugly spirit of a lynching mob.

—Albert Castel, "The Fort Pillow Massacre," pp. 46–47

PLAGIARISM: UNACCEPTABLE BORROWING

Albert Castel suggests that much of the brutality at Fort Pillow can be traced to racial attitudes. Fifty percent of the troops holding Fort Pillow were Negroes, former slaves who had joined the Union Army. Toward them Forrest's soldiers displayed the savage hatred of men who had been taught the inferiority of blacks and who for the first time had confronted them armed and fighting against white men. The vision angered and perhaps frightened the Confederates and aroused in them the ugly spirit of a lynching mob.[3]

To avoid plagiarizing an author's language, set the source aside, write from memory, and consult the source later to check for

accuracy. This strategy prevents you from being captivated by the words on the page.

ACCEPTABLE PARAPHRASE

Albert Castel suggests that much of the brutality at Fort Pillow can be traced to racial attitudes. Nearly half of the Union troops were blacks, men whom the Confederates had been raised to consider their inferiors. The shock and perhaps fear of facing armed ex-slaves in battle for the first time may well have unleashed the fury that led to the massacre.[3]

ON THE WEB > dianahacker.com/writersref
Research exercises > E-ex CMS 2–1 through CMS 2–5

CMS-3

Integrating sources

Quotations, summaries, paraphrases, and facts will support your argument, but they cannot speak for you. You can use several strategies to integrate information from research sources into your paper while maintaining your own voice.

CMS-3a Limit your use of quotations.

Using quotations appropriately

Although it is tempting to insert many quotations in your paper and to use your own words only for connecting passages, do not quote excessively. It is almost impossible to integrate numerous long quotations smoothly into your own text.

It is not always necessary to quote full sentences from a source. At times you may wish to borrow only a phrase or to weave part of a source's sentence into your own sentence structure.

As Hurst has pointed out, until "an outcry erupted in the Northern press," even the Confederates did not deny that there had been a massacre at Fort Pillow.[4]

Union surgeon Dr. Charles Fitch testified that after he was in custody he "saw" Confederate soldiers "kill every negro that made his appearance dressed in Federal uniform."[20]

USING THE ELLIPSIS MARK   To condense a quoted passage, you can use the ellipsis mark (three periods, with spaces between) to indicate that you have omitted words. What remains must be grammatically complete.

> Union surgeon Fitch's testimony that all women and children had been
> evacuated from Fort Pillow before the attack conflicts with Forrest's report:
> "We captured . . . about 40 negro women and children."[6]

The writer has omitted several words not relevant to the issue at hand: *164 Federals, 75 negro troops, and.*

When you want to omit a full sentence or more, use a period before the three ellipsis dots. For an example, see the long quotation on page 510.

Ordinarily, do not use the ellipsis mark at the beginning or at the end of a quotation. Readers will understand that the quoted material is taken from a longer passage.

USING BRACKETS   Brackets allow you to insert words of your own into quoted material, perhaps to explain a confusing reference or to keep a sentence grammatical in your context.

> According to Albert Castel, "It can be reasonably argued that he [Forrest]
> was justified in believing that the approaching steamships intended to aid
> the garrison [at Fort Pillow]."[7]

NOTE: Use [*sic*] to indicate that an error in a quoted sentence appears in the original source. (An example appears on p. 510.) However, if a source is filled with errors, as is the case with many historical documents, this use of [*sic*] can become distracting and is best avoided.

SETTING OFF LONG QUOTATIONS   CMS style allows you some leeway in deciding whether to set off a long quotation or run it into your text. For emphasis you may want to set off a quotation of more than four or five lines of text; almost certainly you should set off quotations of ten lines or more. To set off a quotation, indent it one-half inch (or five spaces) from the left margin and use the normal right margin. Double-space the indented quotation.

Long quotations should be introduced by an informative sentence, usually followed by a colon. Quotation marks are unnecessary because the indented format tells readers that the words are taken directly from the source.

In a letter home, Confederate officer Achilles V. Clark recounted what happened at Fort Pillow:

> Words cannot describe the scene. The poor deluded negroes would run up to our men fall upon their knees and with uplifted hands scream for mercy but they were ordered to their feet and then shot down. The whitte [*sic*] men fared but little better. . . . I with several others tried to stop the butchery and at one time had partially succeeded[,] but Gen. Forrest ordered them shot down like dogs[,] and the carnage continued.[8]

CMS-3b Use signal phrases to integrate sources.

The information you gather from sources cannot speak for itself. Whenever you include a paraphrase, summary, or direct quotation of another writer in your paper, prepare your readers for it with an introduction called a *signal phrase*. A signal phrase names the author of the source and often provides some context for the source material.

When the signal phrase includes a verb, choose one that is appropriate for the way you are using the source (see CMS-1c). Are you arguing a point, making an observation, reporting a fact, drawing a conclusion, or refuting an argument? By choosing an appropriate verb, you can make your source's role clear. See the chart on page 511 for a list of verbs commonly used in signal phrases.

In a CMS-style paper, use the present tense or present perfect tense in phrases that introduce quotations or other source material from nonfiction sources: *Foote points out that* or *Foote has pointed out that* (not *Foote pointed out that*). If you have good reason to emphasize that the author's language or opinion was articulated in the past, however, the past tense is acceptable.

The first time you mention an author, use the full name: *Shelby Foote argues.* . . . When you refer to the author again, you may use the last name only: *Foote raises an important question.*

Marking boundaries

Readers should be able to move from your words to the words of a source without feeling a jolt. Avoid dropping direct quotations into your text without warning. Instead, provide clear signal phrases, including the author's name, to prepare readers for the quotation. A signal phrase indicates the boundary between your words and

Using signal phrases in CMS papers

To avoid monotony, try to vary the language and placement of your signal phrases.

MODEL SIGNAL PHRASES

In the words of historian James M. McPherson, ". . ."[1]

As Dudley Taylor Cornish has argued, ". . ."[2]

In a letter to his wife, a Confederate soldier who witnessed the massacre wrote that ". . ."[3]

". . .," claims Benjamin Quarles.[4]

". . .," writes Albert Castel, ". . ."[5]

Shelby Foote offers an intriguing interpretation: ". . ."[6]

VERBS IN SIGNAL PHRASES

admits	compares	insists	rejects
agrees	confirms	notes	reports
argues	contends	observes	responds
asserts	declares	points out	suggests
believes	denies	reasons	thinks
claims	emphasizes	refutes	writes

the source's words and can also tell readers why a source is trustworthy.

DROPPED QUOTATION

Not surprisingly, those testifying on the Union and Confederate sides recalled events at Fort Pillow quite differently. Unionists claimed that their troops had abandoned their arms and were in full retreat. "The Confederates, however, all agreed that the Union troops retreated to the river with arms in their hands."[9]

QUOTATION WITH SIGNAL PHRASE

Not surprisingly, those testifying on the Union and Confederate sides recalled events at Fort Pillow quite differently. Unionists claimed that their troops had abandoned their arms and were in full retreat. "The Confederates, however," writes historian Albert Castel, "all agreed that the Union troops retreated to the river with arms in their hands."[9]

Introducing summaries and paraphrases

As with quotations, you should introduce most summaries and paraphrases with a signal phrase that mentions the author and places the material in context. Readers will then understand where the summary or paraphrase begins.

Without the signal phrase (underlined) in the following example, readers might think that only the last sentence is being cited, when in fact the whole paragraph is based on the source.

> According to Jack Hurst, official Confederate policy was that black soldiers were to be treated as runaway slaves; in addition, the Confederate Congress decreed that white Union officers commanding black troops be killed. Confederate Lieutenant General Kirby Smith went one step further, declaring that he would kill all captured black troops. Smith's policy never met with strong opposition from the Richmond government.[10]

Putting source material in context

Readers need to understand how your source is relevant to your paper's argument. It's a good idea, in other words, to embed your quotation—especially a long one—between sentences of your own, introducing it with a signal phrase and following it up with interpretive comments that link the source material to your paper's argument.

QUOTATION WITH INSUFFICIENT CONTEXT

> In a respected biography of Nathan Bedford Forrest, Hurst suggests that the temperamental Forrest "may have ragingly ordered a massacre and even intended to carry it out--until he rode inside the fort and viewed the horrifying result" and ordered it stopped.[11]

QUOTATION WITH EFFECTIVE CONTEXT

> In a respected biography of Nathan Bedford Forrest, Hurst suggests that the temperamental Forrest "may have ragingly ordered a massacre and even intended to carry it out--until he rode inside the fort and viewed the horrifying result" and ordered it stopped.[11] While this is an intriguing interpretation of events, even Hurst would probably admit that it is merely speculation.

Integrating statistics and other facts

When you are citing a statistic or another specific fact, a signal phrase is often not necessary. In most cases, readers will understand that the citation refers to the statistic or fact (not the whole paragraph).

> Of 295 white troops garrisoned at Fort Pillow, 168 were taken prisoner.
> Black troops fared worse, with only 58 of 262 captured and most of the rest
> presumably killed or wounded.[12]

There is nothing wrong, however, with using a signal phrase.

> Shelby Foote notes that of 295 white troops garrisoned at Fort Pillow, 168 were
> taken prisoner but that black troops fared worse, with only 58 of 262 captured
> and most of the rest presumably killed or wounded.[12]

ON THE WEB > dianahacker.com/writersref
Research exercises > E-ex CMS 3–1 through CMS 3–4

CMS-4

Documenting sources

Professors in history and some humanities courses often require
footnotes or endnotes based on *The Chicago Manual of Style.* When
you use CMS-style notes, you will usually be asked to include a bibliography at the end of your paper (see CMS-4b).

TEXT

> A Union soldier, Jacob Thompson, claimed to have seen Forrest order the
> killing, but when asked to describe the six-foot-two general, he called him
> "a little bit of a man."[13]

FOOTNOTE OR ENDNOTE

> 13. Brian Steel Wills, *A Battle from the Start: The Life of Nathan
> Bedford Forrest* (New York: HarperCollins, 1992), 187.

BIBLIOGRAPHY ENTRY

> Wills, Brian Steel. *A Battle from the Start: The Life of Nathan Bedford Forrest.*
>   New York: HarperCollins, 1992.

CMS-4a First and subsequent notes for a source

The first time you cite a source, the note should include publication
information for that work as well as the page number on which the
passage being cited may be found.

1. Peter Burchard, *One Gallant Rush: Robert Gould Shaw and His Brave Black Regiment* (New York: St. Martin's, 1965), 85.

For subsequent references to a source you have already cited, you may simply give the author's last name, a short form of the title, and the page or pages cited. A short form of the title of a book is italicized; a short form of the title of an article is put in quotation marks.

4. Burchard, *One Gallant Rush,* 31.

When you have two consecutive notes from the same source, you may use "Ibid." (meaning "in the same place") and the page number for the second note. Use "Ibid." alone if the page number is the same.

5. Jack Hurst, *Nathan Bedford Forrest: A Biography* (New York: Knopf, 1993), 8.

6. Ibid., 174.

CMS-4b CMS-style bibliography

A bibliography, which appears at the end of your paper, lists every work you have cited in your notes; in addition, it may include works that you consulted but did not cite. For advice on constructing the list, see page 525. A sample bibliography appears on page 530.

NOTE: If you include a bibliography, *The Chicago Manual of Style* suggests that you shorten all notes, including the first reference to a source, as described in CMS-4a. Check with your instructor, however, to see whether using an abbreviated note for a first reference to a source is acceptable.

CMS-4c Model notes and bibliography entries

The following models are consistent with guidelines set forth in *The Chicago Manual of Style,* 15th ed. For each type of source, a model note appears first, followed by a model bibliography entry. The model note shows the format you should use when citing a source for the first time. For subsequent citations of a source, use shortened notes (see CMS-4a).

ON THE WEB > dianahacker.com/writersref
Research exercises > E-ex CMS 4–1

Directory to CMS-style notes and bibliography entries

ON THE WEB > dianahacker.com/writersref
Research and Documentation Online > History: Documenting sources (*Chicago*)

Books (print and online)

1. BASIC FORMAT FOR A PRINT BOOK

1. William H. Rehnquist, *The Supreme Court: A History* (New York: Knopf, 2001), 204.

Rehnquist, William H. *The Supreme Court: A History*. New York: Knopf, 2001.

1. Suzanne L. Bunkers, *In Search of Susanna* (Iowa City: University of Iowa Press, 1996), 13.

Bunkers, Suzanne L. *In Search of Susanna*. Iowa City: University of Iowa Press, 1996.

■ 2. BASIC FORMAT FOR AN ONLINE BOOK

2. Heinz Kramer, *A Changing Turkey: The Challenge to Europe and the United States* (Washington, DC: Brookings Press, 2000), 85, http://brookings.nap.edu/ books/0815750234/html/R1.html.

Kramer, Heinz. *A Changing Turkey: The Challenge to Europe and the United States.* Washington, DC: Brookings Press, 2000. http://brookings.nap.edu/books/ 0815750234/html/R1.html.

■ 3. TWO OR THREE AUTHORS

3. Michael D. Coe and Mark Van Stone, *Reading the Maya Glyphs* (London: Thames and Hudson, 2002), 129-30.

Coe, Michael D., and Mark Van Stone. *Reading the Maya Glyphs.* London: Thames and Hudson, 2002.

■ 4. FOUR OR MORE AUTHORS

4. Lynn Hunt and others, *The Making of the West: Peoples and Cultures,* 2nd ed. (Boston: Bedford/St. Martin's, 2005), 541.

Hunt, Lynn, Thomas R. Martin, Barbara H. Rosenwein, R. Po-chia Hsia, and Bonnie G. Smith. *The Making of the West: Peoples and Cultures.* 2nd ed. Boston: Bedford/St. Martin's, 2005.

■ 5. UNKNOWN AUTHOR

5. *The Men's League Handbook on Women's Suffrage* (London, 1912), 23.

The Men's League Handbook on Women's Suffrage. London, 1912.

■ 6. EDITED WORK WITHOUT AN AUTHOR

6. Jack Beatty, ed., *Colossus: How the Corporation Changed America* (New York: Broadway Books, 2001), 127.

Beatty, Jack, ed. *Colossus: How the Corporation Changed America.* New York: Broadway Books, 2001.

■ 7. EDITED WORK WITH AN AUTHOR

7. Ted Poston, *A First Draft of History,* ed. Kathleen A. Hauke (Athens: University of Georgia Press, 2000), 46.

Poston, Ted. *A First Draft of History.* Edited by Kathleen A. Hauke. Athens: University of Georgia Press, 2000.

■ 8. TRANSLATED WORK

8. Tonino Guerra, *Abandoned Places,* trans. Adria Bernardi (Barcelona: Guernica, 1999), 71.

Guerra, Tonino. *Abandoned Places.* Translated by Adria Bernardi. Barcelona: Guernica, 1999.

■ 9. EDITION OTHER THAN THE FIRST

9. Andrew F. Rolle, *California: A History,* 5th ed. (Wheeling, IL: Harlan Davidson, 1998), 243.

Rolle, Andrew F. *California: A History.* 5th ed. Wheeling, IL: Harlan Davidson, 1998.

■ 10. VOLUME IN A MULTIVOLUME WORK

10. James M. McPherson, *Ordeal by Fire,* vol. 2, *The Civil War* (New York: McGraw-Hill, 1993), 205.

McPherson, James M. *Ordeal by Fire.* Vol. 2, *The Civil War.* New York: McGraw-Hill, 1993.

■ 11. WORK IN AN ANTHOLOGY

11. Zora Neale Hurston, "From *Dust Tracks on a Road,*" in *The Norton Book of American Autobiography,* ed. Jay Parini (New York: Norton, 1999), 336.

Hurston, Zora Neale. "From *Dust Tracks on a Road.*" In *The Norton Book of American Autobiography,* edited by Jay Parini, 333-43. New York: Norton, 1999.

■ 12. LETTER IN A PUBLISHED COLLECTION

12. Thomas Gainsborough to Elizabeth Rasse, 1753, in *The Letters of Thomas Gainsborough,* ed. John Hayes (New Haven: Yale University Press, 2001), 5.

Gainsborough, Thomas. Letter to Elizabeth Rasse, 1753. In *The Letters of Thomas Gainsborough,* edited by John Hayes, 5. New Haven: Yale University Press, 2001.

■ 13. WORK IN A SERIES

13. R. Keith Schoppa, *The Columbia Guide to Modern Chinese History,* Columbia Guides to Asian History (New York: Columbia University Press, 2000), 256-58.

Schoppa, R. Keith. *The Columbia Guide to Modern Chinese History.* Columbia Guides to Asian History. New York: Columbia University Press, 2000.

■ 14. ENCYCLOPEDIA OR DICTIONARY

14. *Encyclopaedia Britannica,* 15th ed., s.v. "Monroe Doctrine."

14. Bryan A. Garner, *Garner's Modern American Usage* (Oxford: Oxford University Press, 2003), s.v. "brideprice."

Garner, Bryan A. *Garner's Modern American Usage.* Oxford: Oxford University Press, 2003.

The abbreviation "s.v." is for the Latin *sub verbo* ("under the word").

Well-known reference works such as encyclopedias do not require publication information and are usually not included in the bibliography.

■ 15. SACRED TEXT

15. Matt. 20.4-9 (Revised Standard Version).

15. Qur'an 18:1-3.

Sacred texts are usually not included in the bibliography.

Articles in periodicals (print and online)

■ **16. ARTICLE IN A JOURNAL**   For an article in a print journal, include the volume and issue numbers and the date; end the bibliography entry with the page range of the article.

16. Jonathan Zimmerman, "Ethnicity and the History Wars in the 1920s," *Journal of American History* 87, no. 1 (2000): 101.

Zimmerman, Jonathan. "Ethnicity and the History Wars in the 1920s." *Journal of American History* 87, no. 1 (2000): 92-111.

For an article accessed through a database service such as *EBSCOhost* or for an article published online, include a URL. If the article is paginated, give a page number in the note and a page range in the bibliography. For unpaginated articles, page references are not possible, but in your note you may include a "locator," such as a numbered paragraph or a heading from the article, as in the example for an article published online.

Journal article from a database service

16. Eugene F. Provenzo Jr., "Time Exposure," *Educational Studies* 34, no. 2 (2003): 266, http://search.epnet.com.

Provenzo, Eugene F., Jr. "Time Exposure." *Educational Studies* 34, no. 2 (2003): 266-67. http://search.epnet.com.

Journal article published online

16. Linda Belau, "Trauma and the Material Signifier," *Postmodern Culture* 11, no. 2 (2001): par. 6, http://www.iath.virginia.edu/pmc/text-only/issue.101/11.2belau.txt.

Belau, Linda. "Trauma and the Material Signifier." *Postmodern Culture* 11, no. 2 (2001). http://www.iath.virginia.edu/pmc/text-only/issue.101/11.2belau.txt.

▨ **17. ARTICLE IN A MAGAZINE** For a print article, provide a page number in the note and a page range in the bibliography.

17. Bissell, Tom. "Improvised, Explosive, and Divisive." *Harper's,* January 2006, 42.

Bissell, Tom. "Improvised, Explosive, and Divisive." *Harper's,* January 2006, 41-54.

For an article accessed through a database service such as *FirstSearch* or for an article published online, include a URL. If the article is paginated, give a page number in the note and a page range in the bibliography. For unpaginated articles, page references are not possible.

Magazine article from a database service

17. David Pryce-Jones, "The Great Sorting Out: Postwar Iraq," *National Review,* May 5, 2003, 17, http://newfirstsearch.oclc.org.

Pryce-Jones, David. "The Great Sorting Out: Postwar Iraq." *National Review,* May 5, 2003, 17-18. http://newfirstsearch.oclc.org.

Magazine article published online

17. Fiona Morgan, "Banning the Bullies," *Salon,* March 15, 2001, http://www.salon.com/news/feature/2001/03/15/bullying/index.html.

Morgan, Fiona. "Banning the Bullies." *Salon,* March 15, 2001. http://www.salon.com/news/feature/2001/03/15/bullying/index.html.

▨ **18. ARTICLE IN A NEWSPAPER** For newspaper articles — whether in print or online — page numbers are not necessary. A section letter or number, if available, is sufficient.

18. Dan Barry, "A Mill Closes, and a Hamlet Fades to Black," *New York Times,* February 16, 2001, sec. A.

Barry, Dan. "A Mill Closes, and a Hamlet Fades to Black." *New York Times,* February 16, 2001, sec. A.

For an article accessed through a database such as *ProQuest* or for an article published online, include a URL.

Newspaper article from a database service

18. Gina Kolata, "Scientists Debating Future of Hormone Replacement," *New York Times,* October 23, 2002, http://www.proquest.com.

Kolata, Gina. "Scientists Debating Future of Hormone Replacement." *New York Times,* October 23, 2002. http://www.proquest.com.

Newpaper article published online

18. Phil Willon, "Ready or Not," *Los Angeles Times,* December 2, 2001, http://www.latimes.com/news/la-foster-special.special.

Willon, Phil. "Ready or Not." *Los Angeles Times,* December 2, 2001. http://www.latimes.com/news/la-foster-special.special.

▓ **19. UNSIGNED ARTICLE** When the author of a periodical article is unknown, treat the periodical itself as the author.

19. *Boston Globe,* "Renewable Energy Rules," August 11, 2003, sec. A.

Boston Globe. "Renewable Energy Rules." August 11, 2003, sec. A.

▓ **20. BOOK REVIEW**

20. Nancy Gabin, review of *The Other Feminists: Activists in the Liberal Establishment,* by Susan M. Hartman, *Journal of Women's History* 12, no. 3 (2000): 230.

Gabin, Nancy. Review of *The Other Feminists: Activists in the Liberal Establishment,* by Susan M. Hartman. *Journal of Women's History* 12, no. 3 (2000): 227-34.

Web sites and postings

▓ **21. WEB SITE** Include as much of the following information as is available: author, title of the site, sponsor of the site, and the site's URL. When no author is named, treat the sponsor as the author.

21. Kevin Rayburn, *The 1920s,* http://www.louisville.edu/~kprayb01/1920s.html.

Rayburn, Kevin. *The 1920s.* http://www.louisville.edu/~kprayb01/1920s.html.

NOTE: *The Chicago Manual of Style* does not advise including the date you accessed a Web source, but you may provide an access date after the URL if the cited material is time-sensitive: for example, http://www.historychannel.com/today (accessed May 1, 2006).

■ **22. SHORT DOCUMENT FROM A WEB SITE**   Include as many of the following elements as are available: author's name, title of the short work, title of the site, sponsor of the site, and the URL. When no author is named, treat the site's sponsor as the author.

22. Sheila Connor, "Historical Background," *Garden and Forest,* Library of Congress, http://lcweb.loc.gov/preserv/prd/gardfor/historygf.html.

Connor, Sheila. "Historical Background." *Garden and Forest.* Library of Congress. http://lcweb.loc.gov/preserv/prd/gardfor/historygf.html.

22. PBS Online, "Media Giants," *Frontline: The Merchants of Cool,* http://www.pbs.org/wgbh/pages/frontline/shows/cool/giants.

PBS Online. "Media Giants." *Frontline: The Merchants of Cool.* http://www.pbs.org/wgbh/pages/frontline/shows/cool/giants.

■ **23. AN ENTRY IN A WEBLOG (BLOG)**   Treat an entry for a Weblog as you would a short document from a Web site, including as many of the following elements as are available: the author's name; the title of the entry; the title of the blog; the sponsor, if any; and the URL.

23. Andrew Reeves, "Electoral Politics and FEMA's Poor Performance in the Aftermath of Hurricane Katrina," *Political Behavior Blog,* Institute for Quantitative Social Science at Harvard University, http://www.iq.harvard.edu/blog/pb/2005/09/electoral_politics_and_femas_p.html.

Reeves, Andrew. "Electoral Politics and FEMA's Poor Performance in the Aftermath of Hurricane Katrina." *Political Behavior Blog.* Institute for Quantitative Social Science at Harvard University. http://www.iq.harvard.edu/blog/pb/2005/09/electoral_politics_and_femas_p.html.

■ **24. ONLINE POSTING OR E-MAIL**   If an online posting has been archived, include a URL, as in the following example. E-mails that are not part of an online discussion are treated as personal communications (see item 27). Online postings and e-mails are not included in the bibliography.

24. Janice Klein, posting to State Museum Association discussion list, June 19, 2003, http://listserv.nmmnh-abq.mus.nm.us/scripts/wa.exe?A2=ind0306c&L=sma-l&F=lf&S=&P=81.

Other sources (print, online, multimedia)

■ **25. GOVERNMENT DOCUMENT**

25. U.S. Department of State, *Foreign Relations of the United States: Diplomatic Papers, 1943* (Washington, DC: GPO, 1965), 562.

U.S. Department of State. *Foreign Relations of the United States: Diplomatic Papers, 1943.* Washington, DC: GPO, 1965.

▦ 26. UNPUBLISHED DISSERTATION

26. Stephanie Lynn Budin, "The Origins of Aphrodite (Greece)" (PhD diss., University of Pennsylvania, 2000), 301-2.

Budin, Stephanie Lynn. "The Origins of Aphrodite (Greece)." PhD diss., University of Pennsylvania, 2000.

▦ 27. PERSONAL COMMUNICATION

27. Sara Lehman, e-mail message to author, August 13, 2003.

Personal communications are not included in the bibliography.

▦ 28. PUBLISHED OR BROADCAST INTERVIEW

28. Ron Haviv, interview by Charlie Rose, *The Charlie Rose Show,* PBS, February 12, 2001.

Haviv, Ron. Interview by Charlie Rose. *The Charlie Rose Show,* PBS, February 12, 2001.

▦ 29. PODCAST Treat an entry for a podcast as you would a short document from a Web site, including as many of the following elements as are available: the author's (or speaker's) name; the title of the podcast, in quotation marks; the title of the site on which it appears; the sponsor of the site; and the URL.

29. Chris Patterson, "Will School Consolidation Improve Education?" *Texas PolicyCast,* Texas Public Policy Foundation, http://www.texaspolicy.com/texaspolicycast.php.

Patterson, Chris. "Will School Consolidation Improve Education?" *Texas PolicyCast.* Texas Public Policy Foundation. http://www.texaspolicy.com/texaspolicycast.php.

▦ 30. VIDEO OR DVD

30. *The Secret of Roan Inish,* DVD, directed by John Sayles (1993; Culver City, CA: Columbia TriStar Home Video, 2000).

The Secret of Roan Inish. DVD. Directed by John Sayles. 1993; Culver City, CA: Columbia TriStar Home Video, 2000.

▦ 31. SOUND RECORDING

31. Gustav Holst, *The Planets,* Royal Philharmonic, André Previn, Telarc compact disc 80133.

Holst, Gustav. *The Planets.* Royal Philharmonic. André Previn. Telarc compact disc 80133.

▓ **32. SOURCE QUOTED IN ANOTHER SOURCE**

32. Adam Smith, *The Wealth of Nations* (New York: Random House, 1965), 11, quoted in Mark Skousen, *The Making of Modern Economics: The Lives and the Ideas of the Great Thinkers* (Armonk, NY: M. E. Sharpe, 2001), 15.

Smith, Adam. *The Wealth of Nations,* 11. New York: Random House, 1965. Quoted in Mark Skousen, *The Making of Modern Economics: The Lives and the Ideas of the Great Thinkers* (Armonk, NY: M. E. Sharpe, 2001), 15.

ON THE WEB > dianahacker.com/writersref
Electronic research exercises > E-ex CMS 4–2 through CMS 4–6

CMS-5

Manuscript format; sample pages

CMS-5a Manuscript format

The following guidelines for formatting a CMS paper and preparing its endnotes and bibliography are based on *The Chicago Manual of Style,* 15th ed. For pages from a sample paper, see CMS-5b.

Formatting the paper

CMS manuscript guidelines are fairly generic, since they were not created with a specific type of writing in mind.

TITLE PAGE Include the full title of your paper, your name, the course title, the instructor's name, and the date. Do not number the title page but count it in the manuscript numbering; that is, the first page of the text will be numbered 2. See page 526 for a sample title page.

PAGINATION Using arabic numerals, number all pages except the title page in the upper right corner. Depending on your instructor's preference, you may also use a short title or your last name before the page numbers to help identify pages in case they come loose from your manuscript.

MARGINS AND LINE SPACING Leave margins of at least one inch at the top, bottom, and sides of the page. Double-space the entire manuscript, including long quotations that have been set off from the text. (For line spacing in notes and the bibliography, see the bottom of this page and p. 525.) Left-align the text.

LONG QUOTATIONS When a quotation is fairly long, set it off from the text by indenting (see also pp. 509–10). Indent the full quotation one-half inch (five spaces) from the left margin. Quotation marks are not needed when a quotation has been set off from the text.

VISUALS *The Chicago Manual* classifies visuals as tables and illustrations (illustrations, or figures, include drawings, photographs, maps, and charts). Keep visuals as simple as possible. Label each table with an arabic numeral (Table 1, Table 2, and so on) and provide a clear title that identifies the subject. The label and title should appear on separate lines above the table, flush left. Below the table, give its source in a note like this one:

Source: Edna Bonacich and Richard P. Appelbaum, *Behind the Label* (Berkeley: University of California Press, 2000), 145.

For each figure, place a label and a caption below the figure, flush left. The label and caption need not appear on separate lines. The word "Figure" may be abbreviated to "Fig."

In the text of your paper, discuss the most significant features of each visual. Place visuals as close as possible to the sentences that relate to them unless your instructor prefers them in an appendix.

Preparing the endnotes

Begin the endnotes on a new page at the end of the paper. Center the title Notes about one inch from the top of the page, and number the pages consecutively with the rest of the manuscript. See page 529 for an example.

INDENTING AND NUMBERING Indent the first line of each note one-half inch (or five spaces) from the left margin; do not indent additional lines in the note. Begin the note with the arabic numeral that corresponds to the number in the text. Put a period after the number.

LINE SPACING Single-space each note and double-space between notes (unless your instructor prefers double-spacing throughout).

Preparing the bibliography

Typically, the notes in CMS-style papers are followed by a bibliography, an alphabetically arranged list of all the works cited or consulted (see p. 530 for an example). Center the title Bibliography about one inch from the top of the page. Number bibliography pages consecutively with the rest of the paper.

ALPHABETIZING THE LIST Alphabetize the bibliography by the last names of the authors (or editors); when a work has no author or editor, alphabetize it by the first word of the title other than *A, An,* or *The.*

If your list includes two or more works by the same author, use three hyphens instead of the author's name in all entries after the first. You may arrange the entries alphabetically by title or by date; be consistent throughout the bibliography.

INDENTING AND LINE SPACING Begin each entry at the left margin, and indent any additional lines one-half inch (or five spaces). Single-space each entry and double-space between entries (unless your instructor prefers double-spacing throughout).

CMS-5b Sample pages from a research paper: CMS style

Following are sample pages from a research paper by Ned Bishop, a student in a history class. (The complete paper is available on the *Writer's Reference* Web site.) Bishop was asked to document his paper using CMS-style endnotes and a bibliography. In preparing his manuscript, Bishop also followed CMS guidelines.

ON THE WEB > dianahacker.com/writersref
Model papers > *Chicago* (CMS) paper: Bishop

Title of paper.

The Massacre at Fort Pillow:

Holding Nathan Bedford Forrest Accountable

Writer's name.

Ned Bishop

Title of course,
instructor's name,
and date.

History 214

Professor Citro

March 22, 2001

Marginal annotations indicate CMS-style formatting and effective writing.

Bishop 2

Although Northern newspapers of the time no doubt exaggerated some of the Confederate atrocities at Fort Pillow, most modern sources agree that a massacre of Union troops took place there on April 12, 1864. It seems clear that Union soldiers, particularly black soldiers, were killed after they had stopped fighting or had surrendered or were being held prisoner. Less clear is the role played by Major General Nathan Bedford Forrest in leading his troops. Although we will never know whether Forrest directly ordered the massacre, evidence suggests that he was responsible for it.

What happened at Fort Pillow?

Fort Pillow, Tennessee, which sat on a bluff overlooking the Mississippi River, had been held by the Union for two years. It was garrisoned by 580 men, 292 of them from United States Colored Heavy and Light Artillery regiments, 285 from the white Thirteenth Tennessee Cavalry. Nathan Bedford Forrest commanded about 1,500 troops.[1]

The Confederates attacked Fort Pillow on April 12, 1864, and had virtually surrounded the fort by the time Forrest arrived on the battlefield. At 3:30 p.m., Forrest demanded the surrender of the Union forces, sending in a message of the sort he had used before: "The conduct of the officers and men garrisoning Fort Pillow has been such as to entitle them to being treated as prisoners of war. . . . Should my demand be refused, I cannot be responsible for the fate of your command."[2] Union Major William Bradford, who had replaced Major Booth, killed earlier by sharpshooters, asked for an hour to consider the demand. Forrest, worried that vessels in the river were bringing in more troops, "shortened the time to twenty minutes."[3] Bradford refused to surrender, and Forrest quickly ordered the attack.

The Confederates charged to the fort, scaled the parapet, and fired on the forces within. Victory came quickly, with the Union forces running toward the river or surrendering. Shelby Foote describes the scene like this:

> Some kept going, right on into the river, where a number drowned and the swimmers became targets for marksmen on the bluff. Others, dropping their guns in terror, ran back toward the Confederates with their hands up, and of these some were spared as prisoners, while others were shot down in the act of surrender.[4]

Thesis asserts writer's main point.

Headings help readers follow the organization.

Statistics are cited with an endnote.

Quotation is cited with an endnote.

Long quotation is set off from text by indenting. Quotation marks are omitted.

Bishop 3

Writer uses a primary source as well as secondary sources.

In his own official report, Forrest makes no mention of the massacre. He does make much of the fact that the Union flag was not lowered by the Union forces, saying that if his own men had not taken down the flag, "few, if any, would have survived unhurt another volley."[5] However, as Jack Hurst points out and Forrest must have known, in this twenty-minute battle, "Federals running for their lives had little time to concern themselves with a flag."[6]

Quotation is introduced with a signal phrase.

The federal congressional report on Fort Pillow, which charged the Confederates with appalling atrocities, was strongly criticized by Southerners. Respected writer Shelby Foote, while agreeing that the report was "largely" fabrication, points out that the "casualty figures . . . indicated strongly that unnecessary killing had occurred."[7] In an important article, John Cimprich and Robert C. Mainfort Jr. argue that the most trustworthy evidence is that written within about ten days of the battle, before word of the congressional hearings circulated and Southerners realized the extent of Northern outrage. The article reprints a group of letters and newspaper sources written before April 22 and thus "untainted by the political overtones the controversy later assumed."[8] Cimprich and Mainfort conclude that these sources "support the case for the occurrence of a massacre" but that Forrest's role remains "clouded" because of inconsistencies in testimony.[9]

The writer draws attention to an important article containing primary sources.

Did Forrest order the massacre?

Topic sentence states the main idea for this section.

We will never really know whether Forrest directly ordered the massacre, but it seems unlikely. True, Confederate soldier Achilles Clark, who had no reason to lie, wrote to his sisters that "I with several others tried to stop the butchery . . . but Gen. Forrest ordered them [Negro and white Union troops] shot down like dogs[,] and the carnage continued."[10] But it is not clear whether Clark heard Forrest giving the orders or was just reporting hearsay. Many Confederates had been shouting "No quarter! No quarter!" and, as Shelby Foote points out, these shouts were "thought by some to be at Forrest's command."[11] A Union soldier, Jacob Thompson, claimed to have seen Forrest order the killing, but when asked to describe the six-foot-two general, he called him "a little bit of a man."[12]

Writer presents a balanced view of the evidence.

Perhaps the most convincing evidence that Forrest did not order the massacre is that he tried to stop it once it had begun. Historian

Bishop 8

Notes

    1. John Cimprich and Robert C. Mainfort Jr., eds., "Fort Pillow Revisited: New Evidence about an Old Controversy," *Civil War History* 28, no. 4 (1982): 293-94.

    2. Quoted in Brian Steel Wills, *A Battle from the Start: The Life of Nathan Bedford Forrest* (New York: HarperCollins, 1992), 182.

    3. Ibid., 183.

    4. Shelby Foote, *The Civil War, a Narrative: Red River to Appomattox* (New York: Vintage, 1986), 110.

    5. Nathan Bedford Forrest, "Report of Maj. Gen. Nathan B. Forrest, C. S. Army, Commanding Cavalry, of the Capture of Fort Pillow," *Shotgun's Home of the American Civil War,* http://www.civilwarhome.com/forrest.htm.

    6. Jack Hurst, *Nathan Bedford Forrest: A Biography* (New York: Knopf, 1993), 174.

    7. Foote, *Civil War,* 111.

    8. Cimprich and Mainfort, "Fort Pillow," 305.

    9. Ibid., 305.

    10. Ibid., 299.

    11. Foote, *Civil War,* 110.

    12. Quoted in Wills, *Battle from the Start,* 187.

    13. Albert Castel, "The Fort Pillow Massacre: A Fresh Examination of the Evidence," *Civil War History* 4, no. 1 (1958): 44-45.

    14. Cimprich and Mainfort, "Fort Pillow," 300.

    15. Hurst, *Nathan Bedford Forrest,* 177.

    16. Ibid.

    17. Dudley Taylor Cornish, *The Sable Arm: Black Troops in the Union Army, 1861-1865* (Lawrence, KS: University Press of Kansas, 1987), 175.

    18. Foote, *Civil War,* 111.

    19. Cimprich and Mainfort, "Fort Pillow," 304.

    20. Quoted in Wills, *Battle from the Start,* 189.

    21. Ibid., 215.

    22. Quoted in Hurst, *Nathan Bedford Forrest,* 177.

Margin annotations:

First line of each note is indented ½" (or five spaces).

Note number is not raised and is followed by a period.

Authors' names are not inverted.

Last name and title refer to an earlier note by the same author.

Notes are single-spaced, with double-spacing between notes. (Some instructors may prefer double-spacing throughout.)

Bibliography

Castel, Albert. "The Fort Pillow Massacre: A Fresh Examination of the Evidence." *Civil War History* 4, no. 1 (1958): 37-50.

Cimprich, John, and Robert C. Mainfort Jr., eds. "Fort Pillow Revisited: New Evidence about an Old Controversy." *Civil War History* 28, no. 4 (1982): 293-306.

Cornish, Dudley Taylor. *The Sable Arm: Black Troops in the Union Army, 1861-1865.* Lawrence, KS: University Press of Kansas, 1987.

Foote, Shelby. *The Civil War, a Narrative: Red River to Appomattox.* New York: Vintage, 1986.

Forrest, Nathan Bedford. "Report of Maj. Gen. Nathan B. Forrest, C. S. Army, Commanding Cavalry, of the Capture of Fort Pillow." *Shotgun's Home of the American Civil War.* http://www .civilwarhome.com/forrest.htm.

Hurst, Jack. *Nathan Bedford Forrest: A Biography.* New York: Knopf, 1993.

McPherson, James M. *Battle Cry of Freedom: The Civil War Era.* New York: Oxford University Press, 1988.

Wills, Brian Steel. *A Battle from the Start: The Life of Nathan Bedford Forrest.* New York: HarperCollins, 1992.

Entries are alphabetized by authors' last names.

First line of entry is at left margin; additional lines are indented ½" (or five spaces).

Entries are single-spaced, with double-spacing between entries. (Some instructors may prefer double-spacing throughout.)

B

Basic Grammar
Index

B Basic Grammar

B1

Parts of speech

Traditional grammar recognizes eight parts of speech: noun, pronoun, verb, adjective, adverb, preposition, conjunction, and interjection. Many words can function as more than one part of speech. For example, depending on its use in a sentence, the word *paint* can be a noun (*The paint is wet*) or a verb (*Please paint the ceiling next*).

ON THE WEB > dianahacker.com/writersref
Grammar exercises > Basic grammar > E-ex B1–1 through B1–7

B1-a Nouns

A noun is the name of a person, place, thing, or an idea. Nouns are often but not always signaled by an article (*a, an, the*).

>   N   N   N
> The *cat* in *gloves* catches no *mice.*

>   N   N   N
> *Repetition* does not transform a *lie* into *truth.*

Nouns sometimes function as adjectives modifying other nouns. Because of their dual roles, nouns used in this manner may be called *noun / adjectives.*

>   N/ADJ   N/ADJ
> You can't make a *silk* purse out of a *sow's* ear.

Nouns are classified for a variety of purposes. When capitalization is the issue, we speak of *proper* versus *common* nouns (see M3-a). If the problem is one of word choice, we may speak of *concrete* versus *abstract* nouns (see W5-b). The distinction between *count nouns* and *noncount nouns* is useful for nonnative speakers of English (see E3-b). Most nouns come in *singular* and *plural* forms; *collective* nouns may be either singular or plural (see G1-f and G3-a). *Possessive* nouns require an apostrophe (see P5-a).

EXERCISE B1–1 Underline the nouns (and noun/adjectives) in the following sentences. Answers to lettered sentences appear in the back of the book. Example:

Idle hands are the devil's workshop.

a. The sun will set without your assistance.   —Hebrew proverb
b. Pride is at the bottom of all great mistakes.   —John Ruskin
c. Success breeds confidence.   —Beryl Markham
d. The ultimate censorship is the flick of the dial.
                                                                —Tom Smothers
e. Our national flower is the concrete cloverleaf.
                                                                —Lewis Mumford

1. Truthfulness so often goes with ruthlessness.   —Dodie Smith
2. Luck is a matter of preparation meeting opportunity.
                                                                —Oprah Winfrey
3. Problems are only opportunities in work clothes.
                                                                —Henry Kaiser
4. A woman must have money and a room of her own.
                                                                —Virginia Woolf
5. Language helps form the limits of our reality.   —Dale Spender

B1-b Pronouns

A pronoun is a word used in place of a noun. Usually the pronoun substitutes for a specific noun, known as its *antecedent*.

When the *wheel* squeaks, *it* is greased.

Although most pronouns function as substitutes for nouns, some can function as adjectives modifying nouns.

PN/ADJ
This bird always catches the worm.

Most of the pronouns in English are listed in this section.

PERSONAL PRONOUNS   Personal pronouns refer to specific persons or things. They always function as noun equivalents.

Singular: I, me, you, she, her, he, him, it

Plural: we, us, you, they, them

POSSESSIVE PRONOUNS   Possessive pronouns indicate ownership.

Singular: my, mine, your, yours, her, hers, his, its

Plural: our, ours, your, yours, their, theirs

Some of these possessive pronouns function as adjectives modifying nouns: *my, your, his, her, its, our, their.*

INTENSIVE AND REFLEXIVE PRONOUNS   Intensive pronouns emphasize a noun or another pronoun (The senator *herself* met us at the door). Reflexive pronouns name a receiver of an action identical with the doer of the action (Paula cut *herself*).

> *Singular:*   myself, yourself, himself, herself, itself
>
> *Plural:*   ourselves, yourselves, themselves

RELATIVE PRONOUNS   Relative pronouns introduce subordinate clauses functioning as adjectives (The man *who helped us* was never identified). In addition to introducing the clause, the relative pronoun, in this case *who,* points back to a noun or pronoun that the clause modifies (*man*). (See B3-e.)

> who, whom, whose, which, that

INTERROGATIVE PRONOUNS   Interrogative pronouns introduce questions (*Who* is expected to win the election?).

> who, whom, whose, which, what

DEMONSTRATIVE PRONOUNS   Demonstrative pronouns identify or point to nouns. Frequently they function as adjectives (*This* chair is my favorite), but they may also function as noun equivalents (*This* is my favorite chair).

> this, that, these, those

INDEFINITE PRONOUNS   Indefinite pronouns refer to nonspecific persons or things. Most are singular (*everyone, each*); some are plural (*both, many*); a few may be singular or plural (see G1-e). Most indefinite pronouns function as noun equivalents (*Something* is burning), but some can also function as adjectives (*All* campers must check in at the lodge).

> all, another, any, anybody, anyone, anything, both, each, either, everybody, everyone, everything, few, many, neither, nobody, none, no one, nothing, one, several, some, somebody, someone, something

RECIPROCAL PRONOUNS   Reciprocal pronouns refer to individual parts of a plural antecedent (By turns, we helped *each other* through college).

each other, one another

NOTE: Pronouns cause a variety of problems for writers. See pronoun-antecedent agreement (G3-a), pronoun reference (G3-b), distinguishing between pronouns such as *I* and *me* (G3-c), and distinguishing between *who* and *whom* (G3-d).

EXERCISE B1–2 Underline the pronouns (and pronoun/adjectives) in the following sentences. Answers to lettered sentences appear in the back of the book. Example:

> Always beware of persons <u>who</u> are praised by <u>everyone</u>.

a. He has every attribute of a dog except loyalty.   —Thomas Gore
b. A fall does not hurt those who fly low.   —Chinese proverb
c. I have written some poetry that I myself don't understand.
                                                            —Carl Sandburg
d. I am firm. You are obstinate. He is a pig-headed fool.
                                                            —Katherine Whitehorn
e. If you haven't anything nice to say about anyone, come and sit by me.
                                                            —Alice Roosevelt Longworth

1. Men are taught to apologize for their weaknesses, women for their strengths.   —Lois Wyse
2. Nothing is interesting if you are not interested.
                                                            —Helen MacInness
3. We will never have friends if we expect to find them without fault.
                                                            —Thomas Fuller
4. The gods help those who help themselves.   —Aesop
5. I awoke one morning and found myself famous.   —Lord Byron

B1-c Verbs

The verb of a sentence usually expresses action (*jump, think*) or being (*is, become*). It is composed of a main verb possibly preceded by one or more helping verbs.

                    MV
The best fish *swim* near the bottom.

            HV   MV
A marriage *is* not *built* in a day.

Notice that words can intervene between the helping and the main verb (*is* not *built*).

Helping verbs

There are twenty-three helping verbs in English: forms of *have, do,* and *be,* which may also function as main verbs; and nine modals, which function only as helping verbs. The forms of *have, do,* and *be* change form to indicate tense; the nine modals do not.

FORMS OF *HAVE, DO,* AND *BE*

have, has, had

do, does, did

be, am, is, are, was, were, being, been

MODALS

can, could, may, might, must, shall, should, will, would

The verb phrase *ought to* is often classified as a modal as well.

Main verbs

The main verb of a sentence is always the kind of word that would change form if put into these test sentences:

BASE FORM	Usually I (*walk, ride*).
PAST TENSE	Yesterday I (*walked, rode*).
PAST PARTICIPLE	I have (*walked, ridden*) many times before.
PRESENT PARTICIPLE	I am (*walking, riding*) right now.
***-S* FORM**	Usually he/she/it (*walks, rides*).

If a word doesn't change form when slipped into these test sentences, you can be certain that it is not a main verb. For example, the noun *revolution,* though it may seem to suggest an action, can never function as a main verb. Just try to make it behave like one (*Today I revolution . . . Yesterday I revolutioned . . .*) and you'll see why.

When both the past-tense and the past-participle forms of a verb end in *-ed,* the verb is regular (*walked, walked*). Otherwise, the verb is irregular (*rode, ridden*). (See G2-a.)

The verb *be* is highly irregular, having eight forms instead of the usual five: the base form *be;* the present-tense forms *am, is,* and *are;* the past-tense forms *was* and *were;* the present participle *being;* and the past participle *been.*

NOTE: Some verbs are followed by words that look like prepositions but are so closely associated with the verb that they are a part of its meaning. These words are known as *particles*. Common verb-particle combinations include *bring up, call off, drop off, give in, look up, run into,* and *take off.*

> A lot of parents *pack up* their troubles and *send* them *off* to camp.
> —Raymond Duncan

NOTE: Verbs cause many problems for writers. See active verbs (W3), subject-verb agreement (G1), standard English verb forms (G2-a through G2-e), verb tense and mood (G2-f and G2-g), and ESL problems with verbs (E1).

EXERCISE B1–3 Underline the verbs in the following sentences, including helping verbs and particles. If a verb is part of a contraction (such as *is* in *isn't* or *would* in *I'd*), underline only the letters that represent the verb. Answers to lettered sentences appear in the back of the book. Example:

> A full cup <u>must be carried</u> steadily.

a. I can pardon everyone's mistakes except my own. —Cato
b. There are no atheists on turbulent airplanes. —Erica Jong
c. One arrow does not bring down two birds. —Turkish proverb
d. Keep your talent in the dark, and you'll never be insulted.
   —Elsa Maxwell
e. Throw a lucky man into the sea, and he will emerge with a fish in his mouth. —Arab proverb

1. Do not scald your tongue in other people's broth.
   —English proverb
2. Wrong must not win by technicalities. —Aeschylus
3. Love your neighbor, but don't pull down the hedge.
   —Swiss proverb
4. I'd rather have roses on my table than diamonds around my neck.
   —Emma Goldman
5. He is a fine friend. He stabs you in the front.
   —Leonard Louis Levinson

B1-d   Adjectives and articles

An adjective is a word used to modify, or describe, a noun or pronoun. An adjective usually answers one of these questions: Which one? What kind of? How many?

ADJ
the *lame* elephant [Which elephant?]

ADJ   ADJ
valuable old stamps [What kind of stamps?]

ADJ
sixteen candles [How many candles?]

Adjectives usually precede the words they modify. However, they may also follow linking verbs, in which case they describe the subject. (See B2-b.)

ADJ
Good medicine always tastes *bitter.*

Articles, sometimes classified as adjectives, are used to mark nouns. There are only three: the definite article *the* and the indefinite articles *a* and *an.*

ART   ART
A country can be judged by *the* quality of its proverbs.

Some possessive, demonstrative, and indefinite pronouns can function as adjectives: *their, its, this* (see B1-b).

NOTE: Writers sometimes misuse adjectives (see G4). Multilingual speakers often encounter problems with the articles *a, an,* and *the* and occasionally have trouble placing adjectives correctly (see E3 and E4-b).

B1-e Adverbs

An adverb is a word used to modify, or qualify, a verb (or verbal), an adjective, or another adverb. It usually answers one of these questions: When? Where? How? Why? Under what conditions? To what degree?

ADV
Pull *gently* at a weak rope. [Pull how?]

ADV
Read the best books *first.* [Read when?]

Adverbs modifying adjectives or other adverbs usually intensify or limit the intensity of the word they modify.

ADV   ADV
Be *extremely* good, and you will be *very* lonesome.

The negators *not* and *never* are classified as adverbs.

EXERCISE B1–4 Underline the adjectives and circle the adverbs in the following sentences. If a word is a pronoun in form but an adjective in function, treat it as an adjective. Also treat the articles *a, an,* and *the* as adjectives. Answers to lettered sentences appear in the back of the book. Example:

> A wild goose (never) laid a tame egg.

a. General notions are generally wrong.
> —Lady Mary Wortley Montagu

b. The American public is wonderfully tolerant.
> —Anonymous

c. Wildflowers sometimes grow in an uncultivated field, but they never bloom in an uncultivated mind.
> —Anonymous

d. I'd rather be strongly wrong than weakly right.
> —Tallulah Bankhead

e. Sleep faster. We need the pillows. —Yiddish proverb

1. Success is a public affair; failure is a private funeral.
> —Rosalind Russell

2. Their civil discussions were not interesting, and their interesting discussions were not civil. —Lisa Alther

3. Money will buy a pretty good dog, but it will not buy the wag of its tail.
> —Josh Billings

4. We cannot be too careful in the choice of our enemies.
> —Oscar Wilde

5. Feelings are untidy. —Esther Hautzig

B1-f Prepositions

A preposition is a word placed before a noun or pronoun to form a phrase modifying another word in the sentence. The prepositional phrase nearly always functions as an adjective or as an adverb. (See B3-a.)

> The road *to* hell is paved *with* good intentions.

The words *to hell* and *with* above are marked with a "P."

To hell functions as an adjective modifying the noun *road*; *with good intentions* functions as an adverb modifying the verb *is paved*.

There are a limited number of prepositions in English. The most common are included in the following list.

about	beneath	for	out	to
above	beside	from	outside	toward
across	besides	in	over	under
after	between	inside	past	underneath
against	beyond	into	plus	unlike
along	but	like	regarding	until
among	by	near	respecting	unto
around	concerning	next	round	up
as	considering	of	since	upon
at	despite	off	than	with
before	down	on	through	within
behind	during	onto	throughout	without
below	except	opposite	till	

Some prepositions are more than one word long. *Along with, as well as, in addition to,* and *next to* are common examples.

NOTE: Except for certain idiomatic uses (see W5-d), prepositions cause few problems for native speakers of English. For multilingual speakers, however, prepositions can cause considerable difficulty (see E5).

B1-g Conjunctions

Conjunctions join words, phrases, or clauses, and they indicate the relation between the elements joined.

COORDINATING CONJUNCTIONS   A coordinating conjunction is used to connect grammatically equal elements. (See S1-b and S6.)

and	but	or	nor	for	so	yet

CORRELATIVE CONJUNCTIONS   Correlative conjunctions are pairs of conjunctions that connect grammatically equal elements. (See S1-b.)

either . . . or   neither . . . nor   not only . . . but also
whether . . . or   both . . . and

SUBORDINATING CONJUNCTIONS   A subordinating conjunction introduces a subordinate clause and indicates its relation to the rest of the sentence.

after, although, as, as if, because, before, even though, how, if, in order that, once, rather than, since, so that, than, that, though, unless, until, when, where, whether, while, why

CONJUNCTIVE ADVERBS   A conjunctive adverb is used to indicate the relation between independent clauses. (See P3-b.)

> accordingly, also, anyway, besides, certainly, consequently, conversely, finally, furthermore, hence, however, incidentally, indeed, instead, likewise, meanwhile, moreover, nevertheless, next, nonetheless, once, otherwise, similarly, specifically, still, subsequently, then, therefore, thus

NOTE: The ability to distinguish between conjunctive adverbs and coordinating conjunctions will help you avoid run-on sentences and make punctuation decisions (see G6, P1-a, and P3-b). The ability to recognize subordinating conjunctions will help you avoid sentence fragments (see G5).

B1-h Interjections

Interjections are words used to express surprise or emotion (*Oh! Hey! Wow!*).

B2

Parts of sentences

Most English sentences flow from subject to verb to any objects or complements. *Predicate* is the grammatical term given to the verb plus its objects, complements, and modifiers.

ON THE WEB > dianahacker.com/writersref
    Grammar exercises > Basic grammar > E-ex B2–1 through B2–5

B2-a Subjects

The subject of a sentence names who or what the sentence is about. The simple subject is always a noun or a pronoun; the complete subject consists of the simple subject and any words or word groups modifying the simple subject.

To find the complete subject, ask Who? or What?, insert the verb, and finish the question. The answer is the complete subject.

┌── COMPLETE SUBJECT ──┐
The purity of a revolution usually lasts about two weeks.

Who or what lasts about two weeks? *The purity of a revolution.*

┌─────── COMPLETE SUBJECT ───────┐
Historical books that contain no lies are extremely tedious.

Who or what are extremely tedious? *Historical books that contain no lies.*

COMPLETE SUBJECT
┌──────┐
In every country the sun rises in the morning.

Who or what rises in the morning? *The sun.* Notice that *In every country the sun* is not a sensible answer to the question.

The simple subject

To find the simple subject (ss), strip away all modifiers in the complete subject. This includes single-word modifiers such as *the* and *historical,* phrases such as *of a revolution,* and subordinate clauses such as *that contain no lies.*

A sentence may have a compound subject containing two or more simple subjects joined with a coordinating conjunction such as *and* or *or.*

┌─ SS ─┐   ┌─ SS ─┐
Much industry and little conscience make us rich.

In imperative sentences, which give advice or issue commands, the subject is an understood *you.*

[*You*] Hitch your wagon to a star.

Although the subject ordinarily comes before the verb, occasionally it does not. When a sentence begins with *There is* or *There are* (or *There was* or *There were*), the subject follows the verb. The word *There* is an expletive in such constructions, an empty word serving merely to get the sentence started.

┌─ SS ─┐
There is *no substitute* for victory.

Sometimes a writer will invert a sentence for effect.

┌─ SS ─┐
Happy is *the nation that has no history.*

In questions, the subject may appear before the verb, after the verb, or between the helping verb (HV) and main verb (MV).

S ┌—V—┐
Who will take the first step?

V ┌—S——┐
Why is the first step so difficult?

HV   S   MV
Will you take the first step?

NOTE: The ability to recognize the subject of a sentence will help you edit for a variety of problems such as sentence fragments (G5), subject-verb agreement (G1), and choice of pronouns such as *I* and *me* (G3-c). If English is not your native language, see also E2-b and E2-c.

EXERCISE B2–1 In the following sentences, underline the complete subject and write *SS* above the simple subject(s). If the subject is an understood *you,* insert it in parentheses. Answers to lettered sentences appear in the back of the book. Example:

SS   SS
Fools and their money are soon parted.

a. Sticks and stones may break my bones, and words can sting like anything.   —Anonymous

b. In war, all delays are dangerous.   —John Dryden

c. Speak softly and carry a big stick.   —Theodore Roosevelt

d. There is nothing permanent except change.   —Heraclitus

e. Most of the disputes in the world arise from words.
                                              —Lord Mansfield

1. The structure of every sentence is a lesson in logic.
                                              — J. S. Mill

2. Don't be humble. You're not that great.   —Golda Meir

3. In the eyes of its mother, every beetle is a gazelle.
                                              —Moorish proverb

4. The burden of proof lies on the plaintiff.   —Legal maxim

5. There are no signposts in the sea.   —Vita Sackville-West

B2-b   Verbs, objects, and complements

Section B1-c explains how to find the verb of a sentence, which consists of a main verb possibly preceded by one or more helping verbs. A sentence's verb is classified as linking, transitive, or intransitive, depending on the kinds of objects or complements the verb can (or cannot) take.

Linking verbs and subject complements

Linking verbs (v) link the subject to a subject complement (sc), a word or word group that completes the meaning of the subject (s) by renaming or describing it.

```
┌─────────────── S ───────────────┐ ┌─V─┐ ┌─SC─┐
The handwriting on the wall may be a forgery.
```

```
S    V   SC
Love is blind.
```

When the simple subject complement renames the subject, it is a noun or noun equivalent (sometimes called a *predicate noun*), such as *forgery*. When it describes the subject, it is an adjective or adjective equivalent (sometimes called a *predicate adjective*), such as *blind*.

Linking verbs are usually a form of *be: be, am, is, are, was, were, being, been.* Verbs such as *appear, become, feel, grow, look, make, prove, remain, seem, smell, sound,* and *taste* are linking when they are followed by a word group that names or describes the subject.

Transitive verbs and direct objects

A transitive verb takes a direct object (DO), a word or word group that names a receiver of the action.

```
┌─────S─────┐  V  ┌──────────── DO────────────┐
The little snake studies the ways of the big serpent.
```

The simple direct object is always a noun, such as *ways,* or a pronoun. To find it, simply strip away all modifiers.

Transitive verbs usually appear in the active voice, with the subject doing the action and a direct object receiving the action. Active-voice sentences can be transformed into the passive voice, with the subject receiving the action instead.

ACTIVE VOICE	The early bird sometimes catches the early worm.
PASSIVE VOICE	The early worm is sometimes caught by the early bird.

What was once the direct object (*the early worm*) has become the subject in the passive-voice transformation, and the original subject appears in a prepositional phrase beginning with *by*. The *by* phrase is frequently omitted in passive-voice constructions: *The early worm is sometimes caught.* (See also W3-a.)

Transitive verbs, indirect objects, and direct objects

The direct object of a transitive verb is sometimes preceded by an indirect object (IO), a noun or pronoun telling to whom or for whom the action of the sentence is done.

```
 S    V      IO  ┌─DO─┐   S┌─ V ─┐    IO  ┌─DO─┐
You show [to] me a hero, and I will write [for] you a tragedy.
```

Transitive verbs, direct objects, and object complements

The direct object of a transitive verb is sometimes followed by an object complement (OC), a word or word group that completes the direct object's meaning by renaming or describing it.

```
┌───S───┐  V ┌─DO─┐┌────────OC────────┐
Some people call a spade an agricultural implement.
```

```
 S     V    ┌───DO───┐   OC
Love makes all hard hearts gentle.
```

When the object complement renames the direct object, it is a noun or pronoun (such as *implement*). When it describes the direct object, it is an adjective (such as *gentle*).

Intransitive verbs

Intransitive verbs take no objects or complements.

```
  S    V
Money talks.
```

```
   S          V
Revolutions never go backward.
```

Nothing receives the actions of talking and going in these sentences, so the verbs are intransitive. Such verbs may have adverbial modifiers. In the preceding sentence, *never* and *backward* are adverbs modifying *go*.

NOTE: The dictionary will tell you whether a verb is transitive or intransitive. Some verbs have both transitive and intransitive functions.

TRANSITIVE   Sandra flew her Cessna over the canyon.

INTRANSITIVE   A bald eagle flew overhead.

In the first example, *flew* has a direct object that receives the action: *her Cessna*. In the second example, the verb is followed by an adverb (*overhead*), not by a direct object.

EXERCISE B2–2 Label the subject complements and direct objects in the following sentences, using these labels: *SC, DO*. If a subject complement or direct object consists of more than one word, bracket and label all of it. Example:

> ┌─── *DO* ───┐
> You can fool most of the people most of the time.

a.	Talk is cheap.	—English proverb
b.	An elephant never forgets an injury.	—American proverb
c.	A runaway monk never praises his convent.	—Italian proverb
d.	Religion is the opium of the people.	—Karl Marx
e.	Good medicine always tastes bitter.	—Japanese proverb

1. You can say the nastiest things about yourself without offending anyone.   —Phyllis Diller
2. The quarrels of friends are the opportunities of foes.   —Aesop
3. Art is the signature of civilization.   —Beverly Sills
4. You can tell the ideals of a nation by its advertising.
   —Norman Douglas
5. You can never be too rich or too thin.
   —Wallis Warfield Simpson

EXERCISE B2–3 Each of the following sentences has either an indirect object followed by a direct object or a direct object followed by an object complement. Label the objects and complements, using these labels; *IO, DO, OC*. If an object or complement consists of more than one word, bracket and label all of it. Example:

> ┌── *DO* ──┐   *OC*
> Every man thinks his own geese swans.

a. Sorrow makes us wise.   —Alfred Lord Tennyson
b. Too many people make money their primary pursuit.
   —Anonymous

c. Make us happy and you make us good. — Robert Browning
d. Ask me no questions, and I will tell you no lies. — Anonymous
e. Show me a good loser, and I will show you a failure.

— Paul Newman

1. Give the devil his due. — English proverb
2. God gives every bird its proper food, but all must fly for it.

— Dutch proverb
3. A wide screen makes a bad film worse. — Samuel Goldwyn
4. Trees and fields tell me nothing. — Socrates
5. Necessity can make us surprisingly brave. — Latin proverb

B3

Subordinate word groups

Subordinate word groups cannot stand alone. They function only within sentences, usually as adjectives, adverbs, or nouns.

ON THE WEB > dianahacker.com/writersref
Grammar exercises > Basic grammar > E-ex B3–1 through B3–9

B3-a Prepositional phrases

A prepositional phrase begins with a preposition such as *at, by, for, from, in, of, on, to,* or *with* (see B1-f) and usually ends with a noun or a noun equivalent called the *object of the preposition.*

Prepositional phrases function as adjectives or adverbs. When functioning as an adjective, a prepositional phrase nearly always appears immediately following the noun or pronoun it modifies.

Variety is the spice *of life.*

Adjective phrases answer one or both of the questions Which one? and What kind of? If we ask Which spice? or What kind of spice? we get a sensible answer: *the spice of life.*

Adverbial prepositional phrases that modify the verb can appear nearly anywhere in a sentence.

Do not *judge* a tree *by its bark*.

Tyranny will *in time lead* to revolution.

To the ant, a few drops of rain *are* a flood.

Adverbial word groups usually answer one of these questions: When? Where? How? Why? Under what conditions? To what degree?

Do not judge a tree *how? By its bark*.

Tyranny will lead to revolution *when? In time*.

A few drops of rain are a flood *under what conditions? To the ant*.

EXERCISE B3–1 Underline the prepositional phrases in the following sentences. Be prepared to explain the function of each phrase. Answers to lettered sentences appear in the back of the book. Example:

Communism is fascism <u>with a human face</u>. *(Adjective phrase modifying fascism)*

a. On their side, the workers had only the Constitution. The other side had bayonets. —Mother Jones
b. Any mother could perform the job of several air traffic controllers with ease. —Lisa Alther
c. To my embarrassment, I was born in bed with a lady.
   —Wilson Mizner
d. Language is the road map of a culture. —Rita Mae Brown
e. In France, cooking is a serious art form and a national sport.
   —Julia Child

1. We know that the road to freedom has always been stalked by death.
   —Angela Davis
2. A society of sheep produces a government of wolves.
   —Bertrand de Jouvenal
3. Some people feel with their heads and think with their hearts.
   —G. C. Lichtenberg
4. By a small sample, we may know the whole piece.
   —Cervantes
5. You and I come by road or rail, but economists travel on infrastructure.
   —Margaret Thatcher

B3-b Verbal phrases

A verbal is a verb form that does not function as the verb of a clause. Verbals include infinitives (the word *to* plus the base form of the verb), present participles (the *-ing* form of the verb), and past participles (the verb form usually ending in *-d, -ed, -n, -en,* or *-t*). (See G2-a.)

Verbals can take objects, complements, and modifiers to form verbal phrases. These phrases are classified as participial, gerund, and infinitive.

Participial phrases

Participial phrases always function as adjectives. Their verbals are either present participles, always ending in *-ing,* or past participles, frequently ending in *-d, -ed, -n, -en,* or *-t* (see G2-a).

Participial phrases frequently appear immediately following the noun or pronoun they modify.

Truth kept in the dark will never save the world.

Unlike other adjectival word groups, however, which must always follow the noun or pronoun they modify, participial phrases are often movable. They can precede the word they modify.

Being weak, foxes are distinguished by superior tact.

They may also appear at some distance from the word they modify.

History is *something* that never happened, *written by someone*

who wasn't there.

Gerund phrases

Gerund phrases are built around present participles (verb forms ending in *-ing*), and they always function as nouns: usually as subjects, subject complements, direct objects, or objects of the preposition.

Justifying a fault doubles it.

Kleptomaniacs can't help helping themselves.

Infinitive phrases

Infinitive phrases, usually constructed around *to* plus the base form of the verb (*to call, to drink*), can function as adjectives, adverbs, or nouns. When functioning as a noun, an infinitive phrase may appear in almost any slot in a sentence, usually as a subject, subject complement, or direct object.

We do not have the *right to abandon the poor.* [Adjective]

He *cut off* his nose *to spite his face.* [Adverb]

To side with truth is noble. [Noun]

NOTE: In some constructions, the infinitive is unmarked; in other words, the *to* does not appear: *No one can make you [to] feel inferior without your consent.*

EXERCISE B3–2 Underline the verbal phrases in the following sentences. Be prepared to explain the function of each phrase. Answers to lettered sentences appear in the back of the book. Example:

> Do you want to be a writer? Then write. *(Infinitive phrase*
>
> *used as direct object of Do want)*

a. Concealing a disease is no way to cure it. —Ethiopian proverb
b. The trouble with being punctual is that nobody is there to appreciate it. —Franklin P. Jones
c. Fate tried to conceal him by naming him Smith.
—Oliver Wendell Holmes Jr.
d. Being weak, children quickly learn to beguile us with charm.
—Anonymous
e. Wrestling with words gave me my moments of greatest meaning.
—Richard Wright

1. The thing generally raised on city land is taxes. —C. D. Warner
2. Do not use a hatchet to remove a fly from your friend's forehead.
—Chinese proverb
3. He has the gall of a shoplifter returning an item for a refund.
—W. I. E. Gates
4. Tact is the ability to describe others as they see themselves.
—Mary Pettibone Poole
5. He could never see a belt without hitting below it. —Harriet Braiker

B3-c Appositive phrases

Appositive phrases describe nouns or pronouns. In form they are nouns or noun equivalents.

> Politicians, *acrobats at heart,* can sit on a fence and yet keep both ears to the ground.

B3-d Absolute phrases

An absolute phrase modifies a whole clause or sentence, not just one word. It consists of a noun or noun equivalent usually followed by a participial phrase.

> *His words dipped in honey,* the senator mesmerized the crowd.

B3-e Subordinate clauses

Subordinate clauses are patterned like sentences, having subjects and verbs and sometimes objects or complements, but they function within sentences as adjectives, adverbs, or nouns. They cannot stand alone as complete sentences.

Adjective clauses

Adjective clauses modify nouns or pronouns, usually answering the question Which one? or What kind of? They begin with a relative pronoun (*who, whom, whose, which,* or *that*) or a relative adverb (*when, where,* or *why*).

> The *arrow that has left the bow* never returns.

In addition to introducing the clause, the relative pronoun points back to the noun that the clause modifies.

> The *fur that warms a monarch* once warmed a bear.

Relative pronouns are sometimes "understood."

> The things [*that*] *we know best* are the things [*that*] *we haven't been taught.*

The parts of an adjective clause are often arranged as in sentences (subject/verb/object or complement).

S   V DO
We often forgive the people who bore us.

Frequently, however, the object or complement appears first, violating the normal order of subject/verb/object.

DO   S V
We rarely forgive those whom we bore.

NOTE: For punctuation of adjective clauses, see P1-e and P2-e. If English is not your native language, see E2-d for a common problem with adjective clauses.

Adverb clauses

Adverb clauses modify verbs, adjectives, or other adverbs, usually answering one of these questions: When? Where? Why? How? Under what conditions? To what degree? They always begin with a subordinating conjunction (*after, although, as, as if, because, before, even though, if, in order that, once, rather than, since, so that, than, that, though, unless, until, when, where, whether, while*).

When the well is dry, we *know* the worth of water.

Venice *would be* a fine city *if it were only drained.*

Noun clauses

A noun clause functions just like a single-word noun, usually as a subject, subject complement, direct object, or object of a preposition. It usually begins with one of the following words: *how, that, which, who, whoever, whom, whomever, what, whatever, when, where, whether, whose, why.*

————S————
Whoever gossips to you will gossip of you.

————DO————
We will never forget that we buried the hatchet.

The word introducing the clause may or may not play a significant role in the clause. In the preceding example sentences, *Whoever* is the subject of its clause, but *that* does not perform a function in its clause.

As with adjective clauses, the parts of a noun clause may appear out of their normal order (subject/verb/object).

DO   S   V

Talent is what you possess.

The parts of a noun clause may also appear in their normal order.

S   V   DO

Genius is what possesses you.

EXERCISE B3–3 Underline the subordinate clauses in the following sentences. Be prepared to explain the function of each clause. Answers to lettered sentences appear in the back of the book. Example:

Dig a well **before you are thirsty**. *(Adverb clause modifying Dig)*

a. It is hard to fight an enemy who has outposts in your head.
—Sally Kempton
b. A rattlesnake that doesn't bite teaches you nothing.
—Jessamyn West
c. If love is the answer, could you please rephrase the question?
—Lily Tomlin
d. Dreams say what they mean, but they don't say it in daytime language.
—Gail Godwin
e. I generally avoid temptation unless I cannot resist it.   —Mae West

1. What history teaches us is that we have never learned anything from it.   —Georg Wilhelm Hegel
2. When the insects take over the world, we hope that they will remember our picnics with gratitude.   —Anonymous
3. A woman who will tell her age will tell anything.   —Rita Mae Brown
4. If triangles had a god, it would have three sides.
—C. L. de Montesquieu
5. He gave her a look that you could have poured on a waffle.
—Ring Lardner

B4

Sentence types

Sentences are classified in two ways: according to their structure (simple, compound, complex, and compound-complex) and according to their purpose (declarative, imperative, interrogative, and exclamatory).

ON THE WEB > dianahacker.com/writersref
Grammar exercises > Basic grammar > E-ex B4–1

B4-a Sentence structures

Depending on the number and types of clauses they contain, sentences are classified as simple, compound, complex, or compound-complex.

Clauses come in two varieties: independent and subordinate. An independent clause contains a subject and a predicate, and it either stands alone or could stand alone. A subordinate clause also contains a subject and a predicate, but it functions within a sentence as an adjective, an adverb, or a noun; it cannot stand alone.

SIMPLE SENTENCE   A simple sentence is one independent clause with no subordinate clauses.

┌──────────INDEPENDENT CLAUSE──────────┐
Without music, life would be a mistake.

COMPOUND SENTENCE   A compound sentence is composed of two or more independent clauses with no subordinate clauses. The independent clauses are usually joined with a comma and a coordinating conjunction (*and, but, or, nor, for, so, yet*) or with a semicolon.

┌── INDEPENDENT CLAUSE──┐   ┌── INDEPENDENT CLAUSE──┐
One arrow is easily broken, but you can't break a bundle of ten.

COMPLEX SENTENCE   A complex sentence is composed of one independent clause with one or more subordinate clauses.

     SUBORDINATE
┌──   CLAUSE   ──┐
If you scatter thorns, don't go barefoot.

COMPOUND-COMPLEX SENTENCE   A compound-complex sentence contains at least two independent clauses and at least one subordinate clause. The following sentence contains two independent clauses, each of which contains a subordinate clause.

┌──────IND CLAUSE──────┐   ┌──────IND CLAUSE──────┐
   ┌─SUB CLAUSE─┐   ┌─SUB CLAUSE─┐
Tell me what you eat, and I will tell you what you are.

EXERCISE B4–1 Identify the following sentences as simple, compound, complex, or compound-complex. Be prepared to identify the subordinate clauses and classify them according to their function: adjective, adverb, or noun. (See B3-e.) Answers to lettered sentences appear in the back of the book. Example:

> **The frog in the well knows nothing of the ocean.** *(Simple)*

a. People who sleep like a baby usually don't have one.   —Leo Burke

b. My folks didn't come over on the *Mayflower;* they were there to meet the boat.   —Will Rogers

c. The impersonal hand of the government can never replace the helping hand of a neighbor.   —Hubert Humphrey

d. If you don't go to other people's funerals, they won't go to yours.
      —Clarence Day

e. Tell us your phobias, and we will tell you what you are afraid of.
      —Robert Benchley

1. The tragedy of life is that people don't change.   —Agatha Christie

2. Those who cannot remember the past are condemned to repeat it.
      —George Santayana

3. The best mind-altering drug is truth.   —Lily Tomlin

4. Morality cannot be legislated, but behavior can be regulated.
      —Martin Luther King Jr.

5. Science commits suicide when it adopts a creed.   —T. H. Huxley

B4-b Sentence purposes

Writers use declarative sentences to make statements, imperative sentences to issue requests or commands, interrogative sentences to ask questions, and exclamatory sentences to make exclamations.

> **DECLARATIVE**   The echo always has the last word.
>
> **IMPERATIVE**   Love your neighbor.
>
> **INTERROGATIVE**   Are second thoughts always wisest?
>
> **EXCLAMATORY**   I want to wash the flag, not burn it!

Answers to Tutorials and Lettered Exercises

Tutorial 1, page xii

1. A verb has to agree with its subject. (G1-a)
2. Each pronoun should agree with its antecedent. (G3-a)
3. Avoid sentence fragments. (G5)
4. It's important to use apostrophes correctly. (P5-c and P5-e)
5. Check for *-ed* verb endings that have been dropped. (G2-d)
6. Discriminate carefully between adjectives and adverbs. (G4)
7. If your sentence begins with a long introductory word group, use a comma to separate the word group from the rest of the sentence. (P1-b)
8. Don't write a run-on sentence; you must connect independent clauses with a comma and a coordinating conjunction or with a semicolon. (G6)
9. A writer must be careful not to shift his or her [*not* their] point of view. *Or* Writers must be careful not to shift their point of view. (S4-a)
10. Watch out for dangling modifiers. (S3-e)

Tutorial 2, page xiii

1. The index entry "*each*" mentions that the word is singular, so you might not need to look further to realize that the verb should be *has,* not *have.* The first page reference takes you to the entry for *each* in the glossary of usage, which directs you to G1-e and G3-a for details about why *has* is correct. The index entry "*has* vs. *have*" leads you to the chart in G1-a.
2. The index entry "*lying* vs. *laying*" takes you to section G2-b, where you will learn that *lying* (meaning "reclining or resting on a surface") is correct.
3. Look up "*only,* placement of" and you will be directed to section S3-a, which explains that limiting modifiers such as *only* should be placed before the words they modify. The sentence should read *We looked at only two houses before buying the house of our dreams.*
4. Looking up "*you,* inappropriate use of" leads you to the glossary of usage (W1) and section G3-b, which explain that *you* should not be used to mean "anyone in general." You can revise the sentence by using *a person* or *one* instead of *you,* or you can restructure the sentence completely: *In Saudi Arabia, accepting a gift is considered ill mannered.*
5. The index entries "*I* vs. *me*" and "*me* vs. *I*" take you to section G3-c, which explains why *me* is correct.

Tutorial 3, page xiii

1. Section P1-c states that, although usage varies, most experts advise using a comma between all items in a series — to prevent possible misreadings or ambiguities. To find this section, Ray Farley would probably use the menu system.

557

2. Maria Sanchez and Mike Lee would consult section E3, on articles. This section is easy to locate in the menu system.
3. Section G3-c explains why *Sophia and me* is correct. To find section G3-c, John Pell could use the menu system if he knew to look under "Problems with pronouns." Otherwise, he could look up "*I* vs. *me*" in the index. Pell could also look up "*myself*" in the index or he could consult the glossary of usage (W1), where a cross-reference would direct him to section G3-c.
4. Selena Young's interns could turn to sections G1 and G2-c for help. Young could use the menu system to find these sections if she knew to look under "Subject-verb agreement" or "Standard English verb forms." If she wasn't sure about the grammatical terminology, she could look up "-*s,* as verb ending" or "Verbs, -*s* form of " in the index.
5. Section G4-b explains why *I felt bad about her death* is correct. To find section G4-b, Owen Thompson could use the menu system if he knew that *bad* versus *badly* is a choice between an adjective and an adverb. Otherwise he could look up "*bad, badly*" in the index or the glossary of usage (W1).

Tutorial 4, page xiv

1. Changing attitudes toward alcohol have *affected* the beer industry.
2. It is *human* nature to think wisely and act foolishly.
3. Correct
4. Our goal this year is to *increase* our profits by 9 percent.
5. Most sleds are pulled by no *fewer* than two dogs and no more than ten.

Tutorial 5, page xv

Alim, H. Samy. "360 Degreez of Black Art Comin at You: Sista Sonia Sanchez and the

Dimensions of a Black Arts Continuum." BMa: The Sonia Sanchez Literary Review

6.1 (2000): 15-33.

Chang, Jeff. Can't Stop, Won't Stop: A History of the Hip-Hop Generation. New York:

St. Martin's, 2005.

Davis, Kimberly. "The Roots Redefine Hip-Hop's Past." Ebony June 2003: 162-64.

Expanded Academic ASAP. InfoTrac. Ray Cosgrove Lib., Truman Coll., Chicago. 13

Apr. 2006 <http://infotrac.galegroup.com>.

Randall, Kay. "Studying a Hip-Hop Nation." University of Texas at Austin. 11 Apr.

2005. 13 Apr. 2006 <http://www.utexas.edu/features/archives/2003/

hiphop.html>.

Sugarhill Gang. "Rapper's Delight." The Sugarhill Gang. LP. Sugarhill, 1979.

EXERCISE S1–1, page 96

Possible revisions:

a. Police dogs are used for finding lost children, tracking criminals, and detecting bombs and illegal drugs.
b. Hannah told her rock-climbing partner that she bought a new harness and that she wanted to climb Otter Cliffs.
c. It is more difficult to sustain an exercise program than to start one.
d. During basic training, I was told not only what to do but also what to think.
e. Jan wanted to drive to the wine country or at least to Sausalito.

EXERCISE S2–1, page 100

Possible revisions:

a. A good source of vitamin C is a grapefruit or an orange.
b. The women entering VMI can expect haircuts as short as those of the male cadets.
c. Ara stopped the car, only to find that one of the new tires had blown.
d. The graphic designers are interested in and knowledgeable about producing posters for the balloon race.
e. Reefs are home to more species than any other ecosystem in the sea.

EXERCISE S3–1, page 104

a. More research is needed to evaluate effectively the risks posed by volcanoes in the Pacific Northwest.
b. Many students graduate from college with debt totaling more than fifty thousand dollars.
c. It is a myth that humans use only 10 percent of their brains.
d. A coolhunter is a person who can find the next wave of fashion in the unnoticed corners of modern society.
e. Not all geese fly beyond Narragansett for the winter.

EXERCISE S3–2, page 107

Possible revisions:

a. When I was ten, my parents took me on my first balloon ride.
b. To replace the gear mechanism, you can use the attached form to order the part by mail.
c. As I nestled in the cockpit, the pounding of the engine was muffled only slightly by my helmet.
d. After studying polymer chemistry, Phuong found computer games less complex.
e. When I was a young man, my mother enrolled me in tap dance classes, hoping I would become the next Savion Glover.

EXERCISE S4–3, page 112

Possible revisions:

a. An incredibly talented musician, Ray Charles mastered R&B, soul, and gospel styles. He even performed country music well.
b. Environmentalists point out that shrimp farming in Southeast Asia is polluting water and rendering farmlands useless. They warn that governments must act before it is too late.
c. We observed the samples for five days before we detected any growth. *Or* The samples were observed for five days before any growth was detected.
d. In his famous soliloquy, Hamlet contemplates whether death would be preferable to his difficult life and, if so, whether he is capable of committing suicide.
e. The lawyer told the judge that Miranda Hale was innocent and asked that she be allowed to prove the allegations false. *Or* The lawyer told the judge, "Miranda Hale is innocent. Please allow her to prove the allegations false."

EXERCISE S4–4, page 112

Possible revisions:

a. Courtroom lawyers have more than a touch of theater in their blood.
b. The interviewer asked if we had brought our proof of birth and citizenship and our passports.
c. Reconnaissance scouts often have to make fast decisions and use sophisticated equipment to keep their teams from detection.
d. After the animators finish their scenes, the production designer arranges the clips according to the storyboard and makes synchronization notes for the sound editor and the composer.
e. Madame Defarge is a sinister figure in Dickens's *A Tale of Two Cities*. On a symbolic level, she represents fate; like the Greek Fates, she knits the fabric of individual destiny.

EXERCISE S5–1, page 116

Possible revisions:

a. Using surgical gloves is a precaution now taken by dentists to prevent contact with patients' blood and saliva.
b. A career in medicine, which my brother is pursuing, requires at least ten years of challenging work.
c. The pharaohs had bad teeth because tiny particles of sand found their way into Egyptian bread.
d. Recurring bouts of flu caused the team to forfeit a record number of games.
e. This box contains the key to your future.

EXERCISE S6–1, page 118

Possible revisions:

a. Williams played for the Boston Red Sox from 1936 to 1960, and he managed the Washington Senators and Texas Rangers for several years after retiring as a player.
b. In 1941, Williams finished the season with a batting average of .406; no player has hit over .400 for a season since then.
c. Although he acknowledged that Joe DiMaggio was a better all-around player, Williams felt that he was a better hitter than DiMaggio.
d. Williams was a stubborn man; for example, he always refused to tip his cap to the crowd after a home run because he claimed that fans were fickle.
e. Williams's relationship with the media was unfriendly at best; he sarcastically called baseball writers the "knights of the keyboard" in his memoir.

EXERCISE S6–2, page 120

Possible revisions:

a. The X-Men comic books and Japanese woodcuts of kabuki dancers, all part of Marlena's research project on popular culture, covered the tabletop and the chairs.
b. Our waitress, costumed in a kimono, had painted her face white and arranged her hair in an upswept lacquered beehive.
c. Students can apply for a spot in the foundation's leadership program, which teaches thinking and communication skills.

d. Shore houses were flooded up to the first floor, beaches were washed away, and Brant's Lighthouse was swallowed by the sea.
e. Laura Thackray, an engineer at Volvo Car Corporation, designed a pregnant crash-test dummy to address women's safety needs.

EXERCISE S6–3, page 122

Possible revisions:

a. These particles, known as "stealth liposomes," can hide in the body for a long time without detection.
b. Irena, a competitive gymnast majoring in biochemistry, intends to apply her athletic experience and her science degree to a career in sports medicine.
c. Because students, textile workers, and labor unions have loudly protested sweatshop abuses, apparel makers have been forced to examine their labor practices.
d. Developed in a European university, IRC (Internet Relay Chat) was created as a way for a group of graduate students to talk about projects from their dorm rooms.
e. The cafeteria's new menu, which has an international flavor, includes everything from enchiladas and pizza to pad thai and sauerbraten.

EXERCISE S6–4, page 123

Possible revisions:

a. Working as an aide for the relief agency, Gina distributed food and medical supplies.
b. Janbir, who spent every Saturday learning tabla drumming, noticed with each hour of practice that his memory for complex patterns was growing stronger.
c. When the rotor hit, it gouged a hole about an eighth of an inch deep in my helmet.
d. My grandfather, who was born eighty years ago in Puerto Rico, raised his daughters the old-fashioned way.
e. By reversing the depressive effect of the drug, the Narcan saved the patient's life.

EXERCISE W1–1, page 145

a. The number of horses a Comanche warrior had in his possession indicated the wealth of his family.
b. The cat just sat there watching his prey.
c. Correct
d. Correct
e. Chris redesigned the boundary plantings to try to improve the garden's overall design.

EXERCISE W2–1, page 149

Possible revisions:

a. Martin Luther King Jr. set a high standard for future leaders.
b. Anita has loved cooking since she could first peek over a kitchen tabletop.
c. Bloom's race for the governorship is futile.
d. A successful graphic designer must have technical knowledge and an eye for color and balance.
e. You will deliver mail to all employees.

EXERCISE W3–1, page 153

Possible revisions:

a. The Prussians defeated the Saxons in 1745.
b. Ahmed, the producer, manages the entire operation.
c. The video game programmers awkwardly paddled the sea kayaks.
d. Emphatic and active; no change
e. Protesters were shouting on the courthouse steps.

EXERCISE W4–2, page 156

Possible revisions:

a. In my youth, my family was poor.
b. This conference will help me serve my clients better.
c. Have you ever been accused of beating a dead horse?
d. Government studies show a need for after-school programs.
e. Passengers should try to complete the customs declaration form before leaving the plane.

EXERCISE W4–4, page 162

Possible revisions:

a. Dr. Geralyn Farmer is the chief surgeon at University Hospital. Dr. Paul Green is her assistant.
b. All applicants want to know how much they will make.
c. Elementary school teachers should understand the concept of nurturing if they intend to be successful.
d. Students of high-tech architecture pick a favorite when they study such inspirational architects as Renzo Piano and Zaha Hadid.
e. If we do not stop polluting our environment, we will perish.

EXERCISE W5–1, page 166

Possible revisions:

a. We regret this delay; thank you for your patience.
b. Ada's plan is to acquire education and experience to prepare herself for a position as property manager.
c. Tiger Woods, the ultimate competitor, has earned millions of dollars just in endorsements.
d. Many people take for granted that public libraries have up-to-date networked computer systems.
e. The effect of Gao Xinjian's novels on Chinese exiles is hard to gauge.

EXERCISE W5–2, page 168

Possible revisions:

a. Queen Anne was so angry with Sarah Churchill that she refused to see her again.
b. Correct
c. The parade moved off the street and onto the beach.
d. The frightened refugees intend to make the dangerous trek across the mountains.
e. What type of wedding are you planning?

EXERCISE W5–3, page 170

Possible revisions:

a. John stormed into the room like a hurricane.
b. Some people insist that they'll always be available to help, even when they haven't been before.
c. The Cubs easily beat the Mets, who were in trouble early in the game today at Wrigley Field.
d. We worked out the problems in our relationship.
e. My mother accused me of evading her questions when in fact I was just saying the first thing that came to mind.

EXERCISE G1–2, page 186

a. One of the main reasons for elephant poaching is the profits received from selling the ivory tusks.
b. Correct
c. A number of students in the seminar were aware of the importance of joining the discussion.
d. Batik cloth from Bali, blue and white ceramics from Delft, and a bocce ball from Turin have made Angelie's room the talk of the dorm.
e. Correct

EXERCISE G2–1, page 192

a. When I get the urge to exercise, I lie down until it passes.
b. Grandmother had driven our new SUV to the sunrise church service on Savage Mountain, so we were left with the station wagon.
c. A pile of dirty rags was lying at the bottom of the stairs.
d. How did the computer know that the gamer had gone from the room with the blue ogre to the hall where the gold was heaped?
e. Abraham Lincoln took good care of his legal clients; the contracts he drew for the Illinois Central Railroad could never be broken.

EXERCISE G2–2, page 196

a. The glass sculptures of the Swan Boats were prominent in the brightly lit lobby.
b. Visitors to the glass museum were not supposed to touch the exhibits.
c. Our church has all the latest technology, even a closed-circuit television.
d. Christos didn't know about Marlo's promotion because he never listens. He is always talking.
e. Correct

EXERCISE G2–3, page 202

Possible revisions:

a. Correct
b. Watson and Crick discovered the mechanism that controls inheritance in all life: the workings of the DNA molecule.
c. When Hitler decided to kill the Jews in 1941, did he know that Himmler and his SS had had mass murder in mind since 1938?
d. Correct
e. Correct

EXERCISE G3–1, page 207

Possible revisions:

a. Every presidential candidate must appeal to a wide variety of ethnic and social groups to win the election.
b. David lent his motorcycle to someone who allowed a friend to use it.
c. The aerobics teacher motioned for all the students to move their arms in wide, slow circles.
d. Correct
e. Applicants should be bilingual if they want to qualify for this position.

EXERCISE G3–3, page 210

Possible revisions:

a. Some professors say that an engineering student should have hands-on experience with dismantling and reassembling machines.
b. Because she had decorated her living room with posters from chamber music festivals, her date thought she was interested in classical music. Actually she preferred rock.
c. In Ethiopia, a person doesn't need much property to be considered well-off.
d. Marianne told Jenny, "I am worried about your mother's illness." [or ". . . about my mother's illness."]
e. Though Lewis cried for several minutes after scraping his knee, eventually the pain subsided.

EXERCISE G3–5, page 216

a. Correct [But the writer could change the end of the sentence: . . . *than he is.*]
b. Correct [But the writer could change the end of the sentence: . . . *that she was the coach.*]
c. She appreciated his telling the truth in such a difficult situation.
d. The director has asked you and me to draft a proposal for a new recycling plan.
e. Five close friends and I rented a station wagon, packed it with food, and drove two hundred miles to Mardi Gras.

EXERCISE G3–7, page 219

a. The roundtable featured scholars whom I had never heard of. [or . . . scholars I had never heard of.]
b. Correct
c. Correct
d. Daniel always gives a holiday donation to whoever needs it.
e. So many singers came to the audition that Natalia had trouble deciding whom to select for the choir.

EXERCISE G4–1, page 224

Possible revisions:

a. Did you do well on last week's chemistry exam?
b. With the budget deadline approaching, our office has hardly had time to handle routine correspondence.
c. Correct
d. The customer complained that he hadn't been treated nicely.
e. Of all my relatives, Uncle Roberto is the cleverest.

EXERCISE G5–1, page 231

Possible revisions:

a. Listening to the CD her sister had sent, Mia was overcome with a mix of emotions: happiness, homesickness, nostalgia.
b. Cortés and his soldiers were astonished when they looked down from the mountains and saw Tenochtitlán, the magnificent capital of the Aztecs.
c. Although my spoken Spanish is not very good, I can read the language with ease.
d. There are several reasons for not eating meat. One reason is that dangerous chemicals are used throughout the various stages of meat production.
e. To learn how to sculpt beauty from everyday life is my intention in studying art and archaeology.

EXERCISE G6–1, page 238

Possible revisions:

a. The city had one public swimming pool that stayed packed with children all summer long.
b. The building is being renovated, so at times we have no heat, water, or electricity.
c. The view was not what the travel agent had described. Where were the rolling hills and the shimmering rivers?
d. All those gnarled equations looked like toxic insects; maybe I was going to have to rethink my major.
e. The city government had good reason to fear a major earthquake: Most [or most] of the business district was built on landfill.

EXERCISE G6–2, page 239

Possible revisions:

a. Wind power for the home is a supplementary source of energy that can be combined with electricity, gas, or solar energy.
b. Correct
c. In the Middle Ages, when the streets of London were dangerous places, it was safer to travel by boat along the Thames.
d. "He's not drunk," I said. "He's in a state of diabetic shock."
e. Are you able to endure boredom, isolation, and potential violence? Then the army may well be the adventure for you.

EXERCISE E1–1, page 247

a. In the past, tobacco companies denied any connection between smoking and health problems.
b. There is nothing in the world that TV has not touched on.
c. I want to register for a summer tutoring session.
d. By the end of the year, the state will have tested 139 birds for avian flu.
e. The benefits of eating fruits and vegetables have been promoted by health care providers.

EXERCISE E1–2, page 250

a. A major league pitcher can throw a baseball over ninety-five miles per hour.
b. The writing center tutors will help you to revise your essay.
c. A reptile must adjust its body temperature to its environment.

    d. Correct

    e. My uncle, a caricature artist, could sketch a face in less than two minutes.

EXERCISE E1–3, page 257

Possible revisions:

    a. The electrician might have discovered the broken circuit if she had gone through the modules one at a time.

    b. If Verena wins a scholarship, she will go to graduate school.

    c. Whenever there is a fire in our neighborhood, everybody comes out to watch.

    d. Sarah will take the paralegal job unless she gets a better offer.

    e. If I lived in Budapest with my cousin Szusza, she would teach me Hungarian cooking.

EXERCISE E1–4, page 259

Possible answers:

    a. I enjoy riding my motorcycle.

    b. The tutor told Samantha to come to the writing center.

    c. The team hopes to work hard and win the championship.

    d. Ricardo and his brothers miss surfing during the winter.

    e. The babysitter let Roger stay up until midnight.

EXERCISE E2–1, page 264

    a. There are some cartons of ice cream in the freezer.

    b. I don't use the subway because I am afraid.

    c. The prime minister is the most popular leader in my country.

    d. We tried to get in touch with the same manager whom we spoke to earlier.

    e. Recently there have been a number of earthquakes in Turkey.

EXERCISE E2–2, page 266

    a. Although freshwater freezes at 32 degrees Fahrenheit, ocean water freezes at 28 degrees Fahrenheit.

    b. Because we switched Internet service providers, our e-mail address has changed.

    c. The competitor confidently mounted his skateboard and expertly executed a kickflip.

    d. My sister performs the *legong*, a Balinese dance, well.

    e. Correct

EXERCISE E3–1, page 276

    a. Doing volunteer work often brings satisfaction.

    b. As I looked out the window of the plane I could see Cape Cod.

    c. Melina likes to drink her coffee with lots of cream.

    d. Correct

    e. I completed my homework assignment quickly.

EXERCISE E4–1, page 279

    a. Listening to everyone's complaints all day was irritating.

    b. The long flight to Singapore was exhausting.

    c. Correct

    d. After several years of painstaking research, the scientist made a fascinating discovery.

    e. That blackout was one of the most frightening experiences I've ever had.

EXERCISE E4-2, page 280

a. an attractive young Vietnamese woman
b. a dedicated Catholic priest
c. her old blue wool sweater
d. Joe's delicious Scandinavian bread
e. many beautiful antique jewelry boxes

EXERCISE E5-1, page 282

a. Whenever we eat at the Centerville Diner, we sit at a small table in the corner of the room.
b. Correct
c. On Thursday, Nancy will attend her first Pilates class at the community center.
d. Correct
e. We decided to go to a restaurant because there was no fresh food in the refrigerator.

EXERCISE P1-1, page 288

a. Correct
b. As an intern, I learned about all aspects of the broadcasting industry and trained specifically in fundraising efforts.
c. J. R. R. Tolkien finished writing his draft of *The Lord of the Rings* trilogy in 1949, but the first book in the series wasn't published until 1954.
d. German shepherds can be gentle guide dogs, or they can be fierce attack dogs.
e. Some former professional cyclists claim that performance-enhancing drug use is widespread in cycling, and they argue that no rider can be competitive without doping.

EXERCISE P1-2, page 290

a. Considered a classic of early animation, *The Adventures of Prince Achmed* used hand-cut silhouettes against colored backgrounds.
b. Correct
c. Correct
d. After retiring from the New York City Ballet in 1965, legendary dancer Maria Tallchief went on to found the Chicago City Ballet.
e. Because the car had been sitting idle for so long, the battery was completely dead.

EXERCISE P1-3, page 291

a. Correct
b. A complete diagnostic of the system revealed that the trouble was neither electrical nor mechanical.
c. Love, vengeance, greed, and betrayal are common themes in Western literature.
d. Correct
e. In Sherman's march to the sea, the Union army set fire to all crops, killed all livestock, and destroyed all roads and bridges in its path.

EXERCISE P1-4, page 292

a. NASA's rovers on Mars are equipped with special cameras that can take close-up, high-resolution pictures of the terrain.

b. Correct
c. Correct
d. Many experts believe that shark attacks on surfers are a result of the sharks' mistaking surfboards for small injured seals.
e. Correct

EXERCISE P1–5, page 295

a. Choreographer Alvin Ailey's best-known work, *Revelations,* is more than just a crowd pleaser.
b. Correct
c. Correct
d. A member of an organization that provides housing for AIDS patients was also appointed to the commission.
e. Brian Eno, who began his career as a rock musician, turned to meditative compositions in the late seventies.

EXERCISE P1–6, page 300

a. Cricket, which originated in England, is also popular in Australia, South Africa, and India.
b. At the sound of the starting pistol, the horses surged forward toward the first obstacle, a sharp incline three feet high.
c. After seeing an exhibition of Western art, Gerhard Richter escaped from East Berlin and smuggled out many of his notebooks.
d. Corrie's new wet suit has an intricate blue pattern.
e. Correct

EXERCISE P1–7, page 301

a. On January 15, 2004, our office moved to 29 Commonwealth Avenue, Mechanicsville, VA 23111.
b. Correct
c. Ms. Carlson, you are a valued customer whose satisfaction is very important to us.
d. Mr. Mundy was born on July 22, 1939, in Arkansas, where his family had lived for four generations.
e. Correct

EXERCISE P2–1, page 305

a. Correct
b. Tricia's first artwork was a big blue clay dolphin.
c. Some modern musicians (trumpeter John Hassell is an example) blend several cultural traditions into a unique sound.
d. Myra liked hot, spicy foods such as chili, jambalaya, and buffalo wings.
e. On the display screen was a soothing pattern of light and shadow.

EXERCISE P3–1, page 310

a. Do not ask me to be kind; just ask me to act as though I were.
b. When men talk about defense, they always claim to be protecting women and children, but they never ask the women and children what they think.
c. When I get a little money, I buy books; if any is left, I buy food and clothes.
d. Correct
e. Wit has truth in it; wisecracking is simply calisthenics with words.

EXERCISE P3–2, page 310

a. Strong black coffee will not sober you up; the truth is that time is the only way to get alcohol out of your system.
b. It is not surprising that our society is increasingly violent; after all, television desensitizes us to brutality at a very early age.
c. There is often a fine line between right and wrong, good and bad, truth and deception.
d. Correct
e. Severe, unremitting pain is a ravaging force, especially when the patient tries to hide it from others.

EXERCISE P4–1, page 313

a. Correct [Either *It* or *it* is correct.]
b. If we have come to fight, we are far too few; if we have come to die, we are far too many.
c. The travel package includes a round-trip ticket to Athens, a cruise through the Cyclades, and all hotel accommodations.
d. The media portray my generation as lazy, although polls show that we work as hard as the twentysomethings before us.
e. Fran Lebowitz has this advice for parents: "Never allow your child to call you by your first name. He hasn't known you long enough."

EXERCISE P5–1, page 317

a. Correct
b. The innovative shoe fastener was inspired by the designer's young son.
c. Each day's menu features a different European country's dish.
d. Sue worked overtime to increase her family's earnings.
e. Ms. Jacobs is unwilling to listen to students' complaints about computer failures and damaged disks.

EXERCISE P6–1, page 323

a. As for the advertisement "Sailors have more fun," if you consider chipping paint and swabbing decks fun, then you will have plenty of it.
b. Correct
c. Accepting the check for her lottery winnings, Juanita said that she would give half the money to charity.
d. After the movie, Vicki said, "The reviewer called this flick 'trash of the first order.' I guess you can't believe everything you read."
e. Correct

EXERCISE P7–2, page 331

a. A client has left his or her cell phone in our conference room.
b. The films we made of Kilauea on our trip to Hawaii Volcanoes National Park illustrate a typical spatter cone eruption.
c. Correct
d. Correct
e. Of three engineering fields — chemical, mechanical, and materials — Keegan chose materials engineering for its application to toy manufacturing.

EXERCISE M2–1, page 342

a. Correct
b. The swiftly moving tugboat pulled alongside the barge and directed it away from the oil spill in the harbor.
c. Correct
d. Your dog is well known in our neighborhood.
e. Roadblocks were set up along all the major highways leading out of the city.

EXERCISE M3–1, page 346

a. Assistant Dean Shirin Ahmadi recommended offering more world language courses.
b. Correct
c. Kalindi has an ambitious semester, studying differential calculus, classical Hebrew, brochure design, and Greek literature.
d. Lydia's aunt and uncle make modular houses as beautiful as modernist works of art.
e. We amused ourselves on the long flight by discussing how spring in Kyoto stacks up against summer in London.

EXERCISE M4–1, page 349

a. Correct
b. Some combat soldiers are trained by government diplomats to be sensitive to issues of culture, history, and religion.
c. Correct
d. How many pounds have you lost since you began running four miles a day?
e. Denzil spent all night studying for his psychology exam.

EXERCISE M5–1, page 352

a. The carpenters located three maple timbers, twenty-one sheets of cherry, and ten oblongs of polished ebony for the theater set.
b. Correct
c. Correct
d. Eight students in the class had been labeled "learning disabled."
e. The Vietnam Veterans Memorial in Washington, DC, had 58,132 names inscribed on it when it was dedicated in 1982.

EXERCISE M6–1, page 355

a. Howard Hughes commissioned the *Spruce Goose,* a beautifully built but thoroughly impractical wooden aircraft.
b. The old man screamed his anger, shouting to all of us, "I will not leave my money to you worthless layabouts!"
c. I learned the Latin term *ad infinitum* from an old nursery rhyme about fleas: "Great fleas have little fleas upon their back to bite 'em, / Little fleas have lesser fleas and so on *ad infinitum."*
d. Correct
e. Neve Campbell's lifelong interest in ballet inspired her involvement in the film *The Company,* which portrays a season with the Joffrey Ballet.

EXERCISE B1-1, page 533

a. sun, assistance; b. Pride, bottom, mistakes; c. Success, confidence; d. censorship, flick, dial; e. flower, concrete (noun/adjective), cloverleaf

EXERCISE B1-2, page 536

a. He, every (pronoun/adjective); b. those, who; c. I, some (pronoun/adjective), that, I, myself; d. I, You, He; e. you, anything, anyone, me

EXERCISE B1-3, page 538

a. can pardon; b. are; c. does bring down; d. Keep, 'll [will] be insulted; e. Throw, will emerge

EXERCISE B1-4, page 540

a. Adjectives: General, wrong; adverb: generally; b. Adjectives: The (article), American, tolerant; adverb: wonderfully; c. Adjectives: an (article), uncultivated, an (article), uncultivated; adverbs: sometimes, never; d. Adjectives: wrong, right; adverbs: rather, strongly, weakly; e. Adjective: the (article); adverb: faster

EXERCISE B2-1, page 544

a. Complete subjects: Sticks and stones, words; simple subjects: Sticks, stones, words; b. Complete subject: all delays; simple subject: delays; c. Complete subject: (You); d. Complete subject: nothing except change; simple subject: nothing; e. Complete subject: Most of the disputes in the world; simple subject: Most

EXERCISE B2-2, page 547

a. Subject complement: cheap; b. Direct object: an injury; c. Direct object: his convent; d. Subject complement: the opium of the people; e. Subject complement: bitter

EXERCISE B2-3, page 547

a. Direct object: us; object complement: wise; b. Direct object: money; object complement: their primary pursuit; c. Direct objects: us, us; object complements: happy, good; d. Indirect objects: me, you; direct objects: no questions, no lies; e. Indirect objects: me, you; direct objects: a good loser, a failure

EXERCISE B3-1, page 549

a. On their side (adverb phrase modifying *had*); b. of several air traffic controllers (adjective phrase modifying *job*), with ease (adverb phrase modifying *could perform*); c. To my embarrassment (adverb phrase modifying *was born*), in bed (adverb phrase modifying *was born*), with a lady (adverb phrase modifying *was born*); d. of a culture (adjective phrase modifying *map*); e. In France (adverb phrase modifying *is*)

EXERCISE B3-2, page 551

a. Concealing a disease (gerund phrase used as subject), to cure it (infinitive phrase modifying *way*); b. being punctual (gerund phrase used as object of the preposition *with*), to appreciate it (infinitive phrase modifying *is*); c. to conceal him (infinitive phrase used as direct object), naming him Smith (gerund phrase used as object of the preposition *by*); d. Being weak (participial phrase modifying *children*), to beguile us with charm (infinitive phrase used as direct object); e. Wrestling with words (gerund phrase used as subject)

EXERCISE B3–3, page 554

a. who has outposts in your head (adjective clause modifying *enemy*); b. that doesn't bite (adjective clause modifying *rattlesnake*); c. If love is the answer (adverb clause modifying *could rephrase*); d. what they mean (noun clause used as direct object of *say*); e. unless I cannot resist it (adverb clause modifying *avoid*)

EXERCISE B4–1, page 556

a. Complex; who sleep like a baby (adjective clause); b. Compound; c. Simple; d. Complex; If you don't go to other people's funerals (adverb clause); e. Compound-complex; what you are afraid of (noun clause)

(Continued from page vi)

Screen shot of database search results Blackwell Synergy Web site, www.blackwell-synergy.com. Reprinted with the permission of Blackwell Publishers, Ltd.

Eugene Boe, excerpt from "Pioneers to Eternity" from *The Immigrant Experience*, edited by Thomas C. Wheeler. Copyright © 1971 by Thomas C. Wheeler. Reprinted with the permission of Doubleday, a division of Random House, Inc.

Albert Castel, excerpts from "The Fort Pillow Massacre: A Fresh Examination of the Evidence" from *Civil War History* 4, no. 1 (1958). Reprinted with the permission of The Kent State University Press.

Columbia University Library. Library Web pages. Copyright © Columbia University Libraries. www.columbia.edu. Reprinted by permission.

EBSCO Information Services. Various screen shots. Reprinted with the permission of EBSCO Information Services.

Google screen shots. Reprinted with the permission of Google, Inc.

Caroline M. Hoxby. "The Power of Peers." Front page of article and the TOC. From *Education Next*, Summer 2002. www.educationnext.org. Reprinted with the permission of *Education Next*.

Lynn Hunt et al., *The Making of the West,* Volume II. Copyright © 2005 by Bedford/St. Martin's. Reprinted by permission of Bedford/St. Martin's.

Henry Jenkins. Excerpted data from "Bearings." Copyright © 2006. The Massachusetts Institute of Technology. Posted online within the *MIT Communications Forum.* Reprinted with permission.

Jill D. Jenson, excerpt from "It's the Information Age, so Where's the Information?" from *College Teaching* (Summer 2004). Copyright © 2004. Reprinted with the permission of the Helen Dwight Reed Educational Foundation. Published by Heldref Publications, 1319 18th Street NW, Washington, DC 20036.

Harvey A. Levenstein. Reprint of the title and copyright pages from *Revolution at the Table: The Transformation of the American Diet* by Harvey A. Levenstein. Copyright © 2003 by the Regents of the University of California. Reprinted with the permission of the University of California Press.

LexisNexis. Screen shots. Copyright © 2006 LexisNexis, a division of Reed Elsevier Inc.

McDonald's Corporation, "What makes your lettuce so crisp?" advertisement. Copyright © 2004 by McDonald's Corporation. Reprinted with permission.

Anne McGrath, "A loss of foreign talent" from *U.S. News & World Report* (November 27, 2004). Copyright © 2004 by U.S. News & World Report, LP. Reprinted with permission. This figure includes a photo by Kenneth Dickerman which is reprinted by permission.

Merriam-Webster Online, screen shot of thesaurus entry for "regard" from www.MerriamWebster.com. Copyright © 2005 by Merriam-Webster Incorporated. Reprinted with permission.

"The Minnesota Annual Summary" or "Minnesota Health Statistics" report. Copyright © 2005 by the Minnesota Department of Health. www.health.state.mn.us.

L. M. Poupart. Page from "Crime and Justice in American Indian Communities." Copyright © 2002. Reprinted with the permission of *Social Justice*. Screenshot copyright © 2006 by ProQuest Information and Learning. Reprinted by permission.

Beth Shulman. Reprint of title and copyright pages from *Betrayal of Work* by Beth Shulman. Copyright © 2005 by Beth Shulman. Reprinted with the permission of The New Press.

Betsy Taylor, "Big Box Stores Are Bad for Main Street" from *CQ Researcher* (November 1999). Copyright © 1999 by Congressional Quarterly, Inc. Reprinted with permission.

United Nations Department of Public Information, *Africa Recovery* (June 2004), www.un.org/ecosocdev/geninfo/afrec/vol15no1/drugpr1.htm. Reprinted with the permission of UN Africa Renewal.

University of Minnesota Libraries, screen shots. Reprinted with permission.

Fred Zwicky, "Tornado Touch." Copyright © 2004. This photograph originally appeared in the *Peoria Journal Star.* Used with permission.

Index

In addition to giving you page numbers, this index shows you which tabbed section to flip to. For example, the entry "*a* vs. *an*" directs you to section **W** (Word Choice), page 131, and to section **E** (ESL Challenges), page 268. Just flip to the appropriate tabbed section and then track down the exact pages you need.

A

N

Documentation Directory: MLA

Directory to MLA in-text citation models

Documentation Directory: MLA

Directory to MLA works cited models

Documentation Directory: APA

Documentation Directory: CMS

Directory to *CMS-style notes and bibliography entries*

BOOKS (PRINT AND ONLINE)

1. Basic format for a print book, 515
2. Basic format for an online book, 516
3. Two or three authors, 516
4. Four or more authors, 516
5. Unknown author, 516
6. Edited work without an author, 516
7. Edited work with an author, 516
8. Translated work, 517
9. Edition other than the first, 517
10. Volume in a multivolume work, 517
11. Work in an anthology, 517
12. Letter in a published collection, 517
13. Work in a series, 517
14. Encyclopedia or dictionary, 518
15. Sacred text, 518

ARTICLES IN PERIODICALS (PRINT AND ONLINE)

16. Article in a journal, 518
17. Article in a magazine, 519
18. Article in a newspaper, 519
19. Unsigned article, 520
20. Book review, 520

WEB SITES AND POSTINGS

21. Web site, 520
22. Short document from a Web site, 521
23. An entry in a Weblog (blog), 521
24. Online posting or e-mail, 521

OTHER SOURCES (PRINT, ONLINE, MULTIMEDIA)

25. Government document, 521
26. Unpublished dissertation, 522
27. Personal communication, 522
28. Published or broadcast interview, 522
29. Podcast, 522
30. Video or DVD, 522
31. Sound recording, 522
32. Source quoted in another source, 523

ESL Menu

H

Extra Help for
ESL Writers

H Extra Help for ESL Writers

H

Extra Help for ESL Writers

Supplement to Accompany
Diana Hacker's

A Writer's Reference

Sixth Edition

Marcy Carbajal Van Horn
Santa Fe Community College

BEDFORD / ST. MARTIN'S   Boston ◆ New York

Manufactured in the United States of America.

2   1   0   9   8   7
f   e   d   c

For information, write: Bedford/St. Martin's, 75 Arlington Street, Boston, MA 02116   (617-399-4000)

ISBN-10: 0–312–45233–0
ISBN-13: 978–0–312–45233–9

Acknowledgments

Averil Coxhead, excerpt from sublist 1 of "A New Academic Word List" published in *TESOL Quarterly* 34. Copyright 2000. Reprinted with permission.
Robert MacNeil and William Cran, excerpt from *Do You Speak American?* Copyright 2005 by Neely Productions, Inc., and William Cran. Reprinted with permission.

H

Extra Help for
ESL Writers

H Extra Help for ESL Writers

No matter what your educational background is, entering a college environment will most likely provide opportunities for new ways of doing things. Even if you speak English fluently, it is possible to find college intimidating at first. Sections H1–H4 focus on ways to make your transition to college smooth and successful.

H1

Understanding college-level expectations

In the United States, college classrooms are interactive—students are expected to participate in discussions and sometimes work together in groups. Students are also treated as adults who are responsible for managing their own course work and schedule. Succeeding in this environment may require you to adjust your habits both inside and outside the classroom.

H1-a Read your syllabus carefully.

At the beginning of the semester, your instructor will give you a syllabus, a document that provides critical information about the course, including assignments, grading policies, and your instructor's contact information. (For a sample syllabus, see p. H-4.) Be sure to read through your syllabus carefully so that you will know your instructor's expectations and refer to it often during the term. College students are usually expected to keep up with the course work outlined in a syllabus without reminders from their instructor.

When you look at the syllabi for all your courses, you may find that you have several major assignments due on the same day. You may also have smaller assignments that overlap. A calendar or a schedule maker can help you keep track of the due dates for all your classes. It is a good idea to check your syllabus or your calendar regularly, especially before each class session, to remind yourself of the readings and other assignments.

H1-b Understand the expectations of American classrooms.

Education is a cultural activity, and classroom emphases and expectations vary across the globe. Some cultures value memorization of traditional texts, while others value creative thinking. Some

SAMPLE SYLLABUS

ENG 1101: College Composition I

Instructor: Dr. Morgan Felix

Phone: (321) 234-5678

E-mail address: mfelix@yourcollege.edu

Office: Anderson Hall, room 312-B

Office hours: Monday, Wednesday, and Friday, 1:00-2:30 p.m., or by appointment

Course Description
College Composition I (ENG 1101) is designed to give you training and practice in developing literacy in academic English. In this course, you will read and analyze academic texts, and you will write about those texts with an analytical purpose. Multiple drafts are expected for each writing assignment.

Course Objectives
1. Students will learn that writing is a process that requires planning, drafting, revising, peer reviewing, and editing.
2. Students will be competent in reading and analyzing college-level texts.
3. Students will be competent in structuring essays appropriate for college courses, using standard English conventions.

Required Textbooks
Kennedy, X. J., Dorothy M. Kennedy, and Jane E. Aaron. *The Bedford Reader*. 9th ed. Boston: Bedford, 2006.

Hacker, Diana. *A Writer's Reference*. 6th ed. Boston: Bedford, 2007.

Grading System
Your final grade will be based on the following:
- Take-home essays, including drafts = 60%
- In-class (timed) essays = 20%
- Attendance and participation = 10%
- Final exam = 10%

Schedule of Readings and Assignments
You are required to complete the assigned readings *before* each class. Major assignments are listed in **bold**.

   BR = Reading assignments from *The Bedford Reader*
   AWR = Reading assignments from *A Writer's Reference*

SAMPLE SYLLABUS (continued)

Week	Day	Class topics	Readings/ assignments due	
1	Tu	Introduction to the course/syllabus		
	Th	In-class diagnostic essay		
2	Tu	Writing description essays	*BR*: pages 135-58 *AWR*: C1 and C2	**5**
	Th	Essay 1 workshop (focus on global revisions)	Essay 1, draft 1 due *AWR*: C3-a and C3-b	
3	Tu	Essay 1 workshop (focus on editing)	Essay 1, draft 2 due *AWR:* C3-c	
	Th	Strategies for taking essay tests	**Essay 1 final draft due**	**6**

1 Instructors want to talk to their students. Often they list contact information and office hours on the course syllabus.

2 A syllabus often includes a list of materials to purchase.

3 Most instructors expect students to participate in class. Participation is often part of the final grade.

4 Abbreviations used in the schedule are explained.

5 Readings for each class are listed in the right-hand column.

6 Major deadlines are listed in bold.

emphasize individual learning; others expect students to work together.

In the United States, college courses typically require creative, original thinking rather than rote memorization. Most courses expect students to work together at least some of the time. Students might learn their course material in the following ways:

- by participating in class discussions
- by learning the rules, patterns, and theories and then applying them to a variety of situations
- by synthesizing (connecting) ideas from multiple sources
- by working with others to develop new approaches or hypotheses

While you might sometimes be required to memorize or learn basic facts and principles, your instructors will most often expect you to move beyond memorization and show original thinking about the content of the course. The following examples are questions from exams in introductory economics classes. The first example is from a class that emphasized memorization of facts; the second is from a class where students were expected to apply concepts to everyday situations.

EMPHASIS ON MEMORIZATION

QUESTION　　　What does "opportunity cost" mean?

ANSWER　　　　"Opportunity cost" is the value of a resource measured in terms of the next-best alternative use of that resource.

EMPHASIS ON ORIGINAL THINKING

QUESTION/TASK　Illustrate the concept of "opportunity cost" with an example from your own life.

ANSWER　　　　The opportunity cost of going to the movies with my roommate last night was the extra time I could otherwise have spent studying for my economics exam. In other words, I gave up extra study time by going to the movies.

To answer the second question, students needed to learn the definition of *opportunity cost*. But they were expected to go beyond the definition and do some creative thinking.

H1-c Participate actively in class and in groups.

Because US colleges value creativity and originality, students (especially in smaller classes or sections) are expected to participate in class—to share their ideas about the course material, to work together in groups, and sometimes even to lead class discussions. Because students' contributions are so highly valued, many instructors devote a portion of the final course grade to "class participation."

Class participation

To increase your chances of success, take an active part in class discussions. Remember that your instructors will not always expect you to merely recall or restate an idea from the text or a previous class. More often, they will ask you to show original thinking (see H1-b). If you sit quietly, your instructor might assume that you don't know the material or that you have come to class unprepared.

If you feel intimidated by class discussions, you can often over-come your fears by preparing well beforehand. Actively read all of the assigned materials before class and try to anticipate some of the discussion topics your teacher might offer. (Many instructors list the class topics for each session in the course syllabus.) Explore your thoughts and reactions to possible topics before class by keep-ing a reading journal or by freewriting after you have finished a portion of the assigned reading. Review your written notes a few minutes before class so that you can share your ideas when discus-sion begins in class.

Working in groups

Group work, or collaborative activity, gives students the chance to learn not only about the assigned course work but also about how to accomplish a task with a variety of team members. An assign-ment for an environmental studies course, for example, might re-quire you to learn about the levels of toxins in the local water sup-ply for the past five years. If the assignment is a group project, it can help build communication and leadership skills. The group members will need to determine what tasks are required to com-plete the assignment, and then they will need to divide those tasks among themselves. They might have to choose leaders to coordinate their efforts. Group work also results in a broader understanding of an issue. The group's final report on the water supply will include contributions from all group members, much more information than a person working alone could gather.

Collaborative work might be difficult to adjust to if you come from a culture that emphasizes individual learning or if your high school teachers did not assign group projects. But be prepared to encounter group work in college: Most instructors feel that it cre-ates an atmosphere in which new ideas can emerge. It also serves as preparation for the professional world, where many jobs require some form of collaborative activity.

Showing respect for your peers

While instructors may encourage you to give your own interpreta-tions of material, to argue a point using information in the text-book, or to apply original thinking to basic concepts, remember that most instructors expect you to respect your peers' ideas. In some cultures where certain types of aggression or exhibitions of author-ity are valued, it may be appropriate to challenge individuals di-rectly by saying that they are wrong or by exposing their personal flaws. In the United States, however, directly challenging a class-mate in this manner is considered rude and inappropriate. If you disagree with someone's opinion, it is often best to state that you disagree with the idea—not with the person who said it—and then to explain your reasons with evidence or examples. Likewise, you should state your own opinions and interpretations in a reasonable tone and expect that other students will want to discuss your ideas or even to politely disagree.

Speaking in English

The ability to speak two or more languages is an asset that you should take pride in, but it is also important to be sensitive to your instructor and classmates in your shared learning environment. Whenever possible, use the language that all participants in the class can understand easily. In US academic settings, this language is English. If you feel the need to discuss or explain an idea in your native language with one of your classmates, be sure to alert your instructor first. If you begin speaking to a friend in a language your instructor does not understand, your instructor may think that you are not paying attention (which is considered rude). Try to think of the class time as a regular opportunity to practice your spoken English.

H1-d Attend classes regularly; arrive a few minutes before each class begins.

Attending class regularly is important for success. Attending class not only will reinforce the material that you have studied on your own but also will provide you with additional opportunities for language practice. You'll have to listen to your instructor and classmates and participate in the discussion. You'll also have to practice reading what your instructor writes on the board (or displays on a screen) and practice writing by taking notes. The classroom experience provides valuable repetition of key ideas and important facts that you will most likely have to recall or apply on tests and assignments.

Your instructors will expect you to arrive at each class a few minutes before the period begins so the discussion can start at the scheduled time. Make a habit of arriving about five minutes before class begins, and use the time to scan your textbook or review your notes from the previous class or from your reading. It is usually much easier to follow the class discussion—especially if your listening skills are not yet fluent—when you review the material first.

H1-e Get extra help when necessary.

If you have questions about the course material or problems with an assignment, do not be afraid to seek extra help. You may get the answers you need from individuals at your school, or you may find useful advice on the Internet.

Writing centers

Most colleges have writing centers (sometimes called *writing labs*) staffed with instructors or experienced students, usually called *writing tutors*. They can assist you at various stages of the writing process. The tutors are typically trained to help in the following areas:

- generating ideas for a writing assignment
- suggesting ways to revise a draft
- identifying areas of a draft that need clarification
- pointing out places in a draft where more development is needed
- diagnosing repetitive mistakes in a paper

It is important to remember that writing center tutors provide guidance, not proofreading services. They are there to help you to grow as a writer—to understand assignments, to learn how to analyze your own writing. They are not there just to "fix" your mistakes. The more prepared you are for your visit and the more willing you are to discuss your problems, the more productive your time with the tutor will be.

Before you visit the writing center, think about specific problems you are having with your assignment. Maybe you don't know what the assignment is asking you to do. Maybe you have a lot of sources but you don't know how to organize them. Maybe you're stuck on one paragraph. Make a list of specific problems and try to organize them into several questions you can ask the tutor. Bring materials related to your assignment to show the tutor as useful background: the assignment itself, an outline if you've done one, notes, drafts, and source materials. Be prepared to discuss your problems actively—to ask the tutor questions and to respond to questions the tutor asks you.

Professor's office hours

In some cultures, visiting a professor's office may be considered disrespectful. However, professors in American colleges usually encourage students to visit them during their office hours. Check your course syllabus to determine when your instructor is available. If you are confused by an assignment or uncertain about any course material, don't be afraid to ask your instructor for help.

Helpful Web sites

Many online writing centers and ESL Web sites provide helpful information and exercises for practice. Here are a few of them.

- *Activities for ESL Students*
  <http://a4esl.org>
  This site, sponsored by the *Internet TESL Journal*, provides quizzes, tests, exercises, and puzzles submitted by ESL teachers.

- *Guide to Grammar and Writing*
  <http://grammar.ccc.commnet.edu/grammar>
  This site includes comprehensive coverage of everything from punctuation to research, using clear examples and detailed explanations. It also includes quizzes on various grammar and writing issues.

- *Randall's ESL Cyber Listening Lab*
  <http://esl-lab.com>
  This site has a wide variety of exercises—from the everyday to the academic—which provide audio files for listening and quizzes to assess comprehension.

- *Ultralingua Online Dictionary*
  <http://ultralingua.com/shared/references/english/index.htm>
  This site is a glossary of grammatical terms. It includes a brief definition and several examples for each term.

- *Voice of America: Wordmaster*
  <http://voanews.com/specialenglish/wordmaster/index.cfm>
  This news and information site allows users to read along as they listen to audio files of articles about English grammar and usage. The site also includes word games and quizzes.

H2

Strategies for improving your academic English

Few residents of the United States speak academic English in all situations every day. Most of us regularly speak an informal variety: We speak in sentence fragments, we use slang, and we use regional forms. However, we must use academic English when we want to reach broader audiences—particularly in college or business settings.

As you aim to improve your performance in academic English, you might need to broaden the range of strategies you use. You might try a number of reading or listening activities, for example, or make an effort to do more grammar exercises. You may decide to consult a dictionary or a thesaurus more regularly or to keep a vocabulary notebook. Such strategies provide practice that can help you gain familiarity with academic English.

H2-a Engage in intensive and extensive language activities.

Languages—including academic English—are learned through both intensive and extensive practice. Intensive practice involves focusing on a small amount of material with a very high level of attention. Completing grammar exercises, for instance, is an intensive activity. A grammar exercise will help you develop control over a very specific grammatical concept, such as past-tense verbs or the use of commas.

Extensive practice involves absorbing a larger quantity of information, typically over a longer period of time. Extensive practices focus less on individual words or forms and more on general comprehension and fluency—your ability to understand, use, and think in English without translating from your native language. Listening to the radio for general understanding is an extensive practice that can help you develop your speed and your grasp of "natural" English forms in various contexts.

The chart on page H-12 gives some everyday examples of intensive and extensive language activities. (Section H4-b provides a list of writing prompts that can be used for both intensive and extensive practice.)

H2-b Read while listening.

If you learned English informally (through conversation rather than in a classroom) or if your middle school and high school classes did not cover English grammar thoroughly, you may need to pay special attention to the differences between spoken English and academic written English. Writing English requires different skills from those used when speaking English. You need to train your *ears* to know what sounds natural, but you also have to train your *eyes* to know what standard English forms look like.

Sample activities for intensive and extensive language practice

	INTENSIVE	EXTENSIVE
READING	■ reading a textbook chapter for content ■ reading difficult material with unfamiliar vocabulary ■ reading essays to understand different organizational styles or grammatical patterns	■ reading novels or nonfiction books for pleasure ■ reading newspapers or magazines regularly ■ reading Web sites or blogs for entertainment
WRITING	■ writing an essay for class or for a test ■ writing a formal letter, application, or résumé ■ completing grammar exercises that focus on specific grammatical concepts	■ e-mailing friends, chatting online, blogging ■ keeping a journal or diary regularly ■ freewriting or fiction writing for enjoyment
LISTENING	■ listening to take notes or to follow directions (in class) ■ listening to dictation to record text accurately ■ listening for specific words, sounds, or intonations	■ listening to friends talk ■ listening to TV shows or movies to get a general idea ■ listening to the radio
SPEAKING	■ giving a formal speech ■ practicing careful pronunciation ■ emphasizing or focusing on specific grammatical forms (such as the past tense) while speaking	■ having a conversation with English-speaking friends ■ chatting on the phone ■ participating in class discussions

If you speak English well but are having trouble using standard forms or correct English spelling when you write, try reading and listening at the same time. Most libraries carry books on CD or tape, and some libraries even package the paper and audio books together. If you read a book while you listen to the audio version of the book, your brain will begin to connect the visual forms with words you've already heard before. If you purchase a paper copy of the book, you can also underline or highlight new words—or words that look different from how they sound—while you listen. After finishing a few pages or a chapter, stop the tape or CD and review the new forms you've marked. Combined reading and listening practice can help you understand standard English forms and use them in your own writing.

The following Web sites provide text and audio—you can listen to someone speak the words as you read along.

- *American Stories on VOA Special English*
  <http://voanews.com/specialenglish/amer-stories-page.cfm>
  Listen to and read short stories by American authors.

- *VOA Special English News Radio for English Learners*
  <http://voanews.com/specialenglish>
  Listen to current global news (broadcast by the US government) while reading the text.

- *The Poets.org Listening Booth*
  <http://poets.org/audio.php>
  Hear famous poets read their own works as you read along.

- *Global English Salon*
  <http://globalenglishsalon.com>
  Listen to and read short editorials and conversations that focus on business English.

H2-c Use an English-English dictionary or a thesaurus.

Many students who learn English in their home country before coming to the United States use bilingual dictionaries, which list words in English with native-language translations or vice versa. By now, you have probably noticed that some words in these dictionaries do not have appropriate translations for academic work. While the dictionaries can help you understand as you read and may help beginning writers, they are not always the best resource for college writing.

Since you are now a college-level writer, consider investing in an English-English dictionary that is designed for multilingual writers. These dictionaries typically provide not only definitions but also sample sentences for each word. Many of these dictionaries also provide information that is not readily available in dictionaries for native speakers. For example, they usually note whether a noun is count, noncount, or both, and they often provide information about the word's level of formality. The following are some dictionaries and thesauri (books that provide lists of synonyms, words with similar meanings) designed for multilingual writers.

DICTIONARIES

- *Cambridge Advanced Learner's Dictionary*
- *Collin's COBUILD Advanced Learner's English Dictionary*
- *Longman Advanced Dictionary of American English*
- *Oxford ESL Dictionary for Students of American English*
- *Random House Webster's Dictionary of American English: ESL / Learner's Edition*

THESAURI

- *Longman's Language Activator*
- *Webster's New Explorer Thesaurus*

H2-d Become familiar with the Academic Word List.

The Academic Word List, compiled by one linguist, contains almost six hundred of the most frequently used academic words. (The charty on p. H-15 presents the sixty most commonly used words.) Since you will encounter these words regularly both in textbooks and in class, it's a good idea to familiarize yourself with them early in your college experience if you don't know them already.

H2-e Learn how prefixes and suffixes affect a word's meaning.

A prefix is added to the beginning of a word to expand or change the word's core meaning (its *root* or *stem*). The prefix *non-*, for instance, added to the root word *toxic* changes the meaning of the word from "poisonous" to "not poisonous." The chart on page H-16

Academic Word List

analyze	define	indicate	proceed
approach	derive	individual	process
area	distribute	interpret	require
assess	economy	involve	research
assume	environment	issue	respond
authority	establish	labor	role
available	estimate	legal	section
benefit	evident	legislate	sector
concept	export	major	significant
consist	factor	method	similar
constitute	finance	occur	source
context	formula	percent	specific
contract	function	period	structure
create	identify	policy	theory
data	income	principle	vary

Source: Averil Coxhead, "A New Academic Word List," *TESOL Quarterly* 34 (2000): 213–38, app. A, sublist 1. The entire Academic Word List is available at <http://language.massey.ac.nz/staff/awl/headwords.shtml>.

will help you become familiar with some common prefixes, their meanings, and some words in which you might encounter them.

Suffixes are word endings that indicate a word's part of speech (noun, verb, adjective, adverb, and so on). Some languages, such as Chinese and southeastern Asian languages, use word order rather than suffixes to convey a word's grammatical function; pay particular attention to suffixes if your language is one of them.

Consider the English noun *democracy*, for example, which has many related forms: *democrat* (a noun), *democratize* (a verb), *democratic* (an adjective), and *democratically* (an adverb). If you were to switch any of these two words in a sentence, your readers might become confused:

We live in a ~~democratic.~~ democracy.

The chart on page H-17 will help make you more aware of how a word's suffix determines its part of speech. For descriptions of the parts of speech, see B1 in *A Writer's Reference*.

Prefixes and their meanings

PREFIX	BASIC MEANING	EXAMPLES
a-, an-	without, not	apolitical (not political); anaerobic (without oxygen)
ante-	before	antecedent (an element that comes before something); antebellum (before war, particularly the US Civil War)
anti-	against	antibiotic (medicine that works against bacteria); antiwar (against war)
auto-	self	autobiography (biography of oneself); automatic (self-acting)
bi-	two	biannual (occurring every two years); bicultural (being part of two cultures)
co-, col-, com-, con-, cor-	together, with	coincide (happen together); collaborate (work with); commiserate (be unhappy together); congregate (assemble together); correspond (communicate with)
dis-	opposite, not	disagree (not agree); disappear (opposite of appear)
ex-	out, former	exclude (keep out); ex-president (former president)
il-, im-, in-, ir-	not	illegal (not legal); impatient (not patient); incompatible (not compatible); irresponsible (not responsible)
inter-	between	international (between countries)
intra-, intro-	within, inward	intracultural (within one culture); introspective (reflecting, looking within oneself)
intro-	in, into	introduce (bring in)
mis-	wrong, bad	mislead (lead someone in the wrong direction); misuse (use wrongly)
mono-	single, only	monopoly (control by one person or group); monotheism (belief in one God)
non-	not, without	nonverbal (without speech); nontraditional (not traditional)
omni-	all	omniscient (all-knowing); omnivorous (eating all foods)
pan-	all	panacea (cure for all diseases); pantheon (temple of all gods)
poly-	many	polygamy (marriage to more than one person at one time); polyglot (a person who speaks many languages)
post-	after, later	postmodern (after the modern period); postpone (put off till later)
pre-	before	prejudice (judgment before sufficient knowledge); prepare (make something ready)

PREFIX	BASIC MEANING	EXAMPLES
pro-	forward	proceed (go forward); progress (move forward)
re-	again	reappear (appear again); redo (do again)
sub-	under	submarine (underwater vessel); subway (underground train)
super-	over, more than, huge	superimpose (place something over another); superpower (huge power)
un-	opposite, not	unimportant (not important)

Suffixes and their parts of speech

NOUNS

-acy	aristocracy, democracy, privacy, supremacy
-ance, -ence	assistance, dependence, independence, science
-ancy, -ency	emergency, delinquency, infancy, vacancy
-dom	boredom, freedom, kingdom, wisdom
-er, -or	computer, stapler, writer, counselor
-hood	brotherhood, childhood, motherhood, neighborhood
-ism	Buddhism, communism, journalism, perfectionism
-ist	chemist, dermatologist, pianist, socialist
-ity, -ety, -ty	liberty, unity, society, variety
-ment	enjoyment, environment, government, replacement
-ness	forgetfulness, goodness, happiness, sadness
-ship	courtship, friendship, membership, partnership
-sion, -tion, -ion	admission, immigration, pollution, vacation

VERBS

-ate	anticipate, complicate, cooperate, reiterate
-ify	amplify, mystify, quantify, terrify
-ize	computerize, demonize, maximize, publicize

ADJECTIVES

-able, -ible	drinkable, edible, forgivable, legible
-al	functional, legal, physical, visual
-ent, -ient	obedient, salient, sentient, silent
-ful	beautiful, hopeful, powerful, regretful
-ic	automatic, egocentric, poetic, systematic
-ive	active, extensive, passive, productive
-less	fruitless, harmless, homeless, useless
-ous, -ious	delicious, delirious, gracious, mysterious

ADVERBS

-ly	easily, convincingly, hopefully, quickly

H2-f Keep a vocabulary notebook.

Use a vocabulary notebook to keep track of new words—especially those that you have seen more than one time or that you have seen in a few different places. You can make a vocabulary notebook in a binder with loose-leaf paper (single sheets), in a bound journal, or in a simple composition book. While you are reading for your classes, jot down a few new words in your notebook, along with the sentences in which you found the words. After you finish reading, look up each word in an English-English dictionary (see H2-c). Record the word's definition and part of speech, and scan the dictionary page for related words. If you look up the noun *effect*, for instance, you will find in the same entry or on the same page the verb *effect*, the related adjective *effective*, the noun *effectiveness*, and the adverb *effectively*. Keeping track of related words is an easy way to expand your vocabulary with little effort. See the sample vocabulary notebook entry below.

ON THE WEB > dianahacker.com/writersref
    ESL help > Blank vocabulary notebook pages

H2-g Keep an editing log.

As part of the writing process, you will be reading and rereading your own writing to make sure your ideas are clearly stated and to correct any grammatical errors you may have made. Your editing

SAMPLE VOCABULARY NOTEBOOK ENTRY

Word: *civilized*   **Form:** Noun Verb (Adj.) Adv.
                          Other _____

Meaning: **Related words:**
Sophisticated, developed   *civil (adj.)*
                            civilize (v., transitive)
                            civilian (n., person)
                            civilization (n.)

Sentence: *The Romans believed that the Germanic tribes from the north were not <u>civilized</u>.*

SAMPLE EDITING LOG 1: CHECKLIST

Editing log (1/07-5/07)

Issues	Paper 1	Paper 2	Paper 3	Paper 4	Paper 5
Subject-verb agreement	✓✓✓	✓✓✓	✓	✓	
Verb tense	Past ✓✓✓ Future✓✓	Past ✓✓			Past ✓
Verb form	Be + -ing form ✓✓✓	Be + -ing form ✓			
Passive voice	✓✓	✓✓	✓	✓	✓
Comma splice	✓✓✓✓	✓✓			
Fragment	✓				
Missing article	✓✓✓✓✓✓	✓✓✓✓✓	✓✓✓✓	✓✓✓	✓✓
Wrong article	✓✓✓✓	✓✓	✓✓	✓	
Missing plural form	✓✓✓✓✓	✓✓✓	✓✓✓	✓✓	✓

SAMPLE EDITING LOG 2: CORRECTED SENTENCES

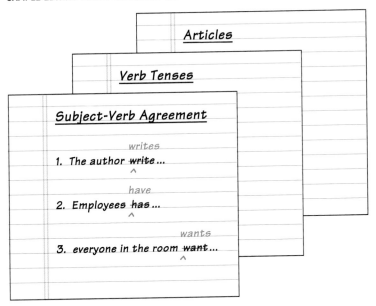

process can be more effective if you keep an editing log or notebook of common errors you make or areas of grammar that give you particular trouble.

When you get a paper back from an instructor, record in your notebook any errors your instructor marked. You might also record any grammatical points that you looked up as you were writing or editing. Your log might be a single chart or checklist, as in sample 1 on page H-19. Or it might consist of sentences with errors and the corrections you make to them, as in sample 2.

Each time you write a new paper, check your editing log during the final stage of your writing process to help you track down and correct your typical mistakes.

H2-h Target specific areas for improvement.

As you master academic English, you will draw on four main skills—reading, writing, speaking, and listening—and you will develop those skills at different rates. At this point, for example, you may have more control over spoken English than formal grammar, or you may have stronger reading skills than listening skills. To increase your chances of success in college, strive to balance out your skills so that you can rely on strengths in not just one or two but all four skill areas.

It may help to work with an instructor or adviser to create a plan that identifies areas for improvement and lists strategies that will help you build your skills.

ON THE WEB > dianahacker.com/writersref
    ESL help > Strategies for improving your academic English

H3

Academic writing and cultural expectations

As you challenge yourself to grow as an academic writer, pay particular attention to your readers' expectations. Some researchers have called English a "writer-responsible" language: The writer (particularly in academic and business settings) is responsible for taking a stand on an issue, stating a clear thesis, and making his or her ideas obvious to readers. Many other languages are "reader-responsible": Writers show many sides to an issue but leave the interpretation entirely to readers.

If you are accustomed to a "reader-responsible" culture, you might find English writing too direct and assertive. Keep in mind, however, that academic readers in the United States will expect you to make a clear point and to convince them with evidence and examples that your ideas are valuable and worthy of their consideration.

H3-a In most academic papers, assert your claim before providing the evidence.

Readers in most academic situations will expect to see your claim — your thesis or main idea — before seeing your evidence or support for the claim (see C2-a and A2-e in *A Writer's Reference*). This is quite different from academic styles in some other languages, which leave the main point open to readers' interpretations or which conclude the essay with the main idea rather than begin with it.

If you're not accustomed to stating a thesis before providing support, you might find it useful to outline your essays carefully before beginning to write. (See also C1-d in *A Writer's Reference* for details on outlining.) Consider using the following steps until you feel comfortable with the academic English style:

1. Outline your ideas in the method with which you are familiar (for example, with the main idea or claim at the end).
2. Read your outline and highlight the main idea and the supporting points in your outline.
3. Rearrange your outline so that the main idea is at the beginning.
4. Use your rearranged outline as a guide when you draft your essay.

Don't be concerned if this planning stage takes time. Remember that the planning stage of writing often takes longer than the writing stage does.

The first sample outline on page H-22 shows several points of support, leading up to the main point in the last sentence. The revised outline shows the preferred organization for an academic English essay, with the main point stated first, followed by the evidence or support.

ORIGINAL: MAIN IDEA LAST

1. In the United States, teenagers often move out of their parents' homes when they turn eighteen.

2. The parents' money is considered only the parents' money--not the money of their adult children.

3. Without their parents' financial help, young American adults often scramble to find affordable housing, transportation, and jobs to pay for all their needs.

4. The fast pace of their daily activities and their lack of job security can be very stressful.

5. So while independence is typically an attractive feature of American culture, it is not always positive.

REVISED: MAIN IDEA FIRST

1. While independence can be an attractive feature of American culture, it can put negative pressure on young people.

2. In the United States, teenagers move out of their parents' homes when they turn eighteen.

3. The parents' money is considered only the parents' money--not the money of their adult children.

4. Without their parents' financial help, young American adults often scramble to find affordable housing, transportation, and jobs to pay for all their needs.

5. The fast pace of their daily activities and their lack of job security can be very stressful.

NOTE: In most cases, paragraphs also should state the main point first, followed by supporting evidence (see C4-a in *A Writer's Reference*). There are, however, some exceptions to this pattern, particularly in the introductory and concluding paragraphs of an essay (see C2-a and C2-c).

H3-b Take a stand on an issue.

As an academic writer, you will need to take a stand, to convince your readers of a particular point of view. Though you must present opposing views fairly, you should clearly state your own view and the evidence to support that view. Your readers will expect you to take one side and to argue reasonably that your view is better or stronger than other views. (See A2 in *A Writer's Reference*.) Here is an example of a paragraph that was revised to stay focused on one side of an issue.

ORIGINAL: DOES NOT TAKE A STAND

Most experts in the United States agree that spanking is not an appropriate form of discipline for children. Some people, however, feel that spanking is acceptable because it can correct behavioral problems such as back-talking. Spanking may lead to larger problems of fear and anxiety. Many children experience no lasting emotional problems from it. Opinions differ on this controversial topic.

REVISED: TAKES A STAND

Most experts in the United States agree that spanking is not an appropriate form of discipline for children. Spanking may temporarily correct a behavioral problem such as back-talking, but it may lead to larger problems such as increased aggression, and it may teach children that violence is an acceptable means of getting what they want ("Guidance" 726). Spanking should be used sparingly as a discipline option.

The original version does not take a stand on the issue of spanking. It only points out that there are differing views on the subject. In the revision, the writer takes a position and uses expert opinion (an article from the journal of the American Academy of Pediatrics) for support.

H3-c Include details that support the main idea directly.

Like busy professionals taking a taxi to the airport, academic readers in the United States prefer that you take the most direct route to your destination, with no detours along the way. They expect your writing to stay focused, each sentence supporting the main point of its paragraph. Your writing should include details, of course, but each detail should directly support your main point. Otherwise readers may think that you have lost your focus or are wasting their time.

If you are accustomed to a writing style that often includes details that are interesting or thought-provoking but not *directly* related to the main idea, you may have a difficult time identifying the difference between necessary and unnecessary details. To recognize what academic English readers consider necessary details, try reading student papers that are considered effective models of academic writing. Often the best way to improve your own writing skills is to review several models.

ON THE WEB > dianahacker.com/writersref
Model papers

In the following paragraph, the writer wanders off the topic (see the highlighted sentence). In the revision, each detail supports the main idea of the paragraph and there are no unnecessary details.

PARAGRAPH WITH UNNECESSARY DETAILS

The gray wolf may not be as harmful to cattle ranching as some believe. Many residents of the western United States are opposed to allowing the gray wolf into western wilderness areas because they believe that the wolves will kill ranchers' herds and ruin their businesses. However, in the last few years, very few cows have been killed by wolves, while thousands of cows have been killed by lightning, storms, and other animals, including coyotes. Although the coyote is related to the wolf and inhabits the same areas, it is lighter in color and smaller in size. While wolves may cause some economic losses, to say that wolves alone will ruin the ranching business overstates the animals' actual impact.

FOCUSED PARAGRAPH

The gray wolf may not be as harmful to cattle ranching as some believe. Many residents of the western United States are opposed to allowing the gray wolf into western wilderness areas because they believe that the wolves will kill ranchers' herds and ruin their businesses. However, in the last few years, very few cows have been killed by wolves, while thousands of cows have been killed by lightning, storms, and other animals, including coyotes. While wolves may cause some economic losses, to say that wolves alone will ruin the ranching business overstates the animals' actual impact.

H3-d Learn to recognize intellectual property and avoid accidental plagiarism.

In some cultures, copying and memorizing texts is a highly valued activity. Using the exact words of scholars in your own writing can be a way of honoring what those scholars have said. In the United States, however, the exact language, images, and original ideas contained in any published work are considered *intellectual property*, which is protected as if it were physical property.

In an academic paper, you are expected to incorporate information and ideas from your sources into your writing. That source material is the intellectual property of its author or publisher, and you must acknowledge your use of that property by following standard academic practices, referred to as *citing your sources* (see R3-c and MLA-2, APA-2, and CMS-2 in *A Writer's Reference*). Even if you do not intend to cheat or steal, you commit a type of theft known as *plagiarism* if you do not properly cite your sources.

Recognizing intellectual property

Recognizing intellectual property can be difficult if you are still becoming accustomed to using the English language. The chart on page H-26 can help you determine whether an idea you have included in your paper is someone else's intellectual property. If you encounter an idea that you think might be intellectual property but is not mentioned in the chart, take a draft of your paper to your instructor or your school's writing center. It is important that you catch cases of accidental plagiarism before you turn in your work.

Avoiding plagiarism by integrating and citing sources

When you use another writer's words or ideas, you must treat that material according to standard academic conventions in the text of your paper, a process called *integrating sources*. The chart on page H-28 will help you determine how to integrate and cite your sources to avoid plagiarism. The examples in the chart are given in MLA style. For more on integrating and citing sources in MLA style, see MLA-2 and MLA-3 in *A Writer's Reference*. For information on APA and CMS styles, see APA-2 and APA-3 and CMS-2 and CMS-3, respectively.

You also must provide a list of your sources at the end of your paper (the list is called Works Cited in MLA, References in APA, and Bibliography in CMS). For details, see MLA-4, APA-4, and CMS-4.

Recognizing intellectual property

Intellectual property

The first column shows the types of information that are considered intellectual property. The second column gives an example from a student essay using and citing a source with the MLA style of documentation (used in English and some humanities). See MLA-4 in *A Writer's Reference* for complete details about citing sources in the text of your paper and in the list of works cited at the end. See APA-4 for details about citation in the social sciences, and see CMS-4 for details about citation in history and other humanities.

TYPE OF INFORMATION	EXAMPLES WITH APPROPRIATE CITATIONS
Any *exact* words from a published source (even if the source provides a fact)	**IN-TEXT CITATION** Luis N. Rivera writes, "Five hundred years ago, thanks to the nautical audacity and cosmographical ignorance of an Italian mariner . . . the Atlantic Ocean ceased to be a divider and became the waterway connection between Europe, Africa, and the Americas" (270). **WORKS CITED ENTRY** Rivera, Luis N. A Violent Evangelism. Louisville: Westminster, 1992.
Any original ideas from a published source— even if you've paraphrased the source (written the information in your own words)	**IN-TEXT CITATION** Historian Paul Gordon Lauren shows that even though the First World War did not seem to be about race at first, a number of racial issues had surfaced by the time the war ended in 1918 (75). **WORKS CITED ENTRY** Lauren, Paul Gordon. Power and Prejudice. 2nd ed. Boulder: Westview, 1996.
Results of a study	**IN-TEXT CITATION** One study showed that cutting down trees that have been burned in forest fires prevents new trees from growing in the area (Donato et al. 352). **WORKS CITED ENTRY** Donato, D. C., et al. "Post-Wildfire Logging Hinders Regeneration and Increases Fire Risk." Science 311 (2006): 352.

Statistics

IN-TEXT CITATION
Gore writes, "In 1988, the EPA reported that the ground water in thirty-two states was contaminated with seventy-four different agricultural chemicals, including one, herbicide atrazine, that is classified as a potential human carcinogen" (xxii-xxiii).

WORKS CITED ENTRY
Gore, Al. Introduction. Silent Spring. By Rachel Carson. Boston: Houghton, 1994. xv-xxvi.

Theories

IN-TEXT CITATION
While many linguists have argued that language is a "cultural invention," Steven Pinker claims that language is an "instinct"; he writes that it is "not a cultural artifact" but "a distinct piece of the biological makeup of our brains" (4).

WORKS CITED ENTRY
Pinker, Steven. The Language Instinct. New York: Perennial, 2000.

Not intellectual property

The first column shows the types of information that are *not* considered intellectual property and that may be used in a paper without citing a source. The second column gives examples of each type.

TYPE OF INFORMATION	EXAMPLES
Well-known historical, scientific, or cultural facts	Christopher Columbus sailed across the Atlantic Ocean in 1492.
	World War I ended in 1918.
	Forest fires are sometimes caused by lightning.
	Rachel Carson wrote Silent Spring.
Broad, general observations	Many languages are spoken in the United States.
	Some students tend to have more motivation than others.
	Many US residents own cars and computers.

NOTE: For types of information not on this list, check with your instructor or your school's writing center to determine whether you need to cite the source. When in doubt, you are always safe to cite the source.

Integrating and citing sources to avoid plagiarism

SOURCE TEXT

Our language is constantly changing. Like the Mississippi, it keeps forging new channels and abandoning old ones, picking up debris, depositing unwanted silt, and frequently bursting its banks. In every generation, there are people who deplore changes in the language and many who wish to stop the flow. But if our language stopped changing it would mean that American society had ceased to be dynamic, innovative, pulsing with life—that the river had frozen up.

—Robert MacNeil and William Cran,
Do You Speak American?, p. 1

NOTE: The examples in this chart follow MLA style (see MLA-4 in *A Writer's Reference*). For information on APA and CMS styles, see APA-4 and CMS-4, respectively.

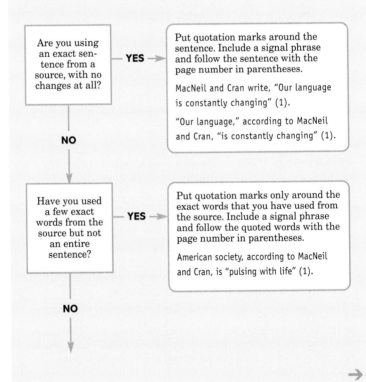

Are you using an exact sentence from a source, with no changes at all? — **YES** →

Put quotation marks around the sentence. Include a signal phrase and follow the sentence with the page number in parentheses.

MacNeil and Cran write, "Our language is constantly changing" (1).

"Our language," according to MacNeil and Cran, "is constantly changing" (1).

NO

Have you used a few exact words from the source but not an entire sentence? — **YES** →

Put quotation marks only around the exact words that you have used from the source. Include a signal phrase and follow the quoted words with the page number in parentheses.

American society, according to MacNeil and Cran, is "pulsing with life" (1).

NO

Are you using some words from the source but changing a few word forms (*I* to *she*, *walk* to *walked*) or adding words to clarify and make the quotation flow with your own text? — **YES** →

Put quotation marks around the quoted words, and put brackets around the changes you have introduced. Include a signal phrase and follow the quotation with the page number in parentheses.

MacNeil and Cran compare the English language to the Mississippi River, which "forg[es] new channels and abandon[s] old ones" (1).

MacNeil and Cran write, "In every generation, there are people who deplore changes in the [English] language and many who wish to stop the flow" (1).

NO

Have you paraphrased or summarized the source, using the author's ideas but not any of the author's exact words? — **YES** →

Introduce the ideas with a signal phrase and put the page number at the end of your sentence. Do not use quotation marks. (See MLA-2c, APA-2c, and CMS-2c.)

MacNeil and Cran argue that changes in the English language are natural and that they represent cultural progress (1).

NO

Have you used the source's sentence structure but substituted a few synonyms for the author's words? — **YES** →

STOP. This is a form of plagiarism even if you use a signal phrase and a page number. Change your sentence by using one of the techniques given in this chart or in MLA-3, APA-3, or CMS-3.

PLAGIARIZED

MacNeil and Cran claim that, like a river, English creates new waterways and discards old ones.

INTEGRATED AND CITED CORRECTLY

MacNeil and Cran claim, "Like the Mississippi, [English] keeps forging new channels and abandoning old ones" (1).

H3-e Sample student essay

The following brief argument paper was written by Amy Zhang, a student in a composition class. The first version (pp. H-30 to H-32) shows Zhang's initial draft with her instructor's comments. The second version (pp. H-33 to H-36) is Zhang's final draft.

ROUGH DRAFT, WITH INSTRUCTOR'S COMMENTS

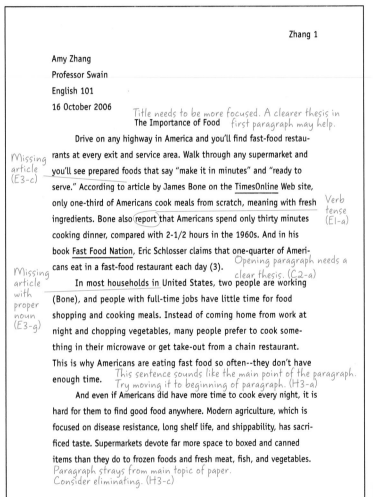

Zhang 1

Amy Zhang

Professor Swain

English 101

16 October 2006

The Importance of Food   *Title needs to be more focused. A clearer thesis in first paragraph may help.*

  Drive on any highway in America and you'll find fast-food restau-

Missing article (E3-c)   rants at every exit and service area. Walk through any supermarket and you'll see prepared foods that say "make it in minutes" and "ready to serve." According to article by James Bone on the TimesOnline Web site, only one-third of Americans cook meals from scratch, meaning with fresh   *Verb tense (E1-a)* ingredients. Bone also report that Americans spend only thirty minutes cooking dinner, compared with 2-1/2 hours in the 1960s. And in his book Fast Food Nation, Eric Schlosser claims that one-quarter of Ameri-   *Opening paragraph needs a clear thesis. (C2-a)* cans eat in a fast-food restaurant each day (3).

Missing article with proper noun (E3-g)   In most households in United States, two people are working (Bone), and people with full-time jobs have little time for food shopping and cooking meals. Instead of coming home from work at night and chopping vegetables, many people prefer to cook something in their microwave or get take-out from a chain restaurant. This is why Americans are eating fast food so often--they don't have enough time.   *This sentence sounds like the main point of the paragraph. Try moving it to beginning of paragraph. (H3-a)*

  And even if Americans did have more time to cook every night, it is hard for them to find good food anywhere. Modern agriculture, which is focused on disease resistance, long shelf life, and shippability, has sacri-ficed taste. Supermarkets devote far more space to boxed and canned items than they do to frozen foods and fresh meat, fish, and vegetables.   *Paragraph strays from main topic of paper. Consider eliminating. (H3-c)*

Zhang 2

Another reason that mealtime has become so short is that many younger adults grew up in what one might call a fast-food culture. In the past thirty years, inventions such as cell phone, fax machine, and computer have increased the pace of life. At the same time, microwave oven, drive-through restaurant, and TV dinner have changed the way Americans eat. Many people now prefer to eat quickly, even in their cars or in front of the television, instead of take time to cook a meal and sit at the table. In this culture of instant gratification, people don't think food is important enough to spend much time on.

Noun ("-ing" form) after preposition (E5-b)

Plural nouns for general categories (E3-f)

Americans' obsession with fast food has caused the quality of their lives to go down. First of all, their health is suffering. As most people know, fast foods and frozen meals generally less healthy than foods made from scratch. They have lots of preservatives, fat, sugar, and salt to hide the fact that they are not fresh. If people will not eat fresh foods that provide necessary vitamins and minerals, they may become tired and sick, and they may miss out on opportunities to enjoy their lives.

Missing linking verb (E2-a)

Possible plagiarism. Check the source. If the words are directly from the source, use quotation marks. (H3-d)

No "will" in "if" clause (E1-e)

Another serious health concern is obesity. Is an obesity epidemic in America today, especially with young people, that is related to the way people are eating. According to Schlosser, "the rate of obesity among American children is twice as high as it was in the late 1970s" (240). Obesity can lead to many health problems, including diabetes, heart disease, and cancer. The United States Department of Health and Human Services notes that deaths due to poor diet and physical inactivity increased 33 percent over the past decade and may soon overtake tobacco as the leading cause of death in this country. Certainly, if fast food causes people to become obese, and then obesity causes them to get sick or die, fast food cannot be consider an "improvement" in Americans' lives.

Place-holder "There" missing (E2-b)

End of essay needs development. Readers expect a strong ending with a clear point, not an open-ended statement.

Passive verb form (E1-c)

The economy causes most people to work long hours, and that leaves little time for cooking, so it is understandable that people rely so much on fast food. It makes life much easier and allows parents to get other things done around the house and spend time with their children. If they try hard enough, people can even find healthy options at fast-food restaurants, such as salads and bottled water instead of fries and sodas. So maybe fast food isn't always a bad thing.

This paragraph may confuse readers—it takes the opposite view of your main point. Revise to acknowledge opposing view without contradicting your main point. (H3-b)

Zhang 3

Works Cited

For an online source, include the URL in your citation.

Bone, James. "Good Home Cooking--Right off the Assembly Line." *TimesOnline* 27 Mar. 2006. 9 Oct. 2006.

Schlosser, Eric. Fast Food Nation: The Dark Side of the All-American Meal. Boston: Houghton, 2001.

United States. Dept. of Health and Human Services. "Citing 'Dangerous Increase' in Deaths, HHS Launches New Strategies against Overweight Epidemic." 9 Mar. 2004. 9 Oct. 2006 <http://www.hhs.gov/news/press/2004pres/20040309.html>.

FINAL DRAFT

Zhang 1

Amy Zhang

Professor Swain

English 101

23 October 2006

Slow Down and Eat Better

Drive on any highway in America and you'll find fast-food restaurants at every exit and service area. Walk through any supermarket and
you'll see prepared foods that say "make it in minutes" and "ready to
serve." According to an article by James Bone on the TimesOnline Web
site, only one-third of Americans cook meals from scratch, meaning with
fresh ingredients. Bone also reports that Americans spend only thirty
minutes cooking dinner, compared with 2-1/2 hours in the 1960s. And in
his book Fast Food Nation, Eric Schlosser claims that one-quarter of
Americans eat in a fast-food restaurant each day (3). Why are Americans
eating so much fast food? The answer is simple: they are willing to trade
quality for speed. While Americans may be attracted to food that is fast
and easy, they are missing some important benefits of slowing down. In
fact, Americans' obsession with fast food is hurting not only their health
but also the quality of their lives.

The main reason that Americans are getting take-out food and
cooking prepared meals is obvious: they don't have enough time. In
more than two-thirds of households in America, two people are working
(Bone). People with demanding work schedules have little time for food
shopping and cooking.

Another reason that mealtime has become so short is that many
younger adults grew up in what one might call a fast-food culture. In the
past fifty years, inventions such as televisions, fax machines, and computers have increased the pace of life. At the same time, microwave
ovens, drive-through restaurants, and TV dinners have changed the way
Americans eat. Many people now prefer to eat quickly, even in their cars
or in front of the television, instead of taking time to cook a meal and
sit at the table. In this culture of instant gratification, people don't
think food is important enough to spend much time on.

Even though Americans think that they are saving time and im-

Marginal annotations:

Zhang opens
with general
observations to
attract readers'
interest.

Zhang states a
clear thesis at
the end of
the opening
paragraph.

Clear topic
sentence helps
guide readers.

Effective transition links
ideas in this paragraph
to those in the previous
paragraph.

Marginal annotations indicate MLA-style formatting **and** effective writing.

Zhang 2

proving their lives by eating precooked and prepackaged food, their obsession with fast food is causing the quality of their lives to go down. First, their health is suffering. As most people know, fast foods and frozen meals are generally less healthy than foods made from scratch. They have lots of preservatives, fat, sugar, and salt to hide the fact that they are not fresh. When people do not eat fresh foods that provide necessary vitamins and minerals, they may become tired and sick, and they will miss out on opportunities to enjoy their lives.

Another serious health concern is obesity. There is an obesity epidemic in America today, especially with young people, that is related to the way people are eating. According to Schlosser, "the rate of obesity among American children is twice as high as it was in the late 1970s" (240). Obesity can lead to many health problems, including diabetes, heart disease, and cancer. The United States Department of Health and Human Services notes that "deaths due to poor diet and physical inactivity increased 33 percent" over the past decade and it cites a study concluding that "poor diet and physical inactivity may soon overtake tobacco as the leading cause of death" in this country. Certainly, if fast food causes people to become obese, and then obesity causes them to get sick or die, fast food cannot be considered an "improvement" in Americans' lives.

In addition to making health problems, fast food hurts people's relationships with their friends and families. In an online interview, John Robbins, author of Diet for a New America and The Food Revolution, comments on the importance of mealtime:

> Throughout history, eating has been a way of bringing people together. It's how parents stay in touch with what's going on in their kids' lives. When people break bread together, it's an act of peacemaking, an act of good will. . . . Dining together can be a deep biological and sacred experience. When we eat, we are connected to all of life. It's a phenomenon found in every culture in the world, except ours. I see the McDonaldization of our food supply as the annihilation of our true relationship to life.

Zhang uses a signal phrase and a parenthetical citation for facts that support her thesis.

No page number is available for this online source.

A long quotation (more than four lines) is indented; quotation marks are omitted. An ellipsis mark indicates that some words from the source have been left out.

Zhang 3

While most Americans will not be able to cook full, fresh meals every day, they can begin to improve the quality of their lives by buying fresh foods when there is an option and by cooking fresh food at least occasionally. For example, people can shop at the farmers' market for fresh local produce instead of buying canned or frozen products. They not only will have a chance to buy foods with more nutrients but also will have the chance to get to know people in their community.

Also, if people slow down to make food with their friends or family, they can enjoy the benefits of good nutrition while they are building stronger relationships. On its Web site, Slow Food, which describes itself as "an international organization whose aim is to protect the pleasures of the table from the homogenization of modern fast food and life," encourages people to make pasta from scratch once in a while. Friends and family can cook meals together so one person isn't doing all the work. And people can try to cook old family recipes the way their grandparents did.

Even though Americans may think they are saving time and improving their lives by eating fast food, they will actually have healthier and more enjoyable lives if they change the way they cook and eat. Making dinner from scratch is much healthier than getting burgers and fries from a fast-food restaurant. And people get more than just a full stomach--they get more time with family and friends and a good feeling from creating something healthy.

Zhang acknowledges the limitations of her argument while maintaining her position.

Zhang offers readers some suggestions for better eating.

Conclusion reminds readers of the essay's main point.

Zhang 4

The works cited
list provides
references for
all the sources
Zhang uses in
her paper.

Works Cited

Bone, James. "Good Home Cooking--Right off the Assembly
    Line." TimesOnline 27 Mar. 2006. 9 Oct. 2006
    <http://www.timesonline.co.uk/article/
    0,,11069-2105427,00.html>.

Robbins, John. "The Common Ground Interview with John
    Robbins." The Food Revolution. 2002. 18 Oct. 2006
    <http://www.foodrevolution.org/commonground.htm>.

Schlosser, Eric. Fast Food Nation: The Dark Side of the All-American
    Meal. Boston: Houghton, 2001.

Slow Food. Slowfood.com. 18 Oct. 2006 <http://www.slowfood.com>.

United States. Dept. of Health and Human Services. "Citing
    'Dangerous Increase' in Deaths, HHS Launches New Strategies
    against Overweight Epidemic." 9 Mar. 2004. 9 Oct. 2006
    <http://www.hhs.gov/news/press/2004pres/20040309.html>.

H4

Practice exercises

This section includes both intensive and extensive grammar and writing exercises. The intensive activities will help you focus on specific areas of grammar such as verb tense and use of articles. The extensive activities will help build your English fluency — your ability to use English quickly and easily without hesitating or translating from your native language.

H4-a Intensive grammar exercises

The intensive exercises in this section can help you improve your awareness and proper use of the English grammar covered in the tabbed section E of *A Writer's Reference*, Sixth Edition. These exercises will also help you strengthen your editing skills when you edit your own writing in English. (For help building fluency rather than grammar and editing skills, see the extensive writing practices in H4-b, starting on p. H-46.) Answers to all the exercises appear at the end of this section.

EXERCISE H1–1 **Verb forms and tenses** Edit the following sentences to correct errors in verb forms and verb tenses. If a sentence is correct, write "correct" after it. (For help, see E1-a in *A Writer's Reference*. You may need to refer to G2-a for help with irregular verbs.) Example:

> *moved*
> I ~~move~~ to Florida three years ago.
> ^

1. When she got home, Mina realize that she had forgotten to buy staples while she was out.
2. Martin Luther King Jr., the famous orator and civil rights activist, deliver his famous "I Have a Dream" speech on August 28, 1963.
3. David was playing soccer for the last fifteen years.
4. Mangoes, which originally grew only in Asia, now grew in the Eastern and Western Hemispheres.
5. Anders has already read *To Kill a Mockingbird* three times.
6. Alexander Fleming discovered penicillin while he was worked at a hospital in London.
7. Moving to a new country often cause people to change their lifestyles.

8. Although anthropologists do not know exactly when the first calendar was invented, they have evidence that solar calendars are existing for at least six thousand years.

9. When they moved here, my husband and his brother open a small restaurant.

10. Professors in the United States often requiring their students to work in groups.

EXERCISE H1–2 Verb forms and tenses Edit the following sentences to correct errors in verb forms and verb tenses. If a sentence is correct, write "correct" after it. (For help, see E1-a in *A Writer's Reference*. You may need to refer to G2-a for help with irregular verbs.) Example:

> *loved*
> Amy ~~was loving~~ Woody Guthrie's songs when she was a child.
> ^

1. Woody Guthrie was being one of the best-known American folk singer–activists.

2. Born in 1912, Guthrie spend his early life surrounded by music in his small hometown of Okema, Oklahoma.

3. Before his twentieth birthday, he was moving to Texas, where he attempted to start a career as a musician.

4. While Guthrie was in Texas, a decade-long period of dust storms began sweeping through the central United States.

5. Guthrie and his family move west to California along with many other Texans and Oklahomans who found employment as farmworkers.

6. While he was traveled, he was exposed to the harsh treatment the migrant workers received.

7. By the time Guthrie arrive in California, he had developed a deep sense of resentment for the rich owners who exploited poor farmworkers.

8. He begin writing and singing more songs about workers' rights and political protest, including his most famous song, "This Land Is Your Land."

9. He continued writing songs with a political edge for the rest of his life and motivate many other popular folk and rock singers to carry on his legacy.

10. Today, Guthrie's music live on in younger generations of people who feel inspired by his words.

EXERCISE H1–3 Verb forms and tenses Edit the following paragraph to correct errors in verb forms and verb tenses. There are ten errors. (For help, see E1-a in *A Writer's Reference*. You may need to refer to G2-a for help with irregular verbs.)

> Since I have been only eight years old, I have dream of becoming a professional baseball player. Trying to develop the skill of a profes-

sional player has been both physically and mentally challenging. One of the greatest difficulties that I have face is fear. When I become the pitcher on my high school team, I was under a lot of pressure; my teammates, coach, and all the students at my school depended on me to win games. The thought of losing terrify me. Before a few games in my first season, I have put so much pressure on myself to win and to be a good leader that I freezed. In time, though, I learn to manage my stress and to make the fear work in my favor. By the time I was a senior, I was transforming the fear into energy that helped me stay alert and quick. Although I know I will have many more challenges to face in pursuit of my dream, I am confident that someday I succeed.

EXERCISE H1–4 **Modal verbs** In the following dialogue, choose the correct modal verb or verb phrase in parentheses. (For help, see E1-b in *A Writer's Reference*.)

HALEY: Good morning, Professor Weil. (May / Would) I ask you for some advice about my course work?

PROFESSOR WEIL: Sure, Haley. What (can / will) I help you with?

H: I (will / would) like to change my major. I'm enrolled as a biology major now, but I am not as interested in science as I thought I (will be / would be).

P: I see. What major are you thinking of?

H: Since I am very good at math, I think I would like to be a business major.

P: That's a good idea, but (can / may) you do well in classes that don't involve math?

H: I think so. Which courses (must I to take / must I take) besides math?

P: You will have to take some communications and writing courses.

H: I (can do / can to do) that. I will go to the registrar and select my courses. Thank you, Professor Weil!

EXERCISE H1–5 **Passive verb forms** Edit the following paragraph to correct errors in passive verb forms. There are ten errors. (For help, see E1-c in *A Writer's Reference*. You may need to refer to G2-a for help with irregular verbs.)

Most people think of a trash bin as a finishing point rather than a starting point. However, a recycling bin can be the start of a new life for a piece of paper. After paper is put into an office bin, it is ship to a recycling center, where it is sorting into types: office paper, cardboard, or colored paper. After it is sorted, it is sended to a paper mill, where it is chop into dry pulp. The pulp is then mixed with water to form a wet substance called "slurry." The slurry is sent through a screen, which removes little bits of excess materials such as glue, plastic, or staples. After it goes through the screen, the slurry is rinse again to remove inks. Then the slurry goes through a machine that makes the paper fibers grow bigger. Next the slurry is water down and place on a screen, where it is press into long, thin sheets and dried on heated rollers. The dried sheets are rolling up and shipped off to other companies where they are process and made into the paper products we use every day.

EXERCISE H1–6 **Negative verb forms** Edit the following sentences to correct errors in the use of negative verb forms. (For help, see E1-d in *A Writer's Reference*.) Example:

>   *not*
> **Even though I was tired, I could ~~no~~ sleep.**
>   ^

1. If the governor is reelected, she not will raise the income tax.
2. I could no park my car next to the library because all of the spaces were taken.
3. Sadly, a cure for AIDS has no been found yet.
4. The book that we have to buy for our ecology class not is very expensive.
5. I tried to make a photocopy, but the copier was no functioning properly.
6. Sunnie did not came with us to the football game last Saturday.
7. Although Omar not like to drive in traffic, he likes to race cars on the weekends.
8. Snow leopards no are extinct, but they are on the endangered species list.
9. Kim could not find no lychees at the supermarket because they are not very common in the United States.
10. I was disappointed that I didn't knew the woman's name.

EXERCISE H1–7 **Conditional sentences** Edit the following conditional sentences to correct any problems with verbs. If a sentence is correct, write "correct" after it. (For help, see E1-e in *A Writer's Reference*.) Example:

> **If the Chargers ~~will~~ win the game tonight, they will move on to the**
>
> **district finals.**

1. If Deborah arrived earlier, she might have found a better parking space.
2. I'll buy you a soda if you will come to the cafeteria with me.
3. The city will not increase the sales tax unless the citizens vote in favor of the new tax law.

4. Most scientists think that if the world does not reduce carbon dioxide emissions, global warming will occur.
5. If I was a famous actor, I would move to Bel Aire and buy a mansion.
6. If you will use aloe on a burn, you can reduce the chances of developing a scar.
7. You would have to pay late charges if you don't return your rental video on time.
8. Unless the Security Council will agree, the UN will not send peace-keeping troops to war-torn countries.
9. When Rosa left for college every September, she closes her summer gardening business.
10. If Kevin would be here with us today, he would be enjoying himself.

EXERCISE H1–8 **Verbs followed by gerunds or infinitives**   Edit the following paragraph to correct problems with verbs followed by gerunds or infinitives. There are eight errors. (For help, see E1-f in *A Writer's Reference*.)

When I was young, my family and I went on an annual camping trip in the canyons of the southwestern United States. One summer, I convinced my family taking a tour of several canyons: the Grand Canyon, Bryce Canyon, and Canyonlands National Park. I remember to be amazed at each stop along the way. I loved looking up at the twisting towers of red rock, wondering how they had avoided to fall down in the last several thousand years. (I can recall to think that some might fall over if someone in the canyon sneezed a little too hard.) Even at that young age, I sensed the power of these remarkable landmarks and understood the spell that they had held over so many generations of residents and visitors. In my heart, I promised going back to the canyons every year. Though I never planned giving up my promise, the commitments of adulthood have prevented me from taking annual trips back to the canyons. I miss to visit the red rocks on a regular basis, but I still manage going back to the Southwest every few years. Breathing in the high desert air while gazing up at the red rock towers never ceases to refresh and rejuvenate me.

EXERCISE H2–1 **Linking verbs**   Add linking verbs where necessary in the following paragraphs. There are seven missing verbs. (For help, see E2-a in *A Writer's Reference*.)

When I only a boy, I was known for being lazy. Every time my parents asked me to clean my room or study for my classes, I always found an excuse to avoid the work. Sometimes I would pretend that I too tired; other times I would pretend that I had simply forgotten their request. Most of the time, however, I would try to approach the situation logically, arguing that since my older brother stronger and had more life experience, he should be responsible for most of the household chores.

However, when I started college, my life changed. I realized that in order to become the successful college student I wanted to be, I would have to take control of my life, change my bad habits, and act responsibly. Now I no longer the lazy boy my parents knew when I was a child. I wake up early, exercise, and go to school. I never late to my classes, and I always turn my assignments in on time. Although I still far from perfect, I try to help others whenever I can. Whenever someone needs me, particularly at school or at home, I never try to hide as I did when I just a boy.

EXERCISE H2–2 Missing subjects   Five sentences in the following paragraph are missing subjects. Add them where they are needed. (For help, see E2-b in *A Writer's Reference.*)

Is common to think that being the oldest child in a family has the most privileges. However, are several advantages to being the youngest child, too. First, is important to note that by the time the youngest child is born, the parents have already had experience as parents. They know how to care for a newborn, and they tend to be more relaxed. Second, the youngest child has the opportunity to learn how to stay out of trouble. If the older children get into trouble, is easy for the youngest child to learn from the older children's mistakes. A third advantage of being the youngest child is that in many cases, the youngest gets extra attention from the older siblings. Is not unusual to see older siblings taking care of their younger siblings at school or protecting them from bullies.

EXERCISE H2–3 Unnecessary words   Edit the following sentences by deleting unnecessary words. (In some cases, more than one correction is possible.) If a sentence is correct, write "correct" after it. (For help, see E2-c, E2-d, and E2-e in *A Writer's Reference.*) Example:

>   *the food*
> ~~The food~~ I ate ~~it~~ very quickly.
>   ^

1. Coming to the United States it changed more than my address. It changed the direction of my career.
2. My life here in Gainesville it's different from the life that I lived in Bolivia.
3. When I was in Bolivia, I was a chef.
4. I attended a culinary school, which it was the best in Bolivia, and I was offered the chance to study for a short time in the United States.
5. When I first came, I met other students who they had different majors.
6. I learned many things from my roommate, Jin, who was a business major.
7. Jin he helped me realize the importance of having business experience.

8. I learned that although I enjoyed being a chef, but I didn't want to be a chef without business knowledge.
9. I decided to stay a bit longer in the United States, where I could study international business here.
10. Someday I will combine both interests and start my own chain of specialized restaurants, which I hope to build them all over the world.

EXERCISE H2–4 **Placement of adverbs**   Edit the following sentences to put adverbs in their proper place. If a sentence is correct, write "correct" after it. (For help, see E2-f in *A Writer's Reference*.) Example:

My roommate likes to play ~~very loudly~~ the drums. *very loudly.*

1. I have never seen a player hit so hard a baseball.
2. Sue cooked very slowly the soup so that the vegetables would be tender.
3. Regular study habits can help students complete all their assignments efficiently.
4. After I finished my workout, I stretched carefully my tender muscles.
5. The professor seemed surprised that the class finished so quickly the exam.
6. After I read the user manual, I installed easily the new hard drive.
7. My mother always told me that she loved equally all her children.
8. As soon as I got the keys to my new car, I drove everywhere my friends.
9. The government found out that the company manufactured illegally the drug.
10. Although she had a difficult time in the past, this year she won very easily the gold medal in cross-country skiing.

EXERCISE H3–1 **Articles**   Edit the following sentences to correct errors in the use of articles (*a, an, the*). (For help, see E3 in *A Writer's Reference*.) Example:

Holly recently bought *a* new sound system for her car.

1. When people move to new place, they definitely have to go through some changes.
2. Temperature dropped twenty degrees in a half hour yesterday.
3. Some governments help couples who have more than two children by giving them the health insurance.
4. When people are too busy, they sometimes forget to eat the dinner.
5. Students are exposed to the new experiences when they move to a new country.
6. I chose to have small family so that I could give my children sufficient attention.

7. Marco became more familiar with the nature when he studied in the rain forests of Brazil.
8. Let me give you an advice: Buy your books early.
9. A common effect of culture shock is the loneliness.
10. Because our school doesn't allow cars within the campus gates, I walk from my parking spot to place where I need to go.

EXERCISE H3–2 Articles Edit the following paragraph to correct errors in the use of articles (*a, an, the*). There are ten errors. (For help, see E3 in *A Writer's Reference.*)

Heifer International is nonprofit organization that provides the animals to poor farmers and families around world. Organization was started in 1940s by man named Dan West, relief worker who gave people food during times of crisis. West realized that he could help people even more by giving them animals that could supply food— such as the milk and cheese— for several years. He wanted to help people for the long term, and he wanted to help them have the pride in themselves. Now Heifer serves communities in more than one hundred countries around world. Its mission is to help families by providing some animals that the families can use to support themselves or start small businesses.

EXERCISE H3–3 Articles Edit the following sentences to correct errors in the use of articles (*a, an, the*). In some cases, more than one revision is possible. (For help, see E3 in *A Writer's Reference.*)

A greeting is the way that the person addresses or acknowledges another person when the two meet. Types of greetings vary in different countries. People in the Japan often prefer to greet nonverbally, with bow and a smile. African would likely greet fellow African with the handshake. For the Maori people of New Zealand, a most common greeting is the *hongi*, which involves rubbing noses. In Poland, kiss on each cheek is customary; but the Dutch custom is to kiss the right cheek, then the left, and then the right again. Traveler to another country would be wise to learn greetings expected by its people.

EXERCISE H4–1 Present and past participles Choose the correct participle in the parentheses in the following sentences. (For help, see E4 in *A Writer's Reference.*) Example:

My (tiring / (tired)) old dog sleeps all day.

1. Charlie thinks I'm (confusing / confused). He says that he doesn't understand me because I talk too fast and never stop to explain my thoughts.

2. My feet still hurt from the long, (tiring / tired) walk we took yesterday.
3. Alex and her boyfriend went to see a really (boring / bored) movie last night.
4. Myrna is always busy. She's a (working / worked) mom with three kids — and she goes to college!
5. Gavin said that Professor Snyder's mythology lecture was (fascinating / fascinated).
6. Is your essay (handwriting / handwritten), or is it (typing / typed)?
7. I will be (satisfying / satisfied) if I can read at least two chapters in my chemistry text over the weekend.
8. This vase is beautiful! Is it (hand-painting / hand-painted)?
9. The commercial claims that this (cleaning / cleaned) product helps kill bacteria.
10. Señora Quiroga put two cups of (peeling / peeled) apples in the bowl.

EXERCISES H5–1 Prepositions showing time and place   Edit the following sentences to correct the use of prepositions. If a sentence is correct, write "correct" after it. (For help, see E5-a in *A Writer's Reference*.) Example:

on
The office will be closed ~~at~~ Memorial Day.
　　　　　　　　　　　　　　　^

1. Does your dance class start in Monday or Wednesday?
2. Fran was working at her desk when the earthquake hit.
3. As soon as Fiona moved into her dorm room, she put a poster of Einstein in the wall for inspiration.
4. My books are a little dusty because they were packed away on the garage for a year.
5. Dr. Horn is taking his students to Ghana for a study trip on early June.
6. My grandmother was born at Los Angeles, but my grandfather was born at Albuquerque.
7. My fraternity brothers like to play loud music at the street in front of our building.
8. My exam begins at two hours, but I'm not nervous at all.
9. Did you read the essay in *The Bedford Reader*, or were you able to find it on the Internet?
10. Bret finished writing his term paper right on midnight.

EXERCISE H5–2 Preposition combinations   Edit the following sentences for errors in preposition combinations (preposition + noun, adjective + preposition, or verb + preposition). If a sentence is correct, write "correct" after it. (For help, see E5-b, E5-c, and E5-d in *A Writer's Reference*.) Example:

about
Sandra has been dreaming ~~with~~ becoming a doctor.
　　　　　　　　　　　　　　^

1. I have trouble concentrating in my homework when my roommate is around.

2. The senator was skilled at delay controversial votes.
3. I'm not worried with our verbs test on Wednesday.
4. While Ellie proofread the group's report, Sam and Tomi worked in the presentation slides.
5. The executives were found guilty of insider trading.
6. The solution consists in sodium and water.
7. I was afraid to board the plane because I'm not accustomed with traveling alone.
8. Shea remained devoted on the teachings of his martial arts master.
9. You can always count with Carole to help out when the office gets busy.
10. Iona wasn't aware of the trouble the manager was experiencing.

H4-b Topics for writing practice

The writing prompts beginning on page H-47 can help you build fluency and confidence in using English grammar in academic situations. Use the prompts in conjunction with the intensive and extensive practice instructions on this page and the next. If you would like to focus on points of grammar, sentence structure, essay development, or editing skills, use the directions for intensive practice. If you would like to develop your fluency—your ability to write in English without translating from your native language—use the directions for extensive practice. Each prompt is accompanied by a suggested writing focus, which can be used with either the intensive or the extensive practice.

Directions for intensive practice (focus on grammar and on writing and editing skills)

1. Write a paragraph or an essay on one of the prompts beginning on page H-47.
2. Edit and revise your work carefully, paying attention to the suggested writing focus (or any other focus your instructor recommends).
3. Take your finished work to your instructor or to the writing center for a conference. If you take your work to the writing center, explain to the tutor that this is a practice exercise and that you would like help with the specific area you focused on.
4. Use your editing log to record any repeated mistakes you've made so that you can be aware of them and try to eliminate them in future writing assignments. (See H2-g for advice about editing logs.)

Directions for extensive practice (focus on fluency and speed)

1. Choose one of the prompts beginning on page H-47 and set aside a specific amount of time to write (fifteen minutes, thirty minutes, or one

hour, for example). Pay special attention to the suggested writing focus in the prompt (or any other focus your instructor recommends).

2. Begin writing and try not to stop until the end of the period you have set. You might find it helpful to set an alarm or a timer.

3. When you are finished, reread your work and highlight the parts of your writing that you like best.

4. If you feel comfortable, read your work to someone else—a roommate, friend, or spouse.

5. Keep your extensive writing in a folder or binder so that you can refer to it as a source of ideas for future writing assignments.

Writing prompts

1. In a paragraph or an essay, discuss the attributes of a person who has had a significant impact on history. *Suggested writing focus:* verb tenses and forms.

2. Write a paragraph or an essay about a time when you were afraid. What did you do? How did you overcome your fear? *Suggested writing focus:* verb tenses and forms.

3. Spend a few minutes reflecting on the last five years of your life. In a paragraph or an essay, describe how you have changed during this time. *Suggested writing focus:* verb tenses and forms.

4. Imagine that you could give advice to any historical figure. To whom would you give advice? What would that advice be? Write a dialogue (a conversation) in which you give this person the advice you think he or she needs. *Suggested writing focus:* modal verbs (for example, "you *could* . . . ," "you *should* . . .").

5. Write a paragraph or an essay that describes your goals in life. Remember to consider not only your educational or career aspirations but your personal and emotional goals as well. *Suggested writing focus:* gerunds and infinitives following verbs (for example, "I would like *to live* . . ." or "I can imagine *working* . . .").

6. Think about some of the English idioms and expressions you know that relate to the concept of time. (*Time is money, Time flies, There's no time like the present, To waste time,* and *To spend time* are just a few.) In a paragraph or an essay, explain what you think these expressions reflect about American culture. (Why, for example, do Americans *not* use the expression *There's no time like the past?*) *Suggested writing focus:* sentence completeness and sentence structure.

7. If you could be invisible for a day, where would you go and what would you do? Write a paragraph or an essay in which you describe your intentions or desires. *Suggested writing focus:* conditional sentences.

8. Visit an art museum or gallery and spend a few minutes looking closely at a piece of art that intrigues you. If that is not convenient, look around your campus for a painting or statue that interests you. Write a paragraph or an essay describing the work of art in detail. *Suggested writing focus:* articles or prepositions.

9. Sit down near a busy place on campus (or any other place you spend much of your time). Take a few minutes to observe the people and things around you. Write a paragraph or an essay describing what you see. *Suggested writing focus:* adjectives and adjective clauses.

10. Skim through the editorials or advice columns of a newspaper or magazine. Choose one that interests you. In a paragraph or a brief essay, write a summary of the article, making sure to include the author's main idea. *Suggested writing focus:* understanding main ideas.

11. In a well-organized essay, discuss the advantages (or disadvantages) of living with a roommate. Include a thesis statement and at least three supporting paragraphs. *Suggested writing focus:* thesis and support.

12. In a well-organized essay, discuss the *negative* impacts of a particular invention that is usually considered positive (such as the cell phone, the computer, or the microwave oven). *Suggested writing focus:* paragraph development.

13. In a well-organized essay, compare your personality to the personality of a close friend. (Who is more introverted, for example? Who takes more risks?) *Suggested writing focus:* using transitions between ideas.

14. Think about a social problem that bothers you or a social issue that you feel strongly about. In a well-organized essay, discuss the problem or issue and explain what should be done to improve the situation. Use information from two or three sources. Document your sources with in-text citations and include a works cited page. *Suggested writing focus:* citing sources in MLA style (see MLA-4 in *A Writer's Reference*).

15. Most colleges in the United States value creative thinking over memorization (see H1-b). In a well-organized essay, compare the negative aspects and positive aspects of these two ways of learning and then explain which one you think is preferable. Ask two friends or classmates what they think. Use their responses and your own reasons as evidence to support your position. Be sure to integrate the words or ideas of others into your essay. *Suggested writing focus:* integrating sources (see MLA-3 in *A Writer's Reference*).

Answers to exercises

Exercise H1–1, page H-37

1. When she got home, Mina realized that she had forgotten to buy staples while she was out.
2. Martin Luther King Jr., the famous orator and civil rights activist, delivered his famous "I Have a Dream" speech on August 28, 1963.
3. David has played [*or* has been playing] soccer for the last fifteen years.
4. Mangoes, which originally grew only in Asia, now grow in the Eastern and Western Hemispheres.
5. Correct
6. Alexander Fleming discovered penicillin while he was working at a hospital in London.
7. Moving to a new country often causes people to change their lifestyles.
8. Although anthropologists do not know exactly when the first calendar was invented, they have evidence that solar calendars have existed for at least six thousand years.
9. When they moved here, my husband and his brother opened a small restaurant.
10. Professors in the United States often require their students to work in groups.

Exercise H1–2, page H-38

1. Woody Guthrie was one of the best-known American folk singer–activists.
2. Born in 1912, Guthrie spent his early life surrounded by music in his small hometown of Okema, Oklahoma.
3. Before his twentieth birthday, he moved to Texas, where he attempted to start a career as a musician.
4. Correct
5. Guthrie and his family moved west to California along with many other Texans and Oklahomans who found employment as farmworkers.
6. While he was traveling, he was exposed to the harsh treatment the migrant workers received.
7. By the time Guthrie arrived in California, he had developed a deep sense of resentment for the rich owners who exploited poor farmworkers.
8. He began writing and singing more songs about workers' rights and political protest, including his most famous song, "This Land Is Your Land."
9. He continued writing songs with a political edge for the rest of his life and motivated many other popular folk and rock singers to carry on his legacy.
10. Today, Guthrie's music lives on in younger generations of people who feel inspired by his words.

Exercise H1–3, page H-38

Since I was only eight years old, I have dreamed of becoming a professional baseball player. Trying to develop the skill of a professional player has been both physically and mentally challenging. One of the greatest difficulties that I have faced is fear. When I became the pitcher on my high school team, I was under a lot of pressure; my teammates, coach, and all the students at my school depended on me to win games. The thought of losing terrified me. Before a few games in my first season, I put so much pressure on myself to win and to be a good leader that I froze. In time, though, I learned to manage my stress and to make the fear work in my favor. By the time I was a senior, I had transformed the fear into energy that helped me stay alert and quick. Although I know I will have many more challenges to face in pursuit of my dream, I am confident that some day I will succeed.

Exercise H1–4, page H-39

Haley: Good morning, Professor Weil. May I ask you for some advice about my course work?

Professor Weil: Sure, Haley. What can I help you with?

H: I would like to change my major. I'm enrolled as a biology major now, but I am not as interested in science as I thought I would be.

P: I see. What major are you thinking of?

H: Since I am very good at math, I think I would like to be a business major.

P: That's a good idea, but can you do well in classes that don't involve math?

H: I think so. Which courses must I take besides math?

P: You will have to take some communications and writing courses.

H: I can do that. I will go to the registrar and select my courses. Thank you, Professor Weil!

Exercise H1–5, page H-39

Most people think of a trash bin as a finishing point rather than a starting point. However, a recycling bin can be the start of a new life for a piece of paper. After paper is put into an office bin, it is shipped to a recycling center, where it is sorted into types: office paper, cardboard, or colored paper. After it is sorted, it is sent to a paper mill, where it is chopped into dry pulp. The pulp is then mixed with water to form a wet substance called "slurry." The slurry is sent through a screen, which removes little bits of excess materials such as glue, plastic, or staples. After it goes through the screen, the slurry is rinsed again to remove inks. Then the slurry goes through a machine that makes the paper fibers grow bigger. Next the slurry is watered down and placed on a screen, where it is pressed into long, thin sheets and dried on heated rollers. The dried sheets are rolled up and shipped off to other companies where they are processed and made into the paper products we use every day.

Exercise H1–6, page H-40

1. If the governor is reelected, she will not raise the income tax.
2. I could not park my car next to the library because all of the spaces were taken.
3. Sadly, a cure for AIDS has not been found yet.
4. The book that we have to buy for our ecology class is not very expensive.
5. I tried to make a photocopy, but the copier was not functioning properly.
6. Sunnie did not come with us to the football game last Saturday.
7. Although Omar does not like to drive in traffic, he likes to race cars on the weekends.
8. Snow leopards are not extinct, but they are on the endangered species list.
9. Kim could not find lychees [or any lychees] at the supermarket because they are not very common in the United States.
10. I was disappointed that I didn't know the woman's name.

Exercise H1–7, page H-40

1. If Deborah had arrived earlier, she might have found a better parking space.
2. I'll buy you a soda if you come to the cafeteria with me.
3. Correct
4. Correct
5. If I were a famous actor, I would move to Bel Aire and buy a mansion.
6. If you use aloe on a burn, you can reduce the chances of developing a scar.
7. You will have to pay late charges if you don't return your rental video on time.
8. Unless the Security Council agrees, the UN will not send peacekeeping troops to war-torn countries.
9. When Rosa left for college every September, she closed her summer gardening business. *Or* When Rosa leaves for college every September, she closes her summer gardening business.
10. If Kevin were here with us today, he would be enjoying himself.

Exercise H1–8, page H-41

When I was young, my family and I went on an annual camping trip in the canyons of the southwestern United States. One summer, I convinced my family to take a tour of several canyons: the Grand Canyon, Bryce Canyon, and Canyonlands National Park. I remember being amazed at each stop along the way. I loved looking up at the twisting towers of red rock, wondering how they had avoided falling down in the last several thousand years. (I can recall thinking that some might fall over if someone in the canyon sneezed a little too hard.) Even at that young age, I sensed the power of these remarkable landmarks and understood the spell that they had held over so many generations of residents and visitors. In my heart, I promised to go back to the canyons every year. Though I never planned to give up my promise, the commitments of adulthood have prevented me from taking annual trips back to the canyons. I miss visiting the red rocks on a regular basis, but I still manage to go back to the Southwest every few years. Breathing in the high desert air while gazing up at the red rock towers never ceases to refresh and rejuvenate me.

Exercise H2–1, page H-41

When I was only a boy, I was known for being lazy. Every time my parents asked me to clean my room or study for my classes, I always found an excuse to avoid the work. Sometimes I would pretend that I was too tired; other times I would pretend that I had simply forgotten their request. Most of the time, however, I would try to approach the situation logically, arguing that since my older brother was stronger and had more life experience, he should be responsible for most of the household chores.

However, when I started college, my life changed. I realized that in order to become the successful college student I wanted to be, I would have to take control of my life, change my bad habits, and act responsibly. Now I am no longer the lazy boy my parents knew when I was a child. I wake up early, exercise, and go to school. I am never late to my classes, and I always turn my assignments in on time. Although I am still far from perfect, I try to help others whenever I can. Whenever someone needs me, particularly at school or at home, I never try to hide as I did when I was just a boy.

Exercise H2–2, page H-42

It is common to think that being the oldest child in a family has the most privileges. However, there are several advantages to being the youngest child, too. First, it is important to note that by the time the youngest child is born, the parents have already had experience as parents. They know how to care for a newborn, and they tend to be more relaxed. Second, the youngest child has the opportunity to learn how to stay out of trouble. If the older children get into trouble, it is easy for the youngest child to learn from the older children's mistakes. A third advantage of being the youngest child is that in many cases, the youngest gets extra attention from the older siblings. It is not unusual to see older siblings taking care of their younger siblings at school or protecting them from bullies.

Exercise H2–3, page H-42

Possible revisions:
1. Coming to the United States changed more than my address. It changed the direction of my career.
2. My life here in Gainesville is different from the life that I lived in Bolivia.
3. Correct
4. I attended a culinary school, which was the best in Bolivia, and I was offered the chance to study for a short time in the United States.
5. When I first came, I met other students who had different majors.
6. Correct
7. Jin helped me realize the importance of having business experience.
8. I learned that although I enjoyed being a chef, I didn't want to be a chef without business knowledge.
9. I decided to stay a bit longer in the United States, where I could study international business.
10. Someday I will combine both interests and start my own chain of specialized restaurants, which I hope to build all over the world.

Exercise H2–4, page H-43

1. I have never seen a player hit a baseball so hard.
2. Sue cooked the soup very slowly so that the vegetables would be tender.
3. Correct
4. After I finished my workout, I carefully stretched my tender muscles.
5. The professor seemed surprised that the class finished the exam so quickly.
6. After I read the user manual, I easily installed the new hard drive.
7. My mother always told me that she loved all her children equally.
8. As soon as I got the keys to my new car, I drove my friends everywhere.
9. The government found out that the company manufactured the drug illegally.
10. Although she had a difficult time in the past, this year she very easily won the gold medal in cross-country skiing.

Exercise H3–1, page H-43

1. When people move to a new place, they definitely have to go through some changes.
2. The temperature dropped twenty degrees in a half hour yesterday.
3. Some governments help couples who have more than two children by giving them health insurance.
4. When people are too busy, they sometimes forget to eat dinner.

5. Students are exposed to new experiences when they move to a new country.
6. I chose to have a small family so that I could give my children sufficient attention.
7. Marco became more familiar with nature when he studied in the rain forests of Brazil.
8. Let me give you some advice: Buy your books early.
9. A common effect of culture shock is loneliness.
10. Because our school doesn't allow cars within the campus gates, I walk from my parking spot to the place where I need to go.

Exercise H3–2, page H-44

Heifer International is a nonprofit organization that provides animals to poor farmers and families around the world. The organization was started in the 1940s by a man named Dan West, a relief worker who gave people food during times of crisis. West realized that he could help people even more by giving them animals that could supply food — such as milk and cheese — for several years. He wanted to help people for the long term, and he wanted to help them have pride in themselves. Now Heifer serves communities in more than one hundred countries around the world. Its mission is to help families by providing some animals that the families can use to support themselves or start small businesses.

Exercise H3–3, page H-44

Possible revisions:

A greeting is the way that a person addresses or acknowledges another person when the two meet. Types of greetings vary in different countries. People in Japan often prefer to greet nonverbally, with a bow and a smile. An African would likely greet a fellow African with a handshake. For the Maori people of New Zealand, the most common greeting is the *hongi*, which involves rubbing noses. In Poland, a kiss on each cheek is customary; but the Dutch custom is to kiss the right cheek, then the left, and then the right again. A traveler to another country would be wise to learn the greetings expected by its people.

Exercise H4–1, page H-44

1. confusing
2. tiring
3. boring
4. working
5. fascinating
6. handwritten, typed
7. satisfied
8. hand-painted
9. cleaning
10. peeled

Exercise H5–1, page H-45

1. Does your dance class start on Monday or Wednesday?
2. Correct

3. As soon as Fiona moved into her dorm room, she put a poster of Einstein on the wall for inspiration.
4. My books are a little dusty because they were packed away in the garage for a year.
5. Dr. Horn is taking his students to Ghana for a study trip in early June.
6. My grandmother was born in Los Angeles, but my grandfather was born in Albuquerque.
7. My fraternity brothers like to play loud music on the street in front of our building.
8. My exam begins in two hours, but I'm not nervous at all.
9. Correct
10. Bret finished writing his term paper right at midnight.

Exercise H5–2, page H-45

1. I have trouble concentrating on my homework when my roommate is around.
2. The senator was skilled at delaying controversial votes.
3. I'm not worried about our verbs test on Wednesday.
4. While Ellie proofread the group's report, Sam and Tomi worked on the presentation slides.
5. Correct
6. The solution consists of sodium and water.
7. I was afraid to board the plane because I'm not accustomed to traveling alone.
8. Shea remained devoted to the teachings of his martial arts master.
9. You can always count on Carole to help out when the office gets busy.
10. Correct

Index

Revision Symbols

Letter-number codes refer to sections of this book.

abbr	faulty abbreviation **M4**	¶	new paragraph **C4**
ad	misuse of adverb or adjective **G4**	*p*	error in punctuation
add	add needed word **S2**	⌃ ⸴	comma **P1**
agr	faulty agreement **G1, G3-a**	*no* ⸴	no comma **P2**
appr	inappropriate language **W4**	;	semicolon **P3**
art	article **E3**	:	colon **P4**
awk	awkward	⸴ᵛ	apostrophe **P5**
cap	capital letter **M3**	" "	quotation marks **P6**
case	error in case **G3-c, G3-d**	. ? !	period, question mark, exclamation point,
cliché	cliché **W5-e**	— ( )	dash, parentheses,
coh	coherence **C4-d**	[ ] ...	brackets, ellipsis mark,
coord	faulty coordination **S6-c**	/	slash **P7**
cs	comma splice **G6**	*pass*	ineffective passive **W3**
dev	inadequate development **C4-b**	*pn agr*	pronoun agreement **G3-a**
dm	dangling modifier **S3-e**	*proof*	proofreading problem **C3-c**
-ed	error in *-ed* ending **G2-d**	*ref*	error in pronoun reference **G3-b**
emph	emphasis **S6**	*run-on*	run-on sentence **G6**
ESL	ESL grammar **E1, E2, E3, E4, E5**	*-s*	error in *-s* ending **G2-c**
exact	inexact language **W5**	*sexist*	sexist language **W4-e**
frag	sentence fragment **G5**	*shift*	distracting shift **S4**
fs	fused sentence **G6**	*sl*	slang **W4-c**
gl/us	see glossary of usage **W1**	*sp*	misspelled word **M1**
hyph	error in use of hyphen **M2**	*sub*	faulty subordination **S6-d**
idiom	idiom **W5-d**	*sv agr*	subject-verb agreement **G1, G2-c**
inc	incomplete construction **S2**	*t*	error in verb tense **G2-f**
irreg	error in irregular verb **G2-a**	*trans*	transition needed **C4-d**
ital	italics (underlining) **M6**	*usage*	see glossary of usage **W1**
jarg	jargon **W4-a**	*v*	voice **W3**
lc	lowercase letter **M3**	*var*	sentence variety **S6-b, S6-c, S7**
mix	mixed construction **S5**	*vb*	verb error **G2**
mm	misplaced modifier **S3-b**	*w*	wordy **W2**
mood	error in mood **G2-g**	//	faulty parallelism **S1**
nonst	nonstandard usage **W4-c**	⌃	insert
num	error in use of number **M5**	x	obvious error
om	omitted word **S2**	#	insert space
		⌒	close up space

Detailed Menu